Methods

DOING SOCIAL RESEARCH

FOURTH EDITION

Winston Jackson

St. Francis Xavier University

Norine Verberg

St. Francis Xavier University

Methods

DOING SOCIAL RESEARCH

FOURTH EDITION

PEARSON

Prentice
Hall

Toronto

Library and Archives Canada Cataloguing in Publication

Jackson, Winston
    Methods : doing social research / Winston Jackson, Norine
Verberg. — 4th ed.

Includes bibliographical references and index.
ISBN 0-13-187925-1

    1. Social sciences—Research—Methodology. I. Verberg, Norine,
1959–. II. Title.

H62.J29 2007   300.7'2   C2006-903162-2

ISBN 0-13-187925-1

Editor-in-Chief, Vice-President of Sales: Kelly Shaw
Senior Acquisitions Editor: Ky Pruesse
Executive Marketing Manager: Judith Allen
Associate Editor: Rachel Stuckey
Production Editor: Kevin Leung
Copy Editor: Trish O'Reilly
Proofreader: Colleen Ste. Marie
Production Coordinator: Janis Raisen
Composition: Debbie Kumpf
Art Director: Julia Hall
Cover Design: Suzanna Brusikiewicz
Cover Image: Getty Images

Printed and bound in Canada.

For Ben, Danielle, and Meaghan

BRIEF CONTENTS

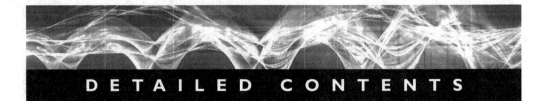

DETAILED CONTENTS

PREFACE

The fourth edition of *Methods: Doing Social Research* attempts to be inclusive. The underlying message is that there are a variety of methodologies and theoretical orientations within the social science community and we should attempt to appreciate the value each has in furthering our knowledge of social behaviour. No one theory, research design, measurement procedure, or statistical approach can provide a satisfactory answer to all research questions. Simply put, we need to develop an appreciation of the diversity of approaches available to the social scientist.

Students are encouraged to do research projects. And to help them, many Rules, Tips, Steps, and Cautions are presented to facilitate the completion of a project. We believe that students learn most by doing projects. The task of the instructor is to help the student through the often intimidating process of completing a project.

While an effort has been made to cover the main contemporary methodological approaches, many had to be omitted. It is no longer possible to write a comprehensive social science methods textbook. Preparing a methodological encyclopedia would be the only approach to listing all the available methods. The text therefore has a bias towards featuring those methods that are most popular in contemporary usage. Many less frequently used techniques, or techniques that were considered too complex for the beginning researcher, simply did not survive the selection process.

The enormous expansion in the social sciences over the past three decades has seen an increase in the variety of theoretical, methodological, and pragmatic concerns of social science practitioners. There is much debate and discussion about the appropriate role of social scientists in bringing about social change, or in resisting it, and about what kinds of evidence are appropriate for what kinds of questions. In addition, there are competing ideological pressures to do one kind of social science or another, to use one technique or another. Students will encounter much mystification in the areas of design, statistics, and measurement, and also about what are the appropriate kinds of questions to be researched by social scientists. This text tries to demystify these and other topics. Rules and Steps are provided to help the student complete a first project in social science research. While only the basics are covered here, sufficient information is provided to give the student an inclusive, generous view of the full range of social science approaches.

The fourth edition of *Methods: Doing Social Research* incorporates a number of enhancements. We maintained the ordering of the chapters to follow the stages of the research process. Part 1 (Chapters 1 and 2) reviews the basic methodological approaches and discusses a variety of theoretical perspectives that social scientists use to explain human behaviour. Part 2 (Chapters 3 to 7) explores alternative research designs. There is some reorganization of Part 2 for this edition. The methods more closely associated with quantitative methods are presented first: experiments, surveys, and nonreactive designs, followed by the chapter on qualitative methods and a chapter on critical approaches to research. The latter chapter incorporates much of the material that was covered in the chapter on applied methods in the third edition. All the chapters in this section have been revised and include examples of current research projects published by Canadian scholars.

Part 3 (Chapters 8 and 9) presents a review of elementary statistical procedures used by social science researchers. Part 4 (Chapters 10 to 15) begins by pointing out sources of bias and discusses ethical concerns in order to prepare the beginning researcher for designing a study. Chapters 12, 13, and 14 deal with how to get a project started, and include discussions of measurement, questionnaire construction, and sampling. Part 5 (Chapters 16 to 18) deals with issues of data analysis, the testing of causal models, and a presentation of frequently used analysis procedures. Chapter 18 discusses the writing of a research report. Part 6 includes Appendix A, which explains how to process data using SPSS. This section walks the first-time user through the various steps in analyzing a project. Sample jobs that cover the basic procedures required to complete a project are included.

Regardless of how we present the chapters, professors are free to decide what order suits them. If the book is being used as a text in a course for which research projects are required, it is recommended that the review of statistical matters be started early in the course, along with any computer labs (a set of training labs is included in the Instructor's Manual), so that by the time students have their studies designed and their data collected, they will be ready to commence analysis. Some instructors find it best to present the statistical chapters in every other lecture, using the interim lectures for the discussion of the material included in the first six chapters.

Some of the features included in this text but not typically found in other Canadian methods texts are:

- an emphasis on practical, down-to-earth steps, rules, and procedures that help to guide students through a project, from framing the question to designing the study, collecting the data, analyzing the data, and reporting the results;

- a demystification of the research process by explaining as simply as possible how research is done;

- a presentation of research bias problems early in the text, alerting students to be strong critics of research and to recognize its limitations;

- a presentation of Milgram's (obedience to authority) and Humphreys' (observations of bisexual males in public washrooms) research, thus alerting students to two key studies that raised important ethical dilemmas and that helped shape the development of contemporary ethical guidelines;

- the use of computational methods that are kept as simple as possible and notations that can be followed easily;

- a section on analyzing data without using a computer for those researchers who do not have access to a computer or for problems that do not require computer analysis;

- an appendix providing instructions and illustrations for the use of SPSS;

- boxes that illustrate material in the text—most of the authors cited in these boxes are Canadian;

- lists of projects completed by students;

- a presentation of original views in the areas of measurement, the problem of grouping data, and the impact that grouping has on results;

- encouraging the use of 9-point Likert-type items;

- interpreting three-variable relations. We present a rule of thirds, which is easier to learn than the traditional approach;

- techniques for visually estimating correlations and simple linear equations.

INSTRUCTOR'S SUPPLEMENTS

The **Instructor's Supplement** package includes an Instructor's Manual with training labs, PowerPoint slides, and an international data set (an SPSS export file) that can be used to learn how to analyze data with SPSS. These supplements are available on the Pearson Education Canada online catalogue (vig.pearsoned.ca) to instructors who have adopted the text. And for a modest additional cost, **SPSS 14.0 Student Version for Windows** (CD-ROM) (ISBN: 0-13-228307-7) can be packaged with this text, providing students with the software at a fraction of the standard price. Instructors may contact their Pearson Education Canada representative for more details.

ACKNOWLEDGMENTS

Many individuals have freely given their advice about the development of this textbook. We would especially like to thank the many students who have challenged and stimulated us with interesting research problems.

We would like to thank those individuals who provided feedback on this edition of the text, including Dean Behrens, Phillipe Couton, Catherine Krull, Mark Lowes, Ming Ouyang, Harry Rosenbaum, and Nikki Thompson. We also thank Richard Myles and Richard Helmes-Hayes who provided helpful information for this edition.

We wish to acknowledge Brian E. Butler, Linda Christiansen-Ruffman, Sandra Kirby, Michael Kompf, Murray Knuttila, Clayton Mosher, Chris Szafnicki, Paul Wong, Udo Staber, Peter M. Butler, James Teevan, Karen March, Gwen Reimer, and J.P. Chartrand, for the invaluable suggestions they provided when reviewing earlier editions of the text.

Many people at St. Francis Xavier University helped in a variety of ways. In particular we would like to mention Carla Haley-Baxter, Angela Gillis, Yvon Grenier, Gary Brooks, Sergei Aalto, Diane Giroux, Marlies Jackson, Jason Ryan MacLean, Barbara Phillips. We owe thanks to all of them. Allan Rankin, a student intern, helped enormously.

SPSS Inc. was kind enough to provide us with the SPSS to help develop Appendix A. They also have been most helpful and cooperative.

Finally we wish to acknowledge the Pearson Education Canada staff whose hard work and scheduling helped get the project completed on time. In particular we would like to thank Patti Riediger, Rachel Stuckey, and Kevin Leung. Thanks also to Trish O'Reilly, our copy editor, for her painstaking attention to detail and for the clarity of thought she brought to the material.

Winston Jackson and Norine Verberg

Methods

DOING SOCIAL RESEARCH

FOURTH EDITION

PRELIMINARIES

The first chapter introduces the reader to three basic approaches to social science methodology, distinguishes between qualitative and quantitative strategies in understanding human behaviour, and introduces some of the key terms used in talking about research methods. The second chapter introduces the reader to social science theories, arguing that theories are general explanations of social behaviour. Approaches to testing theories are presented.

APPROACHES TO METHODS

Western cultures share a great confidence in and respect for science as the way to truth. Science is seen as a powerful tool—a tool that can help solve social problems. And contemporary societies have enormous problems: profound challenges posed by poverty, environmental degradation, and uneven regional development and inequalities in education, employment, and health care.

The challenge for social science is to live up to the expectations the larger society has of it. Social scientists are attempting to understand phenomena that are extremely complex and subject to many interpretations. While there are elements of human behaviour that may be simple, much

of human behaviour cannot be understood satisfactorily with simple, mechanistic models. A *mechanistic model* is one which asserts that a particular behaviour is completely controlled by one or more external actions or events. In most cases, human behaviour is much more complicated. Many factors are usually involved, and involved differently, depending on the situation and on the culture. Social scientists come to know and understand the complexity of human behaviour by using a variety of methodologies. This text will introduce the key methodologies that contemporary social scientists use. Some of these methodologies are illustrated in Box 1.1.

BOX 1.1   BIRTHS AND THE VARIETY OF RESEARCH DESIGNS

To illustrate the range in research techniques, let us consider how information related to births in our society might be examined.

Secondary Data

Because of their impact on society, birth rates (along with other demographic patterns) are important to demographers, economists, and sociologists. For example, such researchers might want to find out if birth rates are lowered by structural constraints, such as limited choice in housing, where few inexpensive apartment units have more than two bedrooms, or limited opportunities in the labour market to earn sufficient income; or if they are raised by family allowance programs, such as those in Canada and France. Researchers who wish to monitor shifts in birth rates normally rely on

the analysis of existing government statistics. They rely on *secondary data,* data collected by persons other than the researcher.

Survey

Changes in attitudes toward appropriate family size might be another factor a researcher should examine. A political scientist, historian, or sociologist might wish to explore why the province of Quebec went from having the second highest birth rate in Canada to the lowest within one generation. What factors influenced such a dramatic shift? If changing attitudes were a factor, what changed them? Here a sociologist would probably conduct a *survey* to represent people drawn from different age groups. The questions would address "family size" and seek to measure those factors that the researcher identifies as probable causes of variability in the dependent variable, family size. A political scientist might be particularly interested in the role of the church in the daily lives of Quebecers. The political scientist/historian might conduct a *historical-comparative* study to show how the influence of the Roman Catholic church in Quebec declined.

Experiment

A psychologist might be interested in examining the impact that a film on birth control had on attitudes toward family size. In this case, the psychologist would probably use an *experiment*. Two groups would be established on the basis of random assignment and both would be measured on desired family size. One group (the experimental group) would then be shown a film about family planning, while the other (the control group) would be shown a film unrelated to the issue at hand. Finally, both groups would be remeasured on desired family size. Here the experiment is designed to test whether a film has an impact on an attitude.

Quasi-Experiment

A nursing researcher might be interested in testing a program to increase the parenting confidence of new mothers. In such cases, the researcher might monitor a group of new mothers over a period of time in an attempt to understand the importance of different support systems, education, and other factors in developing parenting confidence. Such an investigation represents a *quasi-experiment* designed to measure the response of new mothers to a training program.

Phenomenological Investigation

A qualitative social researcher might attempt to capture the "lived experience" of mothers giving birth to their first child. This phenomenological investigation would use in-depth interviews to record what it was like to go through the experience of having a first baby. The report would present the themes emerging from the interviews.

Participant Observation

Another social researcher might want to examine how we have institutionalized the birthing process in our society. How do we organize the obstetrics ward? What are the rules of behaviour and rituals surrounding the birth of a child? In this case, the researcher might implement a *participant observation* study, perhaps by working as a ward assistant, in an attempt to describe the various behaviours. Here one would view the ward as a total social system where the needs of mother and her new child are met within the ward. How are crises, such as the death of the child, managed? What are the unwritten tactics used by nurses to manage patients, newborns, doctors, hospital administrators, and visitors?

These approaches to studying aspects of births (see Box 1.1) indicate but a small number of those used to explore social science issues. The complexity of the questions we ask about human behaviour is truly humbling. In attempting to understand them, many theoretical perspectives have been developed, along with a diversity of research techniques. This text will introduce the beginning research methods student to some of the main methodological approaches and techniques used in the social sciences today. A single text cannot adequately cover all available methods, nor is it possible to provide sufficient detail for the more advanced student.

The goals of the social sciences vary from discipline to discipline and from researcher to researcher. Most would agree, however, that one goal is to produce an understanding of social behaviour. Why do we find regularities, or patterns, in human behaviour? Which patterns are unique to a particular culture and which are found in most cultures? We want not only to document these regularities, but also to understand the complexity of human perceptions, values, and motivations. An additional goal shared by many social scientists is to improve our quality of life through the application of the social sciences. All these goals are enormously challenging. There are many different paths we can take to try to attain them.

A. KEY METHODOLOGICAL APPROACHES IN THE SOCIAL SCIENCES

We can identify three important contemporary approaches in the social sciences: the positivist approach, the interpretive approach, and the critical approach. Let us investigate the assumptions that these approaches make about science, human behaviour, and values and also their preferred methodologies and possible weaknesses.

1. THE POSITIVIST APPROACH

A. THE NATURE OF THE POSITIVIST APPROACH

Most people will have some familiarity with the **positivist approach**—for it is the approach used in the physical sciences. In the early development of the social sciences, some theorists attempted to model the new disciplines on the physical sciences. The French scholars Auguste Comte (1798–1857) and Emile Durkheim (1858–1917) were leaders in encouraging positivist approaches to understanding social behaviour.

Often referred to as the father of sociology, Auguste Comte proposed that societies go through three stages in their development: the theological stage (dominated by religion), the metaphysical stage (dominated by abstract speculation), and the positive stage (dominated by scientific thinking). Comte argued that the social sciences should discover the laws that govern the shift from one stage to the next. The positive stage (which Comte thought was emerging in nineteenth-century France) is one where society is organized according to scientific observations and experiments. Comte also proposed a hierarchy of the sciences, with the social sciences at the top because of their greater complexity (reflected by the need to take many factors, such as plans and intentions, into account simultaneously). Ironically, although Comte began his academic writings as a positivist, stressing science over religion, in the latter part of his life he turned to a religion of humanity, advocating a strong role for social scientists in directing the affairs of society and in defining appropriate goals for society (Comte, 1875).

In *The Rules of Sociological Method,* Emile Durkheim attempted to establish methodological principles to guide the new discipline of sociology. In his book, originally published in 1895, he argued that sociology should model itself on the physical sciences. Our knowledge comes from systematically codifying our experience of the social and the physical realities we encounter. Durkheim asserted that sociologists should study social facts. *Social facts* are ways of "acting, thinking, and feeling, external to the individual [i.e., from society], and endowed with the power of coercion [force toward conformity from society], by reason of which they control him [i.e., the individual]." According to Durkheim the social scientist should treat social facts "objectively"—just as the physical scientist treats data. Durkheim argued that social facts are expressed in society by way of patterns. These patterns or regularities (such as marriage rates or suicide rates) can be studied by means of statistics. Social patterns have an independent existence and cannot be understood adequately by studying individual psychology. To demonstrate this position, Durkheim wrote *Suicide* ([1915] 1976) in which he outlined his formal theory of suicide and demonstrated how quantitative research methods could be used to study suicide (e.g., compare suicide rates for people living in different social conditions, such as being married versus divorced). Durkheim argued, and demonstrated with his statistical analysis, that an intensely personal act like suicide is related to social conditions. Chapter 2 refers to a number of ways that Durkheim's formal theory of suicide (i.e., that the degree of social integration varies inversely with the suicide rate) continues to influence research on suicide.

A variety of labels is used to describe the positivist approach in various social science disciplines. Labels such as behaviourist, empiricist, and scientist are attached to the practitioners, along with, of course, some less flattering labels, such as *abstracted empiricist,* a term coined by C. Wright Mills (1959), or *number cruncher,* a term used by many others. These last two labels imply that too much attention is paid to the numbers themselves and not enough to the underlying reality that they reflect. Some critics of the positivist approach claim that positivist researchers have become overly impressed with the numbers and the tools used to process them and have lost sight of the goal of trying to understand human behaviour. In any case, positivism, in some form or other, is the predominant approach across the social science disciplines. But, as we shall see, the interpretive and the critical approaches represent strong alternatives.

Most positivists would agree with Carlo Lastrucci's definition of science and the postulates he outlines. In attempting to state a consensus on the essential attributes of science, he defines science as "an objective, logical, and systematic method of analysis of phenomena, devised to permit the accumulation of reliable knowledge" (1967, p. 6).

An *objective* approach is designed to minimize bias, is impersonal, and seeks its authority in fact, not opinion; a *logical* approach uses deductive rules; and a *systematic* approach is consistently organized and makes use of such techniques as statistical analysis. Finally, *reliable knowledge* refers to knowledge one can count on, knowledge that allows one to predict outcomes accurately: "reliable knowledge is that which is both objectively and empirically verifiable" (Lastrucci, 1967, p. 6). Predictions are empirically verifiable if they can be tested for accuracy by making systematic observations.

B. POSITIVIST ASSUMPTIONS ABOUT SCIENCE AND HUMAN BEHAVIOUR

There are a number of basic postulates, or working assumptions, that positivist social scientists make in approaching their research. Again, following Lastrucci, we can summarize seven of the major postulates as follows (1967, pp. 37–46):

i. All Behaviour Is Naturally Determined

To understand human behaviour, we should look for causes in the natural world. This postulate emphasizes a mechanistic view of the world: each outcome is produced by one or more external causes.

ii. Humans Are Part of the Natural World

Human beings are part of the natural world. Human behaviour can therefore be studied using the methods employed to study the behaviour of other species, although the study of human behaviour is made far more complex by the need to take language into account.

iii. Nature Is Orderly and Regular

The natural world is orderly, predictable, and therefore knowable. The patterns of nature may be identified and observed. Those events which appear to be random may simply reflect our inability to comprehend fully the natural forces at work.

iv. All Objective Phenomena Are Eventually Knowable

There are no intellectual limits on what we may eventually know about nature or about human behaviour.

v. Nothing Is Self-Evident

Our knowledge of behaviour should be demonstrated objectively. And while we may wish to use folk wisdom or "common sense" as a starting point, ultimately we must test ideas systematically.

vi. Truth Is Relative

What is regarded as a scientific truth today may be disproved or modified tomorrow. There is a dynamic element to what we know. Our knowledge is always on the road to some ultimate truth, but never quite reaching it.

vii. Knowledge Comes from Experience

The belief that we need to test our understanding of the world systematically with knowledge gained through our senses is a fundamental principle of science.

Positivists are interested in understanding the patterns of human activity. An emphasis is placed on identifying, measuring, and expressing the relations among variables with mathematical precision. And since cause–effect relations are of central concern to the positivist, it is no surprise that emphasis is placed on prediction.

The positivist searches out ways of testing theories of human behaviour. Typically, this is accomplished by establishing *hypotheses* (predictions) about relationships, measuring the variables, and then analyzing the relationships to see if there is evidence to support or refute the predictions. Efforts are then made to replicate (repeat) the study to see if similar findings result when studying a different population.

A key indicator of an adequate explanation for the positivist is the ability to predict outcomes. Thus, the positivist wishes to identify the key causes in the variation of some variable. For example, the positivist may be interested in identifying the factors that contribute to the incidence of race riots, illegal drug use, job satisfaction, or the choice of nontraditional careers by female students. In each case, the researcher is interested in understanding what factors best predict the phenomenon under investigation. Thus, a study is successful when most of the variation is accounted for and when the causes can be linked to some general theory of social behaviour.

Unfortunately, the reputation of the social sciences is not impressive when it comes to accurate predictions. Generally it is thought that only the physical sciences are sufficiently well developed to predict with mathematical accuracy. Richard Henshel has examined this topic in some detail and notes that where the physical sciences deal with unaltered (natural) phenomena they fare little better than the social sciences. For example, the ability of the geologist to predict when an earthquake is going to occur in a particular area is poor. Indeed, most of the highly predictable outcomes in science are based not on natural, unaltered systems, but rather on engineered systems—systems designed to take into account various influencing factors (Henshel, 1976). For example, you can predict that no matter what the weather, the bridge you drive over every day to work will be there for you tomorrow. It will be there because it is designed to withstand weather and traffic conditions well beyond its normal loads. So unless something catastrophic happens the bridge will be there. In contrast, the leaf that blew off the tree in your yard may or may not have moved since yesterday. To estimate its current location would be foolhardy since so many factors could influence where it has moved to since yesterday. Prediction for the positivist social scientist is

akin to estimating the whereabouts of the leaf. Natural systems pose a tough challenge for the person keen on prediction.

C. POSITIVIST VIEW OF THE ROLE OF VALUES IN RESEARCH

Positivists argue that research should be value-free. Researchers should put their personal values to one side, so as to avoid influencing the outcomes of studies. Positivists maintain that science progresses when researchers systematically test alternative explanations of behaviour (attempting to rule them out) without trying to support some pet theory or favoured project.

D. RESEARCH DESIGNS ASSOCIATED WITH POSITIVISM

The positivist approach relies mainly (but by no means exclusively) on *experiments*, *surveys*, and *secondary data*, or data collected by others. Typically, positivist approaches rely on some form of numerical analysis rather than on verbal descriptions.

E. CRITICISMS OF POSITIVISM

Many criticisms have been levelled against the positivist approach to knowledge. Following are some of the major criticisms:

- Some critics argue that value-free research is an unattainable goal. Some studies have shown that, despite the best intentions, it is extremely difficult for a researcher to prevent his or her biases or expectations from exerting some influence on the results of a study (see Chapter 10; also see Rosenthal and Fode, 1963).

- Some critics argue that the so-called value neutrality of positivism is itself a value.

- Other critics argue that, far from being value-free, positivists do research that helps to support the existing social order. For example, studies designed to help reduce the level of crime may be seen as research intended to help protect the property of the wealthy.

- Some scholars argue that the positivistic view ignores a crucial aspect of social reality—namely, that different people may experience and perceive the same events differently. The subjective experience of the social world is an alternate social reality that may be explored by the social scientist; it is the one emphasized particularly by those who employ the interpretive approach.

2. THE INTERPRETIVE APPROACH

A. THE NATURE OF THE INTERPRETIVE APPROACH

The German scholar Max Weber (1864–1920) was particularly influential in developing methodological approaches that stressed the importance of the interpretation *individuals* put on their actions and on the actions and reactions of others. He emphasized **Verstehen**, the empathetic understanding of behaviour. The researcher should try to imagine how a particular individual perceives social actions. How does the individual feel? What are the individual's motivations? What meaning does the individual attach to a particular event? Besides Weber, other figures important in the development of interpretive perspectives are Mead (1934), Blumer (1951), Schutz (1954), Becker et al. (1961), Goffman (1962), and Glaser and Strauss (1967).

B. INTERPRETIVE ASSUMPTIONS ABOUT SCIENCE AND HUMAN BEHAVIOUR

Rather than confining itself to behaviour alone, the **interpretive approach** examines how people make sense of their lives, how they define their situation, and how their sense of self develops in interaction with others. Humans are always in a process of *becoming*: they are influenced by how they see themselves, by how others see them, and by what they want to become. Symbolic interactionists, for example, would stress the idea of *role modelling*: that is, the extent to which an individual chooses to emulate someone else's attitudes and behaviours. Note that, in this view, the individual is actively choosing to be like someone else. In contrast, most theories that use the positivist or critical approaches emphasize the extent to which individuals are shaped or moulded by the institutions in their society without being aware of it.

Three major theoretical perspectives emerged from the interpretive approach: the *symbolic interactionist perspective*, the *ethnomethodological perspective*, and *grounded theory*. These perspectives all try to provide an adequate understanding of how people see and interpret the events of their everyday lives. How individuals reflect upon and influence one another are issues of concern to interpretive social scientists.

C. INTERPRETIVE VIEWS OF THE ROLE OF VALUES IN RESEARCH

Interpretive social scientists argue that values are relative. That is, they would argue that definitions of what constitutes appropriate or inappropriate behaviour depend on the socialization that one has received from one's society. These definitions will shift over time and across societies.

Researchers should try to understand (empathetically) and explain the values of the people being studied (i.e., the "actors").

D. RESEARCH DESIGNS ASSOCIATED WITH THE INTERPRETIVE APPROACH

The interpretive approach relies mainly on field studies, with an emphasis on *participant observation studies* (joining a group and participating in it), *in-depth interviews* with people, and *ethnomethodology* (typically a detailed examination of a single event or case). Each of these studies typically involves a few cases that are described in detail. A key question for these researchers is: does the explanation offered make sense to the people whose behaviour is being explained? Communication of the results of such studies usually emphasizes verbal descriptions rather than numerical analyses.

E. CRITICISMS OF THE INTERPRETIVE APPROACH

As we have seen, the interpretive approach differs markedly from the positivist approach. Any proponent of the existence of general abstract laws would criticize the interpretive approach for its subjectivity. Moreover, some critics reject the interpretive theorists' assessment that all values are equally valid. Other critics argue that, with its emphasis on field studies, the interpretive approach does not enable the researcher to make clear generalizations. We cannot easily determine whether the findings of a case study are particular to it or more generally applicable. The difficulty is even more acute when studies cannot be replicated— an ethnomethodological study of individual understandings of events would be a good example. The emphasis on the single case gets us into an old dilemma of knowing more and more about less and less, although in fairness this criticism can be levelled in varying degrees against all types of systematic inquiry. Finally, if emphasis is placed on the individual level of analysis, it seems to be difficult to understand social patterns: to what extent can we understand interrelations among social groups by studying interactions among individuals? The response to this criticism may be that no social theory can hope to explain all of human behaviour.

3. THE CRITICAL APPROACH

A. THE NATURE OF THE CRITICAL APPROACH

There are numerous schools to be covered under this heading: the *conflict* schools and sub-schools would be included, such as Ralf Dahrendorf's *dialectical conflict theory* (1958), Lewis Coser's *conflict functionalism* (1956), Randall Collins' *exchange conflict theory* (1975), and Jurgen Habermas' *critical theory* (1984). In many ways, *feminist* theory fits well with the critical approach, although, methodologically, feminism draws much of its inspiration from the interpretive approach. Proponents of the critical approach share a common desire to improve the condition of humanity. The classic theorists in developing this approach are Karl Marx (1818–1883) and Georg Simmel (1858–1918).

B. CRITICAL ASSUMPTIONS ABOUT SCIENCE AND HUMAN BEHAVIOUR

According to the **critical approach** human behaviour consists of different groups attempting to enhance their interests at the expense of less powerful groups. Whether it is the owners of factories exploiting labour, or males exercising dominance over females, this approach stresses that human relations are characterized by conflicting interests. Proponents of the critical approach argue that social scientists have an obligation to act as advocates working for changes in society, changes needed to bring social justice to all. The researcher helps bring about such changes by making us more sensitive to social problems. This knowledge in turn empowers citizens, helping them to become agents of social transformation (Fay, 1987, p. 27). The fundamental goal of the critical approach is to bring about a truly egalitarian society—one where there is an equality of opportunity *and* an equality of result.

C. CRITICAL VIEW OF THE ROLE OF VALUES IN RESEARCH

Critical social scientists forthrightly declare that certain values are correct while others are not. In short, the critical approach takes an absolutist view of values. Researchers working in the critical tradition would argue that the relativist position of mainstream social science has had the consequence of supporting the established order in society, and has had, therefore, little impact on reducing social inequities. Critical social scientists favour imposing moral absolutes in order to deal with inequalities.

D. RESEARCH METHODS ASSOCIATED WITH CRITICAL APPROACHES

The research methods associated with the critical approach span a broad range. Given the interest in understanding the relations between groups in society and in understanding how social change occurs, it is no

surprise that critical social scientists tend to work with historical materials, and thus pay particular attention to comparative studies and analyses of secondary data. This focus tends to emphasize *macrovariables* (properties of societies) as opposed to *microvariables* (properties of individuals).

Research and explanations are judged to be valid if they lead to an improvement in the social condition of humanity. The critical approach has a strong practical orientation. Social science analysis is seen as a means of achieving greater social justice for all.

E. CRITICISMS OF THE CRITICAL APPROACH

Like the positivist approach, the critical approach relies on general theories. But the positivist, as well the interpretive researcher, would reject the imposition of absolute values. The positivist critic would argue that the difficulty with adopting a value position in any scholarly discipline is that it enhances the likelihood of distorting research to promote one's personal values. Critical researchers may be too selective—reporting only those findings that are compatible with their values and ignoring all others. Critics maintain that critical researchers are unlikely to make a rigorous attempt to exclude competing explanations of behaviour or to find support for competing value systems. In fairness, however, this criticism could be levelled at all social science approaches. Turner (1991), in commenting on Dahrendorf's dialectical conflict theory, argues that insufficient attention has been paid to providing clear formal definitions of concepts that would render the various schemes empirically testable. The argument is that if concepts are loosely defined then researchers will have little to guide them in developing measures of concepts and, as a result, will be unable to test theoretical formulations adequately.

Table 1.1 summarizes some of the main ideas of the three major contemporary methodological approaches. Each approach can increase our understanding of human behaviour. Rather than rejecting any one of them outright, we would do well to regard each approach as potentially valuable in our quest for knowledge about human behaviour.

B. SOME IMPORTANT DISTINCTIONS

1. QUANTITATIVE VERSUS QUALITATIVE RESEARCH

Research techniques can be classified as either *quantitative* or *qualitative*. The distinction is based on the degree to which the analysis is done by converting observations

TABLE 1.1	SUMMARY OF THREE KEY METHODOLOGICAL APPROACHES IN THE SOCIAL SCIENCES		
CRITERION	POSITIVIST	INTERPRETIVE	CRITICAL
Major figures	Comte, Durkheim, Skinner	Weber, Mead, Goffman, Becker, Schutz, Turner, Garfinkel	Malthus, Marx, Simmel, Dahrendorf, Coser, Collins, Habermas
Schools associated with	Operant and Classical Conditioning, Behaviourist, Exchange Theory, Functionalist	Symbolic Interactionist, Ethnomethodological, Grounded Theory Phenomenology	Conflict, Critical, Marxist, Segmentation, Feminist
View of science	A tool for uncovering general laws of cause and effect in social behaviour	A tool for understanding the reality experienced by people	A tool that should be used to improve the condition of the oppressed
View of human behaviour	Caused by forces acting on the individual; characterized by regularity and order	Determined by context and individual perception of meaning	Consists of groups attempting to exploit others for their own advantage
Goals of research	To predict behaviour; to test general theories of behaviour by testing of hypotheses	To provide an adequate reflection of people's experience of the social world; testing Grounded Theory	To improve the social conditions of the oppressed; to achieve a just society; advocacy
Role of values in research	Research should be value-free; relativistic	Research should be value-free; relativistic	Research should impose moral absolutes derived from theory; absolutist
Research designs associated with	Surveys, experiments, quasi-experiments, secondary data, historical analysis; tends toward quantitative orientation	In-depth interviews, participant observations, field studies, document analyses; tends toward qualitative orientation	Historical, comparative, interviews, advocacy research; uses both qualitative and quantitative approaches

to numbers. The distinction also reflects differences in the types of questions asked, the kinds of evidence considered appropriate for answering a question, and the methods used to process this evidence. The use of quantitative data fits well with the research goals of positivists' social science, whereas the use of qualitative data is employed by interpretative social scientists. Researchers working within the critical tradition may use either quantitative or qualitative data to achieve their research objectives.

A. QUANTITATIVE RESEARCH

Quantitative research seeks to quantify, or reflect with numbers, observations about human behaviour. It emphasizes precise measurement, the testing of hypotheses based on a sample of observations, and a statistical analysis of the data. The quantitative researcher attempts to describe relationships among variables mathematically and to apply some form of numerical analysis to the social relations being examined. Quantitative researchers, like physical scientists, treat their subject matter like an object. Quantitative research is characteristic of the positivist approach. It is also used (together with qualitative research) in the critical approach.

i. Types of Questions Asked

The questions asked in quantitative research often concern relationships among variables and patterns in social trends. Questions like the ones following would be typical.

- What is the relationship between gender and suicide?

- What factors are most important in determining the level of an individual's job satisfaction?

- Is the popularity of a political leader rising or falling?

- What is the relationship between gender and conformity?

- Is a stay-in-school intervention program effective in diminishing dropout rates?

ii. Types of Analysis

In quantitative research, findings are typically expressed as relationships that are presented in tables and graphs. Variables are sometimes *cross-classified* to show, for example, how average levels of job satisfaction vary by educational achievement. This same finding could also be presented in the form of a graph. A great variety of statistical procedures is available to the quantitative researcher. It is important to learn which procedures are appropriate for a given research problem.

But there are qualitative dimensions in quantitative research. In the process of turning observations into numbers there are typically a number of judgment calls, a number of qualitative decisions that must be made. So, whether the researcher wishes to decide how to design a question to find out how much self-esteem someone has or how to classify student programs as gender-traditional (those typically taken by one gender or the other) or what is a woman's magazine, a number of subjective judgments must be made. And, while these may be defined numerically, there is nonetheless a qualitative dimension to the research decision. Brett Silverstein, who designed a study to investigate the role of the mass media in promoting the belief that women must be thin to be attractive, classified a magazine as a woman's magazine if 75% of its readers were women (Silverstein et al., 1986). Virtually all studies claiming to be quantitative have important qualitative dimensions to them.

B. QUALITATIVE RESEARCH

Qualitative research emphasizes verbal descriptions and explanations of human behaviour. Rather than concerning itself primarily with representative samples, qualitative research emphasizes careful and detailed descriptions of social practices in an attempt to understand how the participants experience and explain their own world. The tools for gaining information include participant observation, in-depth interviews, or an in-depth analysis of a single case. At the macro level, the qualitative researcher tends to look at whole institutions, or organizations; at the micro level, the qualitative researcher focuses on individual behaviours. Qualitative research is characteristic of the interpretive approach. It is also used (together with quantitative research) in the critical approach.

i. Types of Questions Asked

The questions asked in qualitative research often concern how social systems operate, how individuals relate to one another, how individuals perceive one another, and how they interpret their own and others' behaviour. Questions like those listed below are typical:

- What is it like to be a prisoner?

- How do pool hustlers get their opponent to play?

- How do nurses handle patients who refuse to follow instructions?

- What is it like to be mentally ill?

ii. Types of Analysis

In qualitative research, findings are typically expressed by quoting interviews or relating experiences the researcher has had in the field. Most final reports have few, if any, tables or graphs. Since much qualitative research is based on a small number of participants, or on an in-depth examination of one group, it is often inappropriate even to attempt to quantify the results.

Various sections of Chapter 6 will elaborate on the procedures that may be used to conduct different types of qualitative studies and will also present an alternative view to that of quantitative researchers on such issues as the meaning of validity and the goals of research.

While there is considerable debate over the relative merits of quantitative and qualitative research strategies, to a large degree the issue is a false one. It is false because both approaches have their legitimate place in social science research. The choice of strategy is influenced by the following factors:

- The nature of the question asked: if the question has to do with the nature of human experience, a small number of observations, or a single case, then quantitative techniques would probably not be used. If the question has to do with patterns of social behaviour or descriptions of whole populations, the approach will be quantitative.

- The predisposition of the researcher: if the researcher has a preference for qualitative research strategies, the researcher will tend to ask questions best answered by using such methods.

Sometimes the author of a research report will use a qualitative reporting style in order to communicate effectively. Qualitative research uses language and presentations familiar to all educated members of a society.

Table 1.2 lists some distinctions between qualitative and quantitative approaches. These distinctions are helpful in contrasting assumptions and values that are profoundly different in each research tradition. The table

TABLE 1.2 QUALITATIVE AND QUANTITATIVE RESEARCH CONTRASTED

QUALITATIVE	QUANTITATIVE
• Multiple realities	• Single reality
• Reality is socially constructed	• Reality is objective
• Reality is context interrelated	• Reality is context free
• Holistic	• Reductionistic
• Strong philosophical perspective	• Strong theoretical base
• Reasoning is inductive	• Reasoning is deductive and inductive
• Discovery of meaning is the basis of knowledge	• Cause-and-effect relationships are the bases of knowledge
• Develops theory	• Tests theory
• Theory developed during study	• Theory developed a priori
• Meaning of concepts	• Measurement of variables
• Process oriented	• Outcome oriented
• Control unimportant	• Control important
• Rich descriptions	• Precise measurement of variables
• Basic element of analysis is words	• Basic element of analysis is numbers
• Uniqueness	• Generalization
• Trustworthiness of findings	• Control of error

is not intended to be exhaustive; rather it highlights the key differences for each research orientation. Finally, because both traditions have a role to play in helping us to understand human behaviour, qualitative and quantitative research should be seen as complementary to one another.

2. DESCRIPTIVE VERSUS EXPLANATORY RESEARCH

Descriptive research emphasizes the accurate portrayal of a population. A study that is primarily descriptive has as its major concern the accurate description of some aspect of society. A researcher may wish, for example, to assess the current popularity of federal political parties. With the goal of gauging the general sentiments in a society toward each political party, the researcher tries to describe as precisely as possible what proportion of the population supports each party. Similarly, a census of the population is largely a descriptive project. Here, the attempt is to *count* a variety of attributes of the society, whether the count is of people, racetracks, or automobiles. In a sense, a census is a stock-taking of the objects, people, and resources available within a society. It seeks answers to *what* questions.

Fundamentally, the descriptive study is about *what* and how many of *what*. Since the goal is to describe, survey researchers will frequently draw a sample in order to make estimations about some *population*. As used by the researcher, the term *population* refers to that collection of individuals, communities, or nations about which one wishes to make a general statement. In order to save money and time, the researcher draws from the population a *sample* that will be representative of the population as a whole. While including the whole population would prove to be more accurate (as in a census), the costs may be prohibitive. Public opinion pollsters, market researchers, and census takers typically emphasize descriptive accuracy in their research. All explanatory studies will have descriptive dimensions, and some descriptive studies will have explanatory dimensions.

To explore the differences between female students who select gender-nontraditional programs in university and female students who select traditional programs, a researcher would want to describe the characteristics of the two sets of students. Are rural students more likely to opt for traditional programs, such as education, nursing, or home economics? Are females from higher socioeconomic levels more likely to choose nontraditional programs, such as engineering, business, or chemistry?

By contrast, the primary goal of **explanatory research** is to understand or to explain relationships. Why is it that females who pursue nontraditional occupations are more likely to be from higher socioeconomic backgrounds than those who enrol in traditional programs of study? Here the issue is twofold. First, what is the relationship between background and type of program selected? Second, if there is a relationship, why does it exist? Explanatory studies ask *why* questions.

3. PURE VERSUS APPLIED RESEARCH

Social scientists who focus on understanding social relationships are engaging in **pure research**; those who are interested in figuring out how to bring about specific changes in society are engaging in **applied research**.

A. PURE RESEARCH

The social scientist engaged in pure research tries to understand the patterns of social behaviour. However, it is usually pos-sible to devise many different explanations to account for any particular behaviour. A challenge of social science is to determine which, if any, of the possible explanations accounts for any given pattern. Patterns may be understood through a variety of qualitative and quantitative techniques. Whatever the approach, the ultimate goal is to offer better descriptions and better explanations of human behaviour.

Frequently the social scientist is confronted with "interesting" findings that cry out for an explanation. Suppose, for example, that a project measures high school students' socioeconomic statuses (SES) and their aspirations for higher education. And suppose that, during data analysis, a relatively strong relationship emerges indicating that the higher an individual's socioeconomic origin, the greater the likelihood that the individual will aspire to post-secondary education. At this stage, the researcher may wonder what explains the pattern that has emerged. Possibilities such as the following might come to mind:

- Peers of high SES students have high aspirations themselves and the students influence one another in planning to attend post-secondary institutions.

- Parents of high SES students have greater expectations concerning the educational achievements of their children.

- High SES students know that they have the financial backing to attend a post-secondary institution and therefore plan on it.

- Teachers encourage high SES students more because they have higher expectations of them.

- High SES students have been more exposed to high occupational achievers and are more likely to model themselves on such individuals.

We can identify three important goals of pure research:

- Pure research aims to test existing theories of social behaviour.

- It attempts to explain observed patterns of behaviour.

- It tries to document our knowledge of the emergence, modification, and persistence of patterned human behaviour.

B. APPLIED RESEARCH

Simply stated, what distinguishes the two types of researchers is that the pure researcher values knowledge for its own sake, whereas the applied researcher wishes to have an impact on some specific social behaviour. The applied researcher may want to maintain the enrolment in a music school, or eliminate deviance, or assess the popularity of a government, or change people's attitudes toward wearing seat belts, or persuade people to buy a new toothpaste.

On the one hand, pure researchers might be viewed as striving to be value free by not promoting a particular theory or view of the world. On the other hand, applied researchers might be viewed as striving to achieve particular social changes (which they may or may not believe in themselves). In many instances, the applied researcher rents out his or her skills. The service may be to monitor public responses to a new government policy or to measure the impact of an advertising campaign to discourage smoking. In such cases, the researcher wishes to further the goals of an employer. The applied researcher focuses on those variables that can be changed by intervention so as to achieve the desired goals.

4. UNITS OF ANALYSIS: INDIVIDUALS AND AGGREGATIONS

Social scientists study nations, communities, groups, institutions, and individuals. Moreover, an institution such as the family may be studied either across cultures or within a culture. In doing research it is difficult to deal simultaneously with more than one level of analysis. At the outset of a project we should ask ourselves: "Am I studying individuals or aggregations?"

A. THE INDIVIDUAL AS THE UNIT OF ANALYSIS

If we are studying individuals, then we should pose questions that concern individual properties only. All the data collected should measure variations between individuals on a variety of subjects. And any analyses of the data will have individuals as the basic unit. Most surveys and experiments use the individual as the **unit of analysis**, although it is possible to have individuals report on data for other levels of analysis such as communities, companies, or groups. Furthermore, individuals may be counted and used to produce a measure for some aggregation: the proportion of university-educated people in a community would be an example of such a variable.

B. AN AGGREGATION AS THE UNIT OF ANALYSIS

Alternatively, if we are studying **aggregations**, then we should pose questions that concern properties of groups, institutions, communities, or nations. Individual characteristics, such as income, educational level, or ethnic background, will have to be expressed as averages or proportions. If we begin a study using an individual level of analysis, then it is difficult, without careful advance planning, to switch to a different level, such as the community level. With computers it is easy enough to compute average scores. But it is unlikely that we will have sufficient cases to produce meaningful averages for all of the communities. (If you studied 300 people from 25 different communities, then to move from the individual to the community level you would have but 12 people from each community on which to base the average for the community.)

It is important, therefore, when we start designing a study to be absolutely clear about the level of analysis that we plan to use. If we want to use different levels in the same study, then we should think through very carefully how the analysis is to be done in order to ensure that we will

have a sufficient number of cases for the analysis. Table 1.3 summarizes the relation between the unit of analysis used and some of the tendencies related to the use of different levels.

In later chapters we will explore four research designs in more detail: experiments (Chapter 3), surveys (Chapter 4), nonreactive studies (Chapter 5), qualitative studies (Chapter 6), and critical approaches to research (Chapter 7). Each design is legitimate in its own way. The selection of a design should be guided by what is most appropriate for the problem under investigation. No single design covers all problems. Each approach has its unique combination of strengths and weaknesses. We should choose the approach that is feasible and that optimizes our ability to solve the particular research problem under consideration.

TABLE 1.3 UNITS OF ANALYSIS AND RELATED TENDENCIES

| | UNIT OF ANALYSIS | | | |
| | INDIVIDUAL | | AGGREGATION | |
DIMENSION	ONE	SEVERAL/MANY	ONE	SEVERAL/MANY
Tendency in orientation	Qualitative	Quantitative	Qualitative	Quantitative
Types of study	Case study	Survey Experiment Quasi-experiment Participant observation Nonreactive	Case study Participant observation Survey Nonreactive	Comparative Inter-nation Quasi-experiment Survey Nonreactive
Disciplines	Psychiatry Sociology–ethno-methodology Education	Psychology Sociology Criminology Political science Psychiatry Archaeology	Anthropology Sociology Criminology Political science History Archaeology Education	Anthropology Sociology Criminology Political science Education
Illustration	Explaining an individual suicide	Variations in suicide by gender, age	Explaining suicides in one community	Comparing suicide rates across countries/communities

C. TYPES OF VARIABLES

In designing, implementing, and evaluating studies, researchers distinguish various types of variables.

1. DEPENDENT VARIABLES

A **dependent variable** is a variable thought to be influenced by other variables. It is the "effect" in a cause–effect relationship. As its name suggests, it is "dependent" for its variation on other variables. Recall our example of investigating the factors that influence female students to choose gender-traditional programs rather than nontraditional programs. Here, "program choice" would be treated as the dependent variable. However, this would not preclude exploring the possibility that, in turn, variations in program choice have an impact on a variable such as income. In such a case, income would be treated as the dependent variable.

2. INDEPENDENT VARIABLES

An **independent variable** is the "cause" in a cause–effect relationship. It is a variable that has been selected as a possible influence on variations in a dependent variable. Typically, one finds a number of independent variables in a study. Once again, it is how the variable is treated—how it is thought of—that determines whether it is an independent or a dependent variable. The nature of the variable itself does not determine whether it is dependent or independent—it is how the researcher thinks about and uses the variable that counts.

In our example of university program choices by female students, many different factors might be treated as independent variables. We might well include such factors as rural/urban home community, subject preference and performance in high school, types of games and activities preferred in childhood, parental socioeconomic status, measures of mothers' participation in the labour force, and the presence of role models who have opted for nontraditional female occupations.

In experimental designs independent variables are referred to as *treatment variables*. A treatment is a variable whose effect on some dependent variable is being assessed in an experiment. There may be several treatments used simultaneously with their individual and joint effects being assessed.

In general, we should be careful to ensure that the variables we treat as independent are indeed different variables. For instance, if we measured the length of rooms in a building in inches and then repeated the measurements but this time using centimetres, our two sets of measures would lack independence. In short, they would simply represent different measures of the same variable. The researcher must be careful not to fall into the trap of thinking that there is a powerful causal connection between two variables when the measures lack independence and thus represent two different measures of the same thing.

3. CONTROL VARIABLES

A **control variable** is a variable that is taken into account in exploring the relation between an independent variable and a dependent variable. There are three basic types of control variables: the intervening variable, the conditional variable, and the source of spuriousness (or confounding) variable.

A. INTERVENING VARIABLE

An **intervening variable** *(I)* is a variable that links an independent variable (X) to a dependent one (Y). An intervening variable represents an explanation of how the independent variable influences the dependent variable. It may be diagrammed as:

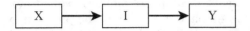

Let us return to our example of investigating the relation between socioeconomic status and preference for a nontraditional program. A possible explanation of how socioeconomic status (SES) influences the type of program preferred would be that high SES students are more likely to be exposed to people in nontraditional occupations. In other words, exposure to people in nontraditional occupations "intervenes" to account for the program preferred.

B. CONDITIONAL VARIABLE

A **conditional variable** *(C)* is a variable that accounts for a change in the relationship between an independent variable (X) and a dependent variable (Y) when the general conditions change. Suppose we are investigating the relationship between socioeconomic status and attitudes toward capital punishment: we might want to find out whether that relationship is fundamentally altered (or is entirely different) for each gender. Accordingly, we might test males and females separately for a relationship between SES and attitudes. Here, gender would be the conditional variable, as in:

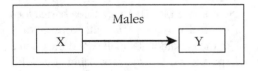

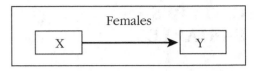

C. SOURCE OF SPURIOUSNESS VARIABLE

A **source of spuriousness variable** *(S/S)* is a variable that is viewed as a possible influence on both the independent (X) and the dependent variable (Y), in such a way that it accounts for the relationship between them. In other words, the relationship between X and Y is "spurious" because it is produced by the influence of S/S on each.

If we were exploring the relation between socioeconomic background and choice of a nontraditional program by female students, we might consider the possibility that rural/urban background is a source of spuriousness. Here the idea is that it may be the type of community that the student comes from that influences the socioeconomic achievement of her parents as well as influencing her own program preferences at university. The relation between socioeconomic status and program choice might therefore be spurious. As in:

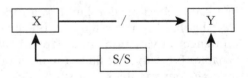

In experimental research a source of spuriousness variable is typically referred to as a confounding variable. A **confounding variable** is one that may be systematically influencing the outcome of an experiment and that, once recognized, is treated in the design and controlled.

D. KEY POINTS

The *positivist approach* is modelled on the physical sciences, treats social behaviour as an object, sees behaviour as a result of forces acting on the individual or society, tries to describe and explain the patterns that characterize social behaviour, and tries to avoid allowing one's values to interfere with one's observations. Knowledge is to be based on testing one's ideas systematically by measuring variables and noting how they are related to one another. Positivists use the ability to predict accurately as a major criterion for judging the soundness of a theory. The research designs most associated with positivism include the use of experimental, survey, and secondary data.

Interpretive approaches ask questions about how people understand their everyday lives, how they define and react to situations. The job of the researcher is to develop an empathetic understanding of behaviour. The research designs most closely associated with an interpretive approach include participant observation studies, in-depth interviews, and the careful analysis of individual cases.

The *critical approach* views conflict as a basic characteristic of the human condition; groups attempt to exploit others for their own advantage. The practical job of critical work is to document social problems and use the knowledge gained in doing so to empower people so that they can become agents of social change. Researchers in this tradition take advocacy positions, particularly with reference to assisting the weak and the powerless in society. The research techniques most associated with the critical approach would include comparative studies, historical analyses, secondary data analyses, and advocacy research.

Quantitative research seeks to quantify, or reflect with numbers, observations about human behaviour. Tables and graphs are incorporated in reports.

Qualitative research uses concepts and classifications in an attempt to interpret human behaviour in a way that rings true to both the analyst and the people whose behaviour is being described. Interview quotations and descriptions of events experienced during observations form key elements of reports written in this tradition.

Descriptive research is about what and how many of what; in polls and in descriptive survey research an emphasis is placed on estimating the extent to which a sample may be taken to represent the population from which the sample was selected.

Explanatory research seeks to provide answers to *why* questions.

Pure researchers attempt to understand human behaviour; the knowledge gained is viewed as important in its own right.

Applied researchers are interested in solving some social problem, in evaluating the extent to which some program is, or is not, effective in bringing about a desired change, or in using social science knowledge to further some goal set by others.

A *unit of analysis* is the element being studied in a research project. Some studies examine individuals, while others study aggregations such as families, communities, or societies. Measures taken reflect qualities of the unit being studied. Beginning researchers, when devising measures, should be careful to ensure that their measures reflect only properties of the unit of analysis they are studying.

A *dependent variable* is the effect in a cause–effect relation; it is the result, the variable one is trying to predict.

An *independent variable* is the cause in a cause–effect relation; it is one of the predictor variables.

A *control variable* is one taken into account in examining the relation between a given independent and dependent variable. There are three basic types of control variables:

1. A *source of spuriousness* variable is one that may be influencing both the dependent and the independent variables, thus rendering any association between them false, only existing because of the common link to the source of spuriousness variable; in experimental research such variables are referred to as *confounding variables*.

2. An *intervening* variable links the independent to the dependent variable.

3. A *conditional* variable is one taken into account to see if the basic relation between the dependent and independent variable is altered under different values of the conditional variable.

E. KEY TERMS

Aggregation

Applied research

Conditional variable

Confounding variable

Control variable

Critical approach

Dependent variable

Descriptive research

Explanatory research

Independent variable

Interpretive approach

Intervening variable

Positivist approach

Pure research

Quantitative research

Qualitative research

Source of spuriousness variable

Unit of analysis

Verstehen

EXPLAINING

A. INTRODUCTION

Humans generalize. We are the generalizing species. In our efforts to understand one another and to anticipate one another's behaviour, we learn rules, or we make them up, and apply them to our everyday activities. All cultures have phrases that attempt to offer general explanations of human behaviour. In English, these are variously referred to as adages, saws, old wives' tales, epigrams, maxims, proverbs, sayings, aphorisms, clichés, folk wisdom, platitudes, and truisms. All of them attempt to provide neat, commonly understood explanations of behaviour.

We could probably not survive well without anticipating the behaviour of others. Smooth social functioning requires us to be able to anticipate the activity of others to some degree. We therefore rely on our everyday generalizations to guide much of our interaction. For example, in greeting your good friend, Sam, you anticipate that you will get an upbeat, positive response rather than a punch in the nose. You have generalized from your previous experiences with him when you conclude that you will be greeted warmly.

But there are problems with nonscientific explanations. Indeed, numerous pairs of contradictory aphorisms can be found: the first explains one result, and a parallel one the opposite result. No matter what happens, a ready explanation is available. This poses a difficulty for the social scientist: many of the conclusions arrived at, after painstaking research, can be dismissed as *obvious*. They seem obvious because there is some saying, some maxim in our folk culture that anticipates the result. All too often, however, folk wisdom accounts for all outcomes. To illustrate the problem, the anecdote in Box 2.1 may help.

Folk wisdom is an important source of ideas for the social researcher. But one must always be careful to distinguish between ideas that have been scientifically tested and those that have not been tested. The social scientist might well ask, "Under what conditions does 'Out of sight, out of mind' apply, and under what conditions are we more likely to feel that 'Absence makes the heart grow fonder'?" The most compelling

---

BOX 2.1 CHARLIE MCMULLIN AND AUNT HAZEL

Charlie McMullin was in love. He had been dating Sally for seven months when she decided to take a trip to Europe. After two weeks, and four letters home to Charlie, the letters stopped. Charlie was in agony. It was then that his dear Aunt Hazel explained the whole thing by saying, "Well, that just proves once again, 'Out of sight, out of mind.'" But after six weeks Sally wrote, full of apologies, and suggesting that they get married on her return. Good old Aunt Hazel understood that too. "Oh," she exclaimed, "that's easy, 'Absence makes the heart grow fonder'!" For a while Charlie thought that his aunt was a first-rate observer of the human scene until he realized that she had an answer for all outcomes.

predictions that the social scientist can make will be those running counter to "common sense." If you are able to make a prediction that goes startlingly against common understandings, and it turns out to be true, you will have a powerfully convincing study. But it is sometimes difficult to find an outcome not covered by some cultural maxim. Box 2.2 lists a few contradictory proverbs. Can you think of other conflicting ones?

Social scientists are interested in understanding social behaviour. In their quest for understanding, they have devoted energy to describing behaviour and to developing and testing general explanations that try to account for the patterns of human behaviour. Perhaps because of its devilish complexity—or perhaps because of the tough standards we set for an adequate explanation—what we miss are well-confirmed, and widely accepted, explanations for behaviour. This chapter explores different types of social science explanations—and insufficient explanations—for human behaviour. Attention will be paid to how quantitative social scientists understand the role of theory in understanding human behaviour. They place an emphasis on theory-testing. This chapter also explores some simple theory-testing techniques that may be applied by the beginning researcher in attempting to understand the elusive

---

BOX 2.2   A FEW CONTRADICTORY SAYINGS

Absence makes the heart grow fonder./
Out of sight, out of mind.

Beauty is as good as ready money./
Beauty buys no beef.

Idleness is the mother of poverty./
It is well to lie fallow for a while.

A farthing saved is twice earned./
Frugality is misery in disguise.

Birds of a feather flock together./
Opposites attract.

Judge not a book by its cover./
Fine feathers make fine birds.

Look before you leap./
He who hesitates is lost.

Two heads are better than one./
If you want something done right, do it yourself.

Nothing ventured, nothing gained./
Better safe than sorry.

Many hands make light work./
Too many cooks spoil the broth.

You can't teach an old dog new tricks./
It's never too late to learn.

Never sweat the small stuff./
God is in the details.

Haste makes waste./
A stitch in time saves nine.

He will shoot higher who shoots at the sun than he who aims at a tree./
Hew not too high lest the chips fall in thine eye.

Better to have loved and lost than never to have loved at all./
Better safe than sorry.

SOURCE: Some of these sayings from Henry Davidoff (1953). *A World Treasury of Proverbs*. London: Cassell & Company.

patterns that characterize the social world. The approach qualitative researchers give to theory development (e.g., grounded theory) is addressed in Chapter 6.

B. THE EXPLANATORY ROLE OF THEORY

What is the function of theory in the social sciences—what is theory supposed to do? The major function of **theory** for social scientists is to *explain* the behaviour of humans, or human institutions. A relationship may be said to be explained once someone has offered a satisfactory explanation for it—offered a satisfactory answer to a *why* question. But what is satisfactory? For some, almost any answer might satisfy. For others, tough rules of **evidence** will have to be followed in order for the explanation to be considered adequate. The social scientist is more likely than the layperson to insist on considerable evidence before accepting an explanation. A simple opinion will not do. "What is your evidence?" is a question that will be asked. Skepticism and curiosity distinguish the scientist from the nonscientist.

Theory is an integral part of research for all social scientists, although the approach to theory varies depending upon the researcher's methodological orientation. For quantitative social scientists, theories guide the development of research hypotheses. The hypotheses are then tested using empirical data. When the data have been analyzed, the researcher then interprets the findings of the study in light of the theory that guided the development of the research hypothesis. Box 2.3 presents the levels in a quantitative research project. This process is called operationalization. It is discussed in greater detail in Chapter 13.

The function of theory is to explain patterns in the world. Theories may be more or

---

BOX 2.3   LEVELS IN QUANTITATIVE RESEARCH

Quantitative research can be conceived of as having three levels: the theoretical, the conceptual, and the operational.

Theoretical Level

The **theoretical level** in a project is the most abstract, general conceptualization of the research problem. Theories propose explanations of phenomena—how things work, how parts are interconnected, and how things influence each other. In the social sciences, theories provide explanations to account for social patterns or for relationships. The more general the theory the greater the number of predictions that can be derived from it. Indeed, the number of predictions that can be derived from a theory is also a measure of the theory's power. Theories may be viewed as lying on a continuum of explicitness. At one end of this continuum, we would place a theory in which there are detailed statements of the relations between the concepts of the theory and a specification of its underlying assumptions (i.e., *formal theories*); at the other end, we would place those theories that offer an explanation of some particular relation (i.e., *partial theories*).

Social scientists use theories to predict behaviour. An important role of the methodologist is to try to refine them, to see if they hold true under all conditions. It is through efforts to *disconfirm* theories that we extend our general knowledge of human behaviour. That is, the hypothesis can be shown to be true or false. One way to test a theory is to derive a prediction (or hypothesis) from it and then test that hypothesis. This chapter will discuss the nature of theories and ways of testing them in greater detail.

Conceptual Level

The **conceptual level** defines the variables that are to be used in the research. A **conceptual variable** is an idea that has a dimension that can vary. Conceptual variables can be relatively simple or quite complex. Examples would include gender, weight, intelligence, peer approval, political orientation, or anxiety. Derivations made at the theoretical level can be formed into conceptual hypotheses. A **conceptual hypothesis** is a statement of the relationship between two or more conceptual variables. Ordinarily, a hypothesis will take the form of *the greater X, the greater Y.* For example, "the higher one's socioeconomic status, the higher one's educational aspirations."

The conceptual definitions of variables serve two important purposes. First, they should provide a clear statement of what is meant by the variables. Second, they should help us decide how each variable should be measured. For example, if we define the concept *socioeconomic status* as "differences in access

to scarce resources," we would then try to measure the variable with *indicators* that reflect this definition as precisely as possible. This brings us to the operational level, which we will consider next.

Operational Level

Operationalization refers both to the selection of indicators (measures) to reflect conceptual variables and to the implementation of a research project. If socioeconomic status is defined as "differences in access to scarce resources," any measurement should attempt to reflect this definition. In this case, a measure of annual income might appropriately reflect the conceptual variable, as defined. And, in the study of program choice, the classification of programs into traditional and nontraditional would constitute a measure of the concept. The **operational level** consists of the measurement of variables as well as the collection and analysis of data. In Chapters 13 and 14 we will provide a number of suggestions for the measurement of variables. And in Chapters 8 and 9, and Chapters 16 and 17, we will discuss procedures for analyzing data.

Linkages between Levels

The theoretical, conceptual, and operational levels do not exist in isolation from one another. The three levels of research are connected by important linkages. Testing a theory properly entails documenting explicitly the connections between the theoretical and the conceptual levels and between the conceptual and the operational levels.

Social researchers use two terms, *validity* and *reliability,* to refer to the connection between the conceptual and the operational levels. **Validity** refers to the extent to which a measure reflects a concept, reflecting neither more nor less than what is implied by the definition of the concept. It is not unusual for researchers to use markedly different "indicators" for similar conceptual variables. While one might define socioeconomic status as "differences in access to scarce resources," another might define it as a "hierarchy of respect and prestige."

Measures are valid to the extent that the chosen indicators reflect the concepts as defined.

Reliability refers to the extent to which, on repeated measures, an indicator will yield similar readings. One can think of reliability as the extent to which a measurement will produce similar readings for similar phenomena. A tire gauge that indicates 26 pounds of pressure now, but 29 pounds a moment earlier,

DEDUCTIVE AND INDUCTIVE REASONING IN RESEARCH DESIGN

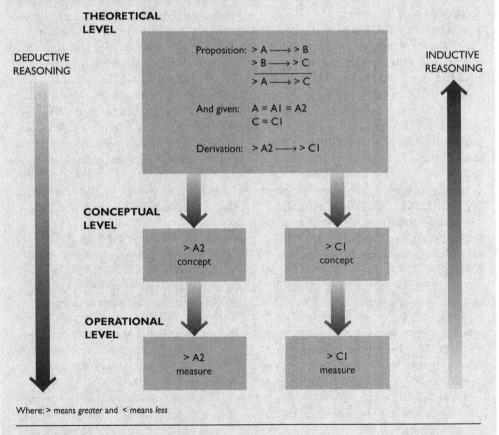

Where: > means *greater* and < means *less*

suggests an unreliable gauge—either that or a bad leak in the tire! In survey research we sometimes repeat a question to test for reliability. Both responses to the question should be the same if the item is generating reliable responses. (The concepts of validity and reliability will be discussed in greater detail in Chapter 13.)

The figure on p. 28 presents the three levels of research. Moving from top to bottom (from the theoretical to the operational), the researcher uses deductive reasoning. Deduction is used to derive testable conceptual hypotheses from theoretical propositions (representing movement from the theoretical level to the conceptual level). And deduction is used to choose the indicators to measure the conceptual variables (representing movement from the conceptual to the operational level). Moving from the bottom to the top of the figure, the researcher employs inductive reasoning. If the results of the data analysis are consistent with the prediction of the conceptual hypothesis, then the researcher has inductive evidence to support the chosen operational methods, the derived conceptual hypothesis, and the theoretical propositions themselves. However, if the results of the data analysis do not accord with the prediction of the conceptual hypothesis, inductive reasoning does *not* enable the researcher to identify the cause of the inconsistency. The problem may lie in the theoretical propositions, the conceptual hypothesis, the operational methods, or even the technique used for selecting the sample, or for analyzing the data.

less explicit. A theory may be highly detailed and explicit, in which case its underlying assumptions will be clearly specified and it will make many specific predictions. On the other hand, a theory may be entirely lacking in detail—it may be a simple explanatory variable. For example, we might include the variable, "variations in socialization patterns," as an explanation of why we get variations in educational aspirations as we move across the SES (socioeconomic status) continuum. What we are proposing by this explanation is that as we move across the SES continuum, we get differences in socialization patterns, which, in turn, account for variations in aspirations. This is a partial theory because it fails to specify the underlying assumptions it makes about human behaviour; it does not tell us anything about how the explanatory variable (variations in socialization patterns) is connected to any other variables. A good deal of theorizing in the social sciences makes use of partial theories. The job of theory is to explain: to offer satisfactory, testable explanations for relationships. A testable explanation is one that can be disconfirmed—one that could turn out to be true or false.

Given the broad range of what may be considered a theoretical explanation, it is instructive to explore the properties of both formal and partial theoretical constructs.

C. FORMAL THEORY

What are the components of formal, explicit theory? According to George Homans

(1964), a **formal theory** consists of three key elements. Firstly, there is a set of concepts or a conceptual scheme. The concepts may be descriptive, serving to identify what the theory is about. In the case of Durkheim's theory of suicide (introduced in Chapter 1), the terms *individualism, social integration, suicide,* and *Protestantism* are some of the key concepts. Other concepts are operatives or properties of nature, and can be expressed as social variables, such as: suicide *rate, degree* of individualism, *incidence* of Protestantism.

A theory consists, secondly, of a set of propositions, each stating a relationship (such as "inversely related to") between some of the concepts. Furthermore, the set of propositions must be interrelated so that one can derive new propositions by combining them deductively. When new propositions are derived they are said to be explained by the previous ones.

Thirdly, Homans argues, some of the propositions must be contingent—that is, they must be amenable to some form of empirical test. A theory, Homans argues, cannot be made up entirely of noncontingent propositions: some, but not necessarily all, must be testable. (For example, is the suicide rate in Spain relatively low?)

The power of a theory refers to the extent and number of propositions that may be derived from it; that is, the greater the number of predictive statements that can be derived from a theory, the more powerful the theory. Powerful theories are general theories. In the case of Durkheim's analysis of suicide, the theoretical formulation is not as general (and hence not as powerful) as it might be. By utilizing the highly specific variable, suicide, he has limited the generalizability of the theory. Had Durkheim used the term "deviance" then the theory would have been more powerful

because one could not only have derived the suicide hypotheses but could also have derived all kinds of other predictions that would be worth testing.

Similar definitions of formal theory are to be found in the work of Braithwaite, Zetterberg, and Gibbs. Braithwaite defines theory as a "deductive system in which observable consequences logically follow from the conjunction of observed facts with the set of fundamental hypotheses of the system" (1960, p. 22). Or, from Zetterberg, theory is defined as a set of "systematically organized, law-like propositions about society that can be supported by evidence" (1965, p. 22). Gibbs defines theory as "a set of logically interrelated statements in the form of empirical assertions about properties of infinite classes of events or things" (1972, p. 5).

In summary, then, one does not have formal, explicit theory "until one has properties, and propositions stating the relations between them, and the propositions form a deductive system—not until one has all three does one have a theory" (Homans, 1964, p. 812). While Homans' minimum requirements for theory are stringent, they nonetheless provide a useful guideline. The essence of formal theories is the precision and explicitness with which they are stated. Assumptions are specified, as are statements of relationship.

However, as any satisfactory answer to a *why* question constitutes an explanation, there may be some advantage to viewing theory as a continuum, ranging from formal theory (such as that defined above by Homans, Braithwaite, Zetterberg, or Gibbs) through to partial theories, such as single intervening variable explanations. (For example: "variations in socialization patterns explain the connection between SES and educational aspirations.") And while these may not meet the requirements of the more formal constructions, they can sometimes be linked to existing formal theory or lead to the development of new ones.

D. PARTIAL THEORY

A **partial theory** attempts to explain an assumed or known relationship by specifying a testable causal model. A good deal of the theoretical research in the social sciences employs partial theories. Their widespread use is perhaps explained by the notion that many researchers begin with a fascination for a relationship that has shown up in the literature. Researchers then wish to understand the pattern that the relationship seems to represent. Thus, partial theories are often grounded in the findings of research and a further elaboration of the findings is sought by the researcher. An earlier illustration (in Chapter 1) concerned the connection between socioeconomic status and educational aspirations; a number of possible explanations were suggested that might account for the relationship. Each of these explanations represents possible answers to the *why* question about the connection between the two. As such, each is a theory. However, such theoretical formulations remain at an implicit level. As worded, they fail to specify what assumptions are being made or articulate the underlying model of human behaviour implicit in the explanation. To illustrate, let us explore two of the explanations.

1. That the reason high SES students are more likely to aspire to higher educational levels is to fulfill their parents' expectations of them.

2. That high SES students have been more exposed to high achievers and are more likely, therefore, to model themselves after such individuals.

A. FULFILLING PARENTAL EXPECTATIONS

This explanation contains two critical elements:

1. High and low SES parents have different educational expectations of their children; and

2. Students try to fulfill the expectations of their parents.

Theoretically, the idea is that people are influenced, or shaped, by the expectations of others. This type of explanation is most consistent with reinforcement theory in psychology (Thibaut and Kelley, 1959) or exchange theory in sociology (Homans, 1961). In this particular case, the child is seen as a rather passive object being shaped or moulded by the expectations of parents and reward systems controlled by parents. Students become what they are rewarded to become.

B. DIFFERENTIAL EXPOSURE TO ROLE MODELS

The second explanation involves at least three assumptions:

1. That there will be differences, correlated with students' SES levels, in the amount of exposure to people in elite occupations;

2. That students recognize the connection between educational and occupational achievement; and

3. That students recognize and desire the rewards that come to people who achieve higher occupational levels.

The implicit model of behaviour here is that individuals aspire to higher educational levels as a vehicle for moving into occupations similar to those of people whose lifestyles they admire. This view of human behaviour suggests that the individual is motivated more by the desire to achieve certain rewards than by the expectations of others. In this case, education is the means used to attain these goals. Role models are copied. This view is most compatible with the ideas expressed by symbolic interactionists (Blumer, 1951) and with the concept of vicarious reinforcement (seeing others being rewarded) in psychology.

Other explanations for the connection between SES and educational aspirations could be developed and connected to existing theoretical perspectives. Frequently it is possible for the researcher to generate theoretical connections by carefully exploring the underlying theory of human behaviour that is being proposed in the research. In short, it is possible to make a backward connection to theory—starting with a partial theory and moving backward to existing formal theories in the discipline. Carefully thought out, such research can contribute to a general understanding of human behaviour.

But what is the use of theory? What do we gain by connecting research to new or existing theoretical perspectives? The answer has to do with power. Research that limits itself to the particular, to the unique, will not contribute to our general understanding of the human condition. General explanations allow research to have implications for our overall understanding of behaviour, as well as for increasing our knowledge of the particular variables involved in a project.

E. THEORY TESTING

As one might expect, there are many examples of theories and partial theories within the social sciences. There is considerable debate in the social sciences as to the proper role of theory and of methods. Most seem to agree that they are best viewed as partners in our attempts to extend our understanding of human behaviour. In that way both theory and methods should be regarded as tools. A theory may be thought of as a cluster of tentative ideas put forward to explain something; research methods are the means we use to test the adequacy of these ideas. Refinements in our theories are neither more nor less important than our refinements in techniques used to test theories. They are equal partners in the knowledge enterprise.

Hypothesis testing is a part of theory testing but, by itself, does not necessarily constitute a test of theory. The fundamental issue in theoretical research is to demonstrate the linkage between a set of theoretical propositions and the conceptual hypothesis that has been selected for examination. Only to the extent that this connection has been articulated successfully can we claim our research has a bearing on theory. This next section will consider methods of testing partial theories, followed by those used to test formal theories.

1. TESTING PARTIAL THEORIES

Previously the argument was made that the testing of alternative explanations is a primitive form of theory testing. This is the case because *theory* and *explanation* do the same thing—provide an answer to some *why* question. The reason we identify the testing of alternative explanations as a primitive form of theory testing is that such formulations typically fail to identify fully the linkages to the model of human behaviour that is being used.

The first thing we need in order to test a partial theory is a relationship that, we feel, needs to be understood. Then we propose a series of alternative explanations for the relationship. After that, all we have to do is to measure the appropriate variables and do the analysis.

For example, if we were to attempt to test an explanation of the connection between the age of initiation into sex and socioeconomic background, we might wish to test:

- whether variations in socialization patterns accounted for conservative attitudes; or

- whether any such connection is simply spurious and conservative attitudes are due to differences in the rural versus urban background of the respondents.

Appropriate research would allow us to evaluate the adequacy of each of the two explanations. The idea here is that size of community (rural versus urban) may be influencing both the SES achievement levels of the parents and the more conservative values found in the rural as opposed to the urban community. Hence, it may be type of community and not SES level that is the key factor in the age of initiation into sex. Note however that, as stated, the first explanation is not well documented. It uses a socialization of values explanation (but connected to what general theory of human behaviour?). Nevertheless, since both explanations are answers to a *why* question, each may be viewed as constituting a theory of human behaviour (albeit an implicit theory).

The advantage of the more formal constructions of social science theory is that we are forced to make explicit our core assumptions about human behaviour. Without such explicitness it is difficult to construct truly general, and therefore powerful, theories of human behaviour. When we seek to explain particular relationships with highly particularized explanations, we do not advance the general state of knowledge much. Hence, more formal approaches to theory construction are to be encouraged. Nonetheless, especially for the beginning researcher, important contributions to the discipline may be made by testing alternative explanations for relationships.

The basic requirements for the testing of alternative explanations are that:

- One has a relationship between two variables which one suspects will be strong (either positive or negative);

- One has a series of alternative explanations for the relationship;

- It is possible to get measures for the appropriate variables; and

- After data are collected suitable procedures are used for the analysis of the data so that an evaluation can be made of the adequacy of the competing explanations.

Box 2.4 on p. 34 illustrates a causal model used by Julian Tanner and Harvey Krahn (1991) in their study of the relationship between deviance and part-time work among high school seniors. Note the arrangement of the variables and how they are linked ultimately to the dependent variable, self-reported illegal activity. Models such as the Tanner/Krahn one are known as *path analysis models*. The arrows and lines represent the causal connections between the variables in the model. (Such models are analyzed using techniques in the correlation/regression family of statistical techniques; a preliminary discussion of these techniques will be introduced later in the text.)

BOX 2.4   SOCIAL RESEARCHERS AT WORK

Julian Tanner and Harvey Krahn: A Path Model of the Determinants of Self-Reported Illegal Activity among High-School Seniors

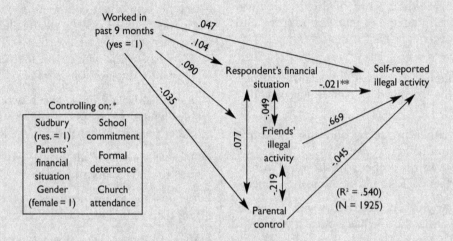

* The six control variables were included in the calculation of each of the four multiple regression equations, although the coefficients for these effects are not displayed. Equations for each of the intervening variables (respondent's financial situation; friends' illegal activity; parental control) did not include the other two intervening variables, because no particular causal order was specified. The bidirectional arrows linking these three intervening variables represent zero-order correlations.

** Path coefficient is not statistically significant (p >.01).

Source: Julian Tanner and Harvey Krahn (1991). "Part-Time Work and Deviance Among High School Seniors." *Canadian Journal of Sociology*, 16(3), 296.

2. TESTING FORMAL THEORIES

Formal theories involve a number of formally stated, interconnected propositions, contain clearly defined variables, and indicate the nature (direct or inverse) and the direction (what is causing what) of the relationships among the variables. The propositions normally take the form of the greater A, the greater B. Not all the concepts in the propositions need to be directly measurable. However, at some point, a connection to measurable variables must be made. It is

BOX 2.5 SOCIAL RESEARCHERS AT WORK

Peter Blau: Social Cohesion

The following five statements are contained in Chapter 2 of his work:

(1) The greater the group cohesion (a), the greater the consensus on normative standards (b).

(2) The greater the group cohesion (a), the greater the effective enforcement of these shared norms (c).

(3) The greater the cohesion (a), the greater the significance of the informal sanctions of the group (d).

(4) The more integrative the bonds of social cohesion (a), the stronger the group in the pursuit of common goals (e).

(5) The greater the cohesion (a), the fewer the proportion of deviants from group norms (f). (Note that "f" is negative.)

Note that the wordings of the "a" variable vary somewhat from proposition to proposition. In doing a propositional inventory of any theoretical work, the student has to decide whether variations of this sort are intended to convey a different meaning, or whether the variations are simply for stylistic considerations.

Source: Adapted from Peter Blau (1964). *Exchange and Power in Social Life*. New York: John Wiley & Sons, Inc.

this link, this connection, that must be specified in order for one's research to have bearing on a theoretical formulation. We will examine two methods used to demonstrate such connections. These are: (a) axiomatic derivations and (b) a replacement of terms.

A. AXIOMATIC DERIVATIONS

Doing **axiomatic derivations** refers to a method of logically deriving new statements of relationship from a given set of assumptions and propositions. Axiomatic derivations are illustrated in Box 2.5 using five statements from Peter Blau (1964).

Let us extend Blau's propositions identified in Box 2.5 using axiomatic derivations.

Suppose that the relationship between "a" and "f" and between "a" and "d" are reversible. This means that we are going to assume that there is a mutual causal link such that "a" influences "f" but also that "f" influences "a." This kind of relationship can be represented as:

Causally, the argument is that the greater a group's cohesion (a), the fewer members will deviate from the group's norms (f). The second argument is that the reverse is also assumed to be true: namely, that having fewer deviants in a group (f) will lead to a strengthening of group cohesion.

Since the original propositions indicated a number of variables to which cohesion is related, we can now suggest some new derived propositions which should be true if the original propositions and a reversibility assumption are correct. They are as follows:

(*Derivation 1*) The smaller the proportion of deviants from group norms (f), the greater the consensus on normative standards (b):

<f ⟶ >b

(*Derivation 2*) The smaller the proportion of deviants from group norms (f), the greater the effective enforcement of shared norms (c):

<f ⟶ >c

(*Derivation 3*) The smaller the proportion of deviants from group norms (f), the greater the significance of the informal sanctions of the group (d):

<f ⟶ >d

(*Derivation 4*) The smaller the proportion of deviants from group norms (f), the stronger the group in the pursuit of common goals (e).

<f ⟶ >e

How are these derivations made? As we have assumed that the "a" to "f" relation is reversible, we are able to argue that "f" leads to "a." And, as we were given the "a" to "b" relation in the original proposition, we can then conclude that "f" leads to "a" and this leads to "b." This may be represented as:

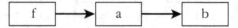

The remaining derivations are made in a similar fashion. In each case, the relationship can be simplified by leaving out the linking, or intervening, variable. Any

time one has a situation such as the following, derivations may be made:

If, > X ⟶ > Y

and, > Y ⟶ > Z

therefore, > X ⟶ > Y ⟶ > Z

or simply, > X ⟶ > Z

The new derived propositions should be true if the assumptions, derivations, and original theoretical propositions are accurate. Derivations are made to locate testable hypotheses, which then constitute a test of the theory. The reason one makes such derivations is to provide many different tests. The reason one wants to do different tests is that ideally one wishes to identify a theoretically predicted relationship, but one that is not obvious.

Box 2.6 on p. 37 identifies the major theoretical propositions, theorems, and a few of the derived hypotheses used by Gibbs and Martin (1964) in their comprehensive study of suicide. The researchers made a total of 676 predictions, of which 58% were correct (1964, p. 197). And of 175 correlation coefficients examined, 91.4% were in the predicted direction, thus lending considerable weight to their argument concerning the impact that status integration has on suicide rates (1964, p. 198). Their study is a brilliant extension of Durkheim's (1951 [1897]) original work.

Why would one want a counterintuitive relationship? Here the answer is psychological rather than scientific. If an unexpected relationship is predicted, and if, indeed, the results of the study confirm it, the evidence is much more convincing. On the other hand, if the predicted relationship is commonsensical, even if it is confirmed, the critic will claim that the results show only what everyone already knew and certainly do not demonstrate any theory. The

BOX 2.6 SOCIAL RESEARCHERS AT WORK

Jack P. Gibbs and W.T. Martin: Status Integration and Suicide: A Sociological Study

The following excerpts illustrate the axiomatic nature of the work done by Gibbs and Martin. In their work hundreds of predictions were made and then tested.

The set of postulates that links status integration to variability in suicide rates is reviewed below.

- *Postulate 1* The suicide rate of a population varies inversely with the stability and durability of social relationships within that population.

- *Postulate 2* The stability and durability of social relationships within a population vary directly with the extent to which individuals in that population conform to the patterned and socially sanctioned demands and expectations placed upon them by others.

- *Postulate 3* The extent to which individuals in a population conform to patterned and socially sanctioned demands and expectations placed upon them by others varies inversely with the extent to which individuals in that population are confronted with role conflicts.

- *Postulate 4* The extent to which individuals in a population are confronted with role conflicts varies directly with the extent to which individuals occupy incompatible statuses in that population.

- *Postulate 5* The extent to which individuals occupy incompatible statuses in a population varies inversely with the degree of status integration in that population.

From the above postulates there follows the major theorem: the suicide rate of a population varies inversely with the degree of status integration in that population. This theorem is central to the present study...examples will be given of the type of hypotheses to be tested in line with the theorem...

Suicide rates by age groups vary inversely with measures of the integration of marital status with age.

In the United States, there will be an inverse relationship by age groups between suicide rates and measures of the integration of marital status with age.

There will be a direct relationship by age groups between the ratio of the suicide rate of widowed persons to married persons and the ratio of the measure of integration with age for the status of married to the status of widowed.

Source: Jack P. Gibbs and W.T. Martin (1964). *Status Integration and Suicide: A Sociological Study*. Eugene Oregon: University of Oregon Press. Reprinted with permission from the University of Oregon.

verification of Albert Einstein's simple but counterintuitive prediction that a rapidly moving clock should run more slowly than a clock that is moving slowly provided powerfully convincing evidence for his theory of relativity.

B. REPLACEMENT OF TERMS

Another way of extending the number of predictions is to use a technique that will be called replacement of terms. **Replacement of terms** refers to replacing general theoretical concepts by specific instances of these concepts. For example, if the general concept is deviance, such a concept could be replaced by a specific instance of deviance—perhaps shoplifting, or burglary, or drunk driving. To the extent that one is able to derive new predictions through such replacements, one can provide a virtually unlimited number of testable relationships. One can then select the better ones—choosing those that are counterintuitive and those that permit one to refine and specify conditions under which the theory does, or does not, hold.

Using a combination of axiomatic derivations and replacement of terms provides powerful, yet simple, methods of deriving interesting testable hypotheses. The student would be well advised, however, to test directly the propositions of a theory and, if that is not possible, to restrict axiomatic steps to a minimum in locating testable hypotheses. Since social relations are complex, and given that few relations are extremely powerful, it is problematic to make a large number of axiomatic steps and still have an iron-clad connection to the original set of propositions. Many factors influence variables in our propositions and it therefore becomes problematic to predict even the sign (+ or −) of derived propositions. (See

also: Costner and Leik, 1964; Gibbs, 1972; Blalock, 1969; and Bailey, 1970.)

F. TYPES OF SOCIAL SCIENCE EXPLANATIONS

We can ask whether there are different kinds of social science explanations. Following the lead suggested by Ernest Nagel (1961) and Gwynn Nettler (1970), five types of explanations will be distinguished.

1. DEDUCTIVE EXPLANATIONS

When social scientists use **deductive explanations**, they try to show that the phenomenon to be explained is a logically necessary consequence of the explanatory premises. For example: if A = B, and B = C, then A = C. Emile Durkheim's analysis (1951 [1897]), for example, of why the suicide rate in Spain will be low is based on the following set of interrelated propositions:

(i)   In any social grouping, the suicide rate (SR) varies directly with the degree of individualism (I). $> I \longrightarrow > SR$

(ii) The degree of individualism (I) varies with the incidence of Protestantism (P). (Untested assumption) $> P \longrightarrow > I.$

(iii) Therefore, the suicide rate (SR) varies with the incidence of Protestantism (P). $> P \longrightarrow > SR$ (Derivation)

(iv) The incidence of Protestantism in Spain is low. (Empirical observation)

(v)   Therefore, the suicide rate (SR) in Spain is low. (Empirically testable hypothesis)

In the above illustration, by combining an untested, but stated assumption, (ii above) with a theoretical proposition (i), along with an empirical observation (iv), and a deductive step (iii), we get a testable hypothesis (v). If, indeed, the data prove to be consistent with the prediction, this would constitute one piece of evidence that is not inconsistent with the theory. We could not claim to have proven the theory correct because alternative theories might also make the prediction that suicide rates will be comparatively low in Spain.

For another illustration, which extends Durkheim's analysis, see the propositions used by Gibbs and Martin (1964). A brief excerpt from their work is featured earlier in Box 2.6.

2. PROBABILISTIC EXPLANATIONS

Probabilistic explanation rests on linking a particular case to its general category. If, when asked to explain why Joe MacDonald (a college student) drinks excessively, you respond by saying, "there's a lot of drinking on campus these days," then you have given a probabilistic explanation. Joe drinks a lot because he is a member of a category of individuals who tend to drink a lot. The explanation suggests that an individual tends to be like others in the same category.

Another illustration of a probabilistic explanation would be the one offered by the neighbour who, in response to my complaint that "I've been buying 6/49 lottery tickets for years, but I never win the big prize," told me that the chances of winning the jackpot are about 1 in 14 million. In other words, he is telling me that the reason I never win is that the odds are against me.

3. FUNCTIONAL EXPLANATIONS

A **functional explanation** explains the presence of some phenomenon by the role it plays in maintaining some system. For example, if the presence of the family unit in all cultures is explained by its role in producing new members for each society, this would be a functional explanation: the family exists to propagate, in order to maintain the social system.

4. CAUSAL EXPLANATIONS

Here we have an event, or sequence of events, leading to something. In a **causal explanation**, an event is explained by making reference to preceding influencing events. The explanation traces the sequence of steps, each influencing the next, that has led to some event. Causal-sequence thinking dominates the thinking of many researchers. Think of a line of dominos falling in sequence after one has been knocked over and you have the idea of a causal sequence. Make a list of all the factors that you think might influence choosing a nontraditional college program: the list should include all the potential causes of those factors that influence program choice.

5. EMPATHETIC EXPLANATIONS

Empathetic explanations are those in which the experience of coming to see, coming to understand, is stressed. At the core is the idea of an *imagined possibility*; the individual feels, "Ah-ha, I've got it— I can see that I would do the same thing in similar circumstances." Everyday life is full of empathetic explanations and understandings. As Nettler points out, the "processes that make human conduct understandable are usually amalgams of feelings, beliefs, and intentions that, from one's own life, seem to provide 'good reasons' for the behaviour" (Nettler, 1970, p. 34). Qualitative researchers pay much attention to empathetic explanations, for, to social scientists working in this tradition, they are the key to adequate explanations. The goal of discerning interpretive understandings of social behaviour is a key goal of the interpretative approach (described in Chapter 1). To come up with an explanation or a description of a behaviour that *rings true* to both the researcher and the person whose behaviour is being revealed is a key element in judging the adequacy of the explanation.

G. THE NATURE OF SOCIAL SCIENCE EVIDENCE

One might argue that social science explanations serve the same function as proverbs, adages, and anecdotes: they attempt to account for some behaviour, or to explain the behaviour. There is a difference, however. Social scientists have developed a variety of research designs and statistical techniques that permit them to test the veracity of their explanations or predictions. The research designs are described in Part Two and the statistical techniques are described in Part Three and Part Five of this text.

Both quantitative and qualitative researchers have developed conventions for collecting and analyzing data. Although their approaches to gathering and analyzing data differ, they both bridge theory and research so that their explanations are anchored in the evidence provided by the data collected and analyzed.

1. QUANTITATIVE EVIDENCE

For the quantitative social scientist an important goal is to arrive at general statements, statements that can be applied to a variety of situations. A **generalization** depicts the typical. The following statements constitute generalizations:

- Among high school students, females achieve higher grades than males.

- Tall people are paid more than short people.

- Students who sit in the middle of the classroom get higher grades than those who sit in the back or to the sides of the classroom.

In contrast to the nonscientist, the evidence a quantitative social scientist would look for would be based on objective, verifiable, controlled observations and communicated in a precise manner (Browne and Keeley, 1990, p. 67). By **objective**, reference is made to observations that are free from bias; by **verifiable**, we mean information that could be confirmed by tests conducted by others; by **controlled observations**, we mean those in which other confounding factors are minimized or taken into account; and by **precise communication**, we mean that the information is unambiguous. In the social sciences many of our generalizations are probabilistic; this means that in most cases (but not all) the statement will be true. Certainly not all tall people are paid more than short people; not all high school females achieve higher grades than their male counterparts; and certainly not all students in the back row get lower grades than those sitting in the middle of the room. (Are you considering changing your seat in Methods?) Since the social scientist's argument must be based on evidence, information must be collected and then appropriately analyzed. The resulting conclusion is then an **informed opinion**: that is, an opinion based on evidence that has been collected under controlled circumstances.

In making probabilistic generalizations, the social scientist has to indicate precisely how the information was collected, what kind of sampling procedures were used, and how the data were analyzed. Sampling refers to the method used to select the research participants. Chapter 15 introduces different sampling strategies and explains why quantitative researchers address the issue of sample size. The researcher should also indicate the procedures used to measure the variables (Chapter 13) and to process the resulting data (Chapters 8 and 9). These procedures, when done properly, allow the research results to be generalized to the population.

2. QUALITATIVE EVIDENCE

For the qualitative social scientist more emphasis is placed on the extent to which explanations and descriptions ring true to both the researcher and to the people who are being described. The evidence itself may be based on a painstaking analysis of documents (see section on content analysis in Chapter 5), on in-depth or focus group interviews (see Chapter 6 for examples), or on lengthy participation in a group (see William Foote Whyte, 1955, and Chapter 6 for examples). But in all cases, the evidence itself, and the interpretations placed on it, is judged by how well it is perceived to deal with the matter at issue.

H. TYPES OF FLAWED EXPLANATIONS AND MISUSES OF EVIDENCE

As a social scientist, one designs studies, makes observations, analyzes them, and then prepares a report on the results. During each stage one must be careful not to fall prey to errors in thinking or in argument. What are some of these errors? Following the arguments presented by Kahane (1988) and by Browne and Keeley (1990), a review will be made of common errors of particular relevance to the social science researcher.

1. ILLEGITIMATE APPEAL TO AN AUTHORITY

Sometimes as researchers we may be tempted to argue that something is bad (for example, capital punishment) by using an **appeal to an authority**. For example, in this case, we could state that capital punishment is bad because physics Nobel Prize winner, Dr. X., claims that it is. In this case, the status of the person expressing the view should not influence our judgment. Legitimate authority, in contrast, is to be found in the literature of the various disciplines. Does the preponderance of evidence in the research literature point to one conclusion? Are the exceptional findings to be explained by quirks in methodology or in the samples studied? In any case, social science proceeds by testing and retesting old ideas under new conditions.

2. PROVINCIALISM

As researchers we carry with us the baggage of our culture. This makes us vulnerable to the danger of **provincialism**, of tending to see things as our culture sees them. Thus, if it is politically correct to view men and women as equally skilled at child rearing, then this may make us reluctant to examine areas in child rearing where this may not be true. Thus Kahane argues provincialism "tends to make us concentrate on our own society...to the exclusion of other cultures...and via *loyalty*, to influence our acceptance or rejection of alleged facts or theories, whatever the nature of the evidence" (1988, p. 47).

3. FALSE DILEMMA

A **false dilemma** is set up when the researcher argues that something is caused either by A or by B. Then, having provided some evidence that B is not responsible, the researcher falsely concludes that A must be the cause. The problem here is that there may be several other possibilities that have not been considered. Kahane cites an example from *Human Nature* (April, 1978) that argues that "Economics, not biology, may explain male domination." In this example, other possible explanations have been omitted, which then paves the way for the inappropriate conclusion that it is economics and not biology that explains male domination (Kahane, 1988, p. 56).

4. MISSING EVIDENCE

Read the reports of researchers carefully to judge the adequacy of the evidence for each point made. While it would be unrealistic to expect all assumptions to be identified and all statements to be demonstrated, watch out for signs of important **missing evidence** and be certain that evidence for key arguments is provided.

Frequently, the social scientist is confronted with "interesting" findings for which an explanation should be offered. Suppose, for example, that a project is being done that measures high school students' socioeconomic status (SES) and relates this variable to the age of first experiencing sexual intercourse. And suppose, during data analysis, that a strong relationship emerges indicating that the higher one's socioeconomic origin, the older the average age of first intercourse. At this stage, the researcher may wonder what explains the pattern that has emerged. Possibilities such as the following might come to mind:

- Peers of high SES students avoid early initiation into sex and influence their friends to do likewise.

- Among high SES students, parental supervision is such that the opportunities to engage in premarital sex are more limited.

- High SES students have higher educational aspirations, and avoid early initiation into sex because they think that to do so would impede their chances of going to university.

Unfortunately, the study may not have been designed to test, and possibly to rule out, competing explanations. Hence, there may be no empirical evidence for the conclusion presented by the researcher. Such explanations may sound good and appear reasonable but lack evidence.

5. INSUFFICIENT EVIDENCE

Suppose an incident concerning a person on a day pass from prison who commits an armed robbery is cited in an attempt to justify the conclusion that the prison system is too lenient: what do you conclude? While this type of **anecdotal evidence** is commonly used, it is hardly sufficient to warrant the conclusion drawn. What are the overall rates of crime being committed by such persons? What are the social and human costs of lengthier sentences? Are lengthier sentences more likely to lead to rehabilitation and decreases in crime rates or provide greater protection, in the long run, to society? Be wary of anecdotal evidence, for it almost always constitutes **insufficient evidence**.

The problem with anecdotal evidence is that it is based on unrepresentative samples. A very small, unrepresentative sample (like an anecdote with one case) should not be used to generalize about all of humankind. You can imagine how inappropriate it would be to generalize about the attitudes of Canadians toward a political leader based on a sample of 74 university students enrolled in a second-year political science class at the University of Calgary. Since the sample appears to be one of convenience (students who were present when the questionnaire was administered), it is not only a small sample, but, since the students were not selected using a strict sampling procedure, one that could not be taken to represent even the students at the university let alone all Canadians. Avoid conclusions that state generalizations that go beyond those justified by the sampling procedure. (Details on sampling procedures will be discussed in Chapter 15.)

6. SELECTED OR SUPPRESSED EVIDENCE

In citing evidence, researchers should attempt to represent the findings in the research literature and their own data fairly. We are all familiar with public debates that have gone on in recent years on such issues as pollution, the dangers of smoking, abortion, and capital punishment. In each case, expert researchers who claim to have

special knowledge on these matters, and claim also to represent the consensus in their discipline, have been called on to testify. The trouble is that each side seems to be able to produce an expert who supports its point of view. These experts are probably presenting **selected evidence**, choosing to report those studies that support a particular point of view and ignoring the evidence that runs counter to what they are attempting to demonstrate. Advocacy is not science: both are legitimate enterprises, but do avoid confusing the two.

7. UNWARRANTED CONCLUSIONS

Sometimes in analyzing data, a researcher will come to an **unwarranted conclusion**. Confusing *correlation* and *cause* is an example of this type of error in reasoning. Researchers take pains to measure variables and to investigate how they are related to one another. However, to show that as A goes up so does B does not demonstrate that A causes B. While this issue will be explored in greater detail later (see Chapter 17, Section A), let us illustrate this point by looking at Max Weber's argument concerning the connection between the Protestant Ethic and the Spirit of Capitalism (1904). He argued that there is a linkage between the emergence of the spirit of capitalism and the work ethic encouraged by the Protestant Reformation. Let us assume that such a correlation, in fact, exists (many would disagree): are we justified in concluding that the Protestant Reformation led to the emergence of work attitudes that helped develop modern capitalism? What are the possibilities when we have a correlation between the two variables?

- Religion has influenced $\quad$ R $\longrightarrow$ C
  capitalism:

- Religion has been influenced by capitalism:

  R ←— C

- They influenced each other:

  R ←——→ C

- Other factor(s) influenced both of them:

  R   C

  ↰ ? ↱

Weber was interested in exploring the first possibility. In doing so, however, he failed to explore the other possibilities sufficiently. R.H. Tawney points out in *Religion and the Rise of Capitalism* (1926) that there was a general secularization going on in society, politics, economics, and the church. Thus, Tawney argues that a third factor—secularization—was the key, influencing both the emergence of capitalism and the Protestant Reformation itself.

Be careful not to confuse association with cause.

I. CONCLUSION

Social scientists have many perspectives available to them, and there is a strong tendency for practitioners to be identified with one school of thought or one methodological approach. And, even if people span a variety of approaches, we tend to label them as members of one school or another. There are squabbles among the various schools over the kinds of evidence that should be used; and, indeed, serious arguments over what questions we should be asking as social scientists.

On occasion, such debate is carried on with a distinct lack of tolerance for differences. Perhaps it is a measure of the immaturity of our disciplines that we are divided into warring camps. By the end of the first year of university, most students will witness at least one professor make an unrelenting attack on some theoretical or methodological perspective not shared by the professor. While debates in the academy can be healthy and invigorating, they can also be destructive and counterproductive if they fail to give the student a balanced view of the various approaches.

Are there points of agreement? Most social scientists would agree on the following.

(i) Study the Full Range of Social Behaviour

It is equally legitimate to study both social constructions of reality (individual subjective perceptions of reality) and objective, measurable structural patterns found in any society. In short, both qualitative and quantitative methodologies have a contribution to make to understanding social behaviour.

(ii) Use the Methodology Appropriate to the Questions Asked

Everyone will agree that the methodology we apply should be appropriate to the question asked. And while we could never agree that either qualitative or quantitative methodologies are better, we could probably agree that both have their place in the various disciplines.

(iii) Systematic Explanation

Explanations offered by the social scientist should be based on a careful, painstaking analysis of the evidence.

(iv) Peer Scrutiny

Whatever our efforts, an important norm is that our scholarly work should be scrutinized by our peers. It is through circulating our analyses that others may criticize them, suggest alternatives, and ultimately, refine the product further.

J. KEY POINTS

The *function of theory* is to answer *why* questions, to explain things.

Formal theories include concepts and interrelated propositions, some of which must be testable.

General theories are powerful because many predictions can be derived from them.

A *partial theory* is a testable causal model with three or more variables in it.

To *test a partial theory* one needs a relationship that is assumed to be true and two or more alternative explanations for why the relationship exists. The test attempts to measure the extent to which the data are or are not consistent with the explanations offered.

Testing derivations from *formal theory* involves deriving a testable hypothesis using axiomatic derivations and/or replacement of terms.

Replacement of terms involves replacing a general concept in a theory with a particular manifestation of that concept. An example would be to replace the term *deviance* with a particular manifestation of deviance, e.g., shoplifting.

Quantitative research projects may be considered to have three levels:
- The theoretical level in a project is the most abstract general conceptualization of the research problem. Theories propose general explanations of phenomena.
- The *conceptual level* involves the definition of variables to be used in a project.
- The *operational level* refers to the indicators (or measures) of the variables and to how the project is to be carried out.

Establishing *linkages* between the conceptual and operational levels of a research project is essential: *validity* is a measure of the extent to which an indicator reflects the concept, reflecting neither more nor less than what is implied by the conceptual definition; *reliability* refers to whether, on repeated measures, an indicator will yield similar readings.

Qualitative social science explanations stress that the social scientist's descriptions of behaviour should be meaningful to the actors involved; *quantitative explanations* emphasize reliable and valid observations, which are objective and verifiable.

A *deductive explanation* is a logically necessary consequence of the explanatory premises.

Probabilistic explanations convey the idea that people behave the way they do because they belong to a category of individuals who behave that way.

Functional explanations convey the idea that any given behaviour pattern exists in order to maintain the social system.

Causal explanations link a particular outcome to a sequence of preceding events.

Empathetic explanations stress the experience of how a person comes to know; these explanations "ring true" to the person who is describing the behaviour and to the person whose behaviour is being described.

Flawed explanations include improper appeals to authority, provincialism, setting up false dilemmas, missing key evidence, or suppressing evidence.

K. KEY TERMS

Anecdotal evidence

Appeal to authority

Axiomatic derivation

Causal explanation

Conceptual hypothesis

Conceptual level

Conceptual variable

Controlled observations

Deductive explanation

Empathetic explanation

Evidence

False dilemma

Folk wisdom

Formal theory

Functional explanation

Generalization

Informed opinion

Insufficient evidence

Missing evidence

Objective

Operational level

Operationalization

Partial theory

Precise communication

Probabilistic explanation

Provincialism

Reliability

Replacement of terms

Selected evidence

Theoretical level

Theory

Unwarranted conclusion

Validity

Verifiable

ALTERNATE RESEARCH DESIGNS

Experiments, field studies, surveys, qualitative research, non-reactive, action, feminist, and critical research will be introduced in Part 2 of this text. The experiment is a good starting point because it offers the most straightforward demonstration of causal links among variables. However, because of practical or ethical reasons, lots of things that social scientists want to study cannot be studied experimentally, so other designs have an important place in social science research. Nonexperimental researchers need to understand the experiment in order to heighten awareness of factors that may be problematic in their own studies.

Chapter 3 introduces the student to the basic principles of experimental design and field studies, Chapter 4 presents survey designs, Chapter 5 covers various nonreactive designs, Chapter 6 includes various qualitative approaches, and Chapter 7 introduces critical research methods.

EXPERIMENTS, QUASI-EXPERIMENTS, AND FIELD OBSERVATIONS

A. EXPERIMENTAL DESIGNS

1. THE RATIONALE OF THE EXPERIMENT

John Stuart Mill (1806–1873) identified the *Method of Difference* (1925, pp. 255–56) as a key tool in understanding causal relations (see Box 3.1). And while Mill's presentation was the first to set out the logic of experimentation systematically, experiments, in fact, go back much earlier. Palys reports that experimentation dates to at least 1648 when Blaise Pascal (1623–1662) had his brother-in-law do an experiment testing for the presence of atmospheric pressure (Palys, 1992, pp. 241–44). A special container was taken up a mountain, and it was noted that the level of mercury in the container declined as it was moved higher. As a control, another mercury dish was not taken up the mountain and its level was monitored; its level remained unchanged throughout the observation period.

BOX 3.1 SOCIAL RESEARCHERS AT WORK

John Stuart Mill: The Method of Difference

"...[W]e require...two instances resembling one another in every other respect, but differing in the presence or absence of the phenomenon we wish to study. If our object be to discover the effects of agent A, we must procure A in some set of ascertained circumstances, as A B C, and having noted the effects produced, compare them with the effect of the remaining circumstances B C, when A is absent. If the effect of A B C is *a b c*, and the effect of B C, *b c*, it is evident that the effect of A is *a*. So again, if we begin at the other end, and desire to investigate the cause of an effect *a*, we must select an instance, as *a b c*, in which the remaining circumstances, *b c*, occur without *a*. If the antecedents, in that instance, are B C, we know that the cause of *a* must be A: either A alone, or A in conjunction with some of the other circumstances present.

It is scarcely necessary to give examples of a logical process to which we owe almost all the inductive conclusions we draw in early life. When a man is shot through the heart, it is by this method we know that it was the gunshot which killed him: for he was in the fullness of life immediately before, all circumstances being the same, except the wound.

The axioms implied in this method are evidently the following. Whatever antecedent cannot be excluded without preventing the phenomenon, is the cause, or a condition of that phenomenon: Whatever consequent can be excluded, with no other difference in the antecedents than the absence of a particular one, is the effect of that one. Instead of comparing different instances of a phenomenon, to discover in what ways they agree, this method compares an instance of its occurrence with an instance of its non-occurrence, to discover in what they differ. The canon which is the regulating principle of the Method of Difference may be expressed as follows:—

If an instance in which the phenomenon under investigation occurs, and an instance in which it does not occur, have every circumstance in common save one, that one occurring only in the former; the circumstance in which

alone the two instances differ is the effect, or the cause, or an indispensable part of the cause, of the phenomenon.

Of these methods, that of Difference is more particularly a method of artificial experiment; while that of Agreement is more especially the resource employed where experimentation is impossible."

Source: John Stuart Mill (1925). *A System of Logic*. 8th ed. London: Longmans, Green and Co., 255–56.

The positivist approach to knowledge (reviewed in Chapter 1) underpins experimental designs. These designs provide evidence for clear interpretations of cause–effect relations: a key feature of the experiment is that measures are taken at different points in time. A well-designed experiment should indicate whether or not a treatment (studying with the radio on) will bring about a change in some dependent measure (grade performance in Methods), *other things being equal*. The last phrase, *other things being equal*, is critical. It means that we must take into account any number of factors (hours of sleep, interest in the subject matter, previous performance) to make certain that it is our treatment and not some other factor that is influencing the dependent variable.

Experimental researchers use the term **internal validity** to refer to the extent to which one can demonstrate that one's treatment is having an impact on a given outcome and that other sources of influence have been controlled. **External validity**, on the other hand, refers to the extent to which one can make extrapolations from the particular study to other groups in general.

2. STANLEY MILGRAM: BEHAVIORAL STUDY OF OBEDIENCE

The "Milgram experiment," as it has become known, is among the most famous experiments conducted in the social sciences. Stanley Milgram was a social psychologist at Yale University when his article "Behavioral Study of Obedience" was published in the *Journal of Abnormal and Social Psychology* in 1963. The experiment is described in Box 3.2. The experiment was designed to measure the extent to which the research "subject" would obey the experimental scientist who instructed each subject to do something that the person knew to be morally wrong. Would they obey the authority figure or act according to their own conscience?

Milgram's experiment began in the year following the trial of Adolf Eichmann. Eichman was on trial for his role in the murder of millions of Jews in Nazi Germany. Eichman, of course, ordered the killings, but it was German soldiers and citizens who committed most of the murders. Milgram wondered whether they did so because they were following orders. Could all individuals

BOX 3.2   SOCIAL RESEARCHERS AT WORK

Stanley Milgram: "Behavioural Study of Obedience"

General Procedure

A procedure was devised which seems useful as a tool for studying obedience (Milgram, 1963). It consists of ordering a naive subject to administer electric shock to a victim. A simulated shock generator is used, with 30 clearly marked voltage levels that range from 15 to 450 volts. The instrument bears verbal designations that range from Slight Shock to Danger: Severe Shock. The responses of the victim, who is a trained confederate of the experimenter, are standardized. The orders to administer shocks are given to the naive subject in the context of a "learning experiment" ostensibly set up to study the effects of punishment on memory. As the experiment proceeds the naive subject is commanded to administer increasingly more intense shocks to the victim, even to the point of reaching the level marked Danger: Severe Shock. Internal resistances become stronger, and at a certain point the subject refuses to go on with the experiment. Behaviour prior to this rupture is considered "obedience," in that the subject complies with the commands of the experimenter. The point of rupture is the act of disobedience. A quantitative value is assigned to the subject's performance based on the maximum intensity shock he is willing to administer before he refuses to participate further. Thus for any particular subject and for any particular experimental condition the degree of obedience may be specified with a numerical value. The crux of the study is to systematically vary the factors believed to alter the degree of obedience to the experimental commands.

The technique allows important variables to be manipulated at several points in the experiment. One may vary aspects of the source of command, content and form of command, instrumentalities for its execution, target object, general social setting, etc. The problem, therefore, is not one of designing increasingly more numerous experimental conditions, but of selecting those that best illuminate the *process* of obedience from the socio-psychological standpoint...

Distribution of Age and Occupational Types in the Experiment

OCCUPATIONS	20–29 YEARS N	30–39 YEARS N	40–50 YEARS N	PERCENTAGE OF TOTAL (OCCUPATIONS)
Workers, skilled and unskilled	4	5	6	37.5
Sales, business, and white-collar	3	6	7	40.0
Professional	1	5	3	22.5
Percentage of total	20	40	40	

Method

SUBJECTS The subjects were 40 males between the ages of 20 and 50, drawn from New Haven and the surrounding communities. Subjects were obtained by a newspaper advertisement and direct mail solicitation. Those who responded to the appeal believed they were to participate in a study of memory and learning at Yale University. A wide range of occupations is represented in the sample. Typical subjects were postal clerks, high school teachers, salesmen, engineers, and labourers. Subjects ranged in educational level from one who had not finished elementary school, to those who had doctorate and other professional degrees. They were paid $4.50 for their participation in the experiment. However, subjects were told that payment was simply for coming to the laboratory, and that the money was theirs no matter what happened after they arrived. The table below shows the proportion of age and occupational types assigned to the experimental condition.

PERSONNEL AND LOCALE The experiment was conducted on the grounds of Yale University in the elegant interaction laboratory. (This detail is relevant to the perceived legitimacy of the experiment. In further variations, the experiment was dissociated from the university, with consequences for performance.) The role of experimenter was played by a 31-year-old high school teacher of biology. His manner was impassive, and his appearance somewhat stern throughout the experiment. He was dressed in a grey technician's coat. The victim was played by a 47-year-old accountant, trained for the role; he was of Irish-American stock, whom most observers found mild-mannered and likable.

PROCEDURE One naive subject and one victim (an accomplice) performed in each experiment. A pretext had to be devised that would justify the administration of electric shock by the naive subject. This was effectively accomplished by the cover story. After a general introduction on the presumed relation between punishment and learning, subjects were told:

But actually we know very little about the effect of punishment on learning, because almost no truly scientific studies have been made of it in human beings.

For instance, we don't know how much punishment is best for learning—and we don't know how much difference it makes as to who is giving the punishment, whether an adult learns best from a younger or an older person than himself—or many things of that sort.

So in this study we are bringing together a number of adults of different occupations and ages. And we're asking some of them to be teachers and some of them to be learners.

We want to find out just what effect different people have on each other as teachers and learners, and also what effect punishment will have on learning in this situation.

Therefore, I'm going to ask one of you to be the teacher here tonight and the other one to be the learner.

Does either of you have a preference?

Subjects then drew slips of paper from a hat to determine who would be the teacher and who would be the learner in the experiment. The drawing was rigged so that the naive subject was always the teacher and the accomplice always the learner. (Both slips contained the word "Teacher.") Immediately after the drawing, the teacher and learner were taken to an adjacent room and the learner was strapped into an "electric chair" apparatus.

The experimenter explained that the straps were to prevent excessive movement while the learner was being shocked. The effect was to make it impossible for him to escape from the situation. An electrode was attached to the learner's wrist and electrode paste was applied "to avoid blisters and burns." Subjects were told that the electrode was attached to the shock generator in the adjoining room.

In order to improve credibility the experimenter declared, in response to a question by the learner: "Although the shocks can be extremely painful, they cause no permanent tissue damage."

Learning task The lesson administered by the subject was a paired-associate learning task. The subject read a series of word pairs to the learner, and then read the first word of the pair along with four terms. The learner was to indicate which of the four terms had originally been paired with the first word. He communicated his answer by pressing one of four switches in front of him, which in turn lit up one of four numbered quadrants in an answer box located atop the shock generator.

Shock generator The instrument panel consists of 30 lever switches set in a horizontal line. Each switch is clearly labeled with a voltage designation that ranges from 15 to 450 volts. There is a 15-volt increment from one switch to the next going from left to right. In addition, the following verbal designations are clearly indicated for groups of four switches going from left to right: Slight Shock, Moderate Shock, Strong Shock, Very Strong Shock, Intense Shock, Extreme Intensity Shock, Danger Severe Shock. (Two switches after this last designation are simply marked XXX.)

Upon depressing a switch: a pilot light corresponding to each switch is illuminated in bright red; an electric buzzing is heard; an electric blue light, labeled "voltage energizer," flashes; the dial on the voltage meter swings to the right; various relay clicks are sounded.

The upper left-hand corner of the generator is labeled Shock Generator, Type ZLB, Dyson Instrument Company, Waltham, Mass. Output 15 Volts–450 Volts.

Details of the instrument were carefully handled to insure an appearance of authenticity. The panel was engraved by precision industrial engravers, and all components were of high quality. No subject in the experiment suspected that the instrument was merely a simulated shock generator.

Sample shock Each naive subject is given a sample shock on the shock generator, prior to beginning his run as teacher. This shock is always 45 volts, and is applied by pressing the third switch of the generator. The shock is applied to the wrist of the naive subject, and has its source in a 45-volt battery wired into the generator. This further convinces the subject of the authenticity of the generator.

Shock instructions The subject is told to administer a shock to the learner each time he gives a wrong response. Moreover—and this is the command—the subject is instructed to "move one level higher on the shock generator each time learner flashes a wrong answer." He is also instructed to announce the voltage level before administering a shock. This serves to continually remind subjects of the increasing intensity of shocks administered to the learner.

Preliminary and regular run Pretests revealed that the procedure of reading words and administering shocks requires some practice before it can be handled smoothly. Therefore, immediately preceding the regular run, the teacher is given a preliminary series of 10 words to read to the learner. There are 3 neutral words in the practice series (i.e., words that the learner answers correctly), so that shocks are administered for 7 of the words, with the maximum shock at 105 volts (moderate shock). Almost all subjects master the procedure by the time the preliminary run is over.

Subjects are then presented with a second list, and are told that the procedure is the same as for the first list; the experimenter adds, however:

> *When you get to the bottom of the list, repeat it over again, and continue giving shocks, until the learner has learned all the pairs correctly.*

The experimenter instructs the subject to:

> *start from 15 volts and increase the shock level one step each time the learner gives a wrong answer.*

Feedback from the victim In all conditions the learner gives a predetermined set of responses to the word pair test, based on a schedule of approximately three wrong answers to one correct answer. In the present experimental condition no vocal response or other sign of protest is heard from the learner until Shock Level 300 is reached. When the 300-volt shock is administered, the learner pounds on the wall of the room in which he is bound to the electric chair. The pounding can be heard by the subject. From this point on, the learner's answers no longer appear on the four-way panel.

At this juncture, subjects ordinarily turn to the experimenter for guidance. The experimenter instructs the subject to treat the absence of a response as a wrong answer, and to shock the subject according to the usual schedule. He advises the subjects to allow 5–10 seconds before considering no response as a wrong answer, and to increase the shock level one step each time the learner fails to respond correctly. The learner's pounding is repeated after the 315-volt shock is administered; afterwards he is not heard from, nor do his answers reappear on the four-way signal box.

Experimenter feedback At various points in the experiment the subject may turn to the experimenter for advice on whether he should continue to administer shocks. Or he may indicate that he does not wish to go on. It was important to standardize the experimenter's responses to these inquiries and reactions.

If the subject indicated his unwillingness to go on, the experimenter responded with a sequence of "prods," using as many as necessary to bring the subject into line.

> *Prod 1: Please continue. Or, Please go on.*
>
> *Prod 2: The experiment requires that you continue.*
>
> *Prod 3: It is absolutely essential that you continue.*
>
> *Prod 4: You have no other choice, you must go on.*

The prods were always made in sequence: Only if Prod 1 had been unsuccessful, could Prod 2 be used. If the subject refused to obey the experimenter after Prod 4, the experiment was terminated. The experimenter's tone of voice was at all times firm, but not impolite. The sequence was begun anew on each occasion that the subject balked or showed reluctance to follow orders.

Special prods If the subject asked if the learner was liable to suffer permanent physical injury, the experimenter said:

> *Although the shocks may be painful, there is no permanent tissue damage, so please go on. [Followed by Prods 2, 3, and 4 if necessary.]*

If the subject said that the learner did not want to go on, the experimenter replied:

> *Whether the learner likes it or not, you must go on until he has learned all the word pairs correctly. So please go on. [Followed by Prods 2, 3, and 4 if necessary.]*

Source: Stanley Milgram (1963). "Behavioral Study of Obedience." *Journal of Abnormal and Social Psychology*, 67, 371–78. Reprinted by permission.

act against their own conscience when given orders? Would people hurt other people simply because they were ordered to do so? What Milgram's experiment suggests is that authority has a powerful influence on individuals, that individuals will inflict great harm upon a person when demanded to follow orders.

Clearly, Milgram's study is of interest for its design and for its unanticipated findings. It is also important because it raised important ethical concerns about the impact of the experiment on the research participants. The ethical issues will be explored further in Chapter 11.

3. KEY ELEMENTS IN THE CLASSIC EXPERIMENTAL DESIGN

Suppose you wish to assess the effectiveness of a film in promoting university attendance. Suppose that some students are exposed to a CD-ROM about university attendance while others see a nature film. Will seeing the CD-ROM about going to university increase the number of high school students wishing to attend university? You decide an experiment would be in order. There are a number of elements to such a study.

A. DEPENDENT VARIABLES

A **dependent variable** is the effect in a cause–effect relation; in this case, the dependent variable would be the subject's desire to attend university. In an experiment, the dependent variable is the phenomenon measured in order to determine if any change has taken place as a result of some experimental intervention.

B. INDEPENDENT VARIABLES

The **independent variables** include all the variables taken into account, or manipulated, by the researcher that can influence the dependent variable. Four types of independent variables can be distinguished:

i. Treatment Variables

In an experiment, the independent variable whose effect is being studied is known as the **treatment variable**. In our example, the type of film or CD-ROM shown—either about nature or about the university—is the treatment variable. An experiment attempts to detect the direct effect of the treatment on the dependent variable. In some experiments there will be more than one treatment variable. In such cases, the experimenter must determine the effects of each treatment used on the dependent variable. (We might consider being exposed to colour versus black-and-white films as an additional treatment variable.)

ii. Control Variables

Control variables are those specifically taken into account in designing a study. In this case, they would include other major factors that could influence a student's plans to attend university, such as gender, academic abilities, and whether the student comes from a family background where university attendance is expected. These variables need to be controlled, or taken into account, in designing the study.

iii. Confounding Variables

Confounding variables are those that can unintentionally obscure or enhance a relationship. For example, one would not want to measure some students' attitudes toward university on Monday morning, and others on Friday afternoon, as it is possible that their interest in attending university varies systematically during the week. If this possibility is not taken into account, it may confound the results of our study.

iv. Random Variables

Since many variables can have an impact on our dependent variable, some may be treated as *random variables*. A **random variable** varies without control but is taken into account by the way groups are set up for the study—by, for example, randomly assigning some students to see the university CD-ROM, and others to see a nature film.

C. LEVELS

Typically, various levels of treatment variables are identified. Often two or three **treatment levels** will be examined. In our example, a two-level study might compare the effect of seeing the university CD-ROM with the effect of seeing the nature film. A study with three treatment levels might compare the effects of seeing a short, medium, or long CD-ROM. The various control and confounding variables are also exposed to the subject at various levels. The simplest multiple-variable design would be a 2 2 one; this refers to a design where there are two levels of the treatment variable (the first two) and two levels in a control (or second treatment) variable. Thus, when experimentalists talk about designs they might talk of a 2 2 2 design. This means that the treatment has two categories; similarly the control variables each have two levels. A 2 3 2 design has two levels in the treatment, a three-level control variable, and a two-level control variable.

4. PSEUDO-EXPERIMENTAL DESIGNS

Pseudo-experimental designs (also called pre-experimental designs) are considered to be of limited scientific merit because they cannot rule out alternative explanations for observed relationships. However, understanding the problems with making causal inferences from data derived from pseudo-experimental studies will help us to better understand the rationale and value of *classic experimental designs*. For this reason pseudo-experimental designs are discussed first in this chapter, as a beginning reference point to illustrate the weaknesses in these designs that lead to threats to the internal validity of the studies and difficulties in interpreting the findings.

A **pseudo-experimental design** is one that does not permit clear causal inferences about the impact of a treatment on the dependent variable. Although these designs share some of the elements of the experiment, their structures inhibit clear causal interpretations. We will examine two pseudo-experimental designs, again using the example of the impact of a CD-ROM on students' desire to attend university.

A. SAME GROUP: PRETEST/ POST-TEST DESIGN

Suppose that you decided that you would need a measure of the students' predispositions toward attending university before seeing the CD-ROM. Having completed this measure, the CD-ROM could then be shown, and the difference between the pretest and post-test scores could be used to measure the change in the desire to attend a university program.

We could diagram the proposed design as shown in Figure 3.1.

Suppose that at Time 1, 57.0% indicated that they wished to attend university, while at Time 2, after seeing the CD-ROM, the percentage increased to 73.0. Could we argue that the CD-ROM produced a 16.0 percentage point increase in those wishing to attend the university (73 − 57 = 16)? The answer is no. There are a number of factors that could render such an interpretation incorrect. Donald T. Campbell and Julian C. Stanley, in their classic work, *Experimental and Quasi-Experimental Designs for Research,* identify threats to internal validity that might confound our interpretations (1966). The reader should note that these threats also apply to non-experimental designs and should be considered when interpreting study findings.

FIGURE 3.1 SAME GROUP: PRETEST/POST-TEST

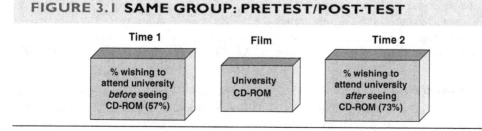

Time 1 — % wishing to attend university *before* seeing CD-ROM (57%)

Film — University CD-ROM

Time 2 — % wishing to attend university *after* seeing CD-ROM (73%)

i. History

Any number of events may have happened in addition to watching of the CD-ROM: the university's basketball team may have won a national championship; the university may have announced a new program in information technology; or a professor may have just won a Nobel prize. In the context of experimental design, **history** refers to concurrent events that, along with the experimental manipulation, may be influencing variation in the dependent variable.

ii. Maturation

People change over time: perhaps the students have become bored with school and, by the time the second measures are taken, systematic changes in attitude may have occurred. Such changes could, in part, be an influence causing the different responses at Time 1 and Time 2. By 3:00 p.m. on Friday, Grade 11 students may experience a profound drop in their motivation to attend university. **Maturation** refers to any changes that occur in an individual subject over the course of an experiment, which can, along with experimental manipulation, influence the outcome of the experiment.

iii. Testing

Even asking identical questions at both tests can influence the responses. Some respondents might want to appear consistent and, therefore, give the same responses in both tests. Others, suspecting that the study is meant to demonstrate how good the CD-ROM is, might want to help the researcher and exhibit **response bias** by being more positive the second time.

iv. Instrument Decay

Suppose we asked students to indicate their preferences by the strength with which they squeezed a hand dynameter. (A dynameter is a mechanical device with a calibrated dial that permits the researcher to read the indicated intensity.) If, for example, the spring in the device has weakened, the second set of readings will be slightly higher. **Instrument decay** refers to the fact that the dynameter no longer measures reliably.

v. Statistical Regression

To explain this idea, we will need to alter the example slightly. Suppose, after our pretest scores had been taken, that we decide to show the CD-ROM just to those with the most negative attitudes toward attending university. Could we legitimately say that any gain in the scores of these students is a result of the CD-ROM? The answer is again no. The reason for this is that when a sample is selected on the basis of extreme scores, retesting will tend to show a **statistical regression** toward less extreme scores. That is, the most negative scores are likely to change in the direction of the mean simply because extreme scores (either positive or negative) are unstable. Even without any CD-ROM, the students' response would, on average, be slightly more positive on the second testing. The explanation is that inaccuracies in measurement at the time of the first measurement have tended to distort the data negatively. In short, those subjects with very low scores might have simply given more negative responses on that day than those subjects with average scores because they were in a bad mood. Box 3.3 presents another example of a regression effect.

B. EXPOSED/COMPARISON GROUP DESIGN

After considering the flaws in the previous design, suppose you alter it to provide for a comparison group, as shown in Figure 3.2.

BOX 3.3

Regression Effect: Reading Scores

Suppose a reading specialist wants to try out a new reading program. If the specialist tests the reading ability of all students in a school and then selects the lowest scoring 10% of students for the program, puts them through it, and then retests them, almost certainly the scores will increase. However, the amount attributable to the program and the amount attributable to regression effects would remain uncertain. In short, the scores would increase, but how much of the increase would be due to the new program would be unclear.

FIGURE 3.2

EXPOSED/COMPARISON GROUP DESIGN: PERCENT PLANNING ON ATTENDING UNIVERSITY

Time 2

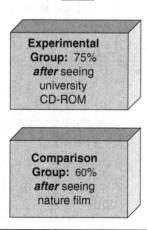

Experimental Group: 75% ***after*** seeing university CD-ROM

Comparison Group: 60% ***after*** seeing nature film

In this design, one group is exposed to the CD-ROM promoting university education and the other is not. Can we legitimately conclude that the difference in attitude between the exposed group and the unexposed group represents the impact of the CD-ROM? (If 75% of the students exposed to the CD-ROM expressed a desire to attend a university program and only 60% of those students who did not see the CD-ROM wished to go to university, could we conclude that the CD-ROM produced this 15-percentage-point difference in measured attitudes?) Again, there are problems. The major difficulty is that we do not know if the groups were the same to start with: any difference in test results may simply reflect initial differences, or differences that emerge during the study but that are unrelated to the impact of the CD-ROM. Two additional confounding factors are noted by Campbell and Stanley (1966):

vi. Selection

It is possible that the students most inclined to go to university choose to go to see the CD-ROM; thus, if they score higher in the test, this result may simply reflect their initial predisposition to study at a university. **Selection** thus refers to subjects selecting themselves *into* a study.

vii. Mortality

Just as people choose to belong to a group, they may choose not to. Some of those who see the CD-ROM may withdraw from the study before their attitude toward attending a university program has been measured. The effect of subjects withdrawing from the experiment may be that those who leave are less interested in higher education and hence the proportion for those who stay in the experiment will be more likely to indicate a desire to attend a university. **Mortality** thus refers to subjects selecting themselves *out* of a study. Therefore, mortality may systematically distort the results of the study.

As we have seen, pseudo-experimental designs have serious problems in making clean causal inferences because of the inherent lack of adequate controls in these designs. Among the problems is whether they have adequately demonstrated: (1) that the test groups were similar prior to the introduction of the treatment variable; (2) that they have a way of dealing with random, confounding, and control variables. Classic experimental designs deal with these issues.

5. CLASSIC EXPERIMENTAL DESIGNS

To solve the problems in making causal inferences using pre-experimental designs, a **classic experimental design** may be used. Two versions of such designs will be presented: the *between-subjects design* and the *within-subject design*.

A. BETWEEN-SUBJECTS DESIGN

A **between-subjects design**, also known as the pretest, post-test **control group design**, contains three crucial elements of the classical experiment: control over extraneous variables, methods of dealing with pre-treatment similarity of groups, and manipulation of a treatment. A between-subjects design involves a *control* and an *experimental* group (see Figure 3.3 below). Measures are taken from members in both groups prior to some treatment and repeated after the treatment has been

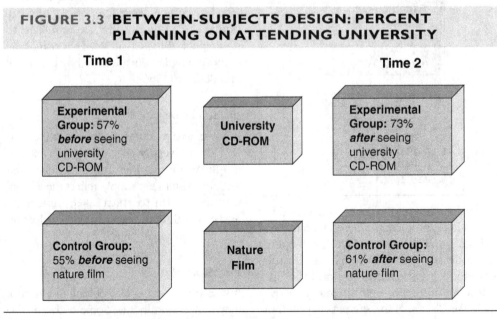

FIGURE 3.3 BETWEEN-SUBJECTS DESIGN: PERCENT PLANNING ON ATTENDING UNIVERSITY

Time 1

Time 2

Experimental Group: 57% *before* seeing university CD-ROM

University CD-ROM

Experimental Group: 73% *after* seeing university CD-ROM

Control Group: 55% *before* seeing nature film

Nature Film

Control Group: 61% *after* seeing nature film

experienced. The control group is exposed to a neutral treatment (seeing the nature CD-ROM in the illustration we have been using) while the experimental treatment is the focus of the study (the university CD-ROM). Data analysis will reveal whether there are differences in the dependent variable as a result of the intervention, while taking into account other factors.

- The **experimental group** is the one that is exposed to the treatment intervention. The researcher attempts to ensure that each subject experiences the intervention in as similar a fashion as possible so as to deal with some extraneous factors that may be influencing the outcome of the study.

- The **control group** is established so that comparisons can be made between the experimental group and the control group. Normally the control group is exposed to a placebo or some neutral treatment that is similar in the time it takes and the kind of experience it represents. In the case of the CD-ROM example, the control group is exposed to a CD-ROM having a nature theme.

i. Achieving Equivalence of Control and Experimental Groups in a Between-Subjects Design

A key factor in the success of a between-subjects design is that the treatment and the control groups (completely different groups) are made as equivalent as possible before the experimental group is exposed to the experimental condition. There are four ways of achieving equivalence:

1. through *randomization*: where individuals are randomly assigned to either the treatment or to the control group; or

2. through *precision matching*: identifying matching pairs according to gender, socioeconomic status, and grades, then randomly assigning one person from each of the matched pairs to the control group and the other person to the experimental group; or

3. through *blocking*: if there is a need to control for a key variable you could select half your sample from one value on the variable (e.g., immigrant status) and the other half from the other category (non-immigrant category); within each block, assignment is made to the treatment and control groups; or

4. through establishing *baseline stability*: sometimes the Time 1 measure on the dependent variable is not taken until it achieves a steady state; after stability is achieved then the treatment and control groups are exposed to their respective treatments (see Figure 3.4 on page 68 for an illustration of baseline stability).

1. RANDOMIZATION is a process of assigning subjects to a treatment or a control group so that each subject has an equal chance of being assigned to either group. This process of random assignment should not be confused with random selection, which will be discussed in Chapter 4. Randomization (if the numbers are large enough) will provide control over both known and unknown factors (the control and random variables). A variety of techniques may be used to accomplish the random assignment. In all cases we avoid allowing subjects to choose their group assignment. The method selected should assure that each subject has an equal chance of being assigned to either the experimental or the control group. Ways of accomplishing random assignment include:

• Random Numbers. Statistical packages have random number generators built into them and these may be used to assign individuals to groups. For example, the statistical package SPSS (see Appendix A) has a procedure for selecting cases at random and can also be used to assign cases to experimental or control groups. The first number shown by the random number generator is used to assign the first person in the subject pool to the experimental or control group. Your rule might be to assign odd numbers to the experimental group and even ones to the control group. Using this rule, if the first number generated was a 7 you would assign the first subject to the experimental group. You would continue through the random numbers and subjects until all are assigned.

• Tables of random numbers may also be used in a similar fashion. Such tables are published in books (e.g., RAND Corporation, [1955] 2001). Here the procedure would be to select a table of random numbers, close one's eyes and, with pencil in hand, make a mark on the table of random numbers, and note the number nearest the mark. You establish a rule for proceeding (perhaps, read down column to bottom of page then start at top of next column and read down). Again, using an odd/even rule you could begin group assignment; if the start number is even, subject 1 is placed in the control group; if the second random number is also even, then subject 2 also goes into the control group. Continue assignment until all subjects are assigned.

Table 3.1 illustrates the use of a table of random numbers or a computer-generated set of random numbers to assign subjects to control and experimental groups. In this case, the rule established was that even numbers lead to an assignment to the control groups, odd ones to the experimental group. Thus, if the numbers were odd, odd, odd, even, odd, even, even, the subjects would then be assigned as shown in Table 3.1.

• A deck of playing cards can also be used to assign subjects to groups. Again establish a set of rules (hearts and diamonds means experimental group, clubs and spades means control group assignment). Shuffle the cards well. Turn cards up one at a time; if the first card is red (hearts or diamonds), the first subject is assigned to the experimental group; if the second card turned over is black, the second subject is assigned to the control group. Continue through the deck assigning each subject.

TABLE 3.1	USING A TABLE OF RANDOM NUMBERS TO ASSIGN SUBJECTS TO TREATMENT AND CONTROL GROUPS	
SUBJECT	ODD/EVEN FROM RANDOM NUMBER TABLE	EXPERIMENTAL CONDITION
Subject #1	Odd	Treatment
Subject #2	Odd	Treatment
Subject #3	Odd	Treatment
Subject #4	Even	Control
Subject #5	Odd	Treatment
Subject #6	Even	Control
Subject #7	Even	Control

- An equal number of slips of paper with Experimental Group or Control Group written on them are placed in a container to be drawn out one at a time. As they are drawn out of the container the subjects are assigned to either the treatment or control group based on the slip of paper.

- Other techniques could also be used, but with caution. You could not, for example, assign every second person to the control group if your sample was made up of married couples with the man's name first. Even if you start randomly, you would end up with an all male experimental group and an all female control group! Be careful that the technique you use provides each individual with an *equal chance* of ending up in the experimental group and that there are no systematic biases built into the order of your subject pool. If you choose a random number (or a heads/tails coin flip) to determine whether the first subject would be placed in the treatment or in the control group, you could then proceed by placing the next subject into the opposite group, altering back and forth as subjects arrive. So long as there are no systematic biases in arrivals this technique should provide each subject with an equal chance of being assigned to the experimental group.

Using one of the above procedures increases the likelihood that the treatment and control groups are *equivalent* prior to the introduction of the treatment. However, because experiments are often carried out on fairly small samples, researchers will often try to enhance the equivalence of the two groups by using a method known as *precision matching.*

2. PRECISION MATCHING is a method of achieving equivalence between control and experimental groups by ensuring that the groups are matched on certain key variables. The key variables will vary depending on the topic being investigated. In the CD-ROM study one might decide to match on previous computer experience and on gender. A preliminary measure would be taken on the subject's computer experience and the subject's gender would be noted. Subjects could then be arranged from highest to lowest computer experience for the females, and then produce a similar listing for the potential male subjects. The top two females on computer experience measure would then be randomly assigned—one to the experimental group, the other to the control group. The next pair of females would then be randomly assigned. And so on through each pair, followed by using the same procedure for the male pairs. Following this procedure will assure equivalence in the average computer experience in the treatment and control groups and will also match them by gender composition. Rather than simply trusting to luck (using the randomization process) to balance the two groups, precision matching assures equivalence on the two key variables. We rely on the random assignment to balance the groups on other control and random variables.

3. BLOCKING. Another technique used in between-subjects designs to reduce within-group variations is blocking. A **blocked design** refers to one where subjects have been grouped together on some variable that needs to be controlled, and subjects are then randomly assigned to treatment and control groups. For example, if you were testing for the effectiveness of a new health promotion program and you were working in an area with many immigrant children, you might want to use blocking in your experimental design. What you would do is assign immigrant children randomly to either the experimental group (new program) or to the control group (old program); you would then do the same for non-immigrant children. The blocking will not allow you to measure the influence of immigration status on learning, but it will increase your chances of detecting a significant effect on your new program. The reason for this is that you have reduced the variation between the treatment and the control groups.

4. BASELINE STABILITY. Another way in which the pretest equivalence is handled is by taking measures of the dependent variable prior to the introduction of the treatment. While the treatment and control groups may be equivalent on many measures as a result of randomization, they nonetheless may be somewhat different in terms of their measures on the dependent variable. Experimenters therefore collect *baseline* data so that we have a stable starting point against which we can make comparisons as we repeat the measures of the dependent variable through the course of the study. Baseline data simply is the score a subject has prior to the introduction of the treatment variable. In some circumstances several

measures are taken and not until the measures achieve stability do we introduce the treatment variable. This is referred to as **baseline stability**. So even if the average baseline scores of the experimental group compared to the control group are somewhat different, we are able to measure how much the scores change from the baseline levels when the measures are repeated after the treatment has been administered.

ii. Analyzing the Data

To estimate the impact of the CD-ROM, we could do the following computation on the percent wanting to attend a university program before and after seeing the CD-ROM (Table 3.2). At Time 1, 57% of the experimental group planned to attend a university program, compared to 55% of the control group members (baseline measures). The Time 2 measures indicate that the experimental group (after seeing the CD-ROM about attending university) now had 73% planning to attend university, compared to 61% for the control group (viewers of a neutral CD-ROM). To estimate the impact of the university CD-ROM on a person's desire to attend university, we subtract the Time 1 percentage from the Time 2 percentage. Here we note a 16-percentage-point difference for those in the experimental group compared to a 6-percentage-point difference among those

TABLE 3.2 PERCENTAGE WANTING TO ATTEND UNIVERSITY BY EXPOSURE AND NON-EXPOSURE TO CD-ROM

GROUP	PERCENTAGE WANTING TO ATTEND UNIVERSITY		
	TIME I	TIME 2	DIFFERENCE
Treatment	57.0	73.0	73 – 57 = 16
Control	55.0	61.0	61 – 55 = 6
		Estimated impact of CD-ROM:	10

in the control group. We then go on to subtract the control difference (6%) from the treatment difference (16%) and arrive at an estimate of the impact of the CD-ROM amounting to some 10 percentage points.

The seven factors Campbell and Stanley (1966) identified as confounding interpretations are dealt with in between-subjects designs through:

- attempting to make certain that the groups are similar to begin with; and

- noting that the various factors should influence the treatment and the control groups equally.

Thus, between-subjects designs rely on establishing pre-treatment similarity of control and experimental groups to minimize the effects of history, maturation, testing, instrument decay, statistical regression, selection, and mortality. Therefore, some form of randomization is a key tool in the experimenter's quest to establish unambiguous causal relationships.

iii. Demonstrating a Causal Relationship in a Between-Subjects Design

To show a causal relationship in any research, three conditions must be demonstrated:

1. CHANGES IN THE TREATMENT VARIABLE MUST OCCUR PRIOR TO CHANGES IN THE DEPENDENT VARIABLE. Because the between-group design involves measures of both the treatment and the dependent variables at two points in time (Time 1, Time 2 measures), the procedure ensures that the measure at Time 1 precedes the one at Time 2. Second, since we introduce the treatment to the experimental group (the CD-ROM about a university nursing program) but not to the control group (who see a nature CD-ROM instead) and follow this by measuring the dependent variable at Time 2, it becomes possible to make an inference about the impact of seeing the university CD-ROM (treatment variable) on the desire to attend a university program (the dependent variable). Thus, since the CD-ROM was shown between the Time 1 and Time 2 measures, if there is a change in the attitudes toward attending a university nursing program among those seeing the university CD-ROM, we will have made the first step in demonstrating that the CD-ROM caused the change in attitude.

2. THE VARIABLES MUST BE ASSOCIATED; AS VALUES ON THE TREATMENT VARIABLE ARE INCREASED, THE DEPENDENT MEASURES VARY CORRESPONDINGLY. A variety of techniques might be used to illustrate that the variables are associated. For example, we might show that those who saw the CD-ROM are more likely to indicate that they are planning to attend a university nursing program than those who did not see the CD-ROM. To say that the dependent variable varies systematically indicates that either:

- the proportion of respondents saying that they plan to attend a university nursing program is higher among those exposed to the university CD-ROM; or

- the proportion of respondents saying that they plan to attend a university nursing program is lower among those exposed to the university CD-ROM; or

- the proportion of students saying that they plan to attend a university nursing program increases as the length of the CD-ROM increases.

However, there may appear, for example, to be a levelling off in the proportion of students planning on attendance when the CD-ROM is longer than 23 minutes.

3. NOTHING BUT THE TREATMENT VARIABLE CAN HAVE INFLUENCED THE DEPENDENT VARIABLE. To ensure that it is only the treatment variable that is causing variation in the dependent variable, steps must be taken to rule out, or control, various sources of contamination:

STEP 1 ENSURE THAT THE CONTEXT IN WHICH THE EXPERIMENT IS CARRIED OUT IS THE SAME FOR ALL SUBJECTS.

To guarantee the similarity of the experimental situation, researchers take great pains to ensure that physical conditions (temperature, humidity, lighting) all remain the same; similarly, instructions to the subjects are standardized, even recorded, to be certain that each respondent gets the same information in the same manner. As much as possible, all subjects should have a similar experience in participating in the experiment.

STEP 2 BALANCE THE BACKGROUND CHARACTERISTICS OF THE SUBJECTS.

Typically this control is accomplished through some combination of precision matching (matching a female with a female; high computer experience person with another who also has high computer experience) and randomly assigning each person to the control or to the experimental groups. The goal is to try to populate both groups with similar kinds of people.

STEP 3 NEUTRALIZE ANY CONFOUNDING VARIABLES.

The researcher must be careful that the experience of the experiment is not having an impact on the results. For example, if you were testing the impact the intensity of colour (treatment variable) has on the speed of recovery from a major depressive episode, you should not simply move systematically from low colour intensity (soft white, beige) through to intense colour (bright yellows, bright pinks, lime greens). Subjects will probably recover from their depressive reaction as they go through their regular treatment regime, and you would therefore want to vary the presentation of different colour conditions for each subject randomly. In this way, the order of presentation would not in itself systematically influence the speed of recovery. If you do not deal with this potential confounding factor, you would not be able to tell how much of the increase of speed in recovery was due to increasing the intensity of colour in the clients' environment and how much was due to a response effect to the regular protocol of care for depressive clients. Confounding variables of this sort are dealt with by:

- varying the way the treatment is administered to the subjects: one strategy for doing this is known as **counterbalancing**. Here a treatment level is introduced, changed, maintained, and then returned to the first level to control for effects of learning on the subject's performance; and

- using statistical controls so that subgroups are analyzed separately to take into account potential confounding variables (perhaps analyzing the male subjects separately from the female subjects).

STEP 4 DEAL WITH RANDOM VARIABLES

Random variables include all those other unknown factors that might be influencing the dependent variable, none of which you can control. Subjects are assumed to be different on all dimensions. Knowing this, experimenters do not let subjects choose which group they will go into (they might think it more fun to be in a experimental group than in a boring control group; or they might choose to be in the same group as their friends). The randomization process used in the assignment of subjects to groups increases the likelihood that the two groups are similar on both known and unknown variables prior to the introduction of the treatment variable. When sample sizes exceed 30 in each group, random assignment is likely to result in reasonable balancing of the groups on random factors.

B. WITHIN-SUBJECT DESIGN

An alternative to the between-subjects design is a **within-subject design**. Sometimes these designs use a single subject, sometimes just a few subjects, and sometimes large samples. What is the idea behind this kind of design?

The previous section stressed the importance of controlling possible sources of contamination. Matching groups or randomly assigning subjects to treatments were noted as ways of ensuring pre-treatment similarity. Without such controls, it would be impossible to distinguish treatment effects from the effects of other factors.

Sometimes one can employ an alternative strategy that provides for the ultimate in control of extraneous factors: suppose that instead of assigning people to different treatments, we instead expose one subject to the different treatments. Since the subject is the same person, background characteristics, attitudes, and intelligence are all perfectly controlled. In a control-group design, on the other hand, the researcher counts on randomized assignment to groups (or precision matching) to adjust for known and unknown variations between the two groups. With large samples the assumption that sources of contamination have been satisfactorily addressed is

reasonable; with smaller samples one has less faith in the ability of randomization to deal with such contamination.

Suppose we were interested in the relation between the frequency with which subjects win a video-poker game and the speed with which they play. Will the subjects play faster after being rewarded and then gradually play more slowly as they fail to win? This experiment could be set up by having a rigged poker video machine designed so that the frequency with which subjects won could be controlled by the experimenter. A subject would be introduced to the game, play for some time, and be allowed to win, on average, every tenth trial. The speed of play would be monitored and, after a stable speed-of-play baseline had been established, the conditions of the game would be changed so that the subjects won, on average, every fifth trial. These trials would go on for some time; finally, the experimenter would change the game again so that subjects won with the original frequency and the speed with which the game was played would be recorded again. This kind of experiment is known as a within-subject, ABBA design. The ABBA refers to four conditions: the first A refers to the reward condition (the subject, on average, wins every tenth trial) associated with the initial baseline speed; B refers to a period when the new reward condition is introduced; the second B refers to a continuation of the B reward condition; finally, reward condition A is repeated to see if the subjects play at a speed similar to that at which they played before the introduction of reward condition B. Suppose we measured the number of games played per minute in all conditions. The reference to counterbalance indicates that we revert to the original reward condition to ensure that it is the reward condition and not a confounding factor such as learning or boredom that influences the speed at which the game is played. If the confounding variables are having an effect, then the speed of play will not return to the original condition. Figure 3.4 shows a graph of what we might expect for results.

Figure 3.4 shows considerable instability at the beginning of the experiment. The speed of play gradually increases and then levels off to a baseline. A **baseline measure** is taken once stability has been achieved in the dependent variable at the beginning of a set of observations; after a new experimental condition is introduced, measures of the dependent variable will be taken and compared to the baseline values. There will be some learning at the beginning and so play will be a little slower at the very start. After the reward condition is introduced, we expect that there will be a gradual increase in the speed of play which, again,

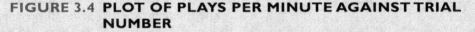

FIGURE 3.4 PLOT OF PLAYS PER MINUTE AGAINST TRIAL NUMBER

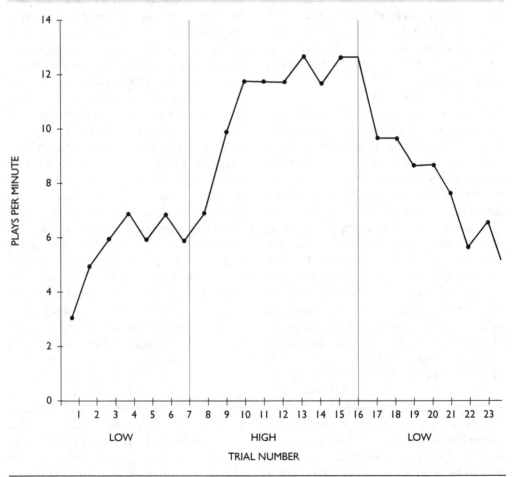

will level off; the acid test comes at the end when we see if the speed of play declines when we revert to the original reward condition (subject wins one game in ten). The return to the original condition is important because we want to make certain that it is not learning, skill, or heightened interest that are controlling speed; we want to measure the impact of the frequency of reward on the speed of play. If the effect is not reversible, then we would have grounds for believing that other factors are influencing the speed of play.

When an effect is not reversible we may have what is known as a **Hawthorne effect**: this effect refers to any variability in the dependent variable that is not the direct result of variations in the treatment variable. The effect is named after one of the experiments done in the Hawthorne Western Electric plants in Chicago by Roethlisberger and Dickson (1939). In their study, workers' output was monitored under varying intensities of lighting. (The hypothesis was that worker productivity would increase with increasing levels of illumination.) The experimenters noted that as lighting intensity increased, worker output increased. It looked as if simply brightening the lights in the workplace would be the way to increase productivity. However, when the experimenters then decreased lighting intensities to the baseline levels, they noted that worker productivity continued to increase. Whoops! Something other than the intensity of illumination was having an impact on the speed of work. A possible interpretation of this result is that the workers knew that they were being observed and that they tried hard to please the observers by increasing their productivity (Roethlisberger and Dickson, 1939). Whenever an effect cannot be reversed, you have to suspect that some factor(s) other than the treatment is

influencing variations in the dependent variable, in this case, the speed of work. ABBA designs return to the baseline levels of the treatment variable in the final stage of the study to detect possible Hawthorne effects.

The key advantage of a within-subject design is that it provides convincing evidence for the impact of the treatment variable on the dependent variable. The evidence is all the more convincing, because, by using the same subject under different levels of the treatment variable, one can be confident that most of the possible extraneous influences, such as gender, age, socioeconomic status, type of background, and values, have been controlled. The control achieved in within-subject designs is sometimes referred to as **control by constancy**. The term stems from the idea that, since the same subject experiences different levels of the treatment, the subject acts as his/her own control. In contrast, the between-subjects design has to try to control these differences by random assignment or precision matching. Especially in studies using relatively small samples, such controls are somewhat suspect, since there are always going to be some random fluctuations, which could mask true effects.

Within-subject baseline studies permit the researcher to determine, for each subject, when baseline stability has been achieved; this permits the researcher to take into account different speeds with which subjects learn to do tasks, and to move to the next stage only when the experimenter is satisfied that a stable baseline has been achieved. Finally, the within-subject design is done when working with special groups that are small in number (e.g., blind students, students with IQs above 150) because there are too few cases to do a between-subject design.

But for some issues these designs are not always possible. Frequently one cannot expect to be able to revert to the baseline level of the treatment and expect the dependent variable to fall to its baseline levels. Studies measuring memory skills, for example, cannot hope to return to baseline abilities because learning has occurred throughout the experimental session.

C. BETWEEN-SUBJECTS AND WITHIN-SUBJECT DESIGNS FOR TESTING TIRES

Table 3.3 presents fictitious data modelled on David W. Martin's illustration of between-subjects and within-subject designs (1991, pp. 66-85). The example evaluates the efficacy of a new racing tire in improving lap times on an oval track.

i. Two Between-Subjects Designs

The idea of a between-subjects design is that we want to establish two (or more) groups to allow us to compare different treatments. In this case, our task is to evaluate the effectiveness of the modified tire compared to the standard racing tire. Let us approach the question by looking at two between-subjects designs.

1. ORDINARY DRIVERS: A BETWEEN-SUBJECTS DESIGN Suppose students in a Methods class are asked to volunteer for an experiment. They are asked to meet at Riverside Speedway on Saturday afternoon. Students are given basic safety instructions and a chance to get the feel of the race cars by driving a few laps. The students are then randomly assigned to drive either a car equipped with standard tires or one with modified tires. Neither the students nor the person recording the lap times is aware of the type of tire on each car. This feature of the design is known as a **double blind**, and is used to minimize the possible effects

on the driver or timer of knowing which tire is being used. Each student drives three warm-up laps and then is timed on lap four. The results are shown in section i of Table 3.3. Note that there is considerable variation in the scores. Even though the average times were better on the modified tires, we are not comfortable in concluding that the modified tires were an improvement on the standard ones—there is simply too much variability in the scores. A change of one or two persons might alter the results substantially. (A test of significance confirms our suspicion, as the difference between the results achieved with standard tires and the results achieved with modified tires is not statistically significant: see Chapter 9 for a discussion of what these tests tell us.)

2. AMATEUR RACE DRIVERS: A BETWEEN-SUBJECTS DESIGN On Saturdays a number of amateur race drivers are available at Riverside. The second experiment is identical to the previous one, except we will use amateur race drivers. Using each driver's record permits us to rank-order all the drivers by skill level. Car assignment is done in pairs: using a coin flip the first- and second-ranked drivers are randomly assigned to drive either a car with the modified tires or one with the standard tires. The third- and fourth-ranked drivers are randomly assigned to drive a car with either type of tire: this procedure is continued until 20 drivers have been assigned. Once again, three untimed practice laps are followed by a timed lap. Section ii of Table 3.3 shows much less variation than was apparent among the student drivers. Nonetheless, some of the variation between the amateur drivers may still be due to differences in driver skill, the cars, or the tires. The results indicate that the lap times of cars with the

TABLE 3.3   RESULTS FROM THREE STUDIES TO TEST RACING TIRES

	STANDARD TIRE		MODIFIED TIRE	
EXPERIMENT	NAME	TIME	NAME	TIME
i. Student drivers: between-subjects design; random assignment to groups	Kathleen	21.4	Paula	20.7
	Li	16.2	Marlies	19.0
	Danielle	18.0	Vanny	16.4
	Kim	16.1	Jacques	16.7
	Kevin	15.9	Sandra	21.6
	Mary	20.3	Marius	20.1
	Yvonne	17.1	Kwami	14.4
	Pierre	21.4	Andrea	16.3
	Ursula	17.7	Tony	15.7
	Hwan	19.8	Carol	19.7
MEANS	18.39		18.06	
STANDARD DEVIATIONS	2.17		2.45	
MEAN DIFFERENCE		.33		
ii. Amateur racers: between-subjects design; pairs matched on known skill level; random assignment to groups	Bob	14.1	Jacob	14.0
	John	14.1	Ravi	13.7
	Fred	14.2	Gary	13.9
	Narinder	13.9	Ron	13.7
	Jim	13.8	Moh	13.8
	Neil	13.3	Emily	13.4
	Hazel	13.7	Sara	13.8
	Iris	13.3	Edward	13.2
	Frank	13.8	Zoe	13.7
	Yvette	13.5	Bruce	13.3
MEANS	13.77		13.65	
STANDARD DEVIATIONS	.32		.26	
MEAN DIFFERENCE		.12		
iii. Amateur racers: within-subject design	James	13.1	James	13.0
	Peter	12.8	Peter	12.9
	Celine	13.5	Celine	13.4
	Jeremy	13.4	Jeremy	13.2
	Stefan	13.5	Stefan	13.5
	Don	13.6	Don	13.3
	Jacques	13.5	Jacques	13.3
	Pierre	12.8	Pierre	12.7
	Linda	12.9	Linda	12.9
	Melanie	13.5	Melanie	13.4
MEANS	13.26		13.17	
STANDARD DEVIATIONS	.32		.28	
MEAN DIFFERENCE		.09		

modified tires are somewhat lower than those of cars with the standard tires. The nagging problem, however, is whether differences in the cars may have been responsible for some of the differences in the times. As there is only a small sample of 10 drivers in each group, we are a little uncomfortable with the results. (The test of significance, however, does indicate a statistically significant difference in lap times for the two tire types.)

ii. Amateur Race Drivers: A Within-Subject Design

Given some uncertainty about the results, could we get even greater confidence in our results by changing our design? In the previous experiment, concern was expressed over the possibility that the differences could be the result of differences in the cars or in the skill of the drivers. However, some control over differences that may have resulted from differences among the drivers was achieved by ranking drivers by skill and then, for adjacent pairs, randomly assigning each driver to either a car with standard tires or a car with modified tires. Could we improve on this design?

Suppose we simply have *each driver run two trials* in the *same car,* once equipped with standard tires and once equipped with the modified tires? We now have control over the quality of the car as well as the skill of the driver. We have control by constancy—the driver and the car are the same for the test with the standard and with the modified tires. As before, the drivers and timer are not aware of which type of tire is on the car (double blind). The results, reported in section iii of Table 3.3, show about the same variability as the results of the previous experiment, but now we have greater confidence that we have controlled both car and driver variability. (The differences by tire type are statistically

significant.) As a tire manufacturer, which of these tests would you trust more?

D. BETWEEN-SUBJECTS AND WITHIN-SUBJECT DESIGNS COMPARED

The goal in experimental research is to isolate and measure treatment effects. To demonstrate an effect convincingly one wants clear differences in the dependent variable (mean lap speed) by treatment categories (standard versus modified tires). To make a study as convincing as possible we would want to have lots of variations between the categories (average lap times should vary consistently by type of tire) but little variation within the category (lap times for those drivers using the same type of tire). In the three designs presented above, note how the first design had a lot of within-group variation (the students varied considerably in their driving skills); the second and third designs, in contrast, had less within-group variation (all amateur race drivers).

While it is not always possible to use a within-subject design, the advantage of such a design over a between-subjects design is that you will need fewer subjects, require less time to train and run your experiment, and that you will exercise almost perfect control over extraneous influences on your dependent variable.

In designing experiments one attempts to reduce the within-group variation. In within-subject designs this is achieved by exposing the same person to different levels of the treatment; between-subjects designs achieve this by using precision matching and/or randomly assigning individuals to be exposed to different treatments. Another technique used in between-subjects designs to reduce within-group variations is blocking. A blocked design refers to one where subjects have been grouped together on some variable that needs to be controlled and subjects are then randomly assigned to treatment and control groups.

6. CONCLUSION

Experimental designs produce the clearest view of causation. This is accomplished through the application of a treatment to subjects under conditions where extraneous variables are controlled. However, there are four special cautions to be taken in evaluating experimental results.

CAUTION 1

Few experiments are done on representative samples and therefore one cannot make extrapolations to the general population. This concern extends to questions about the accuracy of descriptive parameters and questions about whether the causal relationships in an experiment hold true in a larger population. In our racing tire test, even though we find significant differences in the performance of the tires, these differences may well hold true for younger drivers but not older ones (all of the drivers were under 40 years of age in the test); thus we should not conclude that the tires perform better for all drivers.

CAUTION 2

The fact that experimental studies achieve higher explained variances (predictability) than surveys or secondary data analyses should not be misinterpreted. To illustrate: if a treatment variable X controls 10% of the variability in the dependent variable Y, then we should expect an experiment that controls all external factors to explain all variance except that which can be accounted for by measurement error or the application of inappropriate models (for example, using a linear model when the particular relationship to be explained is curvilinear: see Chapter 8). The explained variances of experimental and nonexperimental designs are, therefore, not directly comparable. In principle, experiments should produce higher explained variances than those achieved by nonexperimental designs using the same variables. A robust variable in an experiment might be relatively impotent outside the laboratory setting.

CAUTION 3

There is an element of artificiality in laboratory experiments that is difficult to detect, to interpret, or to control. A "good subject" may try to respond by giving the researcher what the subject thinks the researcher wants; the subject may also be intimidated and act atypically. These problems will be discussed in greater detail in Chapter 10.

CAUTION 4

For practical reasons, experimental designs can deal only with a few variables simultaneously (multiple-variable designs are possible, but with several treatment and control levels one would soon need far too many subjects to run the experiment: a 3 3 3 3 design produces 81 treatment conditions and, if there were 10 subjects per condition, would require 810 subjects). When a large number of variables require simultaneous analysis it is advisable either to use a different experimental design or to simplify the experiment by using fewer variables or fewer levels in each variable.

Despite some inherent weaknesses, experimental designs provide the greatest control and precision in testing causal models and in dealing with many of the worrying sources of bias that plague other approaches. Moreover, through the use of double blind designs, where neither subjects nor researchers know which subjects are under what condition, there is considerable control over bias on the part of subjects and researchers.

Because it is neither practical nor ethical to experiment on all aspects of social behaviour, other designs remain important tools for the social science researcher. The beginning researcher should have some understanding of experimental designs, though, as their great strength is their ability to control many of the confounding factors that influence outcomes. Where experimentation is not possible, it is more difficult to produce convincing inferences about causal relationships. The key strengths and weaknesses of each design will be discussed at the end of this chapter and also in subsequent chapters.

B. QUASI-EXPERIMENTAL DESIGNS

1. THE RATIONALE

Often we want the power of an experimental design in making causal inferences but find that it is not possible to conduct an experiment. Sometimes this happens because for ethical or for practical reasons we cannot manipulate the required variables; in other cases we cannot randomly assign people to different treatments. When these situations arise, researchers modify the experimental approach and design a quasi-experiment. A **quasi-experimental design** is one in which it has not been possible to do any or all of the following:

- randomly assign subjects to a treatment or control group; or

- control the timing or nature of the treatment.

The quasi-experimental design comes as close as possible to the experimental design in order to measure the impact of a treatment. To illustrate this approach, we will examine a study using such a design.

2. FRANCES HENRY AND EFFIE GINZBERG: RACE DISCRIMINATION IN JOB SEARCH

In their imaginative study, Henry and Ginzberg wished to test whether racial discrimination in employment existed in Toronto. They wanted to see if there were differences in the number of job offers to whites and blacks when similarly qualified applicants responded to the same job vacancy. Henry and Ginzberg also wanted to examine whether there would be differences in the treatment accorded to members of different racial groups. Two quasi-experimental designs were used in their study. In the first, similarly qualified white and black applicants applied in person for the same job. In the second approach, applicants using five different ethnic accents made phone inquiries about advertised job vacancies. The accents represented were: white-majority Canadian, Slavic, Italian, Jamaican, and Pakistani. Box 3.4 features a description of the in-person testing phase of the study.

The Henry and Ginzberg study is an important one both for the design and for the findings that it produced. This study is convincing precisely because it was a quasi-experimental field study where the employers were not aware that their hiring behaviours were under scrutiny. The results almost certainly would have been different

BOX 3.4 SOCIAL RESEARCHERS AT WORK

Frances Henry and Effie Ginzberg: "Racial Discrimination in Employment"

In the in-person testing, two job applicants, matched with respect to age, sex, education, experience, physical appearance (dress), and personality, were sent to apply for the same advertised job. The only major difference between our applicants was their race—one was White and the other, Black. We created four such teams: one junior male, one junior female, one senior male, and one senior female. The younger teams applied for semiskilled and unskilled jobs such as gas station attendant, bus boy, waitress, and clerk and sales help in youth-oriented stores. The senior teams applied for positions in retail management, sales positions in prestigious stores, and waiting and hosting positions in expensive restaurants. The senior team members were, in fact, professional actors. Applying for middle-class type jobs meant that they would be required not only to present a sophisticated image but also to participate in a fairly demanding job interview. Professional actors, we believed, would be more convincing in playing the many roles required for this project. The resumes of the team members were carefully constructed to be as alike as possible. In order to further control possible biases, the staff of testers was changed several times so that no individual personality could account for the results.

The younger teams were composed of high-school and university students who would normally be applying for the same types of job that they applied for in the testing situation. Since we were not testing for sex discrimination and did not want this type of discrimination to account for any of our results, the male teams were sent to traditionally male jobs and the women went to jobs traditionally associated with women's work. In some types of jobs, for example waiter/waitress, both men and women were acceptable. Men and women were sent to such jobs but never to the same job. Each tester had a different resume for the various types of positions that he or she was applying for, so each member of the senior female team, for example, carried several resumes, one for a secretary, another for a retail sales assistant, a third for a dental technician, etc. Each resume contained the names of references supplied by business people and friends who had agreed to support our research. Our applicants could thus be checked out by a potential employer who could obtain a reference for the applicant. In actuality, only two employers ever called for references.

Research Procedure

Each evening, a listing of jobs would be selected for the next day from among the classified advertisements. Some types of jobs were excluded, such as those involving driving, where licences could be checked. Jobs which required highly technical skills were also excluded.

The testers were instructed either to go to a certain address or to phone for an appointment. They used standard Canadian accents when phoning since we did not want them to be screened out over the phone. The testers would arrive within approximately one half-hour of each other so that there was little chance that a job had been legitimately filled. In most cases the Black applicant went first. After their interviews the testers completed a summary data sheet especially designed for this project in which they wrote down the details of their treatment and the kinds of information they had been given. Their resumes listed telephone numbers which were in actuality lines connected to the research office. Call-backs for second interviews or with offers of employment were received and recorded by the researchers. On-the-spot offers to the field testers were accepted by them. In the case of call-backs and on-the-spot offers, employers were phoned back, usually within an hour and informed that another position had been accepted, in order to make sure that employer could fill the vacancy as soon as possible.

Research Results:
The In-Person Test

In three-and-one-half months of field testing, the testers were able to apply for 201 jobs for a total of 402 individual applications.

For our purposes, racial discrimination in employment was tested in two ways. First, was an offer of employment made to one of the applicants, both applicants, or neither applicant? Second, during the interview, were there any differences in the treatment of the two applicants? The following tables present the numerical results.

Blacks received fewer job offers than Whites. Of a total of 37 valid job offers,

27 went to Whites, 9 to Blacks, and in one case both were offered the job (Table I). There were an additional 10 cases where both were offered jobs, but these were for commission sales which involved no cost to the employer. Our overall results therefore show that *offers to Whites outweigh offers to Blacks by a ratio of 3 to 1.*

TABLE I   Offer of a Job Versus No Offer

	NUMBER	%
Both offered job	10	5.0
White offered job;		
Black not	27	13.4
Black offered job;		
White not	9	4.5
No offer to either	155	77.1
Totals	201	100.0

We had thought that the nature of the job might influence whether Blacks or Whites would be hired. Only Whites received offers for managerial positions or jobs as waiters and waitresses or hosts and hostesses in the restaurant trade. A Black was offered a job in the kitchen when he had applied for a waiter's job!

As noted above, the second measure of discrimination was whether differential treatment had occurred during the interview. Table II presents the results.

TABLE II   Treatment of Applicants

	NUMBER OF CASES
Treated the same	165
Treated differently	36

Blacks and Whites were treated differently 36 times and in all cases but one the White applicant was preferred to the Black. The ways in which differential treatment took place provide a great deal of insight into the nature of discrimination and its subtleties. Differences in treatment were sometimes very blatant, as the following examples show.

1. Mary, the young Black tester, applied for a sales position in a retail clothing store and was told that the job had already been taken. Sylvia, our White tester, arrived a half-hour later and was given an application form to fill in and told that she would be contacted if they were interested in her.

2. In a coffee shop Mary was told that the job of cashier was taken. Sylvia walked in five minutes later and was offered the job on the spot.

   This pattern occurred five times. Another form of differential treatment was as follows: the Black was treated rudely or with hostility, whereas the White was treated politely. This occurred 15 times.

3. Paul, our White tester, applied for a job as a waiter. He was given an application form to fill out and an interview. He was told that he might be contacted in a week or so. Larry, the Black tester, was also given an application form and an interview. But as the Manager looked over Larry's resume, he asked Larry if he "wouldn't rather work in the kitchen."

4. Applying for a gas station job, the White tester was told that there were no jobs at present but that he could leave a resume. The Black tester was told that there were no jobs, but when he asked if he could leave a resume, he was sworn at: "Shit, I said no, didn't I?"

Another form of differential treatment occurred when the wage offers to Blacks and Whites were different. There were two occasions where the Black tester was offered less money than the White tester for the same job. On a few occasions, derogatory comments were made about Blacks in the presence of our White testers. The Blacks being referred to were our own testers!

These results indicate that Black job seekers face not only discrimination in the sense of receiving fewer job offers than Whites but also a considerable amount of negative and abusive treatment while job hunting. The psychological effects of such experiences became evident in the feelings expressed by the research staff. The Black staff felt rejected and some doubted their own ability: "I was beginning to wonder what was wrong with me and why Jean [the White tester] was so much better than me."

In sum, the findings of the in-person test reveal that in 48 job contacts, or 23.8% of the cases, some form of discrimination against Blacks took place. These findings indicate that Blacks and Whites do not have the same access to employment. *Racial discrimination in employment, either in the form of clearly favouring a White over a Black, even though their resumes were equivalent, or in the form of treating a White applicant better than a Black, took place in almost one-quarter of all job contacts tested in this study.*

Source: Francis Henry and Effie Ginzberg (1990). "Racial Discrimination in Employment." In James Curtis and Lorne Tepperman, *Images of Canada*, 303–306. Scarborough, Ontario: Prentice Hall Canada Inc.

had a mailed survey been done on these same employers measuring their attitudes toward hiring minorities. The Henry and Ginzberg study also is convincing because they took great pains to design the study to test carefully whether employment hiring decisions were biased, while at the same time controlling for such things as the qualifications of the applicants and ensuring that a job vacancy existed with each potential employer. Furthermore, the number of cases was sufficient to provide confidence that the results were not the result of random fluctuations.

3. CONCLUSION

This example shows how the researchers attempted to model their study on an experimental design. The important feature in this study is the attempt to control the qualifications of the job applicants, only allowing their racial background to vary; the same employer was used for each pair of applicants, thus controlling for the employer. The quasi-experimental design employed by the researchers makes the results more convincing.

C. FIELD EXPERIMENTS

There are some studies in which the researcher intervenes in a natural setting and which—in contrast to most participant-observation studies—can be simple and quickly completed. These are called **field experiments** or sometimes **natural setting experiments**. Suppose, for example, that a researcher greets a stranger while walking along a street and then records the type of response (if any) that results. In this case,

the researcher is intervening in a natural environment and is interested in recording the response to a mild form of non-conformity (greeting a stranger). The kinds of observations that can be made in such studies are quite limited. However, as in most observational studies, fairly accurate measures can be recorded concerning the subject's age, sex, dress, and type of response. But the key point is that the observation is being made in a natural environment.

Earlier, we pointed out that laboratory experiments attempt to maintain as much control as possible over the treatment variable(s) and over the conditions under which the experiment takes place. In field experiments, the researcher cannot exercise as much control. But what is given up in control may be compensated for by the fact that the subjects are probably not aware that they are part of an experiment and hence react normally. Both field and laboratory experiments attempt to understand the relationship between some treatment variable and some measurable outcome, exercising as much control over conditions as possible. A researcher conducting a field experiment simply takes conditions and events as they occur naturally, intervenes in some way, and observes the response to the intervention.

Investigations of *proxemics* can also provide some good illustrations of field experiments. **Proxemics** refers to the norms surrounding personal space and the conditions under which such space will or will not be violated. For example, a researcher might position two confederates (people who, unknown to the people under observation, are cooperating with the researcher) facing one another, apparently discussing some issue, in a narrow corridor. Perhaps a 50 cm space is left between the wall and the back of one of the confederates; the other confederate stands against the opposite wall. As people pass through the corridor, an observer will record information about the subjects: perhaps their age, sex, whether they are alone or with others, and whether they walk between the confederates or squeeze through the 50 cm space. If the subjects cut through, do they acknowledge this by saying "excuse me" or bowing their heads slightly as a non-verbal apology? Following a number of observations of this sort, the distance between the confederates could be increased or decreased. As a control, the confederates could be replaced by large ash cans separated by the same distance as the experimenter's confederates (Cheyn, 1972). The above is a simple illustration of a field experiment: an environment is set up under controlled conditions and systematic observations are made of the people who pass through the space.

The following are two more field experiments involving the violation of personal space: a student research group at St. Francis Xavier University did two studies. In the first, a confederate sits right next to an opposite-sex student working in the library when many other spaces are available. This process is repeated a number of times. The responses of the target students vary, but many erect a barrier with books to mark off territory; only rarely do the "subjects" flee. In a related study, a female research student invades a group of male students, who do not know the female, standing in a public area chatting between classes. Once again, this intrusion is repeated with a number of all-male groups. Typically these violations produce a moment of silence; the males would look at one another in bewilderment, and then they would turn and flee! So far, no group of male students has volunteered to see if the same phenomenon occurs with female target groups.

The major advantage of the above studies is that behaviour is observed in natural settings and, thus, not distorted by the artificiality of laboratory experiments. Such studies can be relatively inexpensive to do and, since conditions can be altered systematically by the researcher, some control can still be maintained over the experimental conditions.

One of the disadvantages of these studies is that only a limited number of variables can be measured. In addition, the samples used are usually not representative and one cannot, therefore, generalize the findings.

The reader is asked to recall the study conducted by Henry and Ginzberg (1990). In their study (featured in Box 3.4), the researchers examined racial discrimination in employment in Toronto. Their research is an excellent example of a quasi-experimental field study. Another well-known example of a field experiment is the series of such experiments done by Jane Allyn Piliavin and Irving M. Piliavin (1972). In this study, students faked various medical problems in a number of public locations and observed the conditions under which bystanders would assist the apparently stricken victim. In one of the studies, which compared trials when the victim was bloodied with trials when the victim did not bleed, the research had to be suspended when it was discovered that bystanders could create a major disruption by pulling an emergency cord on the subway car to alert others of the medical problem. Incidentally, Piliavin and Piliavin found that bystanders were more reluctant to assist someone who had blood coming from the mouth.

Over the past few years a number of our students in a first-level one-semester methods course have completed field experiments. Box 3.5 lists some of these studies, which were completed within the time constraints of a one-term course. In each

BOX 3.5 STUDENT RESEARCHERS AT WORK

Student Field Experiments

Project Racial Discrimination in the Service Industry

Student Alicia Van De Sande

Brief This project compared speed of response by employees in various local stores to a young female black student with the response to a young white female student.

Project Non-Verbal Communication at Public Telephones: The Effects of Personal Space Invasion

Student Mary E. Gillis

Brief This study observed the impact of researchers encroaching upon the personal space of target subjects who were using a public telephone; qualitative responses noted.

Project Proxemic Violations in the Library

Student Corine MacDonald

Brief This study compared qualitative responses to different levels of personal-space violations in a library reading room.

Project Greeting Behaviour

Student Maureen Keough

Brief This study compared the responses of target subjects to a greeting from a 20-year-old female stranger to that from a 38-year-old female stranger.

Project Violating Telephone Proxemic Norms

Student Michelle Chisholm

Brief A male student violated the personal space of target subjects; the study included a before/after qualitative observation of subject's behaviour.

Project Cutting-through Behaviour: Who Cuts between Interacting Pairs?

Student Kelly Hannay; Chris Parsons

Brief Students set up varying gender combinations of interacting pairs and observed who would or would not cut between them.

Project Helping Behaviour: A Left-Behind Envelope

Student Charlotte MacDonald

Brief Student experimenters sat beside someone and then departed, leaving behind an envelope marked "confidential." Observations were made on who tried to "help" by trying to return the envelope.

Project Influence of Appearance on Prosocial Behaviour

Student Nathan Cody Francis

Brief Comparisons were made of social reactions and money received when the student experimenter begged on the street as a clean-shaven, well-dressed university stdent one day and as an unshaven, poorly dressed individual another day.

of the studies, students were encouraged to pay particular attention to the qualitative dimensions of their observations. They were encouraged to describe carefully how various target subjects responded to the situation created by the researchers. The project reports used these qualitative descriptions to add depth to the report. Typically, the reports also tested a number of hypotheses related to differences in response to the situation, such as, Are women more likely to be "helpful" than men?

D. NATURALISTIC OBSERVATIONAL STUDIES

A **naturalistic observational study** may be defined as a study in which the people being studied are unaware that they are being observed. The goal is to observe and to record behaviour that occurs in natural settings. Unlike field experiments, naturalistic observational studies do not attempt to alter the social environment in any way. The researcher observes and records behaviour occurring in natural settings. Like field experiments, naturalistic observational studies have high levels of validity (measuring what they claim to measure). However, with both field experiments and naturalistic observational studies, sampling is almost always haphazard (based simply on who happens to walk by), making it problematic to generalize experimental findings to people other than those actually observed. Nonetheless, naturalistic observational studies can reveal much about human behaviour.

Returning to the area of proxemics, a naturalistic observational study could possibly observe pairs of individuals in conversation (standing position), and note the average toe-to-toe distance that they maintain over a 30-second observational period. The researcher would use a recording form to note information such as the type of interacting pair (male/male, male/female, female/female) and age and status differences (teacher/student, parent/child, employer/employee, peer/peer) between the two. Studies such as the one suggested involve few variables and it is, therefore, possible to analyze them without the help of a computer—a decided advantage for those who do not have access to the technology or students in a first level, single semester course.

Many daily activities can be observed and recorded without making subjects aware that their behaviour is being monitored. Several examples of this type of study are included in Box 3.6. In all of the studies, the student research groups began by defining the conditions under which the subjects would be observed. An introduction to establishing and following rules of observation is provided in Box 3.7. Students conduct this simple door-holding exercise to introduce this methodology. For their group projects, they select a topic and review the literature to determine what researchers had reported on in similar studies. Students are encouraged to link the particular behaviour being observed to some general category of behaviour. For example, could the failure to use a seat belt be viewed as an instance of a minor form of deviance? Also, the variables had to be carefully defined and cut-off points for the various categories determined. For example, to estimate the age of subjects, the following age categories could be used:

(i) under 25 years of age;

(ii) between 26 and 39; and,

(iii) 40 and over.

The observer developed a **tally sheet** to record the observations (see Figure 3.5).

BOX 3.6 STUDENT RESEARCHERS AT WORK

Student Naturalistic Observational Studies

Project Dressing Appropriately for the Winter

Student Tracey MacMillan

Brief This project recorded weather appropriateness of outdoor clothing worn by teenagers during winter conditions.

Project Male and Female Food Preferences

Student Tracey Pye

Brief This study observed the differences in food selections of males and females in a university cafeteria.

Project Parking Violations

Student Steven Hawley

Brief This study compared and recorded differences (age category, gender, group status) between people who parked illegally and those who did not.

Project Gender and Smoking

Student Robyn MacDonald

Brief This study recorded the smoking behaviour (yes/no) of subjects in various settings in a small community. Gender, age category, and number in group were related to whether or not the target subject was smoking.

Project The Effects of the Professor's Gender on Class Participation

Student Jeanne Doiron

Brief A number of class situations were observed, and a comparison made on the over- or underrepresentation of "speaking up in class" by gender of student as related to the gender of the professor.

Project Seat Belt Compliance

Student Lori Kiley

Brief Motorists were observed to discover whether or not they were wearing their seat belts. Age categories, gender of driver, and number in the car were noted.

Project Speeding in a Small Town

Student Gordon Barker

Brief Using a radar device borrowed from the local RCMP detachment, student researchers noted the speed, gender of driver, age category, and number in the car driving on a small-town thoroughfare.

Project Who Purchases "Healthy" Foods at the Supermarket

Student Stephanie Power

Brief Patrons' purchases at a local supermarket were observed at the checkout for the amount of junk food included in the cart.

Project Bank Machine Behaviour

Student Kirk D. Bailey

Brief Observers noted whether users of ABMs checked the printed information provided at the machine and counted the cash before leaving the machine.

Project Non-verbal Cues Used to Terminate a One-on-One Conversation

Student Stacey Desmond

Brief Conversations were observed in a mall, and the non-verbal termination cues were noted and related to age category and gender combinations.

Project Drinking Patterns

Student Anne Simpson

Brief Type of alcohol consumed was observed and related to gender composition of drinking group and the age of people at local taverns.

Project Smoking Behaviour in 11- to 19-Year-Old Students

Student Jacques Boudreau

Brief Junior high and high school students were observed as they left school. Smoking (yes/no) was noted, along with the gender, age, and number walking together.

Project Pool Hall Deviance

Student Nadine V.B. Boudreau

Brief Patrons at a youth entertainment establishment were observed; rule-breaking behaviour was noted and related to gender and age.

Project Conformity to Stop-Sign Rule

Students Judith Finn; Patricia Mbowe

Brief Cars were observed as they approached stop signs. The driver's age, gender, and whether he/she was alone in the car were noted by the student researchers.

Project Tipping

Student Jennifer Mercier

Project The tipping patterns of patrons at a local bar were observed and related to gender, age category, and the size and type of group (same or mixed gender).

BOX 3.7 STUDENT RESEARCHERS AT WORK

Rules for Naturalistic Observations of an Everyday Event: Door Holding

1. Student researchers work in pairs. One student acts as leader of the group; the other as checker.

2. Students make observations at *one* of the three mall entrances: #1 East end of mall, #2 Middle entrance, #3 West end of mall. They do not record data if other students are recording data at the entrance.

3. The person playing role of leader stands on one side (looking very casual); the checker stands on the other side of the entrance, looking as inconspicuous as possible. *Do not stand together when doing the observations* as this compromises later exercises based on the data gathered. Observers record the data separately.

4. When researchers are positioned properly and are ready to begin observations, the leader nods indicating that the case should be included (the

checker may veto by a "no" shake of the head, if s/he is not ready or the case does not warrant inclusion); when both agree, the leader and the checker then record the relevant information on the tally sheet.

5. Data are collected only on people *entering* the mall when:

    a. the lead person is located between 2.5 m and 5 m of the second person

    b. there does not seem to be a relationship between holder and holdee (do not include family groups, etc.). Observations should be made only on pairs that appear to be strangers to one another.

6. Door holding involves the first person waiting for the second and holding the door for him/her.

7. The definition of "carrying something" means to be encumbered so that it might be difficult to open the door; normal items such as a handbag or small parcel should not be regarded as encumbrances.

8. Researchers collect data on the same 20 cases (i.e., leader and checker should have information on the same 20 cases).

9. Researchers enter answers to each item on the tally sheet with a check mark. Do not alter answers after data collected; expect differences. These are examined later.

10. Researchers bring tally sheets to class, stapled together along with the information sheet.

After the necessary number of observations had been recorded, the information was transferred from the tally sheets to a *master table* (see Figure 3.6). A **master table** records all the information so that all of the required tables can be derived from it without going back to the tally sheets. Appropriate tables were then constructed to show the relationships between each of the independent variables and the dependent variable.

1. ANDREW HARRELL: CHILD SAFETY IN GROCERY CARTS

Andrew Harrell, a sociologist at the University of Alberta, has conducted several field observation studies on the safety of children in cars, grocery stores, and shopping carts (see Harrell 1994, 2003a, 2003b, 2005, Harrell and Reid, 1990). His most recent study was featured in *Maclean's* magazine in an article called "Unlovely, Unloved" (2005, pp. 48–49) and in the *New York Times* in an article entitled "Ugly Children May Get Parental Short Shrift" (Bakalar, 2005). Harrell found that attractive children were more likely to be buckled up in the child seat of grocery carts than were less attractive children. Harrell, a father and grandfather, said that he is appalled by the findings but not entirely surprised because his research findings confirm what has been found by other researchers: attractiveness influences individuals' social behaviour, even among family members (2005, p. 49). Box 3.8 summarizes Harrell's study, "Are Prettier Kids Protected Better?"

BOX 3.8   SOCIAL RESEARCHERS AT WORK

Andrew Harrell: Are Prettier Kids Protected Better? A Field Observational Study of Child Safety in Grocery Carts

In the present study, we investigate the possibility that parents of unattractive children may be less involved during mundane caretaking activities than they are with attractive children. As noted in the literature review (not reprinted here), evolutionary theory predicts this outcome because beauty may be a marker for reproductive success, whereas socialization theory suggests that this occurs because we learn to value beauty. Evolutionary theory suggests that men may be less attentive caretakers of children than women because of lower perceived genetic relatedness to children in their care while socialization theorists suggest that our culture teaches men that fathers are less involved as parents than are mothers.

Adult monitoring and care for children in grocery stores has been chosen as a setting for investigation. Virtually all parents in North America visit grocery stores with their children at one time or another, in some cases as frequently as once a day. The hazards present in grocery stores and around shopping carts have been well documented. One study estimated that 25,000 to 31,000 children per year in the United States are seriously hurt by falls from shopping carts or tipovers. Harrell (1994) estimates that there are 43 injuries per 1,000 child supermarket visits, though the vast majority of injuries are minor and do not require hospitalization. Previous research demonstrates that parents are not perfect in their monitoring of children in grocery stores and around shopping carts. The typical parent loses sight of his or her child an average of 3.3 times in a 55-minute shopping trip and adults are also likely to be 10 feet or further from their children an average of 2.7 times while shopping (Harrell, 2003a). Eighty percent of parents lose sight of their children at least once and 75% are 10 feet or more away at least once (Harrell, 1994). It is our belief that child attractiveness may impact this caretaking.

Three dependent measures were employed: whether seat belts were used, whether the adult was 10 or more feet away from the child, and whether the adult lost sight of the child. It was hypothesized that more attractive children would be watched more vigilantly (not less than 10 feet from child, not lose sight of child) in grocery stores and would be protected by seat belts. Both evolutionary theory and socialization theory predict that men will be less protective of children—less likely to apply seat belts—and less vigilant than women.

Method

Subjects Subjects were 426 children between the estimated ages of 1 to 7 years who were accompanied by one adult caretaker (and no other children) in supermarkets in Edmonton, Alberta, Canada.

Locations Observations occurred in 14 supermarkets for which permission was received to carry out the research. Shoppers were not interviewed or otherwise interfered with during their shopping trip. Each supermarket had approximately 300–500 shopping carts, all of which were equipped with seat belts for children who were placed in the cart seats. Observations took place seven days a week, from 9 a.m. to 5 p.m. The data were collected by fourteen teams of four persons. Observers were experienced in structured observation on other accident analysis projects and received three hours of orientation for the present study.

Procedure An observer team stood by the entrance of a store until an eligible subject arrived. This was a child able to enter the store on his or her own power, estimated to be between 1 and 7 years of age, and accompanied by only one adult. The decision to confine observations to one child and one adult was made because of the difficulty of recording data for larger groups of subjects and the belief that multiple children and caretakers may have other dynamics beyond the scope of this study. In addition, for a child to be selected for observation the child subject had to be placed in the cart-seat section of the grocery cart. The decision to only observe children placed in the cart seat was made because seat belts are only available in the cart-seat area.

Initially, two members of each team followed the subject and accompanying adult posing as "shoppers." After following the subjects for five minutes, each team member recorded, independently, their ratings of the child's and the adult's physical attractiveness. These observers also recorded the estimated age and gender of the child and adult. At the end of this five minute segment, two observers replaced these two observers. These observers continued following the subjects for an additional five minutes, recording whether or not the child was confined with a seat belt. These observers recorded the measures of parental vigilance (whether or not the adult was ever 10 feet or more from the child and whether or not the accompanying adult was ever out of sight of the child). The decision was made to have the first two observers in the four-observer team record the predictor variables—age, gender, and attractiveness—separately from the two observers who recorded the dependent variables—safety belt use, adult monitoring, and dangerous activities engaged in by the child. It was felt that this separation would prevent the observers who estimated attractiveness from influencing the other two observers.

Measures Attractiveness was measured on a 7-point scale, with 1 indicating least attractive and 7 most attractive. In their training, observers were told to focus on facial attractiveness and to disregard body type, clothing, and grooming. This was an effort to eliminate possible indicia of social or economic class. In the analysis to follow, this attractiveness index was divided into three ordinal rankings that roughly correspond to the breakpoints producing a rectilinear distribution of three equal categories. Caretaker monitoring was measured by recording whether or not the accompanying adult was 10 feet or more from the child and whether the adult lost sight of the child. A composite measure was constructed by combining the two. A score of zero represented a situation in which the adult neither lost sight of the child nor was further than 10 feet away. A score of 1 was received if the adult either was more than 10 feet away or lost sight. A score of 2 indicated that the adult was both 10 feet away and lost sight of the child. These measures of supervision have been used with considerable success in a number of other studies (Harrell and Reid, 1990; Harrell, 1994). It has been shown that adults are less likely to be in a position to protect a child from having an accident if they are more than 10 feet away (Harrell, 1994).

Inter-rater Reliability In previous studies (Harrell & Reid, 1990; Harrell, 1994; Harrell, 2003b), high levels of agreement have been reached on measures of caretaking vigilance, age, gender and dangerous activities, with scores ranging from 80 to 100%. Since there rarely is perfect agreement on estimates of age, a mean age has been calculated for each pair of observers. In the case of the attractiveness judgments, a mean score has been calculated for each observer pair. The correlations between raters on ratings of adult attractiveness were.91 (p <.001) and for children,.86 (p <.001). There were 27 cases of disagreement on caretaker monitoring, i.e., whether or not an adult was 10 feet or more away. There were no disagreements on whether or not a seat belt was used.

Analysis Since the dependent variables, seat belt use, whether or not an adult was 10 feet or more away, and engagement in climbing from or standing in the cart seat, were binomial in nature, a multinomial logistic regression was carried out. This analysis examined the impact of each factor variable—child's and adult's age and gender and child and adult attractiveness—on the three dependent variables. Interaction effects involving child's and adult's sex and attractiveness were also analyzed in cross-tabular analyses. An analysis of variance was carried out for the composite measure of caretaker monitoring.

Results and Discussion

Fifty-one percent of the children in the sample (n= 426) were male, and 48.8% female. The mean age of children was 2.66 years (SD = 1.25 years). Seventy-seven percent of the adults accompanying the children were female, and 23.5% male. On the seven-point Likert scale, the mean level of attractiveness for children was 4.60 (SD = 1.26). Overall, 7.0% of the children were buckled into the child seats; 93.0% were not. Seventy-nine percent of the adults did not lose sight of the children in their care nor were away ten feet or more during the five minute observation period. Twelve percent of adults were either out of sight or ten feet away, and 8.4% were both out of sight and ten feet away. Adults were much more likely to be ten feet away (20.4%) than to lose sight of a child in their care (8.5%).

Seat belt use tended to be greater for more attractive children. Although only 7% of the children in this sample were buckled in with a seat belt, there was a strong linear increase in seat belt use as the rated attractiveness of the child increased. Thus, while only 1% of the least attractive children were buckled in, 10% of the most attractive children were restrained by seat belts. This linear trend was impacted by the sex of the accompanying adult. Male adults did not use seat belts for any of the least attractive children, whereas female adults used seat belts for 4% of the children in this attractiveness category. Female adults were slightly more likely to use seat belts than male adults for the most attractive category of children. Female adults used seat belts in 15% of the cases whereas male adults used seat belts for only 9% of the children in the most attractive category.

Similarly, adults were less likely to be 10 feet away from or to lose sight of attractive children. Attractive adults also tended to be more watchful of the children they accompanied than unattractive adults. These relationships involving attractiveness were stronger for women than for men.

The present study investigated seat belt use in grocery carts and the supervision of children while they were sitting in these carts. Consistent with past research, we found parental safety decisions to be influenced by the attractiveness of the child. It is our belief that the ubiquitous effect of beauty will be found in every instance of child care, including measures taken to prevent injury or harm to children. Conceivably, attractiveness may influence decisions to provide children with bicycle helmets, supervision in dangerous environments such as swimming pools, and possibly vaccinating children to prevent illness.

The field setting in which this study occurred, along with restrictions on our ability to establish the nature of the relationship between adults and the children in their company, did not permit a definitive test of the evolutionary predictions about the importance of child assets such as attractiveness and the quality of parental care. For example, one would expect that the greater the genetic relatedness between the child and the adult, the more conscientious the supervision and the use of safety devices such as seat belts. The fact that in the present study there was not a significantly poorer quality of care by adult males than adult females (assuming that perceived relatedness will be higher for "mothers" than for "fathers") is a strike against the evolutionary approach. Nevertheless, both fitness-related (evolutionary) theory and social learning theory predict and provide some explanation for the differential treatment of children on the basis of beauty.

Source: Andrew Harrell (2005). "Are Prettier Kids Protected Better: A Field Observational Study of Child Safety in Grocery Carts," *unpublished paper*. Printed with permission of author.

2. STEPS IN CONDUCTING A NATURALISTIC OBSERVATIONAL STUDY: SEAT BELT USE

Suppose, for example, that you were doing the "use of seat belt" study and that you wished to relate belt use to the independent variables of the driver's gender, the driver's age, and whether the driver is alone or with others. Let us go through the steps that would be involved in such a study, examining in greater detail how each step would be carried out.

STEP 1 RESTRICTIONS ON OBSERVATIONS

Since this study concerns the use or non-use of seat belts, we would need to restrict observations to those cases in which we can detect whether the driver and/or passengers in a passing vehicle are wearing seat belts. The first restriction, then, would be to limit the observations to recent models of automobiles, since trucks or older cars might be using lap belts which could not be seen as a vehicle passes by. Second, we would do the observations in a place where vehicles are moving fairly slowly so that the observer would have time both to see and to record the information. Finally, a decision would have to be made as to whether observations will be limited to the driver (this will be easiest) or will include other front-seat passengers.

STEP 2 REVIEWING LITERATURE

At this point, a review should be undertaken of the literature to find out what studies, if any, have been done on seat belt use; furthermore, if the failure to use a seat belt is viewed as a form of deviance, the literature on deviance could be reviewed to see what variables are related to deviance. For example, a researcher could check the literature to see if young males show higher levels of deviance for this minor infraction. If use of the seat belt is viewed as a form of conformity, a review could be done on the conformity literature to see what other researchers have found on this subject.

STEP 3 DEVELOPING HYPOTHESES

At this stage, the researcher attempts to make predictions about expected outcomes. Such hypotheses can be derived from:

- common sense;
- what other researchers have found; or
- by relating the specific behaviour (seat belt use) to its general class (deviance) and then making predictions.

The following three hypotheses might be appropriate to the seat belt study:

1. female drivers are more likely to use seat belts than male drivers;
2. older drivers are more likely to use seat belts than younger drivers; and
3. drivers with others in the car are more likely to use seat belts than drivers alone in the car.

By formulating hypotheses prior to collecting data one ensures that one is not inventing the hypotheses after the analysis has been done.

STEP 4 DEFINING TERMS

Prior to collecting the data, a careful definition of each of the variables is required. Seat belt use (or non-use) refers to the apparent use (or non-use) of a shoulder seat belt by the driver (or others if they are included in the study). The observer also records the gender and age (in categories such as under 26, 26 to 39, 40 years of age and over) of the driver. The categories "alone" and "group" are added to classify those drivers who are alone and those drivers accompanied by one or more people.

STEP 5 DEVELOPING A TALLY SHEET

A tally sheet should be developed to record the observations. Generally the first variable listed is the dependent variable (wearing or not wearing a seat belt), followed by the independent variables, gender, age, and alone/in a group. The sheet might look like the one displayed in Figure 3.5. The tally sheet should be designed so that the observer can quickly tick off the categories the individual driver falls into. A check mark is easier than writing the estimated age or writing "female" for a female driver. If conditions or time of day are to be recorded, one can, for instance, place a bracket around a set of observations done during a rainy, cloudy day, or a bracket around those done during rush hour traffic.

FIGURE 3.5 TALLY SHEET FOR RECORDING OBSERVATIONS

ID#	SEAT BELT		GENDER		AGE			GROUP STATUS	
	YES	NO	MALE	FEMALE	16–25	26–39	40+	ALONE	GROUP
1	✔		✔		✔			✔	
2	✔			✔	✔			✔	
3		✔		✔	✔				✔
4	✔		✔			✔			✔
5	✔			✔	✔				✔
6	✔			✔			✔	✔	
7		✔	✔				✔		
8		✔	✔			✔		✔	
9	✔			✔		✔		✔	
10	✔		✔			✔			✔

STEP 6 TRANSFERRING DATA TO THE MASTER TABLE

Once observations have been completed, the tally sheet data are transferred to the master table (see Figure 3.6). Typically, the dependent variable is arranged on the left side of the master table using the categories "wearing belt" and "not wearing belt." Categories of the independent variables are arranged across the top of the master table. In this case we have three independent variables: gender, age, and group size. Each observation ends up in one— and only one—cell of the master table. Thus data about a female driver under 25, who is alone in the car and who does not appear to have her seat belt fastened, would end up in one cell only. Normally each observation is entered into the cell with a short line indicating one observation; these observations are grouped together so that the fifth line entered into a cell has a line across the other four. Each group then reflects five observations falling into the cell. Later these can be counted and a total for each cell entered and circled at the bottom of the cell. Tables 3.4, 3.5, and 3.6 provide examples of summary tables.

FIGURE 3.6 MASTER TABLE FOR SEAT BELT STUDY

	MALE						FEMALE					
	ALONE			GROUP			ALONE			GROUP		
Age/Belt use	Y	M	O	Y	M	O	Y	M	O	Y	M	O
Wearing belt												
Not wearing belt												

Age categories: Y = 16 – 25   M = 26 – 39   O = 40 +

STEP 7 CREATING THE INDIVIDUAL TABLES

At minimum three tables would be created, each showing the relation between the use/non-use of the seat belt and gender, age, and group size. Tables 3.4, 3.5, and 3.6 show the format of the tables. Note that the dependent variable is arranged on the left side of the page and that the categories of the independent variable are arranged across the top of the page. Note also that the percentages are calculated on each of the columns. Details for the construction of such tables are presented in Chapter 16. More complex tables containing control variables can also be created from the master table. However, before constructing such tables, the student should examine the material in Chapter 16.

TABLE 3.4   SEAT BELT USE BY GENDER

| | GENDER | | | | | |
| | MALE | | FEMALE | | TOTAL | |
SEAT BELT USE	N	%	N	%	N	%
Using seat belt	144	75.8	138	79.8	282	77.7
Not using seat belt	46	24.2	35	20.2	81	22.3
Totals	190	100.0	173	100.0	363	100.0

TABLE 3.5   SEAT BELT USE WHEN DRIVER IS ALONE OR WITH OTHERS

| | DRIVER ALONE OR WITH OTHERS | | | | | |
| | ALONE | | GROUP | | TOTAL | |
SEAT BELT USE	N	%	N	%	N	%
Using seat belt	121	76.1	161	78.9	282	77.7
Not using seat belt	38	23.9	43	21.1	81	22.3
Totals	159	100.0	204	100.0	363	100.0

TABLE 3.6 SEAT BELT USE BY AGE

| | AGE CATEGORY | | | | | | | |
| | 16-25 | | 26-39 | | 40+ | | TOTAL | |
SEAT BELT USE	N	%	N	%	N	%	N	%
Using seat belt	87	71.3	110	78.6	85	84.2	282	77.7
Not using seat belt	35	28.7	30	21.4	16	15.8	81	22.3
Totals	122	100.0	140	100.0	101	100.0	363	100.0

STEP 8 WRITING A REPORT

The final step would be to write a report on the research efforts. Chapter 18 presents additional information on report writing.

E. ADVANTAGES AND LIMITATIONS OF EXPERIMENTAL AND FIELD STUDY APPROACHES

The forte of the experiment is in demonstrating that a treatment variable has an impact on some outcome measure. To do this well an experimentalist has to rule out possible sources of contamination and deal with control variables and the effect of random variables. These challenges are met in greater or lesser degrees by experimental designs. The forte of naturalistic and field experiments is that they are conducted in natural settings and hence have greater validity, in that they avoid the artificiality so often found in experimental and survey research. Table 3.7 summarizes the advantages and disadvantages of different types of experimental and field study designs.

1. PSEUDO-EXPERIMENTAL DESIGNS

A. LIMITATIONS

The pre-experimental design involving a *same group: pretest/post-test* discussed earlier in this chapter had problems in that in this design all kinds of other random factors

TABLE 3.7 ADVANTAGES AND LIMITATIONS OF ALTERNATE DESIGNS

RESEARCH DESIGN CATEGORY	GENERAL	VALIDITY	CAUSAL INFERENCE	MULTI-VARIATE	PROBING
EXPERIMENTAL DESIGNS					
Pseudo-experimental	—	—	—	—	—
Experimental	—	—	+	—	—
Quasi-Experimental	±	—	+	—	—
Field Experiments	—	+	+	—	—
Naturalistic Observational	—	+	—	—	—

In each category a "**+**" means that this is an advantage of the technique; a "**–**" means this is a possible limitation; "**±**" means that in some conditions it is a limitation, and in others an advantage.

- **General** refers to the extent to which extrapolations to larger populations may be made using each of the design/data collection procedures.
- **Validity** is the extent to which indicators clearly measure what they are intended to measure.
- **Causal Inference** refers to the ease with which inferences about causal relations among variables may be made.
- **Multivariate** refers to the ease with which information on many variables is collected, leading to the possibility of multivariate analysis.
- **Probing** refers to the extent to which responses may be probed in depth.

may have influenced the change in outcome measures. On the other hand, the *exposed comparison group design* was seen to be flawed because it could not demonstrate that the experimental and control groups were similar prior to the introduction of the treatment. In short, the groups may have been different from one another and the treatment effect cannot be convincingly documented.

2. CLASSIC EXPERIMENTAL DESIGNS

The classic experimental designs seek to remedy the problems of causal inferences by establishing randomly matched comparison groups (experimental and control groups) along with before-treatment and after-treatment measures on the dependent variable. These designs are referred to as *between-subjects designs*. A second approach discussed dealt with problems of causal inference by exposing the same subjects to different treatments. Control over random variables is achieved in the latter design through *control by constancy*—the use of the same subject in the comparisons.

A. ADVANTAGES

The advantage in both these designs is that they can provide powerful, convincing evidence for the effect of a treatment variable. Through statistical analysis and through the use of randomization and precision matching, control over random and confounding variables is enhanced. Thus, classic experimental designs produce the clearest view of causation. This is accomplished through the application of a treatment to subjects under conditions where extraneous variables are controlled. Furthermore, through the use of *double blind* designs, where neither

subjects nor researchers know which subjects are under what condition, there is considerable control over bias on the part of subjects and researchers. However, there are some limitations of experimental designs.

B. LIMITATIONS

i. External Validity

Few experiments are conducted using samples that can be viewed as representative of a larger population and therefore one cannot make extrapolations to the general population—this is the issue of *external validity*. In short, can the findings of a study based on sociology students at Mount Allison University be extrapolated to university students across the country? Clearly one would need to repeat the study in many different locales to determine the extent to which valid generalizations can be drawn from a single study.

ii. The Limits to Predictability in Experimental Studies

The fact that experimental studies do a better job than surveys in predicting outcomes should not be misinterpreted. For example suppose that a treatment variable X (therapeutic touch) controls 10% of the variability in the dependent variable Y (stress level). Ideally an experiment is designed to control all external factors that influence the dependent variable. Surveys can exercise such control only through statistical adjustments. Thus the ability of experimental and nonexperimental designs to predict outcomes is not comparable. In principle, experiments should produce higher predictability than that achieved by nonexperimental designs using the same variables. A robust variable in an experiment, however, may be relatively impotent outside the laboratory setting.

iii. The Artificiality Issue

The third major concern is that there is an element of artificiality in laboratory experiments that is difficult to detect, to interpret, and to control. In the nursing world, for instance, the natural environment in which the client is situated bears heavily on health outcomes. Controlling all factors as you do in a classic experiment may not, however, yield results that are applicable in the real world, where you are unable to control the same set of factors.

In addition, a "good subject" may try to respond by giving the researcher what the subject thinks the researcher wants; the subject may also be intimidated and act atypically. To what extent do people modify their behaviour when they know that they are being studied? While more will be said about this topic in Chapter 10, researchers need to, and frequently do, take into account the effects of expectations on the response of subjects. Since subjects can manage their presentation-of-self to the experimenter, questions can be raised about the validity (are you measuring what you claim to measure?) of some experimental results.

iv. Limitations on Number of Variables

For practical reasons, experimental designs can deal only with a few variables simultaneously (multiple-variable designs are possible, but with several treatment and control levels one would soon need far too many subjects to run the experiment: a 3 x 3 x 3 x 3 design produces 81 treatment conditions and, if there were 10 subjects per condition, would require 810 subjects). When a large number of variables require simultaneous analysis, it is advisable either to use a different experimental design or to simplify the experiment by using fewer variables or fewer levels in each variable.

v. Experiments Cannot Study All Topics

It is neither practical nor ethical to experiment on all aspects of human behaviour and therefore other designs remain important tools for the researcher. For example, in a study exploring the effectiveness of a new birth control method, it would be impractical and entirely unethical to randomly assign half the clients at a well-women's clinic to use no birth control while the other half would be assigned to use the new method.

The beginning researcher should have some understanding of experimental designs, as their great strength is the ability to control many of the confounding factors that influence outcomes. Where experimentation is not possible, it is more difficult to produce convincing inferences about causal relationships.

3. QUASI-EXPERIMENTAL DESIGNS

A. ADVANTAGES

Quasi-experimental designs are typically done when the topic dictates that an experiment is not possible. Thus they are often the best that can be done given certain ethical or practical constraints.

Sometimes quasi-experimental designs involve representative samples. In such studies a group of individuals (usually called a panel) is monitored over time. The panel may have been selected as a representative one and thus the results may enable the researcher to make sound causal arguments that can, at the same time, lead to extrapolations to the larger population. Quasi-experimental designs thus can sometimes fuse strong causal inferences with strong external validity.

B. LIMITATIONS

Given limited control over the context in which the study is conducted, quasi-experimental studies lack the causal inference power of the classic experiment. It is sometimes not possible to control the treatment variable or to place individuals in experimental and control groups. Thus these studies often represent a compromise between what the ideal study would look like and what is feasible.

4. FIELD EXPERIMENTS AND NATURALISTIC OBSERVATIONAL STUDIES

A. ADVANTAGES

Field experiments facilitate making causal inferences, are strong on validity, and are often relatively inexpensive to complete. For example, observing "cutting through between two people carrying on a conversation" can be done cheaply and the distances between the interacting pair can be changed easily to vary the condition presented to the researcher. Similarly, naturalistic observational studies are typically inexpensive to complete and have high levels of validity since normal everyday behaviour is being observed and recorded— subjects are not typically aware that they are being observed as they go about their public behaviour. Observing spontaneous social behaviour in everyday situations provides convincing evidence.

B. LIMITATIONS

A notable limitation of field experiments and naturalistic observational studies is the number of variables that can be observed. We are often limited to such observable variables as gender, age category, whether the subject is alone or with others, as well as the dependent variable of the study. Causal inferences may be difficult because of the inability to control relevant causal factors.

F. CONCLUSION

The strength of experimental designs is their ability to clarify causal inferences. Classic experimental designs have a high level of internal validity because the researcher can demonstrate that the treatment (manipulation of the independent variable) alone produced changes in the dependent variable. The design is intended to control for the effects of possible confounding variables. The two types of classic experimental designs are the between-subjects design and the within-subject design. The typical between-subjects design involves randomly assigning research participants to experimental and control groups and taking pre-treatment and post-treatment measures. The within-subject design exposes the same subject to different treatments in different sequences. Because experiments tend to take place in laboratory settings, it is difficult to know whether the same outcomes would occur in a social context. Given this, experiments are said to have low external validity.

Some natural settings lend themselves well to quasi-experimental designs and field experiments. These types of designs have stronger external validity because the behaviour is measured in real life settings. Because experiments are typically conducted on small, unrepresentative samples, however, their results cannot be generalized to larger populations. And, while this is also a problem with many other designs, there is a sense that the bulk of experimental studies have used undergraduates as subjects (not a representative sample of the population). Quasi-experimental designs, often using panels who are interviewed over time, can more feasibly use representative samples.

Field experiments facilitate making causal inferences, are strong on validity, and are often fairly inexpensive to complete. Naturalistic observational studies, like field experiments, are inexpensive and have high validity since actual behaviour is being observed in a natural setting. In such studies, subjects are not even aware that they are being observed.

The nature of experimental design makes it difficult to take into account a large number of variables at one time systematically. For example, in a 3 x 3 x 2 between-subjects design, the researcher is facing 18 cells, and to run a modest 15 subjects per condition would take 270 subjects. Apart from the treatment variable, we are dealing with only three other variables simultaneously. And while there are experimental designs that make more efficient use of subjects, it is not easy to take even seven or eight variables into account simultaneously.

In naturalistic observational studies, the subjects are observed unobtrusively and are not aware that they are part of a study. A notable disadvantage of such studies is the limits on what can be observed. Since subjects are not asked questions, the variables observed are limited to gender, age, and other characteristics that are manifested during the time of observation. For example, a researcher examining the impact of group size on smoking would not know whether it is group size or the fact that an observed individual subject is a non-smoker that has inhibited smoking.

Even though experiments provide the clearest view of causation, it is often not possible to experiment on all topics. As a result, other research designs—some incorporating different orientations to knowledge—have developed to enhance our understanding of the complexity of human behaviour.

G. KEY POINTS

Experimental designs provide the most convincing evidence for demonstrating causal relations among variables. There are two basic types of experiments: *between-subjects designs,* in which each group of subjects is exposed to only one level of the treatment, and *within-subject designs,* in which each subject is exposed to all levels of the treatment variable.

In an experiment, the independent variable, whose effect is being studied, is known as the *treatment variable.*

A *control variable* is a variable that is specifically taken into account in designing the study.

A *confounding variable* is one that can either obscure or enhance a relationship and must be taken into account in designing an experiment.

A *random variable* is allowed to vary without control, but is taken into account by the way groups are set up for the study.

In a between-subjects design, *treatment and control groups are to be as equivalent as possible before the treatment begins.* There are three ways of achieving equivalence:

1. through precision matching (matching on sex, socioeconomic status, grades—or whatever factors are felt to be important for the study);

2. through randomization (whereby individuals are randomly assigned either to the treatment or to the control group); or

3. through a combination of the previous two techniques. Randomization (if the numbers are

large enough) will provide control over both known and unknown factors (the control and random variables).

To show a causal relationship in any research, three conditions must be demonstrated:

1. changes in the independent variable must occur prior to changes in the dependent variable;

2. the variables must be associated—as values on the independent variable are increased, the dependent measures vary systematically; and

3. nothing but the treatment variable must influence the dependent variable.

A *Hawthorne effect* refers to any variability in the dependent variable that is not the direct result of variations in the treatment variable.

In a *within-subject design* each subject is exposed to all levels of the treatment variable. Control over random and control variables is achieved by control by constancy—by having each subject act as his or her own control.

Natural setting experiments can be done when everyday situations can be manipulated in such a way as to allow the researcher to observe the reactions of people to the intervention.

Naturalistic observational studies are those in which the researcher records observations without the subjects being aware that they are being observed and in which there is no experimental manipulation on the part of the researcher.

Experimental designs produce the clearest view of causation. This is accomplished through the application of a treatment to subjects under conditions in which extraneous variables are controlled.

A *quasi-experiment* is one in which it has not been possible to do any or all of the following:

(i) randomly assign subjects to a treatment or control group; or

(ii) control the timing or nature of the treatment.

The quasi-experiment comes as close as possible to experimental design in order to measure the impact of a treatment.

The particular *strength* of experimental and quasi-experimental designs is their ability to clarify causal inferences.

H. KEY TERMS

Baseline measure	Experimental group	Proxemics
Baseline stability	External validity	Pseudo-experimental design
Between-subjects design	Field experiment	Quasi-experimental design
Blocked design	Hawthorne effect	Random variable
Classic experimental design	History	Response bias
Confounding variable	Independent variable	Selection
Control by constancy	Instrument decay	Statistical regression
Control group	Internal validity	Tally sheet
Control group design	Master table	Treatment levels
Control variable	Maturation	Treatment variable
Counterbalancing	Mortality	Within-subject design
Dependent variable	Naturalistic observational study	
Double blind	Natural setting experiments	

C H A P T E R   F O U R

SURVEY DESIGNS

A. INTRODUCTION

In contrast to the experiment, the survey emphasizes making extrapolations from samples to whole populations. Also in contrast to an experiment, a survey typically measures many variables. Surveys include censuses, polls, and a whole range of situations in which respondents are asked to provide answers to a set of fixed questions.

1. A SHORT HISTORY OF THE SURVEY

Surveys have been around for a long time— there are biblical references to the counts of the children of Israel, Napoleon did surveys, and censuses were taken of the population of ancient Egypt. However, the foundations of the modern survey were laid in nineteenth-century England by Charles Booth who conducted three major London surveys. He was the first to work out operational definitions (the indicators he used to measure poverty); the first to draw colour maps to reflect the social characteristics of an area; and the first to attempt to show how variables were related to one another, thus beginning efforts to understand the association between social variables. Booth was concerned with providing an accurate count and description of poor people living in London. The claim has been made that Booth was "the first empirical sociologist" (Easthope, 1974, p. 57).

In Canada, Herbert Ames conducted a survey of poverty in Montreal and published the results in *The City Below the Hill* (1897). Like Booth, Ames derived his ideas about conducting a survey from European social reformers who believed that surveying the poverty of working people would expose poverty and encourage social reform. The

survey method was practiced by Robert Ezra Park who founded the first American sociology department at the University of Chicago in the 1920s and by Leonard Marsh and Everett Hughes, who founded the first Canadian sociology department at McGill University in Montreal. Park extended Booth's idea of using "ecological maps" to describe social patterns in urban areas.

The link between political interests and survey research is strong, and, just as Booth's work in England had political relevance, so too did the work of another person who lived in England at the time. In 1880, Karl Marx attempted to survey some 25,000 French workers to gauge how badly they were being exploited. The questionnaire included 108 questions, many of which would take considerable time to answer. For example, questions 59 and 100 asked:

59. Have you noticed that the delay in paying your wages makes it necessary for you to resort frequently to the pawnbroker, paying a high rate of interest, and depriving yourself of things which you need; or to fall into debt of shopkeepers, becoming their victim because you are their debtor? Do you know any instances in which workers have lost their wages through the bankruptcy of their employers? (Bottomore and Rubel, 1988, p. 215)

100. What is the general physical, intellectual, and moral condition of the men and women workers employed in your trade? (Bottomore and Rubel, 1988, p. 218)

It would take a thoughtful respondent indeed to respond adequately to these questions! The analysis of such responses would pose enormous difficulties and, judged by contemporary standards, some of Marx's questions seem to have a built-in bias:

56. If you are paid piece rates, how are the rates fixed? If you are employed in an industry in which the work performed is measured by quantity or weight, as in the case of the mines, does your employer or his representative resort to trickery in order to defraud you of your earnings? (Bottomore and Rubel, 1988, p. 215.)

57. If you are paid piece rates, is the quality of the article made a pretext for fraudulent deductions from your wages? (Bottomore and Rubel, 1988, p. 215)

Apparently few questionnaires were returned (Bottomore and Rubel, 1988, p. 211). And although the questions Marx raised were both interesting and important, it would have been difficult to do a meaningful analysis of the responses, given the complexity of some of the questions and the likelihood that many questions would not receive complete answers from the respondents.

Survey research developed in the twentieth century, partly through the efforts of pioneer pollsters George Gallup and Elmo Roper to provide an accurate profile of Americans, partly from efforts of market researchers to understand consumer behaviour better, and partly from the interests of journalists, government agencies, and political organizations, all of whom understood the advantages that could be gained if one could gauge public opinion accurately. Survey research was just too powerful a tool to be left to the scholars alone.

During the post–World War Two era, it was Samuel A. Stouffer and Paul F. Lazarsfeld who did much to make survey research a legitimate academic and practical pursuit. *The People's Choice* (Lazarsfeld, Berelson, and Gaudet, 1968) was a sophisticated analysis of voting intentions and behaviour. It was the first study to interview members of a panel several times in the period leading up to an election. *The People's Choice* marks the beginning of voting studies in political science, and it was the first study to take control variables into account systematically. In 1985, Alfred Hunter published an essay entitled "Doing It with Numbers" in a special edition of the *Canadian Review of Sociology and Anthropology* focused on "The State of the Art and New Directions." In it, he argued that quantitative methods had been institutionalized in Anglo-Canadian sociology. He noted the importance of survey research, particularly among social stratification researchers.

Survey research continues to be a key approach in several social science disciplines including psychology, political science, economics, criminology, education, and nursing. (This point is reflected in Box 4.4 on page 121.) Public opinion pollsters, community groups, and professionals doing evaluations of applied programs all make frequent use of survey methods. Indeed, major surveys have been designed and conducted by political scientists and sociologists working in Canadian universities. Social scientists sometimes employ survey data collected by other researchers or by Statistics Canada, the federal department charged with collecting relevant Canadian statistics on a broad range of topics (e.g., fertility, mortality, labour force participation, unemployment, consumer behaviour, family, health and well-being, and so on).

Many universities support survey research centres, such as the Institute for Social Research at York University in Toronto **www.isr.vorfiu.ca/home.html**, and the Population Research Laboratory at the University of Alberta in Edmonton **www.uofaweb.ualberta.ca/prl/**. Centres like these archive survey data and they provide technical support to researchers developing new surveys. Also, since January

1996, Statistics Canada data has been made available through data resource centres in universities across the country as part of a program called the Data Liberation Initiative (DLI). The objective of the DLI was to make Statistics Canada data more accessible to researchers working in universities and communities. (Prior to the DLI program, universities and colleges had to purchase Statistics Canada data file by file, and when the cost of Statistics Canada data went up in the 1980s, researchers began relying increasingly on data from other countries [Statistics Canada, 2005].) In addition to Statistics Canada data, the centres provide statistical support. An evaluation study of the success of the DLI has demonstrated an increase in the volume of research publications based on Statistics Canada data since the DLI program was launched (Humphrey and Hamilton, 2004).

This chapter will discuss the major types of surveys and provide practical guidelines for using them. Let us first examine the rationale of the survey to see how it contrasts with that of the experiment.

2. THE RATIONALE OF THE SURVEY

Surveys are a method of collecting information by having respondents complete a questionnaire. A **questionnaire** is made up of a series of set questions and either provides a space for an answer or offers a number of fixed alternatives from which the respondent makes a choice. Questionnaires can be completed in group settings, mailed to respondents, or read to respondents by interviewers either over the phone or in person.

As indicated in Chapter 1, surveys are typically associated with the positivist approach to knowledge. But it is to be noted that both Marx (conflict approach) and Weber (interpretive approach) used surveys. Marx developed a questionnaire to measure French worker experiences (Bottomore and Rubel, 1988, pp. 210–18), while Weber surveyed attitudes toward work.

Surveys can be a relatively inexpensive method of collecting a lot of information from a large number of people. Survey researchers will frequently draw a sample in order to make estimations about some population. As used by the researcher, the term **population** refers to that collection of individuals, communities, or nations about which one wishes to make a general statement. In order to save time and money, the researcher draws a **sample** from the population, which will be interpreted to represent the population. While including the whole population could prove to be more accurate (as in a census), the costs may be prohibitive. If the researcher wishes to make extrapolations from a sample to a larger population, then a fairly large sample will be required and hence it is likely that a survey design will be used. Since social behaviour is often highly complex—subject to the simultaneous impact of many variables—a research strategy that measures many variables simultaneously can often be appropriate.

With both experimental and survey designs there can be difficulty in establishing the validity of the measures used. In the case of surveys, respondents are asked to report their own attitudes, behaviour, and backgrounds. Some of the data requested will require respondents to recall episodes from their past ("How happy were you when you were first married?"). And since questionnaires probe into sensitive areas, they permit respondents to manage their responses so as to appear in a favourable light. Suppose one was attempting to measure attitudes toward minorities: in such cases one has to understand that some people may try to appear tolerant—perhaps more tolerant than they actually are. There is not a one-to-one relationship between what people say they believe and how they will actually behave when confronted with real situations. An initial field study conducted by Richard T. LaPiere (1934) showed that only one establishment out of 251 would refuse accommodations to LaPiere and a Chinese couple. Yet when LaPiere asked the same businesses the same question some six months later in a mailed questionnaire, only one business indicated that

it would accept members of the Chinese race as guests of the establishment. In his analysis, encapsulated in Box 4.1, Deutscher (1966) reminds us to consider the relation between attitudes expressed on a questionnaire and subsequent behaviour as problematical. Sometimes there may be little relation between the two.

Nonetheless, surveys can produce reliable and valid responses on many issues. And, if one wishes to measure attitudes, there is no good alternative to asking people about them. One simply has to live with the problems of measurement if the variables are to be measured at all. According

---

BOX 4.1   SOCIAL RESEARCHERS AT WORK

Irwin Deutscher: "Words and Deeds"

Deutscher argues that social-policy analysts are concerned with altering social behaviour. And much of our work as social scientists has to do with simply predicting behaviour. However, the predictions we make are derived from responses that interviewed people have made or to answers prompted by questionnaire items. The key issue is the extent to which we can rely on such responses to accurately reflect behaviour.

In his review of the relation between attitudes and behaviour, Deutscher identifies considerable evidence frequently showing an inverse relation between the two. Deutscher notes that:

> . . .this discrepancy between what people say and what they do is not

limited to the area of racial or ethnic relations: it has been observed that trade union members talk one game and play another, that there is no relationship between college students' attitudes toward cheating and their actual cheating behavior, that urban teachers' descriptions of classroom behavior are sometimes unrelated to the way teachers behave in the classroom, that what rural Missourians say about their health behavior has little connection with their actual health practices, and that the moral and ethical beliefs of students do not conform to their behavior. (Deutscher, 1966, p. 246)

Source: Irwin Deutscher (1966). "Words and Deeds: Social Action and Social Policy," *Social Problems*, 235–54. Reprinted by permission of the publisher.

to conventional wisdom, surveys provide **point-in-time data** and are therefore poor at measuring changes over time. While it is no doubt risky to assume that people will recall their past reliably, most surveys in fact do ask questions about a variety of points in time, such as the year of the respondent's birth, the type of community the respondent grew up in, or how old the respondent was at the time of his or her first full-time job. Once again, while there are problems with recall data, sometimes there is no practical alternative to the survey for measuring some variables.

Questionnaires are restrictive because they can be used only with a literate population, unless the researcher can afford to have the questionnaire read to the respondent in a face-to-face interview format. The wording of questions must be straightforward so that all—or at least most—of the respondents will be able to handle the language. Computer software programs are used to identify any words in the survey that exceed a Grade 8 level. Also, the requirement that all respondents be able to understand the questions prevents certain areas from being probed in depth. Everyone is given the same set of questions, and while it is advantageous to have all respondents reply to the same question, it does mean that interesting responses cannot be pursued. For in-depth probes, a personal interview is necessary.

This chapter will provide a general orientation to survey research. Anyone who wishes to know how to carry out a survey will need to consult two additional chapters in the book: Chapter 14 provides guidelines for developing a questionnaire, and Chapter 15 talks about how to go about selecting a sample and determining how large it should be. You may also wish to consult Chapter 13, which introduces measurement.

B. GUIDELINES FOR THE ADMINISTRATION OF SURVEYS

In this section, general rules will be provided for administering surveys. In all cases, the suggestions should be used with common sense, since there will be times when they should be violated. The following rules are intended to increase response rates for all types of surveys. The **response rate** is the percentage of delivered questionnaires that are completed and returned. The response rate does vary depending upon the type of survey conducted. This is discussed in greater detail in the following section.

RULE 4.1 MAKE PERSONAL CONTACT WITH THE RESPONDENT.

Where feasible, contact respondents in person to explain the survey to them and let them know when you will pick up the completed form. In a door-to-door survey, it should be possible to get over 80% to agree to complete the form. Avoid having third parties hand out your questionnaires: a member of the research team can explain the survey better and answer any questions that might be raised. In particular, avoid having teachers, workers' supervisors, or co-workers hand out questionnaires. The extra effort needed to have a member of the research team hand out the questionnaires will avoid many problems associated with a third-party delivery. For mailed surveys, personalize the letter of invitation by signing each letter sent. The greater the personal contact, the greater the response rate.

RULE 4.2 ESTABLISH LEGITIMACY.

Establish the legitimacy of the research by telling potential respondents who is sponsoring it and why it is being done. It is important to make the survey appear credible and to appear competent yourself; the covering letter and the questionnaire must look professional.

RULE 4.3 PAY RESPONDENTS.

Where reasonable and financially possible, pay respondents for their time and cooperation. The fee helps establish the legitimacy of the study as well as establishing a reciprocal relationship with the respondent. Such payments appear to have a modest impact on the willingness of respondents to participate (Heberlein and Baumgartner, 1978: Senn, Verberg, Desmarais and Wood, 2000). Payments help establish reciprocity between researcher and respondents and help to avoid the respondents' feeling that they have been "ripped off" for their data.

RULE 4.4 DO NOT PRESSURE RESPONDENTS TO PARTICIPATE.

Although the researcher has a powerful interest in getting everyone selected to complete the survey, it must always be made clear that while cooperation in completing the questionnaire or interview is appreciated, it is, nonetheless, optional. Particularly in face-to-face encounters, considerable pressure can be placed on individuals to participate in the study. In the case of questionnaires administered to a gathering of individuals, there is considerable informal pressure on those present to cooperate by staying in the room and completing the survey. The researcher must exercise self-discipline and avoid putting undue pressure on individuals in an attempt to coax participation. (See the discussion on research ethics in Chapter 11.)

RULE 4.5 KEEP IT SIMPLE.

Keep questionnaires, interview guides, or phone interviews as simple and as nonthreatening as possible. Questionnaires should be easy to respond to and should avoid asking questions that pry unnecessarily into the respondent's personal affairs. (Chapter 14 provides additional ideas for making questionnaires easy to complete.)

RULE 4.6 DO QUALITY CONTROL SPOT CHECKS.

It is critical to do spot checks to ensure that administrative procedures are being followed. Research directors are sometimes negligent on this point. Doing interviews, or even handing out questionnaires, is not many people's idea of fun. Research assistants will occasionally cut corners. These may range from ignoring the random-sampling procedures, which should be used to select which person in a household is to complete the questionnaire, to inventing respondents and their answers. Checks can be run on the representativeness of the sample (to see how well the respondents and their answers match known characteristics of the target population) or to see if the person who was supposed to have been interviewed actually was. However, by the time checks are run, field research funds may be expended and you may not be able to redo the work. And if any data have been faked, it will take a lot of time to distinguish the genuine data from the bad. Be cautious of interviewers who are completing far more surveys than other interviewers. Watch out for systematic differences in response rates to sensitive questions. If an interviewer is missing data, try to go through the part of the questionnaire affected by this absence to see if the presentation can be improved. The quality of one's research can be no better than the quality of the data collected; monitor the process carefully.

RULE 4.7 PROVIDE A REPORT TO THE RESPONDENT.

When individuals are to be interviewed more than once during the course of a study (as in a panel study), report findings to respondents. In all cases when a report has been promised to the respondents, it must be provided, otherwise it is less likely that respondents will cooperate in future.

Typically, when questionnaires are administered to groups, probability sampling procedures (see Chapter 15) are not employed, and therefore the data collected cannot be used to extrapolate to some larger population.

C. TYPES OF SURVEYS

There are many variants of the survey, with the main difference being how the data are collected. We will consider three types: self-administered questionnaires, telephone interviews, and face-to-face (in-person) interviews. Each method has a distinctive set of advantages and disadvantages. The type of data collection method employed can influence the response rate as well as the quality of responses. Time and expense are also key factors to consider when selecting which type of survey to use. For example, it is considerably more costly to hire interviewers to conduct face-to-face interviews that take place in the respondent's home than to send mailed questionnaires to people to be completed on their own.

Regardless of the type of survey used, survey researchers typically measure the response rate because it influences their ability to generalize the results of the data. (This is discussed in greater detail in Chapter 15.) It is for this reason that many survey researchers employ **multiple methods**. That is, they may begin with a mailed survey, and follow-up with a telephone interview to encourage those who have not completed the survey with the option of doing so on the telephone.

1. SELF-ADMINISTERED QUESTIONNAIRES

A **self-administered questionnaire** is a questionnaire that is completed by the survey respondent without any interaction with the researcher who designed the questionnaire. There are four types of self-administered questionnaires that are introduced here: **individually delivered questionnaires**, group-administered questionnaires, mailed questionnaires, and **internet-based** (email or web) **surveys**.

A. INDIVIDUALLY DELIVERED QUESTIONNAIRES

Individually delivered questionnaires are delivered to a respondent by a researcher. A brief explanation is offered, any questions are answered, and arrangements are made for the return of the completed questionnaire. This method of handing out questionnaires will typically be used in community surveys, where the questionnaire is dropped off at specific locations such as selected houses, campus dormitories, or work stations. The choice of location is made on the basis of the target sample (e.g., households, students living in residence, municipal employees, etc.). The delivered questionnaires are handed to selected respondents at the target locations. For surveying students, usually the researcher tries to obtain a systematic sample of campus dormitory rooms. For studies in organizations (such as surveys of hospital staff, university faculty, or employees of a private firm), the target respondents are approached individually.

In cases in which a survey of a systematic sample of students in residence is being conducted, care should be taken to provide everyone with an equal chance of participating in the survey if there is a mixture of single and double rooms. This will mean that, in the case of double rooms, both residents should be asked to complete the questionnaire. In this way, all students will have an equal chance of being selected to participate in the survey. (See more details on the systematic sampling procedure in Chapter 15.)

Here are some tips for conducting an individually delivered survey:

TIP 1

Where possible, avoid mailed returns or having respondents drop their completed questionnaires into a box left in a dormitory or other convenient spot. If at all possible, completed forms should be picked up by the researcher at a time agreed to with the respondent. Such arrangements will encourage the respondent to complete the form by the pre-arranged time. Do not be tempted to violate this rule: if you do, you will pay a heavy price in lost and missing questionnaires.

TIP 2

It is critical to record where questionnaires have been dropped off and when they are to be picked up. Pick up the questionnaire on time: respondents will be annoyed if it is not picked up. A form for recording this information should be developed and then used faithfully. (See Table 4.) As well as information on pick-up place and time, the form should also have space to list dates when an attempt was made to contact the individual and to record times when it would be convenient to return to meet the person. After the data have been collected, these sheets will prove invaluable in calculating the response rate to the survey and in identifying what problems were encountered.

TIP 3

Generally it is a good idea to provide respondents with an envelope into which they can seal their completed questionnaire. This simple, inexpensive step helps maintain the respondent's privacy. Sometimes questionnaires are left around waiting to be picked up and unwanted eyes may peruse the responses. A sealed envelope will foil most snoopers. In introducing the survey to the respondent, the researcher can indicate that the envelope is a means of protecting the confidentiality of the answers. This helps make respondents feel safe.

TIP 4

A slotted return box can also be used to help convey the sense of anonymity. Use a box with

TABLE 4.1   SAMPLE DROP-OFF FORM

#	ADDRESS	TRY 1 DATE	TRY 2 DATE	TRY 3 DATE	PICK-UP DATE	PICK-UP TIME	D O N E	NOTES
1								
2								
3								
4								
5								
6								

a slot cut in one end (a box measuring 23 × 30.5 cm is a good size) Respondents' questionnaires can be slipped into the box as they are returned. In especially sensitive studies, this return procedure can be pointed out when the questionnaire is delivered to the respondent.

B. GROUP-ADMINISTERED QUESTIONNAIRES

Group-administered questionnaires are questionnaires delivered to a group of people (such as students in a classroom setting or employees attending a meeting). Group-administered questionnaires almost always have good response rates because there is considerable informal pressure on individuals to cooperate with the researcher. Normally, between 90 and 100% of potential respondents will complete questionnaires in group settings. Group-administered surveys have the advantage of a high response rate and they are fast and easy to administer. There are, however, some concerns that the results of group-administered surveys cannot be generalized to the broader population.

Here are some tips for conducting a group-administered survey:

TIP 1

When you ask a group to complete a survey, it is important to begin by explaining the survey to those present. Tell them who is doing the research and why it is being done. The researchers should encourage respondents to ask any questions about the survey in general or about particular questions.

TIP 2

For practical reasons, it is usually best to administer questionnaires at the end of a meeting or class rather than at the beginning. If, for example, one goes into a classroom with a questionnaire at the beginning of a class, problems will arise because not all the students will finish at the same time. Hence, from the teacher's point of view, valuable class time will be wasted as the researcher waits for the last forms to be completed. Similarly, at a meeting, avoid handing out a questionnaire before the meeting begins; administer it at the end or before a break during the meeting. This will allow people who work at different speeds to complete the questionnaire without feeling rushed. However, in administering a questionnaire at the end of a meeting or class, we probably lose a little in the quality of replies. At the end of sessions respondents may be tired or bored and wish to leave as soon as possible. But, given the researcher's desire to maintain cordial relations with those giving permission to administer the questionnaires, it is generally less disruptive to administer them at the end of the session.

C. MAILED QUESTIONNAIRES

Mailed questionnaires are questionnaires delivered to respondents through the postal system. If the goal of the survey is to solicit information and opinions from the general public, individually delivered or group-delivered surveys are not suitable. Rather, the researcher may wish to use a probability sampling strategy to try to have a final sample that is representative of the population being considered. Mail surveys are popular because they provide a relatively cheap and reasonably fast way of contacting a large number of respondents. And despite the reputation mail surveys have for producing low response rates, it is possible to have the majority of questionnaires returned. In mail surveys we normally deduct from the total number of questionnaires sent out the number that are returned because respondents sent them to a wrong address. Therefore, the number of delivered questionnaires is equal to the number sent out, minus the number returned as undeliverable.

Since our major concern with the mail survey is the response rate, we will consider the factors that influence whether a questionnaire will be returned. There are two factors involved: those largely beyond the control of the researcher, and those the researcher can control.

i. Factors Beyond the Control of the Researcher

These factors are of interest in trying to predict the likely response rate to a mailed questionnaire. The type of respondent receiving the questionnaire is important: as Heberlein and Baumgartner have noted (1978), students, employees, and military personnel are more inclined to return a mailed questionnaire than are members of the general public. The type of sponsoring agency also has an impact: people favour government-sponsored research over market research. (Perhaps the response rates in government-sponsored projects are higher because some citizens may believe that they are legally required to participate in the same way that they are required to participate in the census.) Finally, we need to consider the **salience of the topic** to the respondent; subjects important to the respondent are more likely to produce a positive response than those of lesser importance to the respondent.

ii. Factors Under the Control of the Researcher

The legitimacy of the survey is enhanced if the questionnaire is well presented, the sponsoring agency identified, and the worthiness of the research established. Every effort should be made to make the questionnaire look as professional as possible. A cover letter on official letterhead should be sent prior to the mailing of the survey. It should be signed by the researcher. The purpose of the letter of invitation is to explain that a survey will be sent, tell the respondents what the survey is about, and provide a telephone number for survey respondents to call if they have questions. When the survey is mailed (about a week later) a stamped and addressed return envelope should be provided for the convenience of the respondent.

Among the variables examined, the evidence indicates that monetary incentives do increase response rates (Senn, Verberg, Desmarais, and Wood, 2000). Follow-up contacts in the form of letters, postcard reminders, registered mail, and long-distance phone calls all enhance the likelihood of a positive response. However, with each contact, one can expect slightly reduced effectiveness. Registered mail and long-distance phone calls seem to impress on respondents the importance of the study and their role in it: using these approaches pays off well in increased participation. One of the follow-up contacts should contain a replacement copy of the questionnaire in case the first one has been "misplaced." Although follow-up contacts are worthwhile, one must always be careful not to harass potential respondents.

Given the many factors involved, it is difficult to estimate a response rate with precision before the survey is undertaken. However, a first-round response rate of about 50% should be considered average; three follow-up contacts can be expected to increase the response rate to about 75% (Dillman, Christenson, Carpenter, and Brooks, 1974; Heberlein and Baumgartner,

1978). Any response rate above 75% should be considered excellent. In Canada, Austria, and West Germany, one can expect somewhat lower response rates (Eichner and Habermehl, 1981; Goyder, 1982). John Goyder has suggested that there may well be cultural factors working to lower response rates to mail questionnaires in Canada. His research indicates that in Canadian studies the researcher should anticipate a response rate about 7% lower than is likely in the United States (Goyder, 1982, 1985).

Meeting the predicted response rate should be considered an excellent result. To be within 20% of the predicted response rate should be considered acceptable. If the researcher thinks that the estimated response rate will be insufficient, then additional steps should be taken to increase the likelihood of a response. Goyder's research suggests that the two most important factors in determining response rate are:

- the number of contacts the researcher has with the respondents; and

- the importance of the subject matter to the respondent.

One might wish to consider trying to make the questionnaire more salient for the respondents or consider using phone-call follow-ups or include a $1 or $2 coin as a token of appreciation. While many researchers would feel uneasy (myself included) about sending money to try to encourage a positive response (some potential respondents would be insulted by the gesture), it would, nonetheless, probably be effective in increasing the response rate. It has been shown, for example, that the use of incentives as small as 10 cents will increase the response rate: in one study of top corporate executives, 40% of those receiving no incentive responded, 54% of those receiving 10 cents responded, while among those who received a 25 cent piece, 63% returned their questionnaires (Erdos, 1983, p. 97). Would you have guessed this result if you knew that the value of the token sent was all that differentiated the various surveys, and that the respondents were among the highest-paid executives in North America?

Here are some tips for increasing the likelihood of response to a mailed questionnaire:

TIP 1

Be certain to send a letter of notification a week in advance to sending the questionnaire and be certain that the questionnaire has a professional appearance and follows the rules for questionnaire development (Chapter 14).

TIP 2

The letterhead and envelope should identify the sponsoring organization's name, in order to increase the perceived legitimacy of the project.

TIP 3

The respondent's name should be typed, or even handwritten, using the full name rather than initials.

TIP 4

The mailing should be sent by first-class mail, and should also use stamps rather than metered postage. The idea is to make the package seem as personal as possible. Avoid the mass-produced look; do not use mailing labels.

TIP 5

Enclosed with the original material should be a stamped envelope for the return of the completed questionnaire.

In a recent study of university graduates (2001) a comparison was made of the response rates for graduates whose return envelopes were either *postage-paid* ones or *not postage-paid* ones. The difference in response rate suggests that it is cost effective to provide postage-paid return envelopes. Table 4.2 shows the response rates under the two conditions.

Calculations suggest that the cost per mailing was $1.87 each with a postage-paid envelope included. The cost per mailing was $1.33 when return postage was not provided. However, to get a return of 300 questionnaires, if you used the no-return-postage approach you would need to send out 1,288 questionnaires for a total cost of 1,288 x $1.33 = $1,712.45 ($5.71 per returned questionnaire). To get a return of 300 questionnaires using the return postage paid approach you would need to mail out 809 questionnaires for a total cost of 809 x $1.87 = $1,512.83 ($5.04 per returned questionnaire)—a saving of $200.

The conclusion here is that it would have been cheaper to use postage-paid return envelopes. And you would also avoid having miffed the respondents!

TIP 6

If the questionnaires are to have identification codes placed on them, place them on the top right-hand corner of the first page, and indicate in the accompanying letter that the number is there to assist in following up on those respondents who have not returned the questionnaire. Do not use secret codes.

TIP 7

If an incentive is being used, use new currency, enclosed in a plastic envelope.

TIP 8

You can follow up by sending a postcard, thanking respondents if they have returned the questionnaire and reminding them that returning the form would be much appreciated if this has not already been done.

TIP 9

A second follow-up, including a copy of the questionnaire, may be sent three weeks after the original has been mailed.

TIP 10

A third follow-up after six or seven weeks, using either registered mail or a phone call, is worthwhile and increases the response rate. Most researchers do not go beyond the third follow-up.

TABLE 4.2 THE EFFECT OF PROVIDING RETURN POSTAGE ON RETURN RATES

RETURN STATUS	POSTAGE PAID		POSTAGE NOT PAID		TOTAL	
	NUMBER	PERCENT	NUMBER	PERCENT	NUMBER	PERCENT
Returned	82	37.1	218	23.3	300	26.0
Not Returned	139	62.9	717	76.7	856	74.0
TOTAL	221	100.0	935	100.0	1,156	100.0

Chi-Square = 17.60 df = 1 Prob <.05

Source: Winston Jackson

Generally, returns will be quicker at first and then slow down. After one week expect to get about 30% of those questionnaires that will be returned, and about 85% within two weeks. By the end of four weeks about 96% of those questionnaires that will be returned should have arrived (Erdos, 1983, p. 263).

Box 4.2 presents a list of survey research projects done by students. The students conducted either an individually delivered survey or a group-delivered survey. As the project titles suggest, survey research is suitable for the study of social attitudes and experiences.

D. INTERNET-BASED SURVEYS

With the growing popularity and accessibility of the internet, researchers have been exploring the use of web pages and email to administer a survey. It was hoped that the internet would create new, fast, and inexpensive ways to survey individuals and organizations. In the early 1990s, researchers experimented with different strategies for using the internet for survey purposes, such as sending the survey embedded in an email message. Recipients of the message were asked to fill out the survey embedded in the message and return it by email. A second strategy involved attaching a file copy of the survey. Recipients were asked to open and print the document, then fill out and return the paper copy by regular mail. This method made many demands of the respondent in terms of time and money (for mailing). In addition, people have become increasingly concerned about the use of email to spread computer viruses, which can damage or destroy personal computers. As a result, individuals and organizations

---

BOX 4.2 STUDENT RESEARCHERS AT WORK

Student Survey Research

Project Social Correlates of Religiosity
Student Christopher A. Cook

Project Fear of Rape versus Awareness of Risk of Sexual Assault: Methodological and Conceptual Issues
Student Alicia Van de Sande

Project Looking through the Educational Lens: University Students' Attitudes towards Mental Illness
Student Dennis E. Murphy Odo

Project Water Talk: Examining the Effects of Water Commodification in a Nova Scotian Community
Student Mindy Murphy

Project Call Centres: Where Do Youth Fit In?
Student Sandra P. MacRae

Project Adjustment to Widowhood, Support Systems and Psychological Well-Being: A Study of Pictou County Widows
Student Kirk D. Bailey

Project The Transmission of Political Values: Exploring the Role of Higher Education and Social Class Background
Student Andrew Davidson

have adopted screening systems to detect and screen for viruses and computer "spam." When this happened, email surveys were either not delivered or people were too nervous to open them. Since then, survey researchers have developed "email invitations" in which the recipient is invited to participate in an online survey located on a webpage. The message includes a link to the **web survey** and a password for doing the survey. The recipient completes and delivers the survey online.

Although the latter method seems promising, there are a number of factors that must be considered when deciding if an internet-based survey is suitable for one's project. As with mail surveys, the response rate can be an issue. Research suggests that, in fact, many of the same "rules" that apply to mail surveys apply to internet-based surveys. For example, a relatively high response rate is associated with short questionnaires, vouchers or incentives (especially lotteries), visually appealing surveys (Deutskens, de Ruyter, Wetzels, and Oosterveld, 2004), and advance and reminder notification (Kaplowitz, Hadlock, and Levine, 2004). Research comparing the response rate for web and mailed surveys suggests that there is a comparable response rate for web and mail surveys (Kaplowitz et al., 2004; Campbell, 2003)

A second issue that arises with internet-based surveys is the availability of lists. Email lists and newsgroup lists can be used when surveying a topic that is of particular interest to members of those lists. Indeed, this seems to be where the real potential of web surveys lies—with research topics that pertain to members of available lists. For example, one could potentially survey public libraries using a web survey because all public libraries are online and belong to a formal list. The potential for

the web to be used for major studies of the general population, however, is not within reach at this time. There are two related obstacles to using the internet to survey the general population. First, not everyone has an email account, access to a computer, or the ability to use a computer. Second, it would not be possible to construct random samples, which are essential if one wishes to generalize about the population (Zhang, 2000), because general lists are not available. In spite of the current limitations, strides have been made in developing strategies and tools for making web surveys a viable option for some types of social research.

Brian Campbell wanted to survey the use of technology by post-secondary students. This topic is particularly amenable to web research because many post-secondary institutions are "wired" (i.e., the campus and the residences have computer connections) and because all students are given email accounts, which they use extensively. Because there is both a list of addresses and an email list, Campbell decided to compare the response rate of mailed and web surveys. The results of his study are presented in Box 4.3.

2. TELEPHONE SURVEYS

Telephone surveys are questionnaires administered by an interviewer during a telephone call. Like all types of surveys, the phone survey (as they tend to be called) relies on information reported by the respondent. Yet, there are unique concerns with phone surveys. For example, questions and response categories must be kept simple since they are presented verbally. In-depth probes are difficult and, as with other surveys, it is always difficult to make causal inferences. The interviewer's expectations

BOX 4.3   SOCIAL RESEARCHERS AT WORK

Brian Campbell "Student Technology Use Survey: Comparing the Response Rates for Web and Mailed Formats"

The Study

Paper and web versions of a survey measuring student technology use were conducted at a small undergraduate university in a small town with a wired campus. A mailed paper questionnaire was used in 1998. In 2000, the survey was repeated with parallel paper and web versions. In 2001 the survey was conducted entirely online using email prompts and web forms.

The Survey Protocol

The mailed questionnaires employed a lottery incentive (a draw for $100 selected from participants who returned draw cards with their survey). The invitation to participate in the online surveys was sent to students in an email message that had a link to a web form. The standard protocol was to send out two email prompts. Respondents included their names on the online surveys to enable participants to be included in the lottery, and for survey verification. In the parallel paper and online surveys conducted in 2000, 50% of the population was sent a paper survey while 50% of the population was sent an email with a link to a web form. There was one paper prompt for the paper subjects. This was then followed up with an email prompt to the paper sample offering the option of switching to the online format. There were 52 paper respondents who later took this option. The online sample was given the option of being sent a

paper survey but this option was not exercised by any of the respondents.

The questionnaires covered a broad range of material including:

- Social and personal background
- Program affiliations and level
- Access to computers
- Skill development
- Self-assessment of skill
- Frequency of use across curricular and extracurricular computing
- Computer and educational experiences
- Computer and educational attitudes
- Patterns of cooperation and interaction
- Inventories of learning approaches and styles

The Response Rates for the Paper and Online Surveys

The figure on the following page reports the response rates for the four surveys. The response rate for the paper survey in 1998 was 38.82%. In 2000, the response rate was 39.73% for the online survey and 25.93% for the paper survey. The 2001 online survey had a response rate of 32.7%. Clearly the response rate for the 2000 online survey had a higher response rate than the 2000 paper survey by a considerable margin, yet the response

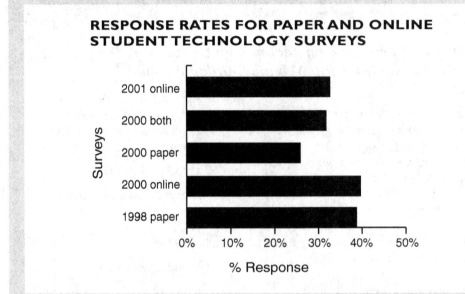

RESPONSE RATES FOR PAPER AND ONLINE STUDENT TECHNOLOGY SURVEYS

rate for the 2001 online survey was considerably lower (by 7%) than the 2000 online survey. Further analyses of the response rate data by year of study and place of residence suggest that the dynamics of online responses are complex.

Year of Study
There are large differences in response rates by student's year of study whereby paper surveys have a higher response rate from third and fourth year students while online surveys have a higher response rate from first and second year students. In 2000 only 1.90% of first year students responded using a paper survey while 58.67% of fourth year students responded on paper. This is a collapse of the paper survey response for first year students. In 1998 the paper response was 31.81% from this group. The reverse pattern holds for online responses in 2000. Although not as dramatic a change as for

first years, fourth year response was cut from 49.75% for paper in 1998 to 12.24% for online in 2000. In 1998 fourth year students were four times more likely to respond to a paper survey. When the survey was run again in 2001 without the paper alternative this collapse rebounded again for fourth year students to 28.43%. When the survey is totally online in 2001 there is a response bias in favour of first year students of 37.07% as opposed to the 28.43% for fourth year students.

Group dynamics appeared to have influenced the response rate of first year students in 2000. We learned that first year students who received the paper version of the survey became aware that other students received the web version. It appears that receiving the paper survey instead of the web survey turned them off responding to the survey, even when given option of switching to the online version. This is reflected in the fact that, of the 52 students who later took the on-line option when presented with the option, only two were first year students. This is the case even though other first year students who were included in the online sample were the highest participators.

Year of Study and Place of Residence

Why does year of study seem to matter so much for the response rate? The answer falls with place of residence. At this university 80% of the first and 68% of second year students live in residence. There is a dramatic drop to about 20% for third year students and less than 10% for fourth year students. Because the residences are wired, the higher response rates for first and second year students living in residence coincide with the high level of accessibility to online resources for these students.

The highest response rate for off-campus respondents in the 1998 paper survey was 45.84%. The on-campus high point is in the 2000 web survey with a 59.06% response rate. However, when

the survey is done totally online in 2001 the on-campus residence online response rate falls to 36.02%. As noted above, the 2000 split survey had response rates that appear to have been affected by the presence of an alternative survey format.

Discussion

This paper reports the response rates for the paper and web version of a parallel survey on student technology use at one undergraduate university. It explored whether year of study and place of residence influence the response rates. The bias in favour of senior students who live off-campus for paper surveys and in favour of first and second year students who live in wired on-campus residences suggest the importance of connectivity. The use of the split method survey formats in 2000 reminds us that surveys are sensitive tools which can be influenced by the group dynamics of the sample. This was an unintended interference, which highlights how sensitive response rates can be to respondents' reaction to aspects of the survey or its delivery format.

Source: Adapted from Brian Campbell (2003). "Student Technology Use Survey: Comparing the Response Rates for Web and Mailed Formats." Unpublished paper. Printed with permission of author.

may inadvertently influence the responses that are recorded into the computer. Most phone interviews now employ computers to present the questions and to provide the response categories into which respondents' answers are to be fitted. Care must be taken, therefore, in monitoring response variations between interviewers.

Phone surveys are gaining in popularity. They are widely used by polling organizations and academic and applied

researchers and represent a technique of data collection that will almost certainly increase in years to come. Phone surveys are a relatively cheap and quick way to collect data. Since there is no travel time, phone interviewers can do many more interviews in a day than would be possible if the interviewer had to travel to each respondent's home. Moreover, according to Sudman (1967, pp. 58–67), phone interviewing can provide cost-effective access to people with whom it is very difficult to arrange interviews (such as physicians), or those that are not concentrated in one area (such as the blind). In national studies, Robert M. Groves and Robert L. Kahn have estimated that phone surveys are about 45% of the cost of personal interviews (1979). Recently, there has been some troubling news regarding the willingness of people to participate in telephone interviews. For example, in one study, some 7 out of 10 respondents in the Toronto area were refusing to cooperate in pre-election polls. If these levels of nonparticipation become widespread it will be more difficult to justify using the phone for collecting such information (Sheppard, 1993; Fisher, 1993).

But there are disadvantages to phone surveys. First, they are not the best means of gathering data if probing is required or if complex response categories are to be presented. Second, respondents interviewed over the phone are slightly less at ease than respondents being interviewed in person. As a result, phone interviews will generally produce slightly higher refusal rates on sensitive issues, such as income or political preference (Groves and Kahn, 1979, p. 98). Sampling is also a key issue because the distribution of phones is uneven. The less well-off and those who are mobile are less likely to have a phone or a listed phone number. And the introduction of cell phones poses new challenges as some telephone consumers use only cell phones, for which a directory is not publicly available. Given these issues, researchers must recognize the possibility of sample distortions when choosing to conduct phone surveys.

Phone interviews also have some special problems related to assessing response rates. It is not always easy to determine how many numbers called are connected to "live" phones; there will also be a fair

number (generally about 20%) of phones attached to businesses. Furthermore, phone interviews have lower completion rates than questionnaires: typically, the completion rate will not exceed 70% (Groves and Kahn, 1979, p. 75). Studies based on rural populations generally have greater success in phone book–based surveys since lower levels of mobility mean that fewer phones will be disconnected.

In conducting a phone survey, one will either be working with a list of potential respondents (such as a list of voters, members of a group or association, or simply the names listed in the phone book). In such cases, one would usually proceed by using a systematic sampling procedure (see Chapter 15 for this sampling method).

It is also possible to create a sample by identifying the various residential phone exchanges in the area and then using a table of random numbers to determine the numbers to be called. Typically phone numbers are assigned in five-digit blocks, the first three determining the exchange. The numbers might start 863-21xx. A table of random numbers can be used to determine the last two digits to be used. If it is possible to get the information from the phone company, one attempts to find out the percentage of phones in each block and then a sample is drawn to represent each block proportionally (Abrahamson, 1983, pp. 225–26).

Computer-assisted telephone interviewing is an important tool for polling organizations and market researchers. The computer dials a sample of respondents and then guides the interviewer through the data collection by presenting the questions on the screen and, depending on the response, proceeds to show the next appropriate question. The answers are then recorded into the machine. Here are some tips for making a telephone survey more successful by increasing the percentage who complete the survey and ensuring that quality data are collected.

TIP 1 BEGIN WITH INTERESTING, SALIENT, AND YET SIMPLE QUESTIONS.

This is a tough rule to follow, but attempt to begin a phone interview with questions that are simple to answer and nonthreatening and that will be considered important. Since phone respondents are slightly more likely than those interviewed in person to terminate the interview, it is especially important to ease them into the discussion. While phone interviews can last up to half an hour, they should be kept as short and as simple as possible.

TIP 2 SUPPLY PHONE INTERVIEWERS WITH RULES FOR DETERMINING WHO IS TO BE INTERVIEWED.

Procedures must be provided for determining who within the household contacted is to be interviewed. It is not acceptable to simply interview the person who happens to answer the phone. If this were done, the survey would overrepresent those who are most likely to answer the phone. The interviewer should not be making decisions based on convenience. Table 4.3 presents such a sample form.

TIP 3 MONITOR QUALITY.

A **quality-control monitoring system** must be in place to ensure that interviewers are following established procedures for selecting respondents, asking questions, and entering the data.

TIP 4 SIMPLIFY RESPONSE CATEGORIES.

Phone interviews must keep the response categories simple. While it is possible to conduct lengthy interviews by telephone, keep the questions simple and, if necessary, break complex questions into smaller simpler ones (Sudman and Bradburn, 1983). Respondents are slightly more likely to select a neutral

TABLE 4.3 CHOOSING PHONE RESPONDENT

#	PHONE #	LIST PEOPLE IN HOUSEHOLD[1]	SKIP[2]	INTER-VIEW NAMES[3]	NAME/ TIME[4]	DONE[5]	NAME/ TIME	DONE	NAME/ TIME	DONE
1										
2										
3										
4										
5										

[1]Get initials of members of household over the age of 19 who normally reside in the household, from oldest to youngest.

[2]Start with person X from this household; if skip interval is 3, do one, skip two, and do one. Carry over skip from interview to interview.

[3]Write down names of persons to be interviewed.

[4]Write down name of first person, and time interview to be done.

[5]Check when interview completed.

response category and there is also a tendency to choose the last response category presented: hence researchers frequently vary the order of the response categories.

Phone interviews are relatively cheap and can be used to generate a representative sample. However, the representativeness of the sample has to be monitored carefully because phones are not evenly distributed among the population and, as mentioned earlier, there is a growing disinclination to agree to be interviewed over the phone.

3. FACE-TO-FACE INTERVIEWS

The final data collection procedure we will consider is the face-to-face interview. Generally there are two kinds of interviews:

1. the structured interview, which is a questionnaire that is read to the respondent; and

2. the interview schedule, which outlines the areas that are to be probed by the interviewer.

A. STRUCTURED INTERVIEW

Structured interviews involve face-to-face interviews where questions are read to the respondents by an interviewer. The literacy level of respondents is less of a concern than for self-administered questionnaires because the research assistant reads the survey and documents the respondent's answer. Such interviews ordinarily will provide for in-depth probes on some of the questions. Interviews also allow the respondents to ask questions to help clarify any ambiguities. Structured interviews are made up of set questionnaire items: the interviewer is expected to read the questions exactly as worded.

B. INTERVIEW SCHEDULE

Interview schedules simply outline the major questions that are to be raised; the interviewer has greater freedom to explore questions in detail than for structured interviews. This kind of interview requires a high level of skill on the part of the interviewer; in particular, care must be taken not to "lead" the respondent. Furthermore, the responses are filtered through the interviewer and, therefore, if there are a number of interviewers, one must realize that some of the variations in response will be due to differences between interviewers and not solely to differences between the respondents. Interview schedules are used for in-depth interviews in field studies (see Chapter 6).

Since face-to-face interviews are expensive, they are normally done when not too many are required and when in-depth information is needed. One major advantage of face-to-face interviews is that good rapport is often built between interviewers and respondents so that if repeated interviews are required, as in a panel study, it will be possible to maintain high response rates. A second major advantage of interviews is that they permit the respondents to clarify any questions that they have about the interview. One of the disadvantages is that interview studies are expensive (more than double the cost of phone interviews) and time consuming (Groves and Kahn, 1979, p. 211).

While it is beyond the scope of this book to discuss the selection and training of interviewers in detail, we will offer some brief comments on this subject. Research done by NORC (National Opinion Research Center) indicates that the quality of work done by interviewers is related to length of time spent working for NORC, high grade averages in high school, liking two or more science subjects, intelligence, and the completion of college. In addition, those who scored high on "need achievement" and manipulativeness (Machiavellianism scale) are more likely to do good interviewing. Of note is that happiness, financial need, religious behaviour, perfectionism, and size of home community were not found to be related to the quality of interviewing that a person does (Sudman, 1967, pp. 100–53).

Interviewers need to be trained. They will need to gain knowledge about ethical issues, the specific survey being conducted, appropriate dress, how to introduce themselves to the respondent, how to gain rapport, how to organize the interview setting, how to present questions, how to react to responses, which issues to probe, how to probe them, how to keep the respondent on topic, and how to end the interview gracefully. In addition to some of the above issues, research directors will need to provide potential interviewers with experience in a few simulated interviews (Weinberg, 1971).

Interviewers are frequently paid on a "per interview" basis. This method is often preferred since it allows the researcher to control costs. Also, it seems to be the case that many interviewers will "burn out" after six or eight weeks. Interviewing is a challenging task requiring great concentration and it is not easy to remain alert after having walked many respondents through the interview. Expect high turnover among interviewing staff.

D. PANEL STUDIES

Panel studies monitor specific organizations or individuals over time. Perhaps it is easiest to think of panel studies as a survey of a particular group supplemented by at least one follow-up interview. Many panel studies request participants to respond to a series of surveys over a specified period of time, such as every May for eight years.

Why would one choose to do a panel study rather than an experiment or a single survey? The answer is that experimentation is frequently not possible, or judged not to be relevant, for the examination of some relationships. Point-in-time surveys, on the other hand, might not provide a sufficient basis for making causal inferences. By documenting attitudes and events over time, we are able to conduct research on how certain social factors influence other social factors.

Suppose, for example, that one was interested in studying the impact of divorce on the children. The survey lends itself well to such a study because you can include multiple dependent variables (e.g., academic performance at school; psychological well-being, such as self-esteem or level of depression; weight; activity level; contact with significant others; and so on). Ideally, however, you would want to assess whether there were changes in these measures over time (e.g., during the years prior to the divorce, during the parents' marital separation, and over the years following the divorce). You would also want to ascertain that the children's well-being was similar to the well-being of other children in the sample in the period prior to the onset of the marital conflict. Thus, you would need **longitudinal data**, defined as data collected from the same sample (i.e., panel) over a period of time. Longitudinal data is also called **time-series data**, especially the sort of data employed by economists.

Although some social scientists conduct panel studies, many Canadian scholars use panel studies conducted by the federal research agency, Statistics Canada. As you can imagine, panel studies require many resources and they cost a great deal of money, particularly when one of the goals of the study is to be able to generalize about the experience of people across the country, in all different walks of life. Consequently, social scientists have urged Statistics Canada to develop and administer panel studies and make the data available to social scientists. Although panel studies are designed and administered by the federal research agency, social scientists are involved in an intensive consultation process, which influences the selection of the variables and the format of the survey. This means that the survey design is informed by social science theory and interests. One such panel study is the National Longitudinal Survey of Children and Youth. It was established by Statistics Canada in 1994, with the original panel of children being re-interviewed every two years. The random sample is made up of 17,000 children ages newborn to eleven. Eighty-eight percent of the original sample were interviewed in the third cycle of data collection, suggesting that every effort was made to achieve a high response rate even in the third interview phase many years later. For this particular study, data is collected from (1) the child, if possible; (2) the person in the child's household who is "most knowledgeable," which is typically the mother, and (3) the child's school teacher, for school-aged children. Once collected, the data are made available to social scientists to test various theories about the well-being of children. Box 4.4 (on page 121) provides a short list of studies based on the National Longitudinal Study on Children and Youth that have been published by social scientists in a wide range of disciplines.

Panel studies pose different challenges than point-in-time surveys. Participants are asked to agree, in principle, to taking part in the survey at different points in time. When the time between contacts is a year or two and the population being studied is

fairly mobile, the challenge for the researcher is simply to keep track of the people in the panel. Here are some tips for keeping track of respondents in a panel study:

TIP 1

At the time of the first interview, request that the name of a relative or friend who will always know how to get in touch with the respondent be provided. These names prove invaluable in later efforts to contact individuals.

TIP 2

Try the original phone number; even though the respondent has moved, the same phone number may have been maintained. If the phone has been disconnected, the operator may be able to provide the new number.

TIP 3

Phone directories for the original year and for the current one are helpful; check how the person was listed in the original directory. If the person is still in the area, the chances are that the name will be listed identically.

TIP 4

Contact the employer of the respondent. Also contact fellow workers in an effort to locate the individual.

TIP 5

Contact neighbours. Especially in smaller cities and towns, neighbours can be helpful in tracing respondents.

TIP 6

Now you are desperate! Call people in the directory with the same last name, hoping to get lucky and find a relative of the person involved, who might be able to give you an address or phone number.

BOX 4.4 SOCIAL SCIENCE STUDIES BASED ON THE NATIONAL LONGITUDINAL SURVEY OF CHILDREN AND YOUTH

Criminology
Jane B. Sprott and Anthony N. Dobb (2000). "Bad, Sad, and Rejected: The Lives of Aggressive Children." *Canadian Journal of Criminology*, 42(2), 123–133.

Economics
Lynn N. Lethbridge and Shelley A. Phipps (2005). "Chronic Poverty and Childhood Asthma in the Maritimes versus the Rest of Canada." *Canadian Journal of Public Health*, 96(1), 18–23.

Education
Clyde Hertzman, Jeanne Brooks-Gunn, and Dafna Kohen (1999). "Neighborhood Affluence and School Readiness." *Education Quarterly Review*, 6(10), 44–52.

Educational Psychology
Tanya N. Beran and Claudio Violato (2004). "A Model of Childhood Perceived Peer Harassment: Analyses of the Canadian National Longitudinal Survey of Children and Youth Data." *Journal of Psychology*, 138(2), 129–147.

Family Studies
Judee E. Onyskiw and Leslie A. Hayduk (2001). "Processes Underlying Children's Adjustment in Families Characterized by Physical Aggression." *Family Relations*, 50(4), 376–385.

Geography
Lisa N. Oliver and Michael V. Hayes (2005). "Neighbourhood Socio-Economic Status and the Prevalence of Overweight Canadian Children and Youth." *Canadian Journal of Public Health*, 96(6), 415–420.

Health Studies and Epidemiology
Lynn McIntyre, Sarah K. Connor, and James Warren (2000). "Child Hunger in Canada: Results of the 1994 National Longitudinal Survey of Children and Youth." *Canadian Medical Association Journal*, 163(8), 961–965.

Kinesiology
Mark S. Tremblay and J. Douglas Willms (2000). "Secular Trends in the Body Mass Index of Canadian Children." *Canadian Medical Association Journal*, 163(11), 1429–1433.

Psychology, Psychiatry, and Mental Health.
Morton Beiser, Feng Hou, Ilene Hyman, and Michel Tousignant (2002). "Poverty, Family Process, and the Mental Health of Immigrant Children in Canada." *American Journal of Public Health*, 92(2), 220–227.

Terrance J. Wade, David J. Pevalin, and Augustine Brannigan (1999). "The Clustering of Severe Behavioural, Health, and Educational Deficits in Canadian Children: Preliminary Evidence from the National Longitudinal Survey of Children and Youth." *Canadian Journal of Public Health*, 90(4), 253–264.

Sociology
Lisa Strohschein (2005). "Parental Divorce and Child Mental Health Trajectories." *Journal of Marriage and the Family*, 67(5), 1286–1301.

E. ADVANTAGES AND LIMITATIONS OF SURVEY DESIGNS

Table 4.4 summarizes the advantages and disadvantages of the first two approaches to research design that we have considered so far: the experiment and the survey. Causal inferences are clearest when experimental and, to a lesser degree, panel data are used. Generalizing about larger populations is the forte of survey designs.

While neither surveys nor experiments rate high on validity, this does not mean that they are, by nature, invalid. The negative sign simply means that this is a problem area in these designs. It is difficult to demonstrate that respondents have not altered their behaviour or their answers on a questionnaire in response to the fact that they know they are being studied. Both experimentalists and survey researchers take the problem of validity seriously and try to minimize distortions. The negative sign for group-administered questionnaires in the generalization column is there because such groups are typically selected in the most convenient way. Probability procedures have therefore not been followed in the way that would be necessary if one wished to make extrapolations to the general population. (See Chapter 15 for details on sampling.)

F. CONCLUSION

Surveys are the major tool in studies attempting to represent large populations. They often deal simultaneously with many variables and attempt to describe the complexity of human behaviour. Surveys also

TABLE 4.4 ADVANTAGES AND LIMITATIONS OF ALTERNATE DESIGNS

RESEARCH DESIGN CATEGORY	GENERAL	VALIDITY	CAUSAL INFERENCE	MULTI-VARIATE	PROBING
SURVEY DESIGNS					
Individual Questionnaire	+	−	−	+	−
Group Administered	−	−	−	+	−
Phone Survey	+	−	−	+	−
Interview	+	−	−	+	+

In each category a "+" means that this is an advantage of the technique; a "−" means this is a possible limitation.

- *General* refers to the extent to which extrapolations to larger populations may be made using each of the design/data collection procedures.
- *Validity* is the extent to which indicators clearly measure what they are intended to measure.
- *Causal Inference* refers to the ease with which inferences about causal relations among variables can be made.
- *Multivariate* refers to the ease with which information on many variables is collected, leading to the possibility of multivariate analysis.
- *Probing* refers to the extent to which responses can be probed in depth.

permit the researcher to construct new variables by combining a number of characteristics—status integration or status crystallization would be an example of such constructed variables. Despite the many advantages of survey research, it is difficult to make clear causal inferences from such data. Most of these difficulties derive from the nature of the data. Survey data are normally based on self-reports and frequently on recollection. While it is probably not difficult to recall factual information (such as reporting the community you were born in or the salary of your first full-time job), it may be very difficult to recall how well you got along with your mother when you were six years old. Another fundamental issue has to do with the connection between words (what people say they will do) and

deeds (what they actually do). There are, therefore, doubts about the extent to which surveys reflect real behaviour as opposed to ideal behaviour. To what extent, then, can we claim to reflect reality with survey data?

Whatever research design is selected, it is important to understand the strengths and weaknesses of each of the approaches. Such knowledge helps the researcher select a design that is appropriate to the study's purpose and to try to deal with the weak points of each design. If a decision has been made to use a survey design, Chapters 13, 14, and 15 contain information of particular relevance to the survey researcher (measurement, questionnaire construction, and sampling methods).

G.   KEY POINTS

Survey designs are important in public opinion polling, census taking, market research, and academic research.

The strength of survey designs is that they offer a way of *estimating characteristics of a population* by studying a sample of that population.

A survey, in contrast to an experiment, typically includes measures of *many variables* and includes *many cases*.

Surveys are often the only *practical* means of measuring variables such as background characteristics of respondents and various attitudes that they express.

Surveys attempt to ensure *standardization* by asking all respondents identical questions.

The *response rate* (the percentage of people who receive a questionnaire who complete and return it) is influenced by the type of organization doing the

research, the length of the questionnaire, the method of delivery, the mode of retrieval, the type and number of follow-up contacts, incentives, and the salience of the topic to the respondent.

The greater the *salience* of the research to the respondent (interest in the topic by the respondent), the higher the response rate.

The greater the *personal contact*, the higher the response rate.

Quality control procedures must be in place to ensure that the questionnaire is being administered properly.

There are several types of surveys: self-administered, telephone, and face-to face surveys. Self-administered surveys can be individually delivered, group administered, mailed out, or completed on the internet. Each method has advantages and disadvantages.

H.   KEY TERMS

Individually delivered
  questionnaires

Internet-based surveys

Interview schedule

Longitudinal data

Multiple methods

Panel study

Point-in-time data

Population

Quality control monitoring system

Questionnaire

Response rate

Salience of topic

Sample

Self-administered questionnaire

Structured interview

Survey

Telephone survey

Time-series data

Web survey

CHAPTER FIVE

NONREACTIVE AND COMPARATIVE RESEARCH

A. AN INTRODUCTION TO NONREACTIVE RESEARCH

While experiments and surveys elicit responses from subjects, **nonreactive studies** involve *indirect data collection*. For example, some kinds of data are not solicited from individuals directly. Rather, certain public institutions are responsible for documenting key events, such as births, deaths, unemployment, diagnoses of diseases, arrests, and so on. Hospitals, for example, are required to register the birth of an infant. Data collected by formal public offices are sometimes called **official statistics**. Official statistics are an important source of data for many social scientists. Print, audio, and audio-visual media also comprise a major source of data for social scientists. Finally, many social scientists use existing survey data. In these cases, the direct data collection was done in the past by other researchers. Studies employing nonreactive data account for a large amount of the work done by social scientists. Illustrations of nonreactive studies would include:

- the political scientist studying the relation between the percentage of people who vote Liberal and the percentage of immigrants registered in each polling station;

- the economist examining trends in unemployment statistics;

- the sociologist analyzing gender stereotyping in primary-school readers;

- the sports psychologist studying the relation between violence in hockey games (as measured by penalty minutes) and audience size (as reported in game summaries in local newspapers);

- the nursing researcher studying trends in the length of time for which children are hospitalized;

- the historian comparing American and Canadian culture;

- the criminologist comparing sentencing decisions for visible minorities and members of the dominant group;

- the social science student employed by the city's traffic safety department to observe how many drivers yield to pedestrians in marked crosswalk zones.

The ability of subjects to modify their answers or reactions because they know that they are being studied is a problem frequently encountered in experiments, surveys, and interviews. A major confounding factor in social research is eliminated in nonreactive studies, because the observed persons or groups are not able to react to the measurement process—they not able to manage their presentation-of-self.

This chapter begins with introductions to two types of nonreactive research: secondary data analysis and content analysis. **Secondary data analysis** involves analyses of data that have already been collected for some other purpose, such as government statistics or previously conducted surveys. Although surveys are not a form of nonreactive research (because respondents can *react* to the questions posed), we mention them here because some secondary analysis research is based on previously collected survey data. **Content analysis** involves analyses of messages conveyed by media such as radio, television, and film, or analyses of various written materials such as plays, poetry, psychiatric interview notes, songs, novels, newspapers, or textbooks. The second section of this chapter introduces **comparative research**, a form of inquiry that often relies on secondary data analysis.

B. SECONDARY DATA ANALYSIS

Economists, political scientists, historians, criminologists, sociologists, and, to a lesser degree, anthropologists and psychologists frequently conduct research based on available material. These sources might include virtually any data—ranging from published statistical, census, or business data to the unpublished diaries of ordinary citizens or important historical figures. With the exception of those who record oral histories, historians rely on secondary data sources and the resulting studies are based entirely on secondary data analysis. The comparative research conducted by political scientists, criminologists, and sociologists often relies on information collected by governments throughout the world or by researchers with similar research interests in different regional settings. This was mentioned in Chapter 4 in the section on panel studies. Box 4.4 on page 121 provided a list of studies based on secondary analysis of the National Longitudinal Survey of Children and Youth. The discussion in the second part of this chapter illustrates the use of secondary data by comparative researchers interested in exploring Canada–U.S. differences. These studies used data collected by social scientists for other purposes.

Secondary analysis of large-scale surveys is not uncommon because archived data sets often include variables that would address research interests that had not been considered by the researchers who conducted the survey originally. For example, Canadian National Election Studies (CNES) covering the federal elections of 1965 through 1988 have been archived and made available to researchers for purposes of secondary analysis. Ronald D. Lambert, the principal investigator for the 1984 CNES, suggests that the national election studies have been an invaluable resource to the scholarly community, noting that approximately two-thirds of scholarly journal articles published using CNES data involved secondary analysis of the data. Lambert sees the merit of making the data available for secondary analyses. "In this way, the social science community is afforded an opportunity to monitor the accuracy and wisdom of published analyses and to initiate research into new problem areas that were perhaps not contemplated by the principal investigators. And, as the series lengthens, temporal analyses have become feasible." (Lambert, 1993, introduction). For the period 1965 to 1993, Lambert cites 126 refereed articles published in Canadian, American, and international sociology, political science, and interdisciplinary journals, "at least 12 books based substantially on CNES data," several book chapters, and 15 Masters theses and 22 Ph.D. dissertations based "in whole or in major part on one or more of the CNES."

1. FREDERICK J. DESROCHES: "TEAROOM TRADE: A RESEARCH UPDATE"

As an example of secondary data analysis, we feature a study by criminologist Frederick J. Desroches, at the University of St. Jerome in the University of Waterloo, in Waterloo, Ontario. In addition, Box 5.2 (on page 129) lists some recent nonreactive projects completed by our students.

Desroches used secondary analysis of police data to replicate the results of a direct observational study conducted by American sociologist Laud Humphreys in the late 1960s. Chapter 11 on research ethics features Humphreys' study on homosexual behaviour in public washrooms (called "tearooms"). That study became a classic, not only for its substantive observations but also for the ethical issues it raised. Desroches attempted to replicate the findings of Humpheys' study, but, unlike Humphreys, Desroches did not do the observations himself. Studying covert deviance raises many practical and ethical issues. Instead, Desroches relied on the reports of observations made by police. Police observations were recorded using video equipment in three communities, while in the remaining two communities direct observations were made through wall-and-ceiling air vents (Desroches, 1990, p. 41). The police surveillance resulted in some 190 arrests. No attempt was made by Desroches to interview any of the arrested men. Box 5.1 outlines the conclusions of Desroches' study.

BOX 5.1   SOCIAL RESEARCHERS AT WORK

Frederick J. Desroches: "Tearoom Trade: A Research Update"

Conclusion

Like many studies of covert deviance, this paper is based upon a captive sample of persons who have come to the attention of law enforcement agencies. The existence of Laud Humphreys' research, however, makes possible a comparison of police generated data with data obtained through observations and interviews with "unapprehended" offenders. Because police observations were so detailed, a rare opportunity to replicate a qualitative study presented itself. This research largely substantiates the picture drawn by Humphreys in his classic study, *Tearoom Trade: Impersonal Sex in Public Places*. Consistent with his observations, most tearoom participants (a) communicate through non-verbal gestures and seldom speak, (b) do not associate outside the tearoom or attempt to learn one another's identity or exchange biographical information, (c) do not use force or coercion or attempt to involve youths or children, (d) are primarily heterosexual and married, (e) depart separately with the insertor leaving first, (f) commit their sex acts out of sight of the entrance and accidental exposure, (g) do not undress or engage in anal sex, (h) break off sexual contact when someone enters the washroom, (i) rarely approach straight men, (j) read and write sexually explicit homosexual graffiti, and (k) linger inside and outside the washroom for someone to appear. In addition, (l) fellatio is generally not reciprocated and fellators are usually older men; (m) most offenders are neat in appearance; (n) some engage in series and simultaneous encounters; (o) encounters are brief, usually not exceeding twenty minutes; and (p) few have criminal records with the exception of those previously convicted of similar offenses.

The behavior of players reveals remarkable consistency over time, from community to community, and across national boundaries. Many men, the majority of them married and primarily heterosexual, continue to visit out-of-the-way public washrooms in search of fast, impersonal, and exciting sex despite the risk to family, friends, job, and reputation. Although shopping malls have usurped public parks as the favorite locale of tearoom participants, the basic rules of the game and profile of the players—as Humphreys contends—remain the same over time and place.

Source: Frederick J. Desroches (1990). "Tearoom Trade: A Research Update." *Qualitative Sociology*, 13(1), 59-60.

BOX 5.2 STUDENT RESEARCHERS AT WORK

Nonreactive Student Research

Content Analysis

Project The *Cosmopolitan* Paradox: The Portrayal of Women's Self-Defense, Violence against Women, and Male/Female Sexual Relationships

Student Tammy MacMillan

Brief The student conducted a content analysis of written articles in *Cosmopolitan* magazine for the years 1975, 1985, and 1995 to assess the impact of the feminist antiviolence campaign. The article was included in the analysis if it referred to women's self-defense or prevention, sexual violence against women, and/or advice on male/female sexual relations.

Project "Men as Success Objects, Women as Sex Objects": A Content Analysis of Personal Advertisements

Student William Peter Gottschall, Jr.

Brief The student conducted a content analysis of 432 personal advertisements drawn from the 3,718 ads placed in the Halifax *Chronicle Herald* over a ten-year period. The code scheme was guided by the literature review and hypotheses drawn from sociobiology.

Secondary Data Analysis of Existing Data

Project Reaching for the Brass Ring: The Consequences of Student Loan Debt

Student Angela Flemming

Brief The student tested the hypothesis that student loan debt will influence graduates' social mobility using longitudinal survey data collected from university graduates 5 and 10 years after graduation from one Nova Scotian university.

Secondary Data Analysis of Government Documents

Project The Impact of Court Decisions and the Charter of Rights and Freedoms on Police Activity

Student Michelle Chisholm

Brief The student examined court decisions dealing with police powers of search and seizure, entrapment, electronic surveillance, arrest, interrogation, and police use of force to assess the prediction that the Charter of Rights and Freedoms will influence police and their decision-making power, especially in the area of proactive policing.

Project Katawapul (Eel Stew): An Anthropological Inquiry of Mi'kmaq Fishing Rights

Student Leslie Jane McMillan

Brief The student conducted a content analysis of government documents, treaties, and court judgments pertaining to the provision of Mi'kmaq fishing rights to examine the role of the state in the formal exclusion of the Mi'kmaq people from participation in the commercial fishery.

Project The Relationship between Gender and Sentencing Outcome for Property-Crime Offenses in a Rural Community

Student Cathy Cameron

Brief The student examined gender differences in sentencing outcomes using data drawn from the Royal Canadian Mounted Police operational statistics on the total number of male and female offenders charged with property crime offenses and the Provincial Court Information Report, which recorded the offense categories ("person," "property," and "criminal other"), the sentence accorded by the court, and the age, marital status, and employment status of the 63 females and 389 males included in the sample.

2. ADVANTAGES AND LIMITATIONS OF SECONDARY ANALYSIS

The major limitation of research based on secondary data is that the necessary information is often unavailable or incomplete. But, with imagination, excellent work can be done. Economists are impressively adept, for example, at locating "indicators" in available data. And, as such data are frequently reported at different points in time, the economist is able to build, and test, elaborate causal models. So, whether attempting to understand the linkage between interest rates and unemployment or between housing starts and the wage level of plumbers, economists make efforts to understand the world by using secondary data.

Secondary data analysis is cost effective and, providing the data are relatively complete, can lead to sound general statements about the social world. As with survey research, however, there can be problems with demonstrating the validity of its indicators. This concern is discussed in greater length in the section on comparative research.

C. CONTENT ANALYSIS

As defined by Holsti and Stone, content analysis is "any technique for making inferences by objectively and systematically identifying specified characteristics of messages" (Holsti, 1969, p. 14). Social scientists frequently wish to examine the messages conveyed by various media. One might wish to understand the frequency with which "sexist" messages are communicated on television or the extent to which traditional sex roles are portrayed in children's school books; or one might wish to compare the number of negative editorials on political officials now to the number fifty years ago. The chances are that if these are the kinds of research questions that are being asked, some form of content analysis will be used. Content analysis may involve examining a sample of films, books, newspapers, or television programs and attempting to categorize the messages that are being conveyed in them. In all cases, one is attempting to assess the "content" of the message that is being communicated.

Content analyses are appropriate for many questions, can be done relatively inexpensively, and, if the material is sampled appropriately, may be taken to represent the material that is available. Furthermore, the validity of the measures used may be fairly high, since direct observations and classifications are being made. However, validity may also be limited because the material presented could be selected for its dramatic impact rather than for its representativeness. For example, we cannot presume that the attitudes of a bigot reported in a story represent the views of the author or of the larger culture.

Content analysis is used in a variety of disciplines and appears to be increasing in popularity (Holsti, 1969, p. 20). Fundamentally, the technique involves evaluating the content of communications—ranging from examining messages conveyed by various media to evaluating written, and even verbal, communications. Central to all researchers using the technique is a concern with analyzing the content of the message.

Sometimes emphasis is placed on understanding what factors influence the content of the message; in other cases, the researcher is concerned with the effects of the message; and in still others, the researcher is concerned with variations in the message itself. In all cases, however, the content of the message is part of what is analyzed.

1. BASIC DECISIONS IN CONTENT ANALYSIS

Typically content analysis, like most social science approaches, has both qualitative and quantitative dimensions. There may be some counting of the frequency with which some phenomena occur. But classifying messages into various categories may involve qualitative choices as to what categories are relevant. Since something about a message is analyzed, the analyst must make a number of fundamental decisions. Some of these are identified below.

A. UNIT OF ANALYSIS

In starting to do content analysis one must first decide on the **unit of analysis**. Is it a speech, is it an issue of a magazine, a story, a book, or a scene in a film, or the whole film?

B. HOW ARE THE UNITS TO BE SELECTED?

Chapter 15 outlines the basic procedures for selecting samples and for deciding on sample size. Standard sampling procedures attempt to remove bias from the choice of materials selected. Since the analyst typically wishes to describe some phenomenon accurately, it is important that the procedures used represent all instances of the phenomenon fairly.

C. WHAT IS TO BE MEASURED AND HOW?

What is being measured? Is it a theme, the presence or absence of some phenomenon, or the frequency with which something is mentioned? And, having decided what is to be measured, how are the classification decisions made? What other pieces of information are to be recorded about the unit being measured? For example, it could be appropriate to record the gender of an author, the type of a magazine, or the name of a program. Suggested strategies for coding (placing into categories) information are discussed in Chapter 13. One of the key issues is to ensure that different people analyzing the same content will agree on the categorization. This can be accomplished by having the coders work through the same items independently and then measure the extent of their agreement. A *coefficient of reliability* may be calculated as follows:

Coefficient of reliability =

$$\frac{\text{Number of units in identical category}}{\text{Total number of units coded}}$$

What the **coefficient of reliability** provides is a measure of agreement between the coders on the categorization of the items being analyzed. The proportion of times there is agreement is reflected in the coefficient. A rule of thumb would be to have a minimum coefficient of .6. Coders need to be trained to achieve this level. Much common sense needs to be shown when adopting the .6 rule since the complexity and subtlety of the categories may influence the outcomes. To assess the gender of a person in an advertisement is one thing (where you would expect a coefficient close to 1.0!), but to decide whether a car is to be categorized as appealing to people in one of the following six categories (old man,

old woman, middle-aged man, middle-aged woman, young man, and young woman) would produce less agreement among coders. If you could not get a .6 reliability coefficient here you would want to review your definition of the different categories to see if they could be refined further.

D. HOW IS INFORMATION TO BE RECORDED?

Before classifying data, a tally sheet should be developed for recording the information. A possible model for such a sheet would be the one used for recording field observations (see Figure 3.5 on p. 84). There should be space on the form to note all the variables, including the exact location of the item being measured.

E. HOW IS THE INFORMATION TO BE ANALYZED?

What techniques are to be used in presenting the information in a report? If the researcher is interested in showing what causes variation in the incidence of the phenomena, how is this analysis to be performed? If computer analysis is anticipated, be certain that coding is done so that transfer to the computer will be easy. If non-computer analysis is anticipated, follow the steps outlined in Chapter 3 (naturalistic observational section) and in Chapter 16.

2. SIMON GOTTSCHALK: "SPEED CULTURE: FAST STRATEGIES IN TELEVISED COMMERCIAL ADS"

Simon Gottschalk did a content analysis of television commercials shown on ABC, CBS, NBC, and Fox during January and February of 1999. Themes were extracted which were intended to provide an answer to three questions:

- *What* do ads communicate about speed?
- *How* are the meanings communicated?
- What *consequences* result from the communication?

Box 5.3 presents an overview of the methods and conclusions of Gottschalk's research.

D. INTRODUCTION TO COMPARATIVE RESEARCH

Most research is comparative. So whether we are doing an experiment comparing Time 1 measures with Time 2 measures or trying to figure out why high socioeconomic background females plan nontraditional

---

BOX 5.3 SOCIAL RESEARCHERS AT WORK

Simon Gottschalk: "Speed Culture: Fast Strategies in Televised Commercial Ads"

Method

A total of 270 commercials were recorded that had been shown on ABC, CBS, NBC, and Fox between 7:00 a.m. and 1:00 a.m. Of these, some 122 communicated something about speed and were then content analyzed in detail for visual, verbal, and aural qualities.

Results

The content analysis leads Gottschalk to the view that these ads normalize and celebrate speed. It becomes virtue, becomes a positive to be encouraged, welcomed. We need things to be fast so that we can become more efficient. The post-modern world celebrates speed, instant gratification, instant solutions to problems.

The *way* in which meanings are communicated is through the combination of visual, verbal, and aural cues. Verbally, "This week only" and "Call right now for a discount" are typical urgings heard. Through the use of heartbeat sounds, ads indicate the urgency and then provide quick solutions. *Fast-acting* Motrin is what you need.

The *consequence* of celebrating speed is to encourage people to have fewer, shorter, and less meaningful interactions with one another. The quest for speed, efficiency, may disrupt healthy social behaviour. As Bertman (1998) reminds us, "the depth of our understanding is inversely proportional to our velocity."

Source: Summarized from Simon Gottschalk (1999). "Speed Culture: Fast Strategies in Televised Commercial Ads." *Qualitative Sociology*, 22(4), 311–29.

careers, we make comparisons. Comparative research is not really a special type of research with its own methodology; it is the research process itself. However, when we think of comparative research, we think of cross-cultural studies or of historical studies. Comparative researchers use the full range of standard techniques, including surveys, interviews, field studies, and experiments, but, in particular, they use published information.

Looking at the similarities and differences between cultures, or within the same culture over time, is the essence of comparative studies (Warwick and Osherson, 1973, p. 8). Such studies began with the Greeks (Herodotus, 495–424 BCE) and have persisted to the present. They are an important approach to the study of human cultures. When the modern social sciences were emerging in the nineteenth century, comparative studies were a central concern of social research. Many scholars pursued comparative studies by pursuing an evolutionary model of societal development. Comte examined the stages societies pass through in their development ([1851] 1875); Durkheim analyzed religion among the Aboriginals of Australia ([1912] 1954); Weber compared religious systems (1964); and Marx analyzed stages in societal development ([1867] 1977).

During the early years of the twentieth century, after arguments were advanced that a **unilineal model**, a model in which the same patterns of development are followed by all societies, was inappropriate, comparative studies shifted to intensive studies of exotic cultures by anthropologists such as Bronislaw Malinowski ([1925] 1954), Ruth Benedict (see Mead, 1966), and Margaret Mead (1935). More recently, the work of George Murdock (1960) emphasized the importance of cross-cultural comparative

research. His work, coupled with the ethnographic information on over 500 cultures included in the *Human Relations Area Files* at Yale University, has encouraged cross-cultural comparative analyses.

There is, then, a long comparative tradition in social science research. And while these studies do not have a distinct methodology associated with them—they use historical material, surveys, secondary data, experiments, and field studies—what they have in common is that they attempt to make comparisons between cultures or within cultures over time. Political scientists, historians, anthropologists, economists, sociologists, and psychologists have all contributed to our knowledge through comparative analyses. Box 5.4 provides some examples of the diversity of comparative research conducted by undergraduate students.

1. THE LIPSET DEBATE ON CANADIAN-AMERICAN DIFFERENCES

The Lipset debate on the differences between Americans and Canadians will be used to illustrate the comparative approach. For over four decades Seymour Martin Lipset has been investigating cultural differences between the United States and Canada (1964, 1986, 1990). In describing the origins of the differences between Canadians and Americans, Seymour Martin Lipset says in *Continental Divide*:

One was Whig and classically liberal... doctrines that emphasize distrust of the state, egalitarianism, and populism—reinforced by a voluntaristic and congregational religious tradition. The other was Tory and conservative in the British and European sense—accepting of the

BOX 5.4   STUDENT RESEARCHERS AT WORK

Nonreactive Student Research

Comparative Research

Project More *Tino Rangatirantanga* for the Maori: A Comparative Analysis of Aboriginal Fishing Rights in Canada and New Zealand

Student Katherine Kennedy

Brief The student compared social science, historical, and empirical case studies to explore why the Maori in New Zealand have greater and more entrenched fishing rights than Canadian Aboriginal peoples.

Project The Impact of Social Policy on Single Mothers: A Comparative Analysis of Pictou and Antigonish Counties

Student Wendy Chisholm

Brief Municipalities in Nova Scotia constructed their own social development policies until the late 1990s. The student conducted a comparative analysis of social welfare policies in the counties of Antigonish and Pictou to assess the extent to which the Nova Scotia welfare policies fell within the neo-conservative or the social corporatist model.

Project The Primacy of Profit or the Welfare of the Worker: Workers' Perceptions of Industrial Ownership in Peru and Canada

Student Tiffany Barrington

Brief The student conducted interviews with retired employees of a smelter facility in La Oroya, Peru, and employees laid off from a closed steel mill in Sydney, Cape Breton, to compare worker perceptions of foreign versus state ownership and management and their beliefs about the position of workers under global industrial trends.

need for a strong state, for respect for authority, for deference—and endorsed by hierarchically organized religions that supported and were supported by the state. (Lipset, 1990, p. 2)

In 1964 Lipset presented an initial analysis of Canadian–American cultural differences. He began by noting the similarities in industrialization; ecology; level of urbanization; political, economic and work conditions; immigration histories; and political stability. Some of the differences noted are summarized in Table 5.1

Lipset traces the differences to Canada's closer ties with Britain and the Anglican church; by contrast, the United States had an anti-British revolution. He notes two revealing phrases: in Canada's *British North America Act* reference is made to "Peace, order, and good government," whereas in the American Declaration of Independence reference is made to "Life, liberty, and the pursuit of happiness." Lipset quite correctly observes that these two phrases say a lot about the differences between the U.S. and Canada.

Lipset's writing reflects a thorough knowledge of North American history: his major concepts are drawn from functionalism, and his measures are gleaned from a diversity of published sources, especially

TABLE 5.1 GENERAL CANADIAN–AMERICAN DIFFERENCES ACCORDING TO LIPSET

CANADA	UNITED STATES
Elitist	Egalitarian
Respect for law	Less respect for law
Collectively oriented	Individualistic
Ascriptive	Achievement-oriented
Traditional/conservative	Less traditional
Not assertive	Assertive

Source: S.M. Lipset (1964). "Canada and the United States: A Comparative View," *The Canadian Review of Sociology and Anthropology*, 1.

government documents. Lipset argues that elitism (*concept*) in Canada is reflected by much lower participation rates in higher education (*measure*). Using 1960 data, he points out that among Americans aged 20–24, 30.2% were attending university, while in Canada the comparable figure was 9.2%. He also points to the paternalistic family pattern in Canada, the greater reverence/respect paid to the clergy, the deference shown to the old and to teachers by the young, and respect for politicians in Canada compared to the U.S.A. (Lipset, 1964).

The greater respect for the law is reflected by the fact that Canada has one-third fewer police per capita. While one police officer was killed per annum in Canada in 1961 and in 1962, 37 police officers were killed in the U.S.A. in 1961, and 55 in 1962. Lipset therefore argues that Canadians use informal controls to a greater degree in controlling behaviour. Greater respect for the law also leads to more freedom for dissent. (See Table 5.2.)

The U.S.A. is a litigious society in which the ratio of lawyers to the general

TABLE 5.2 SPECIFIC CANADIAN–AMERICAN DIFFERENCES ACCORDING TO LIPSET, 1964

	CANADA	U.S.A.	RATIO
Percentage of population aged 20–24 in university	9.2	30.2	3 x
Police per 10,000 population	143.2	193.8	1/3
Police killed by criminals, 1961	1	37	37:1
Police killed by criminals, 1962	1	55	55:1
# Population/Lawyer	1630	868	2 x
Crime rates, 1960 (per 100,000)			
Burglary	46.4	126.7	3 x
Criminal homicide	1.2	7.3	6 x
Forgery	6.4	23.2	3 x
Fraud	13.5	38.8	3 x
Theft/Larceny	87.2	218.1	2 x
Divorce rates 1960 (per 1,000)	53.5	257.5	5 x

Source: S.M. Lipset (1964). "Canada and the United States: A Comparative View," *The Canadian Review of Sociology and Anthropology*, 1.

population is twice as high as in Canada. Crime rates in the United States are two to three times higher than the Canadian rates. In the U.S. everyone must be treated according to the same standard. Newcomers are seen as joining a "melting pot" in which everyone has the same rights and opportunities. (Americans, the argument goes, stress equality of opportunity, not equality of result.) Canadians celebrate a mosaic—the idea that individuals and groups should maintain their distinct identities. For Lipset it is Canada's counter-revolutionary beginnings that led to the continued emphasis on British ascriptive and elitist value patterns (1964). Thus, for example, Lipset would predict that Canadians would be more likely than Americans to make promotions based on whom you know (ascription) rather than on what you know (achievement).

A. IRVING LOUIS HOROWITZ

Irving L. Horowitz, an American sociologist, challenged Lipset's position, arguing that Lipset used old data rather than looking at more recent trends. Horowitz argues that the differences perhaps reflect a "cultural lag." That is, the trends in Canada are in the American direction, just lagging behind a little. In the area of divorce rates, for example, there has been a massive shift toward higher, American-level figures. (Note especially the change after 1968 when the grounds for divorce were extended.) Horowitz points to the boom in post-secondary education in Canada, noting that Canada has a higher number of science Ph.D.s per capita than the U.S.A. And, unfortunately, crime rates are going up in Canada as well (Horowitz, 1973). Like Lipset, Horowitz relies on public statistics to establish his points.

B. CRAIG CRAWFORD AND JAMES CURTIS

Surveys reported by Crawford and Curtis (1979) compare the U.S.A. and Canada in 1969 and 1970. The communities studied were in Oregon and Ontario. The findings indicated that Canadians were *less* collectively oriented than Americans and were also less traditional (in contradiction to Lipset's findings). Americans in these surveys did, however, attach more importance to achievement and were less elitist (Lipset agreement). One interesting part of the analysis shows that among older respondents (61 years plus), the findings tend to support Lipset's predictions. Among the younger age groups, however, the survey's findings on tradition and collectivist orientation suggested the opposite of Lipset's prediction (1979). The above debate shows scholars pursuing comparative questions using survey methodology. (See also Curtis, 1971; Curtis, Lambert, Brown, and Kay, 1989.)

C. STEPHEN ARNOLD AND DOUGLAS TIGERT

Arnold and Tigert (1974) reported on surveys done in the U.S.A. and Canada in 1968 and 1970. The picture is mixed. Some findings support Lipset's analysis; others do not. In summary, their findings show Americans to be:

- higher on five of seven questions on achievement beliefs, such as a belief in equality of opportunity for all people (supporting Lipset);

- higher on all items concerning orientations to the collectivity through voluntary community work (not supporting Lipset);

- less supportive of big government and government income guarantees (supporting Lipset);

- more traditional in their beliefs on moral issues (not supporting Lipset);

- more self-confident (supporting Lipset).

Their findings indicate that Americans are more assertive, self-confident, and optimistic than are Canadians. Americans hold more traditional views on moral issues; Americans are more likely to join organizations.

D. DOUG BAER, EDWARD GRABB, AND WILLIAM A. JOHNSTON

Baer, Grabb, and Johnston (1990) critically reviewed Lipset's work and, in particular, challenged him on a number of methodological issues. They argued that:

- there were inconsistencies in Lipset's characterization of national value differences;

- there were apparent contradictions between Lipset's earlier accounts and his most recent formulations;

- Lipset shifts levels of analysis, when, for example, "structural differences in the two societies or possible differences in the values of elites in both countries are assumed to correspond precisely to value differences between individual citizens in the two nations" (Baer, Grabb, and Johnston, 1990, p. 694);

- Lipset relies at times "on a selective and inconsistent reading of the available evidence in which data that are supportive of the thesis are mentioned but other data that are not supportive of the thesis are either interpreted differently or else placed in a different context" (Baer, Grabb, and Johnston, 1990, p. 694).

Baer, Grabb, and Johnston then go on to test many of Lipset's key arguments empirically. When they do so they find little support for many of the arguments. In particular, and in direct opposition to Lipset, they find Canadians are *less* traditional than Americans about the role of women in society and note that English Canadians are less respectful of government leaders than Americans. Overall, they find little support for Lipset's arguments when the data from national surveys are examined (Baer, Grabb, and Johnston, 1990, p. 708). And so the debate rages on.

E. EDWARD GRABB, JAMES CURTIS, AND DOUGLAS BAER

More recently Grabb, Curtis, and Baer (2000) reexamine the historical evidence for the fifty years immediately following the American Revolution. Their central conclusion is that, contrary to the Lipset thesis, the Loyalists who migrated from the American states to Canada were strikingly similar to the people who remained behind. Their findings provide little support for the Lipset view of the emergence of Canadian–American differences in values. Grabb, Curtis, and Baer claim that only about 40,000 of the antirevolutionaries moved to Canada (60,000 others moving back to Britain or to various Caribbean islands) and, the authors suggest, may have been less well off than those who moved to Britain or to other locations. Furthermore, they were most commonly not newly arrived British migrants but rather individuals who were American born and who had absorbed many key North American values.

F. SEYMOUR MARTIN LIPSET (1990, 2001)

To provide an additional example of the flavour of Lipset's writing, here is his speculation as to how the U.S.A. would be more like Canada had the American Revolution not succeeded:

> ... *the continuing British North American polity would now be more leftist than the revolution's children, more statist, much more social democratic, more disposed to perceive equality in redistributionist rather than meritocratic terms. It would operate under a parliamentary system, more conducive to third parties. It would be less individualistic and more deferential to authority. That hypothetical polity would also be less protective of civil liberties, free speech, and a free press than the actual populist republic, less inclined to place restrictions on the police, less generally inhibitive of the power of government. (1990, pp. 226-27)*

G. EDWARD GRABB AND JAMES CURTIS (2005)

With the publication of *Regions Apart: The Four Societies of Canada and the United States* (2005), Grabb and Curtis propose an alternative interpretation suggesting that Canada–U.S. differences have been exaggerated and that nations have major internal divisions. They use a wide variety of data to demonstrate that the American North and South continue to reveal powerfully different value orientations. They argue that the Civil War represents "the culmination of the divergent evolution of two quite distinct sub-societies growing within the bosom of the early United States, one slave-based, quasi-feudal, and southern, the other more essentially Anglo-American, small-scale capitalist, and northern" (p. 57). In Canada, the distinctiveness of French Canada is revealed in Quebec's greater support for collective rather than individual rights. This orientation, they suggest, is reflected in the actions taken by the Quebec government to promote

Quebec nationalism and to preserve the French language. They develop the position that, historically, English Canada and the American North were the most similar of the four sub-societies.

The debate between Lipset and his critics has been going on for over thirty years and promises to continue. Lipset (2001) has responded to Grabb, Curtis, and Baer (2000), and they (Grabb and Curtis, 2005), in turn, have responded to Lipset. The debate illustrates many of the key challenges in doing comparative studies. Independent of the merits of the case, what are some of the key challenges in doing comparative studies?

2. CHALLENGES IN COMPARATIVE RESEARCH

Comparative research has additional challenges because it deals with different cultures and often a different language. Warwick and Osherson (1973a, pp. 11–40) identify issues concerning equivalence in concepts, indicators, language, and sampling.

A. THE EQUIVALENCE OF CONCEPTS

While ideas such as incest or health are cultural universals, there is no precise agreement about what is meant by these concepts. What is incest in one culture may be defined as a preferred marriage partner in another; what is considered normal, healthy behaviour in one culture may be labelled as bizarre in another. So while we may have similar concepts, their content and meaning may vary considerably from culture to culture. Moreover, even within a culture there may be subtle variations in how concepts are defined.

TIP I DEFINE CONCEPTS CAREFULLY AND FULLY.

In all research, but particularly in comparative research, it is important to define concepts carefully, noting any variations between the cultures being studied. The search for appropriate indicators is facilitated by attention to the definition of the concepts. Only if a researcher is satisfied that there is an **equivalence of concepts** can direct comparisons between cultures be drawn.

B. THE EQUIVALENCE OF INDICATORS

The evidence collected in different countries is rarely based on the identical definitions and collection procedures. For example, if the definitions and collection procedures used to measure unemployment are different, do we dare use the information to compare two societies? What about crime rates: given different definitions, recording methods, and, indeed, the different interests of the parties involved in the data collection (would they benefit by showing an increasing crime rate?), can we legitimately make comparisons across jurisdictions? For virtually every indicator suggested, there are problems with a lack of equivalence in measures.

TIP 2 USE TREND MEASURES RATHER THAN ABSOLUTE MEASURES.

How might we go about limiting the effects of such disparities? One suggestion is that we use data trends rather than absolute measures (like the rate of crime, the unemployment rate, etc.). For example, if you are comparing the United States and Canada in unemployment statistics, minimize the effects of alternate measures by simply using the change in unemployment over periods of time. Then, even if definitions vary between the countries, at least they are comparable across time spans within the country

(unless, of course, definitions or procedures have changed within the country). Just as we standardize data within a country by calculating rates and ratios to deal with units of unequal size, when between-country data are required, consider computing trend data. And while such trend data would not provide the absolute measures desired, at least one should be able to detect whether the rates are converging or diverging.

Most critics would argue that Lipset's use of higher American crime rates as evidence for attaching a greater importance to achievement is dubious. Does the fact that we have fewer police mean we respect the law more, as suggested by Lipset? What else might it mean? (Could such information indicate, among other things, that Canadians have less money for policing, have a less urbanized population, have less fear of crime?)

C. EQUIVALENCE OF LANGUAGE

Box 5.5 presents an anecdote concerning language problems in a research project. Several years ago Jackson and Clairmont conducted a study in Moncton, New Brunswick. They sought to compare people who worked for large companies and government agencies (defined as Central Work World) with a matched sample of workers in smaller companies (defined as Marginal Work World). Since Moncton has a bilingual community, a translator was hired to develop a French version of the interview schedule and a number of bilingual interviewers were employed to conduct the interviews with some 600 residents in Moncton.

D. SAMPLING

Warwick and Osherson (1973a) point out that researchers are often rigorous in the sampling procedures they use within a

BOX 5.5 SOCIAL RESEARCHERS AT WORK

Don Clairmont and Winston Jackson in the Field

There was, alas, some difficulty with the French version of the schedule. Some of our respondents seemed to be having difficulty with it. On checking, we discovered that our translator had done a fine job of converting our simple English version into a Parisian French schedule. Not good. Not Moncton. Our resourceful interviewers, when they found a respondent was having difficulty understanding a question, translated it into English. The respondent would reply (usually in English) and our interviewers would then dutifully translate the answer back into French. Ah, the pleasures and problems of data collection.

Source: Winston Jackson, Memories of the Moncton Project

country but much more opportunistic when it comes to sampling countries themselves. However, it is reasonable for the selection of countries to be driven by pragmatic considerations such as the availability of data. And since a project's cost is often a fundamental issue, there is an understandable tendency for comparative research to be done on those countries where the fewest problems will be encountered in getting the information required. Moreover, since comparative studies typically involve two or three countries, there would be little point in using some form of random sampling to select them; to do so would be an abdication of reason! To compare radically diverse countries would not lead to much understanding, especially if the available data were not comparable. A random sample of two may sound scientific but such a sample would be seriously lacking in other regards.

The development of the *Human Relations Area Files* has been most helpful in providing researchers with inexpensive access to a file on the world's cultures that contains an enormous amount of information. This file is available at most universities.

In choosing to base much of his research on Canada and the U.S.A., Lipset minimized some of the problems that he would encounter. Statistical information is readily available in both countries and, while little comparative research had been done on the two countries prior to his work, a good deal of effort has since been expended, particularly by Canadian scholars attempting to test some of Lipset's hypotheses. And one could identify few countries which would have as much in common as the U.S.A. and Canada, even though available measures are not exactly comparable.

E. THE PROBLEM OF SELECTING EVIDENCE

While the problem of researchers choosing among alternate indicators is relevant to all types of research projects, this is especially the case in comparative studies. (This argument will be treated more fully in Chapter 10.) Given the vast amount of information available, what is the best way, for example, to measure elitism? (Lipset used the percentage of youth participating in post-secondary education in the two countries as one of his indicators.) The problem is that it is possible to demonstrate almost anything if you are free to search around for possible indicators. And while Lipset might well argue that the preponderance of evidence supports his position, his critics might not be so ready to agree (see Baer, Grabb, and Johnston, 1990; Curtis et al., 1989; Grabb, Curtis, and Baer, 2000, 2001; Grabb and Curtis, 2005). The general point here is that the selection of evidence is an especially problematic issue in comparative research. Not only can we question whether the indicators reflect what they are intended to, but we can also question whether the same variable will have the same meaning in different cultural contexts.

It would be difficult for most social scientists to avoid selecting indicators that produce results conforming to the researcher's preferred outcomes, ruling out those indicators not selected as insufficient in some way. There is no easy solution to this problem. One check is simply that researchers be public about which indicators were used—and perhaps even public about which indicators were rejected and why they were rejected. It would not be practical to ask researchers to explain all of their decisions or to list all the alternatives considered. To do so would be akin to asking a chess player to explain all the alternatives considered before making a move. The chess player's information processing is highly complex and the player, in fact, probably could not provide much useful information about how the choice was made. The same would be true of the researcher. But if we are public about what choices have been made, then critics can reexamine the issue using the same or alternate indicators.

TIP 3 INDICATORS, LIKE HYPOTHESES, SHOULD BE IDENTIFIED PRIOR TO COMMENCEMENT OF DATA EXAMINATION.

Social scientists have not always paid sufficient attention to identifying precise indicators before beginning data analysis. Such precision is required, because otherwise the researcher may inadvertently bias the outcome of the study. Moreover, the exact cut-points that are to be used in collapsing categories should also be identified prior to beginning analysis. (For example, where will the line between large and small communities be drawn when looking at the relation between deviance and community size?) Once again, if commitments are not made, the researcher may inadvertently select cut-points that result in an analysis showing what the researcher anticipated or wanted.

Realistically, these two suggestions are unlikely to be applied routinely by social scientists. It is sometimes a challenge to get researchers to state hypotheses formally or provide details of exact operational procedures. However, even getting them to pay "lip service" would be a start. At present, there is little awareness that there is a problem in this area. Issues raised in Chapter 9 (Three Tests of Significance) and in Chapter 10 (Bias) are also related to the issue of committing oneself to operational procedures and operational hypotheses.

E. ADVANTAGES AND LIMITATIONS OF NONREACTIVE STUDIES

Table 5.3 summarizes the advantages and limitations of nonreactive studies. The

TABLE 5.3 ADVANTAGES AND LIMITATIONS OF ALTERNATE DESIGNS

RESEARCH DESIGN CATEGORY	GENERAL	VALIDITY	CAUSAL INFERENCE	MULTI-VARIATE	PROBING
NONREACTIVE DESIGNS					
Comparative Analysis	±	–	–	+	–
Secondary Data	±	–	–	+	–
Content Analysis	±	–	–	–	–

In each category a "**+**" means that this is an advantage of the technique; a "**–**" means this is a possible limitation.

- **General** refers to the extent to which extrapolations to larger populations may be made using each of the design/data collection procedures.
- **Validity** is the extent to which indicators clearly measure what they are intended to measure.
- **Causal Inference** refers to the ease with which inferences about causal relations among variables may be made.
- **Multivariate** refers to the ease with which information on many variables is collected, leading to the possibility of multivariate analysis.
- **Probing** refers to the extent to which responses may be probed in depth.

particular challenges of these types of studies are that it can be challenging to establish the validity of their indicators, causal relations can be difficult to demonstrate, and the researcher cannot easily probe in depth. However, provided adequate sampling techniques are used, nonreactive studies can lead to convincing generalizations. Comparative- and secondary-data studies can yield results that deal with many variables.

F.   KEY POINTS

Nonreactive studies are those in which there is no opportunity for the person (or group) being studied to react to the observations.

A problem encountered in experiments, surveys, and interviews is that *subjects may modify their behaviour* because they are aware that they are being studied. A major confounding factor in social research is eliminated in nonreactive studies because the observed person or group is not able to react to the measurement process—that is, is not able to manipulate presentation-of-self for the researcher.

Comparative research is not really a special type of research with its own methodology; it is the research process itself. Comparative research has additional challenges because it deals with different cultures and often with a different language.

The *evidence collected* in different countries is rarely based on identical definitions and collection procedures.

While the problem of researchers choosing among alternate indicators is relevant to all types of research projects, this is especially the case in comparative studies. The problem is that *it is possible to demonstrate almost anything if you are free to search around for possible indicators.*

Social scientists have not paid sufficient attention to *identifying the precise indicators* that will be used prior to beginning data analysis. Such precision is required because otherwise the researcher may inadvertently bias the outcome of the study.

Economists, political scientists, historians, and, to a lesser degree, sociologists, anthropologists, and psychologists often conduct *research based on available material.* These sources might include virtually any data—ranging from published statistical, census, or business data to the unpublished diaries of important historical figures.

As defined by Holsti and Stone, *content analysis* is "any technique for making inferences by objectively and systematically identifying specified characteristics of messages" (Holsti, 1969, p. 14).

The advantage of *experimental studies* is that they help researchers to make clear-cut causal inferences. *Surveys* are particularly useful for representing populations with samples, and such studies have become associated with complex multivariate analyses. *Field studies'* strengths are in the area of validity and in probing for depth. *Nonreactive studies* are often reasonably cheap to do, can lead to important general statements, and sometimes yield variables that permit the simultaneous treatment of many variables.

G.   KEY TERMS

Coefficient of reliability	Nonreactive study	Unilineal model
Comparative research	Official statistics	Unit of analysis
Content analysis	Secondary data	
Equivalence of concepts	Secondary data analysis	

C H A P T E R   S I X

QUALITATIVE RESEARCH METHODS

WINSTON JACKSON, ANGELA GILLIS, AND NORINE VERBERG

The previous chapters presented introductions to experimental, survey, and nonreactive approaches to social science research. These approaches are predominantly quantitative (using numbers to summarize the findings of the research) and are most associated with the positivist, scientific approach that emphasizes careful measurement (Chapter 13), representative sampling (Chapter 15), and the logic of hypothesis testing (Chapter 2). A vast number of research questions can be posed and answered using these approaches. So whether it is attempting to describe and explain the patterns surrounding the relationship between gender and suicide or trying to determine the effectiveness of a stay-in-school program in decreasing the high school dropout rate, a quantitative approach is likely to be used. When well done, these studies have high levels of credibility because they are using scientific techniques that are fairly well understood and respected in our culture.

The problem with limiting oneself to positivistic approaches is that there is a whole range of human activity that is not adequately understood through these methods. If you wanted to know what it is like to be a psychiatric patient in a hospital, you would be quite limited in getting an adequate understanding of the experience by having patients complete a five-page questionnaire dealing with their perceptions and attitudes toward hospitalization. A certain amount could be gleaned from such a study, but could you really understand the experiences of patients? If you were to limit yourself to a positivist approach, could you make much sense out of how the whole institution works or the complexity of the relations among patients on one ward or how a patient experiences the transition into hospital life? These kinds of questions

beg for a holistic approach—an approach that taps into patients' perceptions of self and how they see others and that describes the process of learning how to act in a hospital ward. Erving Goffman's classic study, *Asylums* (1962), provides a fine example of how such a qualitative study might be conducted.

Fortunately, there are research methods in the social sciences that pay attention to such matters. **Qualitative researchers** emphasize seeing the world from the eyes of the **participants** in the study and are more holistic (studying the whole person, institution, group, or culture rather than one small, measurable aspect of it). Table 1.2 on page 15 summarizes some of the different assumptions and values that distinguish the qualitative and quantitative approaches to social research. Generally, qualitative researchers are associated with the interpretive approach (see Chapter 1); typically they rely more on using words than on numbers to describe findings and emphasize the subjective dimensions of human experience.

Over the past three decades, there has been a marked increase in the number of qualitative studies reported in journals and research textbooks and a tremendous increase in the number of scholarly journals publishing qualitative research. Box 6.1 provides a list of journals that publish *only* qualitative research. This reveals how embedded qualitative research has become in the social sciences.

This chapter defines qualitative research and highlights some of its key characteristics. Three qualitative approaches are featured in this chapter: ethnography, grounded theory, and phenomenology. The chapter introduces three data-collection methods commonly used by qualitative researchers—participant observation, in-depth interviews, and focus group interviews—

BOX 6.1   QUALITATIVE RESEARCH JOURNALS

The following is an abbreviated version of a list of English language qualitative research journals posted on the website of *The Qualitative Report*, an online journal published at the Nova Southeastern University in Florida. At one time, mainstream journals were not welcoming of qualitative research. The growing acceptance of qualitative forms of inquiry has led most of the major journals to begin publishing research based on qualitative methods. Imagine how long this list would be if we added all of the multimethod journals which now publish qualitative research!

Anthropology and Education Quarterly

Constructivism in the Human Sciences

Discourse Analysis Online

Discourse Processes

Discourse Studies

Field Methods (formerly Cultural Anthropology Methods Journal)

Ethnography

Ethnography and Education

The Grounded Theory Review

International Journal of Qualitative Methods

International Journal of Qualitative Studies in Education

International Journal of Qualitative Studies in Health and Well-Being

International Journal of Social Research Methodology Theory & Practice

Journal of Contemporary Ethnography

Journal of Mixed Methods Research

Medical Anthropology Quarterly

Narrative Inquiry

Phenomenology and the Cognitive Sciences

Qualitative Family Research

Qualitative Health Research

Qualitative Inquiry

Qualitative Market Research: An International Journal

Qualitative Methods

The Qualitative Report

Qualitative Research

Qualitative Research in Accounting and Management Journal

Qualitative Research in Organizations and Management: An International Journal

Qualitative Research Journal

Qualitative Research in Psychology

Qualitative Social Work: Research and Practice

Qualitative Sociology

Qualitative Sociology Review

Quality and Quantity: International Journal of Methodology

Research in Phenomenology

Sociological Research Online

Social Research Update

Symbolic Interaction

Visual Anthropology Review

Visual Studies

Source: Adapted from "Qualitative Research Journals," *The Qualitative Report* Home Page, Nova Southeastern University, Fort Lauderdale, FL, online:, posted 5 Nov. 2005, accessed 10 March 2006.

and the approaches to data analysis employed by ethnographers and grounded theorists. Subsequently, we discuss the establishment of criteria to evaluate qualitative research and the strengths and weaknesses of the qualitative approach.

A. ENTERING THE WORLD OF QUALITATIVE RESEARCH

Several leading authors have put forward definitions for qualitative research (Creswell, 1994, 1998; Denzin and Lincoln, 2000; Marshall and Rossman, 1995; Munhall and Oiler, 1986; Parse, Coyne, and Smith, 1985; and Silverman, 1997). Their work has been instrumental in advancing our understanding of qualitative methods.

1. DEFINING QUALITATIVE RESEARCH

Denzin and Lincoln (2000, p. 3) propose the following definition of qualitative research:

Qualitative research is a situated activity that locates the observer in the world. It consists of a set of interpretative, material practices that make the world visible. These practices transform the world. They turn the world into a series of representations, including field notes, interviews, conversations, photographs, recordings, and memos to the self. At this level, qualitative research involves an interpretive, naturalistic approach to the world. This means that qualitative researchers study things in their natural settings, attempting to make sense of, or interpret

phenomena in terms of the meanings people bring to them.

Qualitative research involves the use of a variety of empirical materials—case study; personal experience; introspective; life story; interview; artifacts; cultural texts and productions; observational, historical, interactional, and visual texts—that describe routine and problematic moments and meanings in individuals' lives. Accordingly, qualitative researchers deploy a wide range of interconnected interpretative practices, hoping always to get a better understanding of the subject matter at hand. (pp. 3–4)

Likewise, Creswell's definition emphasizes the complex, holistic picture created by qualitative research (1998, p. 15):

Qualitative research is an inquiry process of understanding based on distinct methodological traditions of inquiry that explore a social or human problem. The researcher builds a complex, holistic picture, analyzes words, reports detailed views of informants, and conducts the study in a natural setting.

This definition incorporates the idea that the researcher is an instrument of data collection focusing on the meaning of participants' experiences in social contexts. The use of descriptive language that emerges from the complex narrative of participants is an important characteristic of qualitative research.

2. CORE ACTIVITIES IN THE QUALITATIVE RESEARCH PROCESS

Like quantitative research, qualitative research involves asking a question or presenting a problem, collecting data, analyzing the data, and presenting findings. Yet there are important distinctions between the manner in which a qualitative investigation is designed and conducted as compared to a quantitative study. Figure 6.1 illustrates the types and order of activities typically found in qualitative versus quantitative studies.

A key to comparing quantitative and qualitative approaches to research is recognizing that the former is *linear*—each

FIGURE 6.1 STEPS IN QUANTITATIVE AND QUALITATIVE STUDIES

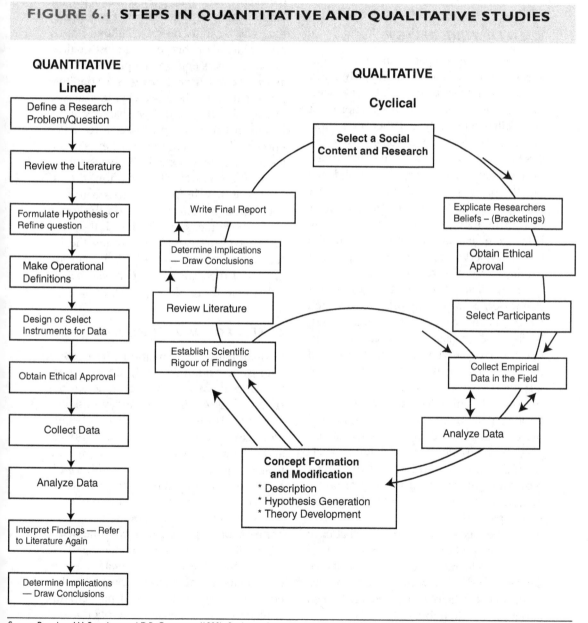

Source: Based on H.J. Streubert and D.R. Carpenter (1999). *Qualitative Research in Nursing: Advancing the Humanistic Imperative*. 2nd ed. Philadelphia: J.B. Lippincott.

step follows a previous one—until the project is completed, while the latter is *cyclical*, with a number of steps repeated as the research process continues and as the researcher tests new ideas as they emerge throughout the project.

A. LITERATURE REVIEW

A quantitative investigation involves an extensive review of the literature early on in the research process to establish the need for the investigation. The researcher must be familiar with different theoretical approaches as well as what other investigators have reported about the research topic. This will give the researcher the confidence that the proposed investigation is the next appropriate one to advance the particular field of knowledge. The literature review helps the quantitative investigator refine the research question and situate the question within a larger theoretical framework.

In qualitative investigations the literature review is carried out *after* the research has been conducted and the data analyzed. While some qualitative investigators accept that a cursory review may be conducted initially to help focus the study, many argue that the review should not occur until completion of the study. The rationale for this is to prevent the researcher from leading participants in the direction of what has already been reported in the literature. This is related to an assumption that the social world is known to the participants. Therefore, the research should be guided by the participants, not the research literature or the theoretical frameworks that have been developed on related topics. The purpose of the literature review in qualitative studies is to show how the current findings fit, or do not fit, into what is already known about the research topic.

B. EXPLICATING RESEARCHER'S BELIEFS

Quantitative researchers often maintain that they can conduct their research without being influenced by cultural values. Qualitative researchers reject this belief, assuming that, as members of the culture, they will be influenced by cultural beliefs and values. For this reason, most qualitative researchers engage in a process known as *bracketing*. **Bracketing** is a cognitive process used by the researcher to set aside biases and personal perspectives about the research topic. Its purpose is to make known what the researcher believes about the research topic honestly. To bracket ideas about the research phenomenon, the investigator may keep a diary to record personal thoughts and feelings on the topic. Once these ideas are disclosed, they can be set aside. Through bracketing the researcher is made aware of when interpretations of the data reflect personal beliefs rather than those of the participants.

C. SUBJECT OR INFORMANT?

In quantitative investigations, individuals who participate in the study are usually referred to as *subjects* (in experimental designs) or *respondents* (in survey designs). The focus is on a narrow range of behaviour (experiments) or answers (surveys) that allow the researcher to test theory. By contrast, the term *participant* or *informant* is employed in qualitative investigations. **Informants** are viewed as *active participants* in the research process and equal partners, or co-participants, with the investigator. Researchers seek to understand the participants' life experiences as they are constructed in their social world. They become deeply involved with participants while trying to understand the phenomena of interest from the participant's perspective. The informant helps the researcher gain an *insider* perspective. To do so, it is essential that participants have first-hand experience with the phenomenon under investigation.

D. SELECTION OF PARTICIPANTS

The quantitative researcher is usually involved as an objective observer, maintaining distance from the research subjects. Data are collected using structured instruments. Random selection or randomization is often used and the number of subjects must be large enough to establish statistical significance (see Chapter 15). Large sample sizes and random selection are not required in qualitative investigations, because the goal is not generalization of the findings but rather the provision of rich descriptions of the phenomena by those who have experienced it. Fundamentally, the emphasis in qualitative research is an in-depth description of the human experience, whether it be of whole cultures (ethnography: the culture of rural Nigeria) or of how individuals experience some life event (phenomenology: the birth of one's first child). Thus, the qualitative researcher selects participants who have experience in the phenomena of interest (member of the rural Nigerian community; first-time mother). This type of sampling is referred to as **purposive sampling**. The purposeful selection of participants in qualitative investigations is a strategically important decision in the study design involving the establishment of clear criteria for the selection of participants.

E. SETTING FOR DATA COLLECTION

In quantitative investigations, standardized data collection tools are employed, such as contrived experimental settings or preformatted questionnaires. The researcher designs the lab study or questionnaire to answer specific research questions or to test a theoretical model. Thus, the data is gathered, usually at a single point in time. The researcher is detached from the subject during the data collection process and the *subject* or *respondent* simply uses the predetermined tools to provide the researcher with data. There is seldom an opportunity for the participant to influence the research process or provide additional data to the researcher. Data collection is a close-ended, terminal process that begins, for example, with the delivery of the survey and ends with the return of the survey. By contrast, data collection in qualitative research is a dynamic, open-ended process.

Data collection in qualitative studies is to be "informant-driven," rather than "theory-driven." The informant teaches the investigator about the culture surrounding the experience being studied. The investigator assumes ignorance of the lived experience of the participants. For example, a researcher studying homelessness would not presume to understand what it is to be homeless or what variety of circumstances influence the experience of homeless people. Rather, the researcher allows the data collection to be guided by that which is highlighted as important by the homeless informants.

Qualitative researchers collect data in natural settings, called *the field*, where people are acting as they usually do. The *field* is the natural world of the participants. It is where they live and experience life. There is considerable onus on the investigator to be as nonintrusive as possible while in the field, while at the same time trying to limit the distance between her/himself and the people being studied. Prolonged time is spent in the field to allow the researcher to learn how things work in the study setting. In this sense, the researcher is described as a tool in the data collection process. Intensive involvement in the natural setting over time is required if the investigator wants to achieve an interpretative understanding of the culture or experience being studied. This is very different from limiting your data to the reactions of subjects in controlled experiments or the answers given by respondents to a questionnaire.

Many qualitative researchers use multiple methods of data collection. The objective is to have the discovery lead the choice of method rather than the method leading the discovery. Researchers often combine methods of data collection such as conducting unstructured in-depth interviews, making observations, and reading pertinent documents. Data-collection strategies may change as the study unfolds because the researcher is committed to using the method that best enables an understanding of the phenomena of interest.

F. DATA ANALYSIS

There are major differences in the data analysis processes of quantitative and qualitative investigations. In quantitative data analysis, the research process is *linear*. The purpose is to answer the research question or to test hypotheses or both. Data analysis does not begin until *after* all data collection is complete. Statistical procedures are used to summarize and analyze data. The research design and the type of data collected determine the appropriate statistical tests to be applied. The researcher must have a thorough knowledge of statistics or access to a statistical consultant to assure that appropriate statistical tests are applied to the data. Inappropriate application of statistics can lead to unjustified results and inappropriate conclusions.

In qualitative research, the investigator is fully immersed in the data in an attempt to bring order and meaning to the vast amounts of narrative that result. This requires that one comes to truly understand what the data are saying. It involves an extensive amount of time spent in dialogue with the data (weeks or months) using inductive reasoning (see Chapter 2). The researcher must decide from day to day which direction to take the method of data collection, based on the ongoing analysis of the data that are collected. In this sense, qualitative data analysis is a *cyclical process* of questioning and verifying the findings. The recursive process of analysis begins *immediately* with the first data-collection episode and continues throughout the study. Reading, rereading, intuiting, analyzing, synthesizing, and reporting on the data are required activities. This is sometimes referred to as **theoretical sampling**, which is a process whereby the researcher collects, codes, and analyzes the data simultaneously and continually decides what additional data are needed to develop the theory. As depicted in Figure 6.1 on page 149, data collected from interviews or observations are continuously reviewed to identify additional questions to be explored with participants. Routinely, data from early analyses are discussed with participants for clarification or elaboration. As the investigators review the data, they must carefully look for *meaning* in the data. At the conclusion of the study there is a protracted period of data immersion during which the investigator reviews all previous conclusions that have emerged, in the context of the whole study. Data that are similar in meaning are clustered together into preliminary categories. Specific techniques for doing this have been developed. Two well established qualitative data analysis strategies are outlined later in the chapter:

ethnographic analysis and the constant comparative method. It should be noted, however, that the specific approach used for the analysis of qualitative data vary by discipline and qualitative school.

G. SATURATION

Saturation is a term used to refer to a situation in data analysis where the participants' descriptions become repetitive and confirm previously collected data. When the researcher believes that data analysis has reached saturation, this is an indication that data collection is complete. It means that data collected from new participants simply confirms previously collected data rather than adding new information. Saturation in qualitative investigations is similar to the determination of adequate sample size in quantitative investigations. Saturation of data gives the researcher confidence that the description of the phenomenon has been captured. This functions in a similar way to the random selection and tests of statistical significance that give the quantitative researcher confidence that his or her results are true and can be generalized to others.

The qualitative research process is well suited to many social investigations where the goal is to develop a deep understanding of human experiences and the meanings that participants attribute to these experiences. Qualitative exploration of socially constructed phenomena can provide social scientists with critical insights and a deeper understanding of participants' experiences. Such insights could not be gleaned by relying exclusively on quantitative approaches.

3. THREE QUALITATIVE RESEARCH APPROACHES

This chapter introduces three qualitative research traditions: ethnography, grounded theory, and phenomenology. They were selected because they move across a continuum in the size of the unit being studied and because they have different research goals. Ethnography is concentrated on larger aggregations of people (up to the study of a whole culture), grounded theorists typically examine smaller aggregations (gangs, work groups, etc.), and phenomenological studies tend to be focused on individual experiences and perceptions. With regard to the focus of the research, anthropological ethnography is the work of describing a culture, grounded theory studies are focused on basic social processes, and phenomenology research is focused on discovering the essence of the lived experience. Table 6.1 presents a comparison of the three qualitative methods.

TABLE 6.1 COMPARISON OF QUALITATIVE METHODS

METHOD	STUDY FOCUS	ANALYTIC FOCUS	DISCIPLINES
Ethnography	culture/cultural group	describe a culture/cultural group	Cultural Anthropology
Grounded Theory	cultural groups	generate theory about a basic social process	Sociology/Symbolic Interaction/ Criminology
Phenomenology	individual experience	discern the essence of the lived experience	Philosophy/ Psychology/Sociology

B. ETHNOGRAPHY

1. WHAT IS ETHNOGRAPHY?

Ethnography is a qualitative research method that attempts to understand human behaviour in the cultural context in which it is embedded. It provides a description of a cultural group that is gleaned from the researcher's prolonged observation of the patterns of behaviour, language, customs, interactions, and ways of life of the culture-sharing group (Creswell, 1998). Ethnography is the work of describing a *culture* (Spradley, 1980). **Culture** may be thought of as a way of life belonging to a designated group of people. It includes all the ways a group of people solves problems, as reflected in their language, dress, food, traditions, and customs. It is a pattern of living that guides the group's thoughts, actions, and sentiments. The purpose of ethnographic research is to make *explicit* what is *implicit* within a culture by studying various cultural characteristics. The ethnographer's role is to paint a portrait of the culture-sharing group.

In cultural anthropology, ethnography once referred to the study of the origin of people, their past ways of living, and their strategies for surviving through time. The philosophical underpinnings of anthropology are still evolving but there is consensus that *culture* remains the central concept; today, however, ethnographers focus on contemporary cultures and subcultures as well as peoples' origins and past ways of living. Anthropologists seek to discover the interrelationships among all the parts that make up a culture or cultural group so that a picture of the wholeness of the culture emerges. These parts include the material culture consisting of man-made objects associated with a given group; the ideas, beliefs, and knowledge expressed in language; social networks; social and political institutions; and the ideals that the group holds as desirable goals (Atkinson and Hammersley, 1994).

Ethnography involves *learning from people* rather than studying people. This important distinction means the researcher must become a student and the participants of the culture become the teachers. By observing and studying what people do (cultural behaviour), what people say and know (cultural knowledge), and the things people use and make (cultural artifacts), the ethnographer comes to learn about the culture by making cultural inferences (Spradley, 1980). The ethnographer attempts to discover the insider's view of the world. To do this the ethnographer must set aside the idea of *naive realism*—the belief that all people define the real world in a similar way. Ethnography requires the researcher to adopt an attitude of *conscious ignorance* about the culture under investigation (Spradley, 1980).

In seeking to describe a culture at a particular moment in time, the ethnographer strives to learn the meanings of life experiences and events to the people studied. This is nicely expressed by Spradley:

> The essential core of ethnography is this concern with the meaning of actions and events to the people we seek to understand. Some of these meanings are directly expressed in language; many others are taken for granted and communicated only indirectly through word and action. But in every society people make constant use of these complex meaning systems to organize their behaviour, to understand themselves and others, and to make sense of the world in which they live. (1980, p. 5)

2. DAVID COUNTS AND DOROTHY AYER COUNTS: AN ETHNOGRAPHY OF RVING SENIORS

Anthropologists David Counts from McMaster University and Dorothy Ayers Counts from the University of Waterloo conducted an ethnography aimed at describing the culture of senior citizens who live and travel extensively in recreational vehicles. In *Over the Next Hill: An Ethnography of RVing Seniors in North America* (2001), the Counts take a close look at the culture of "elderly nomads, RVers." To study the

RVing lifestyle, they bought a 28-foot trailer, joined Escapees, a large organization made up of primarily full-time, year-round RVers, and began a two-stint participant observation study of the "road community" of RVers. In *Over the Next Hill*, the Counts weave together extensive quotations from RVing seniors to provide a rich description of the kinds of people who take up RVing, "what they do all day," the meaning of homes on wheels, the lure of RVing, how RVers build community, and how RVers decide to "hang up the keys."

Box 6.2 provides an excerpt from the chapter on community building among

---

BOX 6.2   SOCIAL RESEARCHERS AT WORK

David Counts and Dorothy Ayer Counts: Over the Next Hill: An Ethnography of RVing Seniors in North America

Metaphors of Community: They're My Family Now

Skips is family. If your husband gets ill, people will come right away and give support. That's family. (A full-timer)

The SKP family is best thought of as siblings—not parents or children. What's at issue is that people help and care for each other. (A full-timer)

What a wonderful world this is with our SKP friends. We call them our new family. (A full-timer)

In the above comments and throughout earlier chapters, RVers frequently use the metaphor of family to describe their feeling of community. To describe the family feeling they use

words such as 'friendship,' 'love,' 'trust,' and 'caring,' to recount the times when other RVers helped and supported them in a crisis. Some, like Polly Neuhaus, use sibling terms to describe their relationship with other RVers. A fellow Skip helped her when she was in hospital. She says of her friend, *"I could not have received better or more loving care from my family, and take her as my 'chosen' sister."* Judy Parrack, who was widowed in 1988 describes a similar experience. Her letter is an eloquent testament to the community feeling among Escapees: *"Family was with me for a week after Ernie died, but it is the continuing support of my SKP Family who write and drop by to visit that keeps me going. I don't think I'd have made it without SKPS! You'll never know how grateful I am."*

The founders of Escapees consciously used the metaphor of family to describe and shape the relationships they hoped to foster among members of the club:

Our main goal has always been to unite SKPs into an RV "family" that cares about each other. Chapters, Co-ops, and BOF groups provide a close "family feeling" in the same way that works with any large family. The family unit consisting of parents and children is closer than the extended family that includes aunts, uncles, and cousins. Yet when the small units come together, they are all part of the larger family unit.

Escapees achieve the "family feeling" through the act of sharing. The Petersons explicitly encourage club members to share with one another *in order* to become like family:

Sharing is the key to all phases of the Escapees Parks from SKP Co-ops to Retreats to the new combination concept. Therefore, it isn't surprising to find members also share rides to town for doing laundry, going shopping, and social events. They are [a] tight-knit group who think of themselves as "family." Because of this, those who are in the park keep a watchful eye over a traveling member's property. Even more

important than the feeling of security for things is the knowledge that there is someone there to help you when you need it.

There is no doubt that RVers are sincere when they use the phrase, "they're my family," to describe their feelings toward their fellows. What do they mean by these words? What *exactly* are they saying when they assert that an organization of RVers is their family now?

Their comments may reflect the North American experience of family and friendship. As Stephanie Coontz says in *The Way We Never Were*, the ideals exemplified by Beaver Cleaver's family never were reality. They were not the typical American family. However, people were raised with this myth and want to believe that sometime in the past this ideal existed, even though it was never part of their experience. Coontz maintains that the family ideal has become the metaphor for evaluating relationships, including relationships of responsibility for others. The family has become a model for public life.

When family relations become "our only model for defining what emotionally 'real' relationships are like," we can empathize and interact only with people whom we can imagine as potential lovers or family members. The choice becomes either a personal relationship or none, a familial intimacy or complete alienation.

Source: David R. Counts and Dorothy Ayers Counts (2001). *Over the Next Hill: An Ethnography of RVing Seniors in North America*, 2nd ed. Toronto: Broadview Press. Reprinted with permission of Broadview Press.

Rvers, especially with other members of the Escapee RV Club. The verbatim statements reveal how club membership influences both the identity of the members and contributes to their ability to build community. For example, the club adopted the letters SKP as its acronym to reflect the members' values. SKP stands for "Sharing, Karing People" and "Special Kind of People." In the quotes, members referred to one another as *Skips*, which suggests that values and membership of the club are meaningful to the members (Count and Counts, 2001, p. 250).

C. GROUNDED THEORY

1. WHAT IS GROUNDED THEORY?

The goal of **grounded theory** is the *development of a theory* that explains underlying social processes. The researcher is interested in understanding how people interact, take action, or engage in the process in response to some phenomenon. Grounded theory is useful in areas in which either little research or extensive research has been conducted. It is particularly appropriate in exploratory and descriptive studies (Glaser and Strauss, 1967). It is now among the most influential and widely used modes of qualitative research when *generating theory* is the researcher's goal (Strauss and Corbin, 1997). It is making an important contribution to knowledge development because of its ability to produce partial theories. Partial theories are useful because they can be empirically tested (see Chapter 2). Glaser and Strauss (1967) made the bold claim that once a grounded theory study has been conducted in an area, little additional research is done because of the density of the theory that emerges. Because the generated theory emerges from the data it is said to be *grounded* in the data and useful to practice.

Grounded theory emerged from the discipline of sociology and has its theoretical foundations in **symbolic interactionism**. Symbolic interactionism focuses on the meaning of events to people in everyday settings. It is this meaning, created by the people in the situation, that guides behaviour, action, and the consequences of that action (Chenitz and Swanson, 1986). At the core of symbolic interaction is an examination of how people define events or reality and how those beliefs shape their actions. George Herbert Mead (1934) and Herbert Blumer (1969) advanced the symbolic interaction tradition. Mead described the process whereby a person develops a sense of self through social interaction with others. Blumer believed symbolic interaction rested on three premises:

1. Humans react to things on the basis of the meanings that the things have for them;

2. Meanings are derived from the social situations that one has with others; and,

3. Meanings are altered and shaped through an interpretive approach used by individuals in dealing with things they encounter (Blumer, cited in Chenitz and Swanson, 1986).

For social life to emerge, group meanings must be shared among the group. Communication provides the mechanism for such sharing. The meaning of the event emerges through both verbal and nonverbal behaviour and hence the interaction becomes the focus of the investigation to discover the true meaning. Through interaction human beings are changed and influence each other and create meaning about life and themselves.

A grounded theory investigation is conducted to identify concepts and propositions about the relationships between them, as they relate to a basic social psychological phenomenon. Unlike most methods, the researcher approaches the study *without* a specific well-defined question in mind. Instead, the question initially is broad and general in nature. It identifies the phenomenon to be investigated in a particular social context. The question emerges, is refined, and may change several times as the data are collected and analyzed. The basic social process is usually a *gerund* (a noun ending in "ing") indicating change across time as a social reality is realized. Table 6.2 presents examples of grounded theory studies. Beside the titles of the studies appear the basic social psychological process that emerged from the research and the stages involved in the process.

TABLE 6.2 SELECTED EXAMPLES OF GROUNDED THEORY STUDIES

TITLE	BASIC SOCIAL PSYCHOLOGICAL PROCESS	STAGES
The Invisible Burden: Women's Lives with Fibromyalgia	Bearing the Invisible Burden	1. Dealing with traumatic life 2. Yearning for affirmation 3. Searching for relief 4. Adjusting to limitations
HIV-Positive Women: Double Binds and Defensive Mothering	Defensive Mothering	1. Preventing 2. Predicting 3. Protecting
Transforming: The Process of Recovery from Schizophrenia	Transforming	1. Battling 2. Connecting 3. Determining 4. Committing
Handling the Hurt: Women Who Use Cocaine and Heroin and Lose Child Custody	Handling the Hurt	1. Numbing out 2. Giving up 3. Running away 4. Cleaning up 5. Dealing with feelings
Inner Strength in Women: A Grounded Theory	Learning to Live a New Life	1. Dwelling in a different place 2. Healing in the present 3. Giving and allowing nurturance 4. Connecting with the future 5. Being spiritual
Loss and Bereavement: HIV/AIDS Family Caregiving Experiences	Personal Work	1. Reconciling 2. Making life-and-death decisions 3. Letting go

The method of data collection used by grounded theorists includes observations, participant observation, and interviews (Dietz, Prus, and Shaffir, 1994, p. 21). In fact, Dietz, Prus, and Shaffir (1994) describe their method as ethnographic because it helps the researcher to reveal the ways in which human group life is accomplished. Similar to other qualitative approaches, data collection, coding, and analysis occur simultaneously from the beginning of a grounded theory study. The process is systematic but fluid, allowing the researcher to respond to new information that emerges from the data.

2. KERRY DALY: GROUNDED THEORY AND THE SOCIAL CONSTRUCTION OF FATHERHOOD

Kerry Daly, a family sociologist at the University of Guelph, employs the principles and practices of grounded theory and the constant comparative method. Box 6.3 presents an excerpt from his study on the meaning and negotiations of time among couples in dual-earner families. He indicates that he employed an "open-ended, discovery-oriented design" to allow him to explore how women and men subjectively experience time negotiations in the household. He interviewed seventeen heterosexual dual-earner couples with at least one child, individually for the first interview, then together as a couple. He found that two central themes emerged: scheduling has become a priority activity in dual-earner families and women were primarily in control of organizing family time. Although women were primarily in control of scheduling family time, negotiations followed two continuums: informal and formal negotiations and accomplishing balance and achieving compliance. The excerpt in Box 6.3 features the first theme of scheduling as a priority activity. You will notice that the researcher provides verbatim quotations of individuals interviewed to illustrate and support the observation being highlighted.

BOX 6.3   SOCIAL RESEARCHERS AT WORK

Kerry Daly: "Time, Gender and the Negotiation of Family Schedules"

Scheduling as a Priority Activity
Because of a perceived escalation of pace, these men and women realized that they spent an increasing amount of time negotiating family schedules. Time, by virtue of its scarcity in their lives, was, as one woman indicated, "the most precious thing that people have these days," and as a result, they saw themselves "talking about it constantly." . . .

Although many of these couples addressed the challenges of trying to fit everything into their schedules, it was clear that time negotiation was routine:

We spend so much time talking about time, you know, Sunday night, what's happening this week and when are you working and what time are you getting home tonight. I don't know what people do.

The apparent lack of awareness of "what people do" suggests that these couples were aware that other families also experience stress about time. However, when it came to devising adaptive responses, other families did not serve as a good source of information. If other families successfully negotiated their schedules, it was not readily visible. As a result, participants treated their scheduling challenges as a private problem that required them to create their own negotiating strategies. A "problem-solving tone" seemed to accompany these negotiations:

When Leo and I do have a chance to talk about it we're always talking about, you know, how can we make more time, more time for the kids, more time for us, but I don't know if it's possible and we're always sort of second guessing ourselves thinking, you know, are we just managing our time poorly, you know, why do the neighbours have so much more time, but I don't know, maybe that's just our perception too and they don't. We certainly don't have time to sit on the driveway and watch the neighbourhood (laughter).

As the above statement suggests, the negotiation of time was embedded in a contradiction between the clear cultural message to spend more time together (fuelled by a belief that others were successful) and uncertainty about how to successfully accomplish this. In addition, the success of this negotiation about time influenced how they perceived themselves as a family. Neighbours appeared to have ample time for family and as a result were perceived as good managers of their time. Scheduling was a priority because they linked it to perceptions of success as a family.

Accordingly, they felt required to give close attention to scheduling, especially during periods of stress:

It's negotiated and when times are really, you know, when things are really stress filled, you know, when we're really pushing things, we do get into discussions all the time over, you know, 'what do you mean you're sitting down and watching TV?, you still have to do this and this,' you know, so that we do have some discussions around that but it is negotiated. I mean, I don't think we really get in to any heavy battles about it or anything. It requires a lot of communication.

Scheduling was not only a priority but an intensively interactive process, and one that was not always entered into on equal terms. Although both women and men expressed an awareness of the central importance of scheduling for the success of their family lives, women appeared to be more invested in the negotiation process. As the passages above indicate (mostly wives' voices), women were more likely to identify and talk about the urgency of scheduling.

Source: Kerry Daly (2002). "Time, Gender and the Negotiation of Family Schedules." *Symbolic Interactionism*, 25(3): 311–331. Reprinted with permission of University of California Press.

D. PHENOMENOLOGY

1. WHAT IS PHENOMENOLOGY?

Phenomenologists seek to reveal the meaning of a *lived experience* from the perspective of the participant. **Lived experiences** are the everyday human experiences that are real to the individuals who experience them. **Phenomenology** seeks to achieve a deep understanding of the phenomenon being studied through a rigorous, systematic examination. Its purpose is to describe the essences of lived experiences. *Essences* are elements related to the true meaning of something that gives common understanding to the phenomenon under study (Spiegelberg, 1975; Fain, 1999). The phenomenologist strives to uncover and convey the true meaning or essence of the experience through the use of descriptive language.

Phenomenology is predicated on the belief that each person has a unique view of the world and that each person's social reality is as valid and true as any other view (Munhall and Boyd, 1993). It focuses on the everyday way in which people make sense of their being in the world. The philosophical basis for phenomenology lies in existentialism, which deals with the way one views the world, stressing the personal "here and now" experiences and the demands they place on the person as a free agent in a deterministic universe (Smith, 1997). Phenomenology is concerned with the nature of being, the here and now as it is—the lived experience.

The development of phenomenology has been affected by philosophers such as Kant, Hegel, Lambert, Husserl, and Heidegger (Schmitt, 1972). Husserl (1859–1938), known as the father of phenomenology, held unique beliefs about what it means to be human. He introduced two ideas that are central to phenomenology: lifeworld and intersubjectivity. **Lifeworld** is the world of lived experience and **intersubjectivity** describes how subjective awareness and understanding can be reached in a common world (Fain, 1999). Phenomenologists believe that whatever is known must appear to consciousness; whatever does not appear to consciousness cannot be known. Consciousness then provides access to the world: to be conscious is to be aware of the lived experience of some phenomenon. Husserl believed consciousness and the lived experience were in relationship—that is, consciousness was the means that constituted the objects of experience. Everything that appears to one's consciousness constitutes an object. This is referred to as *intentionality*. Heidegger (1889–1976) advanced the concept of being-in-the-world from the conception of consciousness as intentionality. He believed that the nature of being human was concern or awareness of one's own being-in-the-world.

Phenomenologists believe in multiple realities that are constructed by individuals within the social context of their lives. Reality is constructed from human experiences that emerge from the relationship between human consciousness and phenomena. The phenomenological view enlarges the experience and tries to understand it in the complexity of its context. Phenomenologists believe that any experience is a valuable and valid source of knowledge. They also believe that intuition (developing one's consciousness through looking and listening) is important in knowledge development (Smith, 1997).

The focus of a phenomenological investigation is to describe the meaning of the lived experience from the perspective of the participants. Any experience that presents itself to consciousness can be a focus of phenomenological investigation. The research question is usually quite broad. This is to allow the participants to provide the answer. It usually takes the form: "What is the meaning of one's lived experience?" From this, the researcher may develop a central overarching question and several subquestions that follow from the central question. Phenomenological researchers avoid using hypothesis statements so as not to sway the participants toward a desired answer.

Suggested steps for formulating the question have been developed by a number of researchers (Munhall and Oiler, 1986; Omery, 1983; Parse, Coyne, and Smith, 1985). The steps may vary depending upon the phenomenological perspective followed. Moustaka (1994, p. 99) suggests four subquestions that may be useful in explicating the meaning of the lived experience. They focus on what is important about the experience to the participant, and how the experience impacts on what it means to be human:

1. What are the possible structural meanings of the experience?

2. What are the underlying themes and context that account for the experience?

3. What are the universal structures that precipitate feelings and thoughts about the experience?

4. What are the structural themes that facilitate a description of the experience?

2. J.E. SOLCHANY: A PHENOMENOLOGICAL STUDY OF WOMEN'S PREADOPTIVE EXPERIENCES

J.E. Solchany's phenomenological study of the experience of mothers-to-be during the child adoption application process is featured in Box 6.4. A phenomenological perspective is particularly appropriate for this study, which sought to gain an understanding of the process of developing a mother–child relationship in the pre-adoptive period from the perspective of women who became mothers through international adoption. Because this process is not well understood and there is little investigation of it, the phenomenological approach is particularly appropriate for exploring people's pre-adoptive experiences from their own perspective. The women in this study recently lived the experience and are a rich source of data.

Solchany used an open-ended interview method to focus the discussion on the mother–child relationship rather than on the adoption process. Data were analyzed inductively using a method developed by Strauss and Corbin (1990). The themes that reflected the experience of the participants in the pre-adoptive stage are presented in Box 6.4. Women's narratives demonstrated the strength, commitment, and resilience inherent in the journey to create a family.

E. DATA-COLLECTION METHODS IN QUALITATIVE STUDIES

Three of the major qualitative approaches to data collection will be considered in this section: participant observation, in-depth interviews, and focus-group interviews. Qualitative researchers frequently use a variety of data-collection methods within one research project. In this section, we describe participant observation as distinct from individual and focus-group interviews, yet

BOX 6.4   SOCIAL RESEARCHERS AT WORK

J.E. Solchany: "Anticipating the Adoptive Child: Women's Preadoptive Experiences: A Phenomenological Study"

This phenomenological pilot study explored the experiences of three women who became mothers through international adoption. The study sought to gain an understanding of the women's experiences of developing a mother–child relationship in the pre-adoptive period.

Findings provided a description of seven themes that describe the process of developing a mother–child relationship in the pre-adoptive period. The themes include: taking control, creating a family, anticipating, celebrating the pictures, honoring the child's origins, investing personally, and bonding.

Taking control encompasses the mother's process of beginning to develop a mother–child relationship. Mothers took control of their lives and their environments in order to make a place in the world for a family purposely created through adoption. All made a conscious decision not to pursue pregnancy, seeing adoption as a natural, proactive choice that put them in control of their reproductive health and desire to be a parent.

Creating a family was the second theme that emerged. All mothers stated clearly that their goal was to create a family, be a parent, and have a child. One mother summed it up nicely:

> *It's a feeling, like you have been on this road all your life and everything that came before was bringing you to this point. These were the kids meant to be in this house, in this*

home, to be our children. I have no doubt about it. This is the way and the time they had to come to us.

Anticipating, the third theme, was charged with emotion, preparation, and expectancy. They prepared for their children by sharing their anticipation and the adoption process with family, friends, acquaintances, and even strangers who were willing to listen.

Celebrating the pictures was a significant component of developing the relationship. All mothers described the pictures of their child as something to hold on to, share with others, and help them prepare for the arrival of their child. The picture became a tangible connection to their baby a world away, like a pregnant belly to rub and smooth.

Honoring the child's origins and learning about their child's land and culture was a way of paying tribute to the country that was giving them their child. They saw the child's time in their country of origin and with their caretakers as worthy beginnings.

Investing personally went beyond money, time, and resources of the mothers. They invested themselves and pursued adoption with blind determination. Once they began, stopping the pursuit to adopt seemed no longer an option.

Bonding was the term used by mothers to describe what they did during the pre-adoption period. It was a significant theme running throughout their experience of developing a relationship with their adopted child. One mother summarized:

The bonding starts with all the preparation you make in your home, just psychologically, all the anticipation, having the pictures. What is that like? Maybe it is like parents who first feel their child kicking. The things that we did to bond, many of them are the same as the couple who are pregnant. I mean you paint a room, you get a crib, you have a baby shower. Many of those things are the same, and then some of the other things are different.

The narratives of the women describe themes in the process of preparing to welcome a child. These were different from those that emerge during pregnancy, yet there are parallels between the pre-adoptive process and pregnancy.

The stories of these women demonstrate the strength, commitment, and resilience inherent in their journey to create a family. Future research might focus on providing adoptive mothers with validation of both their journey and the processes inherent in it, credibility for this alternative but natural path to motherhood, and recognition of the beauty of the adoptive mother's development of a deep, loving, lifelong mother–child relationship.

Source: Adapted from J.E. Solchany (1998). "Anticipating the Adopted Child: Women's Preadoptive Experiences." *Canadian Journal of Nursing Research*, 30(3), 123–129.

conducting interviews with individuals or groups is often part and parcel of doing participant observation research. Also, interview-based studies may involve interviews with both individuals and focus groups. In addition to the three data-collection methods presented here, qualitative researchers might make use of oral histories, secondary data sources such as recorded information about the group, and any number of sources that provide cues as to the experiences of respondents.

1. PARTICIPANT OBSERVATION

The **participant observation** method involves an intensive examination of some culture, community, organization, or group by a researcher who has joined the group for an extended period of time. For example, in studying a pre-literate society by living with the group, the anthropologist is attempting to describe and explain the group's customs and beliefs from within. The researcher becomes a *participant* in the lives of the group's members, sharing their joys and pains. The participant observer *observes* behaviour and engages in a language learning process. These are key activities because language conveys the meaning of the cultural actions the researcher is witnessing. Such studies frequently take much time to complete—not surprising given the need to learn a new language and to absorb the intricacies of the culture.

Classical anthropology led the way in developing participant observation techniques: the names of Bronislaw Malinowski,

Margaret Mead, and Oscar Lewis come immediately to mind. More recently, anthropologists have used participant observation research to study subcultures and groups in western societies. Spradley notes that the language learning process is no less important when conducting research with people who speak the same dominant language. In this situation, the researcher has to pay particular attention to the nuanced ways in which language is used by people who occupy the cultural group being studied because it conveys the meaning system of the group. Working in this qualitative tradition, researchers have studied everything from exotic cultures to prisons (Gresham M. Sykes, 1968), hobos (Nels Anderson, 1961 [1923]), and the world of the punker (Baron, 1989).

Erving Goffman's study on mental institutions, *Asylums* (1962), William F. Whyte's analysis of a street gang, *Street Corner Society* (1955), and Becker, Geer, Hughes, and Strauss' *Boys in White* (1961) are classic studies in sociology using the participant observation method. Elliot Liebow, a graduate student in anthropology who was interested in understanding the world of marginalized blacks in an urban setting, wrote *Tally's Corner* (1967). In psychology perhaps the best-known participant observation study is Festinger, Riehen, and Schachter's *When Prophesy Fails* (1956), a study of a quasi-religious group which had predicted the end of the world. In Canada, Thomas Dunk's (1991) study of the culture of working class men is recognized as an important Canadian ethnography.

Today most ethnographers take the role of an **overt participant**, meaning that their identity as a researcher is known to the people being studied. Some researchers in the past were **covert participants** in the group, meaning that they did not disclose that they were studying the group. Laud Humphreys was a covert participant in his study of impersonal sex between men in public washrooms. Covert research is seldom done anymore, at least not with the approval of the academic community (this is discussed in greater detail in Chapter 11 on research ethics). Some critics suggest that the presence of a researcher (i.e., overt participant observer) in a cultural group will influence the behaviour of the research participants because they know they are being studied. As noted below, however, participant observation researchers work tirelessly to be present in the community of interest long enough to gain an insider perspective. They give considerable attention to gaining entry into the group, building rapport, and developing trust. The lengthy amount of time spent in the field facilitates the development of this rapport-building and trust and, in turn, the trustworthiness of the findings.

There are types of projects where there will be limits placed on the researcher's participant role. For example, Robert Prus wanted to study prostitution, but he did not want to become involved in the sex trade. Prus decided to be himself—a sociologist—and to observe prostitutes as a "bar patron." As such, he simply sat in nightclubs that prostitutes frequented, ordered non-alcoholic beverages, and got down to the work of observing the interactions among the prostitutes, bar staff, and clients. When people spoke with him, he told them that he was a sociologist and that he wanted to learn about how people became involved in the work they were doing. After some time, regulars—including the prostitutes—became accustomed to his routine presence and volunteered to talk with him. He showed a genuine, nonjudgmental interest in people's lives, inquiring about the "what" and "how" of the lifeworld of the participants. The point is that the participant observation method can be adapted so that there is some element of observation and some element of participation in the natural setting of the people being studied.

Given the challenges of doing research in the field, all participant observers must gain entry into the group and develop and establish rapport. An introduction to how this is accomplished is provided below. Because participant observation is used by ethnographers and grounded theorists, their unique approaches to data analysis are included here as well.

A. GAINING ENTRY INTO THE GROUP

Gaining entry is sometimes a simple matter; at other times it is more difficult. For starters, the type of group has to be taken into account: if the researcher wishes to enter a formal organization (religious group, prison, bureaucracy, hospital, school), the entry methods will differ from those used when attempting to study an informal organization (community responding to a crisis, gay and lesbian bar, hobo community, street gang, pool hustler hangout, or business lunches of young executives). But no matter what the researcher studies, entry should be viewed as an ongoing and reciprocal relationship between the researcher and the population being studied. The researcher has to negotiate a relationship with each person in the study population (see particularly Schatzman and Strauss, 1973, pp. 18–34).

Access to the cultural group may be gained through a **gatekeeper**, an individual with special group status who can lead the researcher to other *key informants*. **Key informants** are the group members who are most knowledgeable about the study phenomenon. They are representative of the culture and have potential to yield substantive data about the study phenomenon. Key informants are willing to teach the ethnographer about the study phenomenon and refer him or her to general informants who also have knowledge of the phenomenon.

In entering a formal organization, it is probably best to begin by finding out as much as possible about the organization. Who are the key actors; are there any critical issues currently facing the organization (strike threatened, market disappearing, raw materials becoming increasingly expensive); what are the best times of the week or month to approach the leadership of the organization?

Having determined that the intended study would be appropriate, informal contact should be established with those persons whose permission will be required to gain entry. This initial contact should then be followed by a brief written statement that outlines the goals and methods of the proposed study. The preparation of this document will assist the researcher in defining the problem more clearly (although in participant observation studies the precise problems studied emerge through the research process and are not necessarily present from the beginning of the project). The letter outlining the project should:

- establish the legitimacy of the project: this may be achieved by using the stationery of the sponsoring organization and mentioning the sponsors of the project;

- indicate the goals and methods of the study: this provides the leadership of the target organization with a simple statement that can be used to communicate the project to others in the organization;

- specify the length of time that researchers will be on site and how much time will be spent interviewing various members of the organization: this provides the organization's leaders with important information as to how long the researchers will be present;

- indicate the extent to which anonymity and confidentiality will be possible for various participants; and

- indicate the form in which feedback on the project will be provided to the organization: this may be informal verbal reports, seminars, or formal reports.

Research reports typically mask the location of the site and the names of participants. However, the researcher should assume that published reports circulate among those studied. When studying a group it is difficult to disguise the identity of some of the individuals behind the pseudonyms—especially where a role is occupied by only one person. The writer of a report must bear in mind that damage may be done to the reputations of those being studied. One must be careful, therefore, in promising anonymity before starting a study, for it may not be possible to mask everyone's identity adequately in the final report.

In studying informal organizations, it usually is not necessary to get an official's permission to enter the group; one simply has to establish cordial relations with the people being studied. For example, to do observations among the homeless one would simply need to establish a solid working relationship with them. To keep things simple, one would probably just say that a book (or an article) is being written about the lives of the homeless, that the researcher would be talking to the homeless in the area, and that the identities of individuals will not be revealed in the publication.

There are times when gaining entry is extremely difficult, taking weeks or even months to accomplish. In the case of anthropologist Gerald Berreman (1973), who was studying a Himalayan village, it took four months to begin to have some success in overcoming the fear locals had of outsiders.

B. DEVELOPING AND MAINTAINING RAPPORT

One challenge that the participant-observation researcher faces is to develop good relationships with the people being studied. These relationships are sometimes strained because the subjects may wish to "capture" the researcher to their points of view (Lofland, 1971). The researcher must be careful not to become overly attached to one faction since this would make it more difficult to get information from members of other factions. The researcher may also be blamed for difficulties that the group encounters, and her/his objectivity may be strained if an unequal amount of time is spent with either side. Developing and maintaining rapport is a creative, ongoing process.

C. DEVELOPING A METHOD FOR TAKING FIELD NOTES

Field notes attempt to capture, with as much accuracy as possible, descriptions and interpretations of individuals, interactions, and events. The exact time and location of observations should be recorded, along with other descriptions to help the researcher recall the events (weather conditions, other significant events going on in the community or in the world that day). Emphasis should be placed on reflecting exactly what people say, how they say it, and describing the reactions of others to what is said. As a practical suggestion, Anselm Strauss (1987) used the following method to distinguish types of quotations:

- Words recalled verbatim enclosed within double quotation marks ("......")

- Words recalled with less certainty about the exact wording enclosed within single quotation marks ('......')

- The meaning is clear but wording not exact: no quotation marks.

Field notes should also distinguish clearly between descriptions and interpretations of events and people. One suggestion is to organize field notes so that there is a wide column for descriptions and a narrow column for interpretations. Note, too, that there are two kinds of interpretations:

1. the subjects' own interpretations of their behaviour and the behaviour of others; and

2. the interpretation that the observer places on these same activities.

The emphasis, particularly in the initial stages of research, should be on descriptive accuracy. Field research is a dynamic process whereby ideas develop, are refined, and are then tested and modified throughout the observational period. Thus, the writing of theoretical memos is encouraged to help the observer develop explanations systematically. **Theoretical memos** are tentative interpretations that emerge and are tested during the observational period. Indeed, participant observers do well to carry out both observations and theoretical reflection about these observations concurrently (Corbin and Strauss, 1990, pp. 6–10).

In deciding what situations, or persons, are to be observed, Corbin and Strauss suggest that researchers should sample according to concepts and their properties, and not by trying to locate representative individuals. They argue that in grounded theory "representativeness of concepts, not of persons, is crucial" (1990, p. 9). Thus, if you want to study pool hustlers, you would go to where pool hustlers hang out and watch how they operate. Once at the pool hall, the observer would note events that occur, and begin classifying them according to some general principles. What techniques are used to initiate a game with a mark? How is the bet determined? How is the handicap negotiated? ("I'll play one-handed, make all the balls in the number 4 pocket . . . ten bucks a game, loser pays the table charge.") Perhaps the researcher would then try to observe some of the most highly skilled players, some of moderate skill, and some of the poorer players to note differences in how they operate. And since hustlers often hustle other hustlers, the technique of negotiating the bet is a crucial and complex process (see Prus and Sharper, 1977).

Field notes should be made as soon after field observations as possible, preferably the same day. At the very latest, notes should be made the morning after an evening's observations. Expect to spend as much time writing up field notes as you spent in the field. Three hours of observation will usually be followed by three hours of writing up the observations. The use of a laptop computer is most helpful in compiling field notes. It is also possible to tape field interviews and then have these interviews transcribed. Some researchers even prefer to dictate their observations and then have them transcribed. Field notes will tend to be lengthy. In the case of *When Prophecy Fails*, field notes, combined with transcriptions of recorded information, came to well over 1,000 typewritten pages (Festinger, 1956, p. 251); *Boys in White* produced about 5,000 single-spaced typewritten pages of field notes and interview material (Becker et al., 1961, p. 30). When writing the report, the challenge will be to condense the field notes into a coherent document of reasonable length.

D. INTEGRATING DATA COLLECTION AND DATA ANALYSIS

Some researchers enter field notes using a word processor; others adhere to the pencil and paper strategy. Regardless, researchers are advised to separate their master field files from their analytic files. The **master field file** is made up of the complete journal of the field notes. A copy of the master field file should be placed in a binder and retained. The first step in analyzing the data will be to make several additional copies of the master field file. The copies are used as raw material for building up *analytic files*. **Analytic files** are files relating to a specific topic or relationship explored in the study. For example, you might wish to build up a subfile on interactions between status unequals. You would cut-and-paste all the field notes pertaining to such interactions. Frequently these will be ordered along some dimension (in this case perhaps along the degree of status difference between the two persons interacting). Each piece cut from the copy of the master file should have its original (master copy) page number on it. Various analytic files are made up in this way. There may also be files related to the methodology of the study and the history of the institution or area being studied. It may well be the case that not every part of the master file will make it into any of the subfiles which are created. The files typically will include:

- *Master Field File.* This is the original complete file of the field notes. Pages are numbered and each entry is dated. This represents the raw data to be analyzed.

- *Background, History File.* This subfile contains information drawn from the master field file as well as from other sources.

- *Analytic Files.* Each of these files deals with a particular type of observation or relationship (for example, descriptions of interactions between status unequals, interactions across gender lines, interactions of strangers).

- *Key Character Files.* Individual files may be established on key players in the organization or group being observed. These files attempt to reflect the personality, mannerisms, and typical behaviour of central characters.

If field notes are entered into a computer it will be possible to use special software packages to process the information. Currently a number of such packages are available, such as the Ethnograph (based on ethnographic analytic strategies) and ATLAS.ti (based on Glaser and Straus' constant comparative method). For an excellent review and description of some of these, the reader is referred to special issues of *Qualitative Sociology* that focus on computers and qualitative data. From time to time, this journal provides updates on software packages of particular interest to the qualitative researcher.

If a word processor is used, it is possible to do a significant amount of work simply by entering code words into the word processor's search capability to locate where they appear. The paragraphs associated with the words can then be selected and moved to a separate file. Of course, in doing this, it is crucial to maintain a master copy of the original field notes. And, as always with computer files, be certain to have multiple printed copies and disk copies of the master file. Some word processors also have the ability to number paragraphs and lines; this facility is helpful in keeping track of one's records.

Two specific data analysis strategies will be described in Section F.

2. IN-DEPTH INTERVIEWS

There are types of qualitative research projects that do not permit the researcher to employ a participant observation method of data collection. For example, Frederick Desroches (2002) wanted to study the social processes associated with bank robbery. Bank robbers often work alone and some never disclose to anyone that they have robbed a bank. Even if he were able to locate individuals planning a bank robbery or who had conducted a bank robbery without being caught, clearly it would not be advisable to do participant observation research on bank robbery! Desroches, therefore, decided to interview convicted bank robbers while they were serving prison terms in federal penitentiaries. For his research, Desroches relied on an extremely popular method of data collection: the in-depth interview.

In-depth interviews are used as the sole method of data collection or they can be used along with other methods. They provide a method of collecting respondents' perceptions of their world. Typically, **in-depth interviews** are done to solicit people's descriptions and explanations of events in their world. They are often tape-recorded to preserve the verbatim description of the participants. Quotations from the interviews are used to illustrate the points the author wishes to make in the research report.

An excellent guide to in-depth interviewing is provided by James P. Spradley in his book, *The Ethnographic Interview* (1979). Although Spradley focuses on "ethnographic" interviews conducted in the field, his method has been adapted for interview studies. Three key elements are present in ethnographic interviews: explicit purpose, ethnographic explanations, and ethnographic questions. The *explicit purpose* simply means that both the participant and the interviewer are aware that the discussion has a research purpose and, even though it may be quite conversational, is not to be confused with a casual conversation. *Ethnographic explanations* are those that the researcher tries out on the respondent to see if they make sense. Informants are encouraged to use colloquial language and to become the teacher as they familiarize the researcher with their worlds. *Ethnographic questions* include (i) *descriptive* ones such as "What do you do when you go to a party?"; (ii) *structural* questions having to do with how the respondents organize their world, such as "What kinds of activities generally go on at the parties you attend?"; and (iii) *contrast* questions, which urge the respondent to indicate what is meant by terminology peculiar to the respondent's group, such as "What do you mean when you say someone is *super cool?*"

Although Prus and Grills (2003, p. 25) advocate a multi-method approach to data collection, they suggest that in-depth interviewing, defined as "extended, open-ended inquiries into the experiences (circumstances, viewpoints, dilemmas, activities, adjustments) of others" is the single most important method of gathering data. They caution, however, that the success of the interview method requires the researcher to show genuine interest in learning "the what and the how of other's experiences, . . . which implies that the researchers open themselves to the participants' viewpoints and practices and avoid imposing their own concepts and moralities on the other" (p. 25).

Whether used as the sole method of data-collection or in conjunction with other methods, many qualitative researchers advocate conducting the data analysis during the data collection process. This requires the interviewer to modify the focus and language of the interview to address insights gleaned from earlier interviews. Of course, this is not always done and sometimes it is not possible. The literature shows that the interview method is quite diverse: a researcher may interview several informants once or few informants several times. Phenomenologists, for example, take a different position on interviewing than ethnographers and symbolic interactionists. Thus, the specific assumptions and goals of the research tradition influence the researcher's approach to interviewing.

3. FOCUS GROUP · INTERVIEWS

An approach that is becoming repopularized in academic research is the use of *focus groups*. A **focus group** typically consists of six to twelve individuals who are asked to discuss topics suggested by a facilitator. The idea is for the researcher to observe the interactions among focus-group members and solicit their attitudes, opinions, and solutions to problems. While important information can be revealed in one-to-one interviews, the rationale of focus groups is that they provide a dynamic in which participants learn from one another and develop ideas together. The researcher is able to discern whether there seems to be broad agreement on a point or whether a view being expressed is limited to one or two individuals. The responses may well lead into important issues initially unanticipated by the researcher. Because focus groups can help researchers reach saturation more quickly, they can be cost effective.

Like individual interviews, focus-group discussions will be recorded either manually, by having someone take notes, or by tape-recording the proceedings—or a combination of the two methods. Taped interviews are considered important because of the importance accorded to the verbal descriptions provided by the informants. It is useful to record the names of the speakers in the order that they speak so that the

discussion can be tracked precisely during the analysis stage. It is also useful for the facilitator to note any comments that will help in the evaluation of the discussion. Observational notes on attitudes and interactions are useful additions that can prove helpful in interpreting the results.

The transcript of the discussion, together with the accompanying notes, becomes the data in a focus-group interview. Since the data is the transcript of the discussion, the researcher can use the techniques associated with grounded theory method (discussed following) or content analysis (see Chapter 5). Normally the results will be presented as quotations from the transcript of the discussion(s) to reflect the qualitative dimensions of the participants' interactions.

Although focus groups can be both cost effective and successful in terms of data collection, problems can arise. For example, it is possible for one participant to dominate or discourage other members from expressing their opinions (Sussman, Burton, Dent, Stacy, and Flay, 1991). There may be fewer original ideas expressed than when talking to individuals one-on-one; group members may show how their experiences converge but say less about their unique reactions to an experience (Fern, 1982). While this is true, focus groups can provide a supportive atmosphere for individuals to discuss their common experience.

F. TWO QUALITATIVE APPROACHES TO DATA ANALYSIS

Qualitative researchers have developed a number of different methods of data analysis. Two examples are provided in this chapter: ethnographic data analysis, developed by anthropologists, and the constant comparative method, developed by Glaser and Strauss (1967). Qualitative researchers take an inductive approach to theory development and this is reflected in their data analysis procedures. The two approaches introduced below reflect the inductive strategy typical of qualitative data analysis, because they show that coding strategies facilitate the identification of themes in the data. When choosing a particular method of data analysis, a qualitative researcher is likely to be influenced by the philosophic assumptions and methods employed by researchers in their discipline (e.g., anthropology, criminology, sociology, etc.), the goals of their research, and the challenges posed by their particular research study.

1. ETHNOGRAPHIC DATA ANALYSIS

As noted, the ethnographer analyzes the data in the field on an ongoing basis. This process of integrating data analysis into the data-collection process allows the researcher to know what to look for in the next period of participant observation. For cultural anthropologists, the analysis proceeds through four levels as the researcher learns, describes, and interprets the meaning of cultural symbols in the informants' language. The experienced researcher conducts the four levels of analysis simultaneously throughout the research project; however, it is recommended that the research student learn to do each in sequence before moving on to the next level. The suggested sequence is domain analysis, taxonomic analysis, componential analysis, and theme analysis (Spradley, 1980). Throughout the analysis, the researcher is looking for patterns in the data. The goal is to discover the cultural patterns people are using to

organize their behaviour, to make and use objects, to arrange space, and to make sense out of their experience. These patterns make up the culture (Spradley, 1980).

A. DOMAIN ANALYSIS

In the **domain analysis** the researcher is moving from observing a *social situation* (a set of behaviours carried out by people in a social situation) to discovering a *cultural scene.* **Cultural scene** is an ethnographic term used to refer to the culture under study (Spradley, 1980). Cultural domains are categories of meaning that include other smaller categories. The first step in a domain analysis is to select a situation to observe. In the example in Box 6.2 on page 155, the Counts observed RVing seniors. The category, people who take up RVing, is the first domain to be analyzed. The researcher asks the question, "Who are the people who give up living in their home for most or all of the year to live in a motor home in recreational parks or off-road?" Their field notes document the various categories of people (e.g., full-timers, Escapees, boondockers). Spradley suggests that it is important to identify the *semantic relationships* in the observations made in your particular cultural scene. He identifies a list of universal semantic relationships. For example, x is a kind of y; x is the result of y; x is a part of y. "Full-timers" are one particular type of RVer. Further, another analysis can be done to explore the types of seniors who become full-time and the types who decide that RVing isn't for them. By creating the domain analysis, the researcher identifies additional questions and makes more focused observations that lead to exploring the roles and relationships of other members in the cultural scene.

B. TAXONOMIC ANALYSIS

A *taxonomic analysis* is a more in-depth analysis of the domains. The researcher is searching for larger categories to which the domain may belong. A **taxonomy** is a set of categories organized on the basis of a single semantic relationship. The major difference is that the taxonomy shows more of the relationships among the things inside the cultural domain (Spradley, 1980). You are moving from the general to the particular. For example, the research can explore more closely the lifestyle of the boondockers. Boondockers are RVers who park (dock) anywhere ("even in the boonies") without "hookups" to electricity and water, free of charge. Once this analysis is complete the ethnographer looks for relationships among the parts or relationships to the whole (Streubert and Carpenter, 1999). Based on these new categories additional questions and observations will be made. For example, are there different types of boondockers, and if so, how do they differ? Is their orientation to community-building different from RVers who dock only in parks?

C. COMPONENTIAL ANALYSIS

Cultural meaning comes not only from patterns based on similarities but also from patterns based on contrasts. **Componential analysis** looks for all the contrasts among the cultural categories in the domains. Spradley defines it as "the systematic search for the *attributes* (components of meaning) associated with cultural categories" (1980, p. 131). He uses the domain of mail to exemplify componential analysis. Think about all the different kinds of mail you receive. You get junk mail (flyers, notices, and advertisements), bills, magazines, personal letters, etc. A person from a culture without mail would find it difficult to classify the

mail as you would because they would not see the differences. They would see all the paper as mail. While it is true that there are all kinds of mail, each has a unique cluster of *attributes* that convey the cultural meaning of the mail to you. For example, bills are usually impersonal printed forms, whereas personal letters are often hand addressed and often use your first name. All these different bits of mail have components of meaning (attributes) attached to them that make them meaningful. You act on the implicit cultural meanings without even thinking about it. You know to discard the junk mail, pay your bills, and save your personal letters to respond to them.

The attributes for all the cultural domains are represented in charts known in ethnography as *paradigms*. To complete a componential analysis, the ethnographer should carry out the eight steps outlined by Spradley (1980, pp. 133–139). These include:

1. Select a domain for analysis (RVing seniors).

2. Inventory all contrasts previously listed (some RVers are full-timers, some are boondockers, some are club members, some are club administrators, etc.).

3. Prepare a paradigm worksheet.

4. Identify dimensions of contrast that have binary values.

5. Combine closely related dimensions of contrast into ones that have multiple values.

6. Prepare contrast questions for missing attributes.

7. Conduct selective observations to discover missing information.

8. Prepare a complete paradigm.

The final paradigm may be used as a chart in your ethnography. It enables you to present a great deal of information in a concise manner.

D. THEME ANALYSIS

Cultural themes are recurrent patterns in the data that are used to connect domains. Spradley defines them as:

> . . . *any principle recurrent in a number of domains, explicit or tacit, and serving as a relationship among subsystems of cultural meaning. . . . They usually take the form of an assertion such as men are superior to women. (1980, p. 141)*

Themes are assertions that apply to numerous situations and have a high degree of generality. To identify themes, the ethnographer must immerse her/himself in the data. Spradley suggests that if you are not able to live in another society for a year or two, you can still immerse yourself in the data: block several days to immerse yourself in the cultural setting looking for themes and then take several days to review your field notes in an intensive manner. This type of immersion will often reveal patterns and themes that relate the domains previously identified.

One way to look for themes is to look for similarities and differences across domains. This will focus your attention on the cultural scene as a whole. Another strategy to identify themes is to compare different cultural scenes. A third strategy is to make a schematic diagram of the cultural scene, identifying relationships among the domains. Spradley suggests a list of *universal themes* that may be used as a basis for scrutinizing your data. The list is not intended to be exhaustive: rather it simply suggests possible themes that you may find in studying your cultural scene. The universal themes include:

- Social conflict—in every social situation conflicts emerge, and identifying these conflicts will help interpret the culture.

- Cultural contradictions—every society has contradictory messages. What inherent contradictions have people learned to live with and how?

- Informal techniques of social control—what formal and informal means are used in the group you are observing to get people to conform to the values and norms that make social life possible?

- Managing impersonal social relations—how do people in the cultural scene you are observing deal with people they know well and those they do not know well?

- Acquiring and maintaining status—what cultural symbols and icons convey status and prestige and how are these acquired and maintained?

- Solving problems—a person's cultural knowledge is often designed to solve problems. The ethnographer seeks to discover what cultural problems exist and what knowledge is used to solve them.

The final step of thematic analysis is to write a summary overview of the cultural scene. The goal is to condense everything you know to essentials and to deal primarily with the relationships among the parts of the culture. Although ethnographers examine small details of a cultural scene, at the same time they seek to understand the broader cultural landscape.

Through the analysis process and the writing of the ethnographic report, the researcher is hoping to provide an in-depth study of selected domains, an overview of the cultural scene, and a description that conveys a sense of the whole. Often times, the themes form chapters of the ethnographic report. For example, in *Over the Next Hill* the theme of home is captured in Chapter 7, entitled "Home Is Where I Park

It." In this chapter, the Counts document how RVers make a place home, how the home is a focus of identity, and how RVers personalize space. They note that having a "home on wheels" poses many challenges, such as "living in a sardine can with a partner" and the "three Ms: money, mail and medicine." The chapter provides an exhaustive account of both the joys and challenges of making home on the road on a fixed income, and out of the telling of this chapter, one gains an insight into the culture of developing a sense of home on the road. Clearly the monograph format provides a vehicle for presenting a description of the cultural scene, with chapters presenting different domain summaries.

2. CONSTANT COMPARATIVE METHOD

Consistent with many other qualitative schools, grounded theorists advocate conducting data analysis during the data-collection process. During the data-collection process, grounded theorists generate theory using the **constant comparative method**. As the name suggests, each piece of information is coded and compared to other pieces for similarities and differences in the lives of those interviewed. Figure 6.2 illustrates the fluid and cyclical nature of data analysis in grounded theory research. It requires detailed record keeping of interviews, field notes, and memos. It follows a standard format that has been described by a number of experts in the field (Beck, 1993; Creswell, 1998; Glaser, 1978; Stern, 1980; Strauss and Corbin, 1990; Streubert and Carpenter, 1999; and Chenitz and Swanson, 1986). The steps are briefly summarized below using the process outlined by Stern (1980) and Streubert and Carpenter (1999). Note that the steps in the constant comparative

method can be done using the traditional pencil and paper strategy or by employing computer software (such as ATLAS.ti) to facilitate the coding process.

A. CONCEPT FORMATION: CODING

The researcher reads the transcripts and looks for an underlying pattern in the data. *Coding* occurs at three levels.

i. Level I Coding

Level I coding involves studying the data line by line and identifying key processes in the data. Level I codes are called *substantive codes* because they codify the substance of the data and use the words of participants (Stern, 1980).

ii. Level II Coding

Level II codes assign data to categories according to obvious fit. A *category* is a unit of information composed of events, happenings, and instances (Strauss and Corbin, 1990). Categories emerge through condensing Level I codes by comparing each Level I code with all other Level I codes. Each category is then compared to every other category to assure that they are mutually exclusive.

iii. Level III Coding

Level III codes identify the **core variable** or the *basic social psychological process* (BSP). A core variable is one that focuses the theory and accounts for most of the variation in a pattern of behaviour that is both relevant and problematic for the participants involved. It is central to the other categories (Beck, 1993). BSPs usually represent the title given to the themes that emerge from the data. They are processes that occur over time and that involve changes over time.

FIGURE 6.2 GROUNDED THEORY DATA GENERATION AND ANALYSIS

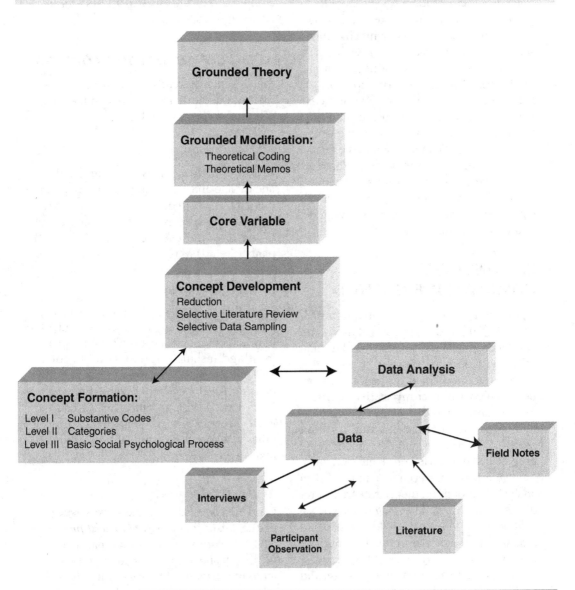

B. CONCEPT DEVELOPMENT

Three steps are involved in the development of the core variable: reduction, selective sampling of the literature, and selective sampling of data.

i. Reduction

Reduction is a vital step in identifying the core variable or BSP. In reduction each category is compared to see if there is a higher order or umbrella category under which a number of the existing categories can be merged. The researcher identifies theoretical linkages among the categories and collapses them to form more general categories.

ii. Selective Sampling of the Literature

Selective sampling of the literature occurs simultaneously with, or follows, data analysis. The literature review is conducted to determine what is known about the concepts that are emerging from the data. The literature is considered data and used to fill in the gaps in the emerging theory and to add completeness and clarity to the theoretical description.

iii. Selective Sampling of the Data

Selective sampling of the data occurs once the main concepts have emerged. At this point additional data are collected in a selective manner to develop the hypothesis statements further, to identify the properties of the main variables, and to ensure saturation of the categories. The researcher generates hypotheses about categories and their relationships and interrelationships and tests these hypotheses with selective data that either support or fail to support the hypotheses. Researchers stop collecting new data when they are satisfied that they are not hearing anything new about the category or the emerging hypothesis. At this point one *core category variable* emerges that can explain the relationships among all of the others. This core variable best explains how a problem is processed (Chenitz and Swanson, 1986).

C. CONCEPT MODIFICATION AND INTEGRATION

This phase of data analysis involves two processes: theoretical coding and memoing.

i. Theoretical Coding

Theoretical coding forms theoretical linkages or connections between the data categories. Whereas the substantive coding that occurred at Level I fractured the data into pieces, theoretical coding helps weave the fractured pieces back together again, by introducing Level II coding (Beck, 1993). Glaser (1978) has identified 18 *families of theoretical codes* to sensitize researchers to the subtleties of their data and the possibilities for integration of data. Three examples of Glaser's coding families (and their constituent members) include:

1. Consequences Family (the six Cs: causes, contexts, contingencies, consequences, covariances, and conditions).

2. Interactive Family (mutual effects, reciprocity, mutual trajectory, mutual interdependence, interaction of effects, and covariance).

3. The Strategy Family (strategies, tactics, mechanisms, manipulations, maneuvering, dealing with handling techniques, ploys, means, and goals).

ii. Memoing

Theoretical memos are the ideas the researcher holds about codes and the relationships as they strike the researcher during analysis. Memos vary in length from one line to several pages. Their purpose is to help the researcher put the fractured data back together. Glaser (1978) identifies three roles for memos: (1) to raise data to a conceptual level; (2) to develop the properties of each category; and (3) to generate hypotheses about relationships between the categories. Memos are sorted into a theoretical outline to assist the researcher in writing up the grounded theory that was discovered. Glaser's rule of sorting memos is to begin sorting categories and their properties *only* as they relate to the core category or BSP. Memos that do not fit are saved until such time as a new focus of the study is considered. Sorted memos become the basis of the research report.

The findings of grounded theory research include a substantive theory that describes the phenomenon under investigation supported by study data. Rich narratives of the study process and findings are provided to show how the theory is embedded in the data.

G. METHODS OF EVALUATING QUALITATIVE RESEARCH

Qualitative researchers have had an uphill struggle to establish the legitimacy of their work. Often it has been seen as overly subjective and lacking the credibility of positivistic approaches, and as a result practitioners have struggled to convince both funding agencies and peers of the value of qualitative research. During the seventies and eighties qualitative researchers tried to show how their work measured up to the standards of quantitative research.

Thus an effort was made to establish parallel criteria to those used by positivists. This approach was ultimately doomed to failure, since qualitative research has different intentions and strengths than those of quantitative research. Recently qualitative researchers are attempting to abandon the notion of parallel criteria and instead to develop their own independent criteria for judging the adequacy of their research. The early and contemporary criteria will now be explored.

1. DEVELOPING STANDARDS OF QUALITY

A. FOUR QUESTIONS FOR ASSESSING QUALITY

Lincoln and Guba (1985) in their classic statement shed some light on the issue of assessing truth in qualitative research. They outlined four questions that any investigation (quantitative or qualitative) into the human condition should consider if the trustworthiness (quality) of the project is to be properly assessed:

1.   How truthful are the particular findings of the study? By what criteria can we judge them?

2.   How applicable are these findings to another setting or group of people?

3.   How can we be reasonably sure that the findings would be replicated if the study were conducted with the same participants in the same context?

4.   How can we be sure that the findings are reflective of the subjects and the inquiry itself rather than the product of the researcher's biases or prejudices?

These questions when appropriately addressed establish the **trustworthiness** of a study, its applicability, its consistency, and its neutrality. These terms are associated with terms from the positivist paradigm of internal validity, external validity, reliability, and objectivity.

B. ALTERNATE TESTS OF QUALITY

Lincoln and Guba are, however, among the many researchers who believe it is *inappropriate* to rely on positivists' concepts of validity and reliability in order to evaluate qualitative research that operates within a different paradigm from the positivist perspective. They identify four alternative concepts that more accurately reflect the assumptions of the qualitative paradigm: *credibility, dependability, transferability, and confirmability* (Lincoln and Guba, 1985, p. 300). These criteria taken together establish the trustworthiness of qualitative findings. Table 6.3 presents concepts used to talk about rigour in quantitative and qualitative research. A discussion of threats to validity and reliability in quantitative and qualitative studies is found in Chapter 13.

i. Credibility

Credibility refers to the accuracy of the description of the phenomenon under investigation. The portrayal of the reality must be faithful and plausible to those who have experienced that reality. Credibility can be enhanced by prolonged time in the field collecting data and repeatedly observing

and interacting with participants. Another strategy for gaining credibility is to use different data sources (which includes different persons, times, places, etc.) and methods (observations, interviews, documents). Doing so enables the researcher to look for patterns of convergence as well as counter patterns or negative cases in the data (Miles and Huberman, 1994). Conducting *member checks* is another technique for ensuring that you have an accurate and true impression of the phenomenon being studied. *Member checks* involve asking the research participants to read the analysis and help to refine it to be congruent with their experience. *Collaborative research* also improves credibility and believability of results. This is accomplished by having other investigators verify the effectiveness of data-collection procedures, the comprehensibility of descriptions, the inclusivity of samples, and the logic of arguments. Credibility is enhanced by an accurate description of the setting, participants, and events observed.

ii. Dependability

Dependability refers to both the stability and the trackability of changes in the data over time and conditions. The issue of dependability in qualitative investigations reflects the reality that situations constantly change and people's realities differ. In assessing dependability, the researcher is

---

TABLE 6.3   PARALLEL CONCEPTS OF RIGOUR IN QUANTITATIVE AND QUALITATIVE RESEARCH

QUANTITATIVE	COMPARISON IN QUALITATIVE
• Validity	• Credibility (Authenticity)
• Generalizability (External Validity)	• Transferability (Fittingness)
• Reliability	• Dependability (Auditability)
• Objectivity	• Confirmability

interested in determining the extent to which another investigator with similar methodological training, rapport with participants, and knowledge of the field would make the same observations. This is determined by an **audit trail**, in which the researcher does an audit of the research process, documenting all the raw data generated as well as the methods and sources of data generation, and analysis decisions. By reading the audit trail another researcher should arrive at comparable conclusions given the same setting.

iii. Transferability

Transferability is concerned with the *generalizability* or *fittingness* of study findings to other settings, populations, and contexts. In assessing transferability of findings the research consumer hopes to show that the results are not context bound. To enable the research consumer to do this, the researcher must provide sufficient detail in the study report so that readers can assess the appropriateness of the findings to other settings. The lack of transferability of findings to other settings is often viewed as a *weakness* of qualitative methods.

iv. Confirmability

Confirmability refers to the objectivity of the data. Meanings emerging from the data have to be tested for their plausibility, their sturdiness, and their "confirmability," so that two independent researchers would agree about the meanings emerging from the data. Otherwise we are left with interesting stories about what happened but they are of unknown truth and utility (Miles and Huberman, 1994). The basic issue here is one of neutrality. In other words, do the conclusions depend upon the subjects and conditions of the inquiry rather than the

researcher (Lincoln and Guba, 1981, 1985)? To assess confirmability, the audit trail is used. The researcher must be explicit about how personal biases, assumptions, and values may have come into play in the study and must consider the plausibility of alternative conclusions and rival hypotheses. To a certain extent the researcher is trying to limit the influence of the Hawthorne effect (see Chapter 3), which is an inevitable part of doing research.

Drawing conclusions from qualitative research data requires careful assessment and involves the processes of forming patterns in the data, looking for contrasts, clarifying relationships, and collecting respondent and peer feedback. Essentially, the investigator ought to ask: do the results of the inquiry fit and make sense and are they true to the understanding of ordinary people in the everyday world?

2. CONTEMPORARY STANDARDS OF QUALITY

More recently Lincoln and Guba (1994) have noted that although the traditional criteria (referred to above) have been well received, their parallelism to positivist criteria make them suspect. Lincoln and Guba continue to call for additional critiques of the issue of quality in qualitative research. While many researchers continue to observe the four traditional criteria (Miles and Huberman, 1994; Streubert and Carpenter, 1999), some argue that there is no longer a need to defend the value and rigour of qualitative research with criteria that parallel those in quantitative research. This has led to an effort to determine more appropriate methods of determining quality in qualitative research (Creswell, 1998; Sandelowski, 1993). Lincoln (1995) traces her own thinking on the issue of quality and the scientific adequacy of qualitative research. She has moved beyond the traditional parallel criteria of the classic work by Lincoln and Guba (1985) to her current perspective. It includes a commitment to emergent relations with respondents, a commitment to a set of stances, and a commitment to a vision of research that promotes justice (Lincoln, 1995). Flowing from these commitments are eight standards found in Box 6.5 for assessing the quality of qualitative research. Adherence to these standards will help the researcher answer the all-important question—"Did we get it right?" And, as Sandelowski noted (1993):

> . . . *we can preserve or kill the spirit of qualitative research; we can soften our notion of rigor to include the playfulness, imagination, and technique we associate with more artistic endeavours, or we can further harden it by the uncritical application of rules. The choice is ours: rigor or rigor mortis.*

BOX 6.5   SOCIAL RESEARCHERS AT WORK

Lincoln's Contemporary Standards of Quality

1. *Diverse inquiry communities* exist with unique traditions of research with their own standards of rigor. These serve to either exclude or legitimize researchers.

2. *Positionality*: a balanced and honest reflection of the participant's and the author's stance.

3. *Community*: all research takes place in a community and serves that community's purposes.

4. *Voice*: qualitative research gives multiple and/or alternative voices to participants that must be "heard" in the text.

5. *Critical subjectivity*: the researcher should have a heightened self-awareness before, during, and after the research encounter leading to personal transformations.

6. *Reciprocity*: the relation between researcher and participant should be one of mutual respect, trust, and intense sharing.

7. *Sacredness of the relationship between researcher and participant*: there is an inviolate relation between the researcher and the participant that is both egalitarian and collaborative.

8. *Sharing privileges*: qualitative researchers share the benefits of their research with the participants. This may take the form of authorship, rights to publication, and royalties.

Source: Adapted from Y. Lincoln (1995). "Emerging Criteria for Quality in Qualitative and Interpretive Research." *Qualitative Inquiry*, 1, 275–289.

H. ADVANTAGES AND LIMITATIONS OF QUALITATIVE RESEARCH

Table 6.4 summarizes the advantages and limitations of the qualitative designs discussed in this chapter. Qualitative research has obvious strengths in the areas of validity and in the ability to probe in depth the human experience.

The author of this text believes that there are advantages to mixing methods as we work toward the common goal for research of understanding the world in which we live. Both quantitative and qualitative methods are *complementary* processes. That is, one perspective completes or makes up for the lack or deficiency in the other perspective.

Hence, by mixing perspectives to address an area of inquiry, the weakness of a single perspective may be overcome or reduced. Neither perspective on its own can establish the truth about phenomena of interest to the social researcher. Rather, each serves a unique purpose, and taken together they can provide a rich repertoire for building knowledge. The successful blending of methods in a single investigation requires resolution of epistemological biases, budgeting for higher costs, and researcher training in both quantitative and qualitative methods. Many believe the benefits to knowledge development that result from integrating methods outweigh the hassles of blending methods and encourage social researchers to make the effort to consider integration if it is appropriate to the study question.

TABLE 6.4   ADVANTAGES AND LIMITATIONS OF QUALITATIVE DESIGNS

RESEARCH DESIGN CATEGORY	GENERAL	VALIDITY	CAUSAL INFERENCE	MULTI-VARIATE	PROBING
QUALITATIVE DESIGNS*					
Phenomenology	−	+	−	−	+
Grounded Theory	−	+	−	−	+
Ethnographic	−	+	−	−	+

In each category a "+" means that this is an advantage of the technique; a "−" means this is a possible limitation.

- *General* refers to the extent to which extrapolations to larger populations may be made using each of the design/data collection procedures.
- *Validity* is the extent to which indicators clearly measure what they are intended to measure.
- *Causal Inference* refers to the ease with which inferences about causal relations among variables may be made.
- *Multivariate* refers to the ease with which information on many variables is collected, leading to the possibility of multivariate analysis.
- *Probing* refers to the extent to which responses may be probed in depth.

*Box 6.5 lists criteria for judging qualitative research designs that are *not parallel* to criteria used to judge quantitative research designs.

I. CONCLUSION

Qualitative research has made an important contribution to knowledge development in social research during the past few decades. Regardless of the particular method employed, qualitative researchers share similar assumptions and characteristics that include:

- Attention to the social context in which events occur and have meaning.

- Emphasis on understanding the social world from the participant's point of view.

- Employing a primarily inductive (theory-generating) perspective.

- Data-collection techniques that include participant observation, in-depth interviews, and focus groups.

- Data-collection tools and procedures that are subject to change in the field. Concern is primarily with discovery and description of phenomena.

- Hypotheses developed during the research rather than a priori.

- Analysis presented in narrative form.

J. KEY POINTS

Qualitative methods are congruent with a philosophy of holistic, humanistic social science. Such methods enable an understanding of the patterns, characteristics, and meanings of the phenomenon under study. They attempt to focus on the experiences of people and seek to describe the uniqueness of participants' human experiences. Because qualitative methods focus on the whole of the human experience and the meanings ascribed to them by respondents, they provide social researchers with deep insights into the experiences of the respondent that would not be possible using exclusively quantitative methods.

In qualitative research, data collection and data analysis are considered recursive, ongoing processes. The methods of data collection are designed to allow researchers to learn to understand the phenomenon from the perspective of the research participants. The primary methods of data collection are participant observation, in-depth interviewing, and, to a lesser extent, focus group interviews. The data collection process is influenced by the data analysis. Researchers continue to collect data until they have reached *saturation*. Saturation refers to new data collection episodes confirming the themes emerging from the data analysis.

There are three schools of qualitative research methods introduced: ethnography, grounded theory, and phenomenology. Ethnography in anthropology has traditionally focused on describing a culture or cultural group, grounded theory in sociology and criminology is typically focused on examining social processes, and phenomenology is typically focused on illuminating the essence of the lived experience. Ethnographers and grounded theorists typically employ participant observation and interview techniques, whereas phenomenologists are more likely to rely on in-depth interviews.

The *major strength* of qualitative research is the validity of the data it produces. Because researchers collect data primarily by means of in-depth interviews and participant observation in natural settings, the participant's true reality is more likely to be reflected in the thick, rich descriptions that result, than in data collected in contrived settings using quantitative instruments. The *major limitation* of qualitative research is its perceived lack of objectivity and generalizability. It is argued that because the qualitative researchers become the research tool, they become so intimately involved with the data-collection process that they cannot be objective. The researcher is likely to be subjective in deciding which participants to select and which data to accept or reject. The small and unrepresentative samples and analytic procedures that rely on subjective judgments make qualitative methods appear to be weak in reliability and generalizability.

Qualitative researchers have devised their own terminology and establish their own procedures to assess the scientific rigour of their work. *Rigour* in qualitative research is less about adherence to rules and more about fidelity to the spirit and standards of qualitative work (Sandelowski, 1993).

Some researchers believe it is appropriate to integrate quantitative and qualitative data within a single study or a cluster of studies on a particular phenomenon. Not everyone agrees, however, that methods can be mixed in the same study. Creswell (1994) suggests that there are three positions on the subject of integration: the purists who believe methods and paradigms should not be mixed, the situationalists who believe certain methods are appropriate for certain situations, and the pragmatists who support integrating methods in a single study.

K. KEY TERMS

Analytic files	Ethnography	Participants
Audit trail	Field notes	Participant observation
Bracketing	Focus group	Phenomenology
Componential analysis	Gatekeeper	Purposive sampling
Confirmability	Grounded theory	Qualitative research
Constant comparative method	In-depth interview	Saturation
Core variable	Informant	Symbolic interactionism
Covert participant	Intersubjectivity	Taxonomy
Credibility	Key character files	Themes
Cultural scene	Key informant	Theoretical coding
Cultural themes	Lifeworld	Theoretical memos
Culture	Lived experience	Theoretical sampling
Dependability	Master field file	Transferability
Domain analysis	Overt participant	Trustworthiness

CHAPTER SEVEN

CRITICAL APPROACHES TO RESEARCH: ACTION AND FEMINIST RESEARCH

WINSTON JACKSON, ANGELA GILLIS, AND NORINE VERBERG

There is a growing trend in the social sciences toward research that empowers participants and leads to improved social conditions for marginalized members of society. These innovative research approaches apply the philosophical tenets associated with the critical approach discussed in Chapter 1. **Critical research** is rooted in the assumption that inequality is rooted in exploitative social relations, and action researchers advocate for sociopolitical and structural change. Lincoln and Guba (1994) identify neo-Marxism, feminism, and participatory action research as following the critical mode of inquiry. Research has a role to play in bringing about social justice by demonstrating how policies and practices produce inequality and by empowering marginalized individuals and groups.

The emancipatory principle of critical research is reflected in the language that has been developed to distinguish it from traditional methods: terms such as *collaborative research* (Parahoo, 1997), *action activist-oriented research* (Denzin and Lincoln, 2000), *new generation research* (Streubert and Carpenter, 1994, 1999), *participatory evaluation* (Feurstein, 1988), and *community reflective action research* (Boutlier, Mason and Rootman, 1997) reflect the social change orientation of the critical approach.

This chapter focuses on the types of methodologies used by researchers working within the critical tradition, and it introduces two types of critical research: action and feminist research. As noted in Chapter 1, feminists locate themselves within the critical tradition. The goal of **feminist research** is to expose the social causes of women's oppression and to empower women. **Action research** has as its primary focus to engage marginalized individuals in a research process aimed at empowering them to affect change. Feminism and action research are similar in that the prime intention of the research is to have an impact on policy-making, be it at the level of the individual, the work unit, the community, or the government. Because they share common assumptions and similar research goals, some feminist research could be described as action research and some action research could be described as feminist research.

A. RESEARCH METHODS IN THE CRITICAL TRADITION

When you read Chapter 1, you may have noticed that quantitative research is associated with the positivist approach while qualitative research is associated with the interpretative approach. Perhaps you wondered about whether critical researchers employ quantitative methods, qualitative methods, or both. In fact, critical researchers employ a variety of methods and research designs. Some critical researchers use exclusively qualitative methods, some use primarily quantitative methods, and still others combine both methods. Regardless of the method employed, critical researchers adapt the research design to make it fit the research goals of exposing the social sources of inequality and/or empowering marginalized individuals and groups. In other words, the research design incorporates the assumption of the critical approach. As such, Berman, Ford-Gilboe, and Campbell (1998, p. 4) suggest that there are five core "methodologic themes" common to all critical approaches. They are:

1. The study addresses an issue that is of concern to a group that is disadvantaged, oppressed, or marginalized in some way.

2. The research process or results have the potential to benefit the group, immediately or in the long term.

3. The researcher's assumptions, motivations, biases, and values are made explicit and their influence on the research process is examined.

4. Prior scholarship is critiqued in an attempt to elucidate the ways in which biases, especially those related to gender, race, and class, have distorted existing knowledge.

5. Interactions between the researcher and participants convey respect for the expertise of the participants.

The explicit focus of the research on social change is reflected in the title of one of the first Canadian books outlining the critical approach to research. *Experience, Research, Social Change: Methods from the Margins* (1989) was written by Sandra Kirby and Kate McKenna, then at the University of New Brunswick. Kirby and McKenna premise their approach with the belief that knowledge is a political process, and that universities play a major role in legitimating the power of dominant groups in society. They argue that the experiences of those on the margins of society have been ignored by researchers, and the people living on the margins have been denied the research tools academics use to produce "legitimate" knowledge. In the opening pages of the book they distinguish critical research from traditional research in this way:

> *We live in a world in which knowledge is used to maintain oppressive relations. Information is interpreted and organized in such a way that the views of a small group of people are presented as objective knowledge, as "The Truth." We believe that Maria Mies was right when she said that "Research, which so far has been*

> *largely the instrument of dominance and legitimation of power elites, must be brought to serve the interests of dominated, exploited, and oppressed groups"* (1983, p. 123). (Kirby and McKenna, 1989, p. 1).

To remedy the exploitative use of research tools they advocate "research from the margins." Two fundamental changes are required to conduct emancipatory research. The first requirement is authentic dialogue with everyone involved in the research: research participants must be respected as "equally knowing subjects." The second requirement is critical reflection of people's social realities. In their words, "Research from the margins is not research *on* people from the margins, but research *by, for,* and *with* them" (p. 28). Thus, before consideration is given to the specific research design employed, the social change goal of the research is brought into focus.

Let's turn to the questions of which "methods" or "research designs" should be used by critical researchers to collect and analyze data. This question has been the subject of considerable debate. Critical researchers reject the philosophic assumptions of positivism; they reject the view that quantitative research is "objective" and value-free or value-neutral. Many critical researchers, in turn, reject quantitative research designs as an extension of their critique of positivism. Yet some critical researchers are not willing to abandon quantitative research methods; they view these methods as an effective tool for exposing inequality. In the end, many critical researchers advocate a multi-method approach, arguing that the purpose of the research should dictate the most appropriate design to be used. There are many celebrated examples of critical research studies that employ either quantitative or qualitative research designs or a combination of the two methods. Given this, the emphasis for many critical researchers is on "methodologies" rather than one unifying method (Eichler, 1997; Reinharz, 1992; Rose, 2001, p. 12–13).

Berman et al. (1998, p. 4) at the University of Western Ontario argue that the most compelling evidence critical researchers can bring to their subject is "a combination of stories and numbers." The relative weight that each method receives should reflect the degree to which the research is intended to bring about personal empowerment or sociopolitical change by influencing attitudes and policy. They contend that "when social and political change is the primary goal, numbers are most appropriately in the foreground, when personal growth or individual or small group empowerment is the central aim, stories may be situated in the foreground, with numbers placed in the background. Alternatively, there may be times when stories and numbers merit an equal place in the study design" (p. 4). They note that there are a number of terms commonly used to reflect their position, including *methodological triangulation* and *multimethod research*.

There are numerous examples of critical research studies that employ traditional designs, such as experiments (Chapter 3), surveys (Chapter 4), nonreactive research (Chapter 5), and qualitative methods (Chapter 6). They use the research design in a way that incorporates the social change orientation of the critical approach. For example, Gina Browne and her colleagues at McMaster University (1998; 1999) used a quasi-experimental design to measure the impact of interventions on parents and children living in single parent families on social assistance. The studies looked at the

effect of various interventions, such as high quality child care and recreation programs for the children and employment counselling, employment retraining, skills development, and health promotion for the parents. The results were compelling. They demonstrated that planned interventions improved the competence of the children with behavioural disorders, improved the health status of both the parents and the children, and contributed to the economic adjustment of the parents. Browne et al. then analyzed whether the interventions were cost effective. They demonstrated that the positive personal and social outcomes experienced by the families in the study are also cost effective for the state (e.g., due to reduced use of hospital services, ability to move from welfare to employment, etc.). In this way, both "numbers" and "quantitative research designs" can have a major impact on policy reform aimed at helping economically marginalized groups.

Like many critical researchers, Browne used the research results to advocate for change. She has campaigned successfully for recreational interventions for at-risk children: seventeen regional governments in Ontario now sponsor recreation programs. In a recent interview, Browne made the following conclusions about the research: "We have learned there is more than 'impact.' There is a 'splash,' a 'ripple,' and continuing 'waves.' Investment in intersectoral, comprehensive, proactive services pays for itself by the reduced use of other publicly funded services. Social entrepreneurship creates social capital! Philanthropy has a major impact." (McMaster University and Affiliated Health and Social Service Agencies, 2005).

Some critical researchers employ traditional qualitative methods, but they are used in an innovative way. One such example is the method developed by Dorothy Smith

(1987; 1999; 2005) called *institutional ethnography.* (Smith is also known for the development of feminist standpoint theory.) **Institutional ethnography** is a multi-method approach used when the research goal is to study social reality as it is constructed in the minds of those who experience it (Campbell and Gregor, 2002). Smith's approach to ethnography is informed by Marxism and **ethnomethodology** (a detailed examination of a single event or case). As such, she gives considerable attention to how everyday life is organized socially. The method she developed differs from traditional qualitative approaches in that there is an explicit focus on the way structural conditions influence interactions and consciousness. Smith advocates studying how *texts* shape and reproduce social relations. **Texts** are organizational features of institutions, such as schools, the workplace, hospitals, and government bureaucracies. Text can be studied to explicate the "ruling relations" that frame the interactions of individuals within organizations. The experience of a student, for example, is mediated by the regulations, scheduling, and organizational features of the school. Smith argues that people's experiences and interactions are mediated by the texts embedded in agencies or institutions. Because of this, she advocates studying how people's experiences are organized by institutional practices that are coded in texts. Kevin Walby notes that institutional ethnography differs from other forms of ethnography because:

> *Institutional ethnography explicates both ethnosocial and structural features of social organizations. Where interpretative forms of ethnography uncritically focus on describing a culture, institutional ethnography focuses on the micro level of the individual to critically analyze the way individual experiences are organized structurally. Thus, institutional ethnography discovers the workings of everyday/everynight lived reality, thereby preserving people's presence as subjects. Texts are not inert, but through activation have the capacity to do untold work upon bodies, consciousness, and social organization. (Walby, 2005, p. 190)*

Institutional ethnography is a relatively new method, yet more Canadian scholars, particularly sociologists, have employed this method in their research in recent years (Campbell and Gregor, 2002). It has been particularly influential among feminist scholars who seek to understand the structural mechanisms that shape women's consciousness and oppress them.

B. ACTION RESEARCH

The term *action research* can be traced back in the literature to the work of Kurt Lewin (1951), who is generally considered the founder of action research and change theory (Hart and Bond, 1998). Lewin, a Prussian psychologist who immigrated to the United States in 1933, introduced the term *action research* as a way of studying a social system while at the same time attempting to change it. Action research is simply defined today as the systematic collection and analysis of data for the purpose of taking action and making change. It provides individuals, organizations, or communities with tools to solve problems (Czerny, Swift, and Clarke, 1994).

1. CHARACTERISTICS

Seven criteria have been identified by Hart and Bond to distinguish action research from other methodologies.

"Action research:

- is educative
- deals with individuals as members of a social group
- is problem-focused, context-specific and future-oriented
- involves a change intervention
- aims at improvement and involvement
- involves a cyclic process in which research, action and evaluation are interlinked
- is founded on a research relationship in which those involved are participants in the change process." (1998, pp. 37–38)

The aim of all action research is the generation of practical knowledge that has the potential to improve a specific social condition. It does not aim to generalize solutions to problems that apply across a range of settings, because the solutions are designed for the particular setting in which the research is conducted. An action researcher would attempt to find a solution to a particular problem by implementing changes in practice and then closely monitoring and evaluating the changes during implementation.

Participatory action research (PAR) is a subset of action research. It consists of three elements—research, adult education, and sociopolitical action (Parahoo, 1997). It emphasizes research for the purposes of both bringing about *change* and encouraging *participation* by community members (either a geographic community or people with common interests and shared experiences). PAR places great emphasis on collaboration with research participants by considering them as co-investigators throughout the entire process, when they become empowered to define their own problems and find solutions. PAR increases

the participants' understanding of the issue they are working on. The research element provides an opportunity for them to test assumptions so that they can be more confident of their ground as they go forward to implement change. The process of participating enables members to build skills, confidence, and knowledge (Barnsley and Ellis, 1992).

2. STEPS IN THE ACTION RESEARCH PROCESS

Action research proceeds in cyclical stages that involve planning, implementing, reflecting, and evaluating, and it involves collaboration between researchers and participants throughout the entire process. Below is a list of some of the steps that are necessary in most action research studies, including participatory action research projects. Action research is described here as if it were a linear process, but in truth it does not follow a series of stages. Rather, it is a dynamic process with a spiral of cycles in which research, action, and evaluation interact with each other at various phases (Waterman, Webb, and Williams, 1995).

STEP I ENTRY INTO THE COMMUNITY AND DEVELOPMENT OF A COLLABORATIVE RELATIONSHIP

In action research the community may represent an actual geographic community or an institution or agency such as a school, health care facility, government department, or grassroots group of people with similar interests and issues. Action research aims to create between the researcher and the researched an equal partnership in which representatives from both come together and form a research team. The extent of the collaboration between the researchers and those researched may vary from review of the problem to diagnosis to full collaboration in all stages of the process. Action researchers who facilitate collaboration at all stages believe that they are able to find the most practical solutions to identified problems (Whyte, Greenwood, and Lazes, 1991).

STEP 2 ASSESSMENT OF THE SITUATION AND IDENTIFICATION OF THE ISSUE

This step involves gathering as much data as possible from a variety of sources in order to identify the problem or issue. At this step you are interested in getting detailed data about the situation as it exists before a change is implemented. Data generation will continue throughout the entire process and involve a wide range of approaches, both qualitative and quantitative. Data collection is usually a collaborative process involving both researchers and participants as members of the research team. At this point steering groups or planning committees may be formed to inform the process. You are concerned with identifying a problem (something that needs changing).

STEP 3 PLANNING FOR RESEARCH AND ACTION

Planning begins with a detailed analysis of the present situation. Researchers and participants decide which data-collection methods are most appropriate to the specific situation. Usually triangulated data generation is recommended, with at least three methods selected, so as to transcend the limitations of each and lead to more effective problem-solving (Streubert and Carpenter, 1999). Participant observation, interviews, focus groups, diaries, questionnaires, and surveys are valuable methods of data generation. At the heart of the planning stage is the development of an action plan that will lead to problem resolution. The action plan will emerge following data analysis.

Analysis will vary depending upon the data-generation techniques used. Quantitative

data will be analyzed in traditional ways using statistical methods and qualitative data using qualitative methods. Researchers and participants work together collaboratively on the data analysis, although the researchers often take the lead in this step because of the knowledge and expertise required for analysis. It is critical, however, to involve participants to make sure that the interpretations of the data fit the reality of the situation. Depending upon the analysis produced, an action plan is developed by the co-researchers. The action plan details the planned change intervention, the implementation process, the plan for facilitating reflection, and the evaluation plan (Streubert and Carpenter, 1999). This stage requires a number of meetings with the co-researchers to discuss and plan the details. Records and detailed notes are made of all meetings and decisions by the researchers, and these are used in the writing of the final plan.

STEP 4 IMPLEMENTATION OF THE ACTION PLAN AND REFLECTION

This stage involves the actual implementation of the planned change. The implementation usually occurs over a specified period of time. At this point the researchers may move into a more peripheral role and community members may be more involved in the actual implementation of change. Researchers remain present, however, to guide and facilitate the reflection that occurs with the implementation (Streubert and Carpenter, 1999).

Reflection is the process of thinking about the implementation of the new change and its impact on the key players. It occurs simultaneously with implementation. Reflection is promoted through group meetings and observation periods during which the participants and co-researchers may record their thoughts and experiences regarding the planned change.

STEP 5 EVALUATION OF THE IMPLEMENTATION

Co-researchers work together to evaluate the implementation according to the action plan. Evaluation can occur at the end of the implementation stage and at various points throughout the implementation stage as well. Evaluation includes data generated during the reflection process as well as additional information that the team decides upon. Evaluation data may be similar to data that was collected in the initial assessment phase. Usually evaluation meetings are held with the research team and key stakeholders to discuss the interpretation of the evaluation data and to verify conclusions.

STEP 6 REPORT AND RE-ASSESSMENT

In action research a report is written by the research team that incorporates a plurality of explanations for events observed as well as questions for future consideration (Streubert and Carpenter, 1999). The report is intended to promote dialogue among participants and stimulate additional courses of action to be taken, with or without the guidance of the researchers. This report on findings and process becomes the initial step in a new cycle of this iterative process.

STEP 7 PLANNING FUTURE ACTION

Based on the report and evaluation data, planning future action continues. The cycle begins again with implementation, reporting, and re-assessment (Deagle and McWilliam, 1992).

3. CHALLENGES IN CONDUCTING ACTION RESEARCH

Action research offers many opportunities to social researchers. An obvious one is the ability to implement change and to evaluate the change simultaneously. Another strength is the ability to empower participants through involvement in the research process. Because research produces knowledge, it empowers those who carry it out or commission it. Action research also provides practical knowledge that enables the social researcher to solve specific problems. Despite these important advantages, action research also presents a number of challenges to the researcher. Some of these include:

- *The challenge of involving community members as part of the research team.* Engaging the appropriate stakeholders and maintaining their commitment to the research project over time requires tact, effort, time, and knowledge of the community. The community must first be appropriately defined and then key stakeholders identified. Decisions must be made as to who will be a research participant (that is, a co-researcher and community member of the research team) and who will be a research respondent (a member of the broader population who provides data and validates results at various stages). The researcher must be sensitive to the participants' agendas.

- *Diversity of values, perspectives, and abilities among community members and researchers must be valued.* On a practical level this often presents difficulties based on the different perspectives of researchers, community members, and academics. One participant, for example, may be interested in broad social change while another may be interested only in a particular practice situation that the project should create. This feature of action research complicates the relationships of collaborators and increases the time required to focus the research project and to complete the action research.

- *Issues of power imbalances and establishment of egalitarian relationships require constant vigilance throughout the research project.* Power balances may shift over the course of the project as various community members may change. Often the commitment to a research project by the community member may not be the same as that of the university-based researcher who participates for the duration of a research grant.

- *All members of the research team must be sensitive and responsive to the need for different forms and types of leadership at different stages of the project* (Lindsey and Stajduhar, 1998). At times community members will take the lead, particularly during the implementation stage, whereas at other times the researcher may take the lead, for example during data analysis.

- *Finally, action research is extremely time consuming.* Identifying and mobilizing participants and, indeed, communities to be involved in the research process is time intensive and requires a high level of negotiation, tact, energy, and commitment on the part of the research team. Time must be provided to train members to be part of the research team, to enable full community participation, and to allow the cyclical, iterative process to work as it is intended.

4. KIM TRAVERS: "REDUCING INEQUITIES THROUGH PARTICIPATORY RESEARCH AND COMMUNITY EMPOWERMENT"

To illustrate action research, let's look at the process of participatory research and community empowerment to reduce nutritional inequities in a group of low-income urban women.

Health-education programs have traditionally focused on providing information to individuals as a way of improving their health through lifestyle modification. This method has lacked demonstrated effectiveness for enhancing health status. Travers (1997) critiques health-education practices and suggests that an alternative orientation is needed. She uses the process of participatory research and community organization to design a project to address the inequities in nutritional practices for a group of low-income urban women. The article highlights the process of social action by monitoring changes associated with the women's experiences and shows how the participatory research experience can be an empowering educational experience for participants. This article demonstrates how the principles of participatory action research emphasize valuing people's knowledge, deriving questions from the perspective of the people, and helping the oppressed to reflect on their situation. It aims to develop critical consciousness and to improve the lives of those involved in the research process. The article also points out the realities and limitations of engaging in this type of research project. Box 7.1 describes the methodology involved in this emancipatory research project and highlights the findings.

C. FEMINIST RESEARCH

Feminist research been defined in many ways, and as it has gained momentum in the past decade and the context and shape

BOX 7.1   SOCIAL RESEARCHERS AT WORK

Kim Travers: "Reducing Inequities through Participatory Research and Community Empowerment"

Background

This study was part of a larger research project the purpose of which was to initiate nutrition education for social change, as well as to explain the social organization which permitted nutritional inequities among socially disadvantaged women and their families. Participatory action research was the methodology used in this study, which attempted to reduce nutritional inequities for a group of low-income urban women and their families. Research participants self-selected to attend a coffee group at a local Parent Centre. A total of 33 women actively participated in the group throughout the duration of the study, but never all at the same time. The group size ranged from 5 to 25 at any given meeting, with a core group of fewer than 10. Although the group was a sample of convenience, it appeared to be representative of the low-income female population in the city in which the research was conducted.

Participant observation was the primary method of data collection. The researcher was a participant observer at the community drop-in Parent Centre in an urban neighbourhood in Nova Scotia. The researcher participated in the life of the centre, serving meals in the soup kitchen, unpacking food from the food bank, and preparing and eating meals with the staff and volunteers.

One month after initiation into the Parent Centre, the researcher initiated a series of group interviews with some of the women to discuss their experiences of feeding themselves and their families. In total, 27 group interviews lasting two

hours each were conducted over a 16-month period. Semi-structured interview guides were used to organize the discussions thematically. Participants also introduced topics through discussion of their relevant experiences. Triangulated data-collection techniques (participant observation and group interviews) were useful as an internal validity/credibility check, as data obtained from one source could be checked against data obtained from another.

Qualitative interview data and field notes were analyzed, not so much for interpretation of data but rather to show the process of emancipatory education for the women's group by organizing the data chronologically into chunks that showed the progression of group activities.

Results

Through the process of participatory research, it was possible to empower research participants to initiate collective action for social change in order to reduce their nutritional inequities. The results section describes the details of the process by which the participants came to understand their experiences and acted on that understanding to create change.

For the first few months of the group meetings, the discussion was unstructured, allowing the women simply to talk about their experiences in trying to feed their families. The women listened to each other's experiences. Suddenly they were not alone. By listening to how others overcame difficulties and similar experiences, they began to learn coping skills from each other and to build hope by working together toward solutions. Almost imperceptibly, the group sessions moved from complaining sessions to consciousness-raising sessions. Consciousness-raising is a practical process that begins with the experience of oppression. Women come together to talk about their experiences and, in doing so, break the culture of silence. They begin to see that their problems are not caused by individual failures but rather by societal structures affecting the lives of all women. They began with their experiences of oppression, by gender, by class, and sometimes by race. They broke the culture of silence by sharing their stories. They came to see the common and political roots of their oppression and thus were able to shed their self-blame and take on a new way of relating to the social world. This was the beginning.

Exploration of women's food-purchasing experiences enabled a process of education leading to community development. At an early meeting one woman discussed her experiences and her perception that food cost more while shopping in low-income neighbourhoods. With pricing inequities brought to the group's attention, the researcher decided to do a comparison of chain stores in low-income and middle-income neighbourhoods. The researcher taught the women to do unit pricing to enable them to make in-store price comparisons. The women split into groups to do the unit-pricing comparison in four stores: two in the inner city and two in the suburbs. Results revealed that prices in inner-city stores were consistently 5%

higher than prices in suburban stores of the same chain. A 10.7% price differential was found between the store most frequently used by the women and the store furthest from their neighbourhood. The women learned that cost savings outweighed transportation costs.

In keeping with participatory action research principles, the women decided to take action to address the inequities. First, they wrote letters to the stores addressing inequities in pricing, quality, and service. Knowledge of the supermarkets' roles in construction of inequities was the catalyst for community action. They confronted both of the local supermarket chains with their findings and recommendations for actions. Both stores changed buying practices to decrease price inequities between locations. One store introduced a bulk-food section in the inner-city store, a move that eliminated price inequities between neighbourhoods. These changes enabled women and socially disadvantaged families to purchase food more affordably. These changes live on long after the research process ended. However, because the women were still dependent upon commercial outlets for the bulk of their food, the researcher worked with a subgroup of women to secure funding for a grassroots co-operative grocery outlet. It is operated out of the Parent Centre and run by a committee composed of women from the community. This process was an empowering learning experience in a personal, political, and economic sense for the women involved. This is emancipatory health education!

Source: Summarized from K. Travers (1997). "Reducing Inequalities through Participatory Research and Community Empowerment." *Health Education and Behavior,* 24(3), 344–356. Reprinted by permission of Sage Publications.

of feminism itself has shifted, so the task of defining feminist research perspectives has become both challenging and exciting. There are many different faces of **feminism**. In the early beginnings of the second phase of the women's movement (1960s onward) one could easily classify feminist researchers by their political views—liberal, radical, or Marxist—or their preferred research styles or their academic discipline. However, these distinctions have become blurred. Political orientations are now blurred by internal divisions in feminist thought; many academic researchers are borrowing from other disciplines, and many are mixing quantitative and qualitative approaches or developing new methods to explore questions of interest (Olesen, 1994). One can no longer speak of *feminism*; one can only speak of *feminisms* and define them by their adherence to four basic principles:

1. valuing women and their experiences, ideas, and needs;

2. seeing phenomena from the perspective of women;

3. recognizing the existence of conditions that oppress women; and

4. desiring to change these conditions through research leading to political action.

Feminist research perspectives use a variety of research methods. Many share the assumptions held by interpretive (qualitative) researchers and by those who adopt a critical perspective. As Reinharz (1992) noted, most feminist scholars use a multiplicity of research methods. They value inclusiveness more than orthodoxy and allow for creativity in all aspects of the research process.

Although feminist researchers use a wide range of quantitative and qualitative methods, most emphasis seems to be on qualitative methods, particularly using in-depth

interviews. Oral histories and comparative and field-study methods are also common. Similar to most interpretive perspectives, feminist research stresses subjectivity and personal experience embedded in the life of the participants. Feminist researchers do not stop here however; they go on and ask the simple but important question, *"and what about the women?"* Where are the women in any situation being investigated? Why are they not present in many situations? If they are present, what exactly are they doing? How do they experience the situation? What do they contribute to it? What does it mean for them? (Ritzer, 1988).

Harding (1987), a feminist philosopher of science, adds clarity to the discussion surrounding definitions of feminist research by providing some simple criteria. She takes the stance that in defining feminist research three aspects of the study should be considered: (1) the purpose of the inquiry; (2) the explanatory hypothesis; and (3) the relationship between the informant or "subject" and the researcher. These three criteria taken together should distinguish feminist research from non-feminist research rather than the methods used to gather data. The purpose of feminist research is to create social change that will benefit women. This is core to any definition of feminist research. Feminist research may also benefit other sectors of society such as children; men; gay, lesbian, and transgendered people; oppressed groups; and others, but it must benefit women. Feminist researchers employ a variety of methods to collect data. These data are analyzed within the context of women's lives in such a way that women are empowered rather than portrayed in ways that stereotype them or reinforce traditional stereotypes. The relationship between the researcher and the participants is a horizontal one in which the participant is a partner in the research process. The participant is a legitimate "knower" of her own experience—an expert.

Feminist research has been defined by some authors in terms of its characteristics. Duffy and Hedin, cited in Bunting and Campbell (1994), provide a useful list of qualities that they attribute to studies conducted from a feminist perspective. These include:

- A feminist consciousness is rooted in an attitude of equality, which replaces the hierarchies of traditional research methods with horizontal relationships. In these relationships, the participants in a study are seen as partners in the research process. The investigator works in partnership with the participants to refine the research question, conduct the research, validate the findings, and disperse the results.

- The aim of feminist research is to include women and to study phenomena of practical concern to women. The focus is always based on women's experiences and the validity of women's perceptions. The research should be for women.

- Feminist perspectives involve "conscious partiality" in which the biases of the researcher are acknowledged and openly discussed. Feminists, like researchers using other qualitative approaches, examine their own values, beliefs, assumptions, and motivations. The researcher's point of view and biases become part of the data. This ensures that the researcher is on a level playing field with the participants.

- Feminist research uses a variety of perspectives and a multiplicity of methods, including both qualitative and quantitative methods, as the complexity and diversity of women's lives require multiple perspectives.

- Feminist research aims to create social change. As noted above, feminism is rooted in the critical approach described in Chapter 1. Feminists argues that science should be used to improve the conditions of the oppressed.

- Feminist research strives to represent human diversity. It includes ethnicity, class, gender, sexual orientation, and culture in designing and conducting the research and interpreting the data. Traditional research sometimes pays insufficient attention to diversity.

- Feminist research critiques prior scholarship, especially looking for androcentric (male) and ethnocentric (race and ethnic) biases.

1. PHILOSOPHICAL TENETS

A philosophical foundation and a uniform methodology have not yet been broadly accepted by feminist scholars; however, many consider it has emerged from the *critical approach*. In keeping with the critical tradition, feminists believe that knowledge is socially constructed and they acknowledge the oppressive nature of social structures. Like other critical researchers, feminists focus on the emancipatory goals of the research. They differ, however, in that the oppression of women is a central concern of feminist research. Some critical theorists write principally for other intellectuals and some maintain power inequalities within their research teams. By contrast, feminist researchers strive to make feminist writing accessible to all and to promote equality within their research teams (Webb, 1993).

Feminist researchers claim that one cannot adequately understand human societies without paying attention to the universal role of **patriarchy**, which refers to the domination of social groups by males, who have greater power and privilege than women and children. Some feminist researchers have argued that inequalities of the sexes emerged because of males' greater physical strength. The control this enabled men to exercise resulted in women playing socially subservient roles and in stereotypes that portrayed women as inferior to men. Sexism is thus fostered and maintained by the transmission of an ideology justifying male domination (Saunders, 1988).

Feminist perspectives stress the idea that inequalities suffered by women stem from an ingrained, systemic patriarchy in societies; this patriarchy pervades many institutions and practices, including, in particular, family socialization. Like researchers who subscribe to one or other of the critical perspectives, feminists see science as a tool that has largely been in the hands of the male oppressor. Feminists take a strong advocacy position in an effort to eliminate sexism from society.

Feminists display a tendency toward synthesizing various critical concepts, symbolic interactionist ideas, and qualitative research styles. Like critical theorists, feminists reject the relativistic stances of positivism and the interpretive approaches, arguing instead that science should be used to achieve gender equality and to improve the conditions of the oppressed. Feminists wish to help eliminate sexism by understanding and documenting its sources. An emphasis on achieving gender equality is central.

Feminist philosophers believe that all women are legitimate "knowers" and that those experiencing particular complexities are the ones who know the most about them. The world of women deals with the particular, with the concrete experiences of child rearing, mothering, parenting, and neighbourhood interactions. Knowledge of

that world should start from the experience of women. Similar to phenomenological researchers, feminist philosophers believe that self-reflection, self-awareness, and purity of language constitute human nature. If this is true, males experience the world differently than females in the everyday experience of friendship, love, sexuality, morality, intellect, conflict, or challenge. Consistent with this point of view, feminist researchers call for research methods that reflect their epistemological beliefs, which emphasize concrete experiences and the particular experiences that comprise the world of women (Rothe, 1994).

2. APPLICATION OF METHOD/METHODOLOGY

Feminist research is not *a* method but rather a multiplicity of methods. The feminist researcher selects a method that is appropriate to answer the research question. Over time feminist researchers have come to a reasoned examination of how all methods can be used to answer feminist questions. Harding (1991) makes an important distinction between *method* (a technique for collecting evidence) and *methodology* (how the methods should be used) in feminist research. She writes that what is important in feminist research is a methodology that is consistent with feminist epistemology (theory of knowledge). This includes a methodology that:

- Places value on women's subjective experiences. Feminist methodology values women as knowers and seeks to reflect with precision women's experiences as viewed by women.

- Values the importance of context in women's lives. Women's experiences are embedded in the context of their everyday lives. It is important that the method chosen provides a rich description of context, including a description of the social and political factors as well as other variables that may influence the phenomenon.

- Values the relationship of the researcher and the participants. This relationship is characterized by respect for the participants, who are viewed as equal partners in the research process.

- Values the inclusion of women from diverse social and ethnic backgrounds in their samples so that perspectives of all women can be exposed and understood.

The diversity of methods used for the collection and analysis of data by feminist researchers is reflected in Box 7.2 on page 200, which provides examples of feminist research conducted by undergraduate students.

A. DEVELOPING THE RESEARCH QUESTION

The purpose of feminist research is to create social change that will enhance the lives of women. Research questions appropriate for a feminist inquiry will vary in focus and form but they will be distinctive in that: (1) the issues will be of primary interest and concern to women, (2) women will report their experiences using their own voices, and (3) the research will allow for a structural analysis of the conditions of women's lives, leading to their improvement. Experiences such as constructing relationships, giving birth, mothering, rape, incest, infertility, poverty, and family violence are topics from which questions appropriate to feminist methods of inquiry could be developed.

B. ROLE OF THE RESEARCHER

One of the defining characteristics of feminist research is the nonhierarchical relationships between the researcher and the participants. Feminist researchers strive for horizontal relationships among members on the research team and participants. They view themselves as partners with the participants and involve them in the generation of the research question, the conduct of the research, and the dissemination of results. Oakley (1981) produced a landmark piece of feminist writing that showed the reciprocity that exists between a feminist researcher and her participants. In her study, Oakley asked questions of the participants and they in turn asked questions of her. She found it impossible not to give her own views, answer participants' questions, and give advice based on her own experience as a woman. Oakley's behaviour reflects the role of the researcher in feminist inquiry. This tendency to treat researcher participants as equals is illustrated in Box 7.3 on page 201.

Like other qualitative approaches, feminist research expects reflexivity of the researcher. **Reflexivity** is defined as the critical thinking required to examine the interaction occurring between the researcher and the data during analyses. The researcher explores personal feelings that may influence the study and integrates her understanding of these feelings into the results of the study. The researcher needs to be reflexive so that she can uncover and provide a full account of her deep-seated views, thinking, and conduct. This openness is necessary so that readers of the research report are aware of how the researcher's values, assumptions, and motivations may have influenced the framework, literature review, design, sampling, data collection, and interpretation of findings. Being explicit about the participation of the

BOX 7.2   STUDENT RESEARCHERS AT WORK

Feminist Research

Project Talking Politics: Language and Gender
Student Myleta Rose Belleville
Brief This study involved a critical examination of the role language plays in the social construction of a gender hierarchy in which males are accorded "superior" status.

Project Adolescent Women as Active Media Users: Resistance and Its Limitations
Student Krista Le Vangie
Brief This student conducted a focus group comprised of five white, middle-class, adolescent women (ages 16–18) to explored women's relationship with television media.

Project An Institutional Analysis of the Lived-Experience of Female Lone Parents Living on Social Assistance
Student Jennifer Hines
Brief The student conducted an institutional ethnography to examine the disjuncture between the dehumanizing and disabling experiences of women living on social assistance and the way their experiences are framed by the "ruling relations" mediated through the textual reality of the welfare policy and service delivery.

Project Text and Content: A Critique of the Smith Report
Student Catherine J. Irving
Brief Using Dorothy Smith's standpoint method, the student explored how women's experiences in university are concealed by the "textual reality" laid out in the *Smith Report on Canadian University Education*.

Project Women's Motivation and Commitment to the Anti–Uranium Mining Movement
Student Tanya Trussler
Brief The student explored women's involvement in grassroots environmental politics using data gathered through semi-structured interviews with eight key women in the anti–uranium mining movement.

Project Herstory: Women, Welfare and Poverty in Canada
Student Faith Scanlon
Brief This student conducted semi-structured interviews with single mothers living on social assistance to illuminate their lived experience of poverty and their resistance to it.

researcher in the generation of knowledge adds to the relevance and accuracy of the results (Webb, 1993).

C. SAMPLE

Sample selection depends upon the research design employed. For studies focused on the lived experience of a particular woman's experience, sampling involves choosing women who have experienced the phenomenon of interest. Feminist researchers embrace the diversity of women's lives and experiences and, therefore, also attempt to include women of diverse social classes, races, ethnic

BOX 7.3   SOCIAL RESEARCHERS AT WORK

Research by, for, and with Participants: Viewing Research Participants as Collaborators

The role assigned to the research participant differs for positivist, interpretative, and critical researchers. Positivists assign a passive role to research participants: they are *subjects* in experiments and *respondents* in survey research. Interpretative researchers view participants as *informants* who possess cultural knowledge that the researcher hopes to learn. Critical researchers view participants as "knowing subjects" with vested interests in the research. As such, they are collaborators.

The following excerpt was drawn from the research article written by Linda Christiansen-Ruffman (which we feature in Box 7.4). In it, she notes her collaborative relationship with women in the coastal communities where she conducted her research. The FishNet organizations she refers to are networks of community-based women's organizations dedicated to studying and taking action around

policy issues impacting coastal communities on Canada's east coast since the closure of the cod fishery in the early 1990s. It is quite common for critical researchers to acknowledge that their analysis is informed by the knowledge shared by research participants.

> *This paper has benefited greatly from my research conducted in coastal communities of Labrador Straits in the 1970s and in Nova Scotia since 1994 in collaboration with the Canadian Research Institute for the Advancement of Women in Nova Scotia, Nova Scotia Women's FishNet, Atlantic Women's FishNet and numerous participatory researchers in coastal communities. I am indebted to the inspiring and intelligent women whom I now have the pleasure of knowing and who have taught me so much.*

Abbreviated from: Linda Christiansen-Ruffman (2002). "Atlantic Canadian Coastal Communities and the Fisheries Trade: A Feminist Critique, Revaluation, and Revisioning." *Canadian Woman Studies/les cahiers de la femme*, 22(1), 56–63.

groups, or cultures in their sample selection. Feminist scholars are critical of the ethnocentric bias in the sampling procedures of many social investigations that fail to report race or ethnicity and make the assumption that a white, Anglo-Saxon perspective on the world is both appropriate and universal (Ford-Gilboe and Campbell, 1996).

D. DATA COLLECTION

As noted in section C, feminist researchers use a variety of methods to collect data.

i. Oral History Interviewing

Oral history interviewing is a participant-guided investigation of a lived experience in which few prepared questions are asked

(Sandelowski and Pollack, 1986). The assumption is that meaning comes from life stories expressed by women in their own way without the use of structured questions.

ii. Multiple In-Depth Interviews

Multiple in-depth interviews are often used to collect rich narrative stories. Because of the close relationship that develops between the researcher and participants, feminist researchers believe that multiple interviews will develop trust among the partners. The researcher shares the transcripts with the participants and invites them to contribute to the analysis and interpretation. The result is more accurate and sensitive descriptions of feelings, emotions, thoughts, and processes as they unfold (Rothe, 1994).

Feminists who focus on gender issues in female-homogenous and heterogeneous settings conduct *participant observation from a feminist perspective*. The process includes the study of women's private domains, workplaces, and organizations, and, according to Reinharz (1992), it attempts to achieve the following goals: (1) view women's behaviour as an expression of social contexts; (2) understand the experience of women from their point of view and correct a bias of traditional participant observation that trivializes female activities and thoughts and/or interprets them from the male researcher's perspective; and (3) document the lives of women to enable the participant observer to see women as full members of their social, economic, and political worlds.

Feminist participant observation generally values intimacy and empathy. The researchers often act on a "nurturing" impulse, which is reciprocated by those observed (Hochschild, 1983). The implication is that only women can understand the meaning of topics which are unique to women (Rothe, 1994).

Feminist researchers use techniques such as *focus group interviews*, and *structured and semi-structured interview guides*, and *documents* such as diaries, letters, journals, photographs, and historical and medical records, to name a few. They also employ quantitative instruments such as *survey questionnaires*.

E. DATA ANALYSIS

The process of analysis in feminist research is similar to the process for quantitative and qualitative procedures in general. Hence, if a feminist researcher is using phenomenology to explore women's lived experiences or grounded theory to develop a theory of empowerment for women, the methods of analysis previously discussed for these perspectives would be followed. The main *distinction* is that the content is likely to be analyzed in terms of artifacts produced by women (or men), about women, for women. The production and perpetuation of patriarchy and ethnocentric bias are major research themes examined in the analyses. Feminists have been vigilant in analyzing text for the presence of gender stereotyping, which limits the opportunities of women, restricts their autonomy, and inhibits female development (Im, 2000; Rothe, 1994).

Many feminist researchers invite participants to be active partners in the data-analysis process. Others have participants "recycle" the analysis and then edit it according to the reactions of participants (Webb, 1993). Not all feminist researchers agree with this practice. Some believe the researcher has access to additional perspectives beyond the immediate research and in order to carry out a structural analysis of the research, as opposed to only reporting women's experiences using their words, the researcher is required to go beyond the immediate data (Ribbens, 1989). Ribbens believes the feminist researcher may interpret data differently than participants do, particularly if the participants do not see themselves as feminists. In such cases researchers must take responsibility for the decisions they make and acknowledge this type of power as a paradox in feminist research.

F. REPORTING ON THE FINDINGS

Reports of feminist inquiry use nonsexist language to portray the everyday lives of women. They are often reported in a user-friendly manner that makes the reports accessible to all, not just to intellectuals. The report is distinctive in that it portrays women's voices, it provides a structural analysis of the conditions of their lives, and the role and influence of the researchers themselves are included in the analysis.

It is as important to the feminist to have her findings published in popular women's magazines as in the most prestigious academic journals. Many feminist projects are published in book form as popular literature, which presents a bit of a dilemma for the academic. Political and prestige issues related to research in academic settings require researchers to modify their writings so that they are acceptable to the academic community that judges the value of knowledge produced through research. Some feminist researchers deal with this dilemma by publishing two different versions of their report: versions reflecting the voices of participants are made available to participants, while more traditional forms of academic writing may be used for submissions to peer-reviewed journals. Such modifications in style increase the likelihood that results will be published in a wide variety of forums.

3. LINDA CHRISTIANSEN-RUFFMAN: "ATLANTIC CANADIAN COASTAL COMMUNITIES AND THE FISHERIES: FEMINIST CRITIQUE, REVALUATION AND REVISIONING"

Linda Christiansen-Ruffman is a feminist sociologist at Saint Mary's University in Halifax, Nova Scotia. The research paper featured in this chapter is a feminist analysis of the crisis that occurred when the Atlantic cod fishery was closed in the 1990s. Christiansen-Ruffman worked alongside women living in coastal communities who became organized to study and respond to the closure of the cod fishery. Together they conducted participatory action research. In addition, Christiansen-Ruffman did participant observation research, interviews, and focus groups, and she examined a wide variety of secondary sources, such as policy statements, government documents, and newspaper reports. Box 7.4 features Christiansen-Ruffman's feminist analysis of the Cashin Task Force on the future of the cod fishery and the direction that might be taken if women's experiences and ways of being guided the future.

Feminist inquiry has empowering potential for women. Through this investigation the women continually alluded to the complementary relationship between their experience of self-definition and their overall experience of health. As the women moved toward discovery, they described feeling more in control of their well-being and beginning to make conscious choices to nurture and care for themselves. It appears the process of self-definition was a health-promoting process whereby women became authors of their own life experience. For

BOX 7.4   SOCIAL RESEARCHERS AT WORK

Linda Christiansen-Ruffman: "Atlantic Canadian Coastal Communities, Women and the Fisheries: Feminist Critique, Revaluation and Revisioning"

Background

In July 1992, dwindling fish stocks led the Canadian government to declare a two year moratorium on harvesting Atlantic Canada's most important commercial fish stock: northern cod. On December 20, 1993, almost all major Canadian cod fisheries were closed. Barbara Neis noted that the crisis "directly affected 40,000 people, touched many others indirectly, and threatened to shut down over a thousand small fishing communities" in what Martha MacDonald says was the "largest mass layoff in Canadian history."

How did government policy-makers respond and in whose interest were new policies developed?

Many Nova Scotian women, who had managed the family fishing business and developed expertise in doing the paperwork, were heavily impacted by rapid changes in government policies and regulations. Women were being effectively "de-skilled"—from this work which was not even recognized as work. As they tried to keep up with the changes, women's "work" stress increased (sometimes to clinical depression), their self-confidence decreased, and their hope was sometimes broken by the profound unfairness which they saw and experienced— and for which they had no names.

While large fishing companies were prospering, fishing communities were dying as families moved away and as fish plants and shops closed. The government's fisheries policies were making people sick, devastating their communities and ways of life. In many families, as Ariella Pahlke, Stella Lord and Linda Christiansen-Ruffman point out, "Fishermen are stressed because they can't work. Women experience the stress of having the men at home 'underfoot' and having to look after them as well as the children, all on a diminished budget." One Nova Scotian woman reported that she could not leave her husband alone for fear he would walk off the end of the wharf and commit suicide. Meanwhile governments cut urgently needed community services as part of cutbacks in social policies and programs in Canada.

Women were excluded from decision-making about their futures. When the (federal) government appointed a Task Force on the fisheries crisis, only men were included. As Vicky Silk has written, "[W]omen's homes and communities were forced onto the bargaining table by exclusively male unions, government and corporate policy-makers." The 1993 Cashin Task Force Report, "Charting a New Course: Toward the Fishery of the Future," extends the corporate agenda by focusing on fish only as an economic commodity, not as food or livelihoods for local communities. Its solution for the future replaces a vision of "fishing as a way of life" in favour of a professionalized, high-tech fishery.

Cashin and others defined the problem as over-capacity which they equated with too many people and boats, not with flawed management strategies or inappropriate technology. Part of the professionalization solution was to ease individuals out of the fishery through programs in which fishers had to give up their future right to participate in the fisheries in exchange for job retraining. Women were not included in conceptions of professionals, either as paid or unpaid employees. In fact, the "professionalization" of the fishery—in both its policies and its rhetoric—might be considered as a mechanism for new forms of discrimination against women. For example, in The Atlantic Groundfish Strategy (TAGS) compensation package, which followed the government's moratorium, many women did not qualify—because their work was not recognized as work, because their work was not recognized as sufficiently at "arm's length" from their employer (their husband), and because their paid work (e.g., baiting trawl) was considered too marginal. This initial failure to qualify for support continues to prevent women's entitlement to training programs and perpetuates their unrecognized unpaid work and associated lack of self-worth—in both their families and their communities.

The professionalization of the fisheries probably failed to include women partly because of women's lack of participation in policy planning and partly because men had envisioned the future professionalized fishery for men, without women; for some men, professionalizing roles of "fishermen" was a way of stopping women's increased participation in the fisheries (both as fish harvesters and fish processors). Ideologically, the patriarchal construction of this male "profession" negated women's traditional work as shore managers, fish processors, and bookkeepers of family businesses. The taken-for-granted male entitlement to this industry, and the utter absence of women and women's interests from consideration, was apparent when a New Brunswick fisheries leader exclaimed: "And then, there are some people who think that women—women!—should sit at the decisions-making table. Well, if this is the case, we might as well invite the Martians to have a seat as well" (this quote was documented on one of the Nova Scotia Women's FishNet Fact Sheets, which are also included in Good Policy, Good Health: An Information and Action Kit for Women in Coastal Communities. In fact, the Cashin Report on the Fisheries paid more attention to female cod than to female persons. Its one mention of women was that middle-aged women would be hardest hit by the crisis. The Report, like government policies, however, assumed women would "cope" and support their families—without needed social development resources and against policies that destroyed their health, their livelihood, and their hope.

Feminist Revaluation and Revisioning

The fisheries crisis in Atlantic Canada could have been an important opportunity for genuine reconstruction and innovation. Women have seen the need for planning by, for, and with the local communities and have identified policy distortions of the current system. Women fishers and policy-makers have potential to fashion an environmentally and economically sustainable, community-based fishery because women are more likely than men to focus on fishing as a way of life and on processing as well as harvesting. Women's more holistic concerns and feminists' more holistic analysis take the needs of life—family members, community, and environment—as their starting point.

This transformative feminist thinking opens up the alternative of societies centered around caring rather than greed and oriented to social development rather than exchange. If participatory, women-centred, environmentally-friendly sustainable social development were to become the core around which a new society were built, a fundamental and radical revaluing of all institutions would be necessary. Social and economic resources would have to be reallocated, the economy transformed to serve societal interests, and a transparent, accountable civil society would have to be created, based on collective as well as individual human rights. This would involve revaluing, recognizing, and rewarding the significant work and responsibilities of women worldwide.

Ultimately, what I am proposing involves profound changes in the very concept of the economy and wealth itself. The new concept would pertain to human potential and relationships rather than commodification and colonization. It would reject reductionism and unilinearity and assumptions of insatiability, and it would embrace the multifaceted, people-centred, and relational reality of women's community work. It would challenge the ideals of exponential growth, revalue economic assumptions, and revise economic institutions, perhaps in ways suggested by Margrit Kennedy's proposal of interest and inflation free money. It might build on women's gift-giving practices and human relationships, rejecting the unequal exchanges of the current so-called level playing field and challenging the very idea of exchange itself in terms proposed by Genevieve Vaughan. If we think about it this way, these feminist conceptions are not so utopian but simply build on values and ethics that are still currencies among the majority of peoples and communities of the world. As Maria Mies suggests, feminists need to recognize that our economy is like an iceberg with only ten percent visible to our policy-makers and people in general. Feminists need to decolonize the iceberg economy, to understand and to build on the whole, prioritizing women's hidden life-sustaining work and concerns.

Source: Abbreviated from Linda Christiansen-Ruffman (2002). "Atlantic Canadian Coastal Communities and the Fisheries Trade: A Feminist Critique, Revaluation, and Revisioning." *Canadian Woman Studies/les cahiers de la femme*, 22(1): 56–63. Reprinted with permission of Linda Christiansen-Ruffman and Canadian Woman Studies.

women in this study, the promotion of self-definition and self-expression simultaneously promoted health. This feminist inquiry revealed how, through the process of self-definition, the women became active participants, experiencing a sense of empowerment in their lives.

D. THE ADVANTAGES AND LIMITATIONS OF DIFFERENT RESEARCH DESIGNS

Table 7.1 summarizes the advantages and limitations of the various research designs presented throughout Part Two of this book. While it is not possible to generalize about all the studies contained within any one type of design, we can conclude that experimental studies have an advantage over other research designs when we need to make clear causal inferences. Surveys are particularly adept at representing populations with samples, and such studies have become associated with complex multivariate analyses. Qualitative and field studies' strengths are in the areas of validity, cost (in some cases), and probing for depth. Applied research is important as a means of bringing about change and improvements in practice and empowering subjects through participation.

E. CONCLUSION

Action research is simply defined today as the systematic collection and analysis of data for the purpose of taking action and making change. It provides practitioners, organizations, or communities with tools to solve their problems.

Feminist research attempts to improve the conditions of the oppressed—particularly women—and to influence public policy in a direction that enhances fairness and justice for all. Just as its goals are diverse, so too are its research methodologies, drawing from positivist, interpretive, and critical approaches.

F. POSTSCRIPT TO PART TWO

While the most common designs used in social research have been reviewed in Chapters 3 through 7, others have been omitted. A discussion of methodological research (controlled investigations for obtaining, organizing, and analyzing data, for example) is not presented in this book. Various kinds of intervention, polls, evaluation models and special-interest approaches to research have also not been included.

As you get ready to design a study, keep in mind that you should choose a design appropriate to the research question you are posing. On occasion, more than one type of design can be used to answer a research question. The question is the key concern. Try to decide precisely what it is you want to accomplish and then figure out the design that is best suited to your needs.

As a postscript to Part Two, Box 7.5 presents Kathleen O'Connell's wry commentary on the dynamic tension between qualitative and quantitative practitioners. We would do well to recognize the gulf between these traditions and to try to build bridges between them. Both have enormous contributions to make to the development of social knowledge in the twenty-first century.

TABLE 7.1 ADVANTAGES AND LIMITATIONS OF ALTERNATE DESIGNS: SUMMARY TABLE

RESEARCH DESIGN CATEGORY	GENERAL	VALIDITY	CAUSAL INFERENCE	MULTI-VARIATE	PROBING
Experimental Designs					
Pseudo-experimental	–	–	–	–	–
Experimental	–	–	+	–	–
Quasi-experimental	±	–	+	–	–
Field Experiments	–	+	+	–	–
Naturalistic Observational	–	+	–	–	–
Survey Designs					
Individual Questionnaire	+	–	–	+	–
Group Administered	–	–	–	+	–
Phone Survey	+	–	–	+	–
Interview	+	–	–	+	+
Qualitative Designs*					
Ethnographic	–	+	–	–	+
Grounded Theory	–	+	–	–	+
Phenomenology	–	+	–	–	+
Nonreactive Designs					
Comparative Analysis	+	–	–	+	–
Secondary Data	+	–	–	+	–
Content Analysis	+	–	–	–	–
Applied and Evaluation					
Action Research	–	–	–	+	+
Evaluation Research	+	±	±	+	±
Feminist Research	±	±	–	±	±

In each category a "**+**" means that this is an advantage of the technique; a "**–**" means this is a possible limitation; "**±**" means that in some conditions it is a limitation, in others an advantage.

- *General* refers to the extent to which extrapolations to larger populations may be made using each of the design/data collection procedures.
- *Validity* is the extent to which indicators clearly measure what they are intended to measure.
- *Causal Inference* refers to the ease with which inferences about causal relations among variables may be made.
- *Multivariate* refers to the ease with which information on many variables is collected, leading to the possibility of multivariate analysis.
- *Probing* refers to the extent to which responses may be probed in depth.

BOX 7.5   SOCIAL RESEARCHERS AT WORK

Kathleen A. O'Connell: "If You Call Me Names, I'll Call You Numbers"

"Some of my best friends are qualitative researchers, but . . . " As that classical bigot's phrase came out of my mouth, I realized that my opinion of qualitative research had taken an unmistakable nosedive. I was writing the final report for a project that included both qualitative and quantitative methodologies. The project concerned coping strategies used during smoking cessation. Reviewing the earlier phases of the project reminded me of my misconceptions and frustrations with our attempts to integrate the two methods . . .

It is important to realize that there's the Quantitative Church and the Qualitative Church. Quantitative and qualitative approaches are not merely research methods. They are liturgies, outward and highly revered forms that represent entire value systems. Although the methods appear to have similar goals, i.e., the explication of new knowledge, they often disagree on everything else, even the definition of knowledge . . .

The first sign of problems emerged when we were gearing up to begin data collection. The qualitative team believed that it would be better to let the participants freely talk into the tape recorder about their experiences, that they should not be given specific directives about what to say, and that follow-up interviews carried out after each day of data collection should be similarly free-flowing. Although I was cognizant that I should be careful about upsetting our collaboration, I had been funded to study coping strategies, and that's what I wanted to study.

While the qualitative team developed a new taxonomy, the quantitative team used a previously developed categorization scheme to classify each strategy. I had hopes of comparing the two systems to determine which was more effective in terms of completeness of coverage and predicting outcome variables, such as whether the participant smoked during the coping episode. Such a comparison would not be possible. Qualitative researchers, it seems, are loathe to predict anything. In addition, the qualitative method was dynamic. The system that was applied to episodes coded early in the process was different and less elaborate than the one used for episodes coded later. Going back and classifying all episodes using the whole system was also out of the question because that's not the way qualitative researchers do it. You cannot, my qualitative research colleague told me, apply a taxonomy on the data set from which it was generated. Well, you can at my church!

The qualitative researcher you collaborate with may have different opinions than the one I collaborated with. It is nevertheless important to realize that such collaborations involve the intersection of two cultures. A final example was the qualitative team's tendency to call the study participants by their first names, a practice that made me surprisingly uncomfortable. The quantitative team referred to the participants by their assigned numbers, a practice that seemed foreign to the qualitative team. I argued that the practice was necessary to protect confidentiality. But in reality, I must admit that it also made our work seem . . . well, more quantitative. In the end they called them names, we called them numbers, and neither knew what the other was talking about.

Source: Kathleen A. O'Connell (2000). "If You Call Me Names, I'll Call You Numbers." *Journal of Professional Nursing*, 16(2), 74, W.B. Saunders Company. Cited with permission.

G. KEY POINTS

Critical research begins with the assumption that inequality is rooted in exploitative social relations. Neo-Marxism and feminism are examples of theoretical frameworks that advocate for a critical mode of inquiry. Critical researchers believe that research should play a role in bringing about social justice by exposing how policies and practices produce inequality and by empowering marginalized individuals and groups.

Many critical researchers advocate a multi-method approach, arguing that the purpose of the research should dictate the appropriate design to be used. Many critical researchers advocate using different methodologies rather than one unifying method. There are many celebrated examples of critical research studies that employ either quantitative or qualitative research designs or a combination of the two methods.

A relatively new method called *institutional ethnography* has been proposed by Dorothy Smith. This multi-method approach is designed to study social reality as it is constructed in the minds of those who experience it. The method differs from traditional qualitative approaches in that there is an explicit focus on the way structural conditions influence interactions and consciousness.

Action research is simply defined today as the systematic collection and analysis of data for the purpose of taking action and making change. The researcher collaborates with individuals, organizations, or communities to solve problems. Action researchers work with individuals, involving them in a reflective process of defining the problems and planning action to remedy the problems.

Feminist research involves valuing women and their experiences, ideas, and needs; seeing phenomena from the perspective of women; recognizing the existence of conditions that oppress women; and desiring to change these conditions through research leading to political action.

These starting points are reflected in the methods employed by feminists, the types of research questions they develop, and their relationships with research participants. For example, feminist researchers promote *intersubjectivity* in their research rather than the one-way communication of traditional methods. They advocate *reciprocity* and acknowledge women's ways of knowing.

H. KEY TERMS

Action research	Feminist research	Reflexivity
Critical research	Institutional ethnography	Texts
Ethnomethodology	Participatory action research	
Feminism	Patriarchy	

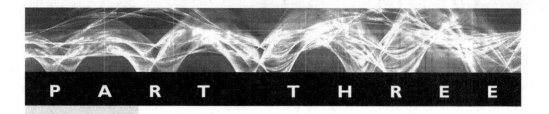

STATISTICS

The two chapters in this section review the statistical concepts necessary for the beginning researcher. While the elementary view presented here will be helpful for the beginning student, a more profound understanding will be necessary for those students attempting more advanced work. (See Blalock, 1979; Siegel, 1956; Mitchell and Jolley, 1992.)

Those with a background in statistics can skip these chapters or review them quickly; those without such a background should work through the material carefully to acquire a foundation upon which they can build an understanding of advanced techniques. A reference to SPSS commands is included after each statistic is introduced so that the reader will be able to find the procedure in Appendix A quickly.

*Chapter 8 reviews elementary **descriptive statistics** (procedures for describing individual variables and for describing the relationship between variables). A second group of statistics is known as **inferential statistics** and deals with making extrapolations from a sample to the population from which it was drawn. Both types of statistics are of relevance to the social researcher. An introduction to inferential statistics will be presented in Chapter 9.*

CHAPTER EIGHT

A STATISTICS PRIMER

The social researcher asks questions about many kinds of phenomena: some of them are about individuals (e.g., age, type of job, income, job satisfaction, and attitudes toward minorities); some questions are about communities (e.g., how much deviance occurs? how many new houses have been built in the past year? has there been a change in the proportion of low-income people living in the community?); and some questions may be about nations (e.g., how many births and deaths were recorded? have the incomes of the people increased or gone down over the past 10 years?).

Typifying a sample's characteristics may be achieved by a variety of *descriptive statistics*. Such statistics include various tools, conventions, and procedures for describing variables. (Means, standard deviations, normal distributions, and Z scores are of particular concern to the social researcher.) Besides describing individual variables, the social researcher is also interested in examining relationships between variables (is there a relationship between gender and income? does this relationship persist when males and females in similar occupations are compared?). Once again, the researcher wishes to decide what relationship exists, and if it does, to determine whether it holds in virtually all circumstances. There are a variety of conventions used to describe relationships. (Cross-classifications, means across categories, and correlations are important tools in describing relationships.)

Keep in mind that statistics are tools to help in describing and understanding social relationships. Be a master of these tools, but treat them as tools. They are no substitute for theory and cannot make up for poorly designed studies or sloppy measurement.

A. LEVELS OF MEASUREMENT

An understanding of levels of measurement is necessary, since how one should go about analyzing a variable is constrained by the measurement level achieved in data collection. As a general rule, one attempts to achieve the most precise measurement possible.

One way to begin to understand levels of measurement is to ask if the variable being measured has an underlying continuum (does it vary from low to high?). If there is no underlying continuum and the variable is made up of a number of discrete categories, then the measurement will be at the nominal level; if the variable has an underlying continuum, then the level of measurement will be either ordinal or a ratio. This text will distinguish between three levels of measurement: nominal, ordinal, and ratio. (See Box 8.1 for an explanation of what happened to the fourth level of measurement typically distinguished in social science texts.)

A. NOMINAL MEASUREMENT

Religious affiliation is a nominal variable. While there may be underlying continua related to religious affiliation (such as degree of religious commitment or frequency of church attendance), by itself the religious organization is a nominal category: it may be, for example, Anglican, United, Roman Catholic, Muslim, Buddhist, or Jewish. When a respondent checks off which (if any) religious affiliations he or she was associated with while growing up, the measurement level attained is nominal. One category is neither higher nor lower than any other—they are simply different categories.

BOX 8.1   TRADITIONAL LEVELS OF MEASUREMENT

Whatever Happened to Equal Interval Measures?

The conventional *equal interval* level of measurement (see S.S. Stevens, 1951) is not presented in this text for the sake of pedagogical simplicity. For those analyses that require equal interval or ratio measurement, in most cases the measurement will be ratio level. Many texts in the social sciences use the temperature measures of Celsius versus Fahrenheit as examples of situations in which the intervals between the points are equal but the zero point is misplaced (absolute zero is about 2273 degrees Celsius). The traditional measurement levels and their associated properties are shown in the table below.

Arguably, most social science measures that meet the equal interval assumption also meet the ratio measurement assumption of a correctly aligned zero point (see Blalock, 1979). Individual variables such as age, weight, height, income, years employed, number of magazines read last week, and the number of dates one had last month all would constitute ratio measures providing the data recorded reflect the charac-teristic being measured and are not placed in some pre-coded set of categories with uneven category sizes.

Similarly, those measures reflecting properties of communities or countries (or other groupings), such as the proportion of non-native-born members, the crime rate, or the number of motor vehicles per person, represent ratio level measures.

While most textbook authors present the four types of measurement, some do not (see Levin and Fox, 1991; Rosenthal and Rosnow, 1991; Jackson, 1988). For the sake of simplicity, equal interval measures will not be identified as such in this text. The reader, then, should be aware that, while the measurement assumptions of various statistics often call for interval level measurement, such measurements will be stated as ratio level measurement in this presentation. Since virtually all the social science measures that are at this level are ratio level measures, this should rarely prove to be a difficulty.

Traditional Levels of Measurement

MEASUREMENT FEATURE	MEASUREMENT LEVEL			
	NOMINAL	ORDINAL	EQUAL INTERVAL	RATIO
Identifies categories?	Yes	Yes	Yes	Yes
Orders observations?	No	Yes	Yes	Yes
Equal intervals between points?	No	No	Yes	Yes
Properly assigned zero point?	No	No	No	Yes

Nominal measurement involves no underlying continuum, and the numerical values assigned are arbitrary and have no arithmetical meaning. Other examples of nominal variables include gender, program of study, political party affiliation, and ethnic origin (see Table 8.1).

B. ORDINAL MEASUREMENT

Ordinal measurement involves an underlying continuum in which the numerical values are ordered so that small numbers refer to lower levels on the continuum and large numbers to higher points; however, the distances between the assigned numbers and the underlying continuum are not in a one-to-one relation with each other.

For example, suppose a statement like the following is presented to respondents:

The United Nations keeps the world safe.

Strongly 1 2 3 4 5 6 7 8 9 Strongly
Disagree   Agree

This kind of item provides ordinal measurement. While we know that high numbers indicate greater agreement with the statement, we do not know that the distances between the values are equal: the distance between 4 and 5 on the scale may not be the same as the distance between 8 and 9. Ordinal measurement orders values, but does not assure equal gaps between the measurement points. Various examples of ordinal level measurement are provided in Table 8.2.

TABLE 8.1 EXAMPLES OF NOMINAL LEVEL MEASUREMENT*

TYPE OF RESEARCH DESIGN	VARIABLE	MEASURE
Experiment	Expectancy created?	Subject run under conditions where outcome is: Expected —— —— 1( ) Not expected —— —— 2( )
Survey questionnaire	Place of residence?	The place where I live now is: Atlantic Canada—— —— 1( ) Quebec —— —— —— 2( ) Ontario —— —— —— 3( ) Western Canada —— 4( ) Other—— —— —— 5( )
Participant observation	Suggests activity?	Decision event: George: Initiates —— —— 1( ) Supports others —— 2( ) Rejects others —— 3( )
Content analysis	Character plays traditional gender role?	Character X plays a gender role which is: Traditional —— —— 1( ) Nontraditional —— 2( )

* Nominal measurement involves no underlying continuum; numeric values assigned have no meaning; values cannot be added, subtracted, or multiplied.

TABLE 8.2 EXAMPLES OF ORDINAL LEVEL MEASUREMENT*

TYPE OF RESEARCH DESIGN	VARIABLE	MEASURE
Experiment	Expectancy level created?	Subject run under conditions of: Low level— — — — — 1( ) Medium level — — — 2( ) High level — — — — 3( )
Survey questionnaire	Size of community?	The place where I live now is: Under 5,000— — — — 1( ) 5,000 to 19,999— — — 2( ) 20,000 to 99,999 — — 3( ) 100,000 to 999,999 — 4( ) 1 million or over — — 5( )
Participant observation	Supportive behaviour?	Support of illegal activity: No support — — — — 1( ) Some support — — — 2( ) Strong support — — — 3( )
Content analysis	Degree of traditional gender role?	Character X plays a gender role which is: Nontraditional — — — 1( ) Neutral — — — — — 2( ) Traditional — — — — 3( )

* Ordinal measurement involves an underlying continuum; numeric values assigned are ordered but intervals are not equal; values may be added or subtracted but not multiplied.

C. RATIO MEASUREMENT

Finally, there is ratio measurement. With **ratio measurement**, the zero point is aligned with true zero and the distances between the intervals are equal. For example, income is a variable whose nature makes it possible to represent an individual's income level exactly with a single number. In this case, it is also possible to use zero to reflect no income and other numerical values to reflect all other income levels. Here it is correct to say that an income of $50,000 is twice as much as an income of $25,000. With ratio level measurement it is possible to add and subtract constants as well as to multiply or divide by them without changing the proportionality among the values.

If a researcher were to have respondents indicate with a check mark which of the magazines on a list they had scanned or read in the previous month and a total was taken of the number ticked off, the result would be a variable that varies from 0 to the number required if a respondent checked off all the items listed: this measure would be a ratio level measure. Similarly, when communities are being studied, measures such as the proportion of visible minorities or the proportion of retired people in the population and various rates and ratios (suicide rate, dependency ratio, sex ratio) are all ratio level measures (see Table 8.3 for additional examples).

TABLE 8.3   EXAMPLES OF RATIO LEVEL MEASUREMENT*

TYPE OF RESEARCH DESIGN	VARIABLE	MEASURE
Experiment	Accuracy of recall	Number of correct answers in trial: _____ _____
Survey questionnaire	Weight?	My weight is: _____ _____ _____ Pounds or _____ _____ _____ Kilos
Participant observation	Community involvement	Number of people at bingo on January 15: _____ _____ _____
Content analysis	Conservative gender portrayals	Ratio of men portrayed in non-traditional gender roles to women portrayed in nontraditional gender roles: _____ : _____

* Ratio measurement involves an underlying continuum; numeric values assigned are ordered with equal intervals; the zero point is aligned with true zero; when different ratio measures are combined, the values may be added, subtracted, multiplied, or divided.

B. DESCRIBING AN INDIVIDUAL VARIABLE

In this first section, we will consider how individual variables may be described. We will look at *measures of central tendency*, how variation within a variable is measured, and approaches to standardizing variables.

1. MEASURES OF CENTRAL TENDENCY

Measures of central tendency use one number to typify a set of values. Just as baseball fans cite the batting average to summarize a player's hitting ability, the social researcher uses various simple statistics to convey a sense of the data. There are three commonly used measures of central tendency.

A. THE MEAN

The *mean* is a measure that typifies a set of observations with a single value. Suppose, for example, we wished to examine grades in two first-year tests. The grades are listed in Table 8.4. Examine the grades. If you were asked to indicate the test on which students did best, what would you say? The task is a frustrating one. It is difficult to answer. The mass of detail is overwhelming. Quickly the need for some method of summarizing the grades becomes apparent. You need a way to compare the results in each of the two tests—a way to simplify the reporting of the numbers contained in Table 8.4. It is too inefficient to read an unordered listing of numbers; to do so would fail to convey to your reader any sense of the results. You would simply have a boring list of numbers. Your job as a data analyst is to put some order into the

TABLE 8.4   TWO SETS OF GRADES FOR A FIRST-YEAR CLASS

TEST A RESULTS

60	60	82	71	60	58	64	81	58	58	70	57	56
56	69	58	55	82	46	54	62	61	77	70	59	74
87	47	57	63	37	67	55	59	63	59	55	52	58
63	72	54	54	62	69	66	58	53	73	57	68	52
75	47	52	73	72	65	64	63	59	57			

TEST B RESULTS

53	64	83	60	61	61	61	83	54	58	68	55	49
60	59	55	53	69	44	56	48	54	74	71	49	54
86	51	67	63	59	63	55	40	65	63	62	55	49
53	72	59	59	54	69	73	57	59	72	26	65	70
60	45	60	69	66	63	51	59	63	63			

data, helping your reader to understand the results in the two tests. Presenting only the grades would not help the reader to detect if the performance in the two tests was very different.

Computing means might be a first step in comparing the grades in the two sections. The **mean** (more formally known as the *arithmetic mean*, less formally known as the *average*) is computed by summing the values of a variable and dividing the result by the total number of cases. A mean is used on ratio level data. To find the mean grade in each test we would simply sum the grades and then divide by the number of students. This would result in a mean grade for each section of the course. Table 8.5 reports the means, showing that the average performance was somewhat higher in Test A. Students scored 2.0 points higher on the first test than on the second one. That difference is not easily apparent in looking at the raw scores.

TABLE 8.5   SUMMARY STATISTICS FOR STUDENT GRADES

SUMMARY STATISTICS	TEST A GRADES	TEST B GRADES
Central Tendency		
Mean	62.02	60.02
Mode	58.00	59.00
Median	60.00	60.00
Variation		
Range	50.00	46.00
Standard deviation	9.53	10.13
Number of cases	62	62

B. THE MEDIAN

The **median** represents the mid-point of a distribution. One-half the cases fall above the median value, one-half below it. The median is used for ordinal-level variables or in cases in which the use of a mean would be problematic because a few extreme values would give an inappropriate impression of the typical case. The steps in determining the median are:

(i) Arrange the cases in order from highest to lowest, or lowest to highest.

(ii) Number the values (ignoring no response or missing data).

(iii) If there are an odd number of cases, then the middle value is identified, and that value is the median for the distribution.

(iv) If, however, there are an even number of cases, then the mean of the middle two is calculated, and that value represents the median.

Table 8.6 illustrates medians on a 9-point attitude item for both odd- and even-numbered sample sizes. Note that the values have been ordered and the middle-most figure identified as the median.

Table 8.7 illustrates a situation in which a median would be a better description of a sample than would a mean. Here the data list the annual incomes of 15 musicians in Montreal. When we compare the extremely high salary of $580,000 with the much more modest incomes of the other musicians surveyed, we realize that citing the mean would give the false impression that the incomes of musicians are quite high. The median value of $18,300 is a much better description of the income distribution than the mean of $54,213. When atypical values are present, the median may provide a better description of the data.

C. THE MODE

The **mode** is the category of a nominal variable with the most cases. If one wishes, for example, to describe "average" respondents in terms of their country, then the mode would be the appropriate statistic. In the

TABLE 8.6 COMPUTING THE MEDIAN

ODD NUMBER OF CASES			EVEN NUMBER OF CASES		
#	VALUE	MEDIAN	#	VALUE	MEDIAN
1.	1		1.	4	
2.	1		2.	4	
3.	1		3.	5	
4.	2		4.	6	
5.	3		5.	6	
6.	3		6.	7	
7.	4	← 4 is	7.	7	
8.	4	median	8.	8	} ← 7.5 is median
9.	5		9.	8	
10.	5		10.	8	
11.	6		11.	9	
12.	8		12.	9	
13.	9		13.	9	
			14.	9	

TABLE 8.7 MEDIAN FOR EXTREME VALUES

CASE #	$ INCOME	
1.	5,400	
2.	6,600	
3.	7,700	
4.	10,200	
5.	13,400	
6.	16,400	
7.	16,700	
8.	18,300	← $18,300
9.	19,000	median value
10.	20,000	
11.	20,500	
12.	22,900	
13.	24,600	
14.	31,500	$54,213
15.	580,000	mean value

case of country, it might be "Canada." This would simply mean that "Canada" was the most frequently occurring response to the question asking respondents to indicate their country. Table 8.8 presents a frequency distribution (simply reports the number of respondents who fall into each category) of respondents who report themselves to be from each of the three countries listed. From Table 8.8 one can identify the modal category by looking at the "Number" column, and picking out the category which has the highest frequency: in this case, the category is "Canada."

2. MEASURES OF DISPERSION

Besides describing a variable's central tendency, it is helpful to know something about the variability of the values. Are most of the values close to one another or spread out? To illustrate, suppose we have two students, Mary and Beth. Their grades are indicated in Table 8.9. While both students have an identical 82% average, the distributions are quite different. Mary's grades vary little; Beth's vary considerably. We will explore three ways of describing the dispersion in the two students' grades.

TABLE 8.8 DISTRIBUTION OF RESPONDENTS BY COUNTRY

COUNTRY	NUMBER	PERCENT	
Canada	65	34.9	← mode
New Zealand	58	31.2	
Australia	63	33.9	
TOTAL	186	100.0	

TABLE 8.9 TWO GRADE DISTRIBUTIONS

SUBJECT	MARY	BETH
Sociology	78	66
Psychology	80	72
Political science	82	88
Anthropology	82	90
Philosophy	88	94
Mean[1]	82	82
Range[2]	10	28
Standard deviation[3]	3.74	12.25
Variance[4]	14.0	150.0

[1]Mean = sum of values divided by number of cases
[2]Range = highest value − lowest value
[3]See computation in Table 8.10 on p. 221.
[4]Variance = sd^2

A. RANGE

The **range** indicates the gap between the lowest and highest value in a distribution. It is computed by subtracting the lowest value from the highest one. Table 8.9 indicates that the range of Beth's grades is 28, while for Mary the range is 10.

B. STANDARD DEVIATION

Researchers rely heavily on the **standard deviation** to give them a sense of how much dispersion there is in a distribution. Essentially, this measure reflects the average amount of deviation from the mean value of the variable. The formula is:

$$sd = \sqrt{\frac{\Sigma (X - \overline{X})^2}{N - 1}}$$

Table 8.10 shows how the standard deviation for Beth's grades could be computed. An examination of Table 8.9 reveals that the standard deviation of Mary's grades

TABLE 8.10 COMPUTATION OF STANDARD DEVIATION, BETH'S GRADES

SUBJECT	GRADE	$X - \overline{X}$	$(X - \overline{X})^2$
Sociology	66	$66 - 82 = -16$	256
Psychology	72	$72 - 82 = -10$	100
Political science	88	$88 - 82 = 6$	36
Anthropology	90	$90 - 82 = 8$	64
Philosophy	94	$94 - 82 = 12$	144
MEAN	82.0	TOTAL	600

$$sd = \sqrt{\frac{\Sigma (X - \overline{X})^2}{N - 1}}$$

$$sd = \sqrt{\frac{600}{4}}$$

$$sd = 12.25$$

Note: The "N–1" term is used when sampling procedures have been used. When population values are used the denominator is "N." SPSS uses "N–1" in calculating the standard deviation in the DESCRIPTIVES procedure.

is 3.7, considerably less than Beth's 12.2. An examination of the actual grades indicates that, indeed, there is much more variability in Beth's than in Mary's grades. The standard deviation reflects the variability in a set of values.

The beginning researcher should be familiar with how standard deviations are computed; this statistic is probably the single most important one that will be encountered. It will also be relevant for a number of other statistics. Once data have been entered into the computer, it will not be necessary to hand-compute standard deviations; nonetheless, it is crucial to understand what they measure.

C. VARIANCE

The third measure of dispersion is **variance**, which is simply the standard deviation squared. Or:

$$\text{Variance} = sd^2 = \frac{\Sigma (X - \overline{X})^2}{N - 1}$$

In the illustration using Mary's and Beth's grades the variances are 14.0 and 150.0 respectively (see Table 8.9).

Table 8.11 summarizes the single-variable statistics that have been presented in this text. Note that it is possible to use all of the summarizing statistics when a ratio level of measurement has been achieved. Indeed, when there are unusual features in the data, such as a few extreme values or a high number of identical scores, it sometimes makes sense to use a summary statistic other than the one highlighted in the table.

3. STANDARDIZING DATA

To standardize data is to make adjustments so that comparisons between units of different size may be made; data can also be standardized to create variables that have similar variability in them (Z scores).

TABLE 8.11 SUMMARY STATISTICS FOR SINGLE VARIABLES

LEVEL OF MEASUREMENT	MEASURES OF CENTRAL TENDENCY	MEASURES OF DISPERSION
Nominal	**Mode***	
Ordinal	Mode **Median**	**Range**
Ratio	Mode Median **Mean**	Range **Standard Deviation** **Variance**

*The statistic that is used under normal circumstances is indicated by bolding.

A. PROPORTIONS

A **proportion** can be calculated to show, for example, how many females there are in a population compared to the total population. Suppose we wished to compute the proportion female in a community:

$$\text{Proportion female} = \frac{\text{Number females}}{\text{Total persons}}$$

$$\text{Proportion female} = \frac{31,216}{58,520}$$

$$\text{Proportion female} = .53$$

The females represent .53 of the population.

B. PERCENTAGES

If we wished to represent a proportion as a **percentage**, we would simply multiply the proportion by 100. In doing this, we note that females constitute 53.3% of the population.

Table 8.12 presents the relationship between size of home community and whether the respondent plans to attend university. It is not adequate simply to say that 69 rural students and 102 small-town students plan on attending university. We report percentages to adjust for the fact that there are different numbers of students involved in each of the categories. By computing the percentages, we are able to say that for every 100 rural students, 52.3 are planning to attend university compared to 73.9 of every 100 high school students from towns over 5,000.

C. PERCENTAGE CHANGE

Often social scientists will compare numbers at one time to those at another one. For example, they might want to measure the percentage increase in the proportion of women in male-dominated professions from one period to the next. Table 8.13 illustrates a problem in which social scientists might wish to calculate the percentage change between 1971 and 1981 in the number of women in economics. The general form of the equation for calculating percentage change would be:

$$\text{Percent change} = \frac{\text{Time 2 Number} - \text{Time 1 Number}}{\text{Time 1 Number}} \times 100$$

To calculate the percentage change, use the following steps:

(i)   Using the general equation, subtract the Time 1 number from the Time 2 number.

TABLE 8.12 PLANS TO ATTEND UNIVERSITY BY SIZE OF HOME COMMUNITY

UNIVERSITY PLANS?	RURAL		TOWN UP TO 5,000		TOWN OVER 5,000		TOTAL	
	N	%	N	%	N	%	N	%
Plans	69	52.3	44	48.9	102	73.9	215	59.7
No plans	63	47.7	46	51.1	36	26.1	145	40.3
TOTAL	132	100.0	90	100.0	138	100.0	360	100.0

If appropriate, test of significance values entered here.

(ii) Divide the above result by the number at Time 1.

(iii) Multiply the above result by 100.

D. RATES

The incidence of a social phenomenon is often presented in the form of a *rate*. A **rate** indicates the frequency of some phenomenon for a standard-sized unit (such as incidence per 1,000 or per 100,000). This allows us to compare easily the incidence of a phenomenon in units of different size. To know, for example, that there were 27 suicides in a city of 250,000 (Middle City) in one year and 13 suicides in another city of 110,000 (Small City), does not allow quick comparison unless we compute a suicide

TABLE 8.13 CALCULATING PERCENTAGE CHANGE: PERCENTAGE CHANGE IN NUMBER OF WOMEN IN SELECTED OCCUPATIONS, 1971 AND 1981

PROFESSION	NUMBER 1971 [Time 1]	NUMBER 1981 [Time 2]	PERCENT CHANGE 1971 TO 1981
Economist	640	2570	301.6
University teacher	5190	9785	88.5
Sociologist and anthropologist	170	540	217.6
Dentist	330	860	160.6
Physician and surgeon	3150	7255	130.3
Lawyer and notary	860	5390	526.7

Source: Derived from Statistics Canada, *Census of Canada*.

Note the method of calculating percentage change:

$$\text{Percent change} = \frac{\text{Time 2 Number} - \text{Time 1 Number}}{\text{Time 1 Number}} \times 100$$

In the case of economists in the above table the calculation would be:

$$\text{Percent change} = \frac{2{,}570 - 640}{640} \times 100$$

Percent change = 301.6

rate. A suicide rate may be computed in the following manner:

$$\text{Suicide rate} = \frac{\text{Number suicides per year}}{\text{Mid-year population}} \times 100,000$$

When calculated, we find that the suicide rate for Middle City is 10.8, while for Small City the rate is 11.8. This means that Middle City has 10.8 suicides in the year for every 100,000 people in the city; in Small City the rate is 11.8 per 100,000. In this case, we see that the smaller of the two cities has a slightly higher suicide rate. Rates can also be computed for specific age categories, or on other bases; the only adjustment required is that we use the number of suicides in the category compared to its total size. Rates are computed for many things including births, marriages, divorces, deaths, and crime.

Table 8.14 presents provincial suicide rates for Canada. Note that rates permit easy comparisons between units of unequal size. The data are standardized, permitting comparison between the units. If the absolute number of suicides were presented, this would create the impression that suicide is a much more serious problem in the larger jurisdictions. This may not be the case. The rates adjust for the differences in size.

E. RATIOS

Ratios are used to compare rates or other measures across categories. For example, suppose one wished to compare American and Canadian crime rates. The burglary rate in the U.S.A. is 200 per 100,000 while the comparable Canadian rate is 57 per 100,000. The American/Canadian burglary ratio could be represented as:

TABLE 8.14 SUICIDE RATES FOR CANADA, 2003

	NUMBER OF SUICIDES	POPULATION	SUICIDE RATE[1]
Newfoundland	48	519,570	9.23
Prince Edward Island	14	137,781	10.16
Nova Scotia	99	936,025	10.57
New Brunswick	91	750,594	12.12
Quebec	1,260	7,487,169	16.82
Ontario	1,038	12,238,300	8.48
Manitoba	165	1,162,776	14.19
Saskatchewan	112	994,843	11.25
Alberta	441	3,153,723	13.47
British Columbia	450	4,146,580	10.85
Yukon	6	31,060	19.31
Northwest Territories	10	41,872	23.88
Nunavut	31	29,384	105.49
Canada	3,765	31,629,677	11.90

[1]Rate per 100,000 people. The data were computed based on data from Statistics Canada. *CANSIM.*

$$\text{America/Canada burglary ratio} = \frac{\text{American burglary rate}}{\text{Canadian burglary rate}}$$

$$\text{America/Canada burglary ratio} = \frac{200}{57}$$

$$\text{America/Canada burglary ratio} = 3.51$$

This ratio suggests that the American burglary rate is 3.51 times higher than the comparable Canadian rate. Many ratios can be computed that, like rates, facilitate comparison between categories.

Table 8.15 presents the ratio between male and female suicide rates for Canadian provinces. Note that, nationally, men commit suicide 3.44 times more frequently than women. The ratios also facilitate comparison between the provinces.

In some cases, ratios are reported so that they are standardized to a base of 100. For example, if we had a community with 27,304 males and 31,216 females, we might compute a sex ratio. The ratio for the community could be calculated as follows:

$$\text{Sex ratio} = \frac{\text{Number of males}}{\text{Number of females}} \times 100$$

$$\text{Sex ratio} = \frac{27,304}{31,216} \times 100$$

$$\text{Sex ratio} = 87.5$$

This sex ratio would indicate that there are 87.5 males in the community for every 100 females. Such a ratio allows us to quickly compare the sex ratios of communities, nations, age groups, or any other category.

TABLE 8.15 MALE/FEMALE SUICIDE RATIOS BY PROVINCE, CANADA, 2003

PROVINCE	SUICIDE RATE MALES	SUICIDE RATE FEMALES	RATIO MALE/FEMALE SUICIDES
Newfoundland	14.47	4.16	3.54
Prince Edward Island	17.9	2.82	6.35
Nova Scotia	17.01	4.39	3.87
New Brunswick	20.23	4.21	3.81
Quebec	26.58	7.32	3.63
Ontario	12.95	4.11	3.15
Manitoba	22.37	6.13	3.65
Saskatchewan	18.60	3.99	4.66
Alberta	20.88	6.92	3.02
British Columbia	16.59	5.21	3.18
Yukon	38.32	—	—
Northwest Territories	46.25	—	—
Nunavut	164.21	42.37	3.88
Canada	18.35	5.39	3.44

In this table the Male/Female suicide ratio is computed for each province by dividing the male suicide rate by the female rate. The result indicates how many male suicides there are for every female suicide.

4. THE NORMAL DISTRIBUTION

The *normal distribution* is another key concept used by researchers. Many of the observations we make on individual or group characteristics will approximate what is referred to as a **normal distribution**. What does this mean?

If a graph is made showing the distribution, for example, of the weight of male university students, it would approximate a bell-shaped curve. There will be few cases on the extremes—the very light and the very heavy; most of the cases will be found clustered toward the middle of the distribution.

Another way to illustrate the normal curve is to plot the outcomes of a series of 10 coin flips. Suppose we flip a coin 10 times, record the number of heads, repeat this operation 1,024 times, and then plot the number of times we got 0, 1, 2,... 10 heads in the trials. The outcome will approximate that shown in Figure 8.1, which is a graph of the theoretical probabilities of getting each of the eleven possible outcomes (i.e., 0 through 10 heads). The result approximates that of a normal distribution.

A further characteristic of the normal distribution is its connection to the standard deviation. By definition, a fixed proportion of cases will fall within given standard deviations of the mean (see Figure 8.2). About two-thirds of the cases will fall within one standard deviation of the mean and just over

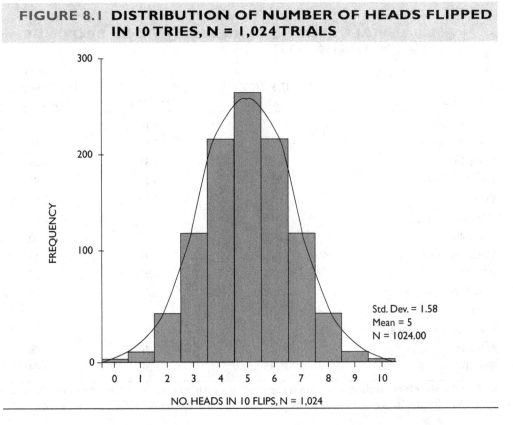

FIGURE 8.1 DISTRIBUTION OF NUMBER OF HEADS FLIPPED IN 10 TRIES, N = 1,024 TRIALS

Std. Dev. = 1.58
Mean = 5
N = 1024.00

FREQUENCY

NO. HEADS IN 10 FLIPS, N = 1,024

FIGURE 8.2 NORMAL DISTRIBUTION CURVE

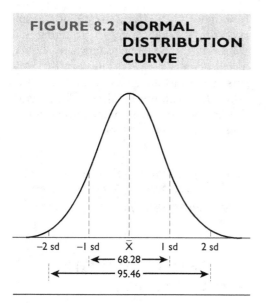

95% of the cases will fall within two standard deviations of the mean. More precisely, the following are some of the properties of a normal distribution:

• It will form a symmetrical, bell-shaped curve.

• The mean, mode, and median values will be the same; half the cases will fall below the mean, the other half above the mean.

• As the number of observations becomes more numerous and the measurement units become finer, the distribution curve will become smoother.

• 68.28% of the observations will be divided equally between the mean and one standard deviation to the right of the mean (34.14) and one standard deviation to the left of the mean (34.14).

• 95.46% of the observations will fall ± two standard deviations from the mean.

• 95% of the cases fall ± 1.96 standard deviation units from the mean.

• 99% of the cases fall ± 2.58 standard deviation units from the mean.

5. Z SCORES

Z scores measure the distance, in standard deviation units, of any value in a distribution from the mean. Thus, if someone's income has a Z score of +1.43, it would indicate that the income is 1.43 standard deviation units above the mean of the distribution. Suppose that the mean income is $65,000 and the standard deviation $22,000: the Z score +1.43 would indicate an income of $96,460. How is this value computed? The formula for Z scores is as follows:

$$Z = \frac{X - \bar{X}}{sd}$$

where: X is the observation;

$\bar{X}$ is the mean of the distribution;

sd is the standard deviation of the distribution.

By plugging the values into the equation, and solving, the value $96,460 is obtained, as in:

$$1.43 = \frac{X - 65,000}{22,000}$$

$$X = (1.43 \times 22,000) + 65,000$$

$$X = 96,460$$

One of the consequences of being able to report a value in terms of its Z score is that we now have a powerful comparative tool. Suppose we wanted to compare individuals' relative income positions in two countries: we could simply report the incomes in Z score terms, and this would tell us where each individual stands in his or her country's income distribution. This would permit us to compare a British family's income of £24,000 pounds to a Canadian family's income of $90,000 dollars.

The student should recognize that whole sets of variables can be standardized by computing Z scores, and the resulting distributions will have means of 0 and standard deviations of 1. Thus, instead of just having variables with income scores, educational levels, and occupational prestige, we might have standardized variables containing the Z scores for each variable. Such standardization can be accomplished easily in SPSS.

To perform this analysis in SPSS use the DESCRIPTIVES procedure; see Appendix A.

Combining indicators to create an index is a major use of Z scores. Suppose, for example, that we have measures on income and years of education and that we wish to combine them to form a socioeconomic index. It would not make sense simply to add a respondent's years of education to his or her annual income: the reason is that incomes might vary from $5,000 to $500,000, while years of education might vary from 0 to 20. By adding them together, the income component would totally dominate the index. Someone earning $50,000 with eight years of education would have a score of 50,008 while a person with a B.A. and $40,000 income would end up with a score of 40,016. Somehow, we need to weight the components so that income and education will equally influence the outcome. Using Z scores is an easy way to do this.

Table 8.16 shows the computation of socioeconomic index scores using Z scores.

Notice how either a lower-than-average income or a lower-than-average education leads to a reduction in the total socioeconomic score. These indexes can be calculated quickly by a computer and the components weighted in any way the researcher likes. The Z scores, for example, can be added together, resulting in a value that can be taken to represent the relative socioeconomic position of the various respondents, with income and education making equal contributions to the final score. Such computations can be done rapidly within SPSS.

To perform this analysis in SPSS use the DESCRIPTIVES and COMPUTE procedures; see Appendix A for details.

6. AREAS UNDER THE NORMAL CURVE

Another useful property of the normal distribution is that it is possible, with the help of a table (see Table 8.17 on p. 230), to work out what proportion of cases will fall between two values or above or below a given value.

To illustrate, suppose we wished to know what percentage of incomes will fall above $100,000, given a population standard deviation of $22,000, and a mean of $65,000. The steps to solve this problem would be as follows.

STEP 1

Draw a normal curve, marking below it the mean and standard deviation values, and drawing a line through the curve at the point where you expect $100,000 to fall. Since the question asks about the percentage above this point, shade the curve to the right of the $100,000 mark.

STEP 2

Calculate the Z score to determine how many standard deviation units $100,000 is above the mean, as in:

$$Z = \frac{X - \overline{X}}{sd}$$

$$Z = \frac{100,000 - 65,000}{22,000}$$

$$Z = 1.59$$

STEP 3

Look up the value 1.59 (in Table 8.17). Move down the Z score column until you come to the value 1.5, then read across the row to the column headed by .09, and read the value. You should have found the number 4441. This number should be understood as ".4441," a proportion.

STEP 4

By definition, we know that one-half of the cases will fall above the mean. Expressed as a proportion, this would indicate that 0.5 of the cases will fall above the mean. The question we are trying to answer is what proportion of the cases fall above $100,000? Looking at the diagram we made in Step 1, we realize that if the right side of the curve contains .5 of all the cases, and, if the value $100,000 is .4441 above the mean, then the cases above $100,000 would have to be:

$$.5000 - .4441 = .0559$$

TABLE 8.16 COMPUTING AN INDEX SCORE USING Z SCORE

	INCOME ($)	YEARS EDUCATION
Given population values:		
Mean	65,000	11
Standard Deviation	22,000	4
Suppose five individuals:		
A.	55,000	7
B.	41,000	12
C.	30,000	8
D.	64,000	16
E.	86,000	9

Compute an Index equally weighting income and years of education. The general equation is:

$$Z = \frac{X - \overline{X}}{sd}$$

Case A.

Income: (55,000 − 65,000) ÷ 22,000	= − .45
Education: (7 − 11) ÷ 4	= −1.00
Socioeconomic index score	−1.45

Case D.

Income: (64,000 − 65,000) ÷ 22,000	= − .05
Education: (16 − 11) ÷ 4	= 1.25
Socioeconomic index score	1.20

Case B.

Income: (41,000 − 65,000) ÷ 22,000	= −1.09
Education: (12 − 11) ÷ 4	= .25
Socioeconomic index score	− .84

Case E.

Income: (86,000 − 65,000) ÷ 22,000	= .95
Education: (9 − 11) ÷ 4	= − .50
Socioeconomic index score	.45

Case C.

Income: (30,000 − 65,000) ÷ 22,000	= −1.59
Education: (8 − 11) ÷ 4	= − .75
Socioeconomic index score	−2.34

TABLE 8.17 AREAS UNDER THE NORMAL CURVE

Fractional parts of the total area (10,000) under the normal curve, corresponding to distances between the mean and ordinates which are Z standard-deviation units from the mean.

Z	.00	.01	.02	.03	.04	.05	.06	.07	.08	.09
0.0	0000	0040	0080	0120	0159	0199	0239	0279	0319	0359
0.1	0398	0438	0478	0517	0557	0596	0636	0675	0714	0753
0.2	0793	0832	0871	0910	0948	0987	1026	1064	1103	1141
0.3	1179	1217	1255	1293	1331	1368	1406	1443	1480	1517
0.4	1554	1591	1628	1664	1700	1736	1772	1808	1844	1879
0.5	1915	1950	1985	2019	2054	2088	2123	2157	2190	2224
0.6	2257	2291	2324	2357	2389	2422	2454	2486	2518	2549
0.7	2580	2612	2642	2673	2704	2734	2764	2794	2823	2852
0.8	2881	2910	2939	2967	2995	3023	3051	3078	3106	3133
0.9	3159	3186	3212	3238	3264	3289	3315	3340	3365	3389
1.0	3413	3438	3461	3485	3508	3531	3554	3577	3599	3621
1.1	3643	3665	3686	3718	3729	3749	3770	3790	3810	3830
1.2	3849	3869	3888	3907	3925	3944	3962	3980	3997	4015
1.3	4032	4049	4066	4083	4099	4115	4131	4147	4162	4177
1.4	4192	4207	4222	4236	4251	4265	4279	4292	4306	4319
1.5	4332	4345	4357	4370	4382	4394	4406	4418	4430	4441
1.6	4452	4463	4474	4485	4495	4505	4515	4525	4535	4545
1.7	4554	4564	4573	4582	4591	4599	4608	4616	4625	4633
1.8	4641	4649	4656	4664	4671	4678	4686	4693	4699	4706
1.9	4713	4719	4726	4732	4738	4744	4750	4758	4762	4767
2.0	4773	4778	4783	4788	4793	4798	4803	4808	4812	4817
2.1	4821	4826	4830	4834	4838	4842	4846	4850	4854	4857
2.2	4861	4865	4868	4871	4875	4878	4881	4884	4887	4890
2.3	4893	4896	4898	4901	4904	4906	4909	4911	4913	4916
2.4	4918	4920	4922	4925	4927	4929	4931	4932	4934	4936
2.5	4938	4940	4941	4943	4945	4946	4948	4949	4951	4952
2.6	4953	4955	4956	4957	4959	4960	4961	4962	4963	4964
2.7	4965	4966	4967	4968	4969	4970	4971	4972	4973	4974
2.8	4974	4975	4976	4977	4977	4978	4979	4980	4980	4981
2.9	4981	4982	4983	4984	4984	4984	4985	4985	4986	4986
3.0	4986.5	4987	4987	4988	4988	4988	4989	4989	4989	4990
3.1	4990.0	4991	4991	4991	4992	4992	4992	4992	4993	4993
3.2	4993.129									
3.3	4995.166									
3.4	4996.631									
3.5	4997.674									
3.6	4998.409									
3.7	4998.922									
3.8	4999.277									
3.9	4999.519									
4.0	4999.683									
4.5	4999.966									
5.0	4999.997133									

Source: Harold O. Rugg: *Statistical Methods Applied to Education*, pp. 889–90. Boston: Houghton Mifflin Company. Copyright © 1917, renewed 1945.

STEP 5

As a proportion, .0559 of the cases will fall above $100,000. Or another way of expressing the same thing is to say that 5.6% of the cases will fall above $100,000 (multiply the proportion .0559 by 100 to get 5.6%).

Suppose we wish to determine the proportion of cases that will fall between $40,000 and $70,000, given the same population mean and standard deviation. We should follow procedures similar to those used in the case above. This time, however, the diagram will show a shaded area between two points on either side of the mean. Two Z scores will need to be computed, the values looked up in Table 8.17, and the proportions between the mean and each cut-point will need to be determined, then added together to get the final answer. The computations may be done as follows:

STEP 1

Proportion between the mean and $70,000:

$$Z = \frac{X - \overline{X}}{sd}$$

$$Z = \frac{70,000 - 65,000}{22,000}$$

$$Z = .23$$

Proportion of normal curve included in Z score of .23 = .0910

STEP 2

Proportion between $40,000 and the mean:

$$Z = \frac{X - \overline{X}}{sd}$$

$$Z = \frac{40,000 - 65,000}{22,000}$$

$$Z = -1.14$$

Proportion of normal curve included in Z score of −1.14 = .3729

STEP 3

Adding the proportions together:

$$.3729 + .0910 = .4639$$

The computation indicates that just under one-half of all the cases, 46.4%, fall between the incomes of $40,000 and $70,000. The proportion between the mean and the respective Z scores is shown in Figure 8.3. In this case, the values are added together to determine the proportion of cases that fall between $40,000 and $70,000.

There are other types of normal curve problems that can be solved. Just keep in mind the above examples, draw a diagram shading in the area you need to determine, and remember that each side of the normal curve contains one-half, or 0.5, of the cases. With these things in mind, it should be possible to solve most normal curve problems.

7. OTHER DISTRIBUTIONS

Not all variables will be normally distributed. If, for example, we were to plot the weights of freshman students, we would almost certainly find that the result would

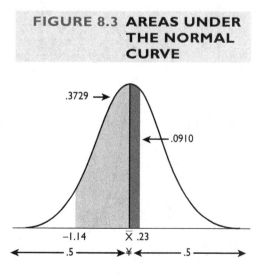

FIGURE 8.3 AREAS UNDER THE NORMAL CURVE

be a **bi-modal distribution**. The reason for this is that female students will have lower average weights than the males. Essentially, we would end up combining two normally distributed plots, one for women and one for men, into one that would have two peaks and considerable overlap between the male and female weights. (See Figure 8.4.)

If a set of values has little variability—a small standard deviation relative to the magnitude of the values—then the distribution will be peaked, and it is said to be **leptokurtic**; on the other hand, if the distribution has a great deal of variability, the distribution curve will tend to be flat and

wide and is called a **platykurtic distribution**. The recognition that distributions can be quite different from one another will be important when the time comes to learn about sampling (Chapter 15) and tests of significance (Chapter 9).

As a review of this first section, before we go on to consider how we analyze relationships between variables, let us examine Table 8.18. Before we begin to analyze any variable, we need to appreciate its level of measurement so that appropriate analyses may be made. The level of measurement attained determines the best ways of summarizing a variable. Note the following points in Table 8.18.

FIGURE 8.4 OTHER DISTRIBUTIONS

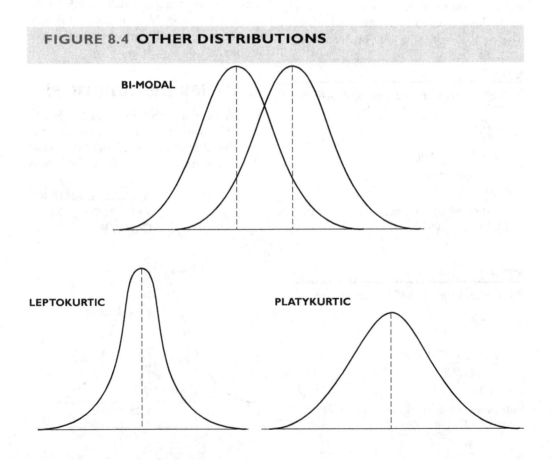

BI-MODAL

LEPTOKURTIC

PLATYKURTIC

TABLE 8.18 LEVELS OF MEASUREMENT AND STATISTICS RELATED TO EXAMINING INDIVIDUAL VARIABLES

DESCRIPTIVE STATISTIC	LEVEL OF MEASUREMENT		
	NOMINAL	ORDINAL	RATIO
Central tendency	Mode	Median	Mean
Dispersion		Range	Standard deviation variance
SPSS	NOMINAL	ORDINAL	RATIO
Commands[1]	FREQUENCIES	FREQUENCIES	DESCRIPTIVES
Options	MODE	RANGE MEDIAN	ALL

[1]See Appendix A for details in running SPSS.

- To provide a measure of central tendency, use the mean (ratio measurement), median (ordinal measurement), or the mode (nominal measurement).

- A frequency distribution is used to reflect dispersion with nominal variables; the range is used as a measure of dispersion with ordinal variables; the standard deviation and variance are used to reflect dispersion of ratio level variables.

> *To perform this analysis in SPSS use the DESCRIPTIVES and/or the FREQUENCIES procedures; see Appendix A for details.*

C. DESCRIBING RELATIONSHIPS AMONG VARIABLES

Researchers are concerned with describing the relationships among variables. In dealing with two-variable relationships, one of the variables will be treated as a dependent variable and the other as an independent variable. Recall that the dependent variable is the effect, the independent variable the cause. If a control variable is used, it will either be an intervening, source of spuriousness, or conditional variable.

This section of the chapter will describe some of the major procedures used to examine relationships among variables. Three basic steps must be taken to begin analyzing any relationship:

1. Decide which variable is to be treated as the dependent variable and which as the independent variable.

2. Decide on the appropriate procedure for examining the relationship.

3. Perform the analysis.

Since the researcher typically is trying to understand what causes variations in a dependent variable, common sense alone can generally determine which variable should be designated as the dependent variable. However, there will be cases where it is not obvious. In such cases, try to decide which variable occurs last in a temporal sequence. It is entirely possible that the two variables mutually influence one another. If this is the case, one will nonetheless have to be designated as the "dependent" variable.

Having decided which variable is to be treated as the dependent variable, one must next identify the level of measurement of each of the variables. Now, using the information provided on the inside front cover of this book, identify which procedure would be most appropriate for the analysis. Let us explore each of the procedures.

1. CONTINGENCY TABLES: CROSSTABS

A **contingency table** presents information so that the relationship between a nominal-level dependent variable can be related to an independent variable. Table 8.19 presents findings on the relationship between the educational plans and the size of the home community for 360 high school students. We will examine this table in detail as it typifies the contingency table.

A contingency table cross-classifies cases on two or more variables. In this example, the data are first sorted into categories representing community size; next, each of these categories is sorted into whether the person does, or does not, plan to attend university. This sorting allows us

to see if those from rural areas are more likely to have university plans than their urban counterparts.

Let us now examine some of the rules for constructing and interpreting cross-tabulation tables.

RULE 8.1 IN TABLE TITLES, NAME THE DEPENDENT VARIABLE FIRST.

Tables must be numbered and be given a title. In providing a title for a table, the dependent variable is named first, followed by the independent variable, followed by any control variables.

RULE 8.2 PLACE DEPENDENT VARIABLE ON VERTICAL PLANE.

Label the categories of the dependent variable and arrange these categories on the left side of the table. If the categories involve some cut-points, these should be specified. (For example, for income, the first two categories might be "Under $5,000" and "$5,000 to $19,999.")

RULE 8.3 PLACE INDEPENDENT VARIABLE ON HORIZONTAL PLANE.

Label the categories of the independent variable and arrange them across the top of the table. Again, if there are cut-points, be careful to specify these.

TABLE 8.19 PLANS TO ATTEND UNIVERSITY BY SIZE OF HOME COMMUNITY

UNIVERSITY PLANS?	RURAL		TOWN UP TO 5,000		TOWN OVER 5,000		TOTAL	
	N	%	N	%	N	%	N	%
Plans	69	52.3	44	48.9	102	73.9	215	59.7
No plans	63	47.7	46	51.1	36	26.1	145	40.3
TOTAL	132	100.0	90	100.0	138	100.0	360	100.0

If a test of significance is appropriate for the table, the values for the raw Chi-Square value (which will be introduced in Chapter 9), the degrees of freedom, whether the test is one- or two-tailed, and the probability level should be indicated.

RULE 8.4 USE VARIABLE LABELS THAT ARE CLEAR.

Avoid the use of computer variable labels that have been designed to meet the space requirements of the statistical program. For example, FAED may have been used to refer to the variable, father's education. Use clear, easily understood labels, such as "Father's Education."

RULE 8.5 RUN PERCENTAGES TOWARD THE INDEPENDENT VARIABLE.

Percentages should be computed so that each column will total 100%. A percentage is computed by dividing the column total into the cell frequency. In the first cell, for example, the computation involves:

$$\text{Cell percentage} = \frac{\text{Cell total}}{\text{Column total}} \times 100$$

$$\text{Cell percentage} = \frac{69}{132} \times 100 = 52.3$$

RULE 8.6 REPORT PERCENTAGES TO ONE DECIMAL POINT.

Percentages should be reported to one significant decimal point. If the total is 99.9 or 100.1%, report it as such.

RULE 8.7 REPORT STATISTICAL TEST RESULTS BELOW TABLE.

Any special information and the results of statistical tests should be reported below the line under the table. (Tests of significance are discussed in Chapter 9.) The preferred method of presenting the probability or significance level is to report the exact value, such as $p = .0037$.

RULE 8.8 INTERPRET THE TABLE BY COMPARING CATEGORIES OF THE INDEPENDENT VARIABLE.

Since we are attempting to assess the impact of the independent variable on the dependent variable (size of community on educational plans), we are interested in the percentage of positive planners for each category of the independent variable. "While about one-half of the rural and small-town students (52.3% and 48.9%, respectively) plan on attending university, some 73.9% of those from communities over 5,000 have such plans." In short, compare percentages in each column. Usually it will be sufficient to use one row (in this case, just the row for those planning on attending university).

RULE 8.9 MINIMIZE CATEGORIES IN CONTROL TABLES.

When control variables are used, it is necessary to minimize the number of categories in the independent and in the control variables. Generally, there should be no more than two or three categories within these variables. There are two major reasons for this limitation: first, the number of cases in each cell will become too small if there are many categories in either the independent or the control variable; second, the interpretation of the table is very difficult if simplicity is not maintained. Chapter 17 discusses interpretations of three-variable contingency tables.

Often it will be necessary to regroup data (code into fewer categories) before contingency tables are produced. This recoding may involve both the independent and the dependent variable. Indeed, some researchers will regroup the scores in a dependent variable measured at the ratio level and do a contingency table analysis. And while researchers generally favour using correlational or analysis of variance techniques (which makes more complete use of information that may be masked when variables are recoded), there are situations when researchers favour proceeding with contingency table analysis with a ratio level dependent variable. This will be done in the following circumstances:

- When the other analyses presented use contingency tables and the researcher does not wish to introduce into the research report a different analytical tool for presenting one or two relationships.

- When a researcher wishes to make comparisons with published reports that have reported the relationships in the form of contingency tables.

A. LAMBDA

Researchers are interested in how closely two variables are related. When analyzing a relation with a nominal dependent variable, a simple measure is **Lambda**. This statistic measures the **proportionate reduction in error** that occurs in estimating a dependent variable, given knowledge of the independent variable. If two variables are strongly associated, then errors in predicting variations in the dependent variable will be considerably reduced if information on the independent variable is taken into account.

The following example shows how Lambda is calculated. Suppose we wish to measure the strength of the association between gender and the ability to become pregnant. Table 8.20 reports the result of the appropriate medical examinations on 140 individuals.

TABLE 8.20 NUMBER OF CASES IN WHICH PREGNANCY IS POSSIBLE

ABLE TO BECOME PREGNANT	TOTAL NUMBER OF CASES
Yes	74
No	66
TOTAL	140

i. Guessing Who Can Become Pregnant

If we were asked to guess whether a person could become pregnant, our best strategy would be to guess the category with the most cases. Each time a case is presented, our best guess is to say "Yes, can get pregnant." (There are more in the sample who can become pregnant than those who cannot become pregnant.) If we went through all the cases, guessing "yes" each time, we would be right 74 times and in error 66 times.

Table 8.21 supplements the material contained in Table 8.20 by adding information on gender. With this additional information, would we be able to make fewer errors?

This time, instead of using the "Total" column and always guessing "yes," we will use the gender information as a basis for our guess: if the case considered is male, we will guess "no, cannot become pregnant." If we do this, we will make 0 errors; if the case is female we will always guess "yes." By following this procedure we will make a total of 6 errors—the cases of females who are not able to conceive. Given the additional information on gender, we will now only make a total of 6 errors (0 + 6 = 6) in estimating whether a respondent could become pregnant.

ii. Proportionate Reduction in Error

Lambda is based on how much error reduction occurs with the additional information provided by the independent variable (gender). Recall that we made 66 errors when we did not have the information on gender. Taking into account the information on gender, we make 6 errors— 60 fewer than we made without the gender information.

TABLE 8.21 RELATION BETWEEN ABILITY TO BECOME PREGNANT AND GENDER

ABLE TO BECOME PREGNANT?	GENDER MALE NUMBER CASES	FEMALE NUMBER CASES	TOTAL NUMBER CASES
Yes	0	74	74
No	60	6	66
TOTAL	60	80	140

$$\text{Lambda} = \frac{\text{Errors not knowing gender} - \text{Errors knowing gender}}{\text{Errors not knowing gender}}$$

$$\text{Lambda} = \frac{66 - 6}{66}$$

$$\text{Lambda} = .909$$

In this case we have reduced the errors in our estimate by 0.909 (proportion) or 90.9%. Lambda varies from 0 to 1. The higher the value of Lambda, the more closely two variables are associated. A high value on Lambda indicates that knowing the additional information about the independent variable (in our example, gender) greatly reduces the number of errors one would make in guessing the value of the dependent variable (in our example, the ability to become pregnant). A value close to zero would indicate that the additional knowledge of the independent variable leads to a slight proportionate reduction in error. In most cases, the reduction in error will not be as dramatic as that found in the illustration used above.

2. COMPARING MEANS: MEANS

When one has a ratio level dependent variable and either a nominal or an ordinal independent variable, then it is appropriate to compute the mean values of the dependent variable for each category of the independent variable. Table 8.22 presents data that would be appropriate for this kind of analysis. Note that the dependent variable (income) is measured at the ratio level, while the independent variable (gender) is nominal.

A. THE MEANS PROCEDURE (SPSS)

The MEANS procedures in SPSS (see Appendix A) require that you move the

TABLE 8.22 MEAN INCOME BY GENDER

GENDER	MEAN INCOME	STANDARD DEVIATION	NUMBER OF CASES
Male	$37,052	12,061	142
Female	$34,706	10,474	37
COMBINED MEAN	$36,567	11,642	179

If a test of significance is appropriate for the table, the values for the t-test or F-test value, the degrees of freedom, whether the test is one- or two-tailed, and the probability level should be indicated.

dependent variable to the top window (marked dependent variable) while the independent variable is moved to the lower pane. Once you click OK, the program will compute the mean value of the dependent variable for each category of the independent variable. In cases in which there are many categories in the independent variable, these will have to be regrouped into two or three categories before the analysis is run (RECODE procedure). The number of categories into which we arrange the variables will depend on the following criteria:

(i)   A reasonable number of cases will appear in each category (often we try to have roughly equal numbers in the various categories).

(ii) The categories used must make theoretical sense (we have to exercise caution to ensure that the categories remain as coherent as possible: thus, if we were recoding religious affiliation from eight categories to three, we would perhaps want to do the grouping so as to reflect the degree to which the religious categories we create either reflect or reject mainstream societal values).

In interpreting the outcome of an analysis, the mean values should be compared. In Table 8.22, for example, the average incomes of the males are compared to those of the females.

3. CORRELATIONAL ANALYSIS: CORRELATION

Correlation analysis is a procedure for measuring how closely two ratio level variables co-vary together. Once the fundamentals of this family of statistical techniques are understood, the beginning researcher is in a position to grasp such procedures as partial correlations, multiple correlations, multiple regression, factor analysis, path analysis, and canonical correlations.

A major advantage of using correlational techniques is that many variables can be analyzed simultaneously without running out of cases. Multivariate (many variable) analysis, whose computations have been made easier through the use of computers, relies heavily on correlational techniques. But the cost of utilizing these powerful statistical tools is that more attention must be paid to measurement. Correlational techniques assume measurement at the ratio level. While this assumption may be relaxed, the cost of doing so is that the strength of the relationships among variables will tend to be underestimated. (See Chapter 13 on this point.)

Given the importance of correlational techniques, it is crucial that the beginning researcher understands the fundamentals of these procedures. Once understood, the more sophisticated procedures are extensions of the simple ones.

We have two basic concerns:

1.   What is the equation that describes the relation between the variables?

2.   What is the strength of the relation between the two?

An attempt will be made to show how each can be visually estimated; in addition, a simple, intuitively obvious approach to each computation will be presented in Boxes 8.2 (p. 241) and 8.3 (p. 246).

A. THE LINEAR EQUATION: A VISUAL ESTIMATION PROCEDURE

Our first concern will be to determine the equation that describes the relation between two variables. The equation is:

$$Y = a + bX$$

The components of the equation are Y, the dependent variable (starting salary to the nearest $10,000), and X, the independent variable (years of post-secondary education); *a* is a constant that identifies the point at which the regression line crosses the Y axis; *b* refers to the slope of the regression line that describes the relation between the variables. The terms "Y axis" and "regression line" are discussed below.

For purposes of illustration we will use the data shown in Table 8.24.

STEP 1

The first step in visually estimating the equation that describes the relation between the variables would be to plot the relation on graph paper. To have fairly accurate estimates, it is necessary to plot carefully and to ensure that units of measurement of the same size are used on both dimensions of the graph. Figure 8.5 shows what such a graph would look like. Note that the dependent variable (Y) is plotted on the vertical axis, and the independent variable (X) on the horizontal axis.

STEP 2

Insert a straight **regression line** such that the vertical deviations of the points above the line are equal to the vertical deviations below the line. There need not be the same number of points above and below the line, nor need any of the points necessarily fall right on the line. The

TABLE 8.24 **SAMPLE DATA SET**	
X	Y
2	3
3	4
5	4
7	6
8	8

regression line offers the best linear description of the relation between the two variables.

From the regression line one can estimate how much one has to change the independent variable in order to produce a unit of change in the dependent variable. The following is a hint to locate where the regression line should be drawn. Turn a ruler on its edge; then move the ruler to achieve both minimal deviations from it and equal deviations on both sides of the ruler. (See Figure 8.6.)

STEP 3

Observe where the regression line crosses the Y axis; this point represents the constant, or the *a* value, in the regression equation. Note that on Figure 8.6 we have estimated that it crosses the Y axis at 1.33.

STEP 4

Draw a line parallel to the X axis and one parallel to the Y axis to form a right-angled

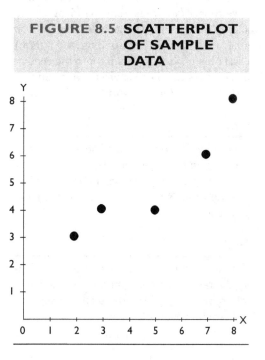

FIGURE 8.5 SCATTERPLOT OF SAMPLE DATA

FIGURE 8.6 INSERTING THE REGRESSION LINE

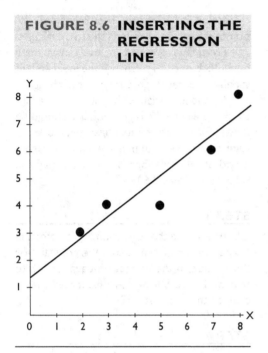

In our illustration the values would be as follows:

$$Y = 1.33 + 0.79(X)$$

The above formula is our *visually estimated equation* of the relation between the two variables. Box 8.2 presents a calculation of the actual equation. After the calculations have been made we can compare the results to those we got using the visual estimation procedure.

Note that we have come fairly close to the computed figures. In a research project we would have the computer generate the *a* and the *b* values using the REGRESSION procedure.

> *To perform this analysis using SPSS see the REGRESSION procedure in Appendix A.*

Estimating equations is a good exercise to become familiar with the different elements involved in **regression analysis**.

triangle with the regression line, similar to that shown in Figure 8.7 (make the triangle fairly large to facilitate measurement). Measure the lines in millimetres. (In Figure 8.7, the vertical measures 72 mm, the horizontal 91 mm.) Divide the horizontal distance into the vertical distance; this computation will provide our estimated *b* value. (In our figure, 72 ÷ 91 = 0.79.)

STEP 5

If the slope of the regression line is such that it is lower on the right-hand side, the *b* coefficient is negative, meaning the more X, the less Y. If the slope is negative, use a minus sign in your equation.

STEP 6

The visual estimation of the equation describing the relation between the variables is determined by simply adding the *a* and *b* values to the general equation:

$$Y = a + bX$$

FIGURE 8.7 ESTIMATING THE EQUATION

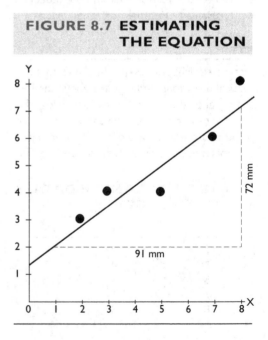

In some cases, the *a* value will turn out to be negative; this simply means that the regression line crosses the Y axis below the X axis. It should be noted as well that, as the *b* value increases, the regression line is steeper. Thus, smaller increments in the X variable lead to increments in the Y variable. A negative value on the *b* indicates a negative slope, a situation in which the data are indicating a relationship where the greater X, the less Y.

The beginning researcher should recognize that, with a linear equation, it is possible to *predict* the value of a dependent variable given a value of the independent variable. When social scientists speak of **prediction** this is usually the sense in which they are using the term. Figure 8.8

BOX 8.2   CALCULATING A LINEAR EQUATION

The Linear Equation: A Simple Computational Procedure

Having estimated the equation describing the relation between the variables, let us now compute the actual equation. The following table presents the data and the computations necessary to determine the equation. The following steps are required:

Step 1 Determine the mean value for the X and Y variables. This can be done by summing the values and dividing by the number of cases.

Step 2 Subtract each value of X from the mean of X.

Step 3 Square the values determined in the previous step.

Step 4 Subtract each value of Y from the mean of Y.

Step 5 Multiply the value determined in Step 2 by those values determined in Step 4.

Step 6 Sum all columns.

Step 7 To determine the *b* value: divide the column total determined in Step 5 by the column total in Step 3. As in:

$$b = \frac{\Sigma\,(X - \overline{X})(Y - \overline{Y})}{\Sigma\,(X - \overline{X})^2}$$
$$b = 19 \div 26$$
$$b = .73$$

Step 8 Inspect the regression line: if it slopes upward (highest on the right side) the sign of the *b* will be positive (+); if it slopes downward (lowest on the right side), then the *b* value will be negative (–).

Step 9 To determine the *a* value apply the formula:

$$a = \overline{Y} - b\overline{X}$$
$$a = 5 - .73(5)$$
$$a = 1.35$$

Step 10 The values can now be applied and the final equation determined. The calculated equation is:

$$Y = 1.35 + .73X$$

Recall that the visual estimation of the formula was:

$$Y = 1.33 + .79X$$

cont'd

Computing a Linear Equation

STEP 1		STEP 2	STEP 3	STEP 4	STEP 5
X	Y	$X - \overline{X}$	$(X - \overline{X})^2$	$Y - \overline{Y}$	$(X - \overline{X})(Y - \overline{Y})$
2	3	−3	9	−2	6
3	4	−2	4	−1	2
5	4	0	0	−1	0
7	6	2	4	1	2
8	8	3	9	3	9
25	25	0	26	0	19

$\overline{X} = 5$
$\overline{Y} = 5$

General equation: $Y = a + b(X)$ where:

$$b = \frac{\sum (X - \overline{X})(Y - \overline{Y})}{\sum (X - \overline{X})^2} = \frac{19}{26} = .73$$

$a = \overline{Y} - b\overline{X}$
$a = 5 - .73(5)$
$a = 1.35$
Hence, $Y = 1.35 + .73(X)$

NOTE: The sign of the *b* coefficient is determined by inspection. If the slope of the regression line is positive (highest on the right side), then the *b* coefficient is positive (+); if it is negative (lowest on the right side), then the *b* coefficient is negative.

on p. 243 shows how one could visually estimate the predicted value of Y (income), given a value of X (years of post-secondary education). The procedure simply involves locating the X value on the X axis, moving vertically to the regression line, then moving horizontally to the Y axis. The point at which the Y axis is intersected represents the visual estimate of the Y variable.

A predicted value is computed using an equation where values of the independent variable(s) are plugged into the equation. Suppose, for example, that we attempted to predict the values of Y given X values of 1, 4, and 6. To solve the problem we would simply use the equation computed above and then determine the predicted values of Y, as in:

Computed equation: $Y = 1.35 + .73(X)$

	Y_p
With X value of 1: $Y = 1.35 + .73(1) = 2.08$	
With X value of 4: $Y = 1.35 + .73(4) = 4.27$	
With X value of 6: $Y = 1.35 + .73(6) = 5.73$	

We use the same procedures in situations in which there are multiple independent variables determining the predicted values of a dependent variable, except that there are more values to be plugged into the equation.

FIGURE 8.8 VISUALLY ESTIMATING Y FROM X

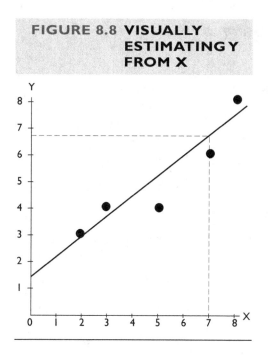

those in which a few deviant cases can radically shift the slope of the regression line. The change of two points in the two plots shifts the sign of the correlation from a positive one (Plot 7) to a negative one (Plot 8).

One reason that it is important to plot out relationships is to permit a visual inspection of the results. If there are extreme values, or if the plot indicates a non-linear relationship, then a linear correlation analysis would be inappropriate.

The **correlation coefficient (r)** is a measure of the strength of association between two variables. The correlation may vary from +1 to -1. Perfect correlations are rare, except when a variable is correlated with itself; hence, almost all of the correlations will be represented by values preceded by a decimal point, as in .98, .37, or –.56. Negative correlations mean that there is a negative slope in the relation.

Let us now develop an intuitively simple way of estimating the strength of the relation between two variables. Examine the first four plots shown in Figure 8.9. Note that the closer the plotted points are to the regression line, the higher the correlation. Conversely, the more points diverge from the regression line, the lower the correlation. In estimating the correlation coefficient, there are two kinds of variability that we have to be concerned with:

1. variations around the regression line; and

2. variations around the mean of Y.

We can determine the ratio between these two types of variability. In essence, the correlation coefficient (r) reflects this ratio so that the higher the ratio, the higher the correlation. Indeed, we can represent the relation as follows:

$$r^2 = 1 - \frac{\text{Variations around regression}}{\text{Variations around mean of Y}}$$

B. CORRELATION COEFFICIENT: A VISUAL ESTIMATION PROCEDURE

In learning to estimate a correlation visually, it is important to develop some sense of what correlations of different magnitude look like. Figure 8.9 presents graphs of eight relationships. In the first four, the correlation coefficients vary from .99 to .36. Note that if the correlation dropped below the .36 level, it would become difficult to determine where the regression line should be drawn. At the other end of the continuum, note that correlations drop fairly slowly as the scatter around the regression line increases. Plot 5 shows a **curvilinear relationship** where the plot goes in one direction and then switches to another one. Plot 6 shows a case where the linear correlation is zero, but where there is a fairly strong association between the variables. Plots 7 and 8 show situations to be wary of—namely,

FIGURE 8.9 EIGHT LINEAR CORRELATIONS

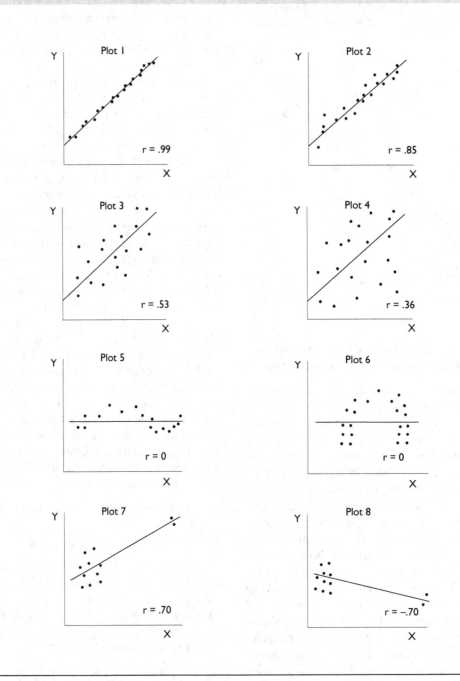

As an exercise in trying to visually estimate the strength of a correlation, the following steps can be taken:

STEP 1

Plot the data on graph paper and draw in an estimated regression line. Again, remember that the same units of measurement must be used on both dimensions of your graph.

STEP 2

Draw in a line, parallel to the X axis, that will cut through the estimated mean value of Y.

STEP 3

To estimate the deviations around the regression line, draw in an additional regression line, parallel to the original one, for the points on or above the existing regression line. (You may want to cover the points below the regression line to avoid confusion.) Now draw in yet another regression line, parallel to the other two, for those points below the original regression line. Measure and record the perpendicular distance between the two new regression lines.

STEP 4

To estimate the deviations around the mean of Y, two additional lines parallel to the mean of Y line must be drawn, the first for those points above the line, the second for those points below the line. Once again, the perpendicular distance between these new lines should be measured and recorded.

STEP 5

At this point you should have drawn a graph similar to the one shown in Figure 8.10.

To estimate the correlation simply enter the values from your graph into the following equation:

$$r^2 = 1 - \frac{\text{Variations around regression}}{\text{Variations around mean of Y}}$$

$$r^2 = 1 - \frac{8}{44}$$

$$r^2 = .82$$

$$r = .91$$

Your estimation is based on the idea that the correlation reflects the ratio of *variations around the regression line* to *variations around the mean of Y*. As the variations around the regression line become relatively smaller, the correlation rises. Conversely, as the two measures of variation approach equality, the correlation approaches zero. Although visually estimated correlations are never reported because they are not exact, the exercise is an excellent one for becoming familiar with the meaning of the correlation coefficient. If you have few cases, it is easy to hand-compute the exact correlation using the steps outlined in Box 8.3. However, with more than 15 or 20 cases you would probably want to have the computations done by a computer.

FIGURE 8.10 ESTIMATING A CORRELATION

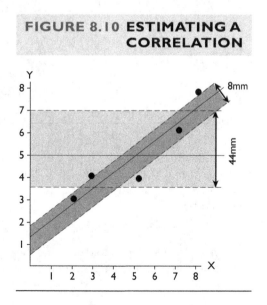

Note that the computations in Box 8.3 have led to results roughly similar to those achieved using the visual estimation procedures. (Usually the results will not be so close.) Having done a few visual estimations and a few hand calculations of correlations, you should have a good understanding of simple correlations. There are many statistical techniques that are extensions of correlational techniques. Once the basics are understood, then the drudgery of computation can be turned over to a computer.

4. PLOTTING THE DATA: GRAPH

It is a good idea to produce a scatterplot of important relationships in your study. A plot will alert you to problems such as:

- A few extreme cases, which may be influencing the correlation between the variables (see Figure 8.9: Plots 7 and 8).

- A strong relationship exists, but it is not linear, and the correlation does not reflect the true strength of the relation (see Figure 8.9: Plots 5 and 6).

BOX 8.3   CALCULATING A CORRELATION

Correlation Coefficient: A Simple Computational Procedure

The following table presents the information necessary to hand-compute a correlation using a method that parallels the estimation procedure outlined above. The steps are simple and can be quickly performed if there are only a few observations.

Computing the Correlation Coefficient

X	Y	$(Y - \overline{Y})^2$	Y_p*	$Y - Y_p$	$(Y - Y_p)^2$
2	3	4	2.81	.19	.0361
3	4	1	3.54	.46	.2116
5	4	1	5.00	−1.00	1.0000
7	6	1	6.46	− .46	.2116
8	8	9	7.19	.81	.6561
		16			$\Sigma = 2.1154$

*The Y_p value is computed by substituting each value of X into the general equation determined in Box 8.2. In the first observation the computation would be:

$$Y_p = 1.35 + .73(2) = 2.81$$

Step 1 The first step is to determine the variation around the regression line. For each observation of X, we will need to compute the predicted value for Y. To do this, we simply go to the equation determined in Box 8.2—the calculated equation (i.e., the first equation) in step ten—plug in the value for X, and solve. The first observation would be done as follows:

cont'd

$$Y_p = 1.35 + .73(X)$$
$$Y_p = 1.35 + .73(2)$$
$$Y_p = 2.81$$

The predicted values for Y are determined for each case in the manner described for the first observation.

Step 2 The second step is to compute how much each observation deviates from its "predicted" value.

$$(Y - Y_p)$$

Step 3 The third step is to square the results of the previous step. After this is completed, this column should be summed.

$$(Y - Y_p)^2$$

Step 4 The previous three steps provide us with a measure of the variations around the regression line. To get an estimate of the deviations around the mean

of Y, we need only look at the sum for the column:

$$(Y - \overline{Y})^2$$

Step 5 We are now able to plug the values into the formula:

$$r^2 = 1 - \frac{\text{Variations around regression}}{\text{Variations around mean of Y}}$$

$$r^2 = 1 - \frac{\Sigma (Y - Y_p)^2 \div N}{\Sigma (Y - \overline{Y})^2 \div N}$$

$$r^2 = 1 - \frac{.423}{3.2}$$

$$r^2 = 1 - .13$$

$$r^2 = .87$$

$$r = .93$$

Note: If the regression line is highest on the right side, the *r* value will be positive; if it is lowest on the right side of the plot, the *r* value will be negative.

- There are a lot of data points with the same value. This lack of variation may alert you to a problem in the measurement of one of the ratio variables involved in the plot.

Many computer programs can produce such plots quickly.

5. COMPUTING SPEARMAN CORRELATIONS

Sometimes researchers might wish to run a correlation on ordinal data without violating the measurement assumptions of correlation. In cases in which one or both of one's variables are ordinal, then a **Spearman correlation** is the appropriate

measure of association. The details of such computations can be checked in any elementary statistics text and will not be presented here. Think of them as being similar to the correlation procedures just discussed. (See Appendix A.)

6. COMPUTING PARTIAL CORRELATIONS: PARTIAL CORR

A **partial correlation** is a special type of correlation that can be used with ratio level variables. It measures the strength of association between two variables while simultaneously controlling for the effects of one or more additional variables. In partial correlations we adjust the values of the dependent and independent variables in order to take into account the influence of other independent variables. The advantage of partial correlations over contingency table analysis is that:

- we make use of all of the data (by not recoding variables into two or three categories as would be done in a contingency table analysis [CROSSTABS]); and

- we can work with fewer cases without running into cell-size problems as happens frequently with contingency table analysis.

Like ordinary correlations, partial correlations take on values from +1.0 through to −1.0. Partial correlations control one or more independent variables. The number of controls determines the order of the partial. A correlation with one control variable is a *first-order partial correlation*; one with two controls is a *second-order partial correlation*, and so forth. Incidentally, ordinary correlations are sometimes referred to as *zero-order correlations*, which simply means that there are no control variables in the analysis.

The strategy involved in partial correlations is that regression equations can be used to express the relation between each pair of variables in the equation. For any value of an independent variable, it is possible to predict the value of the dependent variable, while adjusting for the influence of the control variables.

The idea of residuals is also useful in understanding partial correlations. In the three-variable case, if the possible combinations X-Y, Z-Y, and X-Z are plotted, and a regression line is entered for the X-Y relation, we could argue that the deviations from the line are the result of the influence of factor Z plus that of other known, and unknown, factors. These deviations are *residuals*. They arise when we allow one variable to explain all the variation that it can in another variable; what is left unexplained (deviations from the regression line) are the residuals. By correlating residuals, we can get a measure of the amount of influence a third variable has on the first relationship (X-Y), independent of the second relationship (X-Z).

The notational convention that we use in referring to partial correlations shows the numbers of the two major variables and these are separated from the numbers of the control variables by a "." as in:

$$r_{12.3} = .56$$

In this case, we have a first-order partial reported, with a value of .56. This value represents a measure of the strength of association between variables 1 and 2, controlling for variable 3. A third-order partial simply designates three control variables, as in:

$$r_{12.345} = .28$$

Partial correlations will be used in testing causal models where the variables involved are measured at the ratio level of measurement (see Chapter 17).

Since it is easy to hand-compute a first-order partial, the formula is presented here. It can be used if the researcher has the zero-order correlation matrix.

$$r_{12.3} = \frac{r_{12} - (r_{13})(r_{23})}{\sqrt{1 - r_{13}^2}\ \sqrt{1 - r_{23}^2}}$$

D. KEY POINTS

Researchers use a variety of statistics to describe the central tendency and dispersion of a single variable. It is often necessary to standardize data so that comparisons between groups of different size can be made; thus rates and ratios are calculated along with proportions and percentages.

Many distributions can be described as *normally distributed*. This kind of distribution is bell-shaped, which means that there are fewer observations of extreme values, and more as the middle-range values are examined. A *Z* score expresses an observation's location within a normal distribution.

Relationships between variables are analyzed using contingency tables, by comparing means across categories, and by calculating correlations and regression equations.

E. KEY TERMS

Bi-modal distribution

Contingency table

Correlation analysis

Correlation coefficient (r)

Curvilinear relationship

Descriptive statistics

Inferential statistics

Lambda

Leptokurtic distribution

Mean

Measures of central tendency

Median

Mode

Nominal measurement

Normal distribution

Ordinal measurement

Partial correlation

Percentage

Platykurtic distribution

Prediction

Proportion

Proportionate reduction in error

r^2

Range

Rate

Ratio measurement

Ratios

Regression analysis

Regression line

Spearman correlation

Standard deviation

Variance

Z scores

THREE TESTS OF SIGNIFICANCE

Tests of significance are an aspect of **inferential statistics**. Inferential statistics do two basic things. First, they enable us to make judgments about the accuracy of a given sample in reflecting the characteristics of the population from which it was drawn. In other words, they allow us to "infer" facts about a population based on information provided by a sample of that population. For example, in a random sample of 3,000 men 25 to 45 years of age, 30% of the men were smokers. Inferential statistics allow us to generalize from this limited sample to the larger population and draw conclusions about the percentage of male smokers in the population based on the sample data. Given the size of the sample, we can be 95% certain that the true population mean will be 30%, plus or minus 4%. In other words we can be 95% certain that the true population mean falls between 26 and 34%.

Second, inferential statistics are used in testing hypotheses—that is, statistics to help us make decisions about which study outcomes reflect fluke differences between groups and which ones reflect true differences (those that are statistically significant). An introduction to tests of significance is the focus of this chapter.

A. WHAT DOES "STATISTICALLY SIGNIFICANT" MEAN?

Beneath most tables a number of values are reported. Almost certainly one of these will indicate whether the differences reported in the table are statistically significant. What does this mean? A **test of significance** reports the probability that an observed association or difference is the result of sampling fluctuations and not reflective of some "real" difference in the population from which the sample has been taken.

This chapter will explore three tests of **statistical significance**. Other such tests are based on similar principles and, therefore, need not be explored in detail by the beginning researcher. The three that will be presented include the Chi-Square test, the *t*-test, and the *F*-test. Since tests of significance are often misunderstood, this chapter will also review the conditions under which such tests are not appropriate.

1. RESEARCH HYPOTHESIS AND NULL HYPOTHESIS

Tests of significance are used to test hypotheses. These are set up in a "research" and in a "null" form. The **research hypothesis** (also commonly known as the *alternative hypothesis*) is simply a prediction of the relation between variables; the **null hypothesis** states that there will be no relation between the variables. The following statements illustrate research and null hypotheses:

- Research Hypothesis 1: "The greater the participation, the higher the self-esteem."

- Null Hypothesis 1: "There is no relation between levels of participation and levels of self-esteem."

- Research Hypothesis 2: "Male university faculty members earn more than their female counterparts when statistical controls take into account qualifications, achievements, and experience."

- Null Hypothesis 2: "Controlling for qualifications, achievements, and experience there is no difference in the earnings of male and female faculty members."

It is the null hypothesis that is tested—the proposition that there is no relation between the variables. The test will lead us either to accept or to reject it. If the null hypothesis is accepted, we conclude that the association or the difference may simply be the result of sampling fluctuations and may not reflect an association or difference in the population being studied. The implication is that if we accept the null hypothesis then the research hypothesis is false. If the null hypothesis is rejected, then we argue that there is an association between the variables in the population, and that this association is of a magnitude that probably has not occurred because of chance fluctuations in sampling. If the null hypothesis is rejected, then the data are examined to see if the association is in the predicted direction; if it is, then this is one piece of evidence that is consistent with the research hypothesis. (The finding may be in the opposite direction predicted, in which case the evidence is not consistent with the prediction.)

Positivist social scientists typically avoid expressions such as "proof," or "demonstrates conclusively." Instead they prefer a more tentative phrasing such as "The evidence supports the view that . . . " or "The data are consistent with the research hypothesis." The reason for the cautious wording is that scientists are well aware that future research may well disconfirm, or qualify in important ways, the findings of any research. Hence, when the results of a study lead to the rejection of a null hypothesis, this means only that there is *probably* a relationship between the variables under examination. Simply put, the possibility that the hypothesis is correct has not been ruled out. The point is that empirical scientists can never provide absolute proof of the accuracy of a research hypothesis. It is always possible that some other theory might make the same prediction. That is why the language of science is tentative. (See Box 9.1.)

When a null hypothesis is accepted, however, this is taken to mean that the predicted relationship in the research hypothesis is false. And even this conclusion must remain tentative because of the possibility

---

BOX 9.1

Terminology Conundrum: Do You "Accept" a Null Hypothesis, or Do You "Fail to Reject" a Null Hypothesis?

There appears to be some variation in usage here. The common practice among psychologists is to use the "fail to reject" terminology. And while this is probably the most accurate phrasing, it does carry with it an unfortunate, unintended implication. It conveys the idea that the researcher has somehow failed if a statistically significant association is not found.

For pedagogical reasons, I prefer the "accept the null hypothesis" terminology, since it does not carry with it the idea of failing if no significant association is found. Thus, it is easier to convince students that it is acceptable to have findings that are not statistically significant. Sociologists and political scientists appear to follow the terminological usage recommended here.

that luck or error may have played a role in the results. Nonetheless, the way the positivist proceeds is to test null hypotheses. Evidence leading to the acceptance of the null hypothesis indicates that the research hypothesis is probably in error.

Often new researchers think that they have somehow failed if they do a project and find out that they have to accept the null hypothesis. Such should not be the case. The null hypothesis should be accepted as a research finding because it may well be just as important to find out that two variables are not associated as it is to find out that they are. It might be extremely important to discover, for example, that among people under 25 years of age, there is no significant difference between Roman Catholics and Protestants in their attitude toward the use of birth control; perhaps among those over 50 there is less inclination among Roman Catholics, in comparison to Protestants, to support the use of birth control.

Tests of significance report whether an observed relationship could be the result of sample fluctuations or reflect a "real" difference in the population from which the sample has been taken.

2. THE SAMPLING DISTRIBUTION

Perhaps the best way to begin understanding tests of significance is to recognize that in drawing one sample (containing 50 individuals, for example), we are getting a unique collection of respondents who are assumed to represent the larger population from which the sample was selected. If another sample is drawn from that same population, we would have another unique collection of individuals, slightly different from the first sample. If 1,000 such samples

were drawn and the means of the same variable for each of the samples were plotted, a normal distribution curve would result, albeit a peaked, or leptokurtic, one. (See Chapter 15 for more details.)

Suppose, for example, the means of the weights of respondents are plotted. While these weights might range from 70 kg to 80 kg for the males, the majority of the samples would cluster around the true mean of 75 kg. Note that we are not plotting the weights of the respondents—we are plotting the mean weight of the respondents in *each* of the 1,000 samples drawn. The distribution is quite peaked because we are plotting the *mean weight for each sample*. To measure the dispersion of the means of these samples, we use a statistic known as the **standard error of the means**. If the standard deviation of the population was 7 kg, with repeated samples of size 50, the standard error of the means would be given by the following formula:

$$\text{Standard error of means} = \frac{\text{Sd population}}{\sqrt{N}}$$

$$\text{Standard error of means} = \frac{7}{\sqrt{50}}$$

$$\text{Standard error of means} = .99$$

When a sample is drawn, the sample mean will fall somewhere within a normal distribution curve. In doing tests of significance, we are assessing whether the results of one sample fall within the null hypothesis acceptance zone (usually 95% of the distribution) or outside this zone, in which case we will reject the null hypothesis.

Although the beginning researcher is not likely to be doing methodological research and selecting repeated samples, it is necessary to understand such distributions in order to understand sampling and related tests of significance. There are four key points that can be made about probability sampling procedures where repeated samples are taken:

1. Plotting the means of repeated samples will produce a normal distribution. Note that this distribution, however, will be more peaked than that achieved when raw data are plotted. (See Figure 9.1.)

2. The larger the sample sizes, the more peaked the distribution and the closer the means of the samples to the population mean, as shown in Figure 9.2.

3. The greater the variability in the population, the greater the variation in the samples.

4. When sample sizes are above 100, even if a variable in the population is not normally distributed, the means will be normally distributed when repeated sample means are plotted. For example, weights of a population of males and females will be bi-modal, but if we did repeated samples, the means of sample weights would be normally distributed

FIGURE 9.1 DISTRIBUTION OF RAW DATA VERSUS MEANS OF SAMPLES

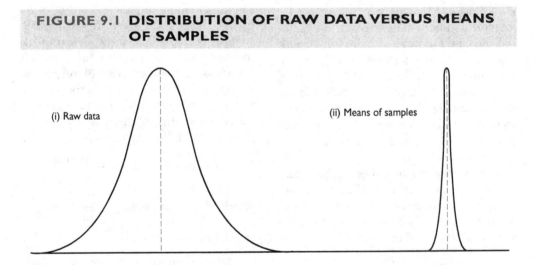

(i) Raw data

(ii) Means of samples

FIGURE 9.2 SAMPLE SIZE AND THE NORMAL DISTRIBUTION

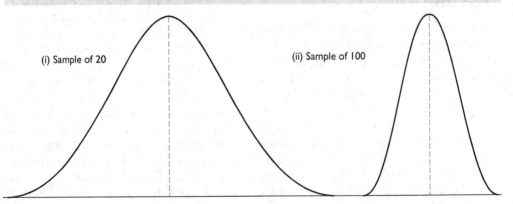

(i) Sample of 20

(ii) Sample of 100

3. ONE- AND TWO-TAILED TESTS OF SIGNIFICANCE

An understanding of tests of significance requires knowledge of the difference between one- and two-tailed tests. If the direction of the relation is predicted in the research hypothesis then the appropriate test will be one-tailed; in such cases we speak of a **one-tailed test** because we are predicting which particular tail of the normal distribution the result will fall into if the null hypothesis is to be rejected. If no prediction about the direction of the relationship is made, then a **two-tailed test** is in order. For example:

- A one-tailed research hypothesis: "Females are less approving of physical conflict than males." (Note that the prediction indicates which gender will be less approving.)

- A two-tailed research hypothesis: "There is a difference between males and females in their approval of physical conflict." (Note that there is no prediction here about which gender will be more approving.)

A test of significance measures the likelihood that an observed difference (for example the difference in "approval of conflict" scores between males and females) falls within normal sampling fluctuations and, therefore, does not reflect a real difference between the males and the females in the population. This means that if there is less than a 5% chance that the magnitude of the observed relationship is the result of sampling fluctuations, then the null hypothesis is rejected: we are concluding that there *probably* is a real difference between the male and female tolerance of conflict. If we predict which "tail" of the normal distribution curve the difference will fall into, then we have made a one-tailed prediction; if we simply predict a difference without specifying into which tail the difference will fall, then we would do a two-tailed test.

Figure 9.3 shows two normal distribution curves; the first one has the 5% rejection area split between the two tails—this would be a two-tailed test; the second one has the 5% rejection area all in one tail, indicating a one-tailed test. The same principle applies to tests at the 1% level—only now the difference between the males and the females would have to be greater in order to fall into the null-hypothesis-rejection area.

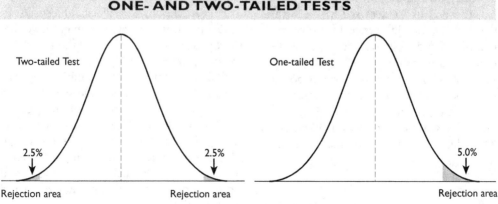

FIGURE 9.3 FIVE PERCENT PROBABILITY REJECTION AREA: ONE- AND TWO-TAILED TESTS

Two-tailed Test

2.5%
2.5%

Rejection area   Rejection area

One-tailed Test

5.0%

Rejection area

4. A SIMPLE PROBLEM: ARE THERE MORE RED BALLS IN THE CONTAINER?

Suppose that we have a huge container filled with a mixture of thousands of red and white balls. Now suppose that we draw a sample of 200 balls from the container and that we get 114 red ones and 86 white ones. Can we safely conclude that there are more red balls in the container than white ones? Perhaps if we drew another sample we would find more white than red balls. Let us introduce the Chi-Square test to try to answer this question.

B. THE CHI-SQUARE TEST OF SIGNIFICANCE (X²): CROSSTABS

The *Chi-Square test* is used primarily in contingency table analysis, where the dependent variable is a nominal one. Essentially, the Chi-Square is based on a comparison of *observed frequencies* that show up in the sample to *expected frequencies* that would occur if there were no difference between the categories in the population.

The null hypothesis we wish to test is that there is no difference in the proportion of red and white balls in the container; here we are testing to see if the sample selected could have come from a population (total contents of container in this case) containing 50% red balls and 50% white ones. The **Chi-Square test** (also known as X²) is defined by the following equation:

$$X^2 = \sum \frac{(f_0 - f_e)^2}{f_e}$$

where f_0 is the frequency observed and f_e is the frequency expected. Note that the formula reflects the amount of deviation from the expected values in relation to the magnitude of the expected values.

1. MANUALLY COMPUTING A CHI-SQUARE FOR THE RED AND WHITE BALL EXAMPLE

Let us now analyze the red and white ball example using the Chi-Square test. Normally, Chi-Squares will be computed by the computer; in the particular example under consideration, however, it is quite simple to compute the required value manually. The computations are shown in Box 9.2.

The results reported in Box 9.2 would lead us to *reject the null hypothesis* since the difference observed would occur by chance less than 5% of the time. We can then conclude that there are more red balls than white balls in the container. The risk we take in making that conclusion is that we may, by chance, just happen to have overselected red balls. A difference of that magnitude, however, would occur in fewer than 5% of the samples we draw. Another way to think about it is to say that we can be confident that we will make the correct decision 19 out of 20 times.

In attempting to understand tests of significance more clearly, one might note that if repeated samples were taken and the results plotted (say, the percentage of red balls), the plot would resemble a normal distribution curve. As sample sizes become larger, a more peaked (leptokurtic) distribution would result. Most times we draw one sample and have no way of knowing if it is a truly representative sample. Perhaps our sample is atypical—we just happened to draw one with a preponderance of red

BOX 9.2

Sample Chi-Square Computation: Red Ball and White Ball Example

COLOUR	STEP 1 f_o	STEP 2 f_e	STEP 3 $f_o - f_e$	STEP 4 $(f_o - f_e)^2$	STEP 5 $\dfrac{(f_o - f_e)^2}{f_e}$
Red	114	100	14	196	1.96
White	86	100	-14	196	1.96
				TOTAL	3.92

Chi-Square = 3.92   df (degrees of freedom) = 1 significant at the 0.05 level

Required critical value to reject the null hypothesis is 3.841 (two-tailed test, 1 degree of freedom, at .05 level); see Table 9.2 on p. 260.

Decision: Since the Chi-Square value is 3.92 and this exceeds the critical value, the null hypothesis is rejected.

The steps in the calculation are as follows:

Step 1 Create a calculation table containing the headings as shown in the above table. Enter the observations that have been made for each of the cells. The convention for naming cells is to label them by starting in the top left corner of the table, and naming them a, b, c, etc., across the table, then continuing at the beginning of the next line.

Step 2 Compute the frequency expected (f_e) for each of the cells. There are four basic techniques for doing this.

1. Determine what the expected frequency would be if the null hypothesis is correct (in the red/white ball example, the theoretical expectation would be that one-half would be red, the other half, white).

2. In a contingency table, a cell's expected frequency can be determined by multiplying the row marginal by the column marginal and dividing this result by the total number of cases.

3. Alternatively, in a contingency table, the expected frequency would have the same number corresponding to the percentage distribution of the margin column.

4. Having computed the expected frequency in some columns, it is possible to compute the remaining ones by subtraction, knowing that the margin totals for expected and observed frequencies must be identical.

Step 3 Subtract the expected from the frequency observed (f_o) for each of the cells.

Step 4 Square the values determined in Step 3.

Step 5 Divide the result of Step 4 by the frequency expected.

cont'd

Step 6 Sum the column of values determined in Step 5. This value is the raw Chi-Square.

Step 7 Determine the degrees of freedom. Count the number of cells where the expected frequencies would have to be computed before the expected frequencies in the remaining cells could be determined by subtraction, given that the total expected must equal the total observed. In the red ball/white ball example, once we determine that we would expect 100 red balls (50% of all balls selected is implied by the null hypothesis), and since there were 200 balls selected in all, then 100 would be expected to be white.

In contingency tables with two or more categories in both the dependent and independent variables, the degrees of freedom can be determined by the following formula:

$$\text{Degrees of freedom} = (\# \text{ rows} - 1) \times (\# \text{ columns} - 1)$$

Step 8 Decide the "level" of risk you wish to take; usually you will choose either the .01 or .05 level. This means that you are willing to accept that a difference is statistically significant with a 1% or 5% chance of being wrong.

Step 9 Determine whether you are doing a one- or two-tailed test of significance. Remember that if the direction of the relation is predicted then the appropriate test will be one-tailed; we are predicting which particular tail of the normal distribution the result will fall into if the null hypothesis is to be rejected. If no prediction about the direction of the relationship is made, then a two-tailed test is required.

Step 10 Look up the raw Chi-Square value found in Table 9.2 on p. 260 to determine if the difference between the expected and the observed frequencies is statistically significant. But note:

- For a two-tailed test, at the .05 level, use the value as indicated in Table 9.2. (For example, with 1 degree of freedom, the value must exceed 3.84 to be statistically significant.)

- For a one-tailed test, at the .05 level, use the value printed under the probability level .05 (with 1 degree of freedom, the value must exceed 2.71 to be regarded as statistically significant).

Step 11 Below the table report the raw Chi-Square value, degrees of freedom (df), and whether the difference observed is statistically significant and at what level (generally .05 or .01).

Step 12 If the null hypothesis is rejected, the data must then be inspected to see if the data are consistent with the research hypothesis. (It is possible, of course, that the difference could be statistically significant but in the opposite direction predicted by the research hypothesis.) If the difference is not statistically significant then the null hypothesis is accepted.

balls and we might, therefore, wrongly conclude that there are more red balls in the container. But since we cannot easily observe all the cases, we simply take the chance of being wrong. We can reduce that risk by changing the probability level at which we will reject the null hypothesis from 0.05 to 0.01 or even to 0.001. That would reduce, but not eliminate, the chance of coming to an incorrect conclusion. If we reject a null hypothesis when it should be accepted, we have made what is referred to as a **Type I error**. If we accept a null hypothesis that should be rejected, we have made a **Type II error**. The probability of making a Type I error is referred to as the significance level of the test.

2. A ONE-SAMPLE CHI-SQUARE TEST: A SOCIAL SCIENCE EXAMPLE

There are situations in which one wishes to compare a cohort of respondents to some known distribution. Table 9.1 reports the family incomes of university students along with the income distribution of all families in the vicinity of the university.

The research hypothesis tested in Table 9.1 is that "university students come from the wealthier families in the region." Note that this hypothesis predicts which group (the wealthy as opposed to the non-wealthy) would be overrepresented, and we therefore use a one-tailed test. The null form of this hypothesis would be that there is no difference between the income distribution of university students' families and that of other families in the region served by the university. Box 9.3 presents the steps in computing the Chi-Square value for this example.

TABLE 9.1 SAMPLE STUDENT AND GENERAL POPULATION FAMILY INCOMES

INCOME	NO. OF STUDENTS (CELL)	% OF SAMPLE	% OF GENERAL POPULATION
Over $100,000	30 (a)	15.0	7.8
$40,000 to $99,999	160 (b)	80.0	68.9
Under $40,000	10 (c)	5.0	23.3
TOTAL	200	100.0	100.0

BOX 9.3

*Computing Chi-Square for Student Family Income Data**

INCOME CATEGORY	f_o	f_e	$f_o - f_e$	$(f_o - f_e)^2$	$\dfrac{(f_o - f_e)^2}{f_e}$
Over $100,000	30	15.6*	14.4	207.36	13.29
$40,000 to $99,999	160	137.8	22.2	492.84	3.57
Under $40,000	10	46.6	−36.6	1,339.56	28.75
TOTALS	200	200			45.61

cont'd

*The expected frequencies are computed on the presumption that if there is no difference between the general population and the families of university students, then the income distribution would have similar proportions in the various categories. In the first cell, where there were 30 students, we would have expected 15.6: (200.078 = 15.6). In the general population 7.8% of the families had incomes above $100,000.

- Degrees of freedom = 2: two cells would have to be computed before

the final one could be calculated by subtraction as in:

$$f_e \text{ cell } c = (200 - (30 + 160))$$

- Required critical value to reject the null hypothesis is 4.605 (one-tailed test, 2 degrees of freedom, at the.05 level); see Table 9.2.

- Decision: Since the Chi-Square value is 45.61 and this exceeds the critical value, the null hypothesis is rejected.

The critical value that must be exceeded in order to reject the null hypothesis is 4.605 (see Table 9.2: note that we look up the value for 2 *degrees of freedom*, under the .05 (one-tailed) column, since we are predicting the direction of the relationship). Since the observed X^2 value is 45.61, we reject the null hypothesis and, after inspecting the data, conclude that university students come from the wealthier families in the region.

3. A TYPICAL CHI-SQUARE ILLUSTRATION

Box 9.4 presents a two-variable contingency table showing the relationship between frequency of drug use by gender. Beneath the table, the procedures are presented for the computation of the Chi-Square. But, before proceeding to Box 9.4, note especially the calculations following on the next page.

TABLE 9.2 CRITICAL VALUES FOR THE CHI-SQUARE DISTRIBUTION, ONE- AND TWO-TAILED TESTS

DEGREES OF FREEDOM	.05 LEVEL OF SIGNIFICANCE		.01 LEVEL OF SIGNIFICANCE	
	ONE-TAILED	TWO-TAILED	ONE-TAILED	TWO-TAILED
1	2.71	3.84	5.41	6.63
2	4.61	5.99	7.82	9.21
3	6.25	7.82	9.84	11.34
4	7.78	9.49	11.67	13.28
5	9.24	11.07	13.39	15.09
6	10.64	12.59	15.03	16.81
7	12.02	14.07	16.62	18.48
8	13.36	15.51	18.17	20.09
9	14.68	16.92	19.68	21.67
10	15.99	18.31	21.16	23.21

Remember that the computed value must equal or exceed the relevant value as shown above if the null hypothesis is to be rejected. Please consult the appendix of any statistics text if you require additional degrees of freedom or other levels of significance.

BOX 9.4

Frequency of Drug Use, by Gender

FREQUENCY OF DRUG USE IN LIFETIME	MALE NO.	CELL	%	FEMALE NO.	CELL	%	TOTAL NO.	%
No experience	47	a	34.8	63	b	49.2	110	41.8
Once or twice	51	c	37.8	39	d	30.5	90	34.2
Three or more times	37	e	27.4	26	f	20.3	63	24.0
TOTALS	135		100.0	128		100.0	263	100.0

Chi-Square = 5.689   df = 2   Not significant at .05 level

The Chi-Square could be hand-computed in the following manner:

CELL	f_o	f_e	$(f_o - f_e)$	$(f_o - f_e)^2$	$\dfrac{(f_o - f_e)^2}{f_e}$
a	47	56.5	–9.5	90.25	1.597
b	63	53.5	9.5	90.25	1.687
c	51	46.2	4.8	23.06	0.499
d	39	43.8	–4.8	23.06	0.526
e	37	32.3	4.7	21.72	0.673
f	26	30.7	–4.7	21.72	0.707
					Σ 5.689

Required critical value to reject the null hypothesis is 5.991 (two-tailed test, 2 degrees of freedom, at the .05 level); see Table 9.2.

Decision: Since the Chi-Square value is 5.689 and this does not equal or exceed the critical value, the null hypothesis is accepted.

A. CALCULATING EXPECTED FREQUENCIES

There are four basic techniques for calculating expected frequencies.

1. Determine what the expected frequency would be if the null hypothesis is correct (in the red/white ball example, the theoretical expectation would be that one-half would be red, the other half, white); this technique would also be used in the example concerning the proportion of students drawn from wealthy families.

2. In a contingency table, a cell's expected frequency can be determined by multiplying the row marginal by the column marginal and dividing this result by the total number of cases; for cell *a* (males, no experience) the computation would be as follows: $(110 \times 135)/263 = 56.5$.

3. Alternatively, in a contingency table, the expected frequency would have the number corresponding to the *proportion* (percentage 100) distribution in the total margin column; for cell *a* (males, no experience) the computation would be as follows: (.418 × 135) = 56.4.

4. Having computed the expected frequency in some columns, it is possible to compute the remaining ones by subtraction, knowing that the margin totals for expected and observed frequencies must be identical. In cell *a* (males, no experience with drugs), by using either method 2 above (110 × 135)/263 = 56.5 or 3 above 135 × .418 = 56.4, it is possible to compute the expected value for cell *b* (females, no experience with drugs) by subtracting the expected frequency of cell *a* from the marginal total: 110 − 56.5 = 53.5. Rounding errors result in a slightly different answer if the other expected frequency is used: 110 − 56.4 = 53.6.

B. CALCULATING DEGREES OF FREEDOM

To determine the **degrees of freedom** in the examples used so far, several approaches can be used.

(i) One method of determining the degrees of freedom in a table is by counting the number of cells where the expected frequency would have to be computed before the remaining cells could be determined by subtraction. The total expected must equal the total observed. In the red ball/white ball example, once we determine that we would expect 100 red balls (50% of all balls selected is implied by the null hypothesis), we would also expect 100 white balls, since

200 balls were selected in all. This method of computing degrees of freedom is used when there is only one column in the table (as in the case of the red ball/white ball example or the example of the proportion of students from wealthy families).

(ii) In contingency tables with two or more categories in both the dependent and independent variables, the degrees of freedom can be determined by the following formula:

$$\text{Degrees of freedom} = (\text{number of rows} - 1) \times (\text{number of columns} - 1)$$

It should be noted that there are two degrees of freedom in Box 9.4. In determining the number of rows and columns, the marginal total column and the total row are not counted. In the table in Box 9.4 there are two degrees of freedom because:

$$\text{Degrees of freedom} = (\text{rows} - 1) \times (\text{columns} - 1)$$

$$\text{Degrees of freedom} = (3 - 1) \times (2 - 1)$$

$$\text{Degrees of freedom} = 2$$

Note that if there are "no response" categories, these are excluded from the computations.

In Box 9.4, since the critical value is not exceeded, the decision is to accept the null hypothesis. (Note, however, that had we been doing a one-tailed test, we would reject the null hypothesis.) The data indicate that there is not a statistically significant association between gender and frequency of drug use. There is a greater than 5% probability that the differences observed in drug use between the genders are the result of chance fluctuations in sampling (assuming the null hypothesis of no difference by gender in drug use in the population).

To perform this analysis using SPSS
see CROSSTABS procedure in
Appendix A.

The next two sections will introduce
tests that involve the comparison of means
between categories. Each test assumes that
the dependent variable is measured at the
ratio level. We will begin with two versions
of the *t*-test.

C. THE *T* DISTRIBUTION: *T*-TEST GROUPS, *T*-TEST PAIRS

Suppose that an experimental/control group
design has been used to measure the acqui-
sition of mathematical skills (measured at
the ratio level) and that the study involves
the comparison of 20 students, 10 taught
in the conventional manner and 10 using
a new methodology. What test would be
appropriate here? We could collapse the
mathematical scores into high and low
scores and then run a Chi-Square. But this
would not make full use of our data. In
effect, we would be throwing out all the
variability within the two grade categories.
Instead, it would make more sense to compare the means of the mathematics scores
of students exposed to the different teaching techniques. And, as we have a small
sample, a *t*-test would do what we want.

The *t*-test is used most often in cases
in which:

- sample sizes are small (under 30 typically);

- the dependent variable is measured at
the ratio level;

- assignment to groups has been done
independently and randomly;

- the treatment variable has two levels:
presence or absence;

- the population from which the sample
was drawn is normally distributed and
therefore, the distribution of sample
means would be normally distributed;

- the researcher wants to find out if there
are statistically significant differences
between the groups.

Two commonly used variants of the *t*-
test will be presented in this section: the
first is appropriate for a between-subjects
experimental design, the second for a
within-subject design.

The **t-test** represents the ratio between
the difference in means between two
groups and the standard error of the difference. Thus:

$$t = \frac{\text{Difference between means}}{\text{Standard error of the difference}}$$

1. A BETWEEN-SUBJECTS *T*-TEST

Box 9.5 shows how one could compute the
t score in a between-subjects design for differences in the tires being used at the
Riverside Speedway reported in Chapter 3,
Table 3.3.

While the student drivers with the modified tires were able to get around the track
slightly faster (on average .33 of a second)
there was a lot of variation within the two
groups. The test of significance leads us to
accept the null hypothesis: there is simply
not enough between-group variation compared to within-group variation to reject the
null hypothesis.

2. A WITHIN-SUBJECT *T*-TEST

A variation of the *t*-test is available for
dependent samples (where the comparison

BOX 9.5

Between-Subjects t-Test for Equal-Sized Groups*

In Chapter 3, data were reported comparing a modified versus standard racing tire. The means and standard deviations were reported for the speeds of drivers using each type of tire. The data were as follows:

	STANDARD TIRE		MODIFIED TIRE	
	DRIVER	TIME	DRIVER	TIME
i. Student drivers:	Kathleen	21.4	Paula	20.7
between-subjects	Li	16.2	Marlies	19.0
design; random	Danielle	18.0	Vanny	16.4
assignment to groups	Kim	16.1	Jacques	16.7
	Kevin	15.9	Sandra	21.6
	Mary	20.3	Marius	20.1
	Yvonne	17.1	Kwami	14.4
	Pierre	21.4	Andrea	16.3
	Ursula	17.7	Tony	15.7
	Hwan	19.8	Carol	19.7
MEANS	18.39		18.06	
STANDARD DEVIATIONS	2.17		2.45	
MEAN DIFFERENCE		0.33		

*From Tire Testing Data, Chapter 3, Table 3.3.

Using the following formula we can quickly compute the *t*-test:

$$t = \frac{\overline{X}_1 - \overline{X}_2}{\text{Standard error of the difference}}$$

The standard error of the difference may be computed using the following formula:

$$\sqrt{\frac{sd_1^2}{N_1} + \frac{sd_2^2}{N_2}}$$

Where: sd_1^2 is the variance for group 1; sd_2^2 is the variance for group 2. N_1 refers to the number of subjects in group 1; N_2 refers to the number of subjects in group 2.

Step 1 Subtract the mean speed of the modified tires test from the mean speed for the standard tires: (18.39 – 18.06 = .33). This is the value we will use in the numerator (the value above the line in the equation).

Step 2 For the denominator (below the line in the equation) we require the variance for each type of tire, and since we have the standard deviations reported in the table, all we have to do is square the standard deviations to get the variances. Hence:

Variance standard tire:
$$sd^2 = 2.17^2 = 4.71$$
Variance modified tire:
$$sd^2 = 2.45^2 = 6.00$$

Step 3 The N (number of cases) for standard tires is 10; the N for modified tires is also 10.

Step 4 Calculate the values for the denominator by using the values calculated in Step 2, using the equation given above.

$$\text{Standard error of difference} = \sqrt{\frac{sd_1^2}{N_1} + \frac{sd_2^2}{N_2}}$$

$$\text{Standard error of difference} = \sqrt{\frac{4.71}{10} + \frac{6.00}{10}}$$

$$\text{Standard error of difference} = 1.03$$

Step 5 Plug the values into the equation for the *t*-test, as in:

$$t\text{-test score} = \frac{.33}{1.03}$$

$$t\text{-test score} = .320$$

Step 6 Determine the degrees of freedom by subtracting number of groups from number of cases (20 − 2 = 18).

Step 7 Decision: Since the *t* value does not exceed the one shown in Table 9.3 on p. 266, we accept the null hypothesis. The differences in the speeds may simply be the result of sampling fluctuations.

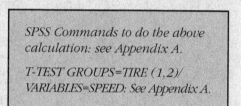

SPSS Commands to do the above calculation: see Appendix A.

T-TEST GROUPS=TIRE (1,2)/ VARIABLES=SPEED: See Appendix A.

groups are not selected independently). The steps for hand-computing a dependent *t*-test are reported for the within-subject design Riverside Speedway data originally reported in Chapter 3 (see Box 9.6 on p. 267).

In the case of the within-subject design to test the efficacy of the different racing tires, we are led to reject the null hypothesis and conclude that, indeed, the modified tires do seem to make a difference. Note that the differences in the speeds achieved on the two different types of tires is slight (0.09 of a second), yet the difference in this case is found to be statistically significant (we reject the null hypothesis). In comparison to the student drivers (see Box 9.5), the amateur drivers show much less variation in lap times (ranging from 12.8 seconds to 13.6 seconds compared to a range of 8.4 to 20.7 seconds for the student drivers).

Where a test of significance is required for a study with a more complex experimental design, such as those with several independent variables or more than two different levels in the treatment or control variable, the researcher typically uses *analysis of variance* techniques. These will now be introduced.

D. THE *F* DISTRIBUTION: MEANS, ANOVA

A second test of significance associated with comparing means involves an *analysis of variance*. The distribution associated with this test is the **F distribution**, and it is used to test whether there is a significant difference in

TABLE 9.3 CRITICAL VALUES FOR THE *T* DISTRIBUTION ONE- AND TWO-TAILED TESTS

DEGREES OF FREEDOM	.05 LEVEL OF SIGNIFICANCE		.01 LEVEL OF SIGNIFICANCE	
	ONE-TAILED	TWO-TAILED	ONE-TAILED	TWO-TAILED
1	6.31	12.71	31.82	63.66
2	2.92	4.30	6.96	9.92
3	2.35	3.18	4.54	5.84
4	2.13	2.78	3.75	4.60
5	2.02	2.57	3.36	4.03
6	1.94	2.45	3.14	3.71
7	1.90	2.36	3.00	3.50
8	1.86	2.31	2.90	3.34
9	1.83	2.26	2.82	3.25
10	1.81	2.23	2.76	3.17
11	1.80	2.20	2.72	3.10
12	1.78	2.18	2.68	3.06
13	1.77	2.16	2.65	3.01
14	1.76	2.14	2.62	2.98
15	1.75	2.13	2.60	2.95
16	1.75	2.12	2.58	2.92
17	1.74	2.11	2.57	2.90
18	1.73	2.10	2.55	2.88
19	1.73	2.09	2.54	2.86
20	1.72	2.09	2.53	2.84
25	1.71	2.06	2.48	2.79
30	1.70	2.04	2.46	2.75
40	1.68	2.02	2.42	2.70
60	1.67	2.00	2.39	2.66
120	1.66	1.98	2.36	2.62
∞	1.64	1.96	2.33	2.58

Remember that the computed value must equal or exceed the relevant value shown above if the null hypothesis is to be rejected. Please consult the appendix of any statistics text if you require additional degrees of freedom or other levels of significance.

the means of various categories. Some of this material will not seem to be new, since similar ideas were presented when discussing both the Chi-Square test and correlation analyses. **Analysis of variance** will typically be used when:

- the dependent variable is measured at the ratio level;

- the treatment variable has two or more levels;

- two or more treatments are used simultaneously;

- it is assumed that the population from which the sample was drawn is normally distributed and, therefore, that the distribution of sample means would be normally distributed;

- the researcher wants to find out if there are statistically significant differences between the groups;

BOX 9.6

Testing Tires: A Within-Subject Design*

	STANDARD TIRE		MODIFIED TIRE	
	DRIVER	TIME	DRIVER	TIME
iii. Amateur racers:	James	13.1	James	13.0
within-subject	Peter	12.8	Peter	12.9
design	Celine	13.5	Celine	13.4
	Jeremy	13.4	Jeremy	13.2
	Stefan	13.5	Stefan	13.5
	Don	13.6	Don	13.3
	Jacques	13.5	Jacques	13.3
	Pierre	12.8	Pierre	12.7
	Linda	12.9	Linda	12.9
	Melanie	13.5	Melanie	13.4

MEANS	13.26		13.17	
STANDARD DEVIATIONS	0.32		0.28	
MEAN DIFFERENCE		0.09		

Calculating a Within-Subject (Dependent Groups) t-Test

SUBJECT	TIME 1 STANDARD	TIME 2 MODIFIED	DIFFERENCE T1-T2 (D)	AVERAGE DIFFERENCE (AD)	AD – D	(AD – D)²
			Step 1	Step 2	Step 3	Step 4
James	13.1	13.0	.1	.1	.0	.00
Peter	12.8	12.9	–.1	.1	–.2	.04
Celine	13.5	13.4	.1	.1	.0	.00
Jeremy	13.4	13.2	.2	.1	–.1	.01
Stefan	13.5	13.5	.0	.1	.1	.01
Don	13.6	13.3	.3	.1	–.2	.04
Jacques	13.5	13.3	.2	.1	–.1	.01
Pierre	12.8	12.7	.1	.1	.0	.00
Linda	12.9	12.9	.0	.1	.1	.01
Melanie	13.5	13.4	.1	.1	.0	.00
Totals			1.0			.12

AVERAGE DIFFERENCE $= 1.0 \div 10$
$= .1$

VARIANCES OF DIFFERENCES $= .12 \div 9$
$= .013$

*From Tire Testing Data, Chapter 3, Table 3.3.   *cont'd*

Step 1 Subtract Time 2 measure from Time 1 measure to get the difference score (D): in the case of James: 13.1 − 13.0 =.1.

Step 2 Calculate the average difference score (AD): sum the values for the 10 subjects (.1 − .1 + .1 + .2 + .0 + .3 + .2 + .1 + .0 + .1 = 1.0); divide sum by number of subjects (1.0 ÷ 10 = .1).

Step 3 Subtract the difference score (D) calculated in Step 1 from the average difference score (AD) calculated in Step 2: in the case of James: .1 − .1 = 0.

Step 4 Square each value calculated in Step 3.

Step 5 Sum the squared values from Step 4 and divide by the number of subjects minus 1 (10 − 1 = 9). The measure of the variance of the differences is .12 ÷ 9 = .013

Step 6 To get the standard deviation of the differences, calculate the square root of the variance of the differences. As in:

Standard deviation = $\sqrt{.013}$ = .115
   of differences

Step 7 Calculate the standard error of the difference by dividing the standard deviation of the differences by the square root of the number of pairs of scores. As in:

Standard error of = .115 ÷ $\sqrt{10}$ = .037
the differences

Step 8 Compute the t-ratio by dividing the average difference (AD) by the standard error of the difference. As in:

$$t = 0.1 \div .037$$

$$t = 2.74$$

Step 9 Determine the degrees of freedom by subtracting 1 from the number of pairs of scores (10 − 1 = 9). Look up the t value in Table 9.3. The two-tailed value with 9 df = 2.262.

Step 10 Decision: Since the t value exceeds that in Table 9.3, we reject the null hypothesis.

> *SPSS commands to do the above calculation: see Appendix A.*
>
> *T-TEST PAIRS TIME1, TIME2: see Appendix A.*

- the researcher wants to check to see if the various treatments may be interacting with one another.

1. ONE-WAY ANALYSIS OF VARIANCE: EGALITARIANISM SCORES BY COUNTRY

Data on egalitarianism scores have been collected and the researcher wants to examine whether they vary significantly from country to country. Egalitarianism was measured using six items that reflect how equally respondents think the wealth of society should be spread among its members. The sample involves a total of 182 respondents from Canada, New Zealand, and Australia. Our research hypothesis is that egalitarianism scores will vary by country. The null hypothesis is that there is no difference in egalitarianism scores across national boundaries.

The procedures used to answer the above question involve:

- determining the appropriate test to run;

- stating the null hypothesis;

- deciding the probability level we want to employ (normally specifying whether we risk being wrong 5% or 1% of the time);

- determining whether the observed difference is, or is not, within the range of normal sampling fluctuations; and

- deciding whether we accept or reject the null hypothesis.

Box 9.7 presents the results from our study of egalitarianism. Various computations are made and the resulting test of

---

BOX 9.7

Analysis of Variance of Egalitarianism by Country

| | EGALITARIANISM SCORES | | |
	CANADA	NEW ZEALAND	AUSTRALIA	TOTAL
	34	36	37	
	28	49	34	
	24	38	33	
	31	33	24	
	30	27	31	
	...	...	...	
	30	34	43	
Sums	1,989	1,559	2,061	5,609
Means	30.60	27.35	34.35	30.82
Number of cases	65	57	60	182

Steps in Computing a Simple Analysis of Variance

Three measures of variation are required to compute the analysis of variance. These are total variation, between variation, and within variation:

$$\underset{\text{variation}}{\text{Total}} = \underset{\text{variation}}{\text{Between}} + \underset{\text{variation}}{\text{Within}}$$

The *total variation* may be computed by summing the squares of all the egalitarian scores and subtracting from that result the square of the sum divided by the total number of cases. As in:

Step 1 $34^2 + 28^2 + \ldots + 43^2 = 186,677$
minus

Step 2 $5,609^2 \div 182 = 172,862$
equals

Step 3 $186,677 - 172,862 = 13,815$

Total variation = 13,815

Step 4 The between variation can be computed by squaring the column totals, dividing this value by the number of cases, then summing the result, and finally subtracting the value in Step 2 above. As in:

$((1{,}989^2 \div 65) + (1{,}559^2 \div 57) + (2{,}061^2 \div 60)) - 172{,}862 = 1{,}437$

Step 5 The *within variation* can be determined by simply subtracting the between variation from the total variation. As in:

$13{,}815 - 1{,}437 = 12{,}378$

Step 6 An *F* ratio table can be computed as follows:

Step 7 To estimate the mean squares (population variance) for the between and within rows, divide the sums of squares for the row by the degrees of freedom for the row, as in:

(i) Between estimate of mean squares: $1{,}437 \div 2 = 718.5$

(ii) Within estimate of mean squares: $12{,}378 \div 179 = 69.2$

	SUMS OF SQUARES	DEGREES OF FREEDOM	MEAN OF SQUARES	F	F. PROB.
Total variation	13,815	N – 1 = 181			
Between variation	1,437	k – 1 = 2	718.4	10.39	.0001
Within variation	12,378	N – k = 179	69.2		

Where k = number of categories in the independent variable.

Step 8 To calculate the *F* ratio, divide the *within variation* (69.2) into the *between variation* (718.4):

$718.4 \div 69.2 = 10.39$

Step 9 If the probability is not calculated for you (in cases when the values are calculated manually or when using some software packages), we will need to determine the value that has to be exceeded in order to reject the null hypothesis by looking up the value on the *F* table (Table 9.4 on p. 272). The *F* table requires the use of two values for degrees of freedom: the *between variation df* is placed across the top of the table (in the sample case df = 2); the *within variation df* is arranged along the vertical column (in our table df = 179). We will test the hypothesis at the .05 level. The critical value given in the table is 3.07. The *F* ratio must equal or exceed this value in order to reject the null hypothesis.

Step 10 Since the *F* ratio for the sample data is 10.39 (exceeding the critical value) the null hypothesis is rejected. Variability of the magnitude reported in the egalitarianism scores is regarded as statistically significant. If the differences between the countries had been smaller and we were led to accept the null hypothesis, we would argue that the differences observed simply reflect sampling fluctuations and we cannot reasonably conclude that there is a "real" difference in the egalitarian scores of the respondents from each of the three countries. (In most software packages the exact probabilities are provided for the researcher, which allows the researcher to skip steps 9 and 10.)

significance, the *F*-test, indicates that the null hypothesis should be rejected. The differences in the mean scores on egalitarianism (27.35 in New Zealand, 30.60 in Canada, and 34.35 in Australia) are more than one would expect from normal sample fluctuations. We conclude, therefore, that there is a statistically significant difference in egalitarianism scores of samples drawn from the three countries.

The test of significance is based on the idea that when a sample is drawn, there will be fluctuations in the mean egalitarian scores. What the test is doing is assessing the chance, if the true difference between the countries in egalitarianism is zero, of getting a sample fluctuation of the magnitude shown in the sample data. In the case under examination, the differences range from a low of 27.35 in New Zealand to a high of 34.35 in Australia on the egalitarianism index. The test of significance reveals that the observed fluctuation is greater than that that would probably be due to normal sample variability. In other words, if there was no "real" egalitarianism difference between the countries, a sample would reveal a difference ± 7.0 points less than 5% of the time simply because of sampling fluctuations. If, however, the observed difference could occur more than 5% of the time, we would accept the null hypothesis, and conclude that there are no statistically significant differences in egalitarianism in the populations studied.

To repeat, a statistically significant relationship is one in which the observed difference would occur by chance less than 5% of the time. If the test were set at the 1% level, it would simply be more difficult to reject the null hypothesis; here the difference would be statistically significant only if it could occur by chance less than 1% of the time.

2. COMPUTATIONAL DETAILS FOR A SIMPLE ANALYSIS OF VARIANCE

Like the computational procedure involved in determining the correlation between two variables, the procedures for an analysis of variance require a measurement of two kinds of variation: variations within a column (for example, differences within each country) and variations between columns (differences that show up between Canada, New Zealand, and Australia). An analysis of variance involves computing a ratio that compares these two kinds of variability—within-column and between-column variability.

On examining the data within column one (Canada data) of Box 9.7, note that country of origin cannot explain variations *within* this column (all cases are Canadian). Differences in egalitarian scores *between* the columns, however, might be explained by the association with the independent variable (country).

Box 9.7 goes through the computation of a one-way analysis of variance for the sample data. In this particular case, the estimates of variance indicate more variation between the columns than within them; as a result, the *F* ratio is more than one. After the *F* ratio is computed and the critical value is looked up in Table 9.4, the decision is made to reject the null hypothesis, since the computed *F* ratio is more than the value looked up in Table 9.4.

A. MEANS: COMPARING A DEPENDENT VARIABLE ACROSS CATEGORIES OF INDEPENDENT VARIABLE(S)

Frequently researchers use multiple independent variables to show how the means on the dependent variable vary across the categories of the independent variables.

TABLE 9.4 CRITICAL VALUES FOR THE *F* DISTRIBUTION, ONE-TAILED TESTS, .05 LEVEL OF SIGNIFICANCE

DF FOR THE DENOMINATOR	DF FOR THE NUMERATOR				
	1	2	3	4	5
2	18.51	19.00	19.16	19.25	19.30
3	10.13	9.55	9.28	9.12	9.01
4	7.71	6.94	6.59	6.39	6.26
5	6.61	5.79	5.41	5.19	5.05
6	5.99	5.14	4.76	4.53	4.39
7	5.59	4.74	4.35	4.12	3.97
8	5.32	4.46	4.07	3.84	3.69
9	5.12	4.26	3.86	3.63	3.48
10	4.96	4.10	3.71	3.48	3.33
11	4.84	3.98	3.59	3.36	3.20
12	4.75	3.88	3.49	3.26	3.11
13	4.67	3.80	3.41	3.18	3.02
14	4.60	3.74	3.34	3.11	2.96
15	4.54	3.68	3.29	3.06	2.90
16	4.49	3.63	3.24	3.01	2.85
17	4.45	3.59	3.20	2.96	2.81
18	4.41	3.55	3.16	2.93	2.77
19	4.38	3.52	3.13	2.90	2.74
20	4.35	3.49	3.10	2.87	2.71
25	4.42	3.38	2.99	2.76	2.60
30	4.17	3.32	2.92	2.69	2.53
40	4.08	3.23	2.84	2.61	2.45
60	4.00	3.15	2.76	2.52	2.37
120	3.92	3.07	2.68	2.45	2.29
∞	3.84	3.00	2.60	2.37	2.21

Remember that the computed value must equal or exceed the relevant value as shown above if the null hypothesis is to be rejected. Please consult the appendix of any statistics text if you require additional degrees of freedom or other levels of significance.

Survey designs often use this procedure to compute results.

3. ANALYSIS OF VARIANCE WITH ADDITIONAL VARIABLES

A. ANOVA

Experimental researchers use analysis of variance (ANOVA) when their design has more than one independent variable or multiple treatment levels. The inclusion of additional complexity is relatively simple and provides an opportunity to explore the interaction of treatment variables (when effects change for different combinations of treatment variables) in influencing the dependent variable. Note that the variations that are compared in an analysis of variance are composed of two elements: random error and possible treatment effects. The test that is done compares the ratio in the following way:

$$F = \frac{\text{Random error} + \text{Possible treatment effects}}{\text{Random error}}$$

The interpretation of the results of an ANOVA test is split between a concern for:

- the main effect of treatment variable A;

- the main effect of treatment variable B;

- an interaction of the treatment variables (A × B);

- an error term (within groups).

Box 9.8 presents the results of an analysis of variance test. To interpret such a table one normally begins with an examination of the main effects; if there are significant main effects, one would then examine whether there are significant interactions.

Analysis of variance is a major analytical tool, used particularly by experimental researchers. Normally, all such computations will be made by computers. The researcher will encounter *F* distributions in using the MEANS, ANOVA, MANOVA, and REGRESSION procedures.

To perform this analysis using SPSS see the ANOVA procedure in Appendix A.

BOX 9.8

Sample ANOVA Results

Suppose we had run a factorial design experiment with one dependent variable and two treatments and we wished to test for possible interactions between the treatments. In such cases, we would perform a two-way analysis of variance with a test for interaction (ANOVA).

The output might be summarized in the following way:

SOURCE OF VARIANCE	SUM OF SQUARES	*DF*	MEAN SQUARE	*F*	SIG. OF *F*
Main effect (A)	1,449.393	2	724.697	10.421	.000
Main effect (B)	12.652	1	12.652	.182	.670
Interaction (A x B)	125.990	2	62.995	.906	.406
Error term—within groups	12,239.591	176	69.543		
Total	13,815.016	181	76.326		

1. Understanding the Values in the Summary Table

i) The degrees of freedom are calculated as follows:

- main effect (A): df = 1 less than number of levels in that factor. [In this case: 3 − 1 = 2]

- main effect (B): df = 1 less than number of levels in that factor. [In this case: 2 − 1 = 1]

- interaction effect (A × B): df = product of the dfs making up the interaction. [In this case: 2 × 1 = 2]

cont'd

- error term: df = total number of cases minus the product of number of levels of A and B. [In this case, $182 - (3 \times 2) = 176$]
- Total df = N − 1 [In this case 182 − 1 = 181]

ii) To compute the mean square for an effect, divide the sum of squares for the effect by its df.

iii) To compute the *F* value for each effect, divide the mean square by the mean square error term.

2. *Interpreting the Results*

You will want to examine two issues as you begin to interpret your results. First, you will want to know if your treatment variables had a significant effect; if either or both did, you will want to see if there is any interaction between the treatments.

A. MAIN EFFECTS

To decide if a treatment was statistically significant you will need to compare the *F* value to the values found in Table 9.4, using the appropriate degrees of freedom. If the value you obtained is larger than the one reported in Table 9.4, you have a statistically significant effect. To use Table 9.4, you will need values for the required degrees of freedom: use the smaller value across the top of the table, and the larger one on the vertical axis.

B. INTERACTION EFFECTS

If you have a significant main effect, you will then want to inspect your results for any interactions between the effects.

Your job is simple if there is no significant interaction effect: you simply report that none was present. It is more complicated with an interaction; in this case, the effect of a treatment is not independent of the other treatment; it may be that under the high condition of Treatment A, we find that Treatment B does not enhance the impact on the dependent variable.

E. WHEN TESTS OF SIGNIFICANCE ARE NOT APPROPRIATE

Tests of significance are often inapplicable. Yet they are widely used, often improperly (Selvin, 1957; Gold, 1958; Beshers, 1958; McGinnis, 1958; Morrison and Henkel, 1970; Skipper, Guenther, and Nass, 1967). Why is this the case?

Performing tests of significance is, no doubt, often motivated by the desire to be scientific—or appear to be scientific. If one's data turn out to be "statistically significant," then that is taken to demonstrate the importance of the finding and to confer scientific legitimacy on one's work. Such tests help to create the impression that the god of science—that independent, unbiased arbiter of truth—has blessed one's research with approval.

A second motivation perhaps has to do with the fact that such tests are routinely—even if inappropriately—reported in the literature. Hence, to produce a report that meets the standards of the discipline, tests of significance are expected.

A third possibility is that tests of significance are poorly understood by social scientists, and that they are inappropriately used because of such misunderstandings.

For a variety of reasons, many studies should not be using tests of significance. The following rules indicate when such tests are inappropriate.

RULE 9.1

Tests of significance are not applicable when total populations are studied. If a study is being done on the wage differences between male and female faculty members and data relating to all faculty members are analyzed, then a test of significance would not be in order. If a $1,500 difference is observed after the appropriate controls are introduced, this difference is absolute. The researcher must decide whether the difference is to be characterized as substantial, modest, or trivial. To say that it is statistically significant is simply wrong!

Arguments have been advanced that a study like the one above represents a sample out of a universe of possible samples that might be taken. The problem with this argument is that not all institutions were given an equal chance to be included; second, if you wish to make the argument that this is but one case among many, then you have shifted the unit of analysis to the institutional level (a university) and now have one case represented by one difference. Here you would be left with a difference of $1,500, but with no knowledge of what differences are present in other institutions.

RULE 9.2

Tests of significance are not appropriate when non-probability sampling procedures are employed. Data gathered using convenience or quota samples are not properly analyzed using tests of significance. Since tests of significance provide only a measure of the probability of a given difference being the result of sampling fluctuations, assuming that probability sampling procedures have been used, such tests are not

appropriate if those methods are not used. If an experimenter asked people to volunteer to be in a treatment group and then wished to compare these individuals to others who agreed to serve as controls, any test of significance on the differences between the groups would be meaningless.

In experimental designs in which volunteers have been sought for participation (convenience sample), but subjects have been assigned to treatment and control groups using random sampling techniques, it is appropriate to use tests of significance to compare the treatment and control groups. However, in such instances the population should be regarded as those who volunteered for participation.

RULE 9.3

Tests of significance are to be considered suspect when there is a substantial nonparticipation rate. If substantial numbers of respondents have refused to participate (for argument's sake, let's say 40%), then tests of significance become problematic, for it is difficult to assume that nonparticipants are similar to those who agree to participate in the study. Hence, the extent to which such data can be considered representative can be called into question.

RULE 9.4

In *nonexperimental research*, if one is exploring a relationship that has been shown to be statistically significant, it is inappropriate to employ a test of significance once again when controls have been applied to check for spuriousness or an intervening variable. The issue in evaluating models is to assess the impact of the control on the original relationship and to observe whether the differences have remained the same, increased, decreased, or disappeared. Frequently, they may change from being statistically significant to being statistically insignificant, but this change could simply represent the fact that the data have been partitioned (perhaps cut in half). If fewer cases are involved, for instance, the switch from significance to nonsignificance might simply reflect that change.

The researcher should note how much the original relationship has shifted, not simply note whether the relationship is still statistically significant. To avoid confusion, do not employ tests of significance when causal models are being evaluated beyond the stage of the initial relationship. For example, if the relationship between X and Y is being explored, and if sampling and other conditions are appropriate, then a test of significance for the relation between X and Y is legitimate. However, having established that there is a statistically significant relation between X and Y, a further test of significance would not be appropriate when testing to ensure that the relationship is not spurious because of its connection to some third variable. (This point is discussed in Chapter 17.)

RULE 9.5

Tests of significance cannot be applied to relationships that were not formulated as hypotheses prior to the collection of data for the study. Researchers routinely collect data on many variables—it is not unusual in a survey, for example, to collect data on 100 or more variables. If we run every variable against every other one, we will not only generate enormous piles of computer output, but we will also generate results for many hundreds of theoretically meaningless relationships—and will also generate many "statistically significant" relationships. Indeed, one would expect that one-in-twenty tables will prove to be significant, providing one is using the .05 level for one's tests. Unfortunately, researchers rarely report how many relationships were analyzed, what confounding data have been discarded, and which causal models were not fully developed prior to data collection.

An exception to the above rule has to be made for those analyzing secondary data. In such cases, hypotheses need to be formulated prior to data analysis. In addition, while not reporting the results of the tests, some researchers find it useful to run tests of significance even in inappropriate situations to help shed light on the relationships explored.

Researchers must use tests of significance with great care. Above all, the beginning researcher must appreciate what such tests really measure. All too often it is not recognized that a finding may be equally important whether the relationship is statistically significant or not. Social scientists are in the business of trying to understand and to describe the social world, and to have discovered that there is no relationship between *A* and *B* is as important as it is to discover that there is a relation between *A* and *B*. And, if one is testing a theory, it is especially important to find that a predicted relationship does not hold, for this will cast doubt on the theory and, perhaps, lead to a refinement or refutation of it. In short, do not despair if your study does not yield statistically significant results. Science proceeds through disconfirmation, through ruling out alternatives, through rejecting, modifying, and continually rethinking theoretical formulations.

F. KEY POINTS

A *test of significance* reports the probability that an observed association or difference is the result of sampling fluctuations and does not reflect some "real" difference in the population from which the sample has been taken.

It is the *null (no relationship) hypothesis* that is tested in a test of significance. The test will lead the researcher to one of two conclusions: either to *reject* the null hypothesis or to *accept* it.

If the nature of the relationship has been specified in the research hypothesis (e.g., "Females are less accepting of physical violence than males"), then a one-tailed test is performed to test the null hypothesis. If the nature of the relationship has not been specified (e.g., "There is a relationship between gender and the acceptance of physical violence"), then a two-tailed test of the null hypothesis is performed.

When researchers talk about sampling distributions, they are talking about how, by drawing repeated samples from the same population and plotting the mean values of some measured variable, the plot of the means from the many samples would result in a normal curve. The *standard error of the means* is a measure of variability in the means of repeated samples.

In doing tests of significance, we are assessing whether the results of one sample fall within or outside the null hypothesis acceptance zone (usually 95% of the distribution). A *Chi-Square test* is a test of significance used with nominal or ordinal data that compares expected frequencies (if there are no differences between categories) and observed frequencies.

T-tests and *analysis of variance* tests of significance compare variability of a ratio-level dependent measure within categories of a treatment variable(s) to the variability between the categories.

Tests of significance are not used when:
- total populations are measured;
- non-probability sampling procedures have been employed;
- the test is for spurious, intervening, or conditional relationships;
- hypotheses have not been formulated prior to data analysis.

G. KEY TERMS

Analysis of variance (ANOVA)	Null hypothesis	Test of significance
Chi-Square test (X^2)	One-tailed test	*t*-test
Degrees of freedom	Research hypothesis	Two-tailed test
F distribution	Standard error of the means	Type I error
Inferential statistics	Statistical significance	Type II error

BEGINNING THE PROJECT

Part Four of the book begins with issues that need to be thought about carefully when commencing a research project. The two main initial areas of concern are the problem of bias (Chapter 10) and ethical questions (Chapter 11). The remaining chapters in Part Four deal with taking the first steps in designing a project (Chapter 12), thinking about measurement issues (Chapter 13), designing questionnaires (Chapter 14), and how to go about sampling (Chapter 15). For some types of research design, of course, you may not need to cover all this material; for a content analysis, for example, Chapter 14 is obviously not relevant. And if you are doing a participant observation study in a hospital, you need not cover Chapters 14 and 15.

BIAS

Chapter 2 argued that humans like to generalize—always trying to come up with rules to understand behaviour. These general rules set up expectations about how things work. These shared understandings may be thought of as biases or sets of predispositions and expectations. If social research is to produce reliable generalizations about human behaviour, we need unbiased evidence—evidence not influenced by what the researcher would like to find. But the tendency to bias conclusions in the direction of expectations—or preferences—is a danger in all research. This chapter will explore the nature of bias and illustrate that, at all stages of the research process, the danger of bias needs to be recognized. The chapter will conclude with some rules for detecting and minimizing bias.

A. THE NATURE OF BIAS

A **bias** may be thought of as a preference—or predisposition—to favour a particular conclusion. **Research bias** may be defined as the systematic distortion of research conclusions. Typically these distortions are inadvertent, but they can also be intentional. They no doubt occur in all disciplines and can influence most phases of a project: from problem selection to the identifying of variables through developing measurements, collecting and analyzing data, and interpreting the results of the research.

To suggest that there is bias, or distortion, implies that there is an underlying truth waiting to be described accurately. For the social scientist this stable, unwavering truth is not so easily described. The reality we study varies according to many conditions

and across individuals, groups, and cultures. Indeed, the questions we ask about social issues are difficult. And the results of any study depend not only on who is studied but on subtle cues that we provide in asking questions. So the results social scientists get are dependent on a whole host of factors. We can only hope to minimize the effects of these factors.

To illustrate this point, recall the experimental work by Stanley Milgram (1963) on obedience to authority. (See Box 3.2 for an excerpt from one of his studies.) His research program involved testing how many subjects would be willing to apply electric shocks to a fellow volunteer in an experiment. (See Chapter 11 for more details on Milgram's studies.) Milgram's research program was an extensive one, involving some 19 different experimental conditions and 616 subjects (Reynolds, 1982, pp. 25–26). By changing the conditions of the study slightly, the percentage of subjects who were prepared to administer strong shocks to fellow participants varied from zero to 92.5%. The variation depended on the instructions, who gave the instructions, the location of the experiment, and so forth. In other words, many factors influenced the level of compliance shown by subjects when ordered to administer electric shocks. So what is the underlying truth? It depends. Many factors seem to be at play here. Indeed, the Milgram research indicates that variations in the results of studies should not be surprising, since relatively small changes in the design of a study can make enormous differences to its results. Each set of conditions has its own truth.

Bias is just one of many factors that could be influencing the outcome of a study. How important bias itself is will vary across many conditions. When we fail to replicate a study (fail to get the same finding as another researcher), we cannot assume that the difference in results is due to bias alone. Many factors, including bias, may have been responsible.

In everyday life we have our likes and dislikes. Often interpretations of our experiences serve to confirm for us what we already knew or thought. In short, bias helps to organize our interpretation of events and make sense of a complex world. So when our good friend John messes up and fails to submit his term paper on time, he interprets this as a sign that he is under a lot of pressure, and, on top of that, his girlfriend just walked out on him. By contrast, an acquaintance of John's sees his failure to submit his work on time as just another indication that John will never amount to much, with all his drinking and womanizing. The point here is that we often find corroborative evidence for our predispositions. John himself finds a justification for his behaviour; the John-basher finds yet another reason why John should be shunned. Sometimes it takes quite powerful contrary evidence to change our minds; and when we must change our minds, we do so unwillingly, with much moaning and groaning.

In theory at least, social research systematically challenges our predispositions. The trouble is that we also take these same predispositions with us to our social research laboratories. Furthermore, as researchers, we tend to incorporate some research findings into our predispositions, and these too may become difficult to change. Science itself is part of the lore of the culture, but it also has a lore all of its own. In a sense, then, the social scientist has a double load of biasing predispositions: one acquired as a member of society and another heaped on by the experience and knowledge acquired as a participant in an academic discipline. Both sources of bias need to be recognized as potential blinders to a clear view of social behaviour, unfettered by expectations or preferences.

The view of women in the development of psychology is an excellent illustration of the problem of bias in a discipline. Shields (1988) argues that much of nineteenth- and early twentieth-century psychology was severely limited because it assumed female intellectual inferiority. Research was devoted not to questioning this assumption but rather to various attempts to understand this inferiority. Thus efforts were made to:

(i) identify those parts of the brain that were more poorly developed in women than in men;

(ii) understand how the greater variability in male skills leads to a higher proportion of male geniuses;

(iii) understand the role of the maternal instinct in maintaining women in passive, subservient roles.

Shields concludes her article by noting:

Graves (1968, p. v) included among the functions of mythologizing that of the justification of existing social systems. This function was clearly operative throughout the evolutionist-functionalist treatment of the psychology of women: the 'discovery' of sex differences in brain structure to correspond to 'appropriate' sex differences in brain function; the biological justification (via the variability hypothesis) for the enforcement of women's subordinate social status; the Victorian weakness and gentility associated with maternity; and pervading each of these themes, the assumption of an innate emotional, sexless, unimaginative female character that played the perfect foil to the Darwin male. That science played handmaiden to social values cannot be denied. Whether a parallel situation exists in today's study of sex differences is open to question. (Shields, 1988, p. 55)

While there can be dangers in the researcher becoming *overly* self-conscious about research procedures and the possibility of unwarranted assumptions—that is, it is possible to get completely bogged down contemplating the difficulties of research and, as a result, not get the job done!—nonetheless it is important to remain aware of the way in which bias can affect the conclusions of a social science report.

B. SOURCES OF BIAS IN THE RESEARCH PROCESS

Frequently the social researcher is confronted with "interesting" findings for which an explanation should be offered. Suppose, for example, that a project measures high school students' socioeconomic statuses (SES) and their aspirations for higher education. And suppose, during data analysis, that a robust relationship emerges indicating that the higher a student's socioeconomic origin, the greater the likelihood that the student will aspire to post-secondary education. At this stage, the researcher might wonder what explains the pattern that has emerged. Possibilities such as the following might come to mind:

- peers of high SES students have high aspirations themselves and influence their friends in such a way that they plan to attend post-secondary institutions;

- the parents of high SES students have higher expectations concerning their children's educational achievements;

- high SES students know that they have the financial backing to attend a post-secondary institution and, therefore, plan to do so;

- teachers encourage high SES students more;

- high SES students have been exposed more frequently to high occupational achievers and are therefore more likely to model themselves on such individuals.

Unfortunately, the study may not have been designed to test, and possibly to rule out, competing explanations. The problem here is that while data documenting a variety of relationships may have been presented, there may be no actual evidence for the particular explanation offered; however, the reader of the report may be convinced, inappropriately, that the researcher has provided evidence: "After all, look at all the tables." Even though the explanation may sound good and appear reasonable, there may be no real evidence to back it up. We need to design studies that systematically test a variety of possible explanations for the relationship under examination. At times the social scientist may feel pressured to provide an explanation even though there is little or no evidence available to check it.

In short, much of what is said about social science research methods describes ideal practices and is not always a good description of what is actually done. Much is not reported. The term *researcher affect* has been used to characterize this phenomenon. **Researcher affect** refers to the danger of researchers falling in love with a particular explanation for some relationship, or some view of the world, and inadvertently using procedures that lead to conclusions supporting the preferred explanation or world view. All stages of the research process can be affected adversely by bias. In this chapter, we will examine how bias can affect the initial selection of the problem to be researched, the sample design, funding decisions, data collection, data analysis, and the reporting and use of research findings.

1. SELECTION OF THE PROBLEM

The issue in problem selection is that some phenomena are judged to be more important than others—some are considered worthy of exploration, others not. Because of this, the choice of subject matter can provide a clue as to the values held by the researcher. Within North American culture, researchers are more likely to study armed robbery than the incidence of friendly greetings on a street corner. The former is viewed as a social problem, the latter not. The researcher is likely to see robbery as a problem with negative consequences, and also as one that should be controlled or eliminated. It could be argued that identifying the most effective variables in reducing robberies can be done without bias. But there is probably no value-free, culture-independent way of choosing variables for a study. Bias will result in the selection of those variables conventionally considered important and the exclusion of those conventionally considered unimportant.

2. SAMPLING DESIGN

Whether one opts for a survey, panel study, case study, or experimental design, there are potential sources of bias in the sample

selected for study. For example, by choosing to survey attitudes toward capital punishment in a community containing a maximum security prison, a researcher will probably produce a study that shows fairly high levels of support for capital punishment. To pursue the example further, a researcher might do a case study of the attitudes of police officers in a rural community on public policy issues. Once again, attitudes favouring capital punishment will probably emerge. Choosing both a rural community and a police organization increases the likelihood that the attitudes expressed will favour capital punishment more than would be the case in most other areas or with many other work groups. The experienced researcher, knowing how different variables usually work out, can choose a research design, sets of variables, and ways of wording questions so as to bias results.

A particular problem that has plagued social science research is sexism. At all stages of research, but especially at the design stage, care must be taken to avoid sexism. Margrit Eichler's *Nonsexist Research Methods* (1988) identifies several types of sexism in research. The major types she identifies include:

A. ANDROCENTRICITY

If someone presents the world from an exclusively male perspective as if this perspective were universal, that person is guilty of **androcentricity**. Eichler uses the example of "intergroup warfare" as a "means of gaining women and slaves." Eichler points out that the real group here is males, since what is gained is women. Here, women are seen as passive objects that are acted upon, not as part of the group being discussed (Eichler, 1988, p. 5).

B. OVERGENERALIZATION

If a study claims to study all people but, in fact, samples only, or largely, males, we have an example of an **overgeneralization**. Eichler uses the example of a sample of males to study social class; she also points out that when one uses the term "parents" to refer to mothers, one is guilty of overgeneralization, since one is ignoring fathers. A parallel problem is **overspecificity**, when single-sex terms are used to describe situations applicable to both sexes: for example "the doctor...he," "the nurse...she" (Eichler, 1988, p. 6).

C. GENDER INSENSITIVITY

To ignore gender as an important variable is to display **gender insensitivity**. Researchers should identify the gender composition of their samples and be sensitive to the different impacts social policies have on men and women (Eichler, 1988, pp. 6–7).

Familism is a special case of gender insensitivity and involves treating the family as the unit of analysis when, in fact, it is individuals within the family unit that engage in a particular activity or hold a certain attitude. Familism is also a problem when we assume that some phenomenon has an equal impact on all members of the family when, in fact, it may affect different family members in different ways.

D. DOUBLE STANDARDS

If a researcher uses different means of measuring identical behaviours, attitudes, or situations for each gender, that researcher would be guilty of using a **double standard**. But note that some qualities may exist only in one gender category (Eichler, 1988, p. 7).

Sex appropriateness is a special case of the double standard and refers to a situation in which "attributes are assigned only to one sex or the other and are treated as more important for the sex to which they have been assigned" (Eichler, 1988, p. 8).

If a researcher treats the sexes as discrete social, as well as biological, cohorts rather than two cohorts with shared characteristics, then the researcher is guilty of **sexual dichotomism** (Eichler, 1988, p. 9).

3. FUNDING

Granting agencies, although they may claim to fund projects on the basis of merit, are themselves subject to bias. In Canada, for example, the Social Sciences and Humanities Research Council (SSHRC) has funds targeted to encourage research in specified areas. The federal government, which provides the funding for SSHRC, may wish to promote scholarly inquiry into some areas. These are designated, and funds are set aside for projects in that area. Projects in such areas are then favoured over other projects.

In addition, scholars in the traditional disciplines are generally more readily funded than those in newer areas. Indeed, in recent years, the SSHRC has set up a special committee to deal with applications for people working in interdisciplinary programs or in newly developing areas. The establishment of the new review committee was a response to the perception that scholars in some areas were at a disadvantage when competing with scholars in traditional disciplines.

The value society places on different kinds of research is also reflected in the relative amounts of research funds made available. The NSERC (Natural Sciences and Engineering Research Council) and the MRC (Medical Research Council) are relatively well funded in comparison to the SSHRC.

Project-funding decisions are adjudicated by peer-review committees. University scholars are appointed to discipline committees and make recommendations on funding. SSHRC committees have an especially difficult time, given the high demand for funds and the severely limited resources available to each committee. These committees more or less represent the collective wisdom of each discipline. They reflect current research trends and views as to what kinds of research should be funded.

Research operates in a social context. The researcher is constrained by peers and granting agencies from engaging in "trivial" research and required to tackle issues that are considered "important." Research is not free of social constraints.

4. DATA COLLECTION

There is an extensive literature in psychology dealing with the influence the experimenter may have on the results of a study. Robert Rosenthal and K.L. Fode (1963, pp. 183–89), for example, did a series of important **experimenter effect** studies in which student researchers were asked to collect data on the number of trials it took rats to learn a maze. The student researchers were informed that a new breed of laboratory rat was being developed and that it had been bred for intelligence; the observations were to see if, in fact, there was any difference between the specially bred "smart" rats and ordinary laboratory rats. And so the students set to work, running the two types of rats through the maze.

It turned out that, indeed, the "smart" rats took fewer trials to learn the maze than the "ordinary" ones. Apparently the breeding program was working. There was just one problem. Dr. Rosenthal did not have any smart rats. The rats were simply

assigned randomly to the "smart" and the "ordinary" categories. It was the students who were the "real" subjects of this study. Somehow their expectations about the outcome of the trials had an impact on the results of the study. If the experimenter expects a rat to learn fast, somehow the data will come out that way. Thus, Rosenthal and Fode's findings indicate that there is a tendency to produce findings consistent with the experimenter's expectations. The explanation of the so-called experimenter effect has been more difficult to identify.

Did the students "fudge" the data to please the professor? Did they perceive "errors" differently for the two groups, perhaps being less likely to note an error made by the "smart" rats? Did they handle the rats differently? The generally accepted view is that experimenter effect occurs because of both the influence of behaviour by expectations and slight, but systematic, recording errors by the observer (Johnson and Adair, 1970, pp. 270–75). But no matter what the explanation, Rosenthal's research is of critical importance to the experimentalist as well as to all social science researchers.

Before discussing the implications of Rosenthal's research, one other illustration is pertinent. A German mathematics teacher had a horse with unusual talents (Rosenthal, 1966). The amazing horse, known as Clever Hans, could solve simple mathematical problems by stamping his foot to indicate his answer. At first, skeptics thought that Clever Hans' trainer was signalling to the horse, thus accounting for the horse's unusual ability. However, it turned out that even when the trainer was removed from the room, the horse could still do the trick for other people posing the same questions.

The horse was, indeed, very smart. It turned out that Clever Hans' mathematical skills declined dramatically when the audience did not know the answer, or when he was blindfolded. Apparently he was watching the audience. If the answer was three, the audience would gaze intently at the hoof of the horse clumping out the answer; after three stomps, members of the audience would raise their heads slightly, focusing their gaze on the horse's head. The horse simply watched the audience—they cued him when to stop. A pretty smart horse. Not much good at mathematics, but an acute observer of body language.

How is Clever Hans relevant to the social scientist? Or, for that matter, what can we learn from Robert Rosenthal's experiments? Suppose you are conducting an interview. And suppose you have just asked the respondent how often she goes to church. The respondent replies: "I don't go to church." You say, raising your eyebrows slightly, "Oh, so you don't go to church?" In all likelihood, your respondent now feels slightly uncomfortable—your eyebrow movement and your comment have communicated a message. After this, future questions about religious issues may well encourage the respondent to express more interest in religion than she actually has. It is as if the interviewer is demanding a pro-religion response. Respondents are often interested in figuring out what the survey is "really" all about. They will therefore be looking for cues and may be influenced by them. If a Clever Hans notes a slight raising of heads in the audience, it is probable that most human subjects will be sensitive to a raised eyebrow, a change in voice tone, or a shift in the body position of the interviewer.

Johnson and Ryan (1976) demonstrated that while experimenters could not intentionally influence a subject's behaviour by using nonverbal cues, the experimenters did err in recording the subjects' responses.

In this study the experimenters were to follow instructions carefully and were specifically told not to tell subjects how to respond. The study shows that while a subject's responses were not significantly altered by the experimenter, the results (because of the recording errors) were nonetheless biased in the direction of the experimenter's preferences.

Given the issue of **expectancy** raised by Rosenthal and the results of the Johnson and Ryan studies, the social researcher should avoid specifying the hypotheses of the study either to the respondents or the research assistants. Sometimes it is difficult, however, to withhold such information from one's research assistants. As a principal investigator, you want to make them feel that they are a part of the study and, therefore, feel that they should know what the study is "really" about. However, if you tell the research assistants what the hypotheses are, they may inadvertently bias results either toward the hypothesis (if they are friendly) or away from it (if they are hostile).

Questionnaires or interview guides can also provide cues to the respondent and, unless one is careful, these can distort responses in the direction that the respondent thinks the researcher prefers. Such distortions are labelled **demand characteristics**. In such situations, test results are distorted because people respond in the way they think they are expected to respond. The term "demand characteristic" was coined by psychiatrist Martin T. Orne, who noted that subjects in experiments will sometimes play the role of "helpful subject" and produce the results they think the researcher desires (Orne, 1962). An illustration drawn from survey research would be the rather obvious attempt by Marx to elicit negative comments from workers when he posed the following question: "If you are paid piece rates, is the quality of the article made a pretext for fraudulent deductions from your wages?" (Bottomore and Rubel, 1988, p. 215).

During the data-collection phase, a research director must ensure that when a selected respondent refuses to participate or is unavailable, the replacement is selected on an equal probability basis (see Chapter 15). If this is not done, there is a danger that the data-collection personnel will simply choose the most convenient replacement, and this will tend to bias the study by overrepresenting those people who spend more time at home.

5. DATA ANALYSIS

At the beginning of an analysis in surveys, interview studies, and participant observation studies, researchers go through a process of coding the information. What this means is that if data are collected in an open-ended format (questions without fixed-response categories), then the information will have to be placed into categories before analysis begins. The process of coding is subject to two kinds of error: random and systematic.

Random error refers to inconsistencies that enter into the coding process but which display no systematic pattern. For example, suppose that you are coding people into the following educational categories: (1) eight or fewer years of formal education, (2) nine to twelve years of formal education, (3) some post-secondary training, or (4) college or university graduation. If you accidentally coded a person with five years of education into category (2), you would have made an accidental or random error. In processing data, one often enters the information twice, comparing the first version with the second in order to locate

such random errors. Occasionally, entry errors will include values that are not within the range of possible values: in the above example, entering a 6 would be an example of such an error. These errors are easiest to spot because, once data analysis begins, an out-of-range value will become apparent as soon as one runs a frequency distribution of the variable. And, since these errors simply represent "noise" in one's data, they are not as threatening to the conclusions of a study as systematic errors.

Systematic errors are especially problematic. These errors are in danger of biasing a study because they are systematic— they distort the data in one particular direction. For example, suppose that any person who does not answer the question on education is assigned to the lowest category, the category representing those people with eight or fewer years of education. In such cases, we would be biasing the data systematically for those who refuse to answer the question by always coding them as if they should fall into the lowest educational category. (Normally those who do not answer a question are assigned a missing value code for the question.) Another kind of systematic error could occur if we discovered, after having developed code categories and starting our work, that another and uncategorized kind of response is occurring halfway through the analysis. If, to save time, we do not go back to the beginning and reexamine all of our cases to see if some of the codings have been inappropriately forced into certain categories, we will have decreased the number of cases that fall into the newly discovered category systematically. This kind of difficulty is likely to pop up in studies with many open-ended questions. (This is one reason, incidentally, why many social researchers avoid using a lot of open-ended questions.)

Particularly in survey and in nonreactive research, a great amount of information is collected on a large number of variables. This data can be treated in a variety of ways—many of which can be viewed as alternative modes of analysis. The researcher can analyze the data in a number of different ways, discarding those results that are "less interesting," and keeping those that make "the most sense." If cross-tabulations are being done, a variety of cut-points might be tried; some will be retained, and others will be discarded. (If you had measured respondents' education by years of formal school completed, and you now wished to group them into two categories, low- and high-education, where would you draw the line between the two groups?) Frequently the data are worked with until the analysis producing the strongest association is identified and retained. Such procedures violate the principles of objectivity but are, nonetheless, practised in all disciplines. Each discipline has a range of approved methods of analysis. Thus, playing with the data seems perfectly legitimate. After all, you want to produce the "best" analysis of the data. For some, the "best analysis" may include only statistically significant, publishable results. In massaging the data, the bias will be to find evidence supporting expected or preferred outcomes. Such **data massaging** is often done, but rarely reported, in formal presentations of the research.

Given the modern computer, it is now possible to run tests for many different relationships. There might be four or five different operationalizations of a concept (such as socioeconomic status, for example) available to the researcher in a data set; perhaps the various hypothesized relationships are run using each of these possibilities. In all likelihood, the one that is most congruent with the researcher's expectations gets reported. A rationale for throwing out some of the results can readily be found by arguing that they represent a "poor measurement" of the relevant variable. Most researchers have, from time to time, engaged in some "selective" use of data. If the researcher "hunts" through a data set long enough, an acceptable—even interesting—finding will surely emerge. At that point, the hunt stops.

In the physical and the social sciences, "hunting" is common (Selvin and Stuart, 1966). What student in a chemistry or a physics laboratory has not checked the results obtained by other students? If unexpected results occur, then the procedure is rerun on the grounds that something must have been done wrong. In short, if anticipated results are not obtained, the results are discarded. Even the mature researcher has a tendency to work with the data until the "right" finding is obtained. The search for "reportable" findings is a continuous process in all science. Yet few papers acknowledge this search. Reading research papers leaves the impression that most projects are easy and straightforward. Few are.

For the survey researcher there is a special problem. Given many variables and observations, it is possible to run any variable against every other variable in a search for "significant findings." If we use the .05 level of significance (see Chapter 9), then we would expect one in twenty of the relationships examined to be statistically significant. Unless the researcher reports the "hunting" that has occurred, the reader of a report will be in no position to regard the conclusions with the skepticism they deserve.

Finally, it should be pointed out that there is nothing inherently wrong with "exploring" data, looking at relationships that have not been hypothesized. But such analyses should not be reported unless it is made clear that no hypothesis has guided the search. At least then, the reader has been cautioned.

6. REPORTING OF FINDINGS

In 1959, T.D. Sterling published an interesting paper that suggested that much of what is being published in learned journals may represent fluke results (Sterling, 1959, pp. 30–34). His argument is that there are a lot of researchers, and many may be working on a similar problem at any time. If the .05 level of significance has been used, one study in twenty, on average, will produce a statistically significant relationship purely by chance, and such studies may even get published (journals ordinarily do not publish papers reporting "no relationship" findings). The obvious question is: what proportion of journal articles are based on these fluke studies? While Sterling's point is an interesting one, it may overstate the problem (Rosenthal, 1979, pp. 638–41). Nonetheless, the argument needs to be kept in mind as one possible source of bias in published studies. In a recent update of the 1959 research, Sterling, Rosenbaum, and Weinkam (1995) note that little has changed in publication decisions with respect to tests of significance. They note that in psychology journals published in 1958 some 97.3% of the articles reporting tests of significance rejected the null hypothesis; in 1986–87, the figure stood at 95.6% rejecting the null hypothesis. Box 10.1 summarizes some of the points raised in the Sterling, Rosenbaum, and Weinkam 1995 article.

Sterling's argument can be extended into another area. There is a selection process, which finds certain findings reportable and others unreportable. Indeed, it is unusual for one's first analysis of the data to make

it through to the final report. While there are many good reasons for analyzing data in different ways, the process of deciding which findings to report may have more to do with aesthetics than science.

The key issue is this: what scientific principle determines when analysis is finished? Do we stop analysis when we get a reportable, respectable finding? If we stop analysis when we get the results we like, the bias will be toward confirming expectations. While some of the data may be consistent with expectations, some may not be. Frequently, inconsistencies are not reported.

The difficulty is that some nonscientific considerations come into play when reports are written. Are the findings culturally acceptable? Are the findings acceptable to one's peers? Since there is pressure to keep papers reasonably short, only the "major" finding is reported: this "major" finding, however, may not be representative of the findings of the whole research project.

The point here is that not only does the choice of subject matter reflect values, but the researcher's theoretical predispositions may influence the conclusions of the study as much as any data collected. Marxists come to Marxist conclusions, functionalists to functionalist ones.

A key decision was made in 2001 when the publishers of 13 medical journals decided that they would not publish material in which the independence of the researcher cannot be assured. This decision was made in recognition of the role pharmaceutical funding plays in supporting clinical trials of drugs under development. The stakes here are very high. It is claimed that it costs as much as $500 million dollars to bring a single drug to market. It is therefore not surprising that the drug companies, who are paying for the research, want researchers to indicate that the drug under

BOX 10.1 SOCIAL RESEARCHERS AT WORK

Sterling, Rosenbaum, and Weinkam: "Scientists Like to Publish the Positive"

The scientific method has traditionally been touted as a model of objectivity, but a team of Simon Fraser University researchers has revealed a significant bias in the way scientific results are reported.

According to their work, published earlier this year in *The American Statistician,* scientists who offer positive findings from their work—such as the verification of a hypothetical experimental outcome—stand a better chance of getting published. Meanwhile, those whose findings indicate the lack of a result—such as the denial of an expected experimental outcome—are unlikely ever to see their conclusions in print.

"You get this idiocy that you don't publish negative results," says computer science professor Ted Sterling, who first noted the trend in a research paper he published in 1959. At that time he analyzed the contents of a selected group of psychology journals and noted the overwhelming prevalence of articles touting positive outcomes. Dr. Sterling says he was disappointed to find out that nothing had changed more than thirty years later.

For his latest article, which Dr. Sterling co-authored with departmental colleague Jay Weinkam and graduate student Wilf Rosenbaum, a wider variety of scientific journals was sampled, but the prevalence of positive results had not changed. The article even cites a rejection letter written by the editor of a major environment and toxicology journal, which states bluntly, "the negative results translate into a minimal contribution to the field."

The Simon Fraser researchers disagree with that observation, suggesting that alerting scientists to negative findings can prevent others from repeating the same experiment and obtaining the same findings, a process that promotes redundant work since few will be aware of the negative result until they find out about it first-hand.

Moreover, the increasing popularity of a statistical method called meta-analysis makes it all the more important to know about negative results. Meta-analysis pools the results of a number of published studies, without bothering to carry out any original research. But that approach assumes all the relevant scientific findings will be available in print, rather than just the positive ones.

"Because access to study results is typically limited to published studies, the question of whether or not published studies constitute a representative sample of relevant studies is of concern," state the researchers in their *American Statistician* paper.

The solution, according to Dr. Sterling, lies with a new strategy for selecting scientific work to publish. He advocates "blind-to-outcome" peer review, which would weigh submitted papers on the basis of the importance and relevance of the work instead of relying on the nature of the outcome. In light of the fact that little about this aspect of scientific publication appears to have changed in thirty years and because the possibly misleading consequences are becoming more serious, he and his colleagues argue that this sort of drastic modification of editorial policy is necessary:

"In short," their study concludes, "more radical measures than public consciousness raising are needed to curtail the influence of publication bias."

Source: T.D. Sterling, W.I. Rosenbaum, and J.J. Weinkam (1996). "Scientists Like to Publish the Positive." *University Affairs*, 1(16). This report was based on T.D. Sterling, W.I. Rosenbaum, and J.J. Weinkam (1995). "Publication Decisions Revisited: The Effect of the Outcome of Statistical Tests on the Decision to Publish and Vice Versa." *The American Statistician*, 49, 108–12.

development produces statistically significant advantages over no treatment, and that the side effects are rare and/or nonthreatening. Researchers dependent on pharmaceutical company support for future projects would do well to please their sponsor. The need to produce positive findings may intentionally or unintentionally bias the outcomes of research. Box 10.2 reveals a bit more of the story behind the important move by medical journals.

Another dimension to the problem is that gradually funding has migrated from university labs to the labs of the pharmaceutical firms. University researchers on the editorial boards of professional journals are likely to have made a difference in arriving at the decision to insist on autonomy for the researcher in publishing the findings of their research. However, it is to be noted that university researchers have a direct interest in seeing that more funding goes to support research conducted in universities as opposed to in-house research conducted by the pharmaceutical firms. The firms and the universities are powerful in this struggle—the firms have the financial resources, but the universities are viewed as producing research findings that are both credible and impartial. The firms and the universities need one another. The authors'

advice to researchers is to "dance carefully with the porcupine, and know in advance the price of intimacy."

Chapter 2 outlined some types of flawed arguments that may find their way into the final report of a study. Included among these were: inappropriate appeals to authority; provincialism; setting up a false dilemma; missing, insufficient, or suppressed evidence; and unwarranted conclusions. The reader should be alert to these flaws in reading a final report on a research project.

In addition to being evident in theoretical predispositions and improper argument, bias can also be reflected by insensitivity to minorities, sexism, or in tendencies to go beyond the limits of one's data when interpreting them. And, while scholars are trained to be cautious in their interpretations, it is difficult to avoid suggesting extrapolations beyond those justified by the data. For example, any suggestion made only on the basis of a study of 63 first-year students in political science at the University of Victoria that there is a relation between social class and political party preference among Canadians would read far more than is justified into such data. Some of these issues will be explored more fully in Chapter 18, which deals with report writing.

BOX 10.2 SOCIAL RESEARCHERS AT WORK

Stricter Rules for Publishing in Medical Journals: Fallout from the Nancy Olivieri Incident?

The editors of 13 leading medical journals, including such prestigious ones as *The Lancet*, the *New England Journal of Medicine*, the *Journal of the American Medical Association*, and the *Canadian Medical Association Journal*, have decided to no longer publish articles whose scientific impartiality is in question. The editors argue that it is the researchers, not sponsors of research, who must control the design, data collection, data interpretation, and the right to publish or not publish findings.

The hope is that by insisting on the right to review study protocols and funding contracts the journals will be able to enhance the credibility and independence of their articles.

It is thought that the decision by the editors was, in part, a response to the Nancy Olivieri incident in which the Toronto hematologist lost her funding from the pharmaceutical firm Apotex,

Inc. after there was a disagreement over the possible risks in taking the drug deferiprone.

Besides their role in achieving regulatory approval, clinical trials increasingly are used in marketing drugs. And given the astronomical costs (estimated to be up to $500 million for one drug) of achieving such approvals, it is no surprise that researchers are under intense pressure to come up with findings supportive of the drug.

Canadian researchers Steven Lewis (University of Calgary), Françoise Baylis (Dalhousie), and Patricia Baird and Robert Evans (UBC) are urging the adoption of tough new rules to prevent our researchers from becoming the handmaids of industry. Their article "Dance Carefully with the Porcupine" is published in the *Canadian Medical Association Journal* (2001).

Source: Summarized from André Picard (2001). "Medical Journals Set Stricter Rules for Studies." *The Globe and Mail*, September 10.

7. THE USE OF FINDINGS

Given the enormous confidence that western culture has in science, it is no surprise that the findings of science are powerful tools. Courts, politicians, the media, and the general public seem to respect science. Increasingly, social scientists are interviewed on radio and television, appear as expert witnesses in courts, and, indeed, provide evidence taken into account when legal and public-policy decisions are made. Scientific evidence is taken seriously.

Unfortunately, the research literature is easily misrepresented. The fact that the research literature contains many findings, some of which support a particular view and some of which do not, is itself a potential source of biased reviews of that literature. The social scientist who is committed to some social cause or to a particular theoretical perspective might select evidence that helps establish a particular position—like a debater seeking support for a particular conclusion. Because of a desire to support a particular position, the debater is not interested in contrary evidence—only preferred evidence is reported. The problem with using the debater's approach is that many people may think that the findings are objective and impartial, that they reflect a dispassionate, scientific view. But they may simply be a conclusion seeking corroborating evidence. Debaters enjoy the credibility of social science while violating the principle of impartiality. When social scientists slip inadvertently into advocacy roles, they compromise their credibility as "impartial social scientists."

An impartial approach would try to disconfirm a theory, try to rule out alternatives, and continually press any given theory hard in an effort to discover the limits under which it is applicable. While this can never be achieved perfectly, those who attempt to follow this approach are, nonetheless, trying to eliminate as much bias as possible in their research or in their reviews of the literature.

Peter W. Huber has explored the problem of the scientist-for-hire as it relates to the American court system in his book *Galileo's Revenge: Junk Science in the Courtroom* (1991). Numerous court cases in which huge sums of money are at stake involve the use of expert scientific witnesses. Huber argues that the system is at fault because it seems unable to distinguish good scientific testimony from that of the science charlatans who make careers out of court appearances. American courts are faulted for setting insufficient standards as to who may testify. Frequently lawyers consider many scientists, settling finally on the

ones who are willing to make "appropriate" testimony and to be coached. As personal injury lawyer Dennis Roberts notes:

> *You get a professor who earns $60,000 a year and give him the opportunity to make a couple of hundred thousand dollars in his spare time and he will jump at the chance . . . They are like a bunch of hookers in June. (quoted in Huber, 1991, p. 19)*

While Huber is concerned primarily with the problem of testimony from practitioners of the medical and the physical sciences, it will be even more difficult to establish the legitimacy of evidence from the social scientists who may be asked to testify on such matters as community standards of morality or on whether there is evidence that our legal and commercial institutions display bias against the poor, minorities, immigrants, or women.

In any case, Huber would argue that courts would do well to adopt the following measures:

- Pay more attention to establishing the consensus on a topic in the research community and rely less on the personal opinion of some expert who has been selected and groomed by a lawyer seeking a favourable outcome.

- Note whether the findings reported have been peer-reviewed (articles judged by a panel of professional scientists).

- Note whether the findings have been replicated (repeated by others).

- Seek out their own independent experts who can testify objectively and impartially (Huber, 1991).

So long as lawyers are doing the hiring, they are likely to "stack the deck" to improve their chances of winning their cases. This practice fails to represent the findings of science objectively and, thus, may compromise the ability of the courts to come to reasonable conclusions.

A Carnegie Commission report suggests that junk science testimony typically does not win in court. The commission recommends that courts ask three questions:

1. Can the scientific claim be tested?
2. Has the test been done? and
3. Was an appropriate scientific methodology used? (Begley, 1993, p. 64).

C. A PERSPECTIVE

As citizens, social scientists belong to a culture, but they are also members of the social science community and of subunits within that community. And just as membership in a culture predisposes one to favour certain beliefs, values, and behaviours, so, too, does membership in the social science community. There are many written and unwritten rules and understandings about what we should believe and how we should go about our work as social scientists.

1. UNDERSTANDING BIAS

Not only do we take the predispositions, or biases, of our culture to our research but we also bring those acquired as members of various social science subgroups. So, regardless of whether we are positivist, interpretive, or critical in our basic perspective, we bring a set of assumptions, beliefs, theoretical orientations, and expectations to our research. Indeed, a text on methods provides sets of techniques for conducting research and attempts to socialize the student into an understanding and acceptance of the latest approaches to research. In their education,

research methods students are provided with a set of dispositions, a set of rules not only for doing research but for judging the work of other scholars. In short, the norms of research are being communicated.

But the ideas conveyed in a methods text focus on the formal system of social science. You learn how to do research "properly." You learn what techniques are appropriate in any given circumstance. And most methods texts will urge you not to fall prey to bias, urge you to be fair and objective, and urge you to exercise great care so that you will do *good*, impartial research. Are there any problems with this?

The problem is that an important part of social research is missed. While most presentations of research sound straightforward, there is much that happens in the course of the research process that never gets reported. In short, the research act itself can be the subject of research. A careful examination of most social science research projects would reveal how bias inadvertently plays a role in research outcomes. There is, then, a formal system of science—somewhat mythical—and there is the real world of social science. The gap between myth and reality exists in all academic disciplines.

Research is social behaviour. There are expectations of others to be met, norms of behaviour to be followed, and findings that are anticipated. This social component of science is frequently at odds with the fundamental canons of science. Science as practised is neither value-free nor wholly objective. If actual research practices are observed, a whole host of nonscientific factors enters the picture. While the achievements of science have, indeed, been impressive, it is nonetheless true that there is a gap between the ideal and actual practices of science. An awareness of this gap, and of the sources of bias in research, can only benefit the beginning research methods student. Just as the good scientist is portrayed as a skeptic, so should we be skeptical of the methods of social science itself. Table 10.1 provides a few examples of gaps between actual and ideal practices in the social sciences.

Projects are rarely as straightforward as the final report on the project implies. Take sampling. It is a rare project that does not run into some difficulties here. First, there are problems with refusals and lost

questionnaires. Some of the responses may not be clear; when comparisons between the sample and the known parameters of the population are compared, there are often uncomfortable disparities. Interviewers may have cut corners in the interest of completing the project (such tactics may range from faking interviews to avoiding the normal random respondent-selection process, even going so far as to include whoever happens to be available in a sample). In

TABLE 10.1 MYTHS AND REALITIES OF THE SOCIAL SCIENCES

CATEGORY	SOCIAL SCIENCE MYTHS	SOCIAL SCIENCE REALITIES
Value free?	Research is objective and value neutral	There are significant subjective elements in all research
Stereotype: Psychology	Psychologists primarily use experimental data	They also do field studies, surveys
Stereotype: Sociology	Sociologists primarily use survey data	They also do field studies, content analysis, experiments
Stereotype: Anthropology	Anthropologists study exotic cultures	They also study many contemporary western societies
Stereotype: Political Science	Political scientists study formal political organization and voting behaviour	They also study many other aspects of political behaviour, using a variety of techniques
Sampling	Most studies involve representative samples	Most studies are based on nonrepresentative samples
Refusals	Most people are willing to participate in studies	Refusals run from 0% to 95%; commercial market researchers have highest nonparticipation rates
Funding	Open to all; based on peer review and an evaluation of the quality of the proposal and the research record of the applicant	Researchers who are not part of the university system have little chance of receiving funding; there are fads that determine what kinds of projects are funded
Measurement	Agreement on appropriate way to measure most variables	Little standardization or agreement on measures
Report writing	Final reports summarize the results of the observations	Evidence is selectively reported; some facts ignored, not reported
Tests of significance	They assess the extent to which results may be due to chance sampling fluctuations	Often inappropriately used when non-probability sampling is used, or when whole populations studied

short, research is inevitably more messy than our reports of it.

In our exploration of sources of bias in the various stages of research, we have noted how the outcomes of research can be distorted inadvertently. Findings tend to move in the direction of the culturally acceptable, in the direction of our expectations, and in the direction of our preferences. And, if the pervasive attitudes of both the relevant scholarly disciplines and the larger society are liberal and inclusive and stress tolerance, then the research outcomes will tend to reflect these views. On the other hand, a more conservative, exclusive, and intolerant society will encourage research outcomes that are supportive of these views. Funding agencies and their selection processes will particularly encourage "mainstream" researchers—those whom referees think meet the standards governing "good" research. A similar argument can be advanced about the publication decisions of journal editors.

In recent decades a blurring of the line between **advocacy research** on the one hand, and **pure/descriptive research** on the other seems to have occurred. One possible explanation is that social science practitioners have become increasingly aware that all research carries cultural baggage with it. So, whether we talk of research design bias, funding decisions, data collection, analysis, interpretation, or publication decisions, research tends to reflect its sociocultural milieu. This realization perhaps helped to legitimize the use of social research to advocate changes or advance the personal or collective agendas of its practitioners. Box 10.3 contains a tongue-in-cheek classification of various diseases found in the social science community.

The challenge to create an impartial social science has been enormous: some would deny its possibility; others would claim that it is difficult, though not impossible; while still others would claim that all we can do is try to minimize bias in social research. Realizing that there are many difficulties in doing research should not lead the student to despair. The social sciences deal with an extremely difficult subject matter. So difficult, in fact, that some would argue that a scientific social science is impossible. However, all disciplines have their difficulties and challenges. A major problem for the social scientist, in addition to the inherent complexity of the subject matter of the social sciences, is that we are part of the subject matter we are trying to study. We are dealing with a subject where the researcher has to deal continually with strongly held beliefs, not only about how society works but about how it ought to work. A science of society is a challenge, indeed.

The degree of bias reflected in research reports ranges across a continuum. On the one hand, there are research reports specifically designed to study bias; the psychology experiments exploring experimenter effects fall into this category (see Rosenthal and Fode, 1963; Rosenthal, 1966; Johnson and Adair, 1970; Johnson and Ryan, 1976, for examples). While there may well be some inadvertent bias to find bias in these studies, great pains are taken to measure the sources and extent of distortions. At the other end of the continuum are the social activists and advocates whose research leaves little doubt as to its underpinning assumptions and preferences. So, whether we are dealing with a community group doing research to block a school closure or a research project to oppose the location of a landfill site, there is no question as to the stance that will be taken in the study. Bias will almost certainly take the form of overstating both the size and social importance of the problem. In between these extremes fall those studies whose distortions are subtle but almost certainly present.

BOX 10.3

Social Science Afflictions

As an exercise in better understanding bias, social science afflictions are classified. All researchers are afflicted to some degree with at least one of these biases. (Let the innocent cast the first stone.) The following diagnostic categories and treatments are offered for your consideration.

THEORETICAL RIGOR MORTIS Characterized by a quest to do research that will support a favoured theory. Those suffering from this affliction, when asked about it, protest their health, and continue to do research that is rigidly interpreted as supportive of a particular theory. The interest appears to be not in testing the theory's limits but in finding additional support for it. *Cure:* Do a project that puts the favoured theory at risk. Publish the results. Use your real name.

METHODOLOGICAL PARALYSIS An inability to move to different research designs, measurement procedures, or analytical techniques. People who suffer from this affliction spend their time locating problems that can be resolved using familiar design and measurement procedures. *Cure:* Conduct a study using a design, measurements, and statistical procedures that you have never used before. Enjoy it. Understand it.

TRUE BELIEVER FEVER These are the people always in search of evidence to support their particular view of the world, whether in a hypothesis or a pet finding. They strongly challenge competing evidence, ruling it as irrelevant. *Cure:* Write a paper enumerating the flaws in your perspective. Mean it.

GOOD CAUSE SYNDROME These are the researchers with a cause: social science is used where its findings can be made to support the preferred view. Evidence to the contrary is dismissed as methodologically or theoretically flawed. These are the researchers who inevitably show up to help the underdog—or the overdog. They may also suffer from terminal liberalism, terminal political correctness, or terminal conservatism—all for a good cause, all in the name of virtue, all in the name of social science. *Cure:* Write an essay defending cannibalism. Try to believe it.

GUERILLA RAIDERS' SYNDROME These patients typically do not do original research. Instead, they fashion a career out of attacking a particular theoretical or methodological approach. This syndrome is often jointly found in those who suffer from *True Believer Fever.* *Cure:* Do a primary research project. High cure rate.

SCIENTISM AILMENT The belief that if we follow the models of the physical sciences we will eventually understand social behaviour and it will become as predictable as are relations in engineered physical systems. *Cure:* For each day during the next month, predict the weather ten days in advance. Check performance.

ANTI-SCIENCE FEVER Characterized by the belief that social behaviour cannot be understood using orientations borrowed from the physical sciences. Anger is directed at the science practitioners who are favoured in our culture. *Cure:* Marriage to someone with the *Scientism Ailment* is recommended. Check frequently: there is a danger of a double murder.

REPLICATIONITIS This terminal boredom condition is characterized by the researcher who keeps replicating the same study—with minor variation in samples or in the variables involved. This is the person who makes a career out of studying the same set of variables. Incessantly. *Cure:* Cut off funds. Get a hobby.

NO AFFLICTION AFFLICTION These are the social scientists who think that their research is unbiased—untainted by brushes with their sociocultural milieu. *Cure:* Not treatable since the patient is in strong denial. Pray.

Social scientists' increasing awareness of the problems of bias in all research has, in some ways, helped to legitimize those who openly devote their research to advocacy. Critics of mainstream social research believe it supports the interests of the established order in society. Thus, those who consider crime worthy of investigation are considered to be responding to middle-class concerns about the security of property; those who study declines in government funding for higher education are perhaps responding to middle-class parents' concerns about the cost of educating their children. Those supporting such advocacy research would argue that if mainstream research has supported the established order in society then there should also be support for those who openly advance the interests of the underclasses. Why should researchers not try to advance the interests of minorities, women, people with disabilities, the working poor, the homeless, or developing countries? Why should social science not apply knowledge to alleviate suffering? Should the pure researcher stop at describing and explaining the incidence of suffering? Should the applied question, the question of alleviating suffering, be addressed directly by the social scientist? Increasingly, social scientists seem to be coming to the view that pure research, while it has its place, does not go far enough; if the social researcher does not press for the applied changes suggested by social research, who will? Thus, the role of the social scientist has broadened to include an applied dimension. But this broadening has led to confusion as to the line between pure research and advocacy.

2. RULES FOR MINIMIZING BIAS

The following sections provide some suggestions for dealing with research bias. There are no easy answers here. These rules are intended to provoke discussion and, since not all of them are acceptable to all social scientists, they should be considered tentative.

RULE 10.1 ALERT KEY PLAYERS TO THE PROBLEM OF BIAS.

We need to alert our society to the idea that much research, in the end, tends to support some interest or interest group. Education about bias needs to be directed to students, research practitioners, public-policy personnel, courts, governments, and the general public. To the extent that research supports some interest or interest group, research activities can have an underlying structural bias that favours doing work on certain types of research questions and arriving at socially acceptable conclusions.

RULE 10.2 AVOID SEXISM.

In all phases of research, avoid sexism.

RULE 10.3 IDENTIFY ROLES PLAYED BY THE RESEARCH PROCESS.

As researchers we need to be honest about the role we are playing. Advocacy research should be identified as such, as this will avoid confusion. In many cases, our role shifts several times while doing a project. For example, the choice of subject matter might be influenced by advocacy interests, the interpretation of the descriptive and pure aspects of the research might be largely impartial and value-neutral, and the policy recommendations might be directed toward bringing about changes meant to benefit a particular social group. Try to be clear about what hat you are wearing and alert the reader when you switch hats. Have the standards of evidence altered as you move from one phase to another?

RULE 10.4 ELIMINATE BIAS IN DESCRIPTIVE PHASE OF RESEARCH.

In the descriptive phase of research, efforts should be made to ensure that the description is not biased by the way questions are asked and that proper sampling procedures

have been followed rigidly. While subjective elements will influence choices about what should be described and how questions should be posed, once such decisions have been made, the collection, analysis, and interpretation of data should be as free of distortion as possible.

RULE 10.5 IN EXPLANATORY RESEARCH, LET DISCONFIRMATION BE YOUR GUIDE.

In pure research, be certain that competing explanations are given a fair chance. Efforts should be made to disconfirm relations, not to support them.

RULE 10.6 POLICY RECOMMENDATIONS SHOULD BE IDENTIFIED AS VALUE-BASED.

In the policy-recommendation phase, it should be made clear that the evaluations and recommendations of the researcher are intended to achieve some end; given this assumption, we should ask if there is any connection between the conclusions of the research and the researcher's assessment of the likely success of the proposed intervention strategy. In some cases, the research has specifically evaluated competing intervention strategies; in other cases, the intervention strategy proposed is purely commonsensical and has not been evaluated. In both cases, the extent to which the research has assessed intervention alternatives should be made clear to the reader. In short, has the research actually tested the likely response to both intervention strategy A and intervention strategy B?

RULE 10.7 BE SKEPTICAL OF RESEARCH FINDINGS.

Be skeptical of all reported research findings, given the many sources of bias that could have influenced the conclusions. A healthy, questioning attitude toward one's own and others' findings is appropriate, particularly in those disciplines in which there is much room for interpretation.

RULE 10.8 READ LITERATURE CAUTIOUSLY.

In reviewing literature, try to distinguish between those conclusions that appear to be demonstrated logically and/or empirically from those that are speculative. To avoid bias is also to recognize it. One must distinguish between conclusions that appear to have a sound basis and those that are speculative and untested.

RULE 10.9 DISTINGUISH ADVOCACY FROM PURE RESEARCH.

Try to identify those researchers who are engaged in advocacy. By being able to identify someone who is mounting evidence to support a position, whether on theoretical or public-policy issues, one can recognize a debater at work. There is nothing inherently wrong with advocacy, but it must be recognized that its conclusions are not impartial. Where it is clear that a case is being mounted, the question to ask is: "But, Sir, what experiment could disprove your hypothesis?" (Platt, 1964, p. 352).

RULE 10.10 ORIENT RESEARCH TO DISCONFIRMATION.

If studies are designed to rule out alternatives, to disconfirm theories, then one is on the road to minimizing bias.

RULE 10.11 USE THEORY TO GENERATE TESTABLE HYPOTHESES.

Use theory as a guide, as a tool for generating testable hypotheses. Theories should be regarded as efficient summaries of findings and as tools for deriving predictions about relationships between variables. Theories are attempts to make general summary statements and are to be revised continually. Remember, theories are for testing, not supporting.

RULE 10.12 BE SENSITIVE TO YOUR OWN OUTCOME PREFERENCES.

Contemplate your own values. Recognizing your own preferences concerning the kind of society you would like to live in will help to alert you to potential biases that you may bring to a research project. Being sensitive to your own biases enables you to design studies that are more value-neutral rather than studies predisposed to generate results favouring your personal preferences.

RULE 10.13 DO NOT DISCLOSE HYPOTHESES TO SUBJECTS OR ASSISTANTS.

Do not reveal hypotheses to research subjects or assistants. It seems safest to follow this rule if expectancy bias is to be reduced. It may, however, be necessary to provide some general idea of what the study is about, but it is best not to provide either research assistants or subjects with the details.

RULE 10.14 COVER THE ATTITUDINAL CONTINUUM.

Where possible, avoid showing your hand by presenting a variety of views. This will give the respondent a sense that all responses are acceptable. Be certain to offer a full range of attitudinal response categories so that no respondent is always forced to the extreme of the continuum.

RULE 10.15 BE ACCEPTING OF ALL RESPONSES.

Interviewers must be trained to appear to ask questions neutrally and to respond in the same way to all respondents' answers. Ideally, the interviewer should convey an impression of neutrality, yet have a keen interest in respondents' answers. Interviewers should avoid coaching responses.

RULE 10.16 SPECIFY DATA ANALYSIS PROCEDURES IN ADVANCE.

Just as hypotheses must be specified in advance, so must data analysis procedures. To avoid bias or playing with the data, analytical procedures must be specified in advance of data collection. While this may be viewed as a restrictive rule, if followed, it prevents unwarranted massaging of the data.

RULE 10.17 CHECK FOR RANDOM AND SYSTEMATIC ERRORS.

Researchers need to be aware of both random and systematic errors and put into place procedures to minimize both types of errors.

RULE 10.18 REPORT EXTENT OF DATA MASSAGING.

Report the number of relationships that have been explored in the course of data analysis. Researchers should clarify the number of relationships that have been examined and the reasons why certain findings have not been reported.

The above section is intended to suggest that we need to be sensitive to bias and to its role in different types of research projects and different phases of a research project. Predispositions to favour certain outcomes will always be present in human activities, including social research. To appreciate that simple idea is a good start.

D. KEY POINTS

A bias may be thought of as a preference—or predisposition—to favour a particular conclusion. *Research bias may be defined as the systematic distortion of research outcomes.* Such distortions occur in all disciplines and in all phases of the research operation from selecting the problem and the variables to be studied, to developing measurements of the relevant variables, to collecting and analyzing data, right through to reporting the results of the research. There are worrying sources of bias in all research and in all disciplines.

Researchers must be careful to avoid bias in the design, execution, and reporting of research.

The term *researcher affect* refers to the tendency of researchers to fall in love with a particular explanation of some relationship or a particular view of the world in a way that inadvertently leads them to use procedures that generate conclusions supporting the preferred explanation or world view.

The term *experimenter effect* refers to a tendency to produce findings consistent with the experimenter's expectations.

E. KEY TERMS

Advocacy research	Expectancy	Pure/descriptive research
Androcentricity	Experimenter effect	Random error
Bias	Familism	Research bias
Data massaging	Gender insensitivity	Researcher affect
Demand characteristic	Overgeneralization	Sexual dichotomism
Double standard	Overspecificity	Systematic error

ETHICAL ISSUES

A. TWO STUDIES ILLUSTRATING ETHICAL DILEMMAS

The decade of the 1960s was a time of enormous growth in the social sciences. University enrolments expanded and the number of social science practitioners grew correspondingly. There were few rules governing research in the burgeoning disciplines.

Several studies conducted in the 1960s raised key ethical issues for social scientists. By the 1990s, many professional associations, all universities, colleges, and hospitals, and most government agencies had in place codes of ethics to guide social researchers. Researchers have obligations to their subjects, to themselves, to their disciplines, and to their society; researchers need to recognize their different roles and role obligations.

Conflicting pressures often emerge in designing studies, as the researcher may be torn between the desire to use the "ideal" design for a study and the desire to use a less effective design that does not entail activities and techniques that go beyond what is "ethically possible" when studying human subjects. What is convenient for research may be unacceptable ethically. This chapter outlines two studies that illustrate some of the ethical dilemmas faced by the social researcher. Following this review, a series of rules will be presented to guide the researcher in resolving ethical problems which may emerge.

There are a number of studies that have become landmarks in the discussion of research ethics. Two major such studies are Stanley Milgram's research on compliance with authority, which had subjects administer electric shocks to victims, and Laud Humphreys' research observing homosexual contacts in a public washroom. Both of these studies had an impact on the development of regulations governing social research. While many studies do not pose serious ethical dilemmas for the social researcher, it is important for the beginning researcher to understand the impetus behind the development of the codes of ethics adopted by various professional and governmental agencies.

1. LAUD HUMPHREYS: *TEAROOM TRADE*

Let us begin this section by examining a study that has been important because of both its subject matter and the ethical issues it raises. Humphreys' classic study, emerging from his doctoral dissertation at Washington University in St. Louis, was based on observations of homosexuals meeting in public washrooms. An excerpt from the methodology section of Humphreys' work is included in Box 11.1.

The publication of Humphreys' book provoked both critical comment and support. Many have opposed Humphreys' research on ethical grounds; the statements by Nicholas Von Hoffman (1970) and by Donald P. Warwick are particularly incisive. The following quotation provides a sense of journalist Von Hoffman's position:

We're so preoccupied with defending our privacy against insurance investigators, dope sleuths, counterespionage men, divorce detectives and credit checkers, that we overlook the social scientists behind the hunting blinds who're also peeping into what we thought were our most private and secret lives. But they are there, studying us, taking notes, getting to know us, as indifferent as everybody else to the feeling that to be a complete human involves having an aspect of ourselves

BOX 11.1 SOCIAL RESEARCHERS AT WORK

Laud Humphreys: Tearoom Trade

The Sociologist as Voyeur

For several months, I had noted fluctuations in the number of automobiles that remained more than fifteen minutes in front of the sampled tearooms. My observations had indicated that, with the sole exception of police cars, autos that parked in front of these public restrooms (which, as has been mentioned, are usually isolated from other park facilities) for a quarter of an hour or more invariably belonged to participants in the homosexual encounters. The same is true for cars that appeared in front of two or more such facilities in the course of an hour . . .

I also noted, whenever possible, a brief description of both the car and its driver. By means of frequent sorties into the tearooms for observation, each recorded license number was verified as belonging to a man actually observed in homosexual activity inside the facilities . . .

The original sample thus gained was of 134 license numbers, carefully linked to persons involved in the homosexual encounters, gathered from the environs of ten public restrooms in four different parks of a metropolitan area of two million people . . .

The tearooms are challenging, not only because they present unusual problems for the researcher but because they provide an extraordinary opportunity for detailed observation. Due to the lack of verbal communication and the consistency of the physical settings, a type of laboratory is provided by these facilities—one in which human behavior may be observed with the control of a number of variables . . .

A sociologist without verbal communication is like a doctor without a stethoscope. The silence of these sexual encounters confounded such research problems as legitimation of the observer and identification of roles . . . the patterns of behavior themselves acquire meaning independent of verbalization . . .

Despite the almost inviolate silence within the restroom setting, tearoom participants are neither mute nor particularly taciturn. Away from the scenes where their sexual deviance is exposed—outside what I shall later discuss as the "interaction membrane"—conversation is again possible. Once my car and face had become familiar, I was able to enter into verbal relationships with twelve of the participants . . .

After the initial contacts with this intensive dozen, I told them of my research, disclosing my real purpose for being in the tearooms. With the help of some meals together and a number of drinks, all agreed to cooperate in subsequent interviewing sessions . . . Apart from the systematic observations themselves, these conversations constitute the richest source of data in the study.

Some may ask why, if nine of these cooperating respondents were obtained without the formal interviews, I bothered with the seemingly endless task of acquiring a sample and administering questionnaires—particularly when

cont'd

interviews with the intensive dozen provided such depth to the data. The answer is simple: these men are not representative of the tearoom population. I could engage them in conversation only because they are more overt, less defensive, and better educated than the average participant.

This suggests a problem for all research that relies on willing respondents. Their very willingness to cooperate sets them apart from those they are meant to represent. *Tally's Corner* and *Street Corner Society* stand high among the classics of social science—and rightly so—but I wonder sometimes how well Tally and Doc represent the apathetic, alienated, uninvolved men of the street corners. When authors such as Liebow and Whyte strive to compensate for this by extending their research throughout the friendship networks, great ethnography results. But the saddest works in the name of social science are those that barrage the reader with endless individual case studies and small samples from private psychiatric practices, few of which can be representative of the vast numbers of human beings who are supposed to be "understood" in terms of these deviant deviants . . .

Identification of the sample was made by using the automobile license registers of the states in which my respondents lived. Fortunately, friendly policemen gave me access to the license registers, without asking to see the numbers or becoming too inquisitive about the type of "market research" in which I was engaged. These registers provided the names and addresses of those in the sample, as well as the brand name and

year of the automobiles thus registered. The make of the car, as recorded in the registers, was checked against my transcribed description of each car . . . Names and addresses were then checked in the directories of the metropolitan area, from which volumes I also acquired marital and occupational data for most of the sample . . .

Like archives, park restrooms, and automobiles, the streets of our cities are subject to public regulation and scrutiny. They are thus good places for nonreactive research (nonreactive in that it requires no response from the research subjects) . . . The first purpose of this survey of homes was to acquire descriptions of the house types and dwelling areas . . . As physical evidence, however, homes provide a source of data about a population that outweighs any failure they may have as a status index. Swing sets and bicycles in the yards indicate that a family is not childless. A shrine to Saint Mary suggests that the resident is Roman Catholic in religious identification. Christmas decorations bespeak at least a nominal Christian preference. A boat or trailer in the driveway suggests love of the outdoor life. "For Rent" signs may indicate the size of an average apartment and, in some cases, the price. The most important sign, however, was the relative "neatness" of the house and grounds . . .

Realizing that the majority of my participant sample were married—and nearly all of them quite secretive about their deviant activity—I was faced with the problem of how to interview more than the nine willing respondents. Formal interviews of the sample were part of the original research design. The little I knew about these covert deviants made me want to know a great deal more. Here was a unique population just waiting to be studied—but I had no way to approach them. Clearly, I could not knock on the door of a suburban residence and say, "Excuse me, I saw you engaging in a homosexual act in a tearoom last year, and I wonder if I might ask you a few questions." Having already been jailed, locked in a restroom, and attacked by a group of ruffians, I had no desire to conclude my research with a series of beatings . . .

About this time, fortunately, I was asked to develop a questionnaire for a social health survey of men in the community, which was being conducted by a research center with which I had been a research associate. Based on such interview schedules already in use in Michigan and New York, the product would provide nearly all the information I would want on the men in my sample: family background, socioeconomic factors, personal health and social histories, religious and employment data, a few questions on social and political attitudes, a survey of friendship networks, and information on marital relationships and sex.

With the permission of the director of the research project, I added my deviant sample to the over-all sample of the survey, making certain that only one trusted, mature graduate student and I made all the interviews of my respondents. Using a table of random numbers, I randomized my sample, so that its representativeness would not be lost in the event that we should be unable to complete all 100 interviews . . .

My master list was kept in a safe-deposit box. Each interview card, kept under lock and key, was destroyed with completion of the schedule. No names or other identifying tags were allowed to appear on the questionnaires. Although I recognized each of the men interviewed from observation of them in the tearooms, there was no indication that they remembered me. I was careful to change my appearance, dress, and automobile from the days when I had passed as deviant. I also allowed at least a year's time to lapse between the original sampling procedures and the interviews.

This strategy was most important—both from the standpoint of research validity and ethics—because it enabled me to approach my respondents as normal people, answering normal questions, as part of a normal survey . . . they were not interviewed as deviants . . .

Once these interviews were completed, preparations could be made for the final step of the research design. From names appearing in the randomly selected sample of the over-all social health survey, fifty men were selected, matched with the completed questionnaires . . .

These last fifty interviews, then, enabled me to compare characteristics of two samples—one deviant, one control—matched on the basis of certain socioeconomic characteristics, race, and marital status.

From a methodological standpoint, the value of this research is that it has employed a variety of methods, each testing a different outcropping of the research population and their sexual encounters. It has united the systematic

cont'd

use of participant observation strategies with other nonreactive measures such as physical traces and archives. The exigencies of research in a socially sensitive area demanded such approaches; and the application of unobtrusive measures yielded data that call, in turn, for reactive methods.

Research strategies . . . are the outgrowth of the researcher's basic assumptions. Special conditions of the research problem itself also exercise a determining influence upon the methods used. This chapter has been an attempt to indicate how my ethnographic assumptions, coupled with the difficulties inhering in the study of covert deviants and their behavior, have given rise to a set of strategies.

With the help of "oddball" measures, the outlines of the portrait of participants in the homosexual encounters of the tearooms appeared. Reactive strategies were needed to fill in the distinguishing features. They are human, socially patterned features; and it is doubtful that any one method could have given them the expressive description they deserve.

that's unknown . . . No information is valuable enough to obtain by nipping away at personal liberty, and that is true no matter who's doing the gnawing, John Mitchell and the conservatives over at the Justice Department or Laud Humphreys and the liberals over at the Sociology Department. (Von Hoffman, 1970, pp. 4–6)

Irving Louis Horowitz and Lee Rainwater (1970) wrote a spirited response to Von Hoffman's article by pointing out that Humphreys was perfectly entitled to be in a public washroom and that the tactics Humphreys used to gain interviews with the participants were necessary if the project was to be completed. Furthermore, they point out that no one has demonstrated that the subjects' right to privacy was violated. Their concluding argument is as follows:

Laud Humphreys has gone beyond the existing literature in sexual behavior and has proven once again, if indeed proof were ever needed, that ethnographic research is a powerful tool for social understanding and policy making. And these are the criteria by which the research should finally be evaluated professionally . . . In other words, the issue is not liberalism vs. conservatism or privacy vs. publicity, but much more simply and to the point, the right of scientists to conduct their work as against the right of journalists to defend social mystery and private agony. (1970, p. 8)

Donald P. Warwick indicates three ethical objections to Humphreys' research:

1. He took advantage of a powerless group of men to pursue the study.

2. The method used to follow up on the tearoom participants reinforces the image that social researchers are "sly tricksters who are not to be trusted."

3. By using deception, Humphreys encourages others in society to follow his lead (1973, p. 37).

Warwick goes on to argue that:

Social research involving deception and manipulation ultimately helps produce a society of cynics, liars and manipulators, and undermines the trust which is essential to a just social order. (1973b, p. 38)

There appear to be four key points in Humphreys' procedures that raise ethical issues:

1. The researcher acted as a lookout, alerting participants engaged in an illegal activity of any impending danger.

2. Unknown to the subjects, the researcher noted the licence numbers of their cars.

3. Licence numbers were traced to reveal the name and address of each car owner.

4. Traced participants were interviewed as part of a larger public health survey.

A. AIDING IN CRIME

Tearoom Trade raises the issue of a social scientist aiding in crime, acting as a lookout to alert people engaged in an illegal activity. When this study was done homosexual activity in Missouri was punishable by a sentence of not less than two years upon conviction (Humphreys, 1970, p. 26). Technically, then, Humphreys was assisting in committing a crime. Should the social scientist ever engage in such activities? Under what conditions does the importance of a project justify an illegal activity?

B. WITHHOLDING INFORMATION

On two occasions, Humphreys withheld information from the police. The first occurred when he was arrested for loitering after refusing to give police officers his name. Humphreys did not give the police the reason for his presence at the public lavatory. In fairness, he did not lie to the police: he just did not tell them what he was doing. Humphreys felt that the police were harassing him and he also wished to protect the identity of the people he was observing. After all, his field notes could have been subpoenaed. (Social researchers' sources are not protected by law in the United States or Canada.) He then not only would have compromised his project but would also have exposed those being observed to possible harassment, arrest, or public humiliation. Should Humphreys have told the police what he was doing?

On another occasion, Humphreys got names and addresses (traced from the licence numbers of participants' cars) from the police department under the guise of doing market research. The ease with which Humphreys was able to get the information might lead one to fault the police department for laxness. Humphreys was careful to make certain that the police did not record the licence numbers or the names he was getting. Indeed, Humphreys took great care to protect the identity of respondents by having the names and addresses locked in a safety deposit box in another state. Should Humphreys have misrepresented his reasons for tracing the licence numbers to get the names and addresses?

C. INFORMED CONSENT

Humphreys did not inform respondents how they had been selected for participation in a health survey. Here Humphreys admits that he was less than candid with his respondents (1970, p. 171). To further ensure that the respondents would not identify the researcher as the lookout, the interviews took place some 18 months after the tearoom observations and the researcher wore a disguise. None of the respondents indicated that they recognized the researcher. Had the respondents known how they were selected for the health survey, many would have refused participation. These men were most secretive about their clandestine tearoom liaisons, and the thought that someone had recorded information about them would have been scary. Was Humphreys justified in not revealing how the respondents were selected for participation in the study?

D. ENDANGERING A RESPONDENT

Humphreys was extremely careful to protect the identity of his respondents. His use of the safety deposit box for storing the names and addresses, his refusal to tell the police when he was arrested that he was a social researcher, and his use of a disguise were all done to reduce the real or perceived dangers of subjects being identified publicly as homosexuals. Nonetheless, there were risks. Was the project justified given the slight possibility that the respondents' names could inadvertently have been revealed, thus exposing the subjects to a heightened risk of arrest or harassment? Could the publication of the book lead morality squads to put even greater pressure on the gay community?

Perhaps all researchers need to try to anticipate possible dangers and then either abandon the project or rethink it in light of its potentially harmful effects. Humphreys was sensitive to the difficult ethical issues involved in his project; indeed, even before much of the furor over his project erupted (see postscript below), he had written a chapter on his view of the issues involved. Box 11.2 excerpts Humphreys' comments on the ethical issues in his study.

As a postscript to the discussion of Humphreys' research, we should note that his work had a positive influence in the development of the gay rights movement in the United States (Reynolds, 1982, p. 69). Nonetheless, his work raised agonizing ethical issues and also had an unfortunate impact on Washington University's sociology program. Ethical questions concerning his research resulted in an attempt to prevent Humphreys from receiving his Ph.D. The resulting battle created problems in the department, placed significant federal funding in jeopardy, led to the departure of several senior faculty members, and, ultimately, was one of the factors that led to the demise of sociology courses at the university. To this day, Washington University does not have a sociology program; this is unfortunate as, in the 1960s, Washington University's sociology program was considered to be in the top twenty in the United States.

Laud Humphreys (1930–1988) did receive his degree and went on to a distinguished research and teaching career at the State University of New York at Albany, School of Criminal Justice.

2. STANLEY MILGRAM: "BEHAVIORAL STUDY OF OBEDIENCE"

In 1963 Stanley Milgram published "Behavioral Study of Obedience." The study was important for a number of reasons.

- Its findings were disturbing to many readers because no one anticipated the extent to which subjects would comply with the request to continue administering electric shocks to fellow participants in an experiment.

- Its findings illustrate vividly the need to take into account the authority of the

BOX 11.2 SOCIAL RESEARCHERS AT WORK

Laud Humphreys: Postscript—A Question of Ethics

So long as we suspect that a method we use has at least some potential for harming others, we are in the extremely awkward position of having to weigh the scientific and social benefits of that procedure against its possible costs in human discomfort . . .

Are there, perhaps, some areas of human behavior that are not fit for social scientific study at all? Should sex, religion, suicide, or other socially sensitive concerns be omitted from the catalogue of possible fields of sociological research? . . .

I believe that preventing harm to his respondents should be the primary interest of the scientist. We are not, however, protecting a harassed population of deviants by refusing to look at them. At this very moment, my writing has been interrupted by a long-distance call, telling me of a man who has been discharged from his position and whose career has been destroyed because he was "caught" in a public restroom. This man, who protests his innocence, has suffered a nervous breakdown since his arrest. Even if acquitted, his personal identity has been damaged, perhaps irreparably, by the professional spy who apprehended him. The greatest harm a social scientist could do to this man would be to ignore him. Our concern about possible research consequences for our fellow "professionals" should take a secondary place to concern for those who may benefit from our research.

Situation Ethics

If it be granted, then, that the sociologist may commit a grave ethical violation by ignoring a problem area, we may consider the methods that should be used in such studies. Let it be noted that any conceivable method employable in the study of human behavior has at least some potential for harming others. Even the antiseptic strategies involved in studying public archives may harm others if they distort, rather than contribute to, the understanding of social behavior. Criminologists may study arrest statistics, as filtered to us through the FBI, without stirring from the safety of their study chairs, but such research methods may result in the creation of a fictitious "crime wave," a tide of public reaction, and the eventual production of a police state—all because the methods may distort reality . . .

The problems facing researchers, then, are of which methods may result in more or less misrepresentation of purposes and identity, more or less betrayal of confidence, and more or less positive or negative consequences for the subjects. Those who engage in the study of deviant behavior—or any behavior, for that matter—must become accustomed to the process of weighing possible social benefits against possible cost in human discomfort . . . The ethics of social science are situation ethics.

Problems of Misrepresentation

At the conclusion of his article, Erikson proposes two rules regarding

cont'd

misrepresentation of the researcher's identity and purposes:

RULE 1 It is unethical for a sociologist to deliberately misrepresent his identity for the purpose of entering a private domain to which he is not otherwise eligible.

RULE 2 It is unethical for a sociologist to deliberately misrepresent the character of the research in which he is engaged.

Since one's identity within the interaction membrane of the tearoom is represented only in terms of the participant role he assumes, there was no misrepresentation of my part as an observer: I was indeed a "voyeur," though in the sociological and not the sexual sense. My role was primarily that of watchqueen, and that role I played well and faithfully. In that setting, then, I misrepresented my identity no more than anyone else. Furthermore, my activities were intended to gain entrance not to "a private domain" but to a public restroom. The only sign on its door said "Men," which makes me quite eligible for entering. It should be clear, then, that I have not violated Erikson's first canon. Although passing as deviant to avoid disrupting the behavior I wished to observe, I did not do so to achieve copresence in a private domain.

The second rule may be applied to the reactive part of my research, when I interviewed persons I had observed in the tearooms under the pretext of a social health survey. Here it should be noted that all interviews were in fact made as part of a larger social health survey, and abstracted data from my interviews are already in use in that study.

The problem then may be viewed in two ways: First, I gave less than full representation of what I was doing, though without giving false representation. I wore only one of two possible hats, rather than going in disguise. Second, I made multiple use of my data. Is it unethical to use data that someone has gathered for purposes one of which is unknown to the respondent? With the employment of proper security precautions, I think such multiple use is quite ethical; it is frequently employed by anyone using such data banks as the records of the Bureau of Census.

Problems of Confidentiality

. . . I have taken every possible precaution to protect the identities of my respondents and the confidential nature of their communication with me . . . I have guarded the names and addresses in my sample and used only strategies that would safeguard all identities. I even allowed myself to be jailed rather than alert the police to the nature of my research, thus avoiding the incrimination of respondents through their possible association with a man under surveillance.

Problems of Consequentiality

Finally, I must weigh the possible results of this research. It is not enough to plead that I am no seer, for I am a sociologist and should have some ability for prediction. If I have been honest enough in my analyses and convincing enough in their presentation, there should be no negative reaction from the forces of social control. I should hope they would have learned something. Perhaps some will move to construct and situate restrooms in such a way as to discourage the tearoom trade. Except where such activity constitutes an obvious public nuisance, I hope there will be no change in the tearoom locale. There is no need to drive this harmless activity underground. Those who deal in the sex market are resourceful, however, and I doubt that anything short of a total police state could erase the search for sex without commitment! . . .

I doubt that this work will have any effect in either increasing or decreasing the volume of homosexual activity in park restrooms. I do hope it will give readers a better understanding of the activity that is already there. I have no moral or intellectual objection to what goes on in the tearooms, and only a mild aesthetic one. I do have a moral objection to the way in which society reacts to those who take part in that action. As a scientist, I must believe that any addition to knowledge, which has suffered as little distortion as possible from the methods used, will help correct the superstition and cruelty that have marked such reaction in the past.

Source: Reprinted with permission from Laud Humphreys (1970). *Tearoom Trade: Impersonal Sex in Public Places.* New York: Aldine de Gruyter. Copyright © 1970, 1975 by R.A. Laud Humphreys.

---

researcher as a possible confounding variable in a social experiment.

- The study raised difficult ethical issues concerning the treatment of experimental subjects.

The ethical issues raised will be of particular concern in this chapter. The Milgram experiment has become, like Humphreys' research, a touchstone when questions of ethics are raised in connection with social research. Virtually all introductory textbooks in psychology use the Milgram study as an illustration when discussing research ethics (see Box 3.2 on p. 51, which presents the design of the Milgram study).

Box 3.2 reports on the procedures used in the original study. Briefly, subjects were fooled into believing that they are administering increasingly powerful shocks to another subject (who was actually a confederate working with the experimenter, faking increasing pain as the intensity of the "shocks" increased). If the subject asked for permission to stop, the experimenter told him to continue. About two-thirds of the subjects administered shocks that were labelled as dangerous to the victim. Following the experimental session, the subject met with the confederate and was then debriefed by the experimenter. In addition, a follow-up survey was made of the various participants in the studies, which indicated that they felt good about their involvement in the experiment (Milgram, 1964).

Diana Baumrind led off the questioning of Milgram's research. Her questions focused on two central points: first she questioned whether the design of the study was appropriate for the study of obedience given the "special quality of trust and obedience with which the subject appropriately regards the experimenter" (1964, p. 421). In short, Baumrind wondered whether the results showed strong compliance because the experiment took place in a laboratory setting in which the subject may have been particularly sensitive to the cues offered by the researcher. The second major point Baumrind raised is the issue of whether it is appropriate to entrap a subject into committing acts which, on later reflection, may lead to a loss of self-esteem and dignity. Could the subject be saying, "My God, on the instructions of another person, I was willing to inflict a dangerous electric shock to someone else participating in a social psychology experiment . . . what a jerk I am."

Does the social researcher have the right to do experiments which may lead to such devastating self-knowledge (Holden, 1979, p. 538)? Should we be in the business of showing people how awful they really are? And, since the study produced a lot of discomfort for the subjects, was Milgram justified in continuing with the work once this became apparent? How much subject discomfort is permissible in social research? (See Kaufmann, 1967; Kelman cited in Holden, 1979, p. 538.) How do we balance important gains in knowledge of human behaviour against the damage we may be doing to the self-esteem of our respondents? On the other hand, perhaps making experimental subjects recognize their flaws is no bad thing, as this may lead them to think more carefully about their own values (Kaufmann, 1967). Indeed, as the psychiatrist Milton Erickson argues in defending Milgram's research, it is important to study undesirable behaviour so that, as a society, we may be able to control the "ugly realities that have characterized human history since its beginning" (1968, p. 278). And, while challenging Milgram about the legitimacy of trying to make inferences about relations among nations from the study of interactions between a researcher and a subject, Amitai Etzioni recommends extending Milgram's research to take up related questions, such as the impact of a liberal education on the likelihood of obeying evil orders, or the effect that seeing a film on a war crimes trial would have on the likelihood of obeying such orders (Etzioni, 1968, pp. 279–80).

The one point that should not be overlooked, and which is taken up by Milgram in later trials, is the effect of different pressure techniques on the likelihood of subjects continuing with the shocks. The way in which subjects are encouraged to continue, or given an "easy out," seems to be critical in determining the percentage of subjects who continue administering shocks to victims.

Milgram responded to Baumrind's arguments by making clear that great care was taken in the post-experiment phase of the study to **debrief** the subjects. The experimenter pointed out to them that the confederate was not really receiving electric shocks, that their behaviour was entirely normal, and that their feelings of tension were also experienced by others. Milgram also provides information on two follow-up studies of the participants. The first was a questionnaire asking about their reaction to the study, which indicated a high level of approval for the study (about 84% claimed to be glad to have participated in the study). The second follow-up was conducted by an impartial medical examiner who concluded that among the 40 experimental subjects "no evidence was found of any traumatic reactions" (Milgram, 1964, p. 850). Unfortunately, in his response, Milgram did not provide a separate breakdown for how the original 40 subjects responded to the questionnaire on their experience with the study.

Milgram also suggests that had fewer subjects complied with the experimenter's request, there would have been much less reaction to his research. Milgram seems to suggest that his critics hated the findings, hated to learn that two-thirds of Americans would provide a lethal electric shock to an innocent participant simply on the instruction of an authority figure. Had most subjects refused to apply the electric shock to the confederate, would there have been much debate about the research?

Milgram's research was extended to include 18 additional experimental conditions. These have been neatly summarized by Reynolds, and his table is reproduced in Box 11.3. Note that the percentage of subjects administering the maximum shock varied from zero percent to 92.5% (Reynolds, 1982, pp. 25–26).

B. CRITERIA FOR ASSESSING ETHICAL ACCEPTABILITY

The studies cited above illustrate a range of ethical dilemmas. What criteria can be used to identify possible problems with a research design? Two approaches to this question have been noted: the *consequentialist* and the *deontological*.

1. THE CONSEQUENTIALIST VIEW

The **consequentialist** view is that ethical judgments about a research project should be made by evaluating its consequences for the subject, for the academic discipline, and for society. A cost-benefit analysis might reveal that the advantages gained because of the resulting advancement of our knowledge justify the violation of some rules: deception may be acceptable if it does not do any long-term damage. In Warwick's view (1973), Humphreys' research procedures do not justify the project because of the negative consequences to the discipline and to society.

The consequentialist view emphasizes anticipating the possibly unfortunate consequences of the research. Thus, one would want to assess the possible dangers to the subjects. (What would happen if the identity of Humphreys' tearoom participants become public or got into the hands of the police?) Will participation in the study be in any way degrading, dangerous, or expose the subject to undue levels of stress? Can these adverse experiences be justified by the study's contributions to our knowledge of human behaviour? Are we in any way entrapping individuals so that they do things that they otherwise might not do? Are we forcing them to take a position on some issue that they have never thought about? Would subjects' participation in the study reveal unpleasant, unsavoury things about them that might otherwise remain hidden? Should research be imposing unpleasant and perhaps unwanted self-knowledge on subjects? And, if this is sometimes the consequence, can it be justified by other payoffs? The consequentialist would permit projects so long as reasonable precautions are taken and subjects are debriefed so that no long-term negative consequences result.

In the biomedical area, permission to use unproven therapies on dying patients is now more readily available. There is pressure to permit the use of unproven drugs or therapies on such patients. In the area of AIDS and cancer treatments, we permit the use of experimental therapies because of the imminent death of the patient.

2. THE DEONTOLOGICAL VIEW

The **deontological** approach to research ethics proposes absolute moral strictures that must never be violated. Absolutes like never using deception, always masking the identity of respondents, and never putting any pressure on respondents to participate

BOX 11.3 SOCIAL RESEARCHERS AT WORK

Major Results of the Obedience to Authority Research Program

PERCENTAGE ADMINISTERING MAXIMUM SHOCK[1]	MEAN SHOCK LEVEL[2]	EXPERIMENT NO.[3]	EXPERIMENTAL CONDITION
Original Condition			
30.00	17.88	4	Touch-proximity (n=40) "Teacher" must hold "pupil's" hand on metal plate to complete circuit and operate equipment simultaneously
40.00	20.80	3	Proximity (n=40) "Teacher" and "pupil" in same room
62.50	24.53	2	Voice-feedback (n=40) "Teacher" hears "pupil" protest over intercom
65.00	27.0	1	Remote (n=40) "Teacher" hears "pupil" bang on wall in protest
Revised Procedure			
.00	10.00	12	"Pupil" demands to be shocked (n=20) Experimenter instructs "teacher" not to go on
.00	10.00	14	Experimenter serves as "pupil" (n=20) Ordinary man instructs "teacher" to go on
.00	10.00	15	Two experimenters give conflicting instructions (n=20) Ordinary man serves as "pupil"
2.5	5.50	11	"Teacher" chooses shock level (n=40) "Pupil" protests coordinated to shock level
10.00	16.45	17	Two peers rebel (n=40) "Teacher" task subdivided into three activities, subject "shocks"

20.00	16.25	13	Ordinary man gives orders (n=40) Experimenter leaves; "ordinary man," an accomplice, suggests increasing shock levels as own idea
20.50	18.2	7	Experimenter absent (n=40) Orders to "teacher" received over telephone
40.00	21.4	9	"Pupil" does not give full informed consent (n=40) Insists on right to terminate at will prior to becoming involved
47.50	20.95	10	Research conducted in commercial building (n=40) All other conditions on campus of major university
50.00	22.20	6	Variation in personnel (n=40) Different experimenter–"pupil" team
65.00	24.55	5	Voice-feedback condition: male subjects (n=40)
65.00	24.73	8	Voice-feedback condition: female subjects (n=40)
65.00	23.50	16	Two experimenters (n=20) One served as "pupil"
65.75	24.90	13a	Subjects as bystander (n=16) "Ordinary man" assumes right to administer shocks on own initiative
92.50	26.65	18	Peer administers shock (n=40) Subject maintains records on "pupil's" performance

[1] Refers to the percentage that administer shocks at the 450-volt level ("Danger," "Severe Shock," and "XXX" labels of equipment). In all but one condition, Ex. No. 12, this reflects obedience to terminate the study; he is always compliant.

[2] Equipment involved 30 levels of shock, labelled from 15 to 450 volts at 15-volt intervals. The shock level, in volts, can be computed by multiplying the level by 15; for example, level 10 was 150 volts.

[3] Indicated the number of the experiment as described in Milgram (1974).

Source: Descriptions based on Milgram (1974). Numbers in parentheses indicate the number of participants in each condition, a total of 636. Except in Exp. No. 8, all participants were male, chosen to represent different ages in the following proportions: 20-29, 20 percent; 30-39, 40 percent; and 40-49, 40 percent. Occupational categories were represented as follows: skilled and unskilled workers; 40 percent; white color, sales, and business, 40 percent; and professionals, 20 percent.

Source: Paul Davidson Reynolds (1982). *Ethics and Social Science Research*. New Jersey: Prentice Hall, pp. 25–26. Reprinted by permission of Prentice Hall, Englewood Cliffs, New Jersey.

in a study might be proposed by someone taking the deontological view. Rather than assessing the consequences of a given social science procedure, the deontological approach might propose, in its most extreme form, that deception in social psychological experiments is never justified, no matter what the positive contributions to our knowledge might be. Alasdair MacIntyre (cited by Holden, 1979, p. 538) argued that one can distinguish between types of harm to a human subject. He distinguishes between:

- harm to a subject's interests (such as reporting a case of venereal disease);

- wrongdoing (for example, lying to someone, which may not cause any damage);

- a moral harm (doing something to make the subject less good, such as encouraging the person to tell a lie).

MacIntyre argues that harms can be compensated for, whereas wrongs cannot be; hence, the argument is that if doing a wrong is essential to conducting a research project, then the project should be banned (cited in Holden, 1979, p. 538). According to this view, neither Milgram's research (because of the deception), nor Humphreys' research (because the health survey was misrepresented) could be condoned as ethically acceptable. Both would be barred, no matter what their importance for increasing our understanding of human behaviour.

C. MONITORING ETHICAL RESEARCH PRACTICES

Concerns about unethical research practices predate the social science research done by Humphreys and Milgram. Sadly, there is documentation of grossly unethical research conducted by social scientists, natural scientists, and medical researchers throughout the nineteenth and twentieth centuries. Awareness of unethical research led to the development of ethical guidelines for research involving humans. In Canada, one document now provides guidelines to encourage ethical research. It is called the *Tri-Council Policy Statement: Ethical Conduct for Research Involving Humans* (TCPS). The TCPS was developed by the Canadian Institute for Health Research (CIHR), the Natural Sciences and Engineering Research Council (NSERC), and the Social Sciences and Humanities Research Council (SSHRC), who collectively have created the Interagency Advisory Panel on Research Ethics to provide them with independent and interdisciplinary advice on the interpretation, evolution, and use of the document. Box 11.4 provides a list of the ethical principles that should guide researchers when they develop their research proposals.

The TCPS has clout because these federal agencies only fund research if the research institutions (like universities and hospitals) demonstrate compliance with the ethical guidelines. Universities and hospitals, as well as other research institutes, have an in-house research ethics board (REB) which reviews research proposals to screen for adherence to ethical principles. Researchers are required to write a formal application to receive "ethical approval" of their research project. The application typically provides a statement of the purpose of the research, the study design and methodology, the target sample and method of sampling participants, potential risks and benefits to the research participants and academic community, notification of any

BOX 11.4

Tri-Council Policy Statement: Ethical Conduct for Research Involving Humans: Guiding Ethical Principles

Research applications are evaluated against a set of guiding principles. The approach taken in this framework is to guide and evoke thoughtful actions based on principles. The principles that follow are based on the guidelines of the Councils over the last decades, on more recent statements by other Canadian agencies, and on statements from the international community. The principles have been widely adopted by diverse research disciplines. As such, they express common standards, values and aspirations of the research community.

GUIDING ETHICAL PRINCIPLES

Respect for Human Dignity: This principle aspires to protecting the multiple and interdependent interests of the person—from bodily to psychological to cultural integrity. This principle forms the basis of the ethical obligations in research that are listed below.

Respect for Free and Informed Consent: Individuals are generally presumed to have the capacity and right to make free and informed decisions. Respect for persons thus means respecting the exercise of individual consent. In practical terms within the ethics review process, the principle of respect for persons translates into the dialogue, process, rights, duties and requirements for free and informed consent by the research subject.

Respect for Vulnerable Persons: Respect for human dignity entails high ethical obligations towards vulnerable persons—to those whose diminished competence and/or decision-making capacity make them vulnerable. Children, institutionalized persons or others who are vulnerable are entitled, on grounds of human dignity, caring, solidarity and fairness, to special protection against abuse, exploitation or discrimination. Ethical obligations to vulnerable individuals in the research enterprise will often translate into special procedures to protect their interests.

Respect for Privacy and Confidentiality: Respect for human dignity also implies the principles of respect for privacy and confidentiality. In many cultures, privacy and confidentiality are considered fundamental to human dignity. Thus, standards of privacy and confidentiality protect the access, control and dissemination of personal information. In doing so, such standards help to protect mental or psychological integrity. They are thus consonant with values underlying privacy, confidentiality and anonymity respected.

Respect for Justice and Inclusiveness: Justice connotes fairness and equity. Procedural justice requires that the ethics review process have fair methods, standards and procedures for reviewing research protocols, and that the process be effectively independent. Justice also concerns the distribution of benefits and burdens of research. On the one hand, distributive justice means that no segment of the population should be unfairly burdened with the harms of research. It thus imposes particular obligations toward individuals who are vulnerable and unable to protect their own interests in order to ensure that they are not exploited for the advancement of knowledge. History has many chapters of such exploitation. On the other hand, distributive justice also imposes duties neither to neglect nor discriminate against individuals and groups who may benefit from advances in research.

Balancing Harms and Benefits: The analysis, balance and distribution of harms and benefits are critical to the ethics of human research. Modern research ethics, for instance, require a favourable harms–benefit balance—that is, that the foreseeable harms should not outweigh anticipated benefits. Harms–benefits analysis thus affects the welfare and rights of research subjects, the informed assumption of harms and benefits, and the ethical justifications for competing research paths. Because research involves advancing the frontiers of knowledge, its undertaking often involves uncertainty about the precise magnitude and kind of benefits or harms that attend proposed research. These realities and the principle of respect for human dignity impose ethical obligations on the prerequisites, scientific validity, design and conduct of research. These concerns are particularly evident in biomedical and health research; in research they need to be tempered in areas such

as political science, economics or modern history (including biographies), areas in which research may ethically result in the harming of the reputations of organizations or individuals in public life.

Minimizing Harm: A principle directly related to harms–benefits analysis is non-maleficence, or the duty to avoid, prevent or minimize harms to others. Research subjects must not be subjected to unnecessary risks of harm, and their participation in research must be essential to achieving scientifically and societally important aims that cannot be realized without the participation of human subjects. In addition, it should be kept in mind that the principle of minimizing harm requires that the research involve the smallest number of human subjects and the smallest number of tests on these subjects that will ensure scientifically valid data.

Maximizing Benefit: Another principle related to the harms and benefits of research is beneficence. The principle of beneficence imposes a duty to benefit others and, in research ethics, a duty to maximize net benefits. The principle has particular relevance for researchers in professions such as social work, education, health care and applied psychology. As noted earlier, human research is intended to produce benefits for subjects themselves, for other individuals or society as a whole, or for the advancement of knowledge. In most research, the primary benefits produced are for society and for the advancement of knowledge.

Source: Canadian Institutes of Health Research, Natural Sciences and Engineering Research Council of Canada, Social Sciences and Humanities Research Council of Canada, *Tri-Council Policy Statement: Ethical Conduct for Research Involving Humans.* 1998 (with 2000, 2002 and 2005 amendments), www.pre.ethics.gc.ca//english/policystatement/context.cfm#C. Reproduced with the permission of the Minister of Public Works and Government Services Canada, 2006.

potential conflicts of interests, and a thorough explanation about what seps the researcher(s) plan to take to protect the participants. Typically the application is required to provide specific information on how the researcher(s) will ensure that the participant knows that their participation in the study is voluntary, any potential costs or risk to the participant, and how the researcher will protect the participant's confidentiality and anonymity. The REB requires the researcher to provide information to participants in written form, and to ask research participants to sign a letter of "informed consent" only after they have received information on the nature of the study, their involvement, and their rights as participants.

D. RULES FOR RESOLVING ETHICAL ISSUES

The following ethical rules are presented as guidelines and are organized around two themes:

1. the researcher's ethical responsibility to respondents; and

2. the social researcher's responsibility to his or her discipline and society.

1. RULES FOR THE TREATMENT OF RESPONDENTS

RULE 11.1 PROTECT THE CONFIDENTIALITY OF RESPONDENTS.

The researcher's promise to respect the confidentiality of responses to a questionnaire or an interview or the identity of a subject in an experiment or field study is to be treated as a sacred trust. Most surveys, interviews, experiments, and field studies are completed on the understanding that individual responses, or information which would permit the identification of the individual, will never be released. Researchers have not only an ethical responsibility to preserve the anonymity of respondents but have also a practical interest in doing so: their ability to collect accurate information would be impaired if the public believed that responses were not kept in confidence.

Where it is necessary to identify individual names with particular questionnaires (as in panel studies, for example) number codes should be used, not names. The questionnaires and a master list with names and identification numbers can then be stored separately. Such master lists should be destroyed after the study has been completed. In Humphreys' case, the identifying information was stored in a safety deposit box in another state.

The location of the research project is frequently masked to further protect the identity of subjects. When Humphreys did his research over a quarter of a century ago, neither his research location (St. Louis) nor the locations of the tearooms were revealed. Social scientists cooperated in the masking, although any vice-squad member would certainly have been able to identify this information quickly had he or she taken a little time. (The supervising professor, Lee Rainwater, was thanked in the preface and he was, during the period of the study, a prominent professor at Washington University in St. Louis.) In any case, vice-squad members were well aware of the activities in the public restrooms.

If data are released to other researchers, steps should be taken to mask the individual identities of respondents. This can be achieved by removing highly specific identifiers such as area of residence, specific job, or employer identifications.

RULE 11.2 DO NOT PLACE PRESSURE ON RESPONDENTS.

No pressure should be placed on the respondent to cooperate in a study. Respondents must feel free to refuse participation, withdraw at any time, or refuse to answer any particular question. Researchers should not put pressure on respondents or cajole or harass them in an effort to coax them into cooperation with the study. While it is appropriate in a mail survey to follow up with a letter or phone call on those who do not respond, these contacts should seek information and provide prospective respondents an opportunity to seek additional information themselves.

The original Milgram study appeared to place a lot of pressure on respondents to continue administering the electric shocks; indeed, as many as four prods were used to "bring the subject into line."

Prod 1: Please continue; or Please go on.
Prod 2: The experiment requires that you continue.
Prod 3: It is absolutely essential that you continue.
Prod 4: You have no other choice, you must go on. (Milgram, 1963, p. 374)

In subsequent experiments, which used weaker prods or gave the subject an easy out, subjects were much less likely to administer the maximum shock (Reynolds, 1982, p. 25).

RULE 11.3 MAKE THE SUBJECT'S PARTICIPATION PAINLESS.

Completing a questionnaire or interview or participating as a subject in an experiment should be a painless experience for the subject. Researchers must not expose subjects to needlessly long experimental trials or questionnaires or ask questions that pry unnecessarily into personal matters. This constraint is

not meant to suggest that the researcher should not examine certain areas of social behaviour but suggests that only relevant information be collected. (Often when people are working on their first project, they will suggest many variables; however, when asked what they would do with the information, they are unable to articulate a meaningful analysis.) Moreover, consideration should be given to using alternate, or indirect indicators, for those questions that may offend respondents. Maintaining the comfort and self-esteem of the subject should be a central concern of the researcher.

The Milgram research has been faulted for its possibly adverse effects on the subjects' self-esteem. We cannot reasonably expect Milgram to have anticipated the high proportion of subjects who would willingly administer the maximum shock (he took steps to estimate how many would do this by asking various students and colleagues); nor can Milgram be faulted for not anticipating the stress subjects would experience. But should the experiment have been aborted once the high stress experienced by the subjects was recognized? Other researchers have decided to abort projects when it was clear that the study had potential dangers.

Piliavin and Piliavin (1972), for example, aborted trials on the bystander intervention studies once it was clear that there were dangers involved in staging phoney emergencies. The researchers stopped one study when it was observed that bystanders, seeing a person fall with blood trickling from his mouth, activated an emergency stop alarm. It was simply too dangerous and disruptive to continue. Should Milgram have aborted his study?

RULE 11.4 IDENTIFY SPONSORS.

There should be no deception concerning the sponsorship of a project. Respondents must be informed about who is doing the study. On this basis alone, they may choose not to participate in the study.

Many people have opened their doors to a person claiming to be doing a survey on educational matters, only to discover that they are not dealing with a reputable social scientist but rather with a door-to-door encyclopedia salesperson. Feel free to encourage the "researcher" to leave rapidly!

Similarly, you might choose not to participate in a study conducted by an organization whose aims and objectives you find unacceptable; but, for you to refuse, you will need to know who is sponsoring the study. Full disclosure about the project is required.

RULE 11.5 DISCLOSE THE BASIS ON WHICH RESPONDENTS HAVE BEEN SELECTED.

The consensus in the social science community is that the respondent has the right to know how he or she was selected for participation in a study. Has the selection been made by means of a probability sampling procedure or has it been based on special characteristics (membership in a particular organization, the job one has, or any other qualities)? The prospective respondent should be given a reasonable amount of information upon which a decision to participate can be made.

This criterion is an interesting one in the case of Humphreys' research: in the "tea-room" observation phase of the research, the participants were engaging in an activity in a public lavatory. So, while they did not agree to participate in a research project, they did engage in an activity with others present. They clearly made the assumption that the observer was a "safe" person—a lookout. In the interview phase of his research, there was a lack of forthrightness in telling respondents how they were selected. The fifty who were interviewed

were selected because they agreed to the interview. However, the respondents did not know that they had been seen using a "tearoom" for sexual purposes.

Since their tearoom activity was clandestine, it is clear that few of the respondents would have agreed to the interview had they known how they had been selected. The dilemma is that the researcher could not have completed the comparison with the "straight" sample without the interviews; and obtaining a sufficient number of interviews was possible only if the researcher did not fully disclose the basis on which the respondents had been selected. Catch 22? Recall that addresses were identified by tracing car licence numbers; Humphreys was also less than candid about how respondents were selected for the health survey (1970, p. 171). Does the anticipated payoff of the research warrant the failure to disclose fully the basis on which the respondent was selected?

RULE 11.6 PLACE NO HIDDEN IDENTIFICATION CODES ON QUESTIONNAIRES.

Researchers should not use hidden codes on questionnaires to assist in the identification of those who have or have not returned questionnaires. Such codes are sometimes used to enable the researcher to find out who has not returned a questionnaire: such subjects may be sent another request. While such codes may save the researcher much time and money, they are unethical. If individuals are to be identified, this information should be placed directly on the questionnaire itself and discussed in a covering letter.

RULE 11.7 HONOUR PROMISES TO PROVIDE RESPONDENTS WITH RESEARCH REPORTS.

Where an offer to provide a research report to respondents has been given, the promise must be fulfilled. The relation between researcher and respondent/subject should be reciprocal. In practice, it is to the advantage of the researcher to fulfill such obligations because doing so will encourage the continued cooperation of respondents in long-term projects.

Where individuals are offered the opportunity of receiving a report on the study, a separate, stamped envelope and request form should be provided for the respondent. The separate return envelope not only keeps the respondent's name disassociated from the questionnaire, but also conveys to the respondent that the researcher takes a promise of confidentiality seriously.

While there may be no ethical responsibility to pay respondents who volunteer their cooperation, such payments are to be encouraged in order to reinforce the idea of a reciprocal contract between researcher and respondent. Participant observation studies frequently involve rather long periods of observation, and it is particularly important to reciprocate by providing a payment or a report on the research project.

RULE 11.8 INFORMED CONSENT IS A KEY CONCERN.

In dealing with competent adults, participation should be based on **informed consent**—that is, potential respondents must be informed about the nature of the study, what kinds of issues will be explored, how respondents were selected, and who is sponsoring the research. Moreover, prospective respondents should be informed that they should feel free to withdraw from the study at any time if they wish to do so. In surveys, respondents should be told to feel free to skip any questions that they consider inappropriate.

When studies involving children, the infirm, or incompetent adults are done, the organization or individual responsible for the prospective respondents should provide consent in writing.

The issue of informed consent may be a problem for researchers doing participant observation studies. It would not be reasonable to insist that all members being observed would have to consent to being observed. The test in such cases perhaps should be:

- whether sufficient steps are taken to protect the anonymity of those who are observed; and

- that no negative consequences could reasonably be seen to result from the activity of the research project.

To put a blanket prohibition on such studies would mean that works such as Erving Goffman's *Asylums* or Margaret Mead's *Sex and Temperament in Three Primitive Societies* could not have been done.

Covert observational studies, such as those observing whether the drivers of automobiles have their shoulder belts fastened, can be performed so long as there is no apparent danger to the subject being observed or to the observer. In such cases it is not practical to attempt to gain the permission of the person being observed. When deciding if the study should be undertaken, the best test the researcher can make is an attempt to balance any good that may come out of the project against its potentially negative consequences.

In experimental studies, particularly those involving some deception, there is a problem concerning informed consent. If the experimental manipulation requires deception, it is not possible to inform the subject fully, in advance, of the deception: to do so would spoil the study. In such cases, Rule 11.9 needs to be applied.

RULE 11.9 DEBRIEF SUBJECTS.

When experiments or field studies involve deception, subjects should have the study explained to them after the session. The researcher should note what deception was used, why it was necessary, and the subjects should be reassured that their participation was appreciated and helpful.

2. ETHICS AND THE SOCIAL RESEARCHER

The social researcher has two special difficulties, which are not experienced to the same degree by researchers in other areas:

1. the researcher frequently has a theoretical and practical "vested interest" in the outcome of a study; and

2. the social scientist, particularly the survey researcher, typically works with a large number of indicators, providing many opportunities for alternative interpretations.

And, given the special difficulties involved in replicating social research, we often have to trust the findings reported by the social researcher. This situation places an even greater ethical responsibility on the social researcher to conduct unbiased studies.

RULE 11.10 RESEARCHERS SHOULD DISTINGUISH BETWEEN SCIENCE AND ADVOCACY.

In your role as social scientist, do not work on projects in which you are asked to develop a "scientific case" for a conclusion. Given the legitimacy of science in western culture, it should be no surprise that both scientists and nonscientists will be tempted to utilize this legitimacy to achieve personal or group goals. Evidence viewed as scientific carries a lot of weight in argument, and hence, when a presentation is being prepared, collecting or referring to scientific evidence is tempting and sensible.

If you are hired to "develop a scientific case for ..." then you have an ethical problem. You are being asked to provide scientific evidence to convince others of some position. You are, in this case, being asked to make others believe that you have scientific evidence for some position. Such research should not be presented as science: to do so would be unethical.

As a citizen-advocate it is perfectly legitimate to comment on the evidence of others and to produce evidence that is appropriate to the issue under dispute. It should be noted, however, that the information is being presented from the perspective of a citizen-advocate not from that of the expert social scientist. We would be well advised to maintain a distinction between citizen-advocate roles and social science roles. Too often the line between them is blurred.

RULE 11.11 DO NOT HUNT THROUGH DATA LOOKING FOR PLEASING FINDINGS.

The surest way to be guilty of misrepresentation is to search for support for your own views. To do so would be both bad science and unethical behaviour. If data are being scanned for interesting findings, these cannot be reported unless the process by which they have emerged is made absolutely clear.

RULE 11.12 BE AWARE OF POTENTIAL SOURCES OF BIAS.

Becoming aware of the sources of bias may help you avoid bias in your own work and spot it in the research reports of others. Researchers have an ethical responsibility to report their work fairly, attempting to avoid bias as much as possible. Review the discussion of sources of bias in Chapter 10.

RULE 11.13 REPRESENT RESEARCH LITERATURE FAIRLY.

In the interest of objectivity and ethics, researchers must attempt to portray accurately the body of literature in their area of research. Reporting findings selectively is not acceptable.

RULE 11.14 DO THE BEST RESEARCH YOU CAN.

Research must strive to be competent and impartial, and its results must be reported objectively. Use qualified personnel and consultants. Keep up with developments in your field and use the best techniques of data collection and analysis. Seek always to do the best research you can; do research with care.

RULE 11.15 ACKNOWLEDGE ALL YOUR SOURCES.

Acknowledge people who have played a role in your research and acknowledge all literature sources that have directly influenced your study.

Excluding the respondents (who have been assured of anonymity), all other people who have assisted in the project should be acknowledged by way of a footnote. Similarly, when literature has been used in developing the project, each source should be cited.

RULE 11.16 SEEK ADVICE ON ETHICAL ISSUES.

If ethical issues arise, seek the advice of appropriate professional bodies or institutions involved in the project. Most studies will not pose difficult ethical issues. However, when the research team identifies an ethical dilemma, outside consultations are appropriate. Such consultations would weigh the benefits of the research to society against the costs that bending ethical guidelines might entail. Before any study begins, all such ethical dilemmas should be resolved by appropriate adjustments to the project (for good discussions on these matters see Nachmias and Nachmias, 1981; and Reynolds, 1982).

E. KEY POINTS

The *consequentialist view* is that ethical judgments about a research project should be made in the light of its consequences for the subject, for the academic discipline, and for society. A cost-benefit analysis might reveal that the advantages gained by the advancement of our knowledge justify the violation of some rules: in this view, deception is okay if it does not do any long-term damage to the subject.

The *deontological view* of research ethics proposes absolute moral strictures that must never be violated.

Maintaining the *comfort and self-esteem* of the subject should be a central concern of the researcher.

Respondents should feel free to refuse participation, withdraw at any time, or to refuse to answer any particular question.

The respondent has a right to know how he or she was *selected for participation* in a study.

There should be *no deception concerning the sponsorship* of a project.

Researchers should *not use hidden codes* to assist in the identification of those who have or have not returned questionnaires. In dealing with competent adults, participation should be based on *informed consent*—that is, the potential respondents must be informed about the nature of the study, what kinds of issues will be explored, how the respondents were selected, and who is sponsoring the research. Where studies are done involving children, the infirm, or incompetent adults, the organization or individual responsible for the prospective respondents should provide consent in writing.

When experiments or field studies involve deception, following the session, subjects should be *debriefed*—that is, they should have the study explained to them, any deceptions should be noted, their necessity explained, and the subjects should be reassured that their participation was appreciated and helpful.

If you are hired to "develop a scientific case for ..." then you have an ethical problem.

The surest way to be guilty of misrepresentation is to *search for support for your own views*; to do so would be both bad science and unethical behaviour.

If ethical issues arise, *seek the advice* of appropriate professional bodies or institutions involved in the project.

As noted above, Canadian social researchers, including students, are required to follow the Tri-Council Policy Statement on Ethical Conduct for Research Involving Humans. Researchers and graduate students are required to have their research proposals vetted by a university Research Ethics Board (REB). Every hospital, college, university, and government agency is required to have an REB that reviews proposed projects prior to implementation.

F. KEY TERMS

Consequentialist	Deontological	Informed consent
Debrief	Ethical guidelines	

CHAPTER TWELVE

GETTING THE PROJECT STARTED

Getting started is sometimes the most difficult part of a project. But care taken during the beginning stages will pay off handsomely. A carefully designed study enabling the researcher to come to conclusions about some social behaviour, including some theory-testing dimensions, and informed by the existing literature will provide the basis for an excellent project.

A. CHOOSING A PROBLEM, A DESIGN, AND VARIABLES

An enormous variety of topics can be studied using social science techniques. To provide some sense of the range of topics that can be treated, a listing of some projects carried out by my students is found in Box 12.1.

BOX 12.1 STUDENT RESEARCHERS AT WORK

These projects were designed by groups of students and were carried out during a year-long methods course. The students were primarily drawn from sociology or nursing classes with a few from business, political science, and anthropology. The students determined the subject matter and the faculty member assisted them in completing their projects. Traditionally the course emphasized survey research methods, so most, but not all, fit into that type of design.

Territorial Invasions among Students

Summer Employment and Economic Need

Community Size and Prejudice Level

Territorial Imperatives: The Elevator

Religiosity and Morality

Conformity among University Students

Status Crystallization and Its Application to Nurses, CNAs, Orderlies, and Aides

Professor–Student Exchange Relations

Energy Crisis: Attitudes and Concerns

Errors in the Self-Administration of Drugs

Desired Family Size

Factors Contributing to Alcohol Consumption

Cigarette Smoking: Patterns of High School and University Students' Use

Religious Participation at Two Universities

Attitudes toward Campus Medical Facilities

Residence Satisfaction: A Comparison of Two Residences

Factors Influencing Academic Achievement

Social Class and Educational Aspirations of Female Students

Spatial Invasion as a Function of Interaction Intensity

The Effect of Threat upon Distance in an Interacting Dyad

University Students and Involvement in Voluntary Associations

Attitudes toward Women and Faculty

Classroom Seating Location and Grade Performance

Dress and Day of the Week

Patterns of Soap-Opera Viewing

Attitudes toward Separation of Québec from Canada

Patterns of Superstitions

Survey of University Graduates

Academic Performance and On- or Off-Campus Residence

Factors Influencing Liberalism

Grade Performance: What Causes Variation?

Factors Influencing Mother's Satisfaction with Birth Experience

Weight Gain among Female University Students

Factors Influencing Program Selection among Females Enrolled in Nursing and Physical Education Programs

Leadership among University- and Hospital-Trained Nursing Students

Attitudes toward Abortion, Euthanasia, and In vitro Fertilization

Relative Status of University Departments

Class Attendance and Grade Performance

Factors Influencing Professional versus Traditional Career Orientations

Participation and Self-Esteem

Effects of Contact and Attitudes toward the Handicapped

Attitudes toward Capital Punishment

High School Students' Attitudes toward Alcohol Consumption

Attitudes toward Abortion

Retirement and Life Satisfaction: A Study of Senior Citizens in Small-Town Nova Scotia

Attitudes toward Pre-Marital Sex among High School Students

Attitudes toward the Elderly

Drug Use among First-Year University Students

Contraception Use: A Study of Female University Students

Attitudes of Nurses toward Student Nurses

Delinquent Compared to Non-Delinquent Females

Attitudes toward Sex Roles

An Analytical Comparison of Attitudes toward Capital Punishment and Abortion

Choice of Nontraditional University Programs by Females

Wage Discrimination: Comparing Salaries of Male and Female Professors

Attitudes toward the Male Nurse

Male Attitudes toward Homosexuality

Factors Influencing Addictive Behaviour

Fertility Expectations and Intended Labour-Force Participation of Nursing Students

Factors Influencing Expected Age of Marriage

Attitudes toward Primary Care Nursing

Comparing the Occupational Aspirations of High-School Students in Antigonish and Dartmouth

Factors Influencing Maternal Confidence

Attitudes toward Euthanasia

Suicidal Thought among University Students

Attitudes toward Homosexuality

Traditional and Nontraditional Program Choices

A Survey of Nursing Graduates of the Eighties

Liberal Attitudes toward Pre-Marital Sex

Shifts Between Freshmen and Seniors' Perceived Role of the Nurse

Attitudes toward AIDS

Factors Influencing Academic Performance

The Effect of Talkativeness on Group Dynamics

Sexual Harassment on Campus

Male Perceptions of Aggression and Date Rape

Analysis of Residence Satisfaction

Cross-Cultural and Sex-Role Comparisons

Factors Affecting RNs' Shift Preference

The Status of Programs

Attitudes toward the Ordination of Gay Clergy

A Study of Basal-Infusion Patient-Controlled Intravenous Analgesic versus Intramuscular Injection of Women in Labour

Males' Attitudes toward Dating Relationships

PMS as It Is Experienced by Female Students

Nurses' Perceptions of Job Satisfaction

Factors Influencing Deviant Behaviour in Adolescents

Unwanted Intimacy

Male Attitudes toward Nontraditional Roles of Women

Evaluation of the Distance Nursing Program

Attitudes toward the Elderly

Heavy Drinking at University

Fear among Female University Students of Being Attacked

Effects of Eating Breakfast on Grade Performance

Attitudes toward Authority

Diploma Students' Attitudes toward Degree Nursing Students

Attitudes toward Contraceptive Use

Female Aggression on Campus

Attitudes toward People in Nontraditional Roles

Incident Reports and Occupational Violence in Nursing

Students' Attitudes toward Interracial Relationships

Alcohol Consumption of Teenagers

Teachers' Attitudes toward Mainstreaming

University Students' Superstition Levels

Sexual Assault at a Maritime University

Rule-Breaking Behaviour

Attitudes toward Police

Attitudes toward Tuition Rates

Perception of Risk of Sexual Assault

Fear of Being Assaulted

Factors Influencing Program Choice at University

Suicide Ideation on Campus

Attitudes toward Euthanasia

Infection Rates in Newborn Infants

The Effects of Gender on Self-Esteem

Eating Disorders: A Study of Teenagers

Attitudes toward Campus Health-Care Facilities

Homesickness among First-Year Students	Attitudes toward Voluntary Active Euthanasia and Physician-Assisted Suicide
Attitudes toward Marriage	
Consequences of Shiftwork: Physical, Psychological, Social, and Economic	Self-Acceptance by Gays and Lesbians
	Assessing Satisfaction with the New Residences
Health Promoting Behaviours among a Student Population	Changes in Generic Skills, Liberal Attitudes, and Self-Esteem among Undergraduates
Attitudes toward Women in Competitive Sports	
How Punitive Are Students?	Does Birth Order Affect Personality Characteristics?
Contraceptive Use among Male Students	Feminist Attitudes and Self-Identification as a "Feminist"

1. CHOOSING A PROBLEM

Given the considerable effort required to complete a project, the single most important consideration in choosing the topic is genuine interest. Some suggestions of how to go about choosing a project are presented below.

A. CURRENT ISSUE

One method of selecting a project is to choose one that is the subject of public debate. Such topics might include capital punishment, abortion, environmental degradation, free trade, religious cults, racial prejudice, gender inequities, population growth, poverty, attitudes toward people with AIDS, date rape, unemployment, or the popularity of a political leader.

B. VARIATION IN A DEPENDENT VARIABLE

Another approach is to try to understand variations in some dependent variable. What

factors influence grade performance? What influences the popularity of a teacher? What variables influence the choice of a nontraditional program among female students? How do people communicate non-verbally to indicate that they wish to terminate an interaction? Here the goal is to understand the factors influencing the dependent variable.

C. TESTING A THEORY

Those researchers who have a theoretical inclination may wish to test a current theory of human behaviour. Chapter 2 outlined methods for generating testable theoretical hypotheses. The challenge is to examine a relationship between variables that is predicted by a theory but which, at the same time, is not obvious to common sense. The most convincing theory-testing projects will be those that will make a counterintuitive (against common sense) prediction, which, if it turns out to be true, will be a convincing demonstration of the theory. (See Chapter 2 for some examples.)

D. TESTING PARTIAL THEORIES

A review of the literature may reveal a consistent relationship between two variables, but alternative explanations for this relationship may not have been carefully tested. In such cases, it is reasonable to propose alternative explanations for the relationship, design a study, and then test which, if any, of the proposed explanations best accounts for the relationship. (See Chapter 2 for some examples.)

E. TESTING FOLK WISDOM

Interesting projects can often be designed to test the accuracy of some taken-for-granted wisdom systematically. To provide a few examples, consider the following:

- In romance, do opposites attract?

- Among 10-year-olds, are males better than females at solving mathematical puzzles?

- Among 10-year-olds, are females better than males at solving crossword puzzles?

- In a classroom setting, do the strongest friendships occur among those who have the most in common: in short, do "birds of a feather flock together?"

- In sports, does playing in front of a home audience provide any advantage?

Spend some time thinking about commonly accepted views of how things work, and then try to think of some way in which the idea could be tested systematically. Ask yourself how experimental, field, survey, or nonreactive designs might be used to study the problem. Which design would be ideal and which one most practical?

F. APPLIED RESEARCH

Another source of projects is to look at some "applied" problem. Perhaps through research the identified problem will be understood better or even resolved. Typically the problem is defined by the sponsor. The researcher must decide, if the project is ethically acceptable (and the fee is right!), how to do the project. The applied researcher might be asked to figure out how to attract more students to a university program, to describe the public's attitude toward some current issue, or to help a political candidate figure out what issues are of concern to voters in a constituency.

Social scientists are frequently called upon to provide an evaluation of some social intervention. Evaluations are often required for social programs. A solid understanding of experimental design and a good deal of imagination and flexibility, are qualities well suited to doing evaluations. There is a demand for people who know how to do evaluation work.

G. REPLICATION STUDY

Finally, one can choose to replicate, or repeat, some earlier study. But even if a replication is attempted, the researcher should attempt to add a new dimension to the study and try to answer some question that was left open by the previous project.

2. CHOOSING A DESIGN

Many factors influence the choice of research design. The nature of the question being asked primarily determines which type of design would be most appropriate. But there are pragmatic considerations too, such as the amount of time and research funds available or the kind of respondents that are available to the researcher.

Assuming you have a rough idea of the problem you wish to investigate, what steps might you take to decide on the appropriate research strategy? Remember, there may be constraints imposed by funding, time, availability of research assistants, ethical issues, computer resources, and technical competence. The following summarizes some steps you might wish to take to decide which research strategy will be followed.

STEP 1 WHAT HAVE OTHERS DONE?

Do a preliminary review of the literature to get some sense of what has been written about the subject you wish to explore. What research designs were employed in these studies? Can you locate any articles that reflect the use of different designs to explore the problem? Tips for locating such articles will be discussed later in this chapter in the Reviewing the Literature section.

STEP 2 CONSIDER ALTERNATIVES.

Consider alternatives when faced with difficulties such as those listed below:

- Time ("Rats, the project report is due in three months!")

- Ethical issues ("The Research Ethics Board probably would not approve of the deception involved in the study.")

- Computer resources ("Our institution does not have the programs that we need to do the analysis.")

- Technical competence ("Regression analysis is beyond me and to replicate the study I would need to understand it.")

- Availability of research assistants ("To do this project properly we would need assistance and there are not enough sufficiently qualified people available to do the interviewing and observations.")

- Funding ("We just don't have enough money to do the project properly.")

Given difficulties such as these, are there alternative strategies that might be employed? It may be possible to:

- Use data that have been generated by other researchers: you will need to get the data and permission to use them; you will also have to live with someone else's operationalizations.

- Use publicly available data: (i) university and college social science departments often maintain data banks; (ii) government agencies sometimes make data of interest available to social scientists; and (iii) other publicly available data sources exist such as the Human Relations Area Files. Typically data sets are available in the form of computer files.

- Use information published in newspapers or books; much secondary data can be gleaned from regularly published information. For example, if you were interested in examining the relation between final score difference and the likelihood of violence in hockey, you could study one NHL hockey season and, from daily-newspaper game summaries, record the final score gap and relate this to the total number of penalty minutes.

STEP 3 REVIEW THE CHAPTER THAT INTRODUCES THE TYPE OF DESIGN TENTATIVELY SELECTED.

The following chapters introduce different types of research designs:

- Chapter 3. Experiments, Quasi-Experiments, and Field Observations

- Chapter 4. Survey Designs

- Chapter 5. Nonreactive and Comparative Research

- Chapter 6. Qualitative Research Methods

- Chapter 7. Critical Approaches to Research: Action and Feminist Research.

STEP 4 BE PREPARED TO RECONSIDER THE RESEARCH DESIGN USED.

Continue developing the project but be prepared to reopen the research design question. As various factors are considered, it may be necessary to consider alternative approaches to the research question. As you review the literature in detail, different questions may come to seem more relevant to the goals of your project. If this happens, be prepared to reconsider the type of research design to be used in the study.

3. DETERMINING THE PRECISE QUESTIONS

Having selected the general area of research and a tentative research design, the next step is to articulate precisely what you wish to investigate. To illustrate the point further, suppose you wished to do a project on capital punishment. As you start to think about the project, determine whether you want to:

- Examine public attitudes toward capital punishment;

- Compare the types of people who support capital punishment with those who do not;

- Examine the relationship between people's other social attitudes (poverty, abortion, people in authority) and their attitude toward capital punishment;

- Determine whether there is a sex difference in support for capital punishment;

- Determine whether women are less inclined to support capital punishment, and if so, determine what accounts for this tendency.

The list of issues you might wish to tackle could be extended. Once a problem has been selected, the work of pinning

down the precise questions begins. Suppose that you decided to focus on the last question (understanding gender differences in attitudes toward capital punishment): a thorough review of the literature should be undertaken to find out what other researchers have discovered. The review will also help you determine more precisely what is to be investigated.

As projects are developed, it is normal for the first ideas to be fuzzy and to seem to require a project of a rather grand scale. As the researcher becomes more familiar with the literature and sensitive to practical considerations, the project will become more focused and specific and move to something that can be accomplished with the resources available. It is necessary to go through a process of "pinning down the project," "focusing the project," and "specifying the hypotheses." It is normal to begin with rather ambitious plans: with time, the project will gradually take shape.

4. REVIEWING THE LITERATURE

In reviewing the literature, you are trying to get a sense of the state of scientific knowledge about the topic. The first question is "Where do I start?"

- If you are part of a university or college, ask instructors who work in the area for any ideas they might have on where to get information.

- Check with a reference librarian for sources that may lead you to research done on your topic.

- Check textbooks for a lead.

- Check the appropriate discipline's abstracts, as they provide brief descriptions of published papers dealing with a variety of topics. Box 12.2 lists some of the relevant abstracts and indexes available in many libraries.

- Check journals that are likely to publish work in the area. It is advisable to begin by checking through the most recent issues: once you have found an article that is close to your topic in either the particular variables treated or the general concepts presented, check it for references to other articles. By starting with the most recent issues, you will identify the latest research; and if an article published in the 1950s is referenced in many of the articles, you will want to read it, since it is still considered to be one of the classics.

- You may not be able to find published results on the specific relationship, or category of individuals, you wish to study. If this is the case, focus on variables that researchers have found to be related to the major dependent variable you propose to examine.

- In many cases, it will be appropriate to review research that uses similar methodologies or theories.

The goals of a review include:

- identifying areas where there seems to be consensus among researchers;

- noting where there are inconsistencies in research findings;

- identifying variables that others have found to be relevant to the problem at hand;

- identifying areas that, if explored, could lead to important new understandings of the phenomenon under examination;

- seeing how other researchers have made connections to theory; and

- seeing how other researchers have measured variables and analyzed their data.

Generally, when reviews are presented in a report, they should try to summarize

---

BOX 12.2

*Sample Abstracts, Indexes, and Websites of Periodicals and Data Sources of Relevance to Anthropology, Education, Nursing, Political Science, Psychology, and Sociology and Criminology**

General Listing (Relevant to Several Disciplines)

Annual Reviews

Canadian Periodical Index (Canadian Content)

CBCA (Canadian Business & Current Affairs)

Google Scholar

JSTOR

PAIS International

Proquest Research Library

Sage Publications

Social Sciences Citation Index

Social Sciences Index

Canadian Government
www.canada.gc.ca/main_e.html

Anthropology

Abstracts in Anthropology

Anthro.Net **www.anthro.net**

Anthrosource

International Bibliography of Social and Cultural Anthropology

Education

Canadian Education on the Web **//oise.utoronto.ca/canedweb/eduweb.html**

CBCA Fulltext Education

Education World **www.education-world.com**

ERIC Online **www.eric.ed.gov**

ProQuest Research Library

Nursing

AIDSLINE **www.aegis.com/aidsline**

BIOETHICSLINE **www.nlm.nih.gov**

CINAHL **www.cinahl.com**

Health A to Z **www.healthatoz.com**

Health Web **//healthweb.org**

ProQuest Research Library

PubMed

Political Science

CBCA (Canadian Business & Current Affairs)

Environics **www.environics.net**

International Bibliography of Political Science

Ipsos **www.ipsos.ca**

Worldwide Political Science Abstracts

Psychology

Child Development Abstracts and Bibliography

Encyclopedia of Psychology **www.psychology.org**

Psychological Abstracts

PsycARTICLES

PsycINFO

Sociology and Criminology

Canadian Social Research Net **www.canadiansocialresearch.net**

Canadian Social Trends

Criminal Justice Abstracts

Social Services Abstracts

Sociological Abstracts

SOSIG: Social Sciences Information Gateway **//sosig.ac.uk**

*With special acknowledgement to Barbara Phillips of the St. Francis Xavier University Library staff, who prepared this list.

---

briefly the areas of agreement and disagreement in the literature. Article summaries may be useful to the researcher but are generally not appropriate in a final report. What is required is a sense of the current state of knowledge on the topic under investigation. Table 12.1 shows one method of summarizing articles: by using such a grid system, you can make additions to the list, and also provide a quick summary of areas of agreement and disagreement among researchers.

In preparing a discussion of the literature reviewed, it generally seems best to report the findings on one variable at a time. Thus, if you were studying attitudes toward the availability of abortions, you might begin by talking about how such

TABLE 12.1 BACKGROUND CHARACTERISTICS ASSOCIATED WITH SMOKING

Variables	RESEARCH AUTHORS											
	1	2	3	4	5	6	7	8	9	10	11	12
Family Members Smoke	+					+			+		–	
Health Problems Reported		+	+	+								
Age					–				–			–
Education		+		–	+	+					–	
Urban Community				+		+	+			+		
Violence in Family	+								+			
Gender (Male)	+					+	+				+	
Year of Report	1993	1991	1988	1996	1992	1997	1991	1997	1997	1995	1995	1995
Number of Subjects	849	NA	5977	1971	8042	2086	NA	NA	627	1320	827	104
Place of Study	U of Conn.	McMaster U.	London	St. John's	New York	U of Surrey	London	Illinois	Scotland	Florida	Norway	Colorado

Legend:

+ indicates variable was positively related to incidence of smoking

– indicates variable was negatively related to incidence of smoking

blank indicates the variable was not reported in the study

Authors list:

(1) DeFronzo and Pawlak (1993); (2) Willms and Stebbins (1991); (3) Grossarth-Matieecek, Eysenck, and Vetter (1988); (4) Aloise-Young and Hennigan (1996); (5) Covey, Zang, and Wynder (1992); (6) Trush, Fife-Schaw, and Breakwell (1997); (7) Pugh, Power, Goldblatt, and Arber (1991); (8) Kaplan and Weiler (1997); (9) Glendinning, Shucksmith, and Hendry (1997); (10) Sun and Shun (1995); (11) Rogers, Nam, and Hummer (1995); (12) Oygard, Kleep, Tell, and Veller (1995).

Source: Adapted from Amy Gillis (1998). "The Trends and Variations in Smoking." Course paper for Nursing 300, St. Francis Xavier University.

attitudes are related to gender, then to age categories, then to rural and urban residence, and so forth. In each case, you would want to summarize the consensus (or lack of it) in the research literature. And, if you have provided a summary grid for the literature, your reader will be able to review the findings quickly.

RULE 12.1 PROVIDE BIBLIOGRAPHICAL REFERENCES.

Record full bibliographic details of each article or book. When the final report is being prepared, all the sources will be cited in the bibliography. If you have not recorded this information in full, you will waste a lot of time retracing your steps to recover the information. Use the latest APA guide for referencing. (Edition 5 is the current one at the time this text was prepared.)

5. USING THE INTERNET AND OTHER ONLINE SOURCES

Increasingly researchers are turning to resources available online in order to do a thorough literature search. Full-text journal articles are available at many libraries through online services. The big advantage to these is that the researcher is able to get a complete copy of the desired article, print it, and not leave her/his computer desk to do it.

- One tip is to visit your library and find out what full-text sources are available on CD-ROMs or directly online.

- Another tip is to review the websites listed in Box 12.2 on p. 336 and decide whether it would be appropriate to visit these websites to find out the latest materials that may be directly available to you.

6. CHOOSING VARIABLES

Variables may be defined simply as concepts that we intend to measure. Variables may be identified by:

- reviewing the research literature and identifying what variables other researchers have used in doing similar research;

- applying relevant theoretical models and identifying the variables that are implied by the theories;

- examining questionnaires for ideas concerning what variables should be measured if a survey is to be conducted;

- developing causal models and figuring out what sources of spuriousness, intervening, or control variables might be relevant for the project; and

- simply thinking about what variables might influence the dependent variable.

At the beginning of the project the researcher should not worry too much about whether the identified variables can be measured. Simply identify relevant variables. The issue of measurement can be confronted later.

B. DEVELOPING CAUSAL MODELS

Clarity and precision are at the core of successful research. A **causal model** is a graphic representation of proposed causal interconnections between variables. In quantitative research, one way to force accuracy is to draw a diagram of the causal connections between variables. The advantage of a diagram is that it forces clear thinking about what you are doing. Thus, drawing a diagram with causal arrows forces you to indicate which variable is causally prior to other variables. You are forced to be specific. Such diagrams can also replace stating formal hypotheses; each hypothesis should be reflected in a properly drawn diagram.

We will begin with the simplest models and gradually move toward the more complex ones. What all models have in common is that each of them can be represented by a diagram: each such diagram shows either a causal direction, a hypothesis, or a set of hypotheses. We begin with the two-variable model. Chapter 16 and Appendix A present procedures for analyzing these models.

1. TWO-VARIABLE MODELS

In Chapter 1 the distinction between a dependent and an independent variable was made: the dependent variable is the "effect" in a cause–effect relationship, or the result of the influence of an independent variable. Conventionally, we refer to the dependent variable as the Y variable, and the independent variable as the X variable. The relationship can be described simply with a diagram:

What does the diagram tell us? First, it describes a relationship between two variables known as X and Y. Note that there is an arrow pointing from X to Y: this tells us that X is the independent variable, and that Y is the dependent variable. The hypothesis reflected by this diagram argues that X influences Y. Next, note the > symbol before the X box. This symbol means "the greater"; the opposite symbol, <, means "the less." Putting all these elements together, the hypothesis can be stated as: "The greater X, the greater Y." Had we wished to express a negative relationship, the first symbol could be reversed. In this case, the hypothesis would be stated as: "The less X, the greater Y."

If the X and Y were replaced with variable names, we might, for example, be talking about the relationship between participation in social activities and self-esteem, suggesting that "The greater the participation in social activities, the greater the self-esteem" (Brennan, 1985). The wording of the hypothesis indicates that participation is the independent variable, self-esteem the dependent variable.

The advantage of drawing a diagram to represent the relationship is that the researcher is forced to:

- indicate causal direction (arrow points to dependent variable); and

- indicate if the relationship is positive (note use of > symbol) or negative (< symbol).

Drawing a picture forces precision. There may be times when you cannot formulate a problem in such a way that you are able to say whether the relation is positive or negative. In these cases you cannot speak in "greater than," "less than" terms.

When you are unable to specify the nature of the relationship use a "?" to indicate that no prediction is being made.

Occasionally, you will not be in a position to set out a causal order: here you may be faced with a situation in which variables exist together and influence one another simultaneously. In this event, you can indicate reciprocal causation by placing arrows at each end of the line linking the two variables.

2. THREE-VARIABLE MODELS

Now let us turn our attention to various three-variable models. Some terms need to be reviewed. Besides independent and dependent variables, there are three additional types of variables that will need to be understood: intervening, source of spuriousness, and conditional variables.

A. AN INTERVENING VARIABLE MODEL

An **intervening variable** (I) is a variable that links an independent variable (X) to a dependent variable (Y). An intervening variable represents an explanation of how the independent variable influences the dependent variable. The interest here is in understanding the relationship between X and Y—understanding the mechanism by which X is connected to Y. Frequently the researcher will be testing a number of alternative explanations of how X influences Y. In the case of one intervening variable, the relationship could be diagrammed as follows:

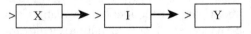

In this diagram, I is the intervening variable, or the linking variable between X and

Y. The hypothesis is that variations in X cause variations in I, which, in turn, influences Y. Typically, one would propose a number of possible intervening variables, so the following diagram would be more appropriate:

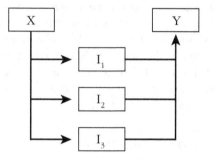

In this diagram, three alternative explanations are suggested for the connection between X and Y. The researcher would collect data that measures each of the variables involved and conduct the appropriate statistical tests to determine which, if any, of the proposed alternative explanations or intervening variables explains the connection between X and Y. These matters will be examined further in Chapter 17.

B. A SOURCE OF SPURIOUSNESS MODEL

A **source of spuriousness model** is one in which a variable is identified as a possible influence on both the independent variable (X) and the dependent variable (Y) in such a way that it accounts for the relationship between them. In other words, the relationship between X and Y may be "spurious" because it is produced by the influence of S/S on each of them. Here, the researcher proposes that, while there is a statistically significant relation between the variables X and Y, this relationship may be non-causal, only existing because some third variable is influencing both X and Y. The argument is

that X and Y are related to one another only because a third factor is influencing both of them. Having observed a statistically significant relation, the researcher will want to ensure that the relationship is not spurious and, therefore, will run a number of spuriousness checks. The source of spuriousness model may be diagrammed as follows:

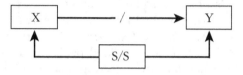

In the source of spuriousness model, the researcher is suggesting that the relation between X and Y may be spurious. The techniques for examining such relations are examined in Chapter 17.

C. AN ANTECEDENT VARIABLE MODEL

An **antecedent variable model** is a causal model that proposes a variable that causes variation in an independent variable, which, in turn, influences the dependent variable in the model. Thus, the antecedent variable is one preceding the main independent and dependent variables. This variable may be having an impact on the independent variable, which, in turn, may be influencing the dependent variable. An antecedent variable may be diagrammed as follows:

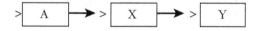

In a sense, an antecedent variable combines one idea from the source of spuriousness model and one from an intervening variable model in that:

- it is causally prior to both the independent and the dependent variables (as in a source of spuriousness model);

- it converts the independent variable into one that intervenes between the antecedent variable and the dependent variable.

D. EXTENDING THE NUMBER OF VARIABLES

It is possible to add variables to three-variable models. In *Causal Inferences in Nonexperimental Research*, Hubert M. Blalock Jr. (1964) outlined partial correlation methods for analyzing relationships when two intervening variables are being evaluated simultaneously. However, it does seem that most researchers have moved toward using regression-based approaches when analyzing such relations rather than using partial correlations, as suggested in Blalock's presentation. A four-variable model such as that suggested by Blalock is shown in the following diagram:

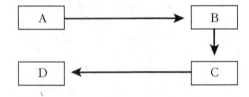

3. MULTIVARIATE MODELS

Models that use numerous variables are known as **multivariate models**. The first we will consider is the candidate variable model.

A. CANDIDATE VARIABLE MODEL

A **candidate variable model** is one that proposes several independent variables as possible causes of variation in a dependent variable. Here the researcher is proposing a number of independent variables that may be influencing the dependent variable. This type of model is illustrated in Figure 12.1.

The variables on the left side of the diagram are the independent variables and are viewed as potential causes of variations in the dependent variable, positive attitudes toward the elderly (MacDonald, 1991). Note that the model uses the symbols > and < to indicate whether the independent variables are positively or negatively associated with the dependent variable. The independent variables will be related to the dependent variable either one at a time or simultaneously, through procedures that are outlined in Chapter 17.

B. PATH MODELS

A **path model** is a graphic representation of a complex set of proposed interrelationships among variables. A model of this type is shown in Figure 12.2 on p. 344 (Jackson and Poushinsky, 1971). (See also Box 2.4 which features Julian Tanner and Harvey Krahn's model of self-reported deviance among high school seniors.)

All the models we have discussed reflect the causal thinking of the researcher in such a way that this reasoning can then be tested in later stages of the project.

1. STATING HYPOTHESES

Good diagrams can replace formal hypotheses statements. By using > and < symbols it is possible to indicate "greater than" and "less than" relations; arrows may be used to indicate causal direction. Particularly in candidate variable models, which include a large number of variables, it is easier to diagram the hypotheses than to present a written version of each one. Similarly, where many alternative explanations are being tested for a particular relationship, a good diagram clearly shows the causal model and the implied research hypotheses.

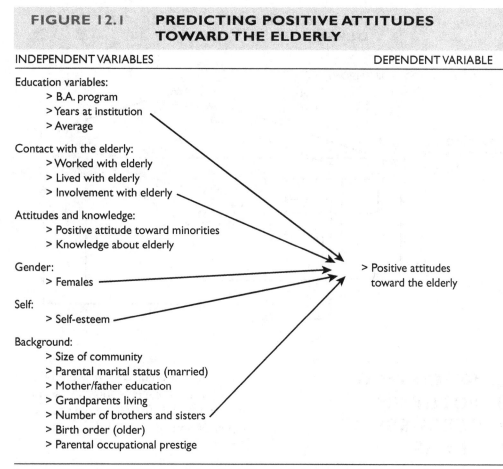

FIGURE 12.1   PREDICTING POSITIVE ATTITUDES TOWARD THE ELDERLY

INDEPENDENT VARIABLES   DEPENDENT VARIABLE

Education variables:
> B.A. program
> Years at institution
> Average

Contact with the elderly:
> Worked with elderly
> Lived with elderly
> Involvement with elderly

Attitudes and knowledge:
> Positive attitude toward minorities
> Knowledge about elderly

Gender:
> Females

Self:
> Self-esteem

Background:
> Size of community
> Parental marital status (married)
> Mother/father education
> Grandparents living
> Number of brothers and sisters
> Birth order (older)
> Parental occupational prestige

> Positive attitudes
  toward the elderly

Source: Lara MacDonald (1991). "Attitudes towards the Elderly." Research Methods paper. Antigonish: St. Francis Xavier University.

In theory-testing projects, it is important not only to state the derived hypotheses but also to indicate the steps that were taken in making the derivation(s). Only to the extent that such derivations can be traced can one claim to have tested a theory.

2. SPECIFYING METHODS OF ANALYSIS

Specifying methods of analysis in advance forces the researcher to be committed to particular procedures. Selecting these procedures also has implications for the way in which variables will be measured. Thus, if contingency tables are to be used exclusively, it will not be necessary to get ratio level measures on the variables. It is probably unreasonable to require a researcher to specify "cut-points" for contingency tables because of the large number of variables that could be involved. However, it is reasonable to indicate the number of categories that will be used and the principle used in making the cut-points (perhaps splitting the sample into thirds, or at the mid-point. See Rule 10.16 on p. 302.).

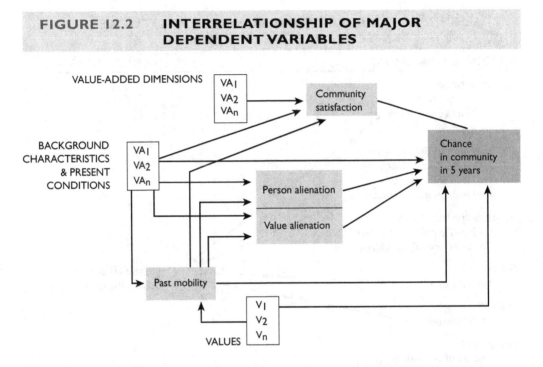

FIGURE 12.2   INTERRELATIONSHIP OF MAJOR DEPENDENT VARIABLES

C. SPECIFYING HYPOTHESES, PROCEDURES OF ANALYSIS

Having developed diagrams for the various relationships that are to be investigated (which imply the hypotheses to be tested), it is now time to indicate formally how the analyses of the data will be done. Proposed methods of analysis are specified in advance to help prevent the researcher from manipulating the data until it conforms to expectations.

We state hypotheses (or diagram them) prior to data analysis to ensure that the researcher is not inventing them after the data have been analyzed. As noted in Chapter 9, developing hypotheses after data are analyzed would render tests of significance meaningless; we would not be able to make judgments about the statistical significance of findings if we did not specify hypotheses in advance of data analysis.

D. HOW TO KNOW WHEN YOU ARE READY TO START THE PROJECT

Table 12.2 provides a check list for items that need to be attended to before beginning a project. Not all items will be relevant to your study. But it is worth going through the list to see if all the things that should be done prior to beginning your project have been completed. Research projects frequently get behind schedule for all

TABLE 12.2 PROJECT INITIATION CHECK LIST

ITEMS TO CHECK	NOT RELEVANT	INITIATED DATE	TARGET DATE	COMPLETED DATE
Preparation of research proposal				
Statement of problem	[ ]	_____	_____	_____
Literature review complete	[ ]	_____	_____	_____
Methodology statement	[ ]	_____	_____	_____
Written formal hypotheses	[ ]	_____	_____	_____
Diagrammed formal hypotheses	[ ]	_____	_____	_____
Ethics review committee submission	[ ]	_____	_____	_____
Funding application	[ ]	_____	_____	_____
Permissions				
From subjects or guardians	[ ]	_____	_____	_____
For use of copyright material	[ ]	_____	_____	_____
For entry into country/group	[ ]	_____	_____	_____
For office/lab space	[ ]	_____	_____	_____
Project staff hired	[ ]	_____	_____	_____
Subjects				
Method of contact established	[ ]	_____	_____	_____
Instruments completed				
Letters to respondents/others	[ ]	_____	_____	_____
Questionnaires	[ ]	_____	_____	_____
Pretesting	[ ]	_____	_____	_____
Pilot study	[ ]	_____	_____	_____
Recording forms	[ ]	_____	_____	_____
Other (list)	[ ]	_____	_____	_____
Equipment				
Tape recorders	[ ]	_____	_____	_____
Computers & programs	[ ]	_____	_____	_____
Other (list)	[ ]	_____	_____	_____
Sampling procedures determined	[ ]	_____	_____	_____
Scheduling, provision for				
Training of staff	[ ]	_____	_____	_____
Holidays, bad-weather days	[ ]	_____	_____	_____
Data collection period	[ ]	_____	_____	_____
Time to get last few cases	[ ]	_____	_____	_____
Data entry time	[ ]	_____	_____	_____
Data analysis time	[ ]	_____	_____	_____
Report-writing time	[ ]	_____	_____	_____

sorts of unanticipated reasons. The check list may help anticipate some of the problems.

The first section deals with the development of a research proposal. Researchers preparing theses will have been told by their supervisor that it is possible to develop a draft of the first three chapters of a thesis before any data are collected. These chapters would include:

- a problem statement,

- a literature review, and

- a methodology section.

RULE 12.2 COMPLETE A RESEARCH PROPOSAL.

The proposal should include a problem statement, a literature review, and a methodology section. These sections should be completed (at least in draft form) before data collection begins.

An exception to this rule would be made for researchers embarking on field studies in which the project will take shape only in the field. Nonetheless, the proposals for such projects can still develop the rationale behind the study and discuss the relevance of the location chosen for the study.

In using Table 12.2, the researcher is encouraged to make realistic estimates of the amount of time it will take to complete various elements. Experienced researchers know that unanticipated delays will often occur, and plan for them by adding in some extra time. The more people involved in the project (either subjects, respondents, or informants), the greater the number of delays that may be anticipated. But even projects that involve few other people, such as a content analysis of children's books, may be delayed—for instance, getting some of the material on interlibrary loan may take longer than anticipated. Try to avoid delays, but it is good advice to assume that they will occur.

So how do you know when you are ready to start the data collection phase of your research? A rule to follow would be:

RULE 12.3

You are ready to commence data collection when all the relevant items noted in Table 12.2 have been realistically planned and when all the necessary written materials, permissions, instruments, and equipment are in place.

E. KEY POINTS

There are researchable problems galore. Some cues to help select one: consider doing something that is currently the subject of public debate; or identify some dependent variable and attempt to understand what factors influence it; or test some aspect of folk wisdom; or perhaps tackle some applied issue (how to reduce shoplifting at the local mall); or replicate a piece of research that someone else has done elsewhere.

Selecting an *appropriate design* requires some knowledge of what the possibilities are, an awareness of how other researchers have tackled similar problems, and a host of practical issues related to what kind of design is feasible.

Reviewing the literature is important to help identify where there are gaps in our knowledge and to find out how other researchers designed their studies and note what their findings were.

Many studies can benefit if the *proposed relationships among variables are diagrammed*, indicating: (i) causal direction (which variable is influencing which); and (ii) whether the relations are positive or negative. That is, are we saying "the greater A, the greater B" or "the less A, the greater B."

An *intervening variable model* suggests possible variables that link an independent and a dependent variable.

A *source of spuriousness model* identifies variables that may be creating a non-causal relation between a dependent and an independent variable.

Candidate variable models simply list a number of independent variables that may be influencing a dependent variable. Normally when such models are tested, a number of variables essentially compete with one another to see which ones best account for variations in the dependent variable.

Path models typically propose an interconnected set of variables with interaction effects in an attempt to understand a system of variables.

F. KEY TERMS

Antecedent variable model

Candidate variable model

Causal model

Intervening variable

Multivariate models

Path model

Source of spuriousness model

Variables

MEASUREMENT

A. THEORETICAL, CONCEPTUAL, AND OPERATIONAL LEVELS

Measurement takes many forms: from unobtrusively observing students and recording which of them remove their dirty plates from dining hall tables, to getting information on suicides from public statistics, observing levels of aggression in people who are frustrated as part of an experiment, classifying television ads according to whether they use sex to sell soap, or having individuals complete questionnaires or undergo personal interviews. Most methods of data collection involve an attempt to measure variables.

We measure things because we wish to describe objects accurately. We wish, for example, to know how popular the prime minister is now as opposed to six months ago, or to describe the prime minister's popularity in various parts of the country, or to see if the prime minister's popularity varies with the gender of the person doing the rating, or to understand what factors explain gender differences in the ratings the prime minister receives. If we pose such questions, we will need to measure the appropriate variables and analyze them. We could make guesses about the answer, but we would not have much confidence in our answer unless the question was tackled seriously and systematically.

As Carmines and Zeller (1979, p. 10) indicate, **measurement** is the "process of linking abstract concepts to empirical indicants." Typically, researchers work from the general to the specific: for each general concept, an indicator is identified. To look for a way of reflecting the idea of social prestige is to ask a measurement question. How might we best measure, or indicate, a person's social prestige? We refer to concepts we intend to measure as *variables*.

Figure 13.1 (on the following page) presents the levels of a research project. To move down the figure is to move from the general to the specific—from the *theoretical level* to the *operational level*, a process referred to as operationalization. At the theoretical level there are a number of interconnected propositions, assumptions, and statements of relationship between concepts. By employing axiomatic derivations and replacement of terms (see Chapter 2), it is possible to derive *conceptual hypotheses*. Such hypotheses may also be identified by reviewing the research literature or by an insightful analysis of the problem. A **conceptual hypothesis** is a statement of the relationship between two or more conceptual variables. An example would be: "the greater the integration into campus life, the less the unemployment experienced after graduation." Having stated the conceptual hypothesis, the researcher would proceed to the operational level, deciding how each of the concepts would be measured and what procedures would be used to collect and analyze the information.

In some approaches the process is reversed and, after doing some observations, the researcher may ask, "Well, what concept does this reflect?" In this case, the researcher begins with observations and then tries to link them to more general ideas. This is the approach recommended by the grounded theory (Glaser and Strauss, 1967). This approach involves a process of discovery in which the researcher begins with observations and tries to make sense of them—to identify the concepts the data seem to reflect. As observations are made, the concepts are continuously identified and refined. Concepts become the basic units of analysis:

In grounded theory, representativeness of concepts, not of persons, is crucial. The

FIGURE 13.1   LEVELS IN RESEARCH DESIGN

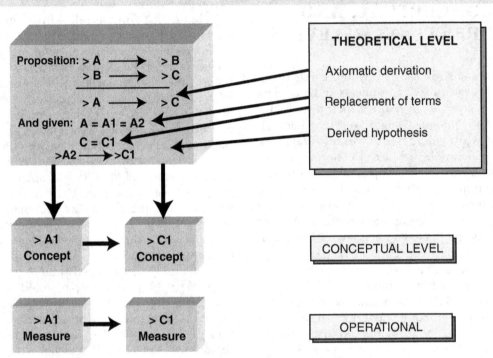

aim is ultimately to build a theoretical explanation by specifying phenomena in terms of conditions that give rise to them, how they are expressed through action/interaction, the consequences that result from them, and variations of these qualifiers . . . For instance, one might want to know how representative 'comfort work' is of the total amount of work that nurses do . . . Do nurses engage in it all of the time or some of the time? What are the conditions that enable them to do it or prevent their doing it? (Corbin and Strauss, 1990, p. 9)

Measurement refers to the process by which categories or numbers are used to reflect, or indicate, concepts. A **concept** is a general idea referring to a characteristic of an individual, a group, or a nation. Concepts help us to organize our thinking about the world. Social scientists use such concepts as socioeconomic status, alienation, job satisfaction, conformity, organizational effectiveness, age, gender, poverty, and political efficacy. There are hundreds of such concepts. It is important that the researcher define precisely what is meant by each concept used. Precision helps to make clear what is included in the idea and also provides a guide as to how it should be measured. The **operational level** of research refers to the indicators used to reflect the concepts as well as to the procedures used to collect and analyze data. *Measurement*, in essence, refers to the linkage between the conceptual and the operational levels. There are two key issues in this linkage: validity and reliability.

1. VALIDITY

In Chapter 1 **validity** was defined as the extent to which a measure reflects a concept, reflecting neither more nor less than what is implied by the conceptual definition. Validity has to do, then, with the congruence of concept and indicator.

A. THE IDEA OF VALIDITY IN QUANTITATIVE RESEARCH

To illustrate, let us examine one possible conceptual definition of socioeconomic status. If SES is defined as a "hierarchical continuum of respect and prestige," and we then choose to operationalize the concept by measuring the annual salary of each individual we study, we will most certainly have problems convincing others of the validity of our measure.

On inspection, it becomes clear that annual salary would not adequately reflect an individual's place on a continuum of respect and prestige. Such inspections are generally referred to as *face validity*. The following are examples of why you might doubt the validity of the proposed measure:

- The local drug dealer is making a fortune but enjoys little respect in the community.

- The best poker player in town always seems to have lots of money, takes expensive trips, and many people admire his worldliness even though his salary at the legion hall is little above the minimum wage.

- The Protestant minister is looked up to by almost everyone even though his salary is a pittance.

- Mrs. Bell Corden, the widow of good Dr. Corden, who served the community with dedication for many years and left his wife a substantial estate, has no salary, but, along with the owner of the hardware store, probably has more prestige than anyone else in the community.

The problem here is that salary does not always capture the concept of social prestige adequately, and even if you could get a measure of annual income rather than salary, you would still not have a valid measure of the concept as defined. (Think of your own home community: can you think of cases in which annual income might not reflect prestige?)

When measuring SES, most social researchers in Canada rely on occupational rating scales that have been based on either:

- the average levels of income and education for people in any given occupation in Canada (see Blishen, 1968; Blishen and McRoberts, 1976); or

- the subjective assessment of the prestige of different occupations in Canada (see Pineo and Porter, 1967; this index is included in Appendix B.)

Both of the above approaches lead to quite similar rankings of the many different occupations in Canada. A major advantage of using such indexes is that it is quite easy to find out a person's occupation and then simply use the score supplied in one of the above indexes to reflect the SES of the individual.

However, one of the problems of using prestige indexes is that such indexes may not reflect the complexity of the organization of the modern household. For example, such indexes traditionally did not produce a prestige score for "homemaker" (researchers would assign a missing value code, or separate special code, to homemakers), and researchers simply tended to use the father's occupational prestige as a measure of the family's socioeconomic level. Given the participation of women in the labour force, this is no longer a satisfactory solution for gauging household socioeconomic status. To avoid the inherent sexism of using the father's occupational prestige rating as a measure of a household's socioeconomic

status, in recent years my students have been basing ratings of a household's socioeconomic status on the *higher* of the two occupational prestige scores in those households where parents are living together and both are employed outside the household. When only one of the parents is employed outside the household, the occupational prestige of that person is used. Simply adding the prestige scores together would result in a prestige score that would not be in line with public perceptions. (For example, the combined prestige scores of parents who are both teachers would be about one and a half times that of a single-earner physician household.) It would be possible to add the values together but weight the lower of the two at a reduced level, perhaps using only one-third of its value (remember, how much you weight it is a judgment call). These calculations are easily done in SPSS, but they are a little tricky (because of the homemaker problem). An example will be shown in Appendix A.

> *To perform this analysis using SPSS see the Creating Indexes section of Appendix A.*

Clearly, however, a definition of socioeconomic status that stresses the relative respect and prestige of members of a community begs for a measure that would get at the extent to which different individuals in the community are looked up to. In a community study, perhaps a panel of local informants could estimate the relative prestige of known members of the community.

When choosing indicators one should, ideally, not select causes, consequences, or correlates of the variable but, instead, get a direct measure of the phenomenon itself. As annual income can be one of several important causes of variation in prestige, it is not adequate to simply measure prestige by income. To do so would be to choose a correlate as the only measure. Similarly, to measure the prestige of Mrs. Bell Corden by the success of her children would be to look at a consequence of her position, and might not adequately reflect her prestige itself. Again the resulting measure might be correlated with her prestige but not reflect it adequately. It is not always feasible, however, to get a direct measure of the concept being studied, and it might, therefore, sometimes be necessary to use indicators that are causes or consequences of it. David Heise and George Bohrnstedt note that:

> *... validity is defined as the correlation between a measure and the true underlying variable. A high validity coefficient does not imply that one has measured that which he set out to measure. It means only that whatever the items are measuring, the composite constructed is highly correlated to it. (Heise and Bohrnstedt, 1970, p. 123; see also Bohrnstedt, 1969)*

Researchers must ensure that measures developed to reflect an independent variable are indeed *independent* of those used to reflect the dependent variable. If care is not taken, a researcher could end up with two different measures of the same phenomenon and, as a consequence, could inappropriately conclude that there is a strong causal relationship between the two variables; instead, there may only be a correlation between two measures of the same underlying phenomenon.

For example, suppose we measured the length of all the classrooms of a college building in inches; suppose we then measured the classrooms again, this time in centimetres. We would then have two measures,

highly correlated, which reflect the same underlying reality. But we would err if we concluded that the length in inches *causes* length in centimetres. These measures lack independence—they both reflect the same underlying variable (the lengths of the rooms). The example is, of course, a simple one and few researchers would be in danger of concluding that variation in inches influences length in centimetres!

But in social science research things are not always so easy. Suppose that you were measuring factors that influence job satisfaction, and that you included the following among the measures of job satisfaction:

INDEPENDENT VARIABLES (CAUSES OF VARIATION IN JOB SATISFACTION)	DEPENDENT VARIABLES (JOB SATISFACTION)
Employee benefits such as retirement benefits	Income
	Satisfaction with income
Hours of work	Satisfaction with being paid the right amount given the contributions you make to the company
Rate of pay	
	Satisfaction, compared to how much others are paid

Clearly there is some overlap between measures of the independent and dependent variables: note that "income" is one of the measures used for dependent variables and that "rate of pay" is one of the measures used for independent variables. You would need to review these indicators to ensure that they are measuring different variables and not simply reflecting the same underlying reality. If you weren't careful you could inadvertently inflate the relationship and come to an inappropriate conclusion. Thus, we can formulate the following rule:

RULE 13.1 MAKE CERTAIN THAT THE INDICATORS OF YOUR INDEPENDENT AND DEPENDENT VARIABLES DO NOT OVERLAP.

This means that the researcher must be careful to ensure that the strength of the association between the independent and dependent variable is not inflated by failing to use measures that reflect different concepts.

Another issue, not typically discussed in methods texts, is the problem of inflating the apparent validity of a measure by choosing a conceptual definition after considering what the most convenient measure would be. What does this mean? In the discussion so far, we have assumed that the researcher is working down from the theoretical to the conceptual and, finally, to the operational level of research. In fact, much research does not follow such a simple path. Before researchers offer conceptual definitions of variables, they often will have given thought to how they will measure the variable.

One way to increase the apparent validity of a measure is to select a conceptual definition that is most congruent with the proposed measure. To go back to the earlier example of measuring socioeconomic status: SES was defined as a "hierarchical continuum of respect and prestige." If the design of the study was to be a door-to-door questionnaire in a community, then the researcher might well reconsider the conceptual definition of SES, since it would be difficult to measure it easily in this way using a questionnaire. It is easier to ask about educational level, occupation, or even income. Knowing this, the researcher might decide that a definition of SES along the lines of "differential access to scarce resources" would be more appropriate: now the researcher can achieve greater face validity by using some combination of education, occupation, and income to reflect SES. Ultimately, in quantitative research, analysis proceeds by examining relationships between indicators. And one must be careful when evaluating such research because, even though two studies might both examine socioeconomic status, the measures used to determine socioeconomic status may differ enormously from one study to another. Is this a shell game? To the extent that conceptual definitions are selected to enhance validity, one could argue that something of a sleight of hand is going on. Thus, even with clearly defined concepts and an indication of the measures used, the research consumer must always be alert to tautologies lurking beneath the surface of a research report.

While techniques for assessing the validity of measures are beyond the scope of this book, the beginning social researcher should, at minimum, be convinced that selected measures have *face validity*. A measure has **face validity** if, on inspection, it appears to reflect the concept that you wish to measure. **Content validity** refers to the extent to which a measure reflects the dimension(s) implied by the concept. Typically content validity requires a more formal assessment including the use of a panel of experts and corroboration of the measurement with the concept's dimensions noted in the literature review and with the study's theoretical framework in order to assure that the content of the measures reflect the framework. There are two types of **criterion validity**: *concurrent* and *predictive*. If you were attempting, for example, to develop a measure to predict success in nurse registration examinations, you could assess the validity of your measure by correlating it with success rates on RN examinations. A high correlation would indicate high **predictive validity**. **Concurrent validity** in the above example would be demonstrated if two different tests were given and the scores correlated highly with each other. If a theoretically derived hypothesis turns out as predicted, this would constitute one piece of evidence for the validity of the measures. This latter type of validity is known as **construct validity**. Another way to think about construct validity is to recognize that it is based on inductive evidence. If one finds evidence to support a theoretically derived hypothesis, then this would indicate that one's measures have construct validity.

Experimentalists in particular distinguish between internal and external validity. **Internal validity** can be taken to mean that the researcher has demonstrated that the treatment, in fact, produced the changes in the dependent variable. **External validity** has to do with the extent to which results can be extrapolated from the particular study to other groups in general.

B. THE IDEA OF VALIDITY IN QUALITATIVE RESEARCH

In qualitative research the issue of external validity perhaps needs to be thought about in a slightly different way. Given the small number of cases typically studied in qualitative projects, the issue of validity is perhaps better thought about in terms of **credibility**. As Margarete Sandelowski has argued, citing Guba and Lincoln (1981) and George Psathas (1973):

A qualitative study is credible when it presents such faithful descriptions or

interpretations of a human experience that the people having that experience would immediately recognize it from those descriptions or interpretations as their own. A study is also credible when other people (other researchers or readers) can recognize the experience when confronted with it after having only read about it in a study. (Sandelowski, 1986, p. 30)

In qualitative studies, the degree to which a description "rings true" to the subjects of the study, to other readers, or to other researchers is an indication of whether you have, in fact, measured what you wished to measure. Furthermore, it has been argued that the closeness of the researcher and the subject being studied should be encouraged rather than discouraged; only through such closeness can the researcher truly penetrate and understand the experiences of the subject (Sandelowski, 1986, pp. 30–31).

As for external validity, the very act of controlling so many extraneous factors (as in an experiment) actually serves to reduce the generalizability of such studies; in qualitative studies such artificiality is reduced given that studies are done in natural settings even though the limited sample sizes mitigate against extrapolations to other populations.

In distinguishing qualitative from quantitative research traditions, Margarete Sandelowski notes:

The artistic approach to qualitative inquiry emphasizes the irreplicability of the research process and product. Every human experience is viewed as unique, and truth is viewed as relative. The artistic integrity, rather than the scientific objectivity, of the research is achieved when the researcher communicates the richness and diversity of human experience in an engaging and even poetic manner . . . qualitative methods such as historical inquiry may employ the methods of science but the presentation or reporting style of art. (Sandelowski, 1986, p. 29)

In order to maximize rigour in qualitative research, Sandelowski makes several suggestions. Note, also, that these suggestions are relevant to the quantitative researcher.

i. Keep Careful Records

The researcher should keep a detailed record of all decisions that have been made, and how they were made. If details are recorded, years later another researcher might be able to repeat the study. Thus, details on how the subject matter was selected, how data were collected, what evidence was deemed unimportant, and the ways in which categories were developed should all be noted. (See Sandelowski, 1986.)

ii. Avoid Holistic Fallacy

This fallacy would make the results of the study look more patterned than they actually are; the researcher should attempt to establish how typical the observations of the study are. Be careful not to report only those events and behaviours that are patterned and consistent; report the exceptions as well (Sandelowski, 1986).

iii. Guard Against an Elite Bias

Elite bias is a danger because informants are more likely to be drawn from the more articulate, high-status elements in a society. Hence, unless care is taken, there is a tendency to represent primarily the views of the elite in one's research (Sandelowski, 1986, p. 32).

iv. Be Wary of Being Taken Over by the Respondent

If the researcher identifies completely with the views of a respondent, it can be difficult to maintain a clear distinction between the researcher's experiences and those of the subject. This can be a problem unless the researcher attempts to record how the respondent and the researcher have mutually influenced one another. If this is done, the report will recognize the reciprocal influence of the respondent on the researcher (Sandelowski, 1986).

The issue of generalizability (external validity) poses difficulties in many research designs, but it presents special challenges in ethnographic studies. Conventional sampling procedures are usually not relevant to ethnographic studies because such studies depend so extensively on case studies. However, it might be possible to argue that the circumstances studied in a particular ethnographic case study are comparable to other situations and that the conclusions of the study can therefore be applied to them. One solution is to carry out research on numerous sites. But, as LeCompte and Goetz point out (1982, pp. 50–53) there are four factors that can influence the credibility of such cross-group comparisons:

v. Selection Effects

The researcher might select sites in which some factors may not be present. A study based on such a site might, therefore, not allow testing of certain ideas.

vi. Setting Effects

Studying a social situation might itself influence the results derived. The impact of the researcher's intrusion might vary from setting to setting, distorting the results more in some settings than in others. Hence, it is difficult to compare the degree to which the researcher influenced the results of different studies conducted at different sites.

vii. History Effects

Each group studied is subject to unique historical influences. When sites are studied at different times, some of the variations between the sites might be explained by history rather than by the interaction of factors within the site.

viii. Construct Effects

Concepts might be regarded differently both by observers in different settings and by those being observed.

2. RELIABILITY

Reliability was defined in Chapter 1 as the extent to which, on repeated measures, an indicator yields similar readings. Reliability issues emerge in both "single-indicator" questions and in those in which a number of indicators are used to reflect a variable.

A. THE IDEA OF RELIABILITY IN QUANTITATIVE RESEARCH

There are both simple and complex ways of assessing reliability. Perhaps the easiest of all is to repeat a question that has been posed. The idea of a *retest procedure* is that if the same question is posed twice and the respondent understands the question identically on both occasions, the response should be identical on both occasions. A second simple approach, though often not feasible, is to verify the answers independently. For example, it might be possible to compare a student's self-reported grade to that "actually" received by the student. Here the issue is the extent to which students systematically over- or underreport grades.

When you are assessing the reliability of the items being used to construct an index (an index represents the combination of several items into a single score), you can randomly split the items into two groups, compute the indexes, and then correlate the resulting scores. Internal reliability would be indicated by a high correlation. This method is known as a **split-half method** for testing reliability. Another procedure is to compare an individual item's correlation to the total index score: if an item is consistent with the total score, it will correlate with it. This technique, known as the **internal consistency approach** to reliability, will be described when index construction is discussed.

> *To perform this analysis using SPSS see the RELIABILITY procedure in Appendix A.*

No matter what indicators are used, the researcher is always trying to accurately reflect both a concept and the reality that is being described.

B. THE IDEA OF RELIABILITY IN QUALITATIVE RESEARCH

When a particular group is studied, there are problems with replication because the circumstances and the individuals can never be the same at some later time.

> What observers see and report is a function of the position they occupy within participant groups, the status accorded them, and the role behaviour expected of them. Direct observer effects can occur when informants become dependent on the ethnographer for status enhancement . . . (LeCompte and Goetz, 1982, p. 46)

Social settings where questions are asked can also be important. So unless the ethnographer fully reports how and where the observations were made, there is little chance of replicating a study.

To increase the chances of replicating a study, LeCompte and Goetz (1982) have suggested the use of five strategies:

1. Focus on verbatim reports—sticking to the facts.

2. Use multiple researchers, as this allows the results of the researchers to be compared.

3. Use participant researchers: this involves training individuals in observational techniques.

4. Use peer examination: when careful descriptions have been made, researchers can check their results against the observations and experiences of fellow researchers.

5. Use mechanical recording devices such as tapes and videos to allow others to check your observations independently at a later date.

Avoiding incorrect conclusions, such as identifying a causal variable incorrectly, is a challenge for the ethnographic researcher. There are three issues of concern:

1. The qualitative researcher must establish that the causal variable precedes the effect; since qualitative researchers make observations over time, establishing the causal ordering of variables is usually not problematical. The researcher is present on the research site over time and is able to observe actions and reactions.

2. The researcher must establish that the variables are related to one another (vary together); the researcher depends, to some degree, on the occurrence of social events that permit him to see whether the variables are varying together. In contrast, the experimentalist creates a situation that systematically varies the intensity of the treatment and observes the reaction to the treatment.

3. The researcher must eliminate rival hypotheses. All researchers who attempt to eliminate rival hypotheses face a challenge, since new hypotheses can always be suggested. The qualitative researcher has to test alternative hypotheses continually as observations are being made. Since observations are made over time, there are opportunities to explore such hypotheses as the study unfolds.

B. MEASUREMENT ERROR

Typically we begin with the assumption that the manifestations of the object we wish to measure have:

- two or more values inherent in them (i.e., we are dealing with a variable, not a constant); and

- that any manifestation has a *true value*.

A **true value** is the underlying exact quantity of the variable at any given time. In measurement, we attempt to reflect this true value as precisely as we can. By specifying "at any given time," we acknowledge that variables change over time and that, consequently, measures might vary from day to day. Just like our weight, anything we measure might vary slightly from one day to the next. And while some variables—like our gender or religious affiliation—remain quite stable, it is possible nevertheless that a change may occur. Sex-change operations and religious conversions are not unknown.

In addition, measurement error will always occur because our instruments are imperfect, because our subjects do not always pay sufficient attention to our instructions, or because we are not careful enough in coding data. **Measurement error** is any deviation from the true value.

Measures are made up from the following components:

$$MEASURE = TV \pm (SE \pm RE)$$

The above equation contains four elements:

- *Measure* This refers to the value that the researcher assigns to the variable in the process of recording the information.

- *TV* The *True Value* is the underlying exact quantity of the variable.

- *SE Systematic Error* is non-random error representing systematic under- or overestimation of the value.

- *RE Random Error* is fluctuation around the "true" value, where higher or lower scores are equally likely (Carmines and Zeller, 1979).

Example: Suppose a male respondent is asked to indicate his weight on a questionnaire. The respondent writes in "70 kilo." Providing that the information is then correctly transcribed in entering the data into the computer, the *MEASURE* is recorded as 70.0 kilograms. Suppose the *TV*, or true value, is 73.367132 kilograms (rounded!). The person usually under-reports his weight by 2 kilograms; this is *SE*, the systematic error. The remaining 1.367132 kilograms is random error (*RE*).

$$MEASURE = TV \pm (SE \pm RE)$$

or

$$70.0 = 73.367132 - (2.0 + 1.367132)$$

The adequacy of a measure is the extent to which the indicator reflects the true value of the variable. All of the above components vary over time and through the various stages of data collection in a research project. Usually we think that measurement errors are made by the subject. But actually the situation is more complex. First, the true value of variables changes over time. If we repeat a measure several times to make certain that we have an accurate reflection of the variable, differences will be due to variations in the true value, random error, and systematic error. (Respondents may change their attitudes over time, hence the true value itself may shift; theoretically, it is fixed only at the time measured.)

1. TIPS FOR REDUCING RANDOM AND SYSTEMATIC ERROR

Researchers can do several things to reduce random and systematic error. Random error refers to those fluctuations that are unsystematic: the respondent who cannot decide whether to rate the quality of lectures in the methods course as a 6 or a 7 on a 9-point scale, and finally decides on a 6, may have made a random choice. Systematic error is error in one direction. For example, if you tell respondents what you expect to find, they may bias their responses to confirm the expectation. Where feasible, consider using some of the following ways of reducing error.

TIP I TAKE THE AVERAGE OF SEVERAL MEASURES.

Sometimes it is possible to repeat a measure several times and then use the average of these measures to reflect the variable. A subject could be weighed on three different scales and the average used. In this way, the researcher hopes to average out random measurement error.

TIP 2 USE SEVERAL DIFFERENT INDICATORS.

In measuring a variable such as attitudes toward abortion, the researcher typically would pose several questions and then combine the responses to form an index. By combining the responses to several questions the researcher hopes to minimize the effect of any one question.

TIP 3 USE RANDOM SAMPLING PROCEDURES.

By giving all people an equal chance of being included in your study, it is possible to minimize distortions that occur when people select themselves. If the goal, for example, was to estimate the popularity of the leader of a country, one would want to reflect the views of the whole country, not special groups within it. By reporting on what the average person thinks about the leader you will minimize the random fluctuations that might occur if you talked to very few, unsystematically selected respondents. By not oversampling those who spend more time at home, for example, you will have avoided systematically biasing the study by overrepresenting the views of people with that characteristic.

TIP 4 USE SENSITIVE MEASURES.

In asking questions, provide respondents with as broad a range of response categories as possible so as not to constrain them. In questions used to create indexes, provide many response categories; in asking respondents to estimate the population of their community, provide many categories. By providing many response alternatives (or, indeed, allowing the respondent simply to respond without using any categories at all), the researcher can decrease the amount of random error in measurement. However, you can go overboard in suggesting increased numbers of response categories: if there are too many response categories, a respondent's ability to make distinctions may be exceeded. To ask someone to report their weight to two-decimal-point accuracy would be silly; few people know their weight with such accuracy.

TIP 5 AVOID CONFUSION IN WORDING QUESTIONS OR INSTRUCTIONS.

Respondents' varied misunderstandings of what is being asked of them is one source of random error. Thus, variation in response may simply be the result of these different understandings. Attempt to develop instructions and questions that are clear and can only have one interpretation.

TIP 6 ERROR-CHECK DATA.

Both systematic and random errors can occur easily. These should be eliminated by conducting error checks on the data. If data are being coded (the process of assigning categories to responses) by several people, inter-rater reliability checks should be carried out in training the individuals to do the work. Only when high levels of inter-rater reliability are achieved should the coding proceed (see Chapter 5). The use of video-recording equipment has permitted those doing observational studies to confirm their data by having other experts examine the work.

TIP 7 REDUCE SUBJECT AND EXPERIMENTER EXPECTATIONS.

As discussed in Chapter 10, subject and experimenter expectations can systematically alter the measures achieved in a research project. Attempt to control these expectations as much as possible.

Precise measurement is indeed a challenge. Any time a measurement is taken, there will be error. The error may be slight or substantial. Measurement should be seen as a matter of probability: most of the time your measurements will fall within a given margin of error. This implies that, some of the time, your measurements will not fall within a given (and acceptable) margin of error. Researchers attempt to estimate the amount of error that is likely in their measurements. The specific procedures for doing this were explained in Chapter 9.

Figure 13.2 presents a target-shooting analogy to help show the relationship between reliability, true value, and validity. In measurement, we attempt to consistently (*reliability*) hit the bull's eye (the *true value*), and if we do so, we have measured what we intended to (*validity*).

An inspection of Figure 13.2 illustrates that a measure can be reliable but lack validity; however, a measure that is valid is also reliable, since measures that hit the bull's eye are closely grouped and, therefore, must be reliable. The three diagrams illustrate the point.

- Diagram 1 depicts measurements that are neither reliable nor valid; the measurements have missed the true value (bull's eye) and produced a lot of scatter.

- Diagram 2 displays a reliable measure, but one that lacks validity. Note that the shots are closely grouped together (hence reliable) but that they are not right on the bull's eye, which represents the true value.

- Diagram 3 displays a valid and reliable measure where the shots are nicely grouped on the bull's eye.

C. LEVELS OF MEASUREMENT

Three levels of measurement were presented in Chapter 8. We will briefly review that discussion to refresh the reader's mind on this important topic. An understanding of levels of measurement is necessary, since the ways in which one should go about analyzing a variable are constrained by the measurement level achieved in data collection. As a general rule, one should attempt to achieve the most precise measurement possible.

One way to begin to understand levels of measurement is to ask if the variable

FIGURE 13.2   BULL'S EYE: TRUE VALUE, RELIABILITY, AND VALIDITY

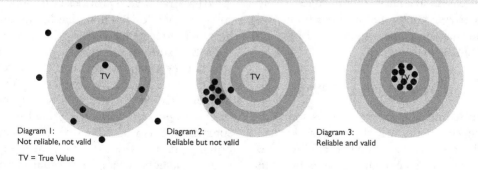

Diagram 1:
Not reliable, not valid

Diagram 2:
Reliable but not valid

Diagram 3:
Reliable and valid

TV = True Value

Source: Adapted from E.R. Babbie (2001). *Practice of Social Research,* 9th ed. Reprinted with permission of Wadsworth, an imprint of the Wadsworth Group, a division of Thomson Learning.

being measured has an underlying continuum (does it vary from low to high?). If there is no underlying continuum, with the variable instead being made up of a number of discrete categories, then the measurement will be at the nominal level; if the variable has an underlying continuum, then the level of measurement will be either ordinal or ratio. This text will distinguish three levels of measurement: nominal, ordinal, and ratio.

1. NOMINAL MEASUREMENT

Examples of **nominal measurement** (those with an arbitrary assignment of numbers to categories) would include measurements of such variables as religious affiliation, gender, program of study, political party affiliation, and ethnic origin. While there may be underlying continua related to religious affiliation (such as degree of religious commitment or frequency of church attendance), by itself the religious organization is a nominal category: it may be Baptist, Lutheran, Roman Catholic, Muslim, Buddhist, or Jewish. When a respondent checks off which (if any) religious affiliations he or she was associated with while growing up, the measurement level attained is nominal. One category is neither higher nor lower than any other—the categories are simply different. Nominal measurement involves no underlying continuum and the numerical values assigned are arbitrary and have no arithmetic meaning.

2. ORDINAL MEASUREMENT

Ordinal measurement involves an underlying continuum with the numerical values ordered so that small numbers refer to lower levels on the continuum and large numbers to higher points; however, the distances between the assigned numbers and the

underlying continuum are not in a one-to-one relation with each other. Note the following questionnaire item asking about the size of a respondent's current home community:

The place where I live now has a population of:

Under 5,000 - - - - - - - - - - - 1 ☐

5,000 to 19,999 - - - - - - - - - 2 ☐

20,000 to 99,999 - - - - - - - 3 ☐

100,000 to 999,999 - - - - - - 4 ☐

1 million or over - - - - - - 5 ☐

Note that the numbers assigned by the researcher (1 through 5) are arranged so that higher numbers refer to larger population centres; but note that the intervals between the numbers are not equal (the second category spans a population range of 15,000, while the fourth category spans a range of 900,000).

Another frequently used type of question would ask respondents to assess their degree of agreement with a statement like the following one:

The United Nations keeps the world safe.

Strongly   1 2 3 4 5 6 7 8 9   Strongly
Disagree   Agree

This kind of item provides ordinal measurement. While we know that high numbers indicate a greater degree of agreement with the statement, we do not know whether the distances between the values are equal: the distance between 4 and 5 on the scale may not be the same size as the distance between 8 and 9. Ordinal measurement orders values but does not assure equal gaps between the measurement points. Additional examples of ordinal level measurement are provided in Table 8.2 (Chapter 8, p. 216).

In conclusion, ordinal measurement involves an underlying continuum; numerical values assigned are ordered but intervals are not equal. The beginning researcher should note, however, that it is common practice for researchers to combine the values of a series of Likert-type questions (Strongly Disagree–Strongly Agree) into an index and then analyze the index, treating it as a ratio variable. Strictly speaking, this practice violates the measurement assumptions, but we all do it in order to use more advanced statistical techniques.

3. RATIO MEASUREMENT

Finally, there is **ratio measurement**. With this level, the intervals between the measurement points are equal and the zero point is aligned with true zero. For example, in the case of income, the nature of the variable is such that it is possible to represent income with a number that reflects the income of a person exactly. In this case, it is also possible to use zero to reflect no income and other numerical values to reflect all other income levels. Here it is correct to say that an income of $50,000 is twice as much as an income of $25,000. With ratio level measurement, it is possible to add and subtract constants as well as to multiply or divide by them without changing the proportionality among the values.

If a researcher were to have respondents indicate with a check mark which of the magazines on a list they had scanned or read in the previous month, and a total was taken of the number ticked off, the result would be a variable that varies from 0 to the number required if a respondent checked off all the items listed: this number would be a ratio measurement. Note that a 0 in this example refers to no exposure to any of the magazines listed, and other values simply

provide a count of the number of the listed magazines that the respondent has scanned or read in the past month. There is a one-to-one relationship between the value assigned by the researcher and the number of listed magazines identified by the respondent.

Similarly, when communities are being studied, measures such as the proportion of visible minorities or the proportion of retired people in the population and various rates and ratios (suicide rate, dependency ratio, sex ratio) are all ratio level measures (see Table 8.3 on p. 217 for additional examples).

In conclusion, ratio measurement involves an underlying continuum: the numerical values assigned are ordered with equal intervals, the zero point is aligned with true zero, and when different ratio measures are combined, the values can be added, subtracted, multiplied, or divided.

D. THE EFFECT OF REDUCED LEVELS OF MEASUREMENT

This chapter has encouraged researchers to achieve the most precise measurements that are practical. To explore the consequences of reducing the level of measurement, the author examined what would happen if a ratio level variable (student's high-school average grade) was regrouped, using random numbers to establish cut-points, into 9, 7, 5, and 3 categories. The new variables were then correlated with unchanged ratio variables (high-school English grade and first-year university grade). As anticipated, the correlations declined further with each succeeding grouping into fewer categories (see Box 13.1).

The analysis suggests that when reduced levels of measurement are achieved, the result will underestimate the strength of association between variables. Furthermore, in doing analyses that permit a comparison of the relative effects of independent variables on a dependent variable (see Multiple Regression, Chapter 17), the effect of an independent variable that has a reduced level of measurement will be underesti-mated. The research suggests the following general principles.

PRINCIPLE 13.1

The greater the reduction of measurement precision, the greater the drop in the correlation between the variables.

BOX 13.1

The Effects of Reduced Level of Measurement

An attempt to examine the consequences of reduced levels of measurement was carried out.

The Hypotheses
The hypotheses that guided this investigation were as follows.

- **Hypothesis 1** The greater the number of categories in a Likert-type variable (i.e., 9 points), the greater the correlation between the variable and other variables.

  In doing a regression analysis:

- **Hypothesis 2** A ratio variable that is measured using a Likert-type question will reduce the amount of variation explained in the analysis in comparison to how much variation would be explained had ratio level measurement been achieved.

- **Hypothesis 3** The beta weights of Likert-type items will be reduced in comparison to those using raw scores.

- **Hypothesis 4** The above effects will be greater for those variables having fewer categories.

- **Hypothesis 5** Beta weights of variables not categorized will be enhanced in comparison to those for which categorization has been done.

A data set containing 3,617 cases was used in this investigation. The variables included university students' high-school average, high-school English grade, and average at the end of their first year of university study. Correlations were calculated (see Table I) for the relation between these variables. The correlation between university average and the English-grade high-school average was .464 and .573 respectively; the high-school English grade and the average high-school grade correlated at .662.

A regression analysis was done by taking the first-year university average as the dependent variable and using the high school English grade and the high-school average grade (excluding the English mark) as independent variables. The results of this analysis are shown in Table II. The R^2 was .341 (34.1% of the variance explained); the beta weight for the English grade was .152, while for high-school average it was .472. The impact of high-school average was about 3 times as great as the English grade alone.

In an attempt to test the hypotheses, a series of trials were done on the data, testing the effect of regrouping the high-school average grade variable. We wanted to compare what would happen if it were collapsed into 3, 5, 7, and 9 categories; we wanted also to observe the impact of such collapsing on the R^2 and the beta weights. A table of random numbers was used to determine the cut-points; a total of 40 variables were cre-ated in this way (10 for 9-category vari-ables, 10 for 7-category variables, 10 for 5-category variables, and 10 for 3-category variables). In all cases, the new variables were used as an independent variable in each trial along with the high-school English grade, and in all cases using the university average as the dependent variable. The results of the correlational analyses are summarized in Table III; Table IV summarizes the results of the 40 regression analyses.

Table I   Correlations Between First-Year University Average, Average High-School Grade, and English High-School Grade (N = 3617)

CORRELATIONS	FIRST-YEAR UNIVERSITY AVERAGE	AVERAGE HIGH-SCHOOL GRADE	ENGLISH HIGH-SCHOOL GRADE
First-year university average	1.000		
Average high school grade	.573	1.000	
English high school grade	.464	.662	1.000

Table II   Regression Analysis Predicting First-Year Average Grade (N = 3617)

VARIABLE	b COEFFICIENT	BETA WEIGHT	PERCENTAGE EXPLAINED
High-school English grade	.16290	.15195	8.30
High-school average*	.54188	.47203	25.78
		% Explained	34.08
CONSTANT	11.08264		
Multiple R	.58383		
R Square	.34085		

*The high-school average was calculated excluding the high-school English grade.

cont'd

Table III   Average Change in Correlations Between High-School Average Grade and First-Year University Grade When Data Are Grouped into 3, 5, 7, and 9 Categories*

NUMBER OF CATEGORIES	AVERAGE DECLINE IN CORRELATION	STANDARD DEVIATION	NUMBER OF RECODINGS
9	−.03810	.03151	10
7	−.05790	.03208	10
5	−.11260	.09623	10
3	−.18240	.16038	10

*The raw data, based on 3,617 cases (St. Francis Xavier University), were used for this analysis. The high-school average grade was recoded into 3, 5, 7, or 9 categories with 10 recodings for each category. For each, the new variable was then correlated with the first-year university average. The above table summarizes the results. For example, when the data were recoded into 3 categories, the average drop in correlation (for the 10 randomly determined cut-points) was .18.

Table IV   Summary of Changes in R^2 and Betas When One Variable Is Grouped into 3, 5, 7, and 9 Categories, Regression Analyses

NUMBER OF CATEGORIES IN RECODED VARIABLE	MEAN CHANGE IN R^2	MEAN CHANGE IN BETA HS*	MEAN CHANGE IN BETA ENG**
9 Categories	−.025	−.067	.059
7 Categories	−.033	−.099	.094
5 Categories	−.055	−.162	.135
3 Categories	−.069	−.217	.179
Probability	.0059	.0039	.0001

*HS refers to high-school average grade; this is the variable that was recoded.

**ENG refers to high-school English grade; this variable was left in its raw form for the analysis.

This analysis summarizes the results of 40 separate regression analyses, 10 for the recoding of each of the four categories. The total N for each analysis is 3,617. Table II presents the results when the high-school average is used in its raw form.

SOURCE: Winston Jackson. The author wishes to thank Dr. Bernard Liengme, Registrar, St. Francis Xavier University, for providing the data for the analysis.

PRINCIPLE 13.2

In analyses comparing relative effects of variables, the effects of those variables with reduced levels of measurement are underestimated by comparison with those whose measurement is more precise.

PRINCIPLE 13.3

Conversely, variables whose measurement is more precise will have their effects overestimated relative to those whose measurement is less precise.

These three principles suggest that we should attempt to reflect the underlying concepts as precisely as possible. But there are constraints. It is foolish to ask people to give us exact answers when there is little likelihood that they will be in a position to make precise estimates. For example, asking anyone on campus to estimate the weight of a school bus would invite highly variable and inaccurate answers. Furthermore, it is sometimes inappropriate to ask for extremely precise information if such information will be considered too personal by a respondent: in some populations, asking someone his or her exact annual income would fall into that category. Sometimes, in order to soften a question—to make it less threatening—we reduce its precision. In asking about age, for example, we sometimes ask people to indicate into which age category they fall, rather than their exact age. So the rule to be followed is:

RULE 13.2 ACHIEVE AS PRECISE MEASUREMENT AS IS PRACTICAL.

Researchers recognize that weaker measurement will typically result in underestimating the importance of a poorly measured variable relative to other more precisely measured variables.

E. INDEXES, SCALES, AND SPECIAL MEASUREMENT PROCEDURES

Readers will be familiar with some indexes in common use. For example, indexes are used to summarize stock market trends: the S&P/TSE-Composite Index, the Dow-Jones 30 Average, and the Nikkei Stock 225 Average each report the value of stocks from a sample of companies drawn to represent different sectors of the economy. Social researchers also use composite measures. Blishen and McRoberts' (1976) occupational rating index and Pineo and Porter's (1967) occupational prestige scale are important examples of widely used Canadian indexes.

Combining several indicators into one score results in an index or scale. While these terms are often used interchangeably, where a distinction is made, an **index** refers to the combination of two or more indicators. A **scale** refers to a more complex combination of indicators where the pattern of the responses is taken into account.

Indexes are routinely constructed to reflect variables such as socioeconomic status, job satisfaction, group dynamics, or an attitude toward some social issue. (For details of many indexes and scales, see Miller, 1977.) Frequently, the researcher will construct sub-indexes that may be treated alone or combined with other sub-indexes to form a composite measure. For example, a researcher measuring attitudes toward abortion might construct a sub-index for "soft reasons" (economically inconvenient, preference for having a baby later, etc.) and "hard reasons" (pregnancy as a result of rape, severely handicapped, etc.). These sub-indexes might also be combined to form an overall index. In each case, however, the researcher will have to ensure that appropriate items are included in each sub-index.

1. ITEM ANALYSIS

It is important that the components of an index discriminate. That is, various elements must discriminate between high scorers and low scorers. To illustrate, suppose that you are attempting to develop a set of multiple-choice questions to measure students' knowledge of the material covered in an introductory course, and you want to identify those items that best measure mastery of the subject matter. Let us suppose that you have 100 questions on the test and that you want to identify the best 50 questions for a future test. The issue is to select those items that best discriminate between high and low performance on the test. Let us suppose that we have given the preliminary test to 200 students enrolled in an introductory course.

We could proceed by grading the test and computing the total correct responses for each student. If the "marking" was done with a computer program, we would have a matrix that has students and questions on the dimensions. Each cell would identify a correct or an incorrect response to each question for a particular student. Now we could order the students by the number of correct responses and then choose the top and bottom quartiles. Table 13.1 shows the percentage from each quartile getting each question correct.

The next step would be to select those items in which the performance of top and bottom students differs most. We assume here that, overall, the questions measure knowledge of the subject matter, and that we are simply choosing those items that discriminate best.

The first two questions discriminate well—the high scorers do considerably better on those items than the low scorers. The third question would be rejected: while 55% of the students in the top quartile gave the right answer, so did 60% of the bottom group. Similarly, question 4 would be dropped because a similar proportion of top and bottom students answered correctly.

Similar procedures can be used to select high-discrimination items for indexes. Suppose, for example, that we had 15 items

TABLE 13.1 DISCRIMINATION ABILITY OF 100 ITEMS: PERCENTAGE CORRECT FOR EACH ITEM, BY QUARTILE

| | PERCENT CORRECT EACH ITEM | |
QUESTION#	BOTTOM 25%	TOP 25%
1	40.0	80.0
2	5.0	95.0
3	60.0	55.0
4	80.0	80.0
5	10.0	40.0
6	20.0	60.0
...	...	...
100	30.0	20.0

for an index measuring job satisfaction, and we wanted to determine which items to include in the index. We want items that do two things:

1. validly reflect the dimension of the concept they are supposed to; and

2. discriminate between high and low scorers.

What we might do is:

• include those items that have face validity;

• add them together, coming up with a total score for each individual;

• split the sample into the top and bottom quartiles in job-satisfaction scores;

• test each item's ability to discriminate between high and low job satisfaction; and

• select those items that best differentiate high scorers from low scorers.

2. SELECTING INDEX ITEMS

Indexes are constructed by combining several individual questions and represent an attempt to summarize, in one score, a measure of a variable. Indexes are constructed in situations in which we have a single-dimension variable, but one question might not adequately measure the variable. Indexes can be constructed by combining a number of similarly formatted questions or combinations of questions with different formats. In all cases, the indicators are combined, and possibly weighted, to sum to a single index score. The steps involved in developing an index are identified below.

STEP 1 REVIEW CONCEPTUAL DEFINITION.

As in developing other measures, the first step is to review the conceptual definition of the variable. Some sense of the "range," or the dimensions, involved in the variable should be developed. The chances are that several questions can then be designed to measure the variable, reflecting each of the dimensions in the conceptual definition.

STEP 2 DEVELOP MEASURES FOR EACH DIMENSION.

Here the same principles apply as for the development of individual measures. For example, in measuring attitudes toward capital punishment, one might identify which, if any, offences would lead a respondent to favour capital punishment. Items can initially be selected on the basis of face validity. That is, if the item appears, on the face of it, to represent a part of the theoretical continuum being measured, then an effort should be made to get a measure of that item. Three capital punishment items that could be part of an index might be:

I support capital punishment for convicted child molesters.

| Strongly Disagree | 1 2 3 4 5 6 7 8 9 | Strongly Agree |

I support capital punishment for a murderer of a police officer.

| Strongly Disagree | 1 2 3 4 5 6 7 8 9 | Strongly Agree |

I support capital punishment for drug smugglers.

| Strongly Disagree | 1 2 3 4 5 6 7 8 9 | Strongly Agree |

STEP 3 PRETEST INDEX.

Index items should always be pretested. A pretest is simple; all you have to do is:

• complete the index yourself;

• sit beside individuals who are within the population being studied and have several complete the index items.

Encourage these pretest respondents to ask questions, telling them in advance that you are trying to find out if all the questions are clear. Reword questions to achieve clarity. Pretests almost always lead to revisions in the wording of index items.

STEP 4 PILOT TEST INDEX.

If time permits, indexes should be pilot tested. A pilot study involves having a number of respondents complete a questionnaire containing the proposed index items. In a pilot study you take what you consider to be the final version of the index to a sample of respondents. The results are analyzed to see if the index items discriminate and if they are internally consistent. Items can be dropped or altered on the basis of a pilot study.

If time is not available to do a pilot test, at least ensure that a full range of possible variability is represented by the index items. When the data are being analyzed, the various items can be evaluated using the SPSS procedure, RELIABILITY. This procedure provides a method of checking the internal consistency of index items. Items can be dropped if they do not prove to be internally consistent.

3. THE RATIONALE FOR USING SEVERAL ITEMS IN AN INDEX

Suppose we are interested in measuring people's attitudes toward abortion. Would it be better to use one question or several questions in our measure? The general consensus among social researchers is that measures with multiple items have an advantage over single-item measures in attaining precise measurement. John McIver and Edward G. Carmines (1981, p. 15) summarize the arguments in favour of using multiple items in measurement.

- An attitude toward abortion would almost certainly be complex, and one would want to reflect this complexity in any measurement (would people have the same attitude toward abortion if the pregnancy threatened the life of the mother, or was the result of a rape, or was economically inconvenient?).

- A single item might lack precision, or might lack a sufficient range in values (a question like "Are you in favour of abortion?" with yes/no response categories would be inadequate. Even with more response categories it would still be weak because the question does not identify conditions when a person might favour or not favour abortion).

- Single items are also less reliable and more prone to random measurement error. If a question like the one above were repeated in a questionnaire, the respondent, having indicated opposition to abortion the first time, might well change her answer the second time, because she thinks: "Well, it depends on the situation; if the female was raped, and is 14 years old, I would be in favour of her right to have an abortion."

- With multiple items it is possible to evaluate the reliability and validity of the index; with single indicators it is more difficult to gauge the amount of measurement error.

4. LIKERT-BASED INDEXES

Rensis Likert (1931) proposed that indexes could be constructed by summing respondents' answers to a number of related items. This type of question is widely used in social science research. In the original format, the respondent is asked to (1) strongly disagree, (2) disagree, (3) be undecided or neutral, (4) agree, or (5) strongly agree with a statement. Such items were, and continue to be, popular in measuring attitudes and perceptions. Box 13.2 illustrates some of these questions.

The reader will note that the items in Box 13.2 deviate somewhat from the original format. Given a preference to increase the variability in such items, the number of response categories has been increased from five to nine. This increase does not take more space on the questionnaire, nor more space when entered into a computer.

Using more response categories (9-point rather than 5-point) should lead to slightly higher correlations between index items, and prove to be somewhat better at reflecting true underlying values. (See the earlier discussion in Section D, p. 363, on the effects of reduced levels of measurement.)

A. TIPS FOR CONSTRUCTING A LIKERT-BASED INDEX

The following tips may be helpful in constructing such items for use in a **Likert-based index**.

TIP I

Avoid the word "and" in Likert items if such usage makes the item multidimensional. In such indexes we are attempting to measure a single variable, so it is important for us not to add a second dimension inadvertently. Suppose we asked a respondent to assess how well he or she gets along at home by making the following statement:

I get along well with my mother and father.
Strongly   1 2 3 4 5 6 7 8 9   Strongly
Disagree   Agree

BOX 13.2

Likert Index Example: Job Satisfaction of Nurses

In the following items, *circle a number* to indicate the extent to which you agree or disagree with each statement.

16. I enjoy working with the types of patients I am presently working with.
  Strongly Disagree   1 2 3 4 5 6 7 8 9   Strongly Agree

29. I would be satisfied if my child followed the same type of career as I have.
  Strongly Disagree   1 2 3 4 5 6 7 8 9   Strongly Agree

30. I would quit my present job if I won $1,000,000 in a lottery.
  Strongly Disagree   1 2 3 4 5 6 7 8 9   Strongly Agree

31. This is the best job that I have had.
  Strongly Disagree   1 2 3 4 5 6 7 8 9   Strongly Agree

32. I would like to continue the kind of work I am doing until I retire.
  Strongly Disagree   1 2 3 4 5 6 7 8 9   Strongly Agree

Source: Clare McCabe (1991). "Job Satisfaction: A Study of St. Martha Regional Nurses." St. Francis Xavier University, Sociology 300 Project. Cited with permission.

What number is the respondent to circle if he or she gets along well with mother but fights continuously with father? The question has to be subdivided into two questions: one asking about relations with mother and one asking about relations with father. Watch out for the word "and" in a Likert item. Most of the time, you will have to change the item.

TIP 2

Place the "Strongly Agree" on the right-hand side of the scale, with 9 indicating strong agreement. Some researchers prefer to vary the response categories by, for example, reversing the side on which the agree/disagree labels are placed. This is done to prevent **response set**, a situation in which the respondent tends to answer similarly to all items. While switching the side on which the agree/disagree categories are placed may reduce the tendency to respond in a set manner, it may also introduce additional errors in response. (Respondents may not notice that you have switched the agree/disagree categories.) This author's preference is to maintain a uniform presentation. Response sets are best avoided by wording some questions positively and others negatively.

TIP 3

Avoid negatives that could confuse respondents (statements such as: "I don't think the university administration is doing a bad job," will almost certainly confuse and slow down respondents).

TIP 4

Vary the "strength of wording" of questions to produce variation in response. Similarly, if there is uncertainty as to where responses will fall, use more than one item with different intensities in the wordings.

TIP 5

Before the first Likert-type item is presented, provide a brief explanation of how respondents are to indicate their answers.

Likert items result in an ordinal level of measurement. Typically such items are combined to form indexes by adding together the values on individual items (after having reversed the scores on the negative measures).

B. EVALUATION OF LIKERT-BASED INDEXES

We have assumed that the summation score reflects the true underlying variable. If an item does not correlate with this score, we assume that the item is not appropriate. It is, however, possible that the other items are in error. If index items are not well thought out, the chances are that the correlations between the items will generally be low and that this information can then be used to reject items.

> *To perform this analysis using SPSS see the RELIABILITY procedure in Appendix A.*

Likert-based indexes are widely used in the social sciences. Their popularity is due to the following factors:

- They are easy to construct.
- There are well-developed techniques for assessing the validity of potential items.
- They are relatively easy for respondents to complete.

C. USING THE INTERNAL CONSISTENCY APPROACH TO SELECTING INDEX ITEMS

Internal consistency refers to the ability of the items in an instrument to measure the same variable. *Homogeneity* is often used to refer to the internal consistency of an instrument. A homogenous instrument contains items that are strongly correlated with each other. The higher the intercorrelations among the items, the greater the internal consistency of the instrument. Homogenous instruments are unidimensional; that is, the items taken together measure one construct. Because all the items reflect the same underlying construct, the researcher can sum the individual item scores to get a total score that reflects the construct. Often social research deals with phenomena that are multidimensional, such as job satisfaction, social support, or attitudes toward various public issues. In these situations the social researcher must establish separate internal consistency estimates for each dimension of the construct.

When you are assessing the *reliability of the items* being used to construct an index (an index represents the combination of several items into a single score), you can randomly split the items into two groups, compute the indexes, and then correlate the resulting two scores. Internal reliability would be indicated by a high correlation between the two groups of items. This method is known as a split-half method and was one of the first methods available for testing reliability (homogeneity). The advantage to this procedure is it allows the researcher to assess test-retest reliability without administering the instrument twice. The Spearman correlation (covered in Chapter 8) is usually used in this procedure.

The most commonly used procedure to assess homogeneity is to compare an individual item's correlation to the total index score: if an item is consistent with the total score, it will correlate with it. This technique is known as the internal consistency approach to reliability. The item–total correlations represent a group of correlations between each item and the total score for the instrument. Item–total correlations are useful in instrument development. They are helpful in determining which items to retain and which ones to discard in creating a final index. The item–total correlations should be high enough to indicate internal consistency but low enough to indicate that they are not redundant. Nunnally (1978) suggests that uncorrected item-to-total correlations above .25 and below .70 are typically acceptable for item retention when developing a new index.

The most common method used by social researchers for assessing internal consistency is **Cronbach's alpha**. This test is based on the strength of the intercorrelations of all the items in the instrument as well as the number of items used (see RELIABILITY procedure in Appendix A). The alpha value ranges from 0 to 1, with 1 indicating perfect internal consistency and 0 no internal consistency. Since the alpha coefficient is dependent on *both* the number of items used in creating the index and the average inter-item correlation, there is no easy answer as to how high a value is required. As a rule of thumb you need average inter-item correlations above .30 and, with 5 items in the index, that would yield an alpha of .682. Normally it seems easiest to judge the adequacy of an index by the *average inter-item correlation* rather than the alpha value itself. Since alpha values increase as a function of the number of items used, one can increase the alpha value simply by adding items. An alpha of .70 means one thing if there are 5 items in the index, but quite another if there are 14 items. Using the ".30 rule" as a minimum average inter-item correlation is recommended so as to provide greater uniformity in the development and assessment of indexes. Table 13.2 indicates the alpha values that are associated with the number of items and the average inter-item correlation.

TABLE 13.2 CRONBACH'S ALPHAS BY MEAN INTER-ITEM CORRELATIONS AND NUMBER OF ITEMS

MEAN INTER-ITEM CORRELATION

# ITEMS	.10	.20	.30	.40	.50	.60	.70	.80	.90
2	.182	.333	**.462**	**.571**	**.667**	**.750**	**.824**	**.889**	**.947**
3	.250	.429	**.562**	**.667**	**.750**	**.818**	**.875**	**.923**	**.964**
4	.308	.500	**.632**	**.727**	**.800**	**.857**	**.903**	**.941**	**.973**
5	.357	.556	**.682**	**.769**	**.833**	**.882**	**.921**	**.952**	**.978**
6	.400	.600	**.720**	**.800**	**.857**	**.900**	**.933**	**.960**	**.982**
7	.438	.636	**.750**	**.824**	**.875**	**.913**	**.942**	**.966**	**.984**
8	.471	.667	**.774**	**.842**	**.889**	**.923**	**.949**	**.970**	**.986**
9	.500	.692	**.794**	**.857**	**.900**	**.931**	**.955**	**.973**	**.988**
10	.526	.714	**.811**	**.870**	**.909**	**.937**	**.959**	**.976**	**.989**
11	.550	.733	**.825**	**.880**	**.917**	**.943**	**.962**	**.978**	**.990**
12	.571	.750	**.837**	**.889**	**.923**	**.947**	**.966**	**.980**	**.991**
13	.591	.765	**.848**	**.897**	**.929**	**.951**	**.968**	**.981**	**.992**
14	.609	.778	**.857**	**.903**	**.933**	**.955**	**.970**	**.982**	**.992**
15	.625	.789	**.865**	**.909**	**.938**	**.957**	**.972**	**.984**	**.993**
16	.640	.800	**.873**	**.914**	**.941**	**.960**	**.974**	**.985**	**.993**

Note: If we set .30 as the minimum average inter-item correlation for an acceptable index, the column headed by .30 would constitute the minimum alphas required. Thus, the bolded values represent those that are acceptable. Unbolded values are below the acceptable level. For example, if you had a 12-item index, and the mean inter-item correlation was .20, the alpha value would be .750 and, since this is in the non-bolded area, the index would not be sufficiently reliable. However, a 3-item index with an alpha of .562 should be treated as an adequate index. Researchers using 5-point Likert items may want to set the minimum average inter-item correlation at .25 given the weaker measurement.

5. SEMANTIC DIFFERENTIAL PROCEDURES

Osgood, Suci, and Tannenbaum (1957) developed the **semantic differential** measurement technique. There are numerous index applications for this type of measurement technique. Originally, these measurement techniques were used to study subjective feelings toward objects or persons. For example, measuring stereotyping behaviour—that is, how respondents view various out-groups—has been investigated using this approach. The format of such questions is shown in Box 13.3. These questions consist of a series of adjectives indicating two extremes placed at the margins of the page; the respondent is asked to indicate where, between the two extremes, he or she would place the group, individual, or object being evaluated. For example, respondents might be asked to indicate where a group would be placed on an honest/dishonest continuum, or on a hot/cold dimension. Respondents are encouraged to answer the questions quickly, letting their guards down, and thus revealing how they "see" various categories of individuals or objects.

There are a variety of traditional and nontraditional uses for such items. An examination of respondents' self-images is certainly possible; items for conducting such

BOX 13.3

Semantic Differential

62. Circle a number to indicate where you think *you* fit on a continuum between the two opposites.

621	Shy	1	2	3	4	5	6	7	8	9	Outgoing
622	Passive	1	2	3	4	5	6	7	8	9	Dominant
623	Cautious	1	2	3	4	5	6	7	8	9	Daring
624	Bookworm	1	2	3	4	5	6	7	8	9	Social Butterfly
625	Quiet	1	2	3	4	5	6	7	8	9	Loud
626	Serious	1	2	3	4	5	6	7	8	9	Humorous
627	Conformist	1	2	3	4	5	6	7	8	9	Leader
628	Cooperative	1	2	3	4	5	6	7	8	9	Stubborn

Source: Winston Jackson (1988–89). *Research Methods: Rules for Survey Design and Analysis.* Scarborough: Prentice-Hall Canada Inc., p. 99.

an examination appear on question 62 of Box 13.3. Such questions can be used to measure individual variables or be combined to create indexes.

6. MAGNITUDE ESTIMATION PROCEDURES

Magnitude estimation procedures are useful when comparative judgments are required. When these procedures are used, a respondent compares the magnitude of a series of stimuli to some fixed standard. These techniques emerged out of work done by S.S. Stevens (1966a, 1966b), who attempted to examine the relation between physical stimuli (e.g., the physically measured roughness of different sandpapers) and respondents' perception of their roughness. This powerful technique is useful when comparative judgments are required (Hamblin, 1971a; Hamblin, 1974; Jackson

and Poushinsky, 1971; Lodge, 1981). The technique results in ratio level measurement and should most definitely be in the arsenal of the social researcher. Box 13.4 presents an illustration of it. This technique is best used in interview or in group-administered questionnaires. The instructions need to be reviewed carefully with the respondents, so it is necessary to have a researcher present when the instrument is administered.

Typically, one of two methods is used to do magnitude estimations. The first is to have respondents provide numerical estimates. If one were estimating the relative popularity of different students in a residence, for example, one might begin by having respondents compare the popularity of each student to that of a student the researcher has identified as being about average in popularity. The researcher would then assign this average student 100 units of popularity. The respondent would be asked to proceed through a list of students,

BOX 13.4

Magnitude Estimation Training: Community Comparisons

We are now going to ask you to make some comparisons between this community and the one you lived in before moving here. We will ask you to draw lines to indicate how you feel about different things.

For example, we might ask you how much you like your neighbours here compared to the ones you had in your last community. We will say you liked your neighbours in your last community this much:

_____

Now we would like you to draw a line indicating how much you like your present neighbours. If you like the present ones about half as much, then draw a line about half as long as the line above; if you like them more than your previous neighbours—say 2½ times as much—then draw a line 2½ times longer than the line above. Could you try it?

Could you compare *this* community to the *last one* you lived in? (Once again, we will draw lines to indicate the differences: if you think your present community is ½ as good as the previous one, draw a line one-half as long as the standard line; if it is 2½ times as good, draw a line two-and-one-half times as long.)

If your last community was: _____

Could you now indicate how satisfied you are with your present community (compared to the last one you lived in) on the following dimensions?

CLIMATE
SCHOOLS
MEDICAL FACILITIES
COST OF LIVING
JOB SECURITY
HOUSING
JOB SATISFACTION

Source: Winston Jackson and Nicholas W. Poushinsky (1971). *Migration to Northern Mining Communities: Structural and Social-Psychological Dimensions.* Winnipeg: Centre for Settlement Studies, University of Manitoba.

indicating in each case the amount of popularity each has, relative to that of the "average student." If the respondent thinks that Joan is two and a quarter times as popular as the average, a value of 225 would be assigned. Alternatively, if the respondent thinks that Joan has three-quarters the popularity of the "average student," then a value of 75 would be assigned.

A second approach is to have respondents draw different length lines to indicate their perceptions of the differences between stimulus objects. In this case, a standard line is given, and the respondent is asked to draw lines relative to the standard line. (Sample instructions for using the "line method" are presented in Box 13.5.)

BOX 13.5

Sample Magnitude Estimation Instructions: Perceptions of Universities

Now we would like to have you rate the various local universities on a number of dimensions. The way you will do it will be to draw different lengths of line to indicate how each of the universities compare to one another. If you draw a line twice as long as the "standard" line, it means you think that a particular university is twice as good as average for the particular dimension being rated. For example, suppose you were asked to indicate how far each institution is from your home. You would then draw lines indicating the relative distances from your home. You might draw the following lines:

IF THE AVERAGE UNIVERSITY IS THIS FAR _____

HOW FAR IS: (suppose you then drew the following lines)

Acadia _____

Dalhousie _____

Mount Allison _____

Mount St. Vincent _____

St. Francis Xavier _____

St. Mary's _____

We would interpret your lines to mean that you think that Acadia is about 1½ times farther than the average Nova Scotia university; Dalhousie, Mount St. Vincent, and St. Mary's about average, while St. Francis Xavier is about one-third as far as the average university.

Now we would like you to give us estimates on the following 25 aspects, using the technique that was described above.

How good are the residence accommodations?

Standard = _____

Acadia

Dalhousie

Mount Allison

Mount St. Vincent

St. Francis Xavier

St. Mary's

How good an academic reputation do you think each university has?

Standard = _____

Acadia

Dalhousie

Mount Allison

Mount St. Vincent

St. Francis Xavier

St. Mary's

Source: Winston Jackson. *University Preferences and Perceptions of Pictou County Students*. Antigonish, Nova Scotia: St. Francis Xavier University.

A. TIPS FOR USING MAGNITUDE ESTIMATION PROCEDURES

Here are some tips for the utilization of magnitude estimations:

TIP 1

Only use magnitude estimations when a researcher is present to explain the method. The mailed questionnaire is not a suitable vehicle for using this technique.

TIP 2

Use magnitude estimations when comparative judgments are required.

TIP 3

Use a stimulus category somewhere near the middle of the range you intend to use as a standard. Avoid choosing a standard that is near the extreme high or low.

TIP 4

After the standard has been assigned, leave the respondent free to assign all other values.

TIP 5

Randomize the order of presentation and avoid starting with the extremes of the continuum.

TIP 6

Before the session begins, tell the respondent how to indicate a "zero" response or a "non-applicable" one.

TIP 7

Data derived from magnitude estimations will generally require three columns of space for each variable entered. When lines or numbers are used, the value "999" is used to indicate an item that has not been answered; "001" generally is used to indicate a zero response. Lines are generally measured in millimetres, while numerical estimates are entered directly without change.

B. EVALUATION OF MAGNITUDE ESTIMATIONS

The exciting part of this technique is its ability to provide ratio level measurement for perceptions about social phenomena. It is possible, for example, to measure: perceptions of the seriousness of different crimes (Sellin and Wolfgang, 1964); the status of occupations and people with different incomes and educations (Hamblin, 1971b); the perceptions of those who have migrated (Jackson and Poushinsky, 1971); and the relative attractiveness of universities to high school students (Jackson, 1973).

In collecting data, respondents will sometimes use numbers incorrectly, rank ordering the stimuli rather than maintaining the proportionality between the stimulus items. One has to be careful to make certain that respondents understand the procedure. A further limitation is that a researcher must be present to train the respondents in the use of the technique and, hence, it is not applicable to mailed questionnaires, or phone interviews.

F. KEY POINTS

If we are to test theories, we must find a way to measure our concepts. Measurement links abstract concepts to indicators. There are two key issues in this linkage: validity and reliability. The issue of *validity* raises concerns about whether a measure reflects the concept; the issue of *reliability* raises concerns about whether the measure consistently reflects the concept.

In *qualitative research* more emphasis is placed on the credibility of analysis. Such research attempts to describe and interpret social behaviour convincingly, in a way that would seem believable to those people engaging in the social behaviour as well as to other researchers.

Measurement error refers to the extent to which indicants fail to reflect the true underlying values of variables. Measurement error comes in two forms: systematic and random. Systematic error refers to biases that go in one direction, systematically distorting research outcomes; random error goes in either direction from the true underlying values of a variable.

There are three relevant *levels of measurement*: nominal, ordinal, and ratio. It is important to know the nature of the variable being measured (is it by nature nominal or ratio?) so that appropriate indicators may be sought. Furthermore, the level of measurement achieved determines what forms of analysis are appropriate for analyzing relationships among variables.

Nominal measurement involves no underlying continuum; numerical values assigned have no meaning and values cannot be added, subtracted, or multiplied.

Ordinal measurement involves an underlying continuum; numerical values assigned are ordered, but intervals are not equal. When ordinal measures are combined, the values may be added, or subtracted, but not multiplied.

Ratio measurement involves an underlying continuum; numerical values assigned are ordered with equal intervals, and the zero point is aligned with true zero. When different ratio measures are combined, the values may be added, subtracted, multiplied, or divided.

Researchers are encouraged to achieve *precise measurement* whenever possible. Reduced levels of measurement lead to underestimations of the strength of the relations between variables, giving undue emphasis to precisely measured variables at the expense of poorly measured variables.

When two or more items are combined to reflect a variable, an index or scale is created. The rationale for using several indicators is that we gain precision and reflect the complexity of the variable more adequately. A number of sociologists have devised different procedures for creating scales and indexes. The easiest index to create is a Likert-based one. It is the most widely used approach. In addition, researchers should be aware of the *semantic differential* and the *magnitude estimation* procedure for measuring variables.

G. KEY TERMS

Concept	Index	Operational level
Conceptual hypothesis	Internal consistency	Ordinal measurement
Concurrent validity	Internal consistency approach	Predictive validity
Construct validity	Internal validity	Ratio measurement
Content validity	Likert-based index	Reliability
Credibility	Magnitude estimation procedures	Response set
Criterion validity		Scale
Cronbach's alpha	Measurement	Split-half method
External validity	Measurement error	True value
Face validity	Nominal measurement	Validity

QUESTIONNAIRE DEVELOPMENT

Questionnaires have many applications: they are used in interview projects, research assessing the effectiveness of different types of programs, experiments, and a host of other situations. A well-designed questionnaire does not impose on the patience of the respondent. It should be possible to move through the questionnaire rapidly, without becoming bored, and without having to reread questions because of ambiguity. An easy-to-complete questionnaire is more likely to be filled out successfully. For those doing a survey, Chapter 4 contains a discussion of how to administer different types of surveys. The present chapter focuses on the development of the questionnaire. We begin our consideration with some general issues, then pay attention to the phrasing of specific questions, and then deal with issues of layout and format.

A. GENERAL GUIDELINES FOR QUESTIONNAIRE DEVELOPMENT

The following list of rules for developing a questionnaire should be regarded as a guideline; there will be situations in which it should not be followed in detail. Use these rules with intelligence and a good dose of common sense.

RULE 14.1 CONSULT THE RESPONDENT.

All surveys are something of an imposition on those who are asked to complete them. It is important, if you wish to have a high completion rate, not to impose unduly on your respondents. Above all, the respondent must be made to feel that he or she is being consulted and can express opinions freely. The questionnaire or interview schedule should be designed to be inclusive—designed to make all respondents feel that their opinions are both valued and acceptable.

RULE 14.2 KEEP IT SHORT.

Frequently projects involve a group of researchers and there can be considerable difficulty in keeping the questionnaire from becoming too long. Asking too many questions not only is an infringement on the respondent's time but also creates additional work in data entry and error detection. To overcome this problem, it takes a careful negotiator to persuade a colleague that some proposed questions be left for a later study. One test when such difficulties arise is to request individuals to indicate precisely how the variable will be used in analysis. Such discussions force some careful thinking about the survey and the analysis that will follow. All too often a number of variables remain unanalyzed, either because they are considered to be poorly measured or because their relationship to the study is unclear.

There cannot be any strict rules for the length of a questionnaire. If the questions are easy to answer and the respondents have a particular interest in the survey, it is possible to extend the length of the survey. It is always wise to use as few questions as possible, never asking questions merely for interest's sake. Table 14.1 suggests guidelines for maximum lengths for typical surveys.

TABLE 14.1
MAXIMUM NUMBER OF QUESTIONS FOR SURVEYS

TYPE OF SURVEY	MAXIMUM LENGTH
Phone survey	20 questions
Mailed survey	50 questions
Group-administered	70 questions
Interview	60 questions

The table can only be approximate, since there can be enormous variations in the complexity of the questions, the sophistication of the respondents, and the respondents' interest in the survey.

Phone surveys have to be particularly easy to respond to. Each question must have simple response options, as the respondent will have difficulty trying to remember all the response categories if many are presented. The rule here is to keep the questionnaire simple and short.

Other surveys can involve more questions and greater complexity. Mailed surveys need to be kept somewhat shorter than the others because the researcher is not present to provide encouragement. Interviews can safely be extended to about 60 questions and take as much as an hour to complete, but it should be remembered that many interviews will take much more time because of the tendency of respondents to stray from the topic. Questionnaires administered to an assembled collection of individuals can involve 70 or more questions. Here, as long as the questions are well designed, respondents can move through the instrument rapidly; because of subtle group pressure, most respondents will complete the form.

But no matter how the data are to be gathered, the researcher should strive for brevity and simplicity. There is no point in gathering data that you do not have the theoretical or analytical skills to process.

RULE 14.3 ACHIEVE PRECISE MEASUREMENT.

Generally, researchers should try to obtain the most precise measurement possible. Collect data in the rawest form: income to the dollar, precise occupation rather than a general category, and age to the year rather than an age category that spans 10 years. This recommendation

has to be moderated when other factors argue against precise measurement. You might avoid precision when it would entail asking for information that is too personal, require respondents to make distinctions beyond those they normally use, or when the methods needed to ensure such precision would be too cumbersome. Arguments in favour of precise measurement were presented in Chapter 13.

B. TYPES OF QUESTIONS ILLUSTRATED

This section will illustrate a variety of formats for typical questionnaire items. While it is not possible to anticipate all types of questions, the same principles can be applied to many questions.

1. PRE-CODED, SINGLE-CHOICE QUESTIONS

In **pre-coded, single-choice questions**, the respondent is asked to indicate with a check mark which category applies to him or her. Box 14.1 provides illustrations of such questions. In the first case (Question 4), note that only the question is numbered; it will look too cluttered if the categories are also numbered. After the category label, a dashed line is used so that the respondent's eye moves laterally to the check-off category; the number beside the square box is the value that will be used when the data are entered into the computer. To avoid a cluttered look, there should be no space between the number and box.

The next items in Box 14.1 illustrate slightly more complex forms of the check-off question. Question 5 illustrates how to accommodate two columns of check-off

BOX 14.1

The Simple Pre-Coded Question

4. What year are you in?

Freshman – – – – – – – – – 1☐
Sophomore – – – – – – – – 2☐
Junior – – – – – – – – – – 3☐
Senior – – – – – – – – – – 4☐

5.1/5.2 What is the highest education completed by your mother and father?

	Mother	Father
Grades 0 - 6	1☐	1☐
Grades 7 - 9	2☐	2☐
Grades 10 - 12	3☐	3☐
Some post-secondary	4☐	4☐
University graduate	5☐	5☐

11. What was the approximate population of your home area prior to attending university?

Rural area – – – – – – – – 01☐
Small town under 999 – – – – – – 02☐
Between   1,000 -   4,999 – – – 03☐
Between   5,000 -   9,999 – – – 04☐
Between   10,000 -   19,999 – – – 05☐
Between   20,000 -   29,999 – – – 06☐
Between   30,000 -   49,999 – – – 07☐
Between   50,000 -   74,999 – – – 08☐
Between   75,000 -   99,999 – – – 09☐
Between 100,000 - 249,999 – – – 10☐
Between 250,000 - 999,999 – – – 11☐
1,000,000 or over   – – – – – – 12☐

categories; in this case, one for the mother's and one for the father's educational level. Once again, the computer codes are placed next to the categories, as this will facilitate data entry. Similar space saving can be achieved by splitting long category lists into two and placing them side by side.

The question on population size simply illustrates that when there are more than 9 categories, it is important to place the leading zero in the computer codes. If the leading zero is omitted, data-entry errors will almost certainly occur. The particular population categories would, of course, have to be altered, depending on the target population.

Two points also need to be mentioned that are not illustrated in Box 14.1. Frequently, it is not possible to name all the possible responses that would be appropriate (religious affiliation, for example), and the researcher will have a final category that says:

Other − − − − − − 12❐

Please specify _____

The most obvious reason for using a "please specify" category is that there would not be sufficient room to list all possible religions. However, even more importantly, you do not wish to insult your respondent by not having included his or her religion. In actual fact, if the major religious groupings of relevance to your study have been included, the person who specifies a category not included in the questionnaire will simply be coded as an "Other."

Finally, note that the response categories provided should cover the full spectrum of possible responses and it should not be possible for a respondent to check off two of the categories. Note in Box 14.1 that the population categories are **mutually exclusive**—no category overlaps another one. A common error is illustrated in Example 1, Box 14.2.

Example 1 illustrates a situation where the researcher has failed to provide mutually exclusive categories; Example 2 corrects the error.

2. OPEN-ENDED QUESTIONS

An **open-ended question** asks the respondent to answer some question or to offer some suggestion or opinion but to do so without any pre-set categories being

---

BOX 14.2

Two Versions of Population of My Home Town

Flawed Version: Not Mutually Exclusive Categories
Example 1.
The population of the place I considered my home town when growing up was:

Rural area − − − − − − − − − 1❐
Town up to 5,000 − − − − − 2❐
5,000 to 20,000 − − − − − − 3❐
20,000 to 100,000 − − − − − 4❐
100,000 to 1,000,000 − − − 5❐
1,000,000 or over − − − − − 6❐

Better Version: Categories Are Mutually Exclusive
Example 2.
The population of the place I considered my home town when growing up was:

Rural area − − − − − − − − − 1❐
Town under 5,000 − − − − − 2❐
5,000 to 19,999 − − − − − − 3❐
20,000 to 99,999 − − − − − − 4❐
100,000 to 999,999 − − − − 5❐
1,000,000 or over − − − − − 6❐

provided for the answer. There are at least six reasons for including some open-ended questions in a survey.

1. Such questions are used when there are too many possible responses (as in year of birth).

2. Open-ended questions are preferable if the researcher does not wish to impose response categories on the respondent.

3. The researcher uses such questions when he or she wants to create the sense that the respondent is really being consulted by being asked to offer his or her opinions.

4. The researcher wishes to provide a qualitative dimension to the study.

Open-ended questions provide this dimension, along with material that can be used as a source of quotations for the final report.

5. A pilot study is being done and the appropriate response categories have not been determined.

6. Such questions are used to provide a change in pace for the reader.

While open-ended data are not always analyzed when writing the final report on a project, they can provide insights for the researcher that might be missed if such questions were not asked.

Box 14.3 illustrates some variations in typical formats. Questions 20 and 22 are

---

BOX 14.3

Sample Open-Ended Questions

20. Approximately, what was your average in your final year of high school?
_____ _____ %

21. What is (or was) your father's occupation (e.g., supervisor, railway machine shop . . . supervises work of about 25 people)?
Job _____
Brief Job Description _____
_____

22. In what year were you born? __ __ __ __ .

23. What is the one thing that you would like to see changed at the university?
_____
_____

24. In your opinion, what was the single best thing about attending university?
_____
_____

simple questions where the space for the response indicates that two numbers are expected. By providing two blanks, the respondent is being prompted to enter two numbers. The % symbol in question 20 also helps to indicate exactly what is expected. This helps to prevent frivolous replies, like writing in "average" in the case of question 20, which asks about the respondent's average in the final year of high school; or writing in "a long time ago" in the case of question 22, which asks about year of birth.

Question 21 illustrates a method of asking about occupation. The additional line (Brief Job Description) is included to ensure that the respondent provides sufficient detail to enable the researcher to attach an occupational rating code to the response. (See Appendix B for the Canadian Occupational Prestige Index.) If such specification is not requested, some respondents will simply indicate the employer (for example, writing in "CNR") and the researcher will not be able to attach an occupational rating to that kind of response. Where detail is required, the researcher must be careful to request it.

Questions 23 and 24 simply seek the opinion of the respondent on two issues. Typically, the responses that are given would either be listed (simply typed) or coded. If they are coded, the categories would be determined after the data have been collected and the responses examined.

RULE 14.4 MINIMIZE NUMBER OF OPEN-ENDED QUESTIONS.

Many researchers minimize the number of opinion-seeking, open-ended questions because they are time-consuming to code, tend to generate responses that are inconsistent, and are more likely to be left blank. Indeed, respondents will frequently fail to complete a questionnaire that has too many such questions. Many respondents appear to feel that asking them to write a sentence or two is too much of an imposition.

When a pilot study is conducted, and the research team is uncertain about the appropriate response categories, it is a good idea to pose the question in an open-ended form, analyze the results, and then base the categories to be used in the final study on those suggested in the pilot study (Schuman and Presser, 1981).

Placing an open-ended question at about the two-thirds mark of a long questionnaire may well provide the relief needed to sustain the respondent's interest and ensure completion of the questionnaire.

If both open-ended and fixed-choice questions are asked, it is advisable to place the open-ended version first so that the respondent is not influenced by the fixed-choice options (Sudman and Bradburn, 1983).

Michael D. Smith (no date) has explored the effectiveness of open versus pre-coded questions in revealing the incidence of physical abuse. Both formats were equally effective in detecting abuse; however it was noted that if questions about abuse were asked a second time, some 21% of the victims revealed their victimization on the second question. The findings suggest that it is a good idea to repeat a question a second time, using a variant of the question, as this may get respondents to reveal their abuse. Some may object that such persistent questioning might create an expectation (demand characteristic) that the respondent should make a positive response. However, if the question is properly worded this should not be a problem.

Use opinion-seeking, open-ended questions sparingly; do keep in mind, however, that they are an excellent vehicle for providing a change in pace for the respondent or for exploring new issues in detail.

3. PRESENCE-ABSENCE QUESTIONS

Presence-absence questions request respondents to check off which items in a list do or do not apply to them. Box 14.4 provides examples of such questions. Of the two versions presented, the second one is preferable. In it, either a "yes" or a "no" is expected for each item. While this is a little more work for the respondent, the researcher can then be more confident that each item has been considered. In question 24, if an item is left blank, does that mean that the respondent is opposed to capital punishment for that crime? Or did the respondent simply fail to consider that item?

In contrast to the questions presented in Box 14.1, where the respondent was asked to check one of a set number of answers, square response boxes are not used for the answer in Box 14.4. Instead,

---

BOX 14.4

Presence-Absence Check-Off Questions

Flawed Version: Possible Ambiguity of Items Left Blank

24. On a guilty verdict, for which of the following situations would you support the use of capital punishment? (Check as many as appropriate.)

Manslaughter	_____	1
Premeditated murder	_____	1
Rape	_____	1
Murder of police officer	_____	1
Murder of prison guard	_____	1

Better Format: Less Ambiguity About Items Left Blank

23. Have you ever had contact with a physically handicapped person in any of these groups? (Circle to indicate "yes" or "no" for each group.)

	1 Yes	0 No
Community	1	0
Family	1	0
Relatives	1	0
Elementary school class	1	0
Junior high-school class	1	0
Senior high-school class	1	0
University class	1	0
As co-worker	1	0

respondents are asked to circle a 1 (Yes) or a 0 (No). The reader should also note that the computer codes used involve "1" for presence and "0" for absence. During analysis a "total experience" variable may be created by simply adding the variables together. A total score of "5," for example, would mean that the individual has had experience with disabled people in five of the settings identified in the question.

4. RANK-ORDERING QUESTIONS

Rank-ordering questions are those for which a respondent is asked to indicate an ordering of response items, usually from most preferred to least preferred. Asking respondents to rank-order a list has to be done with great care. In this case, detailed instructions should be provided for the respondent. Box 14.5 includes an example of such a question.

First, note that the respondent is asked to pick out only the three most important items; in most cases, respondents will not be able to go beyond the top three meaningfully. These are difficult types of questions for respondents, and they should be kept as simple as possible.

Second, it should be noted that the instructions are embarrassingly explicit. While "rank-ordering" may be an obvious and simple idea for many people, the detailed instructions will minimize the number of respondents who will simply place a check mark beside three items or check just one of the items.

Note that the respondents are given a short line on which they are to write their answers. Again, it is important to provide a different look for the item in order to cue the respondent that this is not a "check-one" question. Be assured that if you use a presentation that resembles a "check-one" format, a good number of questionnaires will be returned with one of the items checked.

TIP

One suggestion for coding these responses into the computer is to use the values provided by the respondents (i.e., 1=1, 2=2, and

---

BOX 14.5

Rank-Ordering Questions

31. Rank-order the three most important characteristics you want in the job you make your life's work. (Place a 1 beside the most important one; a 2 beside the next important one; and a 3 beside the next most important one.)

High salary . . . . _____

Security . . . . _____

Continued interest . . . . _____

Power . . . . _____

Prestige . . . . _____

Excitement . . . . _____

3=3) and code all items left blank as a 4. In this way, means can be computed during analysis. (This is a situation in which it seems to make sense to compute a mean using ordinal data.) In the few cases in which respondents simply tick off three items, each one ticked can be given a 2. Of course, if the whole item is left blank, the researcher will be forced to assign the missing-value code to each of the items.

Avoid overusing rank-ordering items in a questionnaire. They slow the respondent down and increase the risk of losing the respondent's cooperation.

5. LIKERT-TYPE QUESTIONS

Chapter 13 presented Likert questions under the discussion on index construction. The reader is referred to that chapter for a more extensive discussion of these items. But since they are used as stand-alone items, a brief comment will be made on them here. **Likert-type questions** are those that ask respondents to indicate the strength of their agreement or disagreement with a statement. This type of question is widely used in social science research. In the original format (Likert, 1931), respondents were asked to react to a statement by indicating whether they (1) strongly disagree, (2) disagree, (3) are undecided or neutral, (4) agree, or (5) strongly agree. Such items were, and continue to be, popular in measuring both matters of fact and attitudinal issues. (Box 14.6 illustrates some of these questions.)

The reader will note that the items in Box 14.6 deviate somewhat from the original format. Given a preference to increase the variability in such items, the number of response categories has been increased from five to nine. This increase does not take more space on the questionnaire, nor more space when coded into the computer.

The following tips might be helpful in constructing such items:

TIP 1

Avoid the word "and" in such items if such usage makes the item multidimensional.

TIP 2

Place the "Strongly Agree" on the right-hand side of the scale, with 9 indicating strong agreement. Some researchers prefer to vary the response categories, such as reversing the side on which the agree/disagree labels are placed. This is done to prevent **response set**, a situation in which the respondent tends to answer similarly to all items. While switching the side on which the agree/disagree categories are placed may reduce the tendency to respond in a set manner, it may also introduce additional errors in response. (Respondents might not notice that you have switched the agree/disagree categories.) My preference is to maintain a uniform presentation. Response sets are best avoided by wording some questions positively and others negatively.

TIP 3

Avoid negatives that could confuse respondents (statements such as "I don't think the university administration is doing a bad job" will almost certainly confuse and slow down respondents).

TIP 4

Select a "strength of wording" to produce variation in response. For example, if you were asking patients about the quality of care given by nurses in a hospital, you might ask several questions, varying the strength of the wording in each item. You might suspect that nursing care will be rated high, so you might want to strengthen the wording from Version 1 to Version 2.

BOX 14.6

Likert-Type Items

In the following items, *circle a number* to indicate the extent to which you agree or disagree with each statement:

52. I believe capital punishment represents the most effective deterrent to murder.

Strongly Disagree   1   2   3   4   5   6   7   8   9   Strongly Agree

53. I believe a murderer can be rehabilitated to become a responsible, functioning member of society.

Strongly Disagree   1   2   3   4   5   6   7   8   9   Strongly Agree

54. I believe a life sentence is a satisfactory penalty for murder.

Strongly Disagree   1   2   3   4   5   6   7   8   9   Strongly Agree

55. I would quit my present job if I won $1,000,000 through a lottery.

Strongly Disagree   1   2   3   4   5   6   7   8   9   Strongly Agree

56. I would be satisfied if my child followed the same type of career as I have.

Strongly Disagree   1   2   3   4   5   6   7   8   9   Strongly Agree

57. My mother would be upset if she knew I did drugs.

Strongly Disagree   1   2   3   4   5   6   7   8   9   Strongly Agree

VERSION 1: The nursing care I received at St. Martha's was good.

Strongly Disagree   1 2 3 4 5 6 7 8 9   Strongly Agree

VERSION 2: The nursing care I received at St. Martha's was perfect in every instance.

Strongly Disagree   1 2 3 4 5 6 7 8 9   Strongly Agree

The *strengthening* of the wording in Version 2 will almost certainly produce more variation in response. Version 1 would be expected to produce 8s and 9s almost exclusively. (A further illustration is provided in Rule 14.7 on p. 394.)

TIP 5

If there is uncertainty about where responses will fall, use more than one item with different intensities in the wordings.

TIP 6

Before the first Likert-type item, provide a brief explanation of how respondents are to indicate their answers.

TIP 7

When respondents fail to answer a question, use the 0 value as a missing-value code. (The 9, which is usually used for missing values, reflects a real value in the case of a 9-point Likert item.)

Likert items result in an ordinal level of measurement. Frequently, such items are combined to form indexes by adding together the values on individual items (after having reversed the scores on the negative measures).

6. INDEX DEVELOPMENT

Indexes are constructed by combining several individual questions and represent an attempt to summarize in one score a measure of a variable. Indexes are constructed when we are dealing with a single-dimension variable, but in contexts where one question might not measure the variable adequately. Indexes can be constructed by combining a number of similarly formatted questions or combinations of questions with different formats. In all cases, the indicators are combined, and possibly weighted, so that they add up to one index score. (See Chapter 13 for details on different methods of constructing indexes. Appendix A contains illustrations for index construction using SPSS.)

C. STEPS AND RULES FOR QUESTIONNAIRE DEVELOPMENT

This section will review the steps that will need to be taken in developing your questionnaire and will present rules to follow.

STEP 1 MAKE A LIST OF VARIABLES.

Questionnaires can be thought of as consisting of four major groupings of variables: background characteristics, the dependent variable(s), the independent variables, and the other types of variables: intervening, antecedent, and sources of spuriousness variables. Questions to measure variables in each of these groups will have to be developed. The first task is to create a list of variables; during this stage it is not necessary to worry about how the variables will be measured—a list is all that is required. The list may be derived by:

- applying relevant theoretical models and identifying variables that should apply;

- reviewing the literature, paying particular attention to which variables were measured by other researchers;

- examining other questionnaires for ideas as to which variables should be included;

- reviewing the causal models that have been developed for the current project; and finally

- thinking about which variables "make sense," given the topic of the research.

STEP 2 ANTICIPATE HOW DATA WILL BE ANALYZED.

After the list of variables is developed, it is important to discuss how the data will be analyzed when they are collected. Indeed, it is possible to set up proposed analysis tables showing what relationships are to be analyzed and indicating what procedures will be used to examine each of them. It is critical to have some understanding of how the analysis is to proceed, since the methods used to examine relationships are constrained by the level of measurement attained in operationalizing each of the variables. This discussion can also include how the analysis will proceed given different outcomes of preliminary runs on the data. Frequently, important new variables will emerge as a result of this process. Table 14.2 indicates the types of procedures that would be appropriate given different levels of measurement of the variables involved in the study.

Suppose that you wished to do regression analyses on the data. In such cases, you would prefer to have ratio-level measurement of all the variables. You might want to figure out how to use magnitude estimation procedures or how to construct indexes that would meet, or be close to meeting, the standard for ratio measurement. On the other hand, if the nature of the dependent variable (nominal measurement) dictates a reliance on crosstabular analysis, then you would be content to get ordinal and nominal level measurements of your variables.

STEP 3 WRITE THE PROPOSED QUESTIONS ON INDEX CARDS.

During the development of a questionnaire it is a good idea to write proposed questions on index cards (usually 8 × 13 cm cards are large enough). Using cards will facilitate both the quick editing of items and rearranging their location in the questionnaire.

STEP 4 DOUBLE CHECK TO MAKE CERTAIN YOU HAVE ALL THE VARIABLES.

It is essential to ensure that all the variables that play a part in the hypotheses and models related to the project have been included. The list of variables must be checked and double checked. It is not unusual for a researcher to discover that some key variable has become lost in the shuffle. With checking completed, it is now time to begin drafting the questionnaire. Once again, there are some rules to keep in mind as this process begins.

STEP 5 REVIEW CONCEPTUAL DEFINITIONS.

When developing the wording for a particular question, it is important to review its conceptual definition. Knowing the conceptual definition provides an important guide as to what the question is to measure. To illustrate,

TABLE 14.2 APPROPRIATE ANALYSIS PROCEDURES BY LEVELS OF MEASUREMENT

Dependent	INDEPENDENT VARIABLE		
	Nominal	Ordinal	Ratio
Nominal	CROSSTABS	CROSSTABS	CROSSTABS MEANS* DISCRIMINANT
Ordinal	CROSSTABS	CROSSTABS NONPAR CORR	CROSSTABS NONPAR CORR DISCRIMINANT
Ratio	MEANS ANOVA	MEANS ANOVA	CORRELATION GRAPH PARTIAL CORR REGRESSION

*In SPSS for this case, run the independent variable as though it were the dependent variable (i.e., name it first); the interpretation of the test of significance would be standard.

suppose one is attempting to measure socioeconomic status. And suppose that, in the conceptual definition of socioeconomic status, reference is made to a hierarchical continuum of respect and prestige. Given this conceptual definition, the researcher might be led to adopt a measure particularly designed to reflect the relative amount of prestige an individual has. In this case, one might opt to use an occupational prestige scale such as the one developed by Featherman and Stevens in the United States (1982), or Pineo and Porter in Canada (1967).

While this procedure might yield a valid measure of the concept in general, the experienced researcher would realize that the measure may be weak on the "respect" aspect of the definition and would also run into some serious difficulties if there were a number of housewives or single stay-at-home parents in the sample—such individuals are not assigned scores in occupational prestige scales. One might, therefore, choose to measure the "respect and prestige" an individual has by getting a number of individuals to rate each individual compared to others. Perhaps the latter approach would yield the most valid measure of the concept, even though it would be rare for a research design (probably a study of a particular group) to allow for the practical use of this method.

Suppose, alternatively, that the proposed conceptual definition of socioeconomic status stressed variations in access to scarce resources. In this case, one might attempt to reflect the variable by getting some indication of the individual's total income. Here the assumption is that an individual's total income would be a good reflection of that individual's ability to buy access to scarce items in the society.

The more general point is that the researcher must pay careful attention to conceptual definitions—they provide invaluable and crucial guides to valid measurement.

STEP 6 DEVELOP WORDING FOR QUESTIONS.

There are a few rules to keep in mind as you commence writing drafts of the questions to be included in your questionnaire.

RULE 14.5 WORDS MUST BE UNDERSTOOD.

The words used in questionnaires must be understood by all respondents. Err on the side of simplicity. If a survey is being done on high school students, play it safe—use words that a Grade 7 student can handle. Furthermore, the words selected should be those that have only one unambiguous meaning. Showing off an impressive vocabulary has no place in a questionnaire that is intended to produce valid and reliable data.

RULE 14.6 PAY ATTENTION TO THE "AND" ALERT.

Individual questions should be unidimensional. Avoid the trap involved in a question such as:

I get along very well with my mother and father.
Strongly   1 2 3 4 5 6 7 8 9   Strongly
Disagree   Agree

The problem with the question, as worded, is that some respondents will not "get along" equally well with both mother and father. As a result, some respondents may indicate a 1 or a 2 if they do not get along well with both; others might indicate a 6 or 7 as a kind of average of the relationship they have with both their parents. The point is that two dimensions have been introduced—the relationship with mother *and* the relationship with father. Such questions should be divided into two separate questions. It is always useful to scan one's questions to eliminate such unwanted confusion: double check any question that has the word "and" in it.

RULE 14.7 VARY WORDING TO PRODUCE VARIABILITY.

It is important that the items in a questionnaire produce variability in response. If most respondents provide similar responses to a question, then the question will have little use during analysis. Try to ensure that the respondents will scatter themselves across the response continuum. A simple example will illustrate the point:

Mothers play an important role in our society.

Strongly	1 2 3 4 5 6 7 8 9	Strongly
Disagree		Agree

Using common sense alone, one could anticipate that most respondents will be in strong agreement with this statement and will circle 8 or 9. If, indeed, respondents do not vary their responses much, the question will not prove useful in discriminating between respondents' views about the role of mothers. In this case, what one does to produce more variability in response is to "strengthen" the wording of the item, so that more respondents will move toward the "disagree" end of the continuum: perhaps a statement such as "Mothers play a more important role in society than fathers" or "Mothers play the single most important role in our society." In both illustrations we have made it less likely that all respondents will remain at the "Strongly Agree" end of the continuum.

In dealing with a variable such as job satisfaction, a review of the literature will reveal that most respondents will report themselves to be relatively satisfied with their jobs. Knowing this, the researcher strives to identify items that will induce some respondents to report that they are less than fully satisfied—perhaps the researcher will ask if the respondent would like his or her child to have a job similar to their own; or ask if they think they are paid the "right amount" for the responsibilities that they have.

Similarly, questions that measure clients' satisfaction with services delivered—for example, the satisfaction of patients with services in a hospital—will need to ensure that the questions ferret out the slightest dissatisfaction. Otherwise it is likely that virtually everyone will rate the service as "good" or "excellent."

When one is phrasing questions so as to ensure that respondents vary in their scores, one is not attempting to distort reality—to show dissatisfaction when none is present—but rather one is attempting to develop measures that are highly sensitive. And, if one is attempting to understand what leads patients to be relatively more, or relatively less, satisfied with their treatment in a hospital, one would need highly sensitive measures, given the fact that respondents generally tend to respond positively. If all respondents simply reported that they were "satisfied," we would not be able to identify what factors influence levels of patient satisfaction.

RULE 14.8 AVOID COMPLEXITY.

Try to keep questions simple; avoid asking respondents to do difficult tasks. When it is necessary, for example, to have respondents rank-order a list, it is usually best to ask them to rank-order the three most important items, rather than asking them to go through the whole list. In most cases, the slight reduction in discriminatory power will be offset by a higher response rate to the question.

RULE 14.9 USE EXISTING WORDINGS FOR COMPARATIVE ANALYSIS.

When a researcher wants to compare data that he or she is generating to data reported by other researchers, it is important that the wording of questions be identical. Here, one has to weigh the advantages of improving the wording of a question against the advantage of maintaining identical wordings to facilitate comparative analyses.

RULE 14.10 TAKE THE EDGE OFF SENSITIVE QUESTIONS.

Using a combination of experience and common sense, the survey researcher soon learns that there are some issues that respondents may be reluctant to report. Illegal activities, evaluating friends or neighbours, and indicating age or income can all be sensitive issues. By asking for the respondent's year of birth rather than age, the researcher makes the question sound scientific and more likely to be answered; if age is asked, the respondent may feel some invasion of privacy is occurring. Similarly with income. Here, many researchers will ask respondents to indicate into which broad category of income they fall. Alternatively, if income is a key question, and if the question is located among those dealing with conditions of work, respondents will generally provide the information. However, if the income question is being used as a measure of socioeconomic status, then other indicators, such as years of education or occupational prestige, might be considered preferable to income itself—simply to avoid prying unnecessarily into what may be perceived to be a highly personal matter.

RULE 14.11 AVOID ASKING RESPONDENTS TO SPECULATE ON WHY THEY ACT THE WAY THEY DO.

Generally we are not interested in polling respondents' opinions on whether certain relationships exist. For example, if you are studying the relationship between participation in student activities and levels of self-esteem, you would normally not ask respondents if they think there is a relationship between these two variables. Instead, the researcher would get separate measures of the two variables (among others) and would then analyze the data to determine if there is any relationship.

RULE 14.12 BE PRECISE, HIGHLY SPECIFIC WHEN CHOOSING WORDINGS.

If you wish to measure, for example, how much people drink, ask questions that pinpoint the type of drink consumed and the time when it was consumed. Here the time period will have to be reasonable. It is silly to ask how many drinks someone has had in the past two years; few people could make a reasonable estimate without considerable thought. Box 14.7 illustrates some possibilities in asking about drinking patterns.

Question 1 suffers because of variations in what respondents consider light, moderate, or heavy drinking. Question 2 is better because it pins down a specific time period, but perhaps it goes overboard: you can become too specific. Question 3 hits a reasonable compromise, being specific and referring to a reasonable and recent time period.

STEP 7 PRETEST THE QUESTIONNAIRE.

It is important to have a few individuals complete the questionnaire or the interview before settling on the final wordings of the questions. Start by filling it out yourself. Make any necessary corrections, then try it on a few other people. Generally it is best to sit with the individuals completing the questionnaire. Before they begin, tell them exactly what you are doing (trying to remove any ambiguity in the questionnaire) and encourage them to ask for any clarifications. Perhaps, as they complete the questionnaire, they might inquire: "When you ask about the size of my family, do you mean the family I was born into or the one I have with my husband? Also in that question, do you want me to include the parents in the count?" If so, clearly you will need to change your wording of the question. With experience, you will learn to be highly specific in your wording of

---

BOX 14.7

Sample Alcohol Consumption Questions

Flawed Version: Fuzzy

1. How would you describe your drinking?

Abstainer ─ ─ ─ ─ ─ ─ ─ ─ ─ 0☐
Light ─ ─ ─ ─ ─ ─ ─ ─ ─ ─ ─ 1☐
Moderate ─ ─ ─ ─ ─ ─ ─ ─ 2☐
Heavy ─ ─ ─ ─ ─ ─ ─ ─ ─ ─ 3☐

Flawed Version: Too Specific; Recall Problem

2. This past New Year's Eve, how many beers did you have?

____ ____ beers

Better Version: Specific

3. In the past seven days, how many beers did you drink?

None ─ ─ ─ ─ ─ ─ ─ ─ ─ ─ ─ 0☐
1 to 3 beers ─ ─ ─ ─ ─ ─ ─ ─ 1☐
4 to 7 beers ─ ─ ─ ─ ─ ─ ─ ─ 2☐
8 to 12 beers ─ ─ ─ ─ ─ ─ ─ 3☐
13 or more ─ ─ ─ ─ ─ ─ ─ ─ 4☐

---

questions. The goal is to minimize variations in respondents' understanding of each question. It is always a good idea to review your questionnaire and search for possible ambiguities. The goal, although impossible to achieve, is to have all respondents understand each and every question in an identical manner.

STEP 8 IF ADVISABLE, DO A PILOT STUDY.

It is recommended that a pilot study be used in a number of situations. A **pilot study** involves having a small sample of respondents complete the questionnaire or undergo the interview. Pilot studies are used to determine items to be included in indexes, and to determine, from open-ended questions, what categories should

be used in a fixed-choice format. Further refinements in a questionnaire can be achieved through the use of a pilot study.

D. RULES FOR ORDERING QUESTIONS, FORMATTING, AND PRESENTATION

1. ORDERING QUESTIONS

RULE 14.13 INTRODUCE SURVEY TO RESPONDENTS.

Normally, questionnaires will contain a brief statement introducing the study to the respondent. It should be short (usually three or four lines is sufficient) and should inform the respondent about who is doing the study, who is sponsoring it, and what the study is about. These few lines should attempt to establish the legitimacy of the project. By identifying who is doing the study and who is sponsoring it, the idea is conveyed that the survey is important. Such identification also provides the respondent with some additional information before deciding whether or not to fill out the questionnaire. The researcher should not identify the specific hypotheses of the study; to do so might well bias the responses. Finally, if the survey is anonymous, respondents should be assured that their anonymity will be protected. A good way to achieve the latter goal is simply to ask respondents not to write their names on the forms. (See Box 14.8 for sample wordings.)

In a mailed questionnaire, a letter describing the project and requesting the cooperation of the recipient is generally included. Ideally, this letter should be written on letterhead stationery and be signed by the head of the organization. One attempts to communicate the importance of the project by identifying its sponsors and by the professional appearance of the mailing. Normally, a stamped return envelope is included for the convenience of the respondent.

RULE 14.14 EASE THEM INTO IT.

In deciding the order of questions, consideration should be given to starting with those questions that are easy to answer. It is important not to start by asking questions that could

---

BOX 14.8

Sample Introductory Questionnaire Statements

The following is a research project regarding attitudes toward some public issues. As all responses are confidential, please do not sign your name. Answer all questions as honestly as possible. Thank you for your co-operation.

* * * * *

This is a survey of Nursing Students with regard to their anticipated plans for managing both fertility and career expectations. The information will be kept confidential and your name is not required.

* * * * *

The following questionnaire has been prepared by students from St. Francis Xavier University to compare the future plans of high-school students. Your co-operation in completing this study by responding to the following questions would be greatly appreciated. Please do not put your name on the questionnaire since all responses are confidential.

* * * * *

This is a survey being conducted by students. We would appreciate your co-operation in filling out this questionnaire to the best of your ability. Since your responses will remain anonymous, please don't write your name on the questionnaire.

be regarded as "too personal." Background information questions are usually placed at the end of questionnaires (Dillman, 1978, p. 125; Erdos, 1983). However, when students are being surveyed, or in situations in which there is little problem with refusals, it is possible to begin with items that reflect the respondent's place of birth, gender, and the size of the community in which the respondent lives. Perhaps then it will be possible to move to issues such as the respondent's year of birth. Whether one begins with background information or other questions, it is important that the respondent be able to move quickly through these first items, creating the impression that it will take only a few minutes to complete the whole questionnaire. Survey researchers are always concerned to do everything that they can to increase the proportion of people who will complete the form successfully. If obtaining the background information involves questions that could be considered highly personal, then it is best to place such items at the end of the questionnaire.

Another suggestion for question ordering is to begin with questions that the respondents will consider important. Respondents are more likely to complete a questionnaire if they view it as salient (Heberlein and Baumgartner, 1978, p. 457; Goyder and Leiper, 1985, pp. 60–65).

RULE 14.15 PLACE KEY AND REPEATED VARIABLES AT ONE-THIRD POINT.

In most projects there will be a few variables that are particularly important to the study. In most cases, there will be a major dependent variable. Ordinarily, it is a good idea to place key variables about one-third of the way through the questionnaire. It is important for the respondent to be fresh and paying maximum attention when these key variables are presented.

If there are to be any "reliability checks" (repeated questions), then there should be as much separation as possible between the first and second presentation of such questions. The first presentation of any repeated questions should also be placed near the beginning of the questionnaire—after the respondent is warmed up—but before fatigue or boredom sets in.

RULE 14.16 GROUP QUESTIONS BY TYPE.

Some grouping by type of item is advisable. Minimize the amount of shifting between open-ended questions and pre-coded questions. If there are a number of Likert-type items, it is a good idea to group some of them together (Likert, 1931). The idea is to get the respondent used to a particular format in order to permit quick movement through the items. Continual shifting between types of questions will only slow the respondent down and increase the risk of error.

2. FORMATTING

RULE 14.17 BEGIN CONDITIONING RESPONDENTS.

The first questions begin a "conditioning" process. By always presenting the "check-one-of-the-following" questions in the same manner, the respondent soon gets the idea that questions presented in this manner are to be responded to by choosing one of the options provided by the researcher. Later, when a "fill-in-the-blank" question is asked, the researcher can draw attention to the fact that something else is required by varying the format. For example, if the respondent is to be asked to rank-order a list, or to choose the three most important items from a list, then a different look should be given to the question by varying the way in which the response categories are set up on the page—perhaps a short line opposite each item rather than a square response box. (See Boxes 14.1 through 14.5

for illustrations.) The key point is that different formats should be used for different types of questions; this will help the respondent answer the questionnaire rapidly.

Note that the format in Box 14.1 on p. 383 requires the respondent to place a check mark in the appropriate space. Check marks are slightly easier than circling responses, so they are preferable. Any device to make the task easy for the respondent should be incorporated.

RULE 14.18 ANTICIPATE COMPUTER DATA ENTRY.

Virtually all surveys of any size will be analyzed using a computer. To simplify the entry of the data into the computer, it helps enormously if the values that are going to be entered are right on the questionnaire. Indeed, it is now quite common for researchers to avoid what was once referred to as "coding the data." By coding, reference is made to researchers going through the questionnaire and assigning values to each response category, recording this information on "code sheets," and then having the data entered into the computer off the code sheets. This process was expensive, time-consuming, and likely to introduce additional errors into the final data set. Where possible, avoid the whole coding process by placing the code values directly on the questionnaire. These numbers can then be used when the data are entered into the computer. They can be placed unobtrusively on the questionnaire and will not distract the respondent when completing the form.

Box 14.1 illustrates a set of questions for which such numbers have been used. The reader should note that there is no blank space between the response category and the check-off space (usually a square box). Note, as well, that only question numbers are used, and that response categories are numbered beside the place where the

respondent makes his or her check mark. As the reader will appreciate, when the data are entered into the computer, it is easy to enter the number immediately adjacent to the check mark made by the respondent.

Box 14.9 on p. 400 shows the formatting style favoured by Earl Babbie, Don A. Dillman, Harvey Krahn, and this author. Babbie does not appear to favour the use of code values, uses square brackets for the check-off responses, and places the response brackets before the category (Babbie, 1992, p. 155).

Dillman favours the use of capital letters to identify response categories, and, in mail surveys, places the code values to the left of the response categories. Dillman recommends placing the code values to the right of the categories in personal interview forms and telephone surveys (1978). Both Babbie's and Dillman's styles are acceptable.

Another formatting style is illustrated by questionnaires developed by the Population Research Laboratory at the University of Alberta. Harvey Krahn and his associates tend to include the actual computer code values on the questions, placing them to the right of the categories. Having respondents circle numbers placed to the right of the category ensures that right-handed respondents do not cover the category label with their hands. This formatting style is simple, uncluttered—and recommended.

My own preference is to include code values and place them to the right of the response categories, using a series of dashes "– – –" to carry the respondent's eye out to the check-off boxes. Note that no space is left between the code value and the box. (The intention is to make the numbers disappear as much as possible; when spaces are left between the number and the box, the number seems to gain prominence.) Because the numbers that will eventually

---

BOX 14.9

Four Format Styles Illustrated

1. Babbie Format Style for Fixed-Choice Responses:

       23. Have you ever smoked marijuana?

               [   ]   Yes

               [   ]   No

2. Dillman Format Style for Fixed-Choice Responses:

       Q-22 Your Sex (Circle number of your answer)

               1   MALE

               2   FEMALE

3. Krahn Format Style for Fixed-Choice Responses:

       54. In the past year, has any member of your immediate family (not counting yourself) been unemployed (out of work and looking for work)?

              No   1

              Yes   2

4. Jackson Format Style for Fixed-Choice Responses:

       4. What year are you in?

          Freshman – – – – – – – – –1☐

          Sophomore – – – – – – – 2☐

          Junior – – – – – – – – – – 3☐

          Senior – – – – – – – – – – 4☐

Sources: Babbie (1992, p. 155); Dillman (1978, p. 134); Krahn (1991, p. 51); Jackson (1995, p. 388).

---

be entered into the computer are right beside the check mark, data entry is simplified and less subject to error.

Some researchers place the computer screen column numbers for each variable on the questionnaire, on the extreme right-hand side. The advantage of this is that errors can be avoided when entering the information into the computer. Certainly, in the case of interviews or phone questionnaires, it is advisable to include such codes. However, in cases in which respondents are filling in the questionnaires themselves, such numbers add to the clutter on the questionnaire and should probably be avoided. (In Chapter 16 additional suggestions will be made to help reduce errors in data entry.)

RULE 14.19 VARY PLACEMENT OF RESPONSE CATEGORIES.

Box 14.1 on p. 383 also illustrates how the appearance of a questionnaire can be improved by varying the placement of the response categories for each question. While this might be an aesthetic rather than a scientific consideration, a questionnaire with the response categories all lined up on the right margin is not pleasing to the eye, nor is it easy to see where one question ends and another begins. The rule, then, is to vary the location of the response category sets.

RULE 14.20 CLEARLY INDICATE ANY BRANCHING.

Some questions are to be answered only by *some* respondents. In such cases, guide your reader clearly by using one of the techniques shown in Box 14.10. Note that those who responded positively to question 9 are directed to question 9.1.

3. PRESENTATION

RULE 14.21 GIVE QUESTIONNAIRE A DISTINCTIVE LOOK.

Besides paying attention to issues of layout, it is also important to give the questionnaire a distinctive appearance. The use of coloured paper is one way to achieve this. Software programs can facilitate the creation of visually clear and well formatted questionnaires.

RULE 14.22 DO NOT SQUEEZE TOO MUCH ONTO ONE PAGE.

Avoid trying to squeeze too much onto a single page: questionnaires should permit the respondent to move through each page rapidly. Squeezing material looks bad and discourages your respondent.

BOX 14.10

A Branching Question Illustrated

9. Have you consumed any beer in the past seven days?

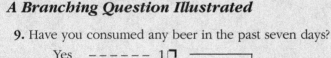

      Yes – – – – – – 1☐

      No – – – – – – 2☐

> **9.1** If Yes: How much did you consume in the past week?
>
> 3 pints or less – – – – 1☐
>
> 4 to 9 pints – – – – – 2☐
>
> 10 or more pints – – 3☐

10. Have you ever been married?

      Yes – – – – – – 1☐ [Answer questions 11–14]

      No – – – – – – 2☐ [Go to question 15]

E. KEY POINTS

A well-designed questionnaire is not only more likely to be answered but is also more likely to generate usable information.

Open-ended questions are used when pre-coding is not a practical option, so as to provide a change of pace for the respondent, to give the respondent a greater feeling of control, and to provide a qualitative dimension to a research project.

Use nine categories for Likert-type questions.

In developing measures, pay close attention to the conceptual definition of the concept you want to reflect. Use easily understood, unambiguous wordings.

Questions should measure one dimension; use indexes to get at multidimensional concepts.

F. KEY TERMS

Likert-type questions

Mutually exclusive categories

Open-ended questions

Pilot study

Pre-coded single-choice questions

Presence-absence questions

Questionnaires

Rank-ordering questions

Response set

SAMPLING AND SAMPLE SIZE

A. THE RATIONALE OF SAMPLING

Social scientists, market researchers, political parties, and media people all need to describe elements of society accurately. One way to approach such problems is to take measures on the relevant variables for all people in the population. While this solution is possible if one is studying a few individuals (perhaps employees who work in a nursing home), when the concern is to understand how people from larger aggregations such as a community, region, or country feel about certain issues, then it is necessary to figure out ways to get a sense of their feelings without having everyone complete a questionnaire or agree to be interviewed. In such cases, a sample that can reflect or represent the views of the larger population can be drawn.

Sampling is done to save time and money. If you can estimate who is going to win an election accurately with a sample of 1,500, why poll two million? And while common sense suggests that larger samples would be more accurate than smaller ones, this is not necessarily the case. The key issue is that a sample must be representative—it must reflect the population accurately. Box 15.1 reports a classic case of an inaccurate sample.

Box 15.1 illustrates a situation in which a large sample failed to predict the winner of the 1936 American presidential election (Simon and Burstein, 1985, p. 108). This is a case in which a huge sample (over two million) did not do the job. The *Literary Digest* needed two key things:

- a more representative sample of the general population; and

- a situation in which circumstances do not alter substantially between the time of data collection and the time of the election.

The lesson to be learned from the *Literary Digest* debacle is that, for reasons of both economy and accuracy, a well-selected small sample is to be preferred to a large, poorly selected sample.

Sampling is used in a great variety of research projects: choosing which children's stories will be subjected to a content analysis, choosing and then assigning subjects to different conditions in experimental designs, or deciding which constituencies are to be included in a voting study—all these studies entail sampling decisions.

B. FUNDAMENTAL SAMPLING PROCEDURES

To begin our discussion, some terms need to be distinguished:

- **Population** The population is the entire group that you wish to describe. In Box 15.1 the population would be the American electors of 1936. If you were studying residence students at a university, the population might be defined as "all students who reside in a university's dormitories during the week of March 22 to March 29." The terms *population* and *universe* are used interchangeably.

- **Sampling frame** This is the list(s) from which you draw a sample. In Box 15.1 the sampling frame included all those people listed as automobile owners as well as all those who had a phone. Ideally, the sampling frame and the population are identical; in practice, however, it is often not possible to get a complete list of the population, so the sampling frame may not reflect the population perfectly. Almost any list will not be up-to-

BOX 15.1

Predicting the 1936 American Election

In 1920, 1924, 1928, and 1932 the New York–based *Literary Digest* conducted polls in an effort to predict the winner and the winning margin in the American presidential elections. The polls were accurate (within 1% in 1932) so it was with considerable confidence that the *Literary Digest* conducted its 1936 poll. And on October 31, 1936, the magazine published its results based on mailings to some ten million Americans. The results are indicated in the table.

Literary Digest *Prediction of Results in 1936 American Presidential Elections**

CANDIDATE	NUMBER OF VOTES	PERCENTAGE OF VOTES
Landon	1,293,669	57.1
Roosevelt	972,897	42.9
TOTAL	2,266,566	100.0

*Responses from over 10,000,000 ballots mailed out (under 23% response rate).

The poll suggested that Landon would easily win the November election. But it turned out that Roosevelt won by a substantial margin. So why, with a sample of over two million, did the *Literary Digest* miss the mark so badly?

The founder of the American Institute, George Gallup, predicted in July of 1936, some months before the *Literary Digest* began mailing out its ballots, that the poll result would not be accurate. Gallup pointed to the flaw of using mailing lists based on telephone listings and listings of automobile owners. Gallup said that such lists largely favoured the more economically prosperous; during the Depression years, new voters came largely from poorer groups (few of whom owned cars or telephones). Gallup also noted that those most likely to return their ballots would overrepresent the better educated and the higher socioeconomic categories.

George Gallup was challenging the *sampling frame* used by the *Literary Digest*. The sampling frame is the target population from which the researcher draws a sample. The sampling frame did not accurately reflect American electors; it favoured the more prosperous elements in society, and Roosevelt's strength was among the poorer elements of American society.

Source: The information on the *Literary Digest*'s attempt to predict the 1936 American election is based on the presentation in Julian L. Simon and Paul Burstein (1985) *Basic Research Methods in Social Science*, 3rd ed. New York: Random House, 107–110.

date; some people will be left off, others perhaps listed twice. The goal is to get as accurate a sampling frame list as possible.

- **Sample** The sample refers to those individuals (or units) selected for a study.

- **Response rate** The response rate refers to the percentage of delivered questionnaires that are completed and returned.

There are two categories of sampling procedures: probability sampling procedures and non-probability sampling procedures.

1. PROBABILITY SAMPLING TECHNIQUES

Probability sampling procedures involve techniques for selecting sampling units so that each unit has a known chance of being included. Because sampling units are selected "at random," the term **random sample** is often subsituted for probability sample. It is important to appreciate that tests of statistical significance assume that sampling has been done using some form of probability sampling (see Chapter 9). If your study involves the use of such tests, be certain to meet the sampling assumption. The sampling units usually are individuals but may also refer to other levels of analysis, such as communities or countries. The procedures for selecting each of the major types are listed below.

A. SIMPLE RANDOM SAMPLE

A simple random sample provides each unit (usually a person) in the population with an equal chance of being selected for participation in a study. This procedure requires that a list of the potential respondents be available to the researcher. Such lists might include student lists, lists of eligible voters used for elections, lists of employees, lists

of companies, and so forth. The following steps are necessary when selecting a **simple random sample**.

STEP 1

Number the units on the list.

STEP 2

Computers are typically used to generate the random numbers used in sample selection. Alternatively, one can use a table of random numbers to select the required number of units. (Sample size determination is discussed later in this chapter.) To use a table of random numbers, shut your eyes and stab a pencil into the table. The point where the pencil has struck is used as the starting point. From this point one reads the numbers systematically (perhaps reading down the column, continuing at the top of the next column and so forth), placing a check mark beside those cases whose number shows up on the random number table. This process continues until a sufficient number of cases for the study has been selected.

In experimental designs, a table of random numbers, or a computer-generated set of random numbers, can be used to assign subjects to treatment or control groups. To do this, simply list the subjects, and then, using odd or even numbers from the table of random numbers or the computer, assign each subject to a condition (perhaps even numbers to control groups, odd ones to the treatment group). Thus, the numbers might be, for instance, odd, odd, odd, even, odd, even, even. The subjects would then be assigned as shown in Table 15.1.

STEP 3

Additional replacement units should be selected and kept on a separate list, so that when a sampling unit cannot be contacted or an individual or company does not participate, then that unit will be replaced by the first replacement unit.

TABLE 15.1 USING A TABLE OF RANDOM NUMBERS TO ASSIGN SUBJECTS TO TREATMENT AND CONTROL GROUPS

SUBJECT	ODD/EVEN FROM RANDOM NUMBER TABLE	EXPERIMENTAL CONDITION
Subject #1	Odd	Treatment
Subject #2	Odd	Treatment
Subject #3	Odd	Treatment
Subject #4	Even	Control
Subject #5	Odd	Treatment
Subject #6	Even	Control
Subject #7	Even	Control
. . .	. . .	. . .

Replacements should be identified and numbered, since they will be used in the order in which they have been selected. R1, R2, and so on is a convenient way of noting them.

B. SYSTEMATIC SAMPLE

A **systematic sample** provides each unit (usually a person) in the population with an equal chance of being selected for participation in a study by choosing every *n*th unit, starting randomly. The systematic sample provides a somewhat easier way of selecting cases from a list of potential respondents. In this case, names listed in phone books, directories, street maps, dormitory diagrams, student lists, or elector lists might all be sources from which one might draw a systematic sample. In the case of systematic samples, it is even possible to proceed with sampling when no list exists prior to sampling. For instance, one could choose students living in every fourth residence room and, so long as one numbers the rooms systematically, one could proceed without a list of the students.

The critical issue is that every person must have a known (usually equal) chance of being selected. The steps in selecting a systematic sample are as follows.

STEP 1

Get a list, map, or diagram as appropriate.

STEP 2

Having determined the sample size required and the additional number for replacements (for the refusals or for those with whom contact cannot be made), add these two figures together; this number will be regarded as the total sample requirement.

STEP 3

Divide the total sample requirement into the total number of units in the population being surveyed. This number should then be rounded to the nearest, but lower, round number. (E.g., if the number you get is 8.73, round it to the nearest, lower, whole number; in this case, 8.) This number represents what is known as the **skip interval**.

One caution that must be mentioned in the use of systematic samples is that if the list is ordered in some fashion there may be a problem; suppose you have a listing of couples, but with the name of the male always listed first. In such a case, if the skip interval was an even number, then all those selected would be females. If the list is patterned, as in the example above, a different sampling procedure will have to be used.

STEP 4

Using a table of random numbers, select a number between 1 and the value of the skip interval. The number selected becomes the starting case, the first one selected to participate in the survey. Suppose we were doing a survey of students living in campus dormitories and we have determined the skip interval to be 8 and the starting case to be 3. In this case, we would develop a systematic procedure for numbering the dormitory rooms and for moving from floor to floor, dormitory to dormitory. We would begin with the 3rd door, then go to the 11th, 19th, and 27th rooms. In rooms with two residents we would ask both students to participate; otherwise students in double rooms would have less chance of being selected for the study. However, caution has to be exercised since, in some universities, students may select their roommates and, if this is the case, there would be a lack of independence in some of the units sampled. If this is a problem, the researcher would be well advised to obtain a list of all students in residence and then use a random sampling procedure.

When systematic samples are being selected from lists, it is a rather straightforward matter to go through the list, placing check marks beside cases that have been selected, perhaps marking every fifth one. Additional units should be selected for use as replacements.

C. STRATIFIED SAMPLE

There are times when a simple random or systematic sample would not provide an appropriate solution to sample selection. Suppose, for example, that you are doing a survey of attitudes toward capital punishment by members of different political parties. While it would be possible to do a random sample of individuals in the community, such a procedure might be somewhat wasteful, because the community might be made up predominantly of those who support one of the parties. As a result, a very large sample would be required to provide a sufficient number of respondents to allow generalizations about supporters of each of the parties. In situations such as the one described above, it is useful to draw a **stratified sample**, a sample that will give supporters within each party an equal chance of selection, but will, at the same time, ensure that an equal number will be selected from each of the parties. As noted earlier, tests of statistical significance (see Chapter 9) assume that a probability sampling procedure was used for sample selection. They also require a sufficient number of cases in categories being compared. Thus, by using a stratified random sample, we are assured of having sampled enough cases to allow comparisons to be made using statistical procedures and we are assured that the sample will be representative of the study population.

You might decide, for example, that you would like to have 150 respondents from each of the political parties. The steps in selecting a stratified sample are:

STEP 1

Determine the sample size required from each of the categories.

STEP 2

Develop a list for each of the categories from which you wish to draw your sample.

STEP 3

Using either a systematic or random sampling procedure, choose the cases for the sample, along with the required number of replacements.

Samples can be stratified by more than one variable. In order to achieve more precise estimates, we might also have stratified the above sample by gender and by socioeconomic level. The procedures are identical: simply identify the stratification dimensions, then, using an equal probability procedure, select respondents. Unless appropriate weighting procedures are used, the results of such surveys can be used only to compare the different subgroups and do not represent the community in general. The reason they do not represent the community is that such samples overrepresent smaller categories and underrepresent the larger ones. Weighting procedures are available

in computer assisted statistical programs, such as SPSS (see Appendix A).

Box 15.2 provides an example of a recent study employing a systematic stratified sample.

D. MULTI-STAGE AREA SAMPLE

When the task involves developing a sample to reflect a large unit such as a state, province, or country, and no list of the population is available, then one develops a **multi-stage area sample**. The key point is that at each stage of the sampling process, every individual (or unit) must have a

A Systematic Stratified Sample by Gender and Practice

Tracey Adams (2005) wanted to explore gender differences in the practice characteristics and attitudes of dentists. Although women have begun to enter the field of dentistry, the profession remains male dominated. Moreover, there are far fewer females in specialized areas of dentistry. For this reason, Professor Adams employed a systematic, stratified sample to oversample female dentists and dental specialists. By doing so, she was assured of having a sufficient number of "cases" to allow a comparison of male and female dentists in general dentistry and dental specialization. Her data were drawn from a mail survey of female and male dentists in Ontario, conducted in 2002. The survey was sent to a systematic, stratified sample of 800

dentists who were registered to practise dentistry in Ontario. She estimated that there were approximately 7,100 dentists in Ontario in 2002, meaning that over 10% of all dentists in the province were surveyed. "The sample was stratified by gender and practice focus to ensure that enough women (who composed only 22% of those registered) and dental specialists (only 15% of those registered) were included for comparative purposes. In effect four samples were drawn and the survey was sent to 350 male general practitioner dentists (sampling interval 1 in 12), 300 female general practitioners (sampling interval 1 in 6), 100 male dental specialists (sampling interval 1 in 8) and 50 female dental specialists (sampling interval 1 in 2)" (pp. 76–77).

Source: Adams, Tracey L. (2005). "Feminization of Professions: The Case of Women in Dentistry." *Canadian Journal of Sociology,* 30(1), 71–94.

known chance of being selected. In a simplified form, the procedures for a national survey may be summarized as follows.

STEP 1

Identify **primary sampling units** (these can be census tract areas or other similar units, normally several hundred of them); these units are numbered and a selection of units is made from them using an equal probability technique.

STEP 2

Within the selected areas, identify the city blocks (in urban areas) or square kilometres (rural areas). From these, using an equal probability technique, choose an appropriate number of units.

STEP 3

Within the selected areas, number the housing units, and select the units that will be used randomly from among these.

STEP 4

For each household, list the people who fall within the desired sampling parameters (for example, adults over the age of 18 who have lived in the community for one month or more). Table 4.3 on p. 117 gives an example of a sample form.

STEP 5

An equal probability procedure is then used to select respondents from a list of those who are eligible.

RULE 15.1 NO SAMPLING CHOICES ARE TO BE MADE BY DATA-COLLECTION PERSONNEL.

All choices are to be made by probability procedures. When a selected participant is not available (moved away, not home after three call-backs, or refuses to cooperate) then replacements are used, in the order selected. It is critical that interviewers not simply replace the unavailable respondent with the nearest, most convenient, replacement. This would bias the sample toward those who are at home or are more cooperative. Whatever rules are established, these should be communicated clearly to those doing the data collection and should also be made clear in any technical reports on the research project. (See Table 4.3 on p. 117 for a sample form that can be used.)

2. NON-PROBABILITY SAMPLING TECHNIQUES

There are three additional **non-probability sampling techniques** that are commonly used by researchers. While these procedures do not provide potential respondents with a known chance of being asked to participate in a study, they are, nonetheless, important to know about.

A. QUOTA SAMPLE

In a **quota sample**, respondents are selected on the basis of meeting certain criteria. No list of potential respondents is required: the first respondent to meet the requirement(s) is asked to participate and sampling continues until all the categories have been filled—that is, until the quota for each has been reached.

Suppose one were asked to compare food preferences of the young versus the elderly. One might do a survey of supermarket customers, selecting the first 75 who meet the "young" criteria, and the first 75 who meet the criteria for inclusion in the comparison group. Note that this sampling procedure is the non-probability twin of stratified sampling.

The steps in selecting a quota sample are as follows:

STEP 1

Define precisely the criteria for inclusion into each of the categories.

STEP 2

Select participants on a first-come first-included basis until the quota for each category has been met.

B. CONVENIENCE SAMPLE

Convenience samples involve selection on the basis of ease or convenience. If you were to "poll" people entering a shopping mall on their attitudes toward an upcoming election, you would be selecting a convenience sample. Such samples may, however, involve particular categories of individuals. For example, by asking a couple of classes of Grade 10 students to complete questionnaires, you would obtain a convenience sample of the students present.

C. SNOWBALL SAMPLING

Snowball sampling is a name for a referral sampling procedure. As you complete one interview you ask if there is anyone else known to the respondent who might be appropriate for the study. This technique is frequently used in situations in which one cannot get a list of the population who share some characteristic. Some examples of when you might choose to use this sampling procedure are:

- a study of the marital adjustment of couples whose first child was born before the couple married. In this case, you would not easily find a list of this population, but through referrals you could

identify individuals who would be appropriate for your study;

- a study of prostitutes who are under the age of 16;

- a study of people convicted of white-collar crimes;

- a study of pool hustlers.

Note that none of these procedures leads to independent or randomly selected units. But, for some research problems, this type of sampling procedure is the only feasible one.

Convenience, quota, and snowball samples are reasonable approaches to sampling when one is investigating relationships among variables (say the relationship between participation and self-esteem) and one is interested in trying to understand the conditions under which there is, or is not, a relation between the major variables rather than generalizing to the entire population. Explanatory studies, in fact, frequently use non-probability sampling procedures. However, when tests of significance are an important tool in one's research, it should be noted that such tests assume that probability sampling procedures have been used. Therefore, tests of significance are not appropriately used when quota, convenience, or snowball samples have been used.

C. SAMPLE SIZE DETERMINATION

A variety of factors influence the size of the sample that is appropriate for any study. No simple rule of thumb is possible in determining an appropriate sample size. So, if someone tells you that samples should be 10% of the population, the advice is not sound. Sample size determination involves a series of trade-offs between precision, cost, and the numbers necessary to do the appropriate analyses. At the same time it is necessary to take into account the amount of variability in the factors studied—and sometimes even the size of the population.

1. STEPS IN DETERMINING SAMPLE SIZE: ESTIMATIONS FOR A RATIO VARIABLE

Sample size determination involves eight basic steps—some statistical, some pragmatic. It is usually best to begin with the statistical ones, estimating the required sample size and then modifying this number to take practical considerations into account.

STEP 1 DECIDE ON THE CONFIDENCE LEVEL TO BE USED.

If you would like to be confident that your result will fall within a given range of precision 95% of the time, use the value 1.96. (Ninety-five percent of the cases fall ± 1.96 standard deviation units from the mean.) If you wish to be 99% confident, a larger sample will be required. (Here the appropriate value will be 2.58.) Most social science researchers use the 95% level in determining sample sizes. With this level you can be confident that your sample mean will be within a given precision 19 out of 20 times.

STEP 2 SELECT A MAJOR VARIABLE TO DETERMINE SAMPLE SIZE.

Normally you focus on the main dependent variable of the study in computing the required sample size. And if the dependent variable is measured at the ratio level, it will be easier to determine sample size requirements. Such a variable might include percentage voting for a given party or an attitude score. You will need to estimate the population standard deviation

(sd pop) for this variable. This estimate can be made by examining results from other surveys, or, failing that, simply by using common sense, noting the mean and the range within which one expects to find two-thirds of the cases. (See illustration in Box 15.3.) Another suggestion for estimating an unknown population standard deviation is to approximate it by taking the range of values (excluding extreme cases) and dividing this value by four. This method will generally provide a reasonable estimate. Finally, it must be acknowledged that, in studies with a large number of variables involved, it is impossible to make claims, with any certainty, about the precision of all the variables. Most of them have unknown sampling distributions. Box 15.3 outlines the steps you should take to estimate the standard deviation of a variable.

STEP 3 DETERMINE THE MINIMUM PRECISION THAT WOULD BE ACCEPTABLE.

Do you want to be within 1.5 kg of the true mean when estimating weight, within two percentage points in predicting a vote, or within three points on a scale with a maximum score of 75? The measure of precision will have to be expressed in the same units as the standard deviation.

STEP 4 COMPUTE SAMPLE SIZE.

Compute the required sample using the following formula:
Required sample size =

$$\left[\frac{(\text{confidence limit}) \ (\text{sd pop})}{\text{Accuracy}} \right]^2$$

Suppose, for example, that you wished to determine the sample size required to estimate the average weight of male university graduates. You wish to be 95% confident (Z = 1.96), and be within 1 kg of estimating the true weight. The estimated standard deviation of the population

BOX 15.3

Estimating the Standard Deviation

Suppose you wanted to estimate the standard deviation of a variable like the weight of male undergraduates. Try doing the following steps:

Step 1 Estimate the average weight of male undergraduates. *Estimate: 70 kg.*

Step 2 Within what weight range would you expect to find about two-thirds of the male students? *Preliminary estimate: 9 kg.*

Step 3 Double the estimate in Step 2 (18 kg). Does it make sense that about 95%

of all cases will fall within the range defined by the mean ± twice the estimate at Step 2? (i.e., 70 ± 18; range = 52 to 88 kg). If the band is not wide enough, how much wider should it be? If it is too wide, how much narrower should it be? Suppose you decide that it should be slightly wider, arguing that about 95% of the cases will fall between 50 and 90 kg. Divide this range by 4 to get the estimated standard deviation. *Standard Deviation Estimate: 10 kg.*

---

is 7 kg. The values would be plugged into the equation, as in:

Required sample size =

$$\left[\frac{1.96\,(7.0)}{1.0}\right]^2 = 188$$

The indicated sample size is 188 and should result in an estimate of the population's average weight within 1 kg, being confident that the estimate will be within this margin 95% of the time.

STEP 5 COMPUTE SAMPLING FRACTION.

The **sampling fraction** is the sample size in relation to the population (see Monette, Sullivan, and DeJong, 1990, p. 149). Thus, if you have a population of 800,000 and a sample of 188, the sampling fraction would be:

Sampling fraction = Sample size/Population
= 188/800,000
= .0002 (.02 percent:
                    go to Step 7)

If the sampling fraction is less than 5%, go to Step 7. Alternatively, if the population was 1,200 residence students, the sampling fraction would be:

Sampling fraction = 188/1200
= .157 (15.7 percent:
                    go to Step 6)

If the computed sampling fraction is more than 5% of the population, an adjustment can be made in your sample size. To compute the adjustment, go to Step 6.

STEP 6 ADJUST FOR SMALL POPULATION.

When the sampling fraction is greater than 5%, the required sample size can be reduced according to the following formula:

Adjusted sample size

$= n \div (1 + (n \div N))$
$= 188 \div (1 + (188 \div 1200))$
$= 188 \div 1.157$
$= 162$

where: n = sample size estimated in Step 4;
         N = estimated size of universe.

(See Monette, Sullivan, and DeJong, 1990.)

STEP 7 DETERMINE WHETHER THERE ARE SUFFICIENT CASES FOR THE ANALYSIS.

The required sample size must now be scrutinized to ensure that it will provide a sufficient number of cases for the most complex analysis that is to be done. For example, if one intends to do a series of cross-tabulation tables with three categories in each of the independent and dependent variables, with a maximum of one control variable with two categories, then one is proposing a number of 18-cell tables ($3 \times 3 \times 2$). With 188 cases, the maximum expected frequencies would be just over 10 cases per cell ($188 \div 18 = 10.44$). This would hardly prove adequate and, therefore, one would want to increase the sample size—or else rethink the proposed types of analyses that are to be performed. Correlational techniques will place less stringent demands on one's sample so that, to the extent that model testing can be done using those techniques, fewer cases will be required.

STEP 8 ADJUST SAMPLE SIZE FOR COST AND TIME FACTORS.

A final step is to adjust the sample to take time and cost into account. If one requires a sample of 3,000 but has the resources to deal with only 1,000, then one will have to do some rethinking on the precision that will be possible. If, on the other hand, one has sufficient resources to increase the sample size, then one usually does so, since some additional precision is likely to result.

2. STEPS IN DETERMINING SAMPLE SIZE: ESTIMATIONS FOR A NOMINAL VARIABLE

A common situation for a researcher is to be trying to estimate a population proportion for a nominal-level variable. Pollsters attempting to predict the vote for a particular candidate in an upcoming election may want to know the required sample size to provide an estimate of the likely vote and to be within perhaps 5% of the percentage likely to support the candidate. Once again, the researcher may want to be 95% certain that the estimate will be within this margin of error. Suppose you believe the support for the given candidate is probably somewhere between 35 and 55%: how might you determine how many must be called in a phone survey to pin the level of support down more precisely?

For nominal or ordinal variables the estimate can be calculated using the following formula:

$$ n = \frac{(Success) \times (failure) \times (confidence\ limit\ Z\ value)^2}{(Accuracy)^2} $$

Where:
n = required sample size;
success is the estimated proportion voting for the candidate;
failure is the estimated proportion not voting for the candidate;
95% confidence limit (Z score: use the value 1.96 for the test; 2.58 for the 99% confidence limit);
accuracy is the range within which you want the estimate to be.

Suppose we thought a reasonable estimate of our candidate's vote would be 40%, we want to be 95% confident (i.e., 19 out of 20 times our population estimate will be within the accuracy parameter), and we want to be within 5% of the vote for the candidate: these values are then plugged into the equation, and the calculation is made. The result indicates that we will need to complete 369 phone surveys to provide our answer.

$$n = \frac{((Success) \times (failure)) \times (confidence\ limit\ Z\ value)^2}{(Accuracy)^2}$$

$$n = \frac{(.40 \times .60) \times (1.96)^2}{.05^2}$$

$$n = \frac{.24 \times 3.84}{.0025}$$

$$n = 369$$

Thus, to be within 5 percentage points it will be necessary to interview 369 persons. If you want to change the parameters, simply adjust the values in the formula accordingly. You will note that gaining accuracy requires substantial increases in sample size.

3. SAMPLE SIZE AND ACCURACY

The relationship between sample size and precision of estimations is a simple one: to double precision, sample size must be quadrupled. In the illustration concerning the weights of graduating university males, if we wanted to be within 0.5 kg of estimating the true value of the population, we would need a sample four times as large as the one proposed for a sample that would get us within 1 kg. For example:

Required sample size =

$$\left[\frac{1.96\ (7.0)}{.5}\right]^2 = 753$$

The original sample size required was 188 or ¼ of 753. "Precision" will be referred to in statistics texts as the confidence interval. In the above illustration, with a sample size of 753 we can be 95% confident that the true population mean weight is within 0.5 kg of the sample mean.

4. SAMPLE SIZE AND CONFIDENCE LIMITS

The relationship between precision and confidence limits means that to move from the 95% confidence limit to the 99% level, one can simply multiply the sample size by 1.73. Thus, in the illustration on graduating males, to be within 1 kg of the average weight but to be 99 per cent confident, one would need to multiply the original sample size of 188 by a factor of 1.73. (188 × 1.73 = 325). A sample of 325 will be required to be 99% confident that the estimate will be within 1 kg of the true population mean. Conversely, to move from the 99% confidence limit to the 95% limit, the sample size determined for the 99% level can be multiplied by .58.

5. THE IMPACT OF REFUSALS

While the evidence from studies examining different response rates under controlled conditions shows little variation in the descriptive accuracy independent of response rate, tests of significance assume probability sampling techniques and also assume that there is no systematic bias in who chooses to complete the form (Erdos, 1983, pp. 146–47). Such tests also assume that any measurement error is random. Since we cannot know what impact refusals and measurement error have on our data, researchers make every effort to get completed questionnaires from all respondents. It is not clear what conclusions one could legitimately arrive at if one had a response rate of 20%. For example, Senn and her colleagues (2000) examined the response rate of men in a sexual coercion study. Previous research indicates that men are less likely to respond to surveys than are women and that individuals are less likely to respond to lengthy surveys and surveys with sensitive topics. Because their study asked men about their sexual attitudes and sexual behaviour, including coercive sexual behaviour, they were not surprised by the low response rate of 20%.

6. CONFIRMING REPRESENTATIVENESS

Steps, however, can be taken to confirm that one's sample is indeed representative of the population about which one is attempting to make generalizations. For example, one might compare the age, gender, and marital status distributions of one's sample to known distributions for the population from census data. If the sample is not wholly representative, there are techniques for weighting results to get a better reflection of the population whose characteristics one is trying to estimate. When, however, there has been a high nonparticipation rate, there is no guarantee that the sample will be representative for other variables, even if it is representative for those age or gender distributions that have been checked. In the study noted above on male sexual coercion, the researchers assessed the representativeness of their sample by comparing the demographic characteristics of the sample to the general population. They learned that there were no significant differences in the ages of the men in the sample and population; however, the sample significantly overrepresented single, more educated, and less religious men. The authors conclude with cautions about the generalizability of the findings and they encouraged researchers to develop better survey strategies to study male sexual coercion across the life span.

D. KEY POINTS

Sampling is used to save time and money. In reflecting characteristics of a population, well-selected small samples are both more economical and more accurate than large, poorly selected samples.

The two categories of sampling techniques are (i) *probability sampling* and (ii) *non-probability sampling*. The former techniques include those sampling procedures for which each unit in the sampling frame has a known chance of being selected; these include *random, systematic, stratified,* and *multi-stage area samples*. Non-probability sampling does not provide all members of the population with any known chance of being selected; non-probability sampling techniques include such approaches as *quota, convenience,* and *snowball* sampling.

Determining sample size requires the researcher to take into account the *precision* required, the *variability* in the phenomenon studied, the *confidence level*, the *size of the population*, the methods that will be used to analyze the data, and the time and resources available for data collection and analysis. A simple eight-step set of procedures is recommended for determining sample sizes for most studies.

E. KEY TERMS

Convenience sample	Probability sampling procedures	Sampling frame
Multi-stage area sample	Quota sample	Simple random sample
Non-probability sampling techniques	Random sample	Skip interval
Population	Response rate	Snowball sampling
Primary sampling units	Sample	Stratified sample
	Sampling fraction	Systematic sample

DATA ANALYSIS

The three chapters in this section deal with aspects of data analysis. Chapter 16 presents various procedures for hand-analyzing data and then various computer concepts are introduced. Chapter 17 deals with the issue of examining three- and four-variable causal models, while Chapter 18 introduces three advanced techniques.

C H A P T E R   S I X T E E N

STARTING THE DATA ANALYSIS

Having collected the data, it is now time to analyze them. We will approach this task in two ways: we begin with a method of hand-tabulating the results; this will be followed by a discussion of how computers can be used to analyze data.

A. ANALYZING DATA WITHOUT USING A COMPUTER

Some analyses that we do with a computer could also be done easily by hand. And sometimes it is even faster to analyze results manually if one does not have easy access to a computer. Chapters 8 and 9 presented a number of statistics that can readily be hand-computed if the data set is small. The following section will provide a method of collecting and processing information from a field study.

1. FIELD STUDY DATA

We will work through a manual analysis of behaviour in a public elevator. These students were interested in whether passengers in an elevator would communicate (signal) the nervousness they felt because of the close proximity forced on people riding in an elevator. Three hypotheses were proposed in that study (Bonnar, 1992):

- Female passengers would be more likely to signal than males.

- The more people present in the elevator, the higher the amount of signalling.

- The higher the status of the person, the lower the amount of signalling.

The data were collected on tally sheets such as the one described in Chapter 3. The student observers indicated on a tally sheet whether or not passengers in the elevator signalled (i.e., did the passengers exhibit any "nervous and/or unnecessary actions performed by people whose personal space is altered in some way" (Bonnar, 1992, p. 7). Signalling included such common behaviours as "staring at the elevator numbers, pushing the elevator buttons for no apparent reason, staring at the floor and subjects shifting their bodies in a nervous manner" (Bonnar, 1992, p. 8). Also entered on the tally sheet was the gender of each new passenger, the person's status (professor, student, other) and the number of people on the elevator.

Figure 16.1 illustrates how the **tally sheet** was set up. Note that each line on the tally sheet records the information for one subject. Column 1 records whether the passenger signalled in some way; column 2 records the gender of the passenger; column 3 records the status of the passenger; and column 4 records the number of passengers present during the observation.

Having recorded the information on the sheets for 150 passengers, the task now is to analyze the results. The best way to do this is to set up a **master table** for the results, enter the observations into the master table, and then derive the results tables from the master table. By using a master table, you will need to make only one pass through the raw data. From the master table you can create any other required tables showing the relation between the independent variables and the dependent variable.

STEP I SET UP A MASTER TABLE.

A master table is generally set up on 11½ by 14" paper. Using the paper so that the long side is across the top, arrange categories of the dependent variable on the left side of the sheet, with the categories *Signal Given* and *No*

FIGURE 16.1 TALLY SHEET FOR RECORDING OBSERVATIONS

ID #	SIGNALLING		GENDER		STATUS			GROUP STATUS	
	YES	NO	MALE	FEMALE	STUDENT	PROFESSOR	OTHER	4 OR FEWER	5 OR MORE
1	✓		✓		✓			✓	
2	✓			✓	✓			✓	
3		✓		✓	✓				✓
4	✓		✓			✓			✓
etc.	✓			✓	✓				✓

Signal Given as labels. Categories of the independent variables are arranged across the top of the master table. In this case we have three independent variables: gender, status, and number on the elevator. Each observation ends up in one—and only one—cell of the master table. Thus, a female student who is the fifth person entering the elevator and pushes the button for the third floor three times would end up in one cell only.

STEP 2 TRANSFER DATA TO THE MASTER TABLE.

Once observations have been completed, the tally sheet data are transferred to the master table. Normally, each observation is entered into the applicable cell with a short stroke; these are grouped together so that the fifth line entered into a cell is a line across the other four. Each group then reflects five observations falling into the cell. Later these can be counted and a total for each cell entered and circled at the bottom of the cell. (See Figure 16.2.)

STEP 3 CREATE THE INDIVIDUAL TABLES.

To test the three hypotheses, three tables would be created, each showing the relation between signalling/non-signalling and each of gender (Table 16.1), status, and group size (Table 16.2). To determine the number of cases

for each cell of the new table you simply add up the count in the appropriate cells of the master table. For example, to find out how many males versus females were seen signalling, simply add together the male cells (the first six cells) and then the female cells (next six cells). These two numbers would then be incorporated into the number of observations of males and females who signalled. Similar procedures are then followed to get the count on the number of males and females not signalling.

STEP 4 FORMAT THE TABLES.

Tables 16.1 and 16.2 show the format for two of the tables. Various features of these tables are to be noted.

Table title The title reports the name of the dependent variable followed by the independent variable. Any control variables would follow. Sometimes it is a good idea to report where and when the observations were made.

Lines to separate sections of the table Following the table title, draw two closely spaced lines to separate the table title from the body of the table. Single lines will be used to separate other sections of the table.

Independent variable across top of page Arrange categories of the independent variable across the top of the table, using easily understood category labels.

FIGURE 16.2 MASTER TABLE FOR ELEVATOR STUDY

Number Present	MALE						FEMALE					
	4 OR FEWER			5 OR MORE			4 OR FEWER			5 OR MORE		
Status/ Signal	S	P	O	S	P	O	S	P	O	S	P	O
Signal given	⊞⊞⊞⊞ (20)	⊞⊞⊞⊞/ (21)	/// (3)	//// (4)	// (2)	/ (1)	⊞⊞⊞/// (18)	⊞⊞/ (9)	/ (1)	⊞⊞⊞ (15)	/ (1)	–
No signal given	⊞//// (9)	⊞// (7)	/ (1)	/ (1)	⊞⊞// (12)	/ (1)	⊞ (5)	//// (4)	// (2)	/ (1)	/ (1)	/ (1)

Status categories: S = Student
P = Professor
O = Other

Source: Adapted from Anne Marie Bonnar (March 1992). "To Signal or Not to Signal: A Study of Personal Space and Behaviour." First-Year Paper for Sociology 100, St. Francis Xavier University, Antigonish. (This project was jointly conducted by Anne Marie Bonnar and Erin Timmons.)

Dependent variable arranged on the vertical axis Note that the dependent variable is arranged along the side of the page. Once again, use labels that are easy to understand and that will communicate clearly to your reader what would be included in each category.

Calculated column percentages Note also that the percentages are calculated on each of

the columns. The rule is to calculate percentages toward the independent variable (adding up to 100% on each category of the independent variable). For example, if we wished to calculate the appropriate percentages for looking at the relation between gender (independent variable) and signalling (dependent variable), we would calculate what percentage

TABLE 16.1 SIGNALLING BEHAVIOUR BY GENDER

SIGNALLING BEHAVIOUR	MALE		FEMALE		TOTAL	
	N	%	N	%	N	%
Signalling	44	75.9	51	55.4	95	63.3
Non-signalling	14	24.1	41	44.6	55	36.7
TOTAL	58	100.0	92	100.0	150	100.0

Chi-Square = 6.449
Degrees of freedom = 1
Probability = <.05 (reject null hypothesis)

Source: Adapted from Anne Marie Bonnar (March 1992). "To Signal or Not to Signal: A Study of Personal Space and Behaviour." First-Year Paper for Sociology 100, St. Francis Xavier University, Antigonish. (This project was jointly conducted by Anne Marie Bonnar and Erin Timmons.)

TABLE 16.2 SIGNALLING BEHAVIOUR BY NUMBER OF PEOPLE ON THE ELEVATOR

| | NUMBER OF PEOPLE | | | | | |
| | 4 OR FEWER | | 5 OR MORE | | TOTAL | |
SIGNALLING BEHAVIOUR	N	%	N	%	N	%
Signalling	72	72.0	23	46.0	95	63.3
Non-signalling	28	28.0	27	54.0	55	36.7
TOTAL	100	100.0	50	100.0	150	100.0

Source: Adapted from Anne Marie Bonnar (March 1992). "To Signal or Not to Signal: A Study of Personal Space and Behaviour." First-Year Paper for Sociology 100, St. Francis Xavier University, Antigonish. (This project was jointly conducted by Anne Marie Bonnar and Erin Timmons.)

of males signal or do not signal. We would then do a similar calculation for the females. In this way, we can compare the percentage of males signalling with the percentage of females doing likewise. The reason you would not calculate the percentage toward the dependent variable is that we are not so much interested in the distribution of signalling by gender (we might have a different proportion of males and females in our sample and therefore more males might signal simply because there might have been more male passengers).

Occasionally tables are created in which the percentages are run across the page. This is usually done to accommodate situations in which there are a number of categories of the independent variable and, in order to have enough space, the table is turned sideways.

To calculate the percentage, divide the cell value by the marginal total (this is the column total if the dependent variable is arranged on the vertical axis) and multiply by 100. In Table 16.1 the first cell percentage would be calculated by $(44 \div 58) \times 100 = 75.9\%$. These percentages should be reported to an accuracy of one decimal point. The total should report the actual total—either 99.9, 100.0, or 100.1.

More complex tables More complex tables containing control variables can also be created from the master table. However, before constructing such tables, the material in

Chapter 17 should be consulted in order to establish what model is being tested and how the results should be interpreted. For ease of interpretation, arrange the dependent variable along the vertical axis, with categories of the independent variables on the horizontal axis.

STEP 5 CALCULATE TESTS OF SIGNIFICANCE AND MEASURES OF ASSOCIATION.

Tests of significance and measures of association can be calculated manually. Chapter 9 provides examples of how such computations can be done. The results of these computations can be entered below the table, as shown in Table 16.1.

STEP 6 INTERPRET THE RESULTS.

In interpreting the results of the analysis, we typically focus on just one of the categories of the dependent variable; in the case of the elevator study, we would simply compare the percentage of males who are seen to signal in the elevator with the percentage of females who are seen to do likewise. In the case of Table 16.1, we would note that "while 75.9% of the males signal, 55.4% of the females signal." It is unnecessary to report the "Not Signal" categories since these are simply the remaining cases adding up to 100.0%. The writer of a report should also note whether the differences between the gender categories are statistically significant and whether the differences observed were in the direction predicted in the hypotheses and report on any measures of the strength of the association.

A Chi-Square test of significance could have been performed on this data using the procedures outlined in Chapter 9 (see Box 9.4 on p. 261).

2. EXPERIMENTAL DATA

Using the procedures outlined in Chapters 8 and 9, it should be possible for the researcher to analyze experimental data without using a computer. Suppose you do a between-subjects experiment: you could compute the dependent variable *means* and *standard deviations* for your treatment group and for your control group. (See Chapter 8 if you do not remember how to calculate means and standard deviations.)

Box 9.5 on p. 264 can be used as a model to calculate a between-subjects *t*-test. If you have a within-subject design, refer to Box 9.6 on p. 267. If you require a one-way analysis of variance, use Box 9.7 on p. 269 as a model. If you require an ANOVA, you will probably find that it will save time to enter the values into a computer and have the machine, equipped with appropriate software such as SPSS, do the calculations.

To perform this analysis using SPSS see the ANOVA procedure in Appendix A.

3. SURVEY AND NONREACTIVE DATA

While survey and nonreactive data could be analyzed by recording the information on a master table (see above), generally the number of variables measured is substantial, and it would usually be advisable to learn how to use a computer to process the information. However, if there are just a few variables measured, even with a large number of cases, it is possible to transfer the information to a master table and then derive cross-tabulation tables from it. But if you wanted to calculate means, standard deviations, or correlations among the variables, the chore of hand-computing the results would be onerous—unless there were few cases in the study. In most situations, the use of computer technology is advised.

B. ANALYZING DATA USING A COMPUTER

For the purpose of this book, we will assume that the computer used by students at most colleges and universities is equipped with a Windows version of SPSS (Statistical Package for the Social Sciences). The Statistical Package for the Social Sciences (**SPSS**) is undoubtedly the most popular and widely available statistical package used by social scientists. It was developed in the 1960s and has gone through a series of embellishments over the years and now contains a great number of statistical and data-manipulation procedures. There are versions for mainframe computers (SPSS^x), versions for personal computers (SPSS/PC+), and versions that take advantage of the capabilities of Microsoft Windows. The version featured in this book is the one designed for Windows and it is known as SPSS for Windows (Versions 10–14).

A number of manuals are available from SPSS that detail the many additional features and options that are available for the various commands. Some of these manuals are listed at the end of Appendix A and you may wish to consult them as you develop your facility in working with SPSS.

1. USING SPSS FOR WINDOWS (VERSIONS 10 TO 14)

You will probably be using the point-and-click method of issuing the various SPSS commands. A few general tips for this method are in order:

- after each procedure is run, the results are sent to the SPSS Viewer which will be displayed on your monitor; you can save, edit, and print your results from the SPSS Viewer;

- to select one variable, simply click on it when it is highlighted;

- to select multiple variables from a list, hold down the Ctrl button and click on all the variables you want to select.

    To start using SPSS, turn on a computer that is using a Windows operating system and is equipped with SPSS for Windows. Once you are logged on you are ready to start.

A. TO BEGIN AN SPSS SESSION

Click on **Start**.

Point to **Programs**.

Point and click on **SPSS**.

A screen similar to the one shown in Figure 16.3 should now appear on your monitor. Note that there are a number of blank cells displayed on the screen. You could start a new SPSS **file** by entering data at this point or you could access an existing SPSS file. We will begin by accessing an SPSS file that has the data entered.

B. TO ACCESS AN EXISTING SPSS FILE

Click on **File**.

Click on **Open**.

FIGURE 16.3 OPENING SCREEN SPSS

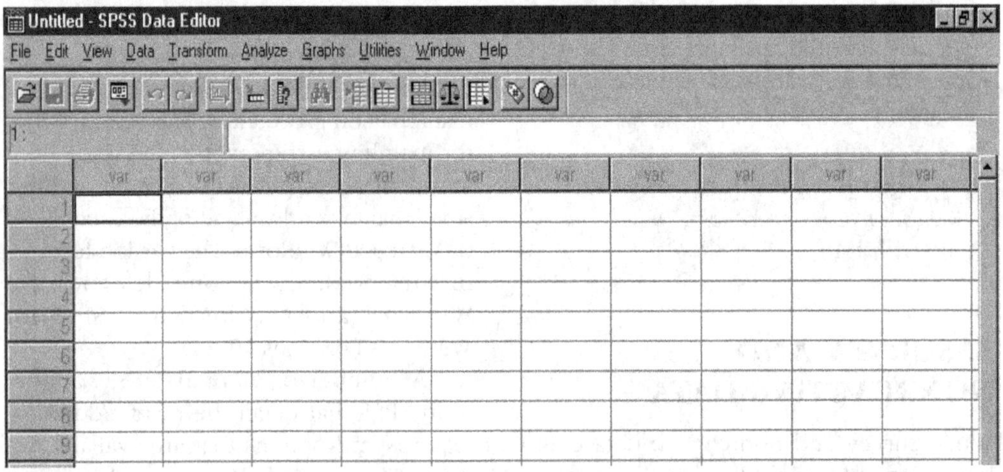

FIGURE 16.4 ACCESS FILE SCREEN

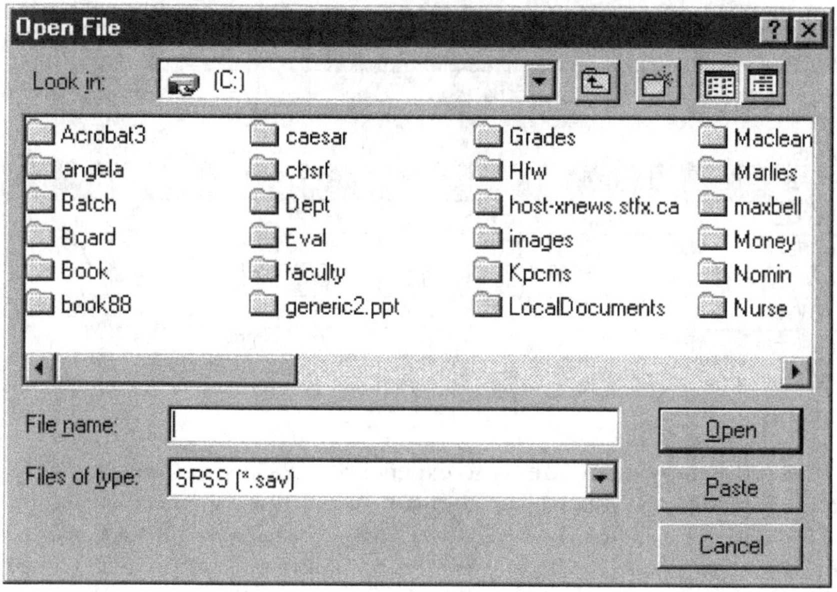

A screen will now appear (see Figure 16.4) and you identify the location of the file and its name. You may need to specify where the file is located as well as its name. For our practice sessions we will assume the file is called "mercy.sav" and it is saved on the C drive. After you enter the name and location of the required file (**C:\mercy.sav**):

Click on **OK**.

The blank boxes on the screen grid will now be filled with numbers and you are now ready to begin analyzing the data set. This is a data set collected from social research methods students in Canada on aspects of mercy killing. Figure 16.5 displays the screen after the system file (a .sav file) is accessed.

There are two methods of using SPSS:

- the **point-and-click** method, which simply involves choosing options from among those provided on a screen menu and clicking on them; or

- the **syntax** method, which involves typing in SPSS commands.

C. USING THE POINT-AND-CLICK MENU METHOD

Assuming you now have the SPSS file loaded (see Figure 16.5), you now must decide what procedures you want to run on the data. The inside of the back cover of the book lists some of the basic things you might want to do (click on that standard toolbar item and then click on each item in the order listed). Appendix A discusses each of the procedures and provides guidelines for interpreting the output that results from each analysis.

Note that the SPSS Windows version uses the following file types:

FIGURE 16.5 SPSS SCREEN AFTER FILE ACCESSED

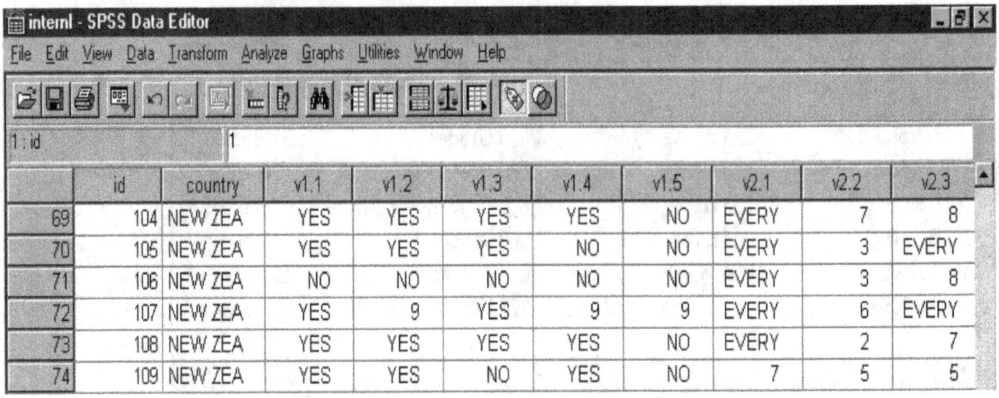

	id	country	v1.1	v1.2	v1.3	v1.4	v1.5	v2.1	v2.2	v2.3
69	104	NEW ZEA	YES	YES	YES	YES	NO	EVERY	7	8
70	105	NEW ZEA	YES	YES	YES	NO	NO	EVERY	3	EVERY
71	106	NEW ZEA	NO	NO	NO	NO	NO	EVERY	3	8
72	107	NEW ZEA	YES	9	YES	9	9	EVERY	6	EVERY
73	108	NEW ZEA	YES	YES	YES	YES	NO	EVERY	2	7
74	109	NEW ZEA	YES	YES	NO	YES	NO	7	5	5

- SAV—an SPSS Windows **system file** (when you access a .sav file, the data will show on the SPSS data editor screen). A system file contains all of your data and all of the labels describing the variables in your file.

- SPS—an SPSS windows **syntax file** (when you access an .sps file, you are automatically in the syntax editor). Syntax files are used to contain instruction commands that are then sent to SPSS for processing. If you are entering data as a numeric file keep it as an .sps file so you can edit it; the added advantage is that each case can be entered on one long line.

- SPO—an SPSS windows **output file** (when you access an .spo file, you are automatically in the SPSS viewer editor). An output file contains the results of your analyses. You can modify, print, or copy these files to a word processor.

D. USING THE SYNTAX METHOD

In the syntax method the user types in the desired commands. This method will appeal

to experienced SPSS users who know SPSS commands and the command structure. New users will probably find it easier to use the point-and-click approach. To use the Syntax method follow these steps:

Click on **File**.

Click on **New**.

Click on **Syntax**.

Now a blank screen should appear and you simply type the commands onto the screen. Remember that after each command is completed you must end the line with a period (.). Having entered the commands you can then position the cursor (the flashing vertical line) where you want SPSS to begin processing. To have SPSS process the commands, do this:

Click on **Run**.

Click to choose from among options shown.

It is a good idea to maintain a copy of the syntax files used. If data errors are found or if additional data are added to the file later, then the syntax files can simply be resubmitted to SPSS without having to think through the whole process a second time.

When you leave the program, you will be asked if you wish to save a copy of the syntax file; if you respond "yes" you will also be given an opportunity to name the file.

2. DATA ENTRY

Data entry is simply the process of transferring the information collected in a study to a computing device. In survey research projects, which include a large number of variables, one may enter the data into a word processor such as Word or WordPerfect. Later you can highlight the text and paste it into an SPSS syntax file. Alternatively, data can be entered directly into the Syntax Editor that is part of SPSS for Windows. Using the Syntax Editor has the advantage of being able to enter all the data on one line for each case as opposed to having to use two or more lines if you have quite a few variables. The Syntax Editor approach is the preferable one, especially if you have a large survey to process.

We will assume that you have figured out how to use one of the above approaches and you are now ready to begin data entry. The following rules provide guidelines for data entry if you are creating a separate raw data file.

A. CREATING A SEPARATE RAW DATA FILE

GUIDELINE 16.1 NUMBER QUESTIONNAIRES, FORMS, AND DATA SOURCES.

Questionnaires or data-collection forms are numbered, normally beginning with 001 (or 0001 if there are more than 1,000 cases). This *ID number* is written on the front page of the instrument (usually in the top right corner). This number will be entered into the computer and provides the only link between the particular form and the data that are entered into the computer file. If an error is found in the data, the original form can be located by using the ID number, and then the information can be checked and the error corrected. Keep the questionnaires or forms sorted by their ID number.

GUIDELINE 16.2 CODE ANY UNCODED QUESTIONS.

If there are questions that have not been pre-coded (such as occupational codes or open-ended opinion questions), they should now be coded and the values written on the questionnaire (or form) in the margin next to the question. In the case of occupational prestige codes, they would be looked up and a value entered onto the questionnaire.

GUIDELINE 16.3 DO A COLUMN COUNT.

Using a blank copy of the questionnaire (or form), go through it and opposite each question indicate where it will be entered onto the terminal screen. Typically, screen widths are 80 columns. This means that you can enter 80 digits across the screen before you run out of space. Thus if you were entering your data into a Word file, you would need to start a second line of data for the questionnaire if it exceeded 80 characters. If you are using SPSS for Windows you need not worry about the screen width: the syntax editor will allow you to use as many columns as is necessary for your data set.

The first three columns will be used for the ID number of the questionnaire; the fourth column will be used to identify the record number for the respondent. (This is required only for questionnaires that require more than 80 columns to enter the data: record #1 refers to the first line of data, record #2 the next set of data for the respondent, and so forth. The ID number is repeated on each line of data, followed by the record number.) If a question can have values between zero and nine, then one column will be required to record the data; if the values range up to 99, then two columns will be required; if the values range up to 999, three columns will be required. These values are recorded on the right-hand margin of the questionnaire (or form). The right-hand margin might look something like this:

Variable	Columns
ID	1–3
Record #	4
Blank	5
Gender	6
Yr. Birth	7–8
Income	9–14
Occupation	15–16

In a short questionnaire the information for all of the variables will fit onto one 80-column line; each questionnaire will occupy one line of data. If more than one record (or line) is required, then a second record is used, with the first three columns being saved for a repeat of the ID number. The fourth column will contain a "2," meaning that it is the second record for the questionnaire. In the case of a questionnaire requiring two records, the data might be set in a way similar to the example in Figure 16.6:

Note the four columns. The first three contain the ID number (which has also been written on the questionnaire), and the fourth column refers to the record number. What we have here is respondent 001 first record; then the same respondent 001, second record; this is followed by respondent 002, first record and respondent 002, second record. It is not critical that the ID numbers be in sequence, but the cases must be together: record one must be followed by record two for each case. The reason we enter the ID number and then the record number is that most computers' sorting routines will be able to sort your file with one simple command. The blanks in the data set are discussed below.

GUIDELINE 16.4 ENTER DATA WITH THE HELP OF A PARTNER.

Inexperienced computer users will find that data entry will be much easier, and be done with fewer errors, if two people work together on entering the data. One person can read the numbers off the questionnaire, with the partner entering the values into the computer.

GUIDELINE 16.5 LEAVE INTERNAL BLANKS TO MARK A NEW PAGE.

Errors can be identified more quickly if, after the end of each page in the questionnaire, a blank is left in the data. The column of blanks must always line up when the data are printed out; if the blanks do not line up then an error has been made and must be corrected. The first six lines of a data set are listed in Figure 16.7, showing how the blanks line up:

FIGURE 16.6   DATA FOR QUESTIONNAIRE REQUIRING TWO RECORDS

0011476989232333 23222111222111 222456345644556666663339
0012453437676767221122211 1122299122876321453213345222
0021456338992212 21222113222112 2233411003344556544432211
0022234343444585746 3748 498505059521122233423334444

FIGURE 16.7	DATA WITH BLANKS BETWEEN QUESTIONNAIRE PAGES

PAGE 1	PAGE 2	PAGE 3	PAGE 4
00112435445523	211212333448976999	123232111123212	23411112
00211231231234	322213222122232212	432235333211232	34532432
00314321234443	233445324433321212	332122341122233	23323222
00413444688822	122221122321233219	234433221222321	34521211
00513335543221	223332221114124211	332111422111212	32121223
00614322345432	231143321122122121	112211222111231	22132454

Note that the fourth line of data contains an error; by examining the listing it becomes apparent that the error is somewhere in the data entered from page two of the questionnaire (there are too many digits in the space reserved for page two). The introduction of blanks to mark the end of pages is enormously helpful in error detection, so be sure to use them.

GUIDELINE 16.6 SIMPLIFY MISSING VALUE CODES.

If respondents do not answer a question, or if the question is not applicable, a **missing value code** is used. These should be kept as simple and as consistent as possible. Where possible, use the values "9," "99," or "999" for variables that require one, two, or three columns respectively. Suppose a respondent is asked to indicate gender as either male or female and leaves the question blank. Instead of leaving the column blank, a "9" would be inserted into the appropriate column. See Appendix A for additional details on missing values.

While it is possible to use alternate codes such as "8" for not answered, and "9" for not applicable, such discrimination should be made only when it is known that the information will be used later; if it is not going to be used, keep matters simple by using the single code "9" to

cover both cases. In occupational codes, it may be necessary to provide special codes for "homemaker" if values are not provided in the occupational code system being used. For the nine-point Likert attitudinal scales, "0" is used for the missing value code.

A code must be entered for every question, even if it is not answered. The reason for this is that, when instructions are given to the computer, each question is identified with particular columns in the data; each question, therefore, must be in the identical position in all lines of data. (Actually most programs allow the use of a space or a comma to separate questions, but since error detection is easiest when questions occupy the identical columns in each question, we will use the same-column method.)

GUIDELINE 16.7 DOCUMENT RESEARCH DECISIONS.

When data are being entered into the computer, a number of decisions will be required. For example, a questionnaire may have a lot of missing data and the person entering the data might decide that it would be better to discard the questionnaire. In that case, set the questionnaire or form to one side and consult with fellow researchers as to whether that data should be used. In another example, cases may arise in which a respondent has checked two items on a question where only one was expected. Generally these discrepancies will be rare enough for it to be appropriate to "flip a coin" to decide which of the two will be taken. (One would not systematically take the highest-placed item on the list since that would systematically bias the results toward those items listed first.) Whatever the case, when such a decision has been made, the decision should be marked clearly on the questionnaire and initialed by the person making the decision. With such documentation, it is then possible for others to check through the data and understand what coding decisions were made and by whom.

GUIDELINE 16.8 CODE FOR INFORMATION NOT ON THE QUESTIONNAIRE.

Frequently there will be information not coded on the questionnaire that should be appended to the data. It is always recommended that provision be made to include a code to identify who collected the original information, who did the coding on the questionnaire, who did the data entry, and any other information that may be useful in the later data analysis or in error checking. The reason it is helpful to code who did the coding is that if there are systematic differences between coders in dealing with different questions, then the cases dealt with by each coder can quickly be identified and compared. Appropriate corrections can then be made without too much fuss.

GUIDELINE 16.9 USE DOUBLE DATA ENTRY.

When resources allow, it is recommended that different individuals enter data twice. A computer program can then be used to compare the two files, flagging any differences between them. This technique is extremely helpful in reducing data-entry errors.

GUIDELINE 16.10 SAVE THE DATA.

When data entry is complete, save the file as an ASCII or DOS file (WordPerfect: Use *Ctrl F5* and *Save*; Microsoft Word: use the *Save As* command; on the *Save as type* window, click on *Text Only*). Alternatively, you can highlight the data and do an *Edit/Copy* on it and then do an *Edit/Paste* of the data into a syntax file. If you have entered the data into a syntax file in SPSS, save it as an .sps file; this will allow for easy entry into the syntax editor. (Saving the file is easy: when you exit from the program, SPSS will ask you if you wish to save the file; simply respond "yes" and provide a name for the file. The machine will automatically append .sps to the file name, indicating that it is an SPSS syntax file.)

GUIDELINE 16.11 CHECK FOR ERRORS.

Error checking is a process for locating and correcting errors in the data prior to data analysis. Programs are available for identifying out-of-range entries and for locating non-numerics (such as O for 0, or an I (lowercase el) instead of a 1 (one)). If you have access to such a utility program use it.

B. POINT-AND-CLICK RAW DATA ENTRY

If the data are being entered directly into SPSS, click on **File/New/Data** and then move the cursor to the cell you wish to start with (the cell will be highlighted) and enter the data for each variable, moving across the row. The value will show on the screen just above the matrix. To move from variable to variable after the value has been entered either hit the Tab key or the right-arrow key; to move from case to case use the down-arrow key after the value has been entered.

i. Inserting a New Case

If you wish to add a new case, position the cursor on the case below where you want to insert the new case. On the toolbar click on **Data** and click on **Insert Case**. Enter the data for the new case.

ii. Inserting a New Variable

If you wish to add a new variable, position the cursor on the variable following the spot where you want to insert the new variable. On the toolbar click on **Data** and click on **Insert Variable.** Enter the data for the new variable for all the cases. Note that if you do not enter any value for a case, the system will add a "." indicating that this case has a MISSING VALUE.

3. CREATING AND SAVING AN SPSS.SAV FILE

If you have a modest to large survey to process, it is probably worth learning how to use the Syntax Editor to enter the commands to define the variables, attach labels, and to indicate the "missing value" codes. Variable lists can be used to give many variables the same labels (yes/no questions for example) and to identify variables with the same missing values. This approach to data entry will be described below in the section called The Syntax Method of Creating and Saving an SPSS System File. If the data being analyzed involve just a few variables (under 10 or 15 perhaps) the direct-entry method can be used comfortably. This approach will be described in the following section.

A. POINT-AND-CLICK METHOD FOR CREATING AND SAVING AN SPSS SYSTEM FILE

Point and Click:

File

New

Data

A screen with blank cells will now appear. Click on *Variable View* tab at the bottom of the data screen. Your first task will be to name each variable. Usually we start with an **ID** as the first variable name and it will give us a place to enter the number for the questionnaire (or observation form): these should correspond to the number written in the top right corner of the questionnaire. Figure 16.8 shows the appropriate window.

i. Defining and Labelling Variables

At the bottom of the Data Editor screen there are tabs for *Variable View* and for *Data View*. Click on the *Variable View* tab and the screen will now display the variables along the vertical axis of the screen. The definable characteristics are arranged along the top of the screen. By clicking on one of the characteristics (Labels, for example) you can then attach the labels for that particular variable. On the gender variable you would attach the labels "Male" and "Female."

> ***Hint:*** *In studies with a lot of variables (as in most surveys), it is a good idea to use the question numbers for variable names. Since the names must begin with an alphabetical character, calling them v1, v2, v3 makes sense. For multi-part questions, use v4.1, v4.2, v4.3, etc. When analyzing data you can quickly find the variable names by just looking at the questionnaire.*

ii. Missing Values

See Guideline 16.6 on p. 429 for suggestions on the treatment of missing values. It is best to use "9," "99," "99.9," etc., to indicate a

FIGURE 16.8 DEFINE VARIABLES SPSS SCREEN

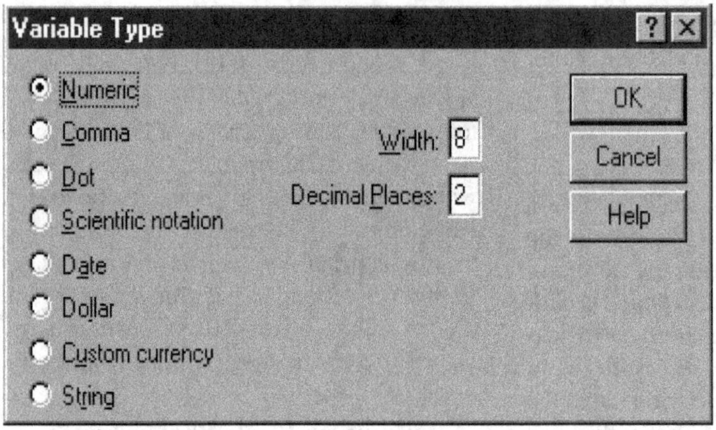

Variable Type [?] [X]

- ⊙ Numeric
- ○ Comma
- ○ Dot
- ○ Scientific notation
- ○ Date
- ○ Dollar
- ○ Custom currency
- ○ String

Width: 8
Decimal Places: 2

OK
Cancel
Help

refusal to answer a question or to indicate a question that does not apply to the respondent. If it is going to be relevant to distinguish the reason for the missing value, other code numbers can be applied. If you are using the syntax approach to defining the missing values, a variable list is made up for each missing value. If the point-and-click approach is used, declare the missing value when the variable labels are attached.

Hint: In large surveys if the point-and-click approach is used to define the variable, you can speed up the process by putting on value labels and missing values after the .sav file has been created. Simply put on the variable names and labels, save the file, then enter the syntax editor, and enter the VALUE LABELS and MISSING VALUES, and then save the output. Since variable lists can be used for VALUE LABELS and MISSING VALUES it is much quicker to do these in the syntax editor.

Hint: You can change the default settings for variables (type of variable, size of field, etc.) by clicking on the Variable View (bottom of screen); select a case with settings you want to duplicate, do an Edit/Copy, then highlight the variables you want it applied to and do an Edit/Paste and those definitions will be applied to the cases that have been highlighted. For example, if you are dealing with survey data, and most variables are 1-character wide, you would reset the defaults to show Numeric 1, MISSING VALUES as 9. Only when you encounter 2-column variables would you have to redefine the settings for these variables.

iii. Saving or Updating the SPSS System File: The .SAV File

Whenever you wish to save or update your SPSS system file, click on the toolbar **File** and click on **Save**. You will be able then to specify where you want it saved and to change the name of the file if you wish. Anytime you compute new variables or transform old ones, you may want to save the changes, so remember to update the file with the Save procedure. Be certain to maintain backup copies of your .sav file on disks as well as on the hard drive of your computer.

iv. The Syntax Method of Creating and Saving an SPSS System File

In order to use the syntax procedure to create a system file, access the Syntax Editor as follows:

>Click on **File.**
>
>Click on **New.**
>
>Click on **Syntax.**

Now a blank screen should appear and you simply type the commands onto the screen. For researchers who are familiar with the SPSS command structure, the main difference between what you are familiar with and the Windows versions is that you have to remember that after each command is completed you must end the line with a period (.). Having entered the commands you can then position the cursor (the flashing vertical line) where you wish SPSS to begin processing. To have SPSS process the commands do this:

>Click on **Run.**
>
>Click to choose from among options shown.

It is a good idea to maintain a copy of the various syntax files used. If data errors are found or if additional data are added to the file later, then the syntax files can simply be resubmitted without having to think through the whole process a second time.

Box 16.1 shows the command structure that will identify, name, and label all the variables in a study. A key shortcut to

---

BOX 16.1

Sample Syntax Commands to Create an SPSS System File

Title system file creation, Social Science Faculty Review, Winston.
Data list file = 'C:\oia\sscience\social science data.SPS' / id 1–5 v1 8 v2 9
  v3 10 v4 12 v4.1 to v4.7 13-19 v5 20 v6 22 v8 23 v9.1 to v9.6 24–29
  v10 to v12 30–32 v13 34 v16 35 v17 36 v18.1 to v18.5 37–41.

variable labels id "identification number" [label up to 40 characters]
 /v1 "Year of Graduation"
 /v2 "Program"
 /v18.5 "Quiet Study Space".

value labels [each label limited to 20 characters]
/v1 0 "1995 or earlier" 1 "1996" 2 "1997"
3 "1998" 4 "1999" 5 "2000" 6 "2001" 7 "2002" 8 "2003"
/v2 1 "Major" 2 "Advanced Major" 3 "Honours"
/v4.1 to v4.5 0 "No" 1 "Yes".

missing values v1, v2, v3, v4, v4.1 to v4.5, v5, v6, v8, v13 (9)
 /v4.5, v4.6, v9.1 to v9.6, v10 to v12, v16, v17, v18.1 to v18.5 (0).
Frequencies var = v1.

remember is that data lists can be used when several variables have the same labels. This saves the researcher entering labels more than once. Examples of the various commands necessary to define an SPSS system file are shown in the box. This method is probably the quickest one for data sets involving many variables and many cases. Smaller data sets can be entered directly using the point-and-click method discussed in the preceding section.

v. Saving or Updating the SPSS System File: The .SAV File

Whenever you want to save or update your SPSS system file, click on the toolbar **File** and click on **Save**. You will be able then to specify where you want it saved and to change the name of the file if you wish. Anytime you compute new variables or transform old ones you may want to save the changes so remember to update the file with the Save procedure. Be certain to maintain backup copies of your .sav file on disks as well as on the hard drive of your computer.

4. DATA CLEANING USING SPSS

After the data have been entered into the computer and saved in a file, it is time to begin the systematic search for errors so that they can be corrected before analysis of the data begins. This process is referred to as **cleaning the data**. If you have specialized software, then you would proceed by using this program. If you do not have access to such data-cleaning programs, the following steps will help you detect errors in the data.

STEP I

Assuming you have entered the data into a file, the first job is to save the file and print out a hard copy. The printout should be examined and any irregularities circled. Check the following:

- All lines must end in the same column. If there are too few or too many columns in a line, it means that questions were either missed or entered twice. Mark discrepant lines so that they can be checked against the original questionnaire and the error(s) can be located. The overall picture of the file must be "rectangular" with no ragged edges.

- Any internal blanks must line up vertically. If end-of-page blanks have been used, one can quickly identify situations where there have been too many, or too few, entries made from a particular page on the questionnaire. Once again, mark any discrepancies.

- When there are two or more files to be checked, ensure that the file lengths are equal. If 165 questionnaires have been completed, there must be 165 lines in each of the files.

- Proofread ID numbers (columns one through three) to ensure that none are repeated or missing. Again, mark any errors. (Some cases may have been withdrawn so those ID values will be missing.)

- Finally, ensure that there are no blank lines or partial lines left in the data set. SPSS will read a blank line as a case and will assign a missing value to all variables. If you find that you always have 1 or 2 missing cases even though you know there should be none on certain variables, your problem may be that you have blank lines somewhere in your data file. Usually the problem is that there are some blank lines at the beginning or end of the file.

STEP 2

When the file that includes the variable labels and other file definition commands is run, SPSS will alert you to any inappropriate non-numerics in your raw data file. The output will indicate which case has the problem. Note the case numbers, examine your data, and make corrections to the data. Sometimes you will have included non-numeric data intentionally but may have forgotten to indicate this on your DATA LIST commands. Remember, you can use non-numerics but when identified on the DATA LIST command you must put an "(A)" following the column numbers for the variable; as in,

    . . . v27 17–18, **v28 19–40 (A),** v29 to v31 41–43

STEP 3

On all nominal and ordinal data, run the frequencies procedure. Examine the output (you need not print it out at this point since you are simply scanning it for errors), looking for any categories that are not labelled or for any out-of-range values for that variable. For example, on the gender variable there should be only two categories, one for male respondents and one for females. If there are any other values included, the case must be identified and the data corrected before you proceed with further analysis. To locate the problem case(s), go to the SPSS grid with your data listed, click on the column (top of grid) where the variable name is identified and the whole column should then be highlighted. If you want to find a 3 in your gender variable, click on the icon for "find" (binoculars) and tell the machine to find "3." The machine will now highlight the problem case. Note the case number listed under ID, go to your sorted pile of questionnaires, and find the questionnaire with the same ID number and note the value that should be included for gender. Correct the value by highlighting the gender cell for the case in error by entering a 2 or a 1 as appropriate. While doing this check make certain that the Missing Values are properly flagged as missing. In the case of the gender variable, 9s probably were used as the missing value code: make certain any 9s are flagged as missing on the frequency

distribution. But note that if there are no missing cases for a variable, the frequencies will not list the category for missing values.

Continue checking the frequency distributions looking for out-of-range entries, correcting them as you go along. It is a good idea to keep a record of these changes and then go back to your raw data file and correct that file as well.

STEP 4

The ratio variables should be listed on the descriptives' window (Analyze/Descriptive Statistics/Descriptives). Check the lowest and highest values for each variable. Are they within range? Note especially that the MISSING value is not listed as the highest value. If it is, you have made an error in your missing values. Problem cases can be identified by bringing up the SPSS data grid: highlight the variable that has an error, and use the binoculars icon to find the value you wish to find. Corrections can be made directly on the SPSS grid but should also be made in the raw data file.

> **Hint:** *If you make the corrections in the raw data file, you can resubmit the MAKER file (the one containing the data list, variable labels, etc.) and this will update your SPSS System file.*

STEP 5

Having corrected the errors you are now ready to proceed with your analysis.

5. STEPS IN ANALYZING DATA FOR A PROJECT

When doing your analysis it is a good idea to use the *Paste* command to save the procedures you have run in a Syntax file. The reason for this is that if you have errors in your data and it becomes necessary to re-run a job after corrections have been made, you can then quickly re-submit your jobs without having to think through your whole analysis anew.

STEP 1

Be certain to have the questionnaire or the recording form on which you have recorded the column numbers for each variable, print-outs of your FREQUENCIES (nominal and ordinal variables), and DESCRIPTIVES (ratio variables) with you. If you have not run these analyses, run them.

STEP 2

If you need to construct any indexes, this should be done at this point. Review the procedures for creating indexes (see Chapter 13); if you are using RELIABILITY, click on the appropriate icons to do the job, and determine the items that are to go into the index. Do a COMPUTE to create the index. Add VARIABLE LABELS (and VALUE LABELS, if appropriate). Save the SPSS (. SAV) file so that the next time you sign on the new variable(s) will be available.

STEP 3

Examine your causal models. Select the appropriate procedures for testing the models. Do the procedures to test the various relationships indicated by the model. Note that you may need to RECODE some variables. If most of the relationships are examined using one method (say MEANS) probably you should do all of them using that procedure, even though a few could be examined using correlations. Enter the commands to do the basic runs and, if recoding of variables has been done, retain the recodes for future use by updating your system file by clicking on FILE/SAVE.

> *Hint: When doing RECODES, create a new variable to contain the information*

and add an 'r' to the name of the original variable. For example if you recode v9, call the new variable v9r; using this method will remind you that any variable name with an 'r' appended to it is a recoded version of the original variable.

STEP 4

If you have any intervening or sources of spuriousness models, these should be processed. Review Chapter 17 for suggestions on interpreting results.

STEP 5

After you have assembled the computer output, you will want to consider how you will present the results. (See various summary tables in Chapter 18 for possible ways of setting up your tables for presentation.) Note that it is helpful, particularly in small sample studies, to indicate whether the trends in various relationships go in the directions predicted.

STEP 6

Write your report in sections, following the outline suggested in Chapter 18.

6. THE 3M APPROACH TO SELECTING ANALYSIS PROCEDURE

As a way to remember how to decide which procedure to use to analyze any relationship, use the three steps in the 3M approach.

STEP 1 MODEL

The first step is to decide which variable is to be treated as the dependent variable and which one as the independent variable. Since the researcher typically is trying to understand what causes variations in a dependent variable, common sense alone can generally determine which variable should be designated as the dependent variable. However, there will be other cases where it is not obvious. In such cases, try to decide which variable occurs last in a temporal sequence. It is entirely possible that the two variables mutually influence one another. If this is the case, one will nonetheless have to be designated as the "dependent" variable. It is a good idea to diagram the relationship using greater than (>) and less than (<) symbols as well as a line with an arrow pointing toward the dependent variable (see Figure 16.9).

STEP 2 MEASUREMENT

The second step is to identify the level of measurement attained in the dependent and in the independent variable. Recall that there are three levels of measurement: nominal, ordinal, and ratio.

STEP 3 METHOD

Having identified the measurement levels, the third step is to examine the inside of the front cover of this book to determine which method should be used to examine the relationship. The methods listed are the names of SPSS procedures.

Having identified the appropriate procedure to use, you are now ready to proceed with the analysis. The reader may wish to review the inside front cover of the book, which indicates the appropriate analysis procedure for given levels of measurement in the independent and dependent variables. Appendix A will present the basic procedures along with the most commonly used options and statistics. For full details of SPSS procedures, consult the appropriate SPSS manual listed in the suggested readings section at the end of Appendix A.

7. WHEN YOU GET ERRORS AND WARNINGS

If you are using the Syntax method of entering SPSS commands, expect to get error and warning messages when you run SPSS jobs. Some of these errors will lead to the termination of the job, other less serious ones (warnings) will simply lead SPSS to ignore an instruction. SPSS has error checking routines that will identify the error immediately following the line on which the error occurs. The following tips are presented to help in detecting some common problems.

TIP 1 EXPECT ERRORS.

The first thing to realize is that you will make errors. Even after many years of using SPSS you will continue to make them. SPSS errors are just part of your life as a data analyst.

FIGURE 16.9 DIAGRAM OF RELATIONSHIP BETWEEN INDEPENDENT AND DEPENDENT VARIABLES

TIP 2 EXAMINE ERROR AND WARNING MESSAGES CAREFULLY.

The errors and warnings will be listed on the output immediately after the problem has been encountered. To assist the researcher, the characters or symbols creating the problem will be quoted. A key point is to examine carefully the description SPSS provides of the error; this will assist you in identifying your mistake.

TIP 3 MAKE CERTAIN SPSS IS ACCESSING THE NECESSARY FILES.

A common error a new user will encounter is that SPSS is not able to access the file(s) required. This means that you may have an error on your GET FILE command line. In SPSS the computer will do an error search and identify all the problems it has with the instructions. Of course if the computer has not been able to find your system file (*.sav), every variable you mention will produce an error since the machine has not found a file containing the named variables. So the first thing to do when you get an error at the beginning of a job is to check to see that the computer was able to access the necessary files for the task.

TIP 4 FIX FIRST ERRORS FIRST.

When correcting errors in a syntax command set, begin with the first errors identified. Often when you fix an error at the beginning (for example you do a COMPUTE to create a new variable known as TOTALS, but on all your subsequent commands you refer to the variable as TOTAL. Each time the machine encounters TOTAL it will give you an error. If you change the name of the variable on the COMPUTE statement to TOTAL and resubmit the job all the subsequent references to TOTAL will be correct. Sometimes it is a good idea to resubmit a job after you have fixed the first few errors to see how many have been eliminated. Proceed then by again fixing the first errors

that show up and then resubmit the job until you get an error-free run.

TIP 5 STUCK? RE-ENTER THE COMMAND LINE.

Sometimes you can stare at an error line and cannot see what is wrong with it. Perhaps you used an 'O' rather than a '0', as in v1O when you meant v10. SPSS does not have a variable called v1O but it is hard to see the difference on some monitors. Do not waste a lot of time; just re-enter the command line.

TIP 6 EXAMINE RESULTS ON SCREEN BEFORE SENDING TO A PRINTER.

Sometimes you may inadvertently do something very silly and produce an enormous, meaningless, output file. Suppose for example that you are running CROSSTABS and you are examining the relationship between two variables with a control for occupational prestige of the respondent. In error you failed to use the recoded version of the occupational prestige variable and you accidentally produced a monster output file because for each occupational code (there may be 70 or 80 distinct numbers) the computer generated a table showing the relationship between your main variables. If you look at the results on the screen before you print them you will avoid wasting computer paper on foolish output.

TIP 7 DOUBLE CHECK VARIABLE LIST.

When the output reflects an inappropriate analysis, check the list of variables submitted. A common mistake is to RECODE a variable for use in an analysis but then use the original form of the variable rather than the recoded one when the variable is mentioned on the command line. This mistake will not generate an error or a warning but it will generate a lot of useless output!

TIP 8 CHECK FOR A PREMATURE FINISH COMMAND.

If part of your job is run but is terminated before all the expected output is completed, check to make certain that you have not left a FINISH command in the middle of your job. Often when previously used .sps jobs are modified and resubmitted we forget to take out the old FINISH command. SPSS will ignore any commands after the FINISH command.

C. KEY POINTS

Many analyses can be carried out without the assistance of a computer. Observational studies that collect information on a few variables (typically five or fewer) and not too many cases can be hand-tabulated readily.

Observational studies frequently proceed by recording information on *tally sheets*. This information can then be transferred to a *master table*. From the master table a number of individual tables, which permit the testing of various null hypotheses, can be calculated.

Typically, tables should include a title, place the independent variable on the horizontal axis, and place the dependent variable on the vertical axis. Percentages should be calculated for the vertical columns and rounded to an accuracy of one decimal point. If applicable, the results of a test of significance should be included, noting the raw Chi-Square, *t*, or *F* score, the degrees of freedom, and whether the results indicate a probability of less than or greater than .05.

In interpreting the results of contingency tables, the researcher compares the percentages of one category of the dependent variable for each category of the independent variable.

If mainframe or personal computers are used in data analysis, the user will have to become familiar with the *operating system* of the computer. *Editors* are programs to provide a way of entering information into the computer. This information is stored in *files*.

In entering data into the computer, one usually numbers the forms (questionnaires) and enters the information into the same columns for each variable, using 9s to indicate missing answers.

The following suggestions will also ease the preparation of data:

- For inexperienced computer operators, it is a good idea to work in teams, one person calling out the numbers to be entered, the other entering the information.

- Leave a blank column at the end of each page of a form or questionnaire (this helps eliminate many errors by making them easier to detect).

- Where coding decisions are made, they should be marked on the form and initialled by the coder.

- Where more than one interviewer, coder, or data entry person is involved, it is a good idea to include, as supplementary information, a code identifying who performed each of these functions for each respondent. This will speed up checking for systematic differences between the decisions of different coders.

- To reduce data-entry errors, it is recommended that data be entered twice and a computer program used to identify discrepancies between the two versions.

Initial cleaning of the data is commenced after data entry has been completed. The steps are:

- Sort and create a file for each record type.

- Print out a copy of the file(s) and check to ensure that there are no ragged edges and that internal blanks line up.

- Check that the files to be merged are the same length.
- Check that no cases are missed and that no cases are entered twice.

- Check that no blank lines are included.
- Use procedures to detect out-of-range values and non-numerics. These should be corrected before data processing begins.

D. KEY TERMS

Cleaning the data	Missing value code	Syntax (.sps) files
File	Output (.spo) files	System (.sav) files
Master table	SPSS	Tally sheet

BASIC MULTIVARIATE TECHNIQUES

A. TESTING THREE-VARIABLE CAUSAL MODELS

In nonexperimental research, how do we test whether a proposed explanation for some relationship has any merit? Suppose, for example, that you want to see if your data support the idea that heightened parental expectations among high SES parents explain the observed link between SES and the educational aspirations of youths. This chapter describes procedures for evaluating causal models such as the one suggested above. First, the type of model being dealt with must be determined: is it a source of spuriousness, an intervening variable, or a candidate variable model? (See Chapter 12 for a description of these models.) Second, the appropriate statistical procedures for the analysis must be determined. This determination will be based on the level of measurement of the variables involved in each of the relevant variables.

To establish a causal relationship, three conditions must be met.

- The variables must be *associated*.

- The variables must be in a plausible *causal sequence*.

- The variables *must not be spuriously connected*.

To show that two variables are *associated*, one has to demonstrate that they vary together. To argue that one variable is producing changes in another, one has to demonstrate that as one variable changes, so does the other. Empirical association is reflected through contingency table analysis (CROSSTABS), differences in means across categories (MEANS, *T*-TEST, ANOVA, MANOVA), and various correlational techniques (CORRELATION, REGRESSION).

To demonstrate a plausible *causal sequence* is largely a matter of theory or of common sense. What is meant here is not only that the independent variable precedes the dependent variable in time, but that the ordering is believable. Usually, giving a little thought to the causal order will provide an answer. For example, it would be foolish to argue that the "size of your present community" influences the size of the "community in which you were born." The causal sequencing is wrong: the present cannot influence the past. The size of community one has chosen to live in may, of course, be influenced by the size of community in which one grew up.

To demonstrate that a relationship is not *spurious* is always a challenge, and one that can never fully be met. (Recall that a spurious relation is one in which some third factor is influencing both the independent and the dependent variables: thus, their covariation may be the result of the common connection to the source of spuriousness.) A critic can always point to some potential **source of spuriousness** for the relation between the variables. The best the first-time researcher can hope to achieve is to deal with the more obvious potential sources of spuriousness. This chapter shows some techniques for testing three- and four-variable causal models.

It turns out that identical analyses can be used to test different three-variable causal models. Such models generally attempt to explain or elaborate on some relationship that is known to exist or that a research project expects to demonstrate. We will use some sample data to illustrate: suppose we have done a survey on 395 senior high-school students concerning their plans for education beyond the high school level. Table 17.1 presents the results.

Table 17.1 is a standard contingency table whose computations could be done

TABLE 17.1 PERCENTAGE OF SENIOR HIGH-SCHOOL STUDENTS WITH PLANS FOR FURTHER EDUCATION BY SOCIOECONOMIC STATUS (SES)

TYPE OF PLAN	LOW SES BACKGROUND		HIGH SES BACKGROUND		TOTAL	
	N	%	N	%	N	%
Some plans	144	73.1	176	88.9	320	81.0
No plans	53	26.9	22	11.1	75	19.0
TOTAL	197	100.0	198	100.0	395	100.0

$X^2 = 16.021$ df = 1   Significant at the .001 level.

with the CROSSTABS procedure (see Appendix A). A shorter version of the table is also possible and will be used to illustrate the model testing to be presented below. The shorter version is illustrated in Table 17.2.

With the information provided, it is possible to reconstruct the original table. As 73.1% of 197 low SES students plan on further education, it is possible to determine the number of students who fall into the category ($.731 \times 197 = 144$). Similar calculations could be done to reconstruct all of Table 17.1.

The much simplified Table 17.2 is easy to read and focuses attention on the two percentage figures that are to be compared: while some 88.9% of the students with high socioeconomic status backgrounds plan on some post-secondary education, 73.1% of those with low SES backgrounds have similar plans. Note that there is a 15.8 percentage point difference by SES categories in those planning on post-secondary education. We will use this table in discussing the first causal model, the intervening variable model.

1. TESTING FOR INTERVENING VARIABLES

A. THE INTERVENING VARIABLE MODEL

In an intervening variable model the interest is in understanding the relationship between X and Y—understanding the

TABLE 17.2 PERCENTAGE OF SENIOR HIGH-SCHOOL STUDENTS WITH PLANS FOR FURTHER EDUCATION BY SOCIOECONOMIC STATUS (SES)

	LOW SES BACKGROUND	HIGH SES BACKGROUND
Percentage who have plans for further education	73.1	88.9
Number of cases	197	198

$X^2 = 16.021$ df = 1   Significant at the .001 level.

mechanism by which X is connected to Y. Frequently the researcher will be testing a number of alternative explanations of how X influences Y. In the case of one intervening variable, the relationship could be diagrammed as follows:

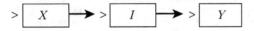

In this diagram, I is the **intervening variable**, or the linking variable between X and Y. The hypothesis is that variations in X cause variations in I, which, in turn, influences Y. Typically, one would propose a number of possible intervening variables, so the following diagram would be more appropriate:

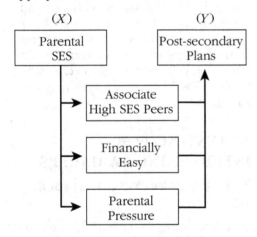

In this diagram, three alternative explanations are suggested for the connection between X and Y. The researcher would collect data that measure each of the variables involved and conduct the appropriate statistical tests to determine, which, if any, of the proposed alternative explanations, or intervening variables, explains the connection between X and Y.

Let us suppose, for example, that three alternative explanations are proposed for the relation between SES and likelihood of post-secondary educational plans.

1. High SES students associate with high SES peers who plan on post-secondary training.

2. High SES students perceive little financial difficulty in attaining a higher education and, therefore, are more likely to plan on such training than are low SES students.

3. High SES parents are more likely to put pressure on their children to participate in post-secondary training.

How would we go about testing these three alternatives?

B. THE RATIONALE BEHIND THE TESTS

The thinking behind the test is as follows: if we have a *causal relationship* between X and Y (SES and Plans) and propose a link to explain how X influences Y, then X (SES) should not be able to influence Y (Plans) if we hold the linking variable constant. The argument is that X influences Y through I. A plumbing analogy may be helpful. Water can flow from X to Y only through a pipe. If you turn off a valve located between X and Y, then increasing the volume of water flowing into the pipe at point X will have no influence on Y, because the valve has been turned off; however, if we open the valve, then changes in the pressure at X will influence the flow at Y. Keeping the analogy in mind, let us now see if we can "control" for the intervening variable.

The first explanation is that high SES students tend to associate more with other high SES students and that this is the link between SES and educational plans. How can we analyze the data to see if the results are consistent with the model we wish to test? Using a contingency table analysis (CROSSTABS), we will run the relation between SES and plans, controlling for the intervening variable, association with high SES peers. We want to see what happens when the control is applied. We want to see whether the original 15.8 percentage-point difference in the relationship between SES and plans (a) increases; (b) stays the same; (c) decreases/disappears; or (d) is mixed.

C. JACKSON'S RULE OF THIRDS

According to **Jackson's rule of thirds**, if the original difference between the categories increases by one-third or more, we will interpret this as an *increase*, or a strengthening, of the original relationship; if the difference remains within one-third of the original, we will interpret this as an indication that the relationship has *remained* the same; if the difference decreases by more than one-third, we will interpret this as a *decrease/disappearance* of the relationship; finally, if the relationship is markedly different when different control categories are compared to one another (e.g., it disappears in one category, but stays the same in the other), the result is *mixed*.

To apply the rule of thirds to the case under examination, we must first decide where the cut-points are between the thirds. To do this we take the original difference of 15.8 and divide by 3; this yields a value of

5.3. Table 17.3 presents these values and shows how the differences would be interpreted.

D. USING CROSSTABS TO TEST FOR AN INTERVENING VARIABLE

But what are our expectations? If the model being tested is correct, we would expect the relationship between SES and plans to decrease/disappear when the relationship is run controlling for the intervening variable. If SES influences plans through the linking variable, then, if we hold the linking variable constant, there should be no relation between SES and plans. Differences in level of planning by SES category should decrease/disappear when the control is applied. All other outcomes are interpreted as not supportive of the model. Table 17.4 presents summary data for five possible outcomes.

To interpret the outcomes it is necessary to determine whether the original relationship has increased, stayed the same, decreased/disappeared, or is mixed. The beginning researcher should keep the interpretation of the data as simple as possible. Only when the difference decreases/disappears do we have possible support for an intervening variable model. Let us look at the five outcomes and suggest an interpretation for each one.

TABLE 17.3 APPLYING JACKSON'S RULE OF THIRDS

SAMPLE DATA RESULTS	INTERPRETATION
Original difference: 88.9 − 73.1 = 15.8	
Determining thirds: 15.8 ÷ 3 = 5.3	
Outcomes:	
a. If new difference is greater than 21.1 (15.8 + 5.3 = 21.1)	Increased
b. If new difference is between 10.5 and 21.1 (15.8 ± 5.3)	Stayed the same
c. If new difference is less than 10.5	Decreased/Disappeared
d. If new differences vary markedly across categories of the control variable	Mixed

TABLE 17.4 **PERCENTAGE OF SENIOR HIGH-SCHOOL STUDENTS WITH PLANS FOR FURTHER EDUCATION BY SOCIOECONOMIC STATUS (SES), CONTROLLING FOR SES OF BEST FRIEND, WITH FIVE POSSIBLE OUTCOMES**

PERCENTAGE PLANNING FURTHER EDUCATION	BEST FRIEND HIGH SES		BEST FRIEND LOW SES*	
	LOW SES BACKGROUND	HIGH SES BACKGROUND	LOW SES BACKGROUND	HIGH SES BACKGROUND
1st outcome	92.0	93.0	71.0	69.0
Difference		1.0		−2.0
2nd outcome	74.0	92.0	71.0	86.0
Difference		18.0		15.0
3rd outcome	85.0	92.0	68.0	76.0
Difference		7.0		8.0
4th outcome	74.0	96.0	61.0	82.0
Difference		22.0		21.0
5th outcome	90.0	92.0	60.0	82.0
Difference		2.0		22.0

*The original difference, with no control for SES of Best Friend, is shown below:

	LOW SES BACKGROUND	HIGH SES BACKGROUND
Percentage who have plans for further education	73.1	88.9
Difference		15.8

OUTCOME 1

According to the rule of thirds, the relationship has decreased/disappeared. The original difference has been reduced to one percentage point in the case of those whose best friends have high SES, and to two percentage points for those whose best friends are classified as low SES. This is the only outcome—one in which the original relationship decreases/disappears—that we consider to be consistent with the intervening variable causal model.

OUTCOME 2

The relationship stays the same, so the intervening variable model is to be rejected.

OUTCOME 3

This outcome supports the intervening variable model: the difference decreases/disappears. The interpretation is that the independent variable influences the dependent variable through the tested intervening variable.

OUTCOME 4

This outcome would lead us to reject the intervening variable model. The relationship is strengthened, so this suggests that the proposed alternative explanation is having an independent influence on the dependent variable.

OUTCOME 5

This outcome would also lead us to reject the intervening variable model: the difference decreases/disappears in one of the control categories, but increases in the other, suggesting a conditional effect—the intervening variable is probably having an independent influence, but only at certain levels of the intervening variable. This is an example of a *mixed* result.

To perform this analysis using SPSS see the CROSSTABS procedure in Appendix A.

E. USING MEANS TO TEST FOR AN INTERVENING VARIABLE

The second explanation proposed for the connection between SES and plans is that high SES students plan on post-secondary education because they know their families can afford it. We will assume that plans are measured by the number of years of post-secondary education planned on (ratio level measurement), permitting the use of the MEANS procedure.

The logic is identical to the previous procedure. We will examine the difference in the number of years planned between SES categories: we will then rerun that relationship, controlling for whether students believe they will have enough financial support to permit them to do some post-secondary training. Once again, we will apply the rule of thirds to provide a guideline for the interpretation of the data. Table 17.5 (bottom) indicates that there is a 1.40 year difference in the number of years of post-secondary education planned by SES categories. The question is: will this difference increase, stay the same, decrease/disappear, or be mixed when the control for perceived financial support is applied?

Table 17.5 shows different outcomes. Once again, we look at the control table, examine the difference between the levels of financial support high and low SES students believe they have available to them and contrast this difference with the original difference of 1.40 years.

OUTCOME 1

For those students who perceive that no financial support will be available for higher education, the data indicate a 1.91 year difference between SES categories in total years of post-secondary education planned. Among those who perceive support, the difference between the categories is 1.96 years. By applying the rule of thirds we see that the difference in both SES categories has increased by more than one-third, and we therefore argue that the relationship has been intensified: we must reject the intervening variable model. The intensification suggests that the perception of financial support has an independent, positive impact on the level of post-secondary planning.

OUTCOME 2

In the second outcome, in both the "No Support" and "Support" categories, the difference between the low and high SES students remains almost the same as the original difference of 1.40. We therefore reject the intervening variable model.

OUTCOME 3

In the third outcome, the difference has been reduced by more than one-third, and we therefore conclude that there is some evidence to support the intervening variable model.

OUTCOME 4

In both the "Support" and "No Support" categories, the differences in years planned have

MEAN YEARS OF FURTHER EDUCATION PLANNED	NO SUPPORT		SUPPORT*	
	LOW SES BACKGROUND	HIGH SES BACKGROUND	LOW SES BACKGROUND	HIGH SES BACKGROUND
1st outcome	1.49	3.40	3.30	5.26
Difference		1.91		1.96
2nd outcome	2.23	3.66	2.55	3.98
Difference		1.43		1.43
3rd outcome	1.56	2.27	3.42	4.10
Difference		0.71		0.68
4th outcome	2.35	2.48	3.77	3.92
Difference		0.13		0.15
5th outcome	1.64	3.13	3.89	4.01
Difference		1.49		0.12

TABLE 17.5   MEAN YEARS OF FURTHER EDUCATION PLANNED BY SOCIOECONOMIC STATUS (SES), CONTROLLING FOR PERCEIVED SUPPORT FOR HIGHER EDUCATION, WITH FIVE POSSIBLE OUTCOMES

*The original difference, with no control for financial support, is shown below:

POST–HIGH SCHOOL PLANS	LOW SES BACKGROUND	HIGH SES BACKGROUND
Mean number of years of further education planned	2.47	3.87
Difference		1.40

decreased/disappeared (dropped by more than two-thirds); this outcome supports the intervening variable model.

OUTCOME 5

The final outcome suggests a mixed result. The difference decreases/disappears within the "Support" category, but remains the same within the "No Support" category. We reject the intervening variable model. The data here suggest that the financial support variable has a conditional impact on years of post-secondary education planned.

F. USING PARTIAL CORR TO TEST FOR AN INTERVENING VARIABLE

Partial correlations are measures of the strength of an association that take into account one or more additional variables. (Refer to Chapter 8 for a more detailed discussion.) Partial correlations measure how closely two variables are associated when the influence of other variables is adjusted for: a first-order partial is one that takes into account one additional variable, and a second-order partial takes into account two additional variables. By combining CORRELATIONS and PARTIAL CORR we can test for an intervening variable.

In this case, we want to test whether parental influence intervenes between SES and plans. Using correlational techniques, we would first establish that there is an association between SES and plans. If there is an association we would then proceed with the analysis to test whether the data are consistent with an intervening variable model.

If the intervening variable model is correct, we should at least expect the following:

- that the correlation between adjacent variables will be greater than between non-adjacent categories ($r_{XY} < r_{XI}$ or r_{IY});

- that if I is controlled, the relation between X and Y should disappear. This could be done with a partial correlation coefficient ($r_{XY.I} = 0$).

The model will be tested using two correlational techniques, CORRELATIONS and PARTIAL CORR. Table 17.6 presents the Pearson correlations between three variables: parental pressure index (I), SES score (X), and years of future education planned (Y).

The first test is to see if the magnitude of the correlations is consistent with the model being tested. The prediction was that adjacent correlations would be higher than non-adjacent ones. The adjacent correlations are I-X and I-Y and the correlations are .31 and .46 respectively. The non-adjacent correlation is X-Y and the correlation is .22.

So far, the data are consistent with the intervening variable model.

The next question is whether the partial correlation will be increased, stay the same, or decrease/disappear when I is controlled. For this analysis, a partial correlation would be computed. When this calculation is done, we find that (see Chapter 8 for the formula) the partial ($r_{XY.I}$) is .10. By applying the rule of thirds, we see that the original relation between X and Y is .22 and, since the partial is about one-half of the original value, we note that the association has decreased/disappeared. We therefore find support for the model.

> *To perform this analysis using SPSS see the PARTIAL CORR procedure in Appendix A.*

2. TESTING FOR SOURCES OF SPURIOUSNESS

A. THE SOURCE OF SPURIOUSNESS MODEL

The next major type of causal model is the source of spuriousness model. Here the researcher proposes that, while there is a statistically significant relation between the variables X and Y, this relationship may be a non-causal one, existing only because some third variable is influencing both X

TABLE 17.6 CORRELATIONS BETWEEN VARIABLES IN MODEL

VARIABLES	PARENTAL PRESSURE (I)	SES SCORE (X)	YEARS OF EDUCATION (Y)
Parental pressure (I)	1.00		
SES score (X)	.31	1.00	
Years of education (Y)	.46	.22	1.00

and *Y*. The argument is that the only reason *X* and *Y* are related to one another is that a third factor is influencing both of them. Having observed a statistically significant relation, the researcher will want to ensure that the relationship is not spurious and, therefore, will run a number of spuriousness checks. The source of spuriousness model can be diagrammed as follows:

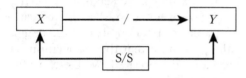

B. THE RATIONALE BEHIND THE TESTS

How do we go about testing a source of spuriousness model? The idea is this: if *X* and *Y* are spuriously associated, the reason they vary together is that a third variable (a source of spuriousness) is influencing both *X* and *Y*. Therefore, if we control for the source of spuriousness (S/S), there should no longer be any association between *X* and *Y*. This suggests that we need the same kind of analysis that we used for testing intervening variables. To test for a potential source of spuriousness, the steps are:

- test the original relation between *X* and *Y*; if this demonstrates a robust relationship (probably statistically significant) then;

- controlling for the source of spuriousness, rerun the relation between *X* and *Y*. As in the intervening variable model, we can then apply Jackson's rule of thirds to determine if the relationship has increased, stayed the same, decreased/disappeared, or become mixed. In order to conclude that the original relation is spurious, the difference between the categories must decrease/disappear.

C. THE DILEMMA: THE MODELS ARE NOT EMPIRICALLY DISTINGUISHABLE

The difficulty is that it is possible for two researchers working with the same data and with the same three variables to establish two different causal models: one proposing that the variables are connected in an intervening variable model, the other proposing that the variables may be associated spuriously. They might then do the identical analysis but come to totally different conclusions. Let us suppose that when the control is applied, the original difference decreases/disappears: one researcher would conclude that the intervening variable model has found support in the data; the other would conclude that the relation is spurious. Both would be right.

Because the two models are not empirically distinguishable, the importance of precisely specifying models in advance becomes clear. If we develop the models after analyzing the data, the interpretation of the data is little more than a flight of fancy.

D. USING MEANS TO TEST FOR SPURIOUSNESS

To illustrate a test for spuriousness, we will use the same variables as last time. Table 17.7 presents sample data showing how the analysis turned out for the relation between SES and plans.

The reader should note that there is a 1.40 year difference between the low and high SES students in the number of years of further education planned (see Table 17.7). Now suppose that we wanted to make certain that this relationship was not caused spuriously by the rural or urban backgrounds of these students. The type of home community (rural versus urban) may be influencing the SES level achieved by

TABLE 17.7 NUMBER OF YEARS OF FURTHER EDUCATION PLANNED BY SENIOR HIGH-SCHOOL STUDENTS, BY SOCIOECONOMIC STATUS (SES)

POST–HIGH SCHOOL PLANS	LOW SES BACKGROUND	HIGH SES BACKGROUND
Mean number of years of further education planned	2.47	3.87
Number of cases	197	198

the families, and may also be influencing the educational plans of the students. It would therefore be the urban or rural location that is influencing both variables rather than the SES level that is influencing the students' plans.

Table 17.8 reports five different outcomes for this analysis. These should be examined carefully and the rule of thirds applied and a decision should be made as to which outcome lends support to the spuriousness model of the relationship between the variables. To apply this rule, simply divide the original difference by 3 (1.40 ÷ 3 = 0.47). Next, one has to compare the difference in years of future education planned by SES categories for each of the rural and urban categories.

OUTCOME 1

Here the differences (2.11 and 1.93) have both grown by more than a third, and we therefore reject the source of spuriousness model. Perhaps the type of background has an independent influence on the number of additional years of education planned.

OUTCOME 2

The original difference between the number of years of education planned by low versus high SES students was 1.4 years. When the control for rural versus urban background is applied, the difference remains much the same,

and we therefore reject rural versus urban background as a source of spuriousness.

OUTCOME 3

The original difference in this result has been reduced to .61 for both categories. Since the difference has decreased/disappeared, we find support for the source of spuriousness model.

OUTCOME 4

In this case, the original difference has been reduced to less than one-third of its original value, and so we cannot reject the source of spuriousness model. Outcomes 3 and 4 both lend support to the spuriousness model.

OUTCOME 5

Here the result is mixed. The difference disappears among the rural students, but is only slightly reduced among the urban students. We reject the source of spuriousness model.

In order to do the analysis, we need a table showing the difference in additional years of education planned, by SES categories. Second, we will need to rerun this relationship, controlling for rural and urban backgrounds.

To perform this analysis using SPSS see the MEANS procedure in Appendix A.

TABLE 17.8 MEAN YEARS OF FURTHER EDUCATION PLANNED BY SOCIOECONOMIC STATUS (SES), CONTROLLING FOR RURAL AND URBAN BACKGROUNDS, WITH FIVE POSSIBLE OUTCOMES

MEAN YEARS OF FURTHER EDUCATION PLANNED	RURAL BACKGROUND		URBAN BACKGROUND*	
	LOW SES BACKGROUND	HIGH SES BACKGROUND	LOW SES BACKGROUND	HIGH SES BACKGROUND
1st outcome	0.87	2.98	3.33	5.26
Difference		2.11		1.93
2nd outcome	2.27	3.67	2.58	3.96
Difference		1.40		1.38
3rd outcome	2.30	2.91	3.71	4.32
Difference		0.61		0.61
4th outcome	1.73	1.91	3.74	3.97
Difference		0.18		0.23
5th outcome	2.16	2.27	2.74	4.04
Difference		0.11		1.30

*The original difference with no control for Urban/Rural backgrounds is shown below:

POST–HIGH SCHOOL PLANS	LOW SES BACKGROUND	HIGH SES BACKGROUND
Mean number of years of further education planned	2.47	3.87
Difference		1.40

E. USING CROSSTABS TO TEST FOR A SOURCE OF SPURIOUSNESS

To use CROSSTABS in a test for a source of spuriousness, one runs the original relationship, then reruns the relationship controlling for the source of spuriousness. The rule of thirds would then be applied and only if the difference decreases/disappears do we consider the original relationship to be spurious.

To perform this analysis using SPSS see the CROSSTABS procedure in Appendix A.

F. USING PARTIAL CORR TO TEST FOR SPURIOUSNESS

This test requires ratio level variables, and simply involves running the zero-order correlation, followed by a partial correlation controlling for the potential source of spuriousness. The analysis should be run and the data interpreted according to the rule of thirds. Only if the relationship decreases/disappears, do we consider the original relationship to be spurious.

To perform this analysis using SPSS see the PARTIAL CORR procedure in Appendix A.

When procedures are being selected for evaluating causal models and the researcher believes that the vast majority will only require one type of procedure, it will, in the interest of simplicity, sometimes be best to use the same procedure throughout rather than shift back and forth between techniques in a way that might confuse the reader. Normally, this will mean some underutilization of the data, since the procedure selected must meet the measurement requirements of the variable with the lowest level of measurement.

B. TESTING FOUR-VARIABLE CAUSAL MODELS

In *Causal Inferences in Nonexperimental Research* (1964), Hubert M. Blalock Jr. presented a number of ideas on testing causal models. These tests parallel the ideas presented in the earlier section of the chapter and should be seen as an extension of them. In the case of four-variable models, there may be two intervening variables (plus an independent and dependent variable). Figure 17.1 illustrates a four-variable model.

Suppose the model that you want to examine is the one presented in Figure 17.1. This model suggests a specific causal ordering of the variables. Or, A→B→C→D. What could one do to test this model? Drawing on the work of Simon (1957) and on Driver and Massey's (1957) North American Indian data, Blalock suggests a number of properties that should hold true if the model is accurate:

- Correlations between adjacent variables should be higher than between non-adjacent variables. If the model is correct, the following should hold:

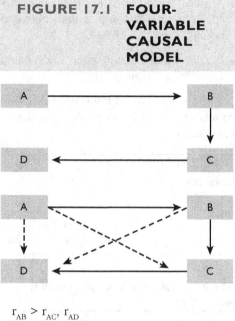

FIGURE 17.1 FOUR-VARIABLE CAUSAL MODEL

$r_{AB} > r_{AC}, r_{AD}$
$r_{BC} > r_{BD}$
$r_{CD} > r_{AC}$

- The weakest correlation in a causal chain should be between the variables furthest apart causally. If the model is correct, the following should hold:

$r_{AD} < r_{AB}, r_{AC}$
$r_{AC} < r_{AB}$
$r_{BD} < r_{AB}, r_{BC}$

- The strength of relationships should diminish if intervening variables are controlled for. If the model is correct, the following partial correlation results should hold:

$r_{AC.B} = 0$
$r_{BD.C} = 0$
$r_{AD.BC} = 0$

As an illustration of the simplest model, we will show the steps necessary to test the model. First, we will examine the magnitude of the various correlations. Are they consistent with the four-variable model? Namely:

- Are the correlations between causally adjacent variables higher than between non-adjacent variables?

- Do correlations drop when intervening variables are controlled?

Suppose that we have the following correlation matrix between the variables A, B, C, and D.

CORRELATION MATRIX:

Variables	A	B	C
B	.56		
C	.21	.61	
D	.10	.18	.63

STEP 1 DOES THE CAUSAL ORDER MAKE SENSE?

The first step in assessing a causal model is to ensure that the causal ordering is plausible. The model should pass a commonsensical test, indicating that the variables are in a temporal sequence that is possible. For example, the first variable in the model should occur before other variables and should represent a possible cause of variation in variables that occur later in the model.

STEP 2 COMPARE THE CORRELATIONS.

Inspect the correlations to see if correlations between adjacent variables are higher than those between non-adjacent variables. In this case we note the following:

MODEL PREDICTS	OBSERVED CORRELATIONS	CON-CLUSIONS
$r_{AB} > r_{AC}, r_{AD}$	.56 .21 .10	Supports model
$r_{BC} > r_{BD}$	.61 .18	Supports model
$r_{CD} > r_{AC}$	.63 .21	Supports model

STEP 3 ELIMINATE CAUSAL LINKS NOT IMPLIED BY THE MODEL.

There are three causal links that are not implied by the model. These include the AB link, the BD link, and the AD link. (These are marked with hatched lines in Figure 17.1.) The first two are tested using first-order (one control) partial correlations, and the last one is tested by means of a second-order partial correlation. The tests reveal the following:

MODEL PREDICTS	OBSERVED PARTIAL CORRELATION	CONCLUSION
i) Testing AC link: $r_{AC.B} = 0^*$	.10	Reduced by more than one-third: supports model**
ii) Testing BD link: $r_{BD.C} = 0$	−.33	Reduced by more than one-third: supports model
iii) Testing AD link: $r_{AD.BC} = 0$	.01	Reduced by more than one-third: supports model

* The formulas used to hand-compute the partials are as follows:

First-order:

$$r_{AC.B} = \frac{r_{AC} - (r_{AC})(r_{BC})}{\sqrt{1 - r_{AC}^2}\ \sqrt{1 - r_{BC}^2}}$$

Second-order:

$$r_{AD.BC} = \frac{r_{AD.B} - (r_{AC.B})(r_{CD.B})}{\sqrt{1 - r_{AC.B}^2}\ \sqrt{1 - r_{CD.B}^2}}$$

** The causal inference uses the rule of thirds, introduced in this text; Hubert Blalock bears no responsibility on this point!

The evidence in this case is consistent with the proposed model. Had any of the results failed the test, then the interpretation would be that the evidence is not consistent with the proposed model.

While it is possible to test complex causal models using contingency tables, the procedure requires a large number of cases as additional control variables are added. Once again, however, the principle remains the same: observe what happens to the original relationship when the control variables are applied simultaneously. Does the original difference increase, stay the same, decrease/disappear, or is it mixed?

To perform this analysis using SPSS see the CORRELATION and PARTIAL CORR procedures in Appendix A.

The next section will introduce some other basic techniques that are used when attempts are made to deal with multiple variables simultaneously.

C. MULTIPLE REGRESSION: REGRESSION

The selection of the appropriate technique should be guided by a consideration of (i) the level of measurement attained in measuring the variables and (ii) what the analysis is attempting to reveal. We will begin this section by exploring multiple regression analysis. An understanding of regression is helpful when examining the other approach featured in this chapter, discriminant analysis. An examination of these two basic multivariate techniques reveals that they have much in common.

1. THE RATIONALE

In **multiple regression analysis** we are attempting to predict variations in a dependent variable from two or more independent variables. As in correlational analysis (see Chapter 8), we are interested in both the equation that describes the relation and a measure of the strength of the association. We will consider only the simplest version of regression—that of an additive or linear relationship among the variables. Regression analysis assumes that the variables are normally distributed and that measurement is at the ratio level. Special procedures, however, do permit the inclusion of variables not achieving ratio measurement.

Regression analysis allows the researcher:

- to estimate the *relative importance* of independent variables in influencing a dependent variable;

- to identify a mathematical *equation* that describes the relation between the independent variables and the dependent variable.

For example, if you are trying to estimate the relative contribution of three variables when predicting the relative prestige of each employee of a company, a regression analysis might indicate that the length of time on the job accounts for 37% of the variation, that educational attainment accounts for 22% of the variation, and that income contributes another 14% of the variation in prestige. Taken together, the three variables account for 73% of the variation in prestige.

Alternatively, the relation between prestige and educational attainment could be analyzed by comparing the average prestige across categories of attainment (MEANS analysis). This would permit the researcher to show a significant relation between prestige and educational attainment but would not enable the researcher to say that educational attainment is about one-half as important as length of time on the job. Because regression analysis provides this additional information it is a powerful tool. Besides allowing the researcher to examine the relative importance of the various factors producing variation in a dependent variable, it also allows the researcher to express the relation in the form of an equation, and hence gives the researcher the ability to predict values for a dependent variable, given values for the independent variables.

Although regression analysis assumes ratio level measurement and normally distributed variables, researchers sometimes include ordinal and even nominal variables. However, the price one pays for reduced levels of measurement is almost certainly a weakened ability to predict variation in the dependent variable, as well as a greater instability in the coefficients associated with the independent variables. (See Box 13.1 on p. 364 for an example of the impact of reduced levels of measurement.)

2. THE LINEAR REGRESSION EQUATION

In Chapter 8 we examined the relationship between two variables using a correlation approach. The equation describing the relation between X (independent variable) and Y (dependent variable) consisted of an a value and a b coefficient as in:

$$Y = a + bx$$

To take into account two or more independent variables, this basic equation is extended as follows:

$$Y = a + b_1 X_1 + b_2 X_2 + \ldots b_k X_k$$

In the equation the a is a constant and, if the values for each case were calculated and plotted, would represent the point where the regression line crosses the Y axis. The **b coefficients** refer to the slopes of the regression lines. If small increases in the X variable lead to large increases in the Y variable, the b value will be higher (see the relation between prestige and years of education shown in Figure 17.2); on the other hand, if it takes large increases in X to produce an increase in Y, the b value will be smaller (see the relation between prestige and annual income shown in Figure 17.4). In the two-variable case (as shown in Figures 17.2 and 17.4), the b value in the case of years of education is higher than the b value for the case of income-predicting prestige. The reason is that the values for years of education have a small range from 0 to 20 years, while the range in the values for income is considerable, perhaps from \$18,000 to \$80,000. Thus, the b values will tend to be much lower. Even though the correlation between prestige and years of education and between prestige and income may be similar (let us say .90 in both cases), the b value for income will be much lower than the b value for years of education.

If standardized slopes are of interest, these will be referred to as β weights or **beta weights**. In this case, think of all the variables in the equation as being standardized—think of them as Z *scores*—so that it does not matter if the independent variables have different ranges (as in the case of income and years of education). Each independent variable is standardized (reassigned values so that each has a mean of zero and a standard deviation of one), which then allows us to compare the beta values directly. The βs represent the amount of change in Y (the dependent variable)

FIGURE 17.2   PRESTIGE AND YEARS OF EDUCATION

Plot of Prestige with Years of Education
(a)

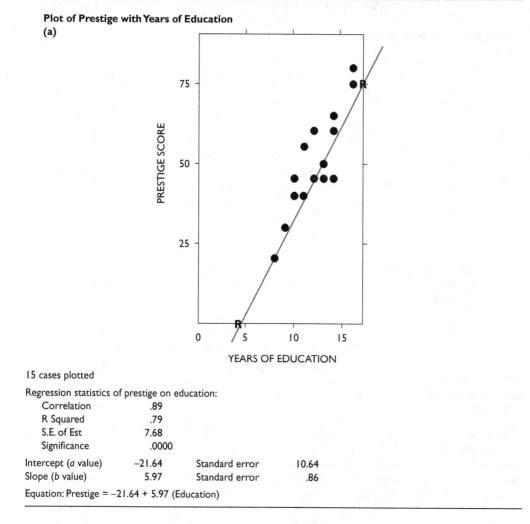

15 cases plotted

Regression statistics of prestige on education:

Correlation	.89		
R Squared	.79		
S.E. of Est	7.68		
Significance	.0000		
Intercept (*a* value)	−21.64	Standard error	10.64
Slope (*b* value)	5.97	Standard error	.86

Equation: Prestige = −21.64 + 5.97 (Education)

---

that can be associated with a given change in one of the Xs, when the influences of the other independent variables are held constant. Regression programs provide the researcher with both the *b* and the *ß* (beta) coefficients (see Figures 17.3 and 17.5).

The strategy of multiple regression involves determining the slopes for each of the independent variables while simultaneously holding constant, or adjusting for, the other independent variables. The slopes (*b* coefficients) are determined so as to maximize our ability to predict variations in the dependent variable. Thus, we may define a **linear regression equation** as one that describes a relationship between a number of independent variables and a dependent variable and that provides for the best linear (additive) weightings of the independent variables and a constant calculated so as to

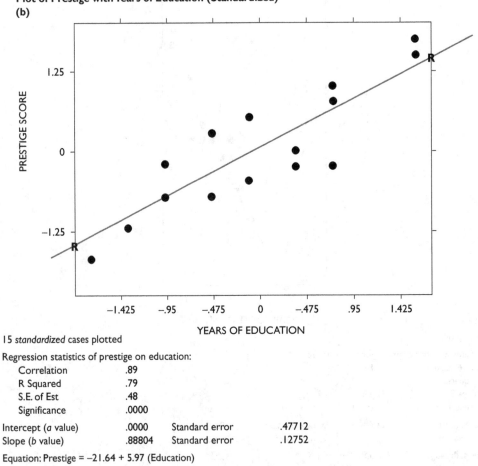

FIGURE 17.3   PRESTIGE AND YEARS OF EDUCATION (CONTINUED)

Plot of Prestige with Years of Education (Standardized)
(b)

15 *standardized* cases plotted

Regression statistics of prestige on education:

Correlation	.89		
R Squared	.79		
S.E. of Est	.48		
Significance	.0000		
Intercept (*a* value)	.0000	Standard error	.47712
Slope (*b* value)	.88804	Standard error	.12752

Equation: Prestige = −21.64 + 5.97 (Education)

maximize the prediction of the dependent variable.

3. THE STRENGTH OF THE ASSOCIATION, R^2

The R^2< is a measure of the amount of variation in the dependent variable that is explained by the combination of independent variables. Recall that when two variables are involved, the measure is r^2 (see Chapter 8). The two statistics are directly comparable and would yield identical results if, in a case in which there are multiple independent variables, one simply took the values for each variable, plugged them into the equation, and then computed the "predicted value" for the dependent variable. If one then correlated the predicted and the observed values of the dependent

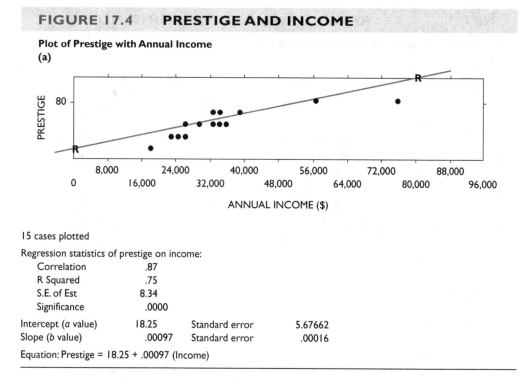

FIGURE 17.4 PRESTIGE AND INCOME

Plot of Prestige with Annual Income

(a)

15 cases plotted

Regression statistics of prestige on income:

Correlation	.87		
R Squared	.75		
S.E. of Est	8.34		
Significance	.0000		
Intercept (*a* value)	18.25	Standard error	5.67662
Slope (*b* value)	.00097	Standard error	.00016

Equation: Prestige = 18.25 + .00097 (Income)

variable, the problem is reduced to a simple two-variable correlation, and the r^2 would equal R^2. Both of these statistics vary from 0 to 1. The higher the value, the higher the explained variance; the higher the value, the higher the predictability of the dependent variable by the independent variables.

Regression analysis is an important technique for both applied and pure research. The applied researcher will be particularly interested in identifying those independent variables that combine:

- importance in influencing the dependent variable; and

- the possibility of manipulation through policy changes.

The applied researcher will be most concerned with the *b* coefficients because they will indicate how much change in the

independent variable will be required for a unit change in the dependent variable. Pure researchers, on the other hand, will usually focus on the *β*s since, generally, the theorist will be more concerned with the relative impact of each independent variable on the dependent variable.

4. USING VARIABLES NOT MEETING THE MEASUREMENT ASSUMPTION

Frequently researchers want to include, along with ratio-level variables, those variables measured at either the ordinal or nominal levels. It is possible to do this, although one must exercise greater caution in interpreting the results.

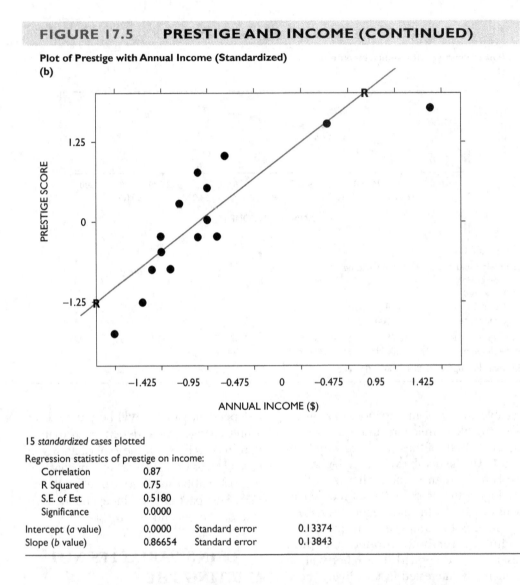

FIGURE 17.5   PRESTIGE AND INCOME (CONTINUED)

Plot of Prestige with Annual Income (Standardized)
(b)

15 *standardized* cases plotted

Regression statistics of prestige on income:

Correlation	0.87		
R Squared	0.75		
S.E. of Est	0.5180		
Significance	0.0000		
Intercept (*a* value)	0.0000	Standard error	0.13374
Slope (*b* value)	0.86654	Standard error	0.13843

A. USING ORDINAL VARIABLES

The price one pays here is generally a weakened ability to predict variations in a dependent variable. In general, the fewer the categories in an ordinal variable, the lower its correlation with other variables. Thus, the more categories in the ordinal variable, the better; if regression analysis is anticipated, using nine-point Likert items rather than five- or seven-point categories is recommended. When ordinal variables are placed into competition with ratio-level variables for explaining variance, the resulting equation will tend to underestimate the relative importance of the ordinal variables. (See Box 13.1 on p. 364 for more details on the effects of using fewer categories.)

B. USING PRESENCE-ABSENCE QUESTIONS

In the case of presence-absence questions, one really has an ordinal variable with two values. Normally such questions are coded so that "0" refers to the absence and "1" refers to the presence of the characteristic. Once again, these variables are at a disadvantage in explaining variation in the dependent variable. Indeed, with only two categories, these variables are at a particular disadvantage (when, for example, compared with another ordinal variable with nine values or a ratio variable). Once again, the coefficients are likely to underestimate the importance of such variables when they are in competition with variables measured at the ordinal or ratio levels.

C. USING DUMMY VARIABLES FOR NOMINAL OR ORDINAL VARIABLES

Suppose you have a religious affiliation variable (nominal) and want to include it in a regression analysis. For purposes of illustration, suppose religion is coded into four categories: (i) Christian, (ii) Jewish, (iii) Muslim, and (iv) Other and None. The dummy-variable procedure involves creating three new variables (one fewer than the number of religious categories) and coding each of them into presence/absence variables. Thus, we will have a "Christian" variable, and it will be coded into presence (1) or absence (0), a "Jewish" variable using 1s for Jews and 0s for non-Jews, and a "Muslim" variable similarly coded 1 and 0 (see Table 17.9). These three new variables would then be entered into the regression analysis as independent variables along with the other relevant independent variables.

Another example of a dummy variable would be the inclusion of a gender variable into a regression analysis. In this case, either the males or the females would be assigned a value of 1, while those not assigned would be given a 0. Thus, if females were assigned the value of 1, then the males would be given the value 0. In this case, only one new variable is needed to represent the two categories of gender (recall that we use one fewer dummy variable than categories of the original variable).

To summarize, then, the newly created *dummy variables* are placed into the regression analysis as independent variables. In each case, there will be one fewer dummy variable than there are categories of the original variable: in the case of the religion variable, there would be three variables to represent the four categories; in the case of gender, only the female variable would be included. The amount of variation explained by each of the new variables is represented by the beta weight associated with the variable. The reason the four categories are represented by three new variables is that the fourth category is taken into account by the combined values in the "absence" category of the three categories. In the case of the gender variable, with females scored as 1 and males as 0, the males are represented as those not scored as 1. A **dummy variable**, therefore, is one that is coded 1 for presence and 0 for absence of a characteristic and represents one category of an independent variable.

5. SOME TIPS FOR USING REGRESSION ANALYSIS

TIP I ENSURE THAT VARIABLES ARE THEORETICALLY INDEPENDENT OF ONE ANOTHER.

What this means is that you cannot use aspects of the dependent variable as independent variables. Ensure that you are including only

TABLE 17.9   RECODING THE RELIGION VARIABLE INTO THREE DUMMY VARIABLES

CASE #	ORIGINAL CODING RELIGION VARIABLE	CODING FOR THREE NEW DUMMY VARIABLES		
		CHRISTIAN	JEWISH	MUSLIM
1	1 (Christian)	1	0	0
2	2 (Jewish)	0	1	0
3	3 (Muslim)	0	0	1
4	3 (Muslim)	0	0	1
5	2 (Jewish)	0	1	0
6	1 (Christian)	1	0	0
7	4 (Atheist)	0	0	0
8	9 (No answer)	0	0	0
9	4 (Buddhist)	0	0	0
10	2 (Jewish)	0	1	0
...				
178	4 (Agnostic)	0	0	0

meaningful potential causes of the dependent variable, *not alternate measures of it.*

TIP 2 WATCH OUT FOR HIGHLY CORRELATED INDEPENDENT VARIABLES.

The weighting attached to the variables will be unstable if the independent variables are highly correlated with one another. The program will print out a warning if there is a problem in this area. The term **multicollinearity** is used to refer to the extent of the correlation among the independent variables. To achieve high predictability of a dependent variable, it is preferable to have the independent variables correlated with the dependent variable but not with one another. If you have a number of highly intercorrelated independent variables, it is usually advisable either:

• to develop an index out of them (if it makes sense to do so); or

• to select one of the measures and use it to represent the others.

TIP 3 TRY TO ACHIEVE RATIO-LEVEL MEASUREMENT.

If you intend to use regression analysis, attempt to collect data in as raw a form as possible, at the ratio level if possible; if ordinal data are collected, use more categories rather than fewer.

TIP 4 USE RAW DATA.

Do not use recoded variables (dummy variables are an exception) in regression analysis. For example, if you have a variable such as age coded as age-at-last-birthday, then use the raw age variable data (such as 24, 19, 37, 54, etc.) rather than recoded age categories that may have used three categories to represent those under 30, those 30 to 49 years of age, and those 50 years of age or over.

TIP 5 USE THE BACKWARD SOLUTION IN THE REGRESSION PROCEDURE.

By using the *BACKWARD (stepwise) solution,* all the variables are included in the regression equation; then the least important variable is dropped, and the equation is recalculated. This procedure is repeated until only significant variables remain. The advantage of this format is that variables that are important when in combination with other variables will remain in the equation; in other formats they might never be included.

TIP 6 INTERPRET WEIGHTINGS WITH CARE.

Understand that the weightings are designed for the particular combination of independent variables in a particular sample and that they may not be reliable if applied to other samples. One has to be particularly cautious in situations where the independent variables are substantially correlated with one another. (In such situations, with another sample, it is quite likely that different variables will be selected as significant predictors of the dependent variable.)

TIP 7 MONITOR NUMBER OF CASES CAREFULLY.

By default (i.e., if you do not provide a specific instruction to the contrary) SPSS deletes a case if it has a missing value in any of the variables in the equation. Thus, if there are a lot of variables in an analysis, there is a danger of losing many cases. And, as the number of cases drops close to the number of variables, the R^2 will increase dramatically. To determine the number of cases used in the analysis, add one to the total degrees of freedom reported in the table.

If a large number of cases have been dropped, one should attempt to detect if there is a pattern to the missing cases. If one subcategory of respondents is more likely to respond to a question, one might wish to analyze the data these respondents provide separately from those subcategories of respondents whose responses are less complete. However,

if it appears that the missing values are random, consider using one or more of the following techniques.

Repeat analysis After an initial regression analysis (using the BACKWARD option) has identified the significant variables, rerun the analysis, naming only the significant variables, plus perhaps two or three that were dropped in the last few steps. This will preserve those cases that were dropped because of missing values in variables that are not in the final equation. Frequently, many fewer cases will be dropped if this procedure is followed.

Pairwise solution Try running the analysis using PAIRWISE treatment of missing cases. In this solution, the correlations are determined for all the pairs of variables for which data are available.

Means solution A third approach is to try the MEANS treatment of missing values, which will substitute the mean of the variable for any missing cases.

TIP 8 DEAL WITH INTERACTIONS AMONG INDEPENDENT VARIABLES.

If you have reason to suspect that the joint effect of two independent variables is important but that, individually, they may not be significant predictors of the dependent variable, there are two relatively easy approaches to take.

* Create a new variable by multiplying the values of the two variables suspected of interaction, and include the new variable in the regression analysis along with the variables from which it was constructed. If the new variable is a significant predictor, it will remain in the equation when the analysis is done; if it is not, it will be dropped.

* Convert all the variables to log function variables (this converts the equation to a multiplicative power function); by doing so any interactions will be taken into account in the weightings of the independent variables.

In this form the equation is:

$$\log Y = \log a + \log X_1 + \log X_2 + \log X_k$$

The consequence of using log transformations is that each independent variable is raised to a power rather than multiplied by the value of the independent variable, as in the linear regression equation.

6. PRESENTING AND INTERPRETING REGRESSION RESULTS

Table 17.10 presents a sample of a regression results table. Note that both the *b* coefficients and the beta weights are reported. It is possible to hand-compute an estimate of the impact of each independent variable, by using the following formula (Hamblin, 1966):

% Variance explained by each variable

$$= \frac{\beta_1 \times R^2}{\Sigma \beta s} \times 100$$

This estimate represents the impact of each variable in the equation. However, if other variables were included, the percentages would change.

The regression equation is included in Table 17.10. This equation will help you identify where each of its elements are found in a printout; note that the *b* coefficients are used (not betas) along with the constant term.

Incidentally, Table 17.10 is based on some research examining possible gender discrepancies in faculty salaries. The question of the research was: given similar levels of qualification, tenure status, experience, age, and academic rank, are female faculty paid less than their male counterparts? The approach taken was to compute a regression equation based on the male faculty. These weightings were then applied to the

female faculty, which gave us a predicted salary which, in turn, allowed us to compare actual salaries to predicted salaries for the female faculty. As is typical in most such studies, the females were found to be paid somewhat less than their male counterparts when adjusting for differences in levels of the independent variables.

D. DISCRIMINANT FUNCTION ANALYSIS: DISCRIMINANT

1. THE RATIONALE

Discriminant function analysis has some similarity to regression analysis. This alternative is used in situations in which:

- the measurement of the dependent variable is at the nominal level; or

- regression analysis is inappropriate because the assumption that the dependent variable is normally distributed is not met.

Discriminant function analysis attempts to predict the category of the dependent variable into which each case falls by using the combined information from the independent variables. For example, suppose you wished to predict whether or not a student will participate in some post-secondary education within five years of completing grade 11. The independent variables include information on final grade 11 average, information on socioeconomic status of family, size of family, and the number of siblings who have engaged in post-secondary education. Based on a study of students who had completed grade 11 a minimum of six years ago, discriminant

TABLE 17.10 MULTIPLE REGRESSION ANALYSIS FACULTY SALARIES

VARIABLE	*b* COEFFICIENT	BETA COEFFICIENT	PERCENT EXPLAINED
Qualifications	794.	.038	3.1
Tenure status	1326.	.065	5.3
Age in current year	94.	.092	7.5
Length in rank	263.	.153	12.5
Professional age	210.	.172	14.0
Years at institution	264.	.250	20.4
Academic rank	-4570.	-.372	30.3
CONSTANT	38504.	% EXPLAINED	93.1
Multiple R	.964		
R Square	.930		

The variables are:

Qualifications	Doctorate = 1; No doctorate = 0
Tenure status	Tenure = 1; No tenure = 0
Age	Age in 1987
Length in rank	Years in rank in 1987
Professional age	Years since highest degree earned
Years at institution	Years teaching at institution
Rank	Professor = 1; Associate = 2;
	Assistant = 3; Lecturer = 4

Salary = 38504 + 794(Qualifications) + 1326(Tenure) + 94(Age) + 263(Rank) + 210(Professional age) + 264(Years) − 4570(Rank).

---

analysis would then be used to predict whether each case would fall into the "participation" or "no participation" categories of post-secondary education.

Discriminant analysis is a valuable tool for the social researcher and can be applied to many situations. To illustrate some of these situations, let us consider applications that might be made of the technique in some of the social science disciplines.

Anthropology Studies of the distribution of neolocal (newly married couple who have established their own residence), patrilocal (newly married couple residing with husband's family), and matrilocal (newly married couple residing with wife's family) residence patterns.

Education Studies of rates of participation and nonparticipation in post-secondary education, of participation in a manual arts elective, or of the rates at which students drop out of school or stay in school.

Political Science Attempts to determine whether individuals are voters or nonvoters, vote switchers or nonswitchers, and the distribution of voters who favour the left, the middle, and the right of the political spectrum.

Psychology Classifying patients as mentally ill or mentally healthy, or differentiating between leaders and nonleaders in group decision-making.

Sociology Attempts to distinguish between delinquent and nondelinquent behaviour.

2. COMPARISON WITH MULTIPLE REGRESSION ANALYSIS

Like multiple regression analysis, discriminant analysis has an ability to deal with multiple independent variables simultaneously. So, if your dependent variable has two, three, or four categories, and your independent variables are ratio variables, and you wish to assess the extent to which you can correctly classify category membership on the dependent measure, consider using discriminant function analysis. And, as with regression analysis, if you wish to use nominal or ordinal independent variables, it is possible to do so (using dummy-coded variables) so long as caution is exercised in interpreting the results.

The coefficients computed are based on a regression-like linear equation:

$$D = B_0 + B_1 X_1 + B_2 X_2 + \ldots + B_k X_k$$

The X values are the values of the independent variables and the B values are the coefficients associated with each independent variable, weighted to maximize the prediction of D, the categories of the dependent variable. The B values are weighted to maximize the ratio of the between-groups sum of squares to the within-groups sum of squares. The output for the analysis will display the discriminant function score for each case. The score for each case is derived by plugging in the observed values for each variable and multiplying it by the coefficient. Suppose the discriminant equation was as follows:

$$D = .013 + .003(X_1) + .004(X_2) + .078(X_3) + .056(X_4)$$

Table 17.11 displays the values for each variable, the coefficients, and the resulting discriminant score for the first case in the file.

Discriminant scores are calculated for each case, and each case is then classified into one of the groups (participating or not participating in post-secondary education). The printed output will indicate the actual

TABLE 17.11	CALCULATING THE DISCRIMINANT SCORE, CASE 1		
	VARIABLE	OBSERVED VALUE	COEFFICIENT	DISCRIMINANT SCORE
D	Dependent variable*	1		
	Constant		.013	.013
X1	Grade 11 average	72.6	.003	.218
X2	Family SES score	47.0	.004	.188
X3	Family size	3	.078	.234
X4	Siblings post-secondary	0	.056	.000
	Sum of values, Case # 1			.653

* Dependent variable is "Participating" or "Not Participating" in post-secondary education.

group each case belongs to, and asterisks are used to indicate those cases that were misclassified.

3. PRESENTING AND INTERPRETING RESULTS

A basic statistic provided by discriminant analysis is the percentage of cases that can be classified correctly using information from the combination of independent variables. The statistic calculated is similar to that of **Lambda**, which was described in the section dealing with contingency table analysis (see Chapter 8). You may recall that Lambda computes the error reduction in estimating a dependent variable, given knowledge of an independent variable. In our example, using the computed discriminant function equation, we determine that 85.2% of the cases were correctly grouped according to the discriminant function analysis.

As with regression analysis, the computed coefficients are available in standardized and unstandardized forms. The unstandardized coefficients are used when calculating the discriminant scores for each case; when the researcher wants to compare the relative impact of each variable, standardized coefficients are used (this is to take into account the different ranges of the variables). Indeed, if there were two categories in the dependent variable, we would have achieved similar results had we used regression analysis. The *b* coefficients in regression analysis will have a similar ratio to the *B* discriminant coefficients. However, where there are three or more categories in the dependent variable, the results are different.

Table 17.12 provides a sample of the way in which discriminant analyses can be presented.

Table 17.13 summarizes some of the characteristics of each of the techniques considered in this chapter.

The table on the inside cover of the text identifies the SPSS techniques and their associated levels of measurement. This table should be consulted when deciding which form of analysis would be most appropriate for your project.

TABLE 17.12	DISCRIMINANT ANALYSIS, SAMPLE PRESENTATION		
ACTUAL GROUP	NUMBER OF CASES	PREDICTED GROUP MEMBERSHIP	
		1	2
Participate (1)	261	221	40
Not participate (2)	83	11	72
TOTAL	344	232	112

Percentage of "grouped" cases correctly classified: 293 out of 344 cases = 85.2%

TABLE 17.13	CHARACTERISTICS OF TWO MULTIVARIATE TECHNIQUES			
TECHNIQUE/ SPSS PROCEDURE	MEASUREMENT/ DISTRIBUTION ASSUMPTIONS	MAJOR STRENGTH	MAJOR WEAKNESS	TYPICAL USE
Multiple Regression REGRESSION	Ratio level on all variables; use dummy variables for nominal independent variables; assumes normal distribution of all variables	Dealing with multiple variables simultaneously, with modest number of cases; predictive equations	Instability of weightings from study to study if independent variables share much common variance	Nonexperimental designs; particularly used in survey research and in nonreactive research designs
Discriminant Function Analysis DISCRIMINANT	Nominal dependent; ratio independent variables; like regression, can use dummy independent variables; normal distribution of independent variables; population covariance matrices must be equal	Does regression-type analysis using a nominal dependent variable; provides a measure of predictive accuracy of model	Like regression, an instability of weightings assigned if the independent variables share much common variance	Nonexperimental designs

E. KEY POINTS

To *establish a causal relationship*, the researcher must demonstrate that:

(i) the variables are associated;

(ii) they are in a plausible causal sequence; and

(iii) they are not spuriously connected.

In *nonexperimental research*, a variety of techniques are used to test for intervening and for source of spuriousness variables. These include the following SPSS procedures: CROSSTABS, MEANS, CORRELATIONS, and PARTIAL CORR.

The procedure for testing models includes:

(i) showing that the original relationship exists (*X-Y* relation);

(ii) rerunning the relationship between *X* and *Y* controlling for either the proposed intervening variable or the source of spuriousness;

(iii) applying Jackson's rule of thirds to the result. Only if the original relationship decreases/disappears is there support for the proposed intervening or source of spuriousness model.

A logic similar to that employed when testing three-variable causal models can be used to test four-variable causal models.

In a causal chain the correlations between adjacent variables should be higher than the correlations between non-adjacent variables; the weakest correlation should be between the variables farthest apart in the chain.

Selection of appropriate multivariate technique should be based on the level of measurement achieved on relevant variables and on what the analysis is attempting to reveal.

Multiple regression provides the researcher with:

(i) estimates of the relative importance of the independent variables in bringing about changes in the dependent variable; and

(ii) an equation that describes the relationship.

Dummy-coded independent variables can be used to include nominal variables in multiple regression analysis.

Beta weights refer to the weightings of standardized variables; *b* coefficients refer to the weightings of non-standardized variables.

Discriminant function analysis is used in situations in which the dependent variable is measured at the nominal or ordinal level. This procedure provides weightings maximizing the likelihood of correctly predicting the category of the dependent variable each case will fall into.

F. KEY TERMS

b coefficient	Jackson's rule of thirds	Partial correlations
Beta weight	Lambda	R^2
Discriminant function analysis	Linear regression equation	Source of spuriousness
Dummy variable	Multicollinearity	
Intervening variable	Multiple regression analysis	

THE RESEARCH REPORT

However well designed and well executed a research project, its impact will depend, above all, on the quality of the written report. This chapter will present some suggestions for the organization and presentation of a research report.

A. GENERAL ORIENTATION

1. AUDIENCE

Reports are written for a variety of audiences, and this fact should be taken into account when preparing one. If a report is intended for a professional journal, then it should be organized in a manner similar to material found in the journal to which the report is to be submitted. If the audience is a nontechnical one, then the report should avoid the use of technical terminology.

Most often, it is best to write for the general audience, to assume no prior knowledge of the project, and to convey ideas clearly and simply. The student submitting a paper for a course requirement is well advised to write not for the professor but in a manner that any intelligent person would be able to follow. One hint is to write for your "Aunt Martha" or your "Uncle John," not for your professor. Your aunt and uncle have no knowledge of your research project, are not social scientists, in fact never went to university, but they are very smart; if you explain things clearly they will understand your project. A side benefit of this is that your professor will also be able to figure it out!

Why would writing for an aunt or uncle be helpful? There is a tendency when preparing a report to use too many computer terms, to use technical jargon, and to fail to explain either the logic behind your

research design or the logic behind the inferences you have made from your data. If you write for Aunt Martha, you will be less likely to fall into some of these traps. And, in the process, you will probably write a better report, whether it is intended for a journal, a term paper, or for the president of your company.

If you know your audience, you will also know what questions will come to their minds and you will be able to address issues of concern to them. Above all, explain your points clearly and fully: do not assume specialized knowledge on the part of your reader.

2. STYLE

Edit your material carefully. Read it slowly, perhaps out loud, and eliminate redundant words, sentences, and paragraphs. Editing should shorten the document considerably. Do not sacrifice readability and brevity for the sake of saving a nice turn-of-phrase. Keep it short.

It is a good idea to provide headings and subheadings to help guide your reader through the material. Footnotes should be used when technical details that would detract from the flow of the main text are nonetheless required.

Tables should include sufficient information to permit the reader to read tables rather than text. Conversely, a reader should be able to get the main points of your findings without studying your tables in detail. Generally, it is preferable to locate tables and figures on separate sheets and place them on the page following the first reference to them in the text. In manuscript preparation, tables are also placed on separate sheets so that the editor can move the material to the nearest convenient spot in the text.

3. AVOIDING PLAGIARISM

In writing papers you must scrupulously avoid plagiarism. **Plagiarism** is the unacknowledged borrowing of other authors' ideas or words. Most academic disciplines have now adopted the method of referencing used by the American Psychological Association. The APA requires you to identify the source from which the material has been taken in the body of the text, and to include the complete bibliographic information in the list of references at the end of the paper. This is the referencing method used throughout this text.

A. SHORT QUOTATIONS

When fewer than forty words are being directly quoted, the material should be enclosed in quotation marks, and, after the quotation, reference is made to the name of the author, year of publication, and the page number. For example: "The difference between mores and folkways lies in the nature of the reaction the violation of the norm produces, and not in the content of the rule" (Teevan, 1989, p. 19).

B. LONG QUOTATIONS

When forty or more words are directly quoted, the material is indented an additional five spaces on both the right and left side of the page, and the material is single spaced, with a reference to the author's name, date, and the page number at the end of the quotation.

C. PARAPHRASED MATERIAL

When using paraphrased material by borrowing ideas that you are not quoting directly, you are nonetheless required to cite your source. Once again, you include the author's name, and the year of publication, but not the page number.

D. MULTIPLE AUTHORS' REFERENCES

When there is more than one author, the first reference includes all the names; subsequent references to their work use only the first author's name, followed by "et al."

E. REFERENCE LIST

At the end of the paper provide a reference list that includes all references cited in alphabetical order. Note how books and articles are cited. Additional examples may be noted in the bibliography included at the end of this text.

> Breton, R. (1989). Quebec sociology: Agendas from society or from sociologists? *Canadian Review of Sociology and Anthropology, 26*(3), 557–570.

> Rosenthal, R. (1966). *Experimenter Effects in Behavioral Research*. New York: Century.

4. AVOIDING SEXIST LANGUAGE

In the last few years, there has been an increasing awareness of sexist language. We will briefly look at some of the major pitfalls in gender references.

A. THE PRONOUN PROBLEM

The **pronoun problem** encourages stereotypic thinking by referring to doctors and managers as *he*, nurses as *she*. There are a number of solutions to the pronoun problem. To illustrate, suppose we have the following sentence:

"A doctor has to be especially careful, otherwise he can be sued for malpractice." (The problem is characterizing the doctor as a male.)

This sentence can be changed in any one of the following ways:

- "A doctor has to be especially careful, otherwise he or she can be sued for malpractice." (A somewhat awkward solution, but all right if not used too frequently.)

- "Doctors have to be especially careful, otherwise they can be sued for malpractice." (This is a common solution: converting to the plural form avoids the use of *he or she*.)

- "If not especially careful, a doctor can be sued for malpractice." (The last sentence avoids the pronoun all together by reconstructing the sentence.)

B. THE MAN PROBLEM

Traditionally, many words and expressions in the English language used *man* or *men* to refer to persons of either gender. In a manner similar to the pronoun problem, such usage may unintentionally suggest, for example, that a *foreman* should be a male. Table 18.1 includes a few examples and some alternative forms that could be considered.

C. THE NON-PARALLEL CONSTRUCTION PROBLEM

Frequently, language can put one gender at a disadvantage. For example, the male can be referred to more formally than the female, suggesting a power or importance differential. More generally, non-parallel constructions can result in confusion or misrepresentation by violating the principle that parts of a sentence that are parallel in meaning should be parallel in structure. Table 18.2 provides some illustrations of non-parallel gender references and more appropriate parallel forms.

TABLE 18.1 NEUTRALIZING GENDER TERMS

TRADITIONAL USAGE	ALTERNATIVE FORMS
Chairman	Chair, chairperson, coordinator, head, leader, moderator, presiding officer
Clergyman	Cleric, member of the clergy, minister
Fisherman	Fisher
Foreman	Boss, supervisor
Mailman	Letter carrier, postal worker
Mankind	Human beings, humanity, people
Manmade	Artificial, manufactured, synthetic
Manpower	Personnel, workers
Salesman	Sales agent, salesperson
To man	To operate, to staff
Workman	Employee, labourer, worker

Source: Modified version of a similar listing found in Diana Hacker (1990). *A Canadian Writer's Reference.* Scarborough: Nelson Canada, p. 103.

TABLE 18.2 NON-PARALLEL AND PARALLEL GENDER REFERENCES

INAPPROPRIATE USAGE (Non-Parallel)	ALTERNATIVE FORMS (Parallel)
Man and wife	Husband and wife
Men and ladies	Men and women
Men's and ladies' teams	Men's and women's teams
Males and women	Males and females

B. ORGANIZATION

A paper should be organized into sections. An effort should be made to cover the material discussed under each of the following headings.

1. INTRODUCTION

The introduction should inform your reader what the project is about, indicate what general approach has been used to solve the problem it tackles, and suggest what critical problems the project raises. Raise interesting questions and unresolved issues that you propose to answer in your research.

2. REVIEW OF THE LITERATURE

The **review of the literature** tries to provide an overview of the "state of scientific knowledge" in your area of study. Consider reviewing the theoretical models that are appropriate and the empirical findings that bear on the particular relationships you will be examining or, if such material is not available, then give the reader some sense of what variables have been related to the major dependent variable in your study. The review should highlight those areas in which there are inconsistencies in the conclusions of other studies and indicate which of these inconsistencies you intend to address.

Generally, it is best not to present summaries of articles, but rather focus on what the consensus is on the relation between particular variables and the dependent variable. For example, suppose that you were examining factors related to "political conservatism." It would be useful for your reader to know whether there is any agreement in the scientific literature on whether "conservatism" is related to such variables as age, sex, rural/urban backgrounds, and socioeconomic status. If there are inconsistencies, have you any observations as to why they emerged? Different regions, different measurement or analytic procedures, or systematic variations in the compositions of the populations studied might all account for the variations between studies. If inconsistencies are present, these can be noted, and you can heighten your reader's interest in your project by proposing to answer some of the questions that have been raised.

Chapter 12 contains a discussion of how a review of literature can be developed and presented. The reader is referred to that chapter for additional suggestions.

3. HYPOTHESES AND RESEARCH DESIGN

The Review of Literature section should lead into a section defining what hypotheses, questions, or relationships are to be examined. These should be precisely stated and connected to the literature of the discipline. It is usually best to diagram the causal models that are being evaluated in the research. Not only does this permit the presentation of hypotheses clearly but, by drawing in causal arrows and "greater than" and "less than" symbols, additional precision is achieved. Figure 18.1 presents the diagrams used by Michelle Broussard (1991) in her study of unwanted intimacy.

The rationale given for the design selected should state the advantages the chosen design has over alternative designs. What designs have typically been used by other investigators looking at similar relationships?

4. DATA-COLLECTION PROCEDURES

Having determined the questions and the design, the next step is to describe the measurement, sample selection, and data-collection procedures. In describing a questionnaire it is not necessary to discuss each question. Rather, focus attention on non-standard items and, if possible, include a copy of the questionnaire in an appendix to the report. Any comments on problems in data collection should be mentioned at this point in the report.

5. DESCRIPTION OF THE SAMPLE

The reader should be introduced to the results by reporting some of the background characteristics of the individuals involved in the study: sex distribution, rural/urban location, and average age might all be reported if judged to be relevant by the

FIGURE 18.1   CAUSAL MODEL FOR UNWANTED INTIMACY STUDY

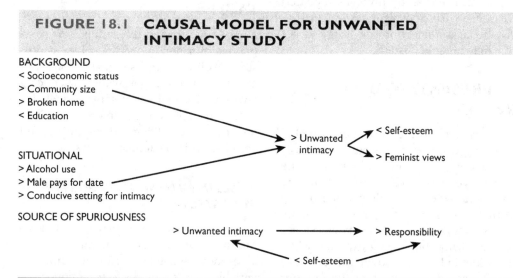

BACKGROUND
< Socioeconomic status
> Community size
> Broken home
< Education

SITUATIONAL
> Alcohol use
> Male pays for date
> Conducive setting for intimacy

> Unwanted intimacy

< Self-esteem
> Feminist views

SOURCE OF SPURIOUSNESS
> Unwanted intimacy → > Responsibility
< Self-esteem

Source: Adapted from Michelle Broussard (1991). "Unwanted Intimacy in Female University Students." Antigonish: St. Francis Xavier University, Research Methods Paper. (Other students who worked on the project were Suzanne Hawco, Marybeth Ryan, and Gertrude Morris). Cited with permission.

researcher. If efforts are to be made to assure the representativeness of the sample, this is the appropriate stage in the report that such material would be introduced. If you know from census material, for example, that 54% of the region's population over the age of 15 is female, and your sample is 59% female, this fact should be noted. In experimental studies a detailed description of the method of randomization used should be included.

6. DESCRIPTION OF INDEXES, MEASUREMENT PROCEDURES

A description and evaluation of indexes constructed and a preliminary report on the mean results should be made at this point. If you have used a previously used index, comparisons can be made between the mean results of your study and those of other researchers. Details for the measurement of other key variables should also be included. If the study involves repeated measures, what steps were taken to assure that the measurement process itself was not contaminating the results?

7. PRESENTING BASIC RESULTS

The variations in the dependent variable should be explored at this point. Any basic runs leading up to an exploration of the formal hypotheses of the study should be presented. Where possible, use **summary tables** to compress the results of many analyses into one table. Remember to focus on the relationships being explored when reporting findings. If you are using tests of significance, report whether the findings are statistically significant; if a particular relationship is not statistically significant, is

there a trend in the data? It is misleading simply to report "significant" findings. As noted earlier, relationships that are not statistically significant may well have substantive significance.

In small sample studies, it is particularly important to report on whether the data trend is in the direction predicted by the various research hypotheses. Generally, SPSS output is not in an appropriate form for presentation. Tables placed in a final report will need to be reformatted, and their format should conform to those shown throughout this book or be modelled on those presented in journal articles or books. While it is possible to control the SPSS output format, the beginning researcher will probably find it easier to retype the tables. In some cases, if the report is being prepared with a word processor, it will be possible to copy the data into a Word document and thus avoid having to re-enter the various numbers.

8. ORGANIZING SUMMARY TABLES

A challenge for the researcher is to compress information into as few tables as possible. Well-designed summary tables can add a lot to your report without sacrificing anything. Let us look at some formats for reporting single-variable information, contingency tables, differences of means, and correlations into summary tables.

A. SUMMARIZING UNIVARIATE STATISTICS

Table 18.3 presents one way of compressing the information on a number of variables into a single table. Note that nominal variables can simply have the frequencies listed for each category. These kinds of listings are useful in summarizing descriptive

TABLE 18.3 SUMMARIZING UNIVARIATE STATISTICS

A. NOMINAL/ORDINAL VARIABLES	NUMBER	PERCENTAGE
Gender		
Male	82	48.0
Female	89	52.0
Status		
Student	26	15.2
Retired	2	1.2
Unemployed, looking for work	13	7.6
Unemployed, not looking for work	4	2.3
Employed part-time	19	11.1
Employed full-time	107	62.6
Size of home community:		
Under 5,000	17	9.0
5,000 – 19,999	24	12.7
20,000 – 99,999	16	8.5
100,000 – 999,999	108	57.1
1,000,000 or more	24	12.7

B. RATIO VARIABLES	MEAN	STANDARD DEVIATION	NUMBER OF CASES
Age	29.60	14.70	183
Income	$43,257.00	16,419.00	77
Seniority	8.87	3.76	104
Number of children	1.37	1.06	78

characteristics of the cohort studied. Ratio variables can be summarized by including the mean values and standard deviations.

B. SUMMARIZING CONTINGENCY TABLES

Table 18.4 shows one method for reporting a series of contingency table results (CROSSTABS procedure in SPSS). Note that only the percentage of smokers is reported, along with the number of cases in the column, the Chi-Square probability, and whether the results have a trend in the predicted direction (+) or in the opposite direction (–).

C. SUMMARIZING MEAN VALUES FOR A DEPENDENT VARIABLE

Table 18.5 provides an illustration of how you can compress a number of analyses of ratio variables into one table. The analysis by Annette Fougere compares the academic performance of Grade 12 students who did or did not regularly eat breakfast. Note that Table 18.5 includes the mean grade performance, standard deviations, number of cases, probability level, and an indication of whether the data have a trend in the predicted direction (+) or in the opposite one (–).

TABLE 18.4   SMOKING BEHAVIOUR BY SELECTED INDEPENDENT VARIABLES

INDEPENDENT VARIABLES	PERCENTAGE OF SMOKERS	NUMBER OF CASES: COLUMN TOTAL	PROBABILITY (CHI-SQUARE)	TREND
Residence				
On campus	19.8	101	.93283	?
Off campus	20.4	54		
SES of Father				
Low SES	22.2	54	.61304	+
Mid to high SES	18.8	101		
Respondent's Age				
19 or younger	19.7	76	.93597	+
20 or older	20.3	79		
Level of Self-esteem				
Low	19.5	77	.87237	−
High	20.5	78		
Level of Stress				
Little	19.4	67	.90052	−
Much	18.6	86		
Home Community				
Under 30,000	17.8	118	.22068	−
30,000 or more	27.0	37		
Gender				
Male	17.6	68	.51734	+
Female	21.8	87		
Type of Program				
Arts	23.3	60	.48859	+
Science	18.7	91		
Exercise/Week				
Less than 3 times	29.6	71	.00613	+
3 or more times	11.9	84		
Father Smokes				
Yes	29.3	41	.08363	+
No	16.7	114		
Mother Smokes				
Yes	45.5	33	.00004	+
No	13.1	122		

Source: Adapted from Michelle Lee (1992). "Smoking Behaviours." Antigonish: St. Francis Xavier University, Research Methods Paper. Cited with permission.

TABLE 18.5	GRADE PERFORMANCE OF GRADE 12 STUDENTS					
INDEPENDENT VARIABLES		MEAN	STANDARD DEVIATION	NUMBER OF CASES	TEST OF SIGNIFICANCE	TREND
Eats breakfast	No	68.9	12.7	46	.0003	+
	Yes	76.3	10.0	95		
Breakfast eaten in last 7 days	No	69.5	9.9	39	.0049	+
	Yes	75.4	11.5	106		
Breakfast maker	Others	72.7	14.4	42	.2731	−
	Self	75.1	10.0	85		
Lunch maker	Others	73.8	11.7	105	.8412	*
	Self	74.3	11.6	29		
Supper maker	Others	74.1	11.6	117	.6416	*
	Self	72.9	10.6	27		
Gender	Male	71.4	11.7	85	.0026	+
	Female	77.2	10.0	58		
Community size	≤5000	73.7	11.9	103	.8024	−
	>5000	74.2	10.2	42		
Career plans	university	78.2	9.0	92	.0000	+
	non-university	66.2	11.1	53		
Extracurricular activities	No	70.9	12.0	70	.0015	−
	Yes	76.8	9.9	74		
After school job	No	73.4	11.8	88	.5825	−
	Yes	74.5	10.8	57		

+ Trend predicted correctly − Trend predicted incorrectly * Trend not predicted

Source: Adapted from Annette Fougere (1992). "Effects of Eating Breakfast on Grade Performance." Antigonish: St. Francis Xavier University, Research Methods Paper. Cited with permission.

D. SUMMARIZING CORRELATIONS

Table 18.6 shows a correlation matrix for variables related to first-year university performance. Note that a report on many relationships can be compressed into such a table. By using asterisks it is also possible to indicate which of the correlations are statistically significant.

9. USING GRAPHS, CHARTS

Where feasible, it is a good idea to present data using graphs and charts to make a greater visual impact on the reader. Figures 18.2 and 18.3 show some alternative forms of reporting information. Figure 18.2 uses a bar graph to show for each gender the relationship between age at first sexual intercourse and country of origin. Respondents' countries of origin are grouped into two categories: respondents from Canada and New Zealand are grouped together and compared to respondents from Australia.

Figure 18.3 uses a plot to show the relation between prestige and income. The visual information conveys much about the

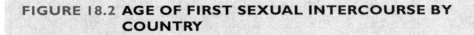

TABLE 18.6 CORRELATIONS BETWEEN FIRST-YEAR UNIVERSITY AVERAGE, AVERAGE HIGH-SCHOOL GRADE, AND ENGLISH HIGH-SCHOOL GRADE (N = 3617)

CORRELATIONS	FIRST-YEAR UNIVERSITY AVERAGE	AVERAGE HIGH-SCHOOL GRADE	ENGLISH HIGH-SCHOOL GRADE
First-year university average	1.000		
Average high-school grade	.573	1.000	
English high-school grade	.464	.662	1.000

Source: Winston Jackson.

FIGURE 18.2 AGE OF FIRST SEXUAL INTERCOURSE BY COUNTRY

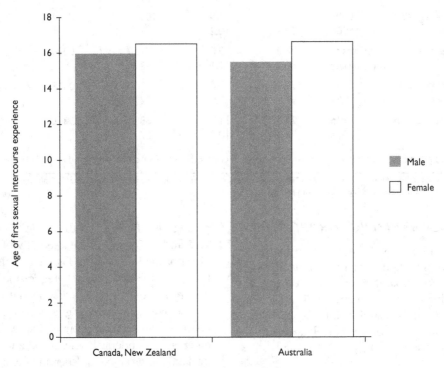

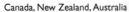

FIGURE 18.3 SAMPLE PLOT

Prestige rating by income

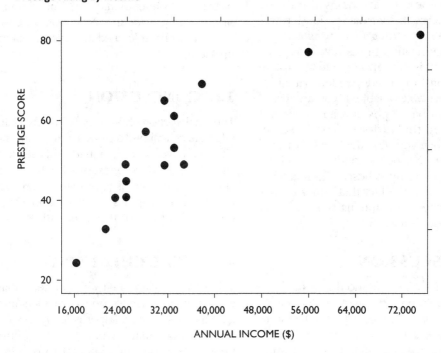

Correlation = .867 (Fictitious data)

strength of the association between the two variables. To the seasoned researcher, the correlation of .87 between the two variables reveals much, but for most readers the plot of the information reveals much more.

> *To perform this analysis using SPSS see the PLOT procedure in Appendix A.*

10. EVALUATING HYPOTHESES, MODELS

The reader should now be well prepared for, and anticipating, the results of the hypothesis/model testing. If diagrams described the original relationships, they should be employed once again when the findings are reported. If you are testing a theory and have derived a hypothesis, then you should report the finding of the test, even if the relationship is not statistically significant. In cases in which you are investigating alternative explanations for some relationship you have initially assumed to be statistically significant, you would continue to test the alternative explanations only if the relationship turned out to be statistically significant. You would, of course, include the intervening variable model in your report; however, if no relationship has emerged, you would not proceed with an evaluation of the alternative explanations—you have no relationship to explain. All you would do is note in your report that the alternative explanations will not be explored, since the original relationship was not sufficiently strong. If it turns out that the primary relationship is not statistically significant, it is then appropriate to explore the relationship of independent variables to the dependent variable. If you are forced to this "fall back" position and have not established the various hypotheses in advance, then you should indicate that your explorations are being conducted without the guidance of hypotheses. The reader is then alerted to the fact that you are on a hunting expedition. Hunting is fine so long as the reader is alerted.

11. DISCUSSION

At this point an effort should be made to tie the whole project together. References should be made to the review of literature section once again, showing how the results of your research fit into the general picture. Such references will also help tie the paper together, reminding the reader of the problems that the project raised initially. In what areas does your research support the general view? In what areas does it not? Where are there discrepancies and what are some of the possible explanations? This discussion should provide the reader with a sense of what has been learned and what remains problematic.

12. CONCLUSION

The final section should try to briefly state what the central problem was and what conclusions have been identified. This section can also include suggestions for how the current project might have been improved and what other issues the researcher identifies as worthy of further exploration.

13. FINAL CHECKLIST

Table 18.7 contains a checklist of items that authors might wish to use to provide some guidance for when a paper is ready to submit. Pay particular attention to transitions between sections, and attempt to provide a succinct summary for the review of literature section and the discussion of findings sections.

TABLE 18.7   CHECKLIST FOR WHEN YOUR PAPER IS READY TO HAND IN

1. Title	Short, informative title should be selected.
2. Abstract	If needed, keep to one-half a page.
3. Introduction	Excite interest of reader; indicate why the topic is of interest; normally the introduction is short; keep literature references to a minimum.
4. Review of Literature	Include summary table if possible. Generally best to organize the review around findings by variable not article summaries. Should anticipate hypotheses (diagrams) to follow.
5. Statement of Hypotheses	Include causal model diagrams or formal statements of hypotheses to be tested. Diagrams force precision.
6. Methodology	Description of variables, measurement procedures, sampling, and analytical procedures identified.
7. Results	Provide a description of sample studied; include summary tables for major hypotheses tested.
8. Discussion	Link findings of study to the body of literature reviewed earlier. What questions remain? Which direction do you see as the most productive for researchers to pursue?
9. Conclusions	Summarize the major findings of the study. Keep this section short.
10. References	Are in-text style references consistent? Are all in-text references included in the "References Cited" section at the end of the paper? Have you consistently used the APA referencing format?
11. Spell Check	Run the paper through a spelling checker to catch any errors.
12. Format	Examine the paper to be certain you are not breaking tables in the middle; use different-sized fonts for subtitles.
13. View Document	Use word processor View Document feature to check on page layout.
14. Print	Print your paper!
15. Proofread	A final check before you submit it.

C. KEY POINTS

Research reports are written for different audiences. Be sensitive to your intended audience so that your organization and language are suitable.

Strive to write crisply, clearly, and briefly.

Be certain to cite sources for your quotations and ideas properly.

Avoid the use of stereotyped gender references. When this may be a problem, consider pluralizing the noun or reconstructing the sentence to avoid the use of the pronoun entirely.

Where appropriate, use diagrams to communicate research hypotheses effectively.

Summary tables and charts should contain sufficient information to permit the reader to reconstruct the original tables from which the summary tables have been constructed. Use summary tables to condense many tables efficiently into a few tables.

Use graphs, charts, and plots to simplify the presentation of your results.

D. KEY TERMS

Plagiarism

Pronoun problem

Review of literature

Summary tables

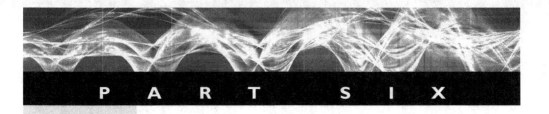

APPENDICES

*Appendix A contains an introduction to analyzing data,
creating new variables, and working with output using SPSS
for Windows (versions 10 to 14).*

USING SPSS FOR WINDOWS

If you are just starting to work with SPSS, it would be a good idea to review the material in Chapter 16 since it includes an introduction to the Statistical Package for the Social Sciences (SPSS) and reviews the procedures for logging onto the computer and accessing an SPSS system file. This Appendix will provide guidelines for the basic procedures most likely to be used by the social science researcher. Sample output will be annotated in the Appendix to assist you in using SPSS.

In addition to the instructions on how to begin an SPSS session included in Chapter 16, you might want to review Chapter 17, which discusses multivariate procedures. There are a number of manuals available from SPSS that present many additional features and options for the various procedures.

A. METHODS OF ISSUING SPSS COMMANDS

SPSS procedures can be run using either a **point-and-click** method or by entering **syntax** commands. Many users find that both techniques are useful. Beginning users typically find the point-and-click method easiest. We will primarily focus on this method in Appendix A.

After each procedure is completed, the results are sent to the Output Viewer that is automatically displayed on your monitor; you can save, edit, and print your output from the Output Viewer. You can also directly copy the output to a word-processor file from the Output Viewer. We will begin by examining the fundamentals of submitting commands to SPSS, then discuss how to work with output, followed by a presentation of the basic procedures that have been covered in this text.

1. POINT-AND-CLICK COMMANDS

The toolbar across the top of the SPSS Data Editor screen provides the starting point for issuing analysis commands to SPSS. One can draw samples, select cases, sort cases, add or delete variables, and initiate a vast range of statistical procedures by clicking on the appropriate toolbar item. The main statistical procedures are listed on the inside back cover of this text. To access each of them, the user simply clicks an item on the toolbar and follows the sequence to identify the desired procedure.

After a procedure has been selected, an SPSS procedure screen will appear and the user simply uses the mouse to select variables and move them into the appropriate analysis boxes shown on the window. A few general tips in using the method are listed below:

- to illustrate an SPSS procedure window, the CROSSTABS one is shown in Figure A.1

- to select one variable, simply click on it

- to select multiple variables from a list, hold down the Ctrl button and click on the variables

- to select several variables in a sequence, click on the first one in the sequence, move the mouse to the last one and, holding the Shift key down, click on that item; all the variables between the two clicked on will then be highlighted and can then be moved to an analysis box by clicking the ▶ key

FIGURE A.1 **CROSSTABS SCREEN**

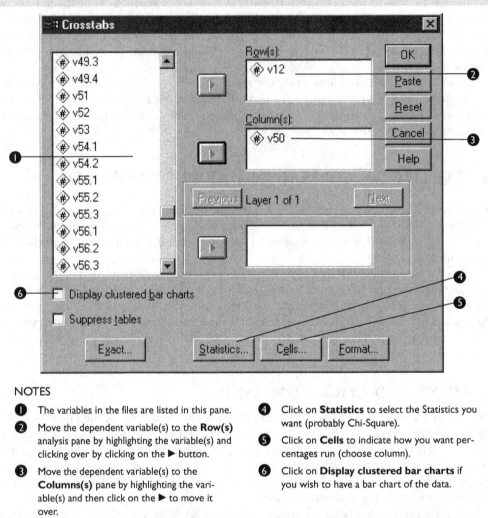

NOTES

❶ The variables in the files are listed in this pane.

❷ Move the dependent variable(s) to the **Row(s)** analysis pane by highlighting the variable(s) and clicking over by clicking on the ▶ button.

❸ Move the dependent variable(s) to the **Columns(s)** pane by highlighting the variable(s) and then click on the ▶ to move it over.

❹ Click on **Statistics** to select the Statistics you want (probably Chi-Square).

❺ Click on **Cells** to indicate how you want percentages run (choose column).

❻ Click on **Display clustered bar charts** if you wish to have a bar chart of the data.

• to move quickly through a variables list, click and hold down the scroll bar button (to the right of the variables list) and slowly drag the scroll bar button down

• click on the various "Options" and "Statistics" boxes to see what additional procedures are available within each procedure

2. SYNTAX COMMANDS

To enter syntax commands, the user brings up a syntax editor screen, types commands into the screen, and then submits the commands to SPSS for processing. To bring up a Syntax Editor screen, click on **File/New/Syntax** on the toolbar. An SPSS Syntax box will appear at the bottom of the screen, and if you click on it, the Syntax Editor screen will appear. You then type SPSS commands into the screen and, when ready to submit, point-and-click on **Run** on the window's toolbar. See Figure A.2 for a copy of the Syntax window.

It is a good idea to retain a copy of the syntax commands used when running an analysis. When you exit from SPSS you will be asked if you want to keep a copy of the syntax file. If you respond **Yes,** then you will be prompted for a name for the file. These files use the file extension .sps.

Another feature of syntax files is that when using the point-and-click method you can also click on **Paste** before you click on **OK** when running procedures, and this will paste into a syntax editor file the syntax commands for the procedure you have just invoked. These syntax files are worth retaining, since if you discover errors in your data, you can fix them and then quickly rerun the analysis by simply resubmitting the commands contained in the syntax file.

If you want to list out several variables for the first 25 cases, this can be done using the LIST command in a syntax file. This procedure is available only as a syntax command and will be useful when confirming that various RECODE, IF, or COMPUTE commands are working properly. (See LIST procedure.)

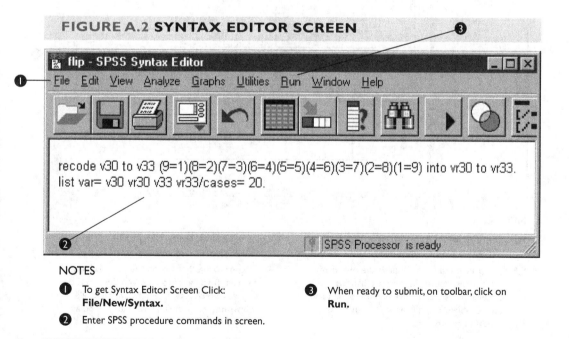

FIGURE A.2 SYNTAX EDITOR SCREEN

```
recode v30 to v33 (9=1)(8=2)(7=3)(6=4)(5=5)(4=6)(3=7)(2=8)(1=9) into vr30 to vr33.
list var= v30 vr30 v33 vr33/cases= 20.
```

NOTES

❶ To get Syntax Editor Screen Click: **File/New/Syntax.**

❷ Enter SPSS procedure commands in screen.

❸ When ready to submit, on toolbar, click on **Run.**

3. WORKING WITH OUTPUT VIEWER

The results of each analysis are sent to the Output Viewer. You can edit, print, and save output from the Viewer. Figure A.3 shows output as it appears in the Output Viewer for an analysis of suicide thoughts by gender. Output Viewer provides two panes: (1) the outline pane, on the left, lists items in the output and you can click on these to move, save, or delete them; and (2) the contents pane, on the right side, shows the output from the analysis.

Some tips for using the Output Viewer are:

• To go directly to a section of the output, simply click on the name of the section on the outline pane (the screen on the left side).

FIGURE A.3 **OUTPUT VIEWER SCREEN**

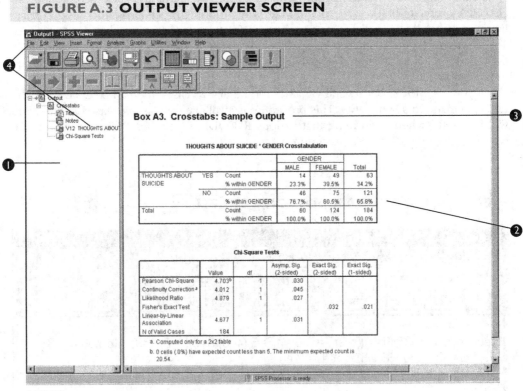

Box A3. Crosstabs: Sample Output

THOUGHTS ABOUT SUICIDE * GENDER Crosstabulation

			GENDER MALE	GENDER FEMALE	Total
THOUGHTS ABOUT SUICIDE	YES	Count	14	49	63
		% within GENDER	23.3%	39.5%	34.2%
	NO	Count	46	75	121
		% within GENDER	76.7%	60.5%	65.8%
Total		Count	60	124	184
		% within GENDER	100.0%	100.0%	100.0%

Chi-Square Tests

	Value	df	Asymp. Sig. (2-sided)	Exact Sig. (2-sided)	Exact Sig. (1-sided)
Pearson Chi-Square	4.703[b]	1	.030		
Continuity Correction[a]	4.012	1	.045		
Likelihood Ratio	4.879	1	.027		
Fisher's Exact Test				.032	.021
Linear-by-Linear Association	4.677	1	.031		
N of Valid Cases	184				

a. Computed only for a 2x2 table

b. 0 cells (.0%) have expected count less than 5. The minimum expected count is 20.54.

NOTES

 The left pane indicates elements; click on an element to have it highlighted.

❷ The pane on the right displays the results of the analysis; to edit the results (changing width of columns, etc., click anywhere on output and then double click on it; now you can change widths of columns, etc.)

❸ To add your table title click on title and then double click; type in new title.

❹ To copy to another file, on left pane click on element(s) you wish to copy, and then on toolbar click **Edit/Copy Objects**; switch to file you wish to copy the material into and do a **Copy/Paste**.

- To delete a section of output, simply click on the item on the left screen and press the delete button. You will generally want to get rid of the "case processing summary."

- To print one or more sections, click on the items on the left pane, and then print the results (you can preview what will be printed by clicking on the preview icon).

- You can move objects around by clicking and dragging to new locations on your output.

- You have various templates available to choose the format of your output; to see options available do the following:

    Double Click on the table (this activates the Pivot Table);

    Click on **Format**;

    Click on **Tablelooks**.

    A number of optional formats will be presented and you can choose from among those presented.

- You can highlight a section(s) on the left pane and then **Edit/Copy** the material into the clipboard, then bring up your word processor and **Edit/Paste** the material into the new file.

- If you want to attach your name as a header for your output, when you are in the Output Viewer, go to **File/Page Setup/Options** and type in what you want in the header panel. Click on **Make Default** and the header will appear on all your subsequent output.

- On lengthy output you might find that not all the output shows. Double click inside the box containing the output; move the cursor to the bottom of the output and drag the bottom margin down. When you do this, the remainder of the output will show on the screen.

- If you find that there are unwanted page breaks in the output, double click inside the output (you should have a thick border now). The little square box marks page breaks, and you can delete these using the delete or backspace key. Recheck your preview to ensure that any unwanted page breaks are gone before you print.

- When you get errors using the syntax procedure, it is a good idea to read the error carefully and then highlight and delete the error message before you resubmit the job. Note that you can run point-and-click procedures without returning to the Data Editor since the analysis toolbar is at the top of the Output Viewer screen.

- When you exit SPSS you will be asked if you want to save your output viewer file. This file will have an .spo file extension.

B. BASIC SPSS PROCEDURES

There are two basic procedures for examining *individual* variables. When you want a count of the number of cases that fall into each category of a nominal or ordinal variable, use the FREQUENCIES procedure described below. If you have a ratio-level variable and you want to calculate the mean and standard deviation, use the DESCRIPTIVES procedure described below.

When analyzing the relationship *between* variables, there are many procedures that can be used. The beginning researcher is advised, however, to apply the 3M approach (Model, Measurement, Method) to determine which procedure is appropriate given the relationship being examined and the level of measurement involved (see Chapter 16).

The following sections of Appendix A present the basic procedures of SPSS. Each procedure is illustrated with annotations on the sample output that should help the researcher understand and interpret the results of the analysis. The procedures are listed alphabetically to make them easier to find.

1. ANOVA: ANALYSIS OF VARIANCE

Experimental researchers use **an**alysis **of va**riance (ANOVA) when their design has more than one independent variable or has more than two treatment levels. (*T*-tests are typically used in studies with fewer than 30 cases in each of the two groups and when there is one treatment level and one independent variable.) The inclusion of additional complexity is relatively simple and provides an opportunity to explore the interaction of treatment variables (when effects change for different combinations of treatment variables) in influencing the dependent variable.

While regression analysis is appropriate in many situations, there are several situations in which analysis of variance (ANOVA or MANOVA) would be more appropriate than regression analysis. For example, if you had predictor variables that have qualitative differences (three different drugs, for example); or if rather than having a ratio variable measuring the amount of time spent in the hospital, we have a variable that indicates whether the person was hospitalized or treated as an outpatient, we again would probably opt for analysis of variance. In short, if an independent variable is made up of values that differ in *kind* rather than in *quantity*, we would opt for analysis of variance.

A second situation that is better handled with analysis of variance is one in which the relationship between the independent and the dependent variable changes over the continuum. Perhaps the relationship is nonlinear; in that case, analysis of variance should once again be considered as an alternative to regression.

Typically, analysis of variance techniques will be used when:

- an experimental design is being used;

- the dependent variable(s) is (are) measured at the ratio level;

- one or more of the treatment variables are measured at the ratio level and others at the nominal or ordinal levels; note that ratio level independent variables can be identified as covariates;

- you have multiple dependent measures that you want to examine simultaneously (MANOVA);

- in nonexperimental designs, you want to examine whether there are significant interactions among independent variables.

i. *Point-and-Click Method*

- Analyze

- General Linear Model

- Univariate or Simple Factorial

Move the dependent variable and then the variables for the various factors and any *covariates* by clicking on them and then clicking them to their appropriate screens by using the ▶ buttons; you will be prompted to identify the lowest and highest values of treatment values, such as: 0, 2. In this case the implied values include 0, 1, and 2. ANOVA assumes that there are no blank categories, so you will have to RECODE values if there are no values in one of the categories implied by the range indicated.

Click **OK** when you are ready to process the data.

ii. *Sample Output: ANOVA*

Note that the variations that are compared in an analysis of variance are composed of two elements: random error and possible treatment effects. The test that is done compares the ratio in the following way:

$$F = \frac{\text{random error} + \text{possible treatment effects}}{\text{random error}}$$

The interpretation of the results of an ANOVA test is split between a concern for:

- the main effect of treatment variable A (Box A.1 indicates that COUNTRY has a statistically significant main effect on egalitarianism);

- the main effect of treatment variable B (Box A.1 indicates that v50 (gender) does not have a statistically significant main effect on egalitarianism);

- an interaction of the treatment variables (A × B) (the interaction between COUNTRY and GENDER is not statistically significant);

- an error term (within groups): this is the "residual source of variation."

2. COMPUTE: CREATING NEW VARIABLES

COMPUTE allows the researcher to create new variables by performing mathematical operations on variables.

BOX A.1   ANALYSIS OF VARIANCE: SAMPLE OUTPUT

BETWEEN-SUBJECTS FACTORS

	Value Label	N
Name of Country	0 Canada	65
	1 New Zealand	57
	2 Australia	60
Gender	1 Male	59
	2 Female	123

TESTS OF BETWEEN-SUBJECTS EFFECTS
Dependent Variable: EGALITARIANISM

Source	Type III Sum of Squares	df	Mean Square	F	Sig.
Corrected Model	1575.426[a]	5	315.085	4.531	.001
Intercept	139602.183	1	139602.183	2007.419	.000
Country	1194.586	2	597.293	8.589	.000
V50	33.219	1	33.219	.478	.490
Country *V50	125.990	2	62.995	.906	.406
Error	12239.591	176	69.543		
Total	186677.000	182			
Corrected Total	13815.016	181			

a. R Squared = .114 (Adjusted R Squared = .089)

NOTES:
- **1** Degrees of Freedom Column
- **2** F test of significance value
- **3** Test of significance results: needs to be .05 or less to be statistically significant

i. Point-and-Click Method

- Transform

- Compute

As illustrated in Figure A.4, enter the name of the new variable you want to create in the Target Variable window (you will now see a window that allows you to place a variable label on the new variable); now move the cursor to the Numeric Expression window and type in the computational formula you want to use. Enter **OK** and the new variable will be created.

Figure A.4 shows the screen illustrating the creation of a new variable, *famsize*, representing the addition of values in two variables (number of brothers plus number of sisters) plus 1 added to the total. Computations within parentheses are performed first and are used to control the order of the mathematical operations. Make certain that there are an equal number of open and closed parentheses. SPSS employs the following symbols to indicate basic functions:

+ Addition

- Subtraction

* Multiplication

/ Division

** Exponentiation

Many other functions are available to the researcher in SPSS; three commonly used ones include:

RND(var)   rounds to whole number

SUM(var list)   sums values in variable list

MEAN(var list)   mean of values

FIGURE A.4 COMPUTE SCREEN

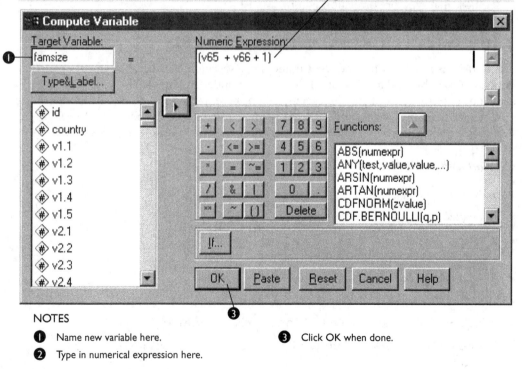

NOTES

❶ Name new variable here.

❷ Type in numerical expression here.

❸ Click OK when done.

3. CORRELATIONS: CORRELATIONAL ANALYSIS

When variables are measured at the ratio level, then various correlational techniques are appropriate. As discussed in Chapter 8, a correlation, or r, measures the strength of an association between two variables. The values can range from +1.00 to –1.00. Typically, they are reported to 2 decimal places, as in .56. Explained variance is the square of the correlation coefficient or r^2.

i. Point-and-Click Method

- Analyze

- Correlate

- Bivariate

The correlation screen will appear. Click on and move variables to the Variable(s) window; for ratio variables you will want **Pearson Correlations**; however if you are using ordinal variables you will use **Spearman Correlations**—click on the appropriate box. You can also specify one- or two-tailed tests; click **OK** when everything is set appropriately.

Box A.2 includes a summary table of correlations. The CORRELATIONS procedure also can be used along with the PARTIAL CORR procedure to test for intervening variables and for sources of spuriousness variables. See the PARTIAL CORRELATION section to see how that type of correlation is run.

4. CROSSTABS: CROSSTABULAR ANALYSIS

CROSSTABS is a procedure used to examine the association between a nominal or ordinal dependent variable and a nominal, ordinal, or ratio independent variable. In order to have sufficient cases in each of the table cells, when there are several categories in the independent variable they would be recoded (a new variable would be created regrouping the categories into two or three *meaningful* categories) prior to the analysis being run.

i. Point-and-Click Method

- Analyze

- Summarize

- Crosstabs
  The crosstabs screen will now appear.

- place the dependent variable(s) in the Row(s) window;

- place the independent variable(s) in the Column(s) window;

- click on **Statistics** and click on **Chi-Square**; click **Continue**;

- click on **Cells** and click on **Column** Percentages; click **Continue**;

- click **OK**.

BOX A.2   CORRELATIONS: SAMPLE OUTPUT

CORRELATIONS ❶

		Government Increase Foreign Aid	More Money Should Be Given to Welfare	Homo-sexuality Okay	Abortion Woman's Personal Choice
Government Increase Foreign Aid	Pearson Correlation	1.000	.323**	.029	−.023
	Sig. (1-tailed)	.000	.000	.347	.379
	N	184.000	183.000	182.000	183.000
More Money Should Be Given to Welfare	Pearson Correlation	.323**	1.000	.272**	.234**
	Sig. (1-tailed)	.000	.000	.000	.001
	N	183.000	184.000	183.000	184.000
Homosexuality Okay	Pearson Correlation	.029	.272**	1.000	.435**
	Sig. (1-tailed)	.347	.000	.000	.000
	N	182.000	183.000	183.000	183.000
Abortion Woman's Personal Choice	Pearson Correlation	−.023	.234**	.435**	1.000
	Sig. (1-tailed)	.379	.001	.000	.000
	N	183.000	184.000	183.000	184.000

** Correlation is significant at the 0.01 level (1-tailed). ❷

❸

NOTES:
❶ Pearson Correlation is the *r* value
❷ One-tailed test requested (** indicates significance at the .01 level)
❸ N = number of cases

ii. Sample Output and Notes

Box A.3 presents the results from a simple CROSSTABS analysis. Note where the Chi-Square value is printed and the probability is identified. Usually CROSSTABS results are reformatted when prepared for presentation in a paper. See Table A.1 (on page 499) for suggestions on how to reformat a CROSSTABS table for presentation in a paper.

Table A.1 presents the relationship between the respondent's country and illegal drug use. Since we are attempting to assess the impact of the independent variable on the dependent one, we are interested in the percentage of drug users in each category of the independent variable. Thus, we might describe the findings as indicating that "while 38.4% of the respondents from Canada and New Zealand report having used illegal drugs, some 60.3% of those from Australia report such usage." In short, we compare percentages in each column. Usually it will be sufficient to use one row (in this case, just the row for those reporting illegal drug use).

BOX A.3   CROSSTABS: SAMPLE OUTPUT

CROSSTABULATION OF THOUGHTS ABOUT SUICIDE AND GENDER

			Gender		Total
			Male	Female	
Thoughts about Suicide	Yes	Count	14	49	63
		% within Gender	23.3%	39.5%	34.2%
	No	Count	46	75	121
		% within Gender	76.7%	60.5%	65.8%
Total		Count	60	124	184
		% within Gender	100.0%	100.0%	100.0%

❶   **❷**   **❸**   **❹**

CHI-SQUARE TESTS

❺

	Value	df	Asymp. Sig. (2-sided)	Exact Sig. (2-sided)	Exact Sig. (1-sided)
Pearson Chi-Square	4.703[b]	1	.030		
Continuity Correction[a]	4.012	1	.045		
Likelihood Ratio	4.879	1	.027		
Fisher's Exact Test				.032	.021
Linear-by-Linear Association	4.677	1	.031		
N of Valid Cases	184.000				

❻   **❼❽**

[a.] Computed only for a 2x2 table

[b.] 0 cells (.0%) have expected count less than 5. The minimum expected count is 20.54.

NOTES:

❶ dependent variable (suicide thoughts)

❷ independent variable (gender)

❸ number of females who have thought about suicide

❹ compare these percentages when discussing results

❺ degrees of freedom

❻ with 2 x 2 tables use this value as the Chi-Square value; if not a 2 x 2 table use the Pearson Chi-Square value

❼ use this value to test null hypothesis (No relationship between suicide thoughts and gender)

❽ since value is < .05 the decision is to reject the null hypothesis; there is a statistically significant relationship between suicide thoughts and gender

TABLE A.1   ILLEGAL DRUG USE BY COUNTRY OF RESPONDENT

COUNTRY

ILLEGAL DRUG USE	CANADA AND NEW ZEALAND		AUSTRALIA		TOTAL	
	N	%	N	%	N	%
Have Used	48	38.4	35	60.3	83	45.4
Have Not Used	77	61.6	23	39.7	100	54.6
TOTAL	125	100.0	58	100.0	183	100.0

Chi-Square = 7.698; 6.838 (corrected for continuity)

Degrees of Freedom = 1

Significance = .006

Number of Missing Observations = 3

For analysis involving three or more variables simultaneously, the procedures are the same, with the control variable identified in the window called **Layer 1 of 1**. (See Box A.4 for sample output.)

When control variables are used, it is necessary to minimize the number of categories in the independent and in the control variables. Generally, there should be no more than two or three categories within each of these variables. There are two major reasons for this limitation: first, the number of cases in each cell will become too small if there are many categories in either the independent or the control variable; second, the interpretation of the table is very difficult if simplicity is not maintained.

Chapter 17 discusses interpretations of three-variable crosstabular tables. Remember that to apply *Jackson's rule of thirds* it is necessary to compare the original difference in the percentages between the categories of the independent variable and to rerun the relation controlling for the intervening (or source of spuriousness) variable. Only if the original difference is reduced by more than one-third *in each category of the control variable* do we have any evidence consistent with the proposed model.

5. DESCRIPTIVES: COMPUTING THE MEAN AND STANDARD DEVIATION

The DESCRIPTIVES procedure computes means and standard deviations and is appropriately used for ratio-level variables. The output will provide the mean, standard deviation, the minimum, and the maximum value for the variable(s) identified on the variable list. In addition, the number of valid (nonmissing) cases is reported. (See Box A.5 for sample output.)

i. Point-and-Click Method

• Analyze

• Descriptive Statistics

• Descriptives

BOX A.4 CROSSTABS: SAMPLE OUTPUT SHOWING A CONTROL VARIABLE

CROSSTABULATION OF THOUGHTS ABOUT SUICIDE, GENDER, AND NAME OF COUNTRY

Name of Country				Gender		Total
				Male	Female	
Canada	Thoughts about Suicide	Yes	Count	8	14	22
			% within Gender	26.7%	40.0%	33.8%
		No	Count	22	21	43
			% within Gender	73.3%	60.0%	66.2%
	Total		Count	30	35	65
			% within Gender	100.0%	100.0%	100.0%
New Zealand	Thoughts about Suicide	Yes	Count	4	16	20
			% within Gender	22.2%	40.0%	34.5%
		No	Count	14	24	38
			% within Gender	77.8%	60.0%	65.5%
	Total		Count	18	40	58
			% within Gender	100.0%	100.0%	100.0%
Australia	Thoughts about Suicide	Yes	Count	2	19	21
			% within Gender	16.7%	38.8%	34.4%
		No	Count	10	30	40
			% within Gender	83.3%	61.2%	65.6%
	Total		Count	12	49	61
			% within Gender	100.0%	100.0%	100.0%

NOTES:

❶ categories of the control variable (country)

❷ to test if country or origin is spuriously influencing relationship between gender and suicide thoughts, compare the percentage difference in suicide thoughts between males and females in each country; have the differences (compared to those shown in Box A3) increased, stayed the same, decreased/disappeared, or are they mixed? See Chapter 17 for details about interpreting this output.

The Descriptives screen will now appear. Identify the variables for which you want DESCRIPTIVES by moving desired variables to Variable(s) window. Click **OK** when ready.

If Optional Statistics are desired click on **Options**. If a standardized (Z score) version of the variable(s) is desired Click **Save Standardized**. SPSS will create a standardized version of the variable and will add a Z to the beginning of the variable name; for example, v24 will become zv24, and the new variable is immediately available for use.

ii. Sample Output: DESCRIPTIVES

Box A.5 shows the output you can expect from a DESCRIPTIVES analysis. See Chapter 18 for suggestions about how to compress the reporting of means and standard deviations for a number of variables.

BOX A.5 DESCRIPTIVES: SAMPLE OUTPUT, INCLUDING Z SCORE VALUES

DESCRIPTIVE STATISTICS ❶

	N	Minimum	Maximum	Mean	Std. Deviation
Egalitarianism	12	10.00	54.00	30.8187	8.7365 ❷
Zscore: Egalitarianism	182	−2.38296	2.65339	−2.9E-16	1.0000000
Valid N (listwise)	182			❸	

NOTES:
❶ shows the mean value for an egalitarianism index score
❷ standard deviation shown
❸ the −2.9E-16 indicates the mean of the scores when converted to Z scores; the value is .0000000000000002.9. Very close to zero!

6. DISCRIMINANT: DOING DISCRIMINANT FUNCTION ANALYSIS

Discriminant function analysis is a procedure for examining the relationship between a nominal dependent variable and ratio independent variables. The basic idea behind discriminant function analysis is to correctly classify into which category of the dependent variable each case will fall. It can also be used to predict which category a case will fall into when measures of the dependent variable are missing. The statistic *Lambda* was discussed in Chapter 8 and the reader should recall that this statistic measures the proportionate reduction in error that is achieved when a variable is added to an analysis. Lambda is used in discriminant function analysis to measure the success in correctly classifying cases. Similar to regression analysis, standardized weightings are provided that permit the researcher to assess the relative impact of independent variables on the dependent one. And, also similar to regression analysis, it is possible to employ *dummy* independent variables. See examples of how to construct these in the Regression Analysis section of this Appendix. And for more details on Discriminant Analysis see Chapter 17.

i. Point-and-Click Method

● Analyze
● Classify
● Discriminant

The Discriminant screen will now appear.

- Click on dependent variable and click ▶ to move to Grouping Variable window;

- Click on **Define Range** to specify minimum and maximum values for the dependent variable (hit Tab key after each entry);

- Click on **Continue**;

- Click on independent variables and click ▶ to move them to the Independent variables window;

- Click on **Analyze**; Click on **Means**;

- Click on **Continue**;

- Click on **Classify**; click on **Summary Table**;

- Click on **Continue**;

- Click **OK**.

- Identify variables for which you want procedure run;

- Click **OK**.

ii. Sample Output and Notes

Box A.6 presents sample output from a discriminant analysis of suicide thoughts (v12) among respondents in an international survey. Selected for independent variables were FAMILY SES (socioeconomic status), v50 (gender, a dummy variable), v58 (size of home community), and EGAL (an index measuring egalitarianism).

The output shown in Box A.6 shows how many cases were used in the analysis, the number of cases who reported that they had thought about committing suicide (60), and the number who reported that they had not had such thoughts (108). The mean scores for each independent variable are then reported for each category of suicide thoughts. Note that those with suicide thoughts had higher mean scores on EGALITARIANISM, FAMILY SES, GENDER, and SIZE OF HOME COMMUNITY.

The last presentation on the output shows the percentage of cases correctly classified. It is reported that 61.3% of the cases were correctly classified using the four independent variables. But how might we have fared if we had just randomly assigned cases to the suicide thought or non-suicide thought categories? To compute the number of correct classifications we would have made using random assignment, the following steps can be taken:

- compute the proportion of cases that fall into each category: in this case, $60 \div 168 = .36$; $108 \div 168 = .64$

- square the proportions and add them together and then multiply by 100: $(.36^2 + .64^2) \times 100 = 53.9\%$

- proportion of errors in random assignment: $1 - .54 = .46$

BOX A.6 DISCRIMINANT ANALYSIS: SAMPLE OUTPUT

GROUP STATISTICS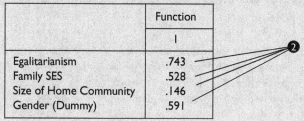

Thoughts about Suicide		Mean	Std. Deviation	Valid N (listwise) Unweighted	Weighted
Yes	Egalitarianism	32.6833	8.9962	60	60.000
	Family SES	68.4190	21.4355	60	60.000
	Size of Home Community	5.2500	2.86560	60	60.000
	Gender (Dummy)	.7667	.4265	60	60.000
No	Egalitarianism	29.0926	8.5002	108	108.000
	Family SES	63.3498	22.6049	108	108.000
	Size of Home Community	5.0093	2.6102	108	108.000
	Gender (Dummy)	.6204	.4876	108	108.000
Total	Egalitarianism	30.3750	8.8241	168	168.000
	Family SES	65.1602	22.2634	168	168.000
	Size of Home Community	5.0952	2.6945	168	168.000
	Gender (Dummy)	.6726	.4707	168	168.000

ANALYSIS I Summary of Canonical Discriminant Functions

EIGENVALUES

Function	Eigenvalue	% of Variance	Cumulative %	Canonical Correlation
I	.091[a]	100.0	100.0	.289

a. First I canonical discriminant functions were used in the analysis.

WILKS' LAMBDA

Test of Function(s)	Wilks' Lambda	Chi-Square	df	Sig.
I	.916	14.307	4	.006

STANDARDIZED CANONICAL DISCRIMINANT FUNCTION COEFFICIENTS

	Function I
Egalitarianism	.743
Family SES	.528
Size of Home Community	.146
Gender (Dummy)	.591

BOX A6. CONTINUED

STRUCTURE MATRIX

	Function
	I
Egalitarianism	.660
Gender (Dummy)	.500
Family SES	.365
Size of Home Community	.142

Pooled within-groups correlations between discriminating variables and standardized canonical discriminant functions

Variables ordered by absolute size of correlation within function

FUNCTIONS AT GROUP CENTROIDS

Thoughts about Suicide	Function
	I
Yes	.403
No	−.224

Unstandardized canonical discriminant functions evaluated at group means

CLASSIFICATION STATISTICS
PRIOR PROBABILITIES OF GROUPS

Thoughts About Suicide	Prior	Cases Used in Analysis	
		Unweighted	Weighted
Yes	.500	60	60.000
No	.500	108	108.000
total	1.000	168	168.000

CLASSIFICATION RESULTS[a]

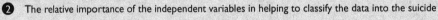

			Predicted Group Membership		
		Thoughts About Suicide	Yes	No	Total
Original	Count	Yes	37	23	60
		No	42	66	108
	%	Yes	61.7	38.3	100.0
		No	38.9	61.1	100.0

a. 61.3% of original grouped cases correctly classified

NOTES:

❶ The mean values for each independent variable is presented for both categories of the dependent variable.

❷ The relative importance of the independent variables in helping to classify the data into the suicide thoughts categories may be measured by the standardized values presented here.

❸ The 103 cases on this diagonal were correctly classified; the other diagonal contains 65 incorrectly classified cases.

- proportion of errors using discriminant analysis–based classifications: 1 − .61 = .39
- the percentage error reduction using the model, compared to random assignment, can be calculated by comparing the proportion of errors in the model compared to random assignment, divided by the proportion of errors using the model, multiplied by 100: $((.46 − .39) ÷ .46) × 100 = 15.2\%$.

The results indicate that we were able to improve our classification of people into the thought-of-suicide category versus the have-not-thought-of-suicide category by 15.2% by using the information on the four independent variables. But how important were each of the independent variables?

There are two basic ways of estimating the relative importance of variables in correctly estimating into which category of the dependent variable a case will fall:

1. Use the DISCRIMINANT procedure including all variables on the first run, then continue to repeat the analysis but exclude a different independent variable each time until you have an analysis excluding each independent variable. The contribution of each independent variable can then be judged by comparing the percentage of correct assignment using the variable to when the variable is not used, as in:

   - Contribution = (% correct with variable included) – (% correct without variable included)

   - The variable that produces the greatest drop in correct assignments is the most important factor, the one with the second greatest drop is the second most important variable, and so forth.

2. Another method to assess the relative importance of factors can be derived by examining the *standardized discriminant function coefficients*. These coefficients are similar to the beta weights in regression analysis in that they are standardized (so that differences in the range and variability of values in a variable do not influence the coefficient; if it helps, think of these as Z scores where each variable has a mean of 0 and a standard deviation of 1). The larger the coefficient, the more importance the variable has in predicting into which group the individual will fall. The relative importance of each variable is directly proportional to its coefficient and can be estimated in a manner similar to that suggested for the beta weights in regression analysis (see Regression Analysis section on p. 518).

Box A.6, Analysis 1, Summary of Canonical Discriminant Functions should be examined. First, it should be noted that the total amount of the variation explained by the combination of variables can be determined by squaring the *canonical correlation*. In our example the canonical correlation is .289, which means that together the four independent variables are accounting for 8.4% of the variance in suicide thoughts ($.289^2 = .0835 × 100 = 8.4\%$).

The *eigenvalue* (.091) represents the ratio of the between-groups variance to the within-groups variance. The higher this value, the greater the ability of the independent variables to discriminate between categories of the dependent variable.

The *Lambda* value varies from 0 to 1.0 and is a direct measure of the discriminating power of the model being tested. That is, the higher the value, the higher the discriminating ability of the model to distinguish between categories of the dependent variable. In this case the Lambda is .916.

A *Chi-Square* value is reported along with the degrees of freedom (DF) and the probability of the difference occurring on a chance basis (Sig.). In our illustration the significance level is .006, which means that only six times in a thousand samples could that much of a difference be observed because of chance factors in sampling.

The number of functions that the DISCRIMINANT procedure will calculate is one fewer than the number of categories in the dependent variable. Thus, as is the case in the example we are using, when there are two categories in the dependent variable, 1 function will be computed; if we had 3 categories, 2 functions would be calculated.

As in regression analysis, if there is a high correlation among the independent variables (say above .70), it is a good idea to either drop one of the highly correlated variables or multiply them together to provide a composite measure of the two variables.

7. FREQUENCIES: HOW MANY CASES IN EACH CATEGORY?

Nominal and ordinal variables are examined using the FREQUENCIES procedure. This procedure provides a count of the number of cases falling into each category. This procedure is also used to check the distribution of a variable before recoding it. FREQUENCIES will also produce Bar Charts and Histograms. Click on **Options** to select whether you want Bar Charts, Pie Charts, Histograms, or none (the default). Various statistics are available on request. By double clicking on the output, various changes can be made to the various charts. (See Box A.7 for sample output.)

i. Point-and-Click Method

- Analyze
- Descriptive Statistics
- Frequencies

The Frequencies screen will now appear. Click on the variables for which you want frequencies run and move them to the Variables window by clicking on the ▶ button on menu. When you have the variables you want listed, click **OK**. The output will be sent to the Output Viewer and displayed on your monitor.

ii. Sample Output: FREQUENCIES

It is often preferable to present nominal/ordinal data in summary tables. Table 18.3 (Chapter 18, p. 477) illustrates such a table for nominal/ordinal data, which is based on information generated using the FREQUENCIES procedure. It is useful in summary tables to report both the numbers and the percentages.

Box A.7 shows what the output will look like from a FREQUENCIES procedure. The circled numbers draw attention to key points on the output.

BOX A.7   FREQUENCIES: SAMPLE OUTPUT

MOTHER'S EDUCATIONAL BACKGROUND

		Frequency	Percent ①	Valid Percent ②	Cumulative Percent ③
Valid	No Education	3	1.6	1.7	1.7
	1–3 Yrs	7	3.8	3.9	5.6
	4–8 Yrs	26	14.0	14.6	20.2
	9–12 Yrs	70	37.6	39.3	59.6
	13–15 Yrs	31	16.7	17.4	77.0
	16+ Yrs	41	22.0	23.0	100.0
	Total	178	95.7	100.00	
Missing	9	8	4.3		
Total		186	100.0		

MOTHER'S EDUCATIONAL BACKGROUND

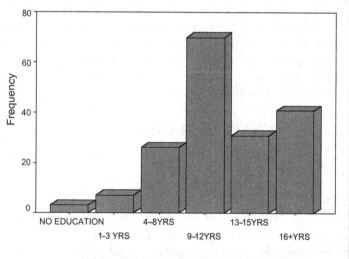

MOTHER'S EDUCATIONAL BACKGROUND

① Percentage calculated including the missing cases
② Percentage calculated excluding the missing cases
③ Cumulative percentage: this column is useful for determining cut-points when recoding ordinal variables
This bar chart was produced using the **Charts** window and then selecting **Bar Chart**.

8. GRAPH: GRAPHING RESULTS

There are a variety of Graph procedures available in SPSS, including bar charts, line charts, pie charts, scatterplots, and histograms, among others. The SCATTER procedure enables the researcher to produce a scatterplot of the relationship between two variables. The researcher can also designate various labels to be placed on the output as well as specify the scale for each dimension of the plot.

i. Point-and-Click Method

- Graphs

- Bar / Line / Area / Pie / High-Low / Scatter / Histogram

- Define

    Identify the variable(s) as appropriate for whichever type of graph you are creating, and then click **OK**.

ii. Sample Output and Notes

The sample output shows the results of a scatterplot of the relationship between two variables, with the dependent variable on the vertical axis (see Box A.8). Various options are available to permit the researcher to control the intervals printed along the two dimensions and to print various statistics. By double clicking on the output in the Output Viewer, the social science researcher can alter various settings on the charts, including such things as the size of the units used for scaling, colours, the format of bars, and so forth. Consult an SPSS manual for other graphics options.

9. IF: CREATING NEW VARIABLES

New variables can be created using IF statements. The simple form of the command (using the Syntax editor) is as follows:

COMPUTE newvar = 0.
IF (v15 LT 25) newvar = 1.

(See footnote to Box A.9 for a list of abbreviations used.)
    Here the new variable is set to 0 initially, and then NEWVAR is set to 1 whenever v15 has a value less than 25.
    More complex uses of the IF statement are illustrated in the following example. Suppose we are studying poverty in a community and we have survey data on 300 people over the age of 18. We want to create a variable identifying different types of poverty, taking into account the variables known as **age** and **income**. The following represents one way of creating the new variable:

BOX A.8

Scatterplot: Mother's Occupation and Family Socioeconomic Status

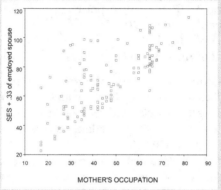

Bar Chart: Father's Education

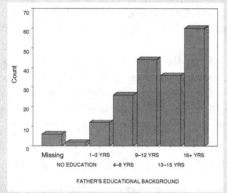

Pie Chart: Father's Education

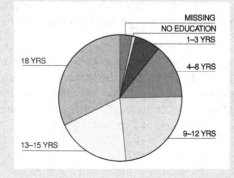

COMPUTE poortype = 0.
IF (age LT 25 AND income LT 20000) poortype = 1.
IF (age GE 25 AND age LT 65 AND income LT 25000) poortype = 2.
IF (age GE 65 AND income LT 20000) poortype = 3.
VARIABLE LABELS poortype "Type of Poor".
VALUE LABELS poortype 0 "all ages, non-poor"
            1 "under 25 under $20 K"
            2 "25–64, under $25 K"
            3 "over 64, under $20 K".

The above set combines age and income levels to create a new variable called POORTYPE, which identifies the non-poor (those with incomes over $20,000 for the young and old, and over $25,000 for the middle-aged respondents) and three categories of the poor: the young, with incomes under $20,000; the middle-aged, with incomes under $25,000; and the seniors, with incomes under $20,000.

Another illustration of the IF statement is the creation of an SES index that identifies for each respondent the higher of the mother's or father's occupational prestige rating. On the assumption that information has been collected on both the mother's and father's occupations and that the prestige scores for the occupations have been entered into the computer, our task is to develop a new variable that will use the higher of the mother's or father's occupational prestige rating to reflect the SES level of the family unit. The challenge here is to have SPSS compute the index. Box A.9 shows how the new variable could be created using SPSS.

Examine Box A.9 carefully. Because "homemaker" (coded as 98) and those who did not answer the question (coded as 99) were both identified as MISSING VALUES, it was necessary to remove the missing-values identifiers before the index could be created. Through the use of IF statements SPSS was then instructed to use the higher of the mother's or father's occupational prestige score to determine the value for the new variable, SES. In this index we have combined several elements:

- selected the higher of the mother's and father's occupational prestige scores;

- if one is not in the labour force, the score for the one who is, is used to indicate the occupational prestige;

- if both are in the labour force, the higher occupational prestige score is used, and then 1/3 of the other person's occupational prestige is added in to derive the "Family SES" score.

It is crucial in creating more complex variables to list a number of cases, to be certain that the values are being properly assigned to the new variable. After the IF statements have been completed, it is necessary to have SPSS do some procedure before the MISSING VALUES for v63 and v64 (the two occupational prestige scores) are reassigned. The syntax commands are illustrated in bold face in Box A.9.

BOX A.9 CREATING AN OCCUPATIONAL PRESTIGE INDEX USING IF STATEMENTS

The following syntax commands were used to create a family socioeconomic index using: (a) the higher of the mother's and father's occupational prestige score plus (2) one-third of the lower spouse's score. In cases of a "housewife" or "house-husband" the score is based on the employed person's occupational prestige. The original data used "99" as a missing value and "98" for housewife or house-husband. The comments to the right side explain the commands.

SYNTAX COMMANDS	COMMENTS
des var= v63 v64.	V63 = father's occupation
	V64 = mother's occupation
missing values v63 v64().	removes missing values; checks
des var= v63 v64.	values before and after removal
if (v64 ge v63 and v64 lt 98) ses = v64.	uses mother's score if higher
if (v63 ge v64 and v63 lt 98) ses = v63.	than father's, etc.
if (v64 ge 98 and v63 lt 98) ses = v63.	
if (v63 ge 98 and v64 lt 98) ses = v64.	if one spouse not in work force
list var = id v63 v64 ses/cases = 25.	other spouse's score is used;
des var = v63 v64 ses.	SES score computed
compute ses1 = ses.	to add 1/3 of lower person's
var labels ses1 "SES + .33 of employed spouse".	score the following is used:
if (v64 ge v63 and v64 lt 98) ses1 = (ses1 + (v63 * .33)).	adds 1/3 of father's score
if (v63 gt v64 and v63 lt 98) ses1 = (ses1 + (v64 * .33)).	adds 1/3 of mother's score
missing values v63, v64 (98,99).	puts missing values back on
des var = v63 v64 ses ses1.	computes new means
list var = v63 v64 ses ses1/cases = 25.	lists 25 cases of confirm data

Note: SPSS recognizes certain abbreviations:
- gt: greater than
- ge: greater than or equal to
- lt: less than
- le: less than or equal to
- eq: equal to
- ne: not equal to
- and: both conditions must be met
- or: either condition must be met

10. LIST: LISTING VARIABLES

After any computation creating or modifying a variable is completed it is a good idea to list some of the cases so that you can confirm that the changes have been properly executed. LIST is available through a syntax command, as follows:

- File

- New

- Syntax

The blank syntax screen should now appear on your monitor. Use the following command format to initiate a listing of cases for each specified variable:

list var = id v1 v1r /cases = 30.

On the toolbar click on **Run** and click on either **All** or **Selection** (if you have highlighted the LIST command line). SPSS will then list the values for the specified variables (id, v1, v1r) for the first 30 cases in the file. The researcher can then check to see that the changes made in v1r are correct. If the "cases" specification is omitted, all the cases will be listed for the variables identified on the variable list.

11. MEANS: COMPARING MEANS

The MEANS procedure is used to compare the mean values of a dependent variable across categories on an independent variable. The test of significance associated with the test is a one-way analysis of variance.

i. Point-and-Click Method

- Analyze

- Compare Means

- Means

Identify the dependent variables for which you want the MEANS procedure run; click them over to the **Dependent List** window by pressing the c button; identify the independent variable list and click those over to the **Independent List** window. Check the Options window to select any statistics you want, clicking them over to the Cell Statistics. When done click **Continue** and then click **OK**.

ii. Sample Output and Notes

Box A.10 presents the results from the use of the MEANS procedure. Note that the average values for all respondents on the egalitarianism index are presented for each country.

When you have a dependent variable measured at the ratio level, and either a nominal or ordinal independent variable, then it is appropriate to compute the mean values of the

BOX A.10 MEANS ANALYSIS: SAMPLE OUTPUT

REPORT

EGALITARIANISM

Country	Mean	N	Std. Deviation
Canada, New Zealand	32.4000	125	8.4204
Australia	27.3509	57	8.4799
Total	30.8187	182	8.7365

ANOVA TABLE

		Sum of Squares	df	Mean Square	F	Sig.
Egalitarianism Canada, New Zealand, Australia	Between Groups (Combined)	998.034	1	998.034	14.016	.000
	Within Groups	12816.982	180	71.205		
	Total	13815.016	181			

❶

❷

MEASURES OF ASSOCIATION

	Eta	Eta Squared
Egalitarianism Canada, New Zealand, Australia	.269	.072

NOTES:

❶ The F statistic here

❷ The significance value here; since it is less than .05 we reject the null hypothesis; there is a statistically significant difference between the countries in their level of egalitarianism.

dependent variable for each category of the independent variable. Table A.2 presents the kind of data that would be appropriate for this kind of analysis. Note that the dependent variable (income) is a ratio-level one, while the independent variable is nominal (gender).

The categories of the table should be carefully labelled. The means and standard deviations of the dependent variable, along with the number of cases, are normally reported in columns across the table. (See Table A.2 for an example.)

A summary table can be used to report the relationship between one dependent variable and a series of independent variables. A sample of such a table is presented in Table 18.6 (Chapter 18, p. 480).

TABLE A.2   MEAN INCOME BY GENDER

GENDER		MEAN INCOME	STANDARD DEVIATION	NUMBER OF CASES
Male		37,052	14,707	142
Female		34,706	11,693	37
	COMBINED MEAN	$36,567	13,474	179

If appropriate, test of significance values entered here.

In cases in which there are many categories in the independent variable, these will have to be regrouped into two or three before the analysis is run (click on the **Transform/Recode/Into Different Variable** procedure).

In interpreting the outcome of an analysis, compare the mean values for each category. In Table A.2 for example, the average incomes of the males are compared to those of the females.

The MEANS procedure can be used to test for intervening variables or for sources of spuriousness models (see Box A.11).

Note that in the test to see if the relationship between egalitarianism and country is spurious, caused by the number of each gender who happened to be in the sample, we first compare the original mean difference between the countries: $32.4000 - 27.3509 = 5.0491$. Second, we now see if the difference holds up when we control for the gender of the respondents: Box A.11 indicates that among the male respondents the difference is 3.1849 ($31.7143 - 28.5294 = 3.1849$) while for the females the difference in egalitarian scores is 5.897 ($32.7470 - 26.8500 = 5.897$). Using *Jackson's rule of thirds*, we note that among the males the difference "decreased" while among the female respondents the difference "remained the same." The result is "mixed" and therefore does not support the spuriousness model.

12. PARTIAL CORR: TESTING FOR AN INTERVENING VARIABLE

The computations for testing for intervening or sources of spuriousness models when you have ratio-level variables involve a combination of CORRELATIONS and PARTIAL CORRELATIONS. Box A.12 shows how such models can be tested. *Jackson's rule of thirds* can be applied (see Chapter 17). And for each, the question is what happens to the original relationship when control variables are applied. Box A.12 indicates that the correlation between v63 and v64 is .45; when "community size" is controlled, the correlation between v63 and v64 drops to .42. Since the partial correlation remains within one-third of the value of the original relationship, this would lead us to argue that the control variable is not a source of spuriousness.

BOX A.11 MEANS ANALYSIS: SAMPLE OUTPUT WITH A CONTROL VARIABLE

REPORT

EGALITARIANISM

Country	Gender	Mean	N	Std. Deviation
Canada, New Zealand	Male	31.7143	42	9.8161
	Female	32.7470	83	7.6602
	Total	32.4000	125	8.4204
Australia	Male	28.5294	17	10.8519
	Female	26.8500	40	7.3504
	Total	27.3509	57	8.4779
Total	Male	30.7966	59	10.1349
	Female	30.8293	123	8.0253
	Total	30.8187	182	8.7365

NOTES:

1. Is gender spuriously causing a false relationship between Country and Egalitarianism?
2. If gender is spuriously causing the relation, then when we control for gender, the difference between the countries should disappear within both of the gender categories.
3. Original difference between countries was 5.0491 (32.4 – 27.3509) see Box A10.
4. Compare these values to get the difference scores.
5. Apply Jackson's Rule of Thirds: 5.0491 ÷ 3 = 1.68
    *   **increased: 5.0491 + 1.68 = 6.7291 and over**
    *   **stayed the same: 5.0491 ± 1.68 = 3.37 to 6.7290**
    *   **decreased/disappeared: <3.37**
    *   **mixed: different category for each cell of control**
6. To find evidence consistent with a source of spurious (or an intervening variable) the results of the test must indicate that the difference falls into the decreased/disappeared category in both categories of the control variable. In the present case, the difference between both the males (in the different countries) and the females (in the different countries) would have to be less than 3.37.
7. Observed differences in males (see ❶ in table) is 3.1849 (decreased/disappeared category); in females (see ❷) the difference is 5.897 (stayed the same category).
8. Conclusion: the relationship is not spuriously caused by gender differences.

Testing for a source of spuriousness using CORRELATIONS and PARTIAL CORR is identical to testing for an intervening variable. And if the results were to come out as shown in Box A.12, we would reject the source of spuriousness model. Remember, to find support for the source of spuriousness model, the partial correlation would have to be less than .30, which would indicate that the original relationship had been reduced by more than one-third (.45 × .33 = .30).

BOX A.12 CORRELATIONS

PARTIAL CORRELATION: SAMPLE OUTPUT
PARTIAL CORRELATION COEFFICIENTS ——————————— ⑤

Controlling for...	v58
①	V63
② V64	.4192
③	(122)
④	P= .000

(Coefficient / (D.F.) / 2-tailed Significance)

"." is printed if a coefficient cannot be computed

NOTES:

❶ V63 = father's occupational prestige; V64 = mother's occupational prestige; V58 = community size

❷ top number is the partial correlation coefficient

❸ middle number refers to the number of cases in the analysis

❹ last number is the test of significance (probability)

❺ the control variable name (V58) is identified

ZERO-ORDER CORRELATION: SAMPLE OUTPUT
CORRELATIONS

		Father's Occupation	Mother's Occupation
Father's Occupation	Pearson Correlation	1.000	.446** — ❷
	Sig. (1-tailed)	.000	.000
	N	179.000	131.000
Mother's Occupation	Pearson Correlation	.446**	1.000
	Sig. (1-tailed)	.000	.000
	N	131.000	133.000

** Correlation is significant at the 0.01 level (1-tailed)

NOTES:

1. Testing to see if size of community is spuriously influencing relation between mother's and father's occupational prestige

2. Original zero-order correlation (shown above) is .45

3. With control for community size (see Partial Correlation table) first-order partial is .42

4. Conclusion: relationship is within 1/3 of its original magnitude, therefore, community size is not spuriously accounting for relationship between mother's and father's occupational prestige

i. Point-and-Click Method

- Analyze

- Correlate

- Partial

Identify variables for which you want Partial Correlations run; click **OK**.

13. RECODE: COLLAPSING AND SWITCHING CATEGORIES

The RECODE procedure is used to temporarily change a variable during analysis or to create a new variable. Primarily, the procedure is used to regroup the values in a variable. Survey researchers in particular have many occasions to use this procedure. For example, you might have eight categories reflecting community size and you might want to regroup the cases into three categories. The best way to proceed with an ordinal variable is to run a FREQUENCIES on the variable, noting on the "Cumulative Frequencies" column where cut-points of 33% and 66% are located. To do this sequentially click on the toolbar:

i. Point-and-Click Method

- Transform

- Recode

- Into Different Variables

A second important use for the RECODE procedure involves reverse-scoring variables. Suppose we have three 9-point Likert-type items we want to reverse score (i.e., change the 9's into 1's, 8's into 2's, etc.) In most cases it is safest to create a new variable containing the new codes.

Hint: *If you are frequently reverse-scoring Likert items, consider doing it in the syntax editor (to get there click on **File/New/Syntax**), and create a template file containing the following:*

RECODE v33 (9=1)(8=2)(7=3)(6=4)(5=5)(4=6)(3=7)(2=8)(1=9) INTO V33R.
VARIABLE LABELS V33R "Reversed V33".

or

COMPUTE V33R = 0.
COMPUTE V33R = 10 – V33.
VARIABLE LABELS V33R "Reversed V33".

Hint: *Save the file with a name like **flip.sps**. In the future when you wish to flip a 9-point scale just access **flip.sps**, change the variable names to the ones you want, and run the job. Note that the new variable names simply have an "R" appended to the original name. It is a good idea to maintain the original name in the new name so that the researcher will know that it is a recoded version of the original variable. Variable labels may be attached as indicated.*

14. REGRESSION: DOING MULTIPLE REGRESSION ANALYSIS

The REGRESSION procedure does various forms of multiple regression analysis. Regression analysis was one of the procedures featured in Chapter 17. Recall that this type of analysis allows the researcher to determine an equation to describe the relationship between a dependent variable and multiple independent variables, as well as to indicate the amount of variation explained by each independent variable.

i. Point-and-Click Method

- Analyze
- Regression
- Linear

Identify the dependent variable, clicking into the Dependent window. Next, move the independent variables over to the Independent(s) window. On the Method window switch to Backward; on the Statistics window click on **Estimates**, **Model fit** and **Descriptives**; click **Continue** and then Click **OK**.

ii. Sample Output and Notes

Box A.13 presents a regression analysis examining the relationship between Family SES and three independent variables: mother's educational background, father's educational back-

---

BOX A.13 REGRESSION ANALYSIS: SAMPLE OUTPUT

DESCRIPTIVE STATISTICS

	Mean	Std. Deviation	N
Family SES	65.4439	22.2776	165
Mother's Educational Background	4.39	1.17	165
Father's Educational Background	4.59	1.30	165
Size of Home Community	5.13	2.72	165

MODEL SUMMARY

Model	R	R Square	Adjusted R Square	Std. Error of the Estimate
1	.390[a]	.152	.136	20.7083
2	.389[b]	.152	.141	20.6460
3	.385[c]	.148	.143	20.6242

a. Predictors (Constant), Size of Home Community, Mother's Educational Background, Father's Educational Background

b. Predictors (Constant), Size of Home Community, Father's Educational Background

c. Predictors (Constant), Father's Educational Background

cont'd

BOX A13. CONTINUED

COEFFICIENTS[a]

Model		Unstandardized Coefficients		Standardized Coefficients	t	Sig.
		B	Std. Error	Beta		
1	(Constant)	33.459	7.230		4.628	.000
	Mother's Educational Background	−.313	1.899	−.016	−.165	.869
	Father's Educational Background	6.739	1.711	.392	3.939	.000
	Size of Home Community	.476	.597	.058	.798	.426
2	(Constant)	32.944	6.504		5.065	.000
	Father's Educational Background	6.546	1.245	.381	5.267	.000
	Size of Home Community	.481	.594	.059	.810	.419
3	(Constant)	35.118	5.918		5.934	.000
	Father's Educational Background	6.610	1.241	.385	5.324	.000

a. Dependent Variable: Family SES

NOTES:

❶ Dependent variable: Family SES. Independent variables: mother's education, father's education, size of home community. All variables entered initially, then dropped one at a time, until only statistically significant variables remain.

❷ SPSS recomputes the model each time a variable is dropped; in this particular case only one statistically significant variable remains at the end of this analysis.

❸ Final equation: Family SES = 35.1 + 6.6 (father's education).

❹ Beta weight show the relative influence of variables.

❺ R^2 is the total explained variance by the formula predicting "Family SES".

ground, and size of home community. Given that we have requested the BACKWARD solution note that all the independent variables are entered into the equation at Step 1, then the variable that is not statistically significant is removed and the equations are recomputed and shown at Step 2. If we had more nonsignificant variables the process would have continued until only statistically significant variables remain. Note that the R Square (explained variance) value, the *b* coefficients (labelled B), and beta weights are all reported on the output (see Model Summary), as well as the test of significance (labelled Sig.). The "model" numbers refer to the steps. In this case, SPSS went through three steps to arrive at the final solution. Only the father's educational level remained as a significant predictor of Family SES.

Table A.3 presents an example of a regression results table. Note that for each model tested the following statistics are presented: the *b* coefficients, the beta weights, and the variance explained (R^2). In cases in which a number of statistically significant predictors survive to the last model, one can use the following formula to compute the percent contribution of each of the independent variables (Gillis and Jackson, 2002):

$$\% \text{ Variance Explained by Each Variable} = \frac{\beta_1 \times R^2}{\Sigma \text{ }\beta\text{'s}} \times 100$$

where:

β_1 is the beta weight for the variable
R^2 is the R Square (explained variance) for the equation
Σ β's   is the sum of the beta weights (ignoring + and – signs)

Table A.4 shows how the above calculations could be presented. Note that the estimate is "rough" because the betas represent the particular variables in the equation and would change if other variables were included.

The pure researcher has a particular interest in the beta weights, for these provide a basis for directly comparing the impact of the different independent variables on the dependent one. Applied researchers are usually more concerned with *b* coefficients, especially those that can be changed through policy alterations. They provide the basis for understanding how much change in the dependent variable can be produced for each change in the independent variable. Variables can be grouped for presentation so as to illuminate the degree to which different variable types influence the dependent variable (for example, how much of the variation in the dependent variable is due to socioeconomic variables in comparison to the variety of experience variables?).

A second method for estimating the relative importance of variables is to calculate a *part correlation coefficient*. This coefficient is calculated for each independent variable and represents the difference in the R^2 when the variable is included versus when it is not included. The variables can then be ordered according to the unique contribution of each independent variable. In regression analysis, to get Part Correlations click on **Statistics** and click on the **part** and **partial correlations** window.

In presenting the results of a regression analysis, most researchers present the final table after the nonsignificant variables have been dropped. But you will want to include the following:

- indicate the names of the variables that remained
- indicate the names of the variables that were dropped
- point out total variation explained (R^2 value)
- note the percentage contribution of each of the statistically significant variables
- discuss the implications of the findings
- in addition, present the formula describing the relationship. In the case presented above, the formula would be as follows: Family SES = 35.1 + 6.6 (Father's Education)
- note that the formula uses *b* coefficients, the *a* value is the constant (General form of the equation is Y = a + b_1X_1 + b_2X_2)

TABLE A.3 SIMPLIFIED TABLE SUMMARIZING RESULTS OF STATISTICALLY SIGNIFICANT VARIABLES IN PREDICTING VARIATIONS IN PRESTIGE RATING, FICTIONAL DATA

MULTIPLE REGRESSION ANALYSIS
DEPENDENT VARIABLE = PRESTIGE RATING

| Multiple R | .91493 |
| R Square | .83709 |

	DF	Sum of Squares	Mean Square
Regression	2	3036.73385	1518.36692
Residual	12	590.99949	49.24996
F = 30.82981		Signif F = .0000	

Variables in the Equation

Variable	B	SE B	Beta	T	Sig T	Percent
		Contribution				
ED	3.65645	1.45103	.54434	2.520	.0269	47.8
INCOME	4.573087E–04	2.42024E–04	.40817	1.890	.0832	35.9
(Constant)	–8.96285	11.81029		–.759	.4626	
			Total Variance Explained			83.7
			Total Variance Unexplained			16.3

Variables not in the Equation

Variable	Beta In	Partial	Min Toler	T	Sig T
EX	–.06440	–.11431	.18567	–.382	.7100

TABLE A.4 CALCULATING THE PERCENTAGE CONTRIBUTION OF EACH INDEPENDENT VARIABLE

VARIABLE	BETA	CALCULATION	PERCENT CONTRIBUTION
ED	.54434	((.54434 * .83709) / .95251) * 100 =	47.8
INCOME	.40817	((.40817 * .83709) / .95251) * 100 =	35.9
		Total Variance Explained	83.7
		Variance Unexplained	16.3

A. DUMMY VARIABLE ANALYSIS

There might be times when a researcher wants to use a nominal variable within a regression analysis. Use dummy variables to do this. Suppose we had three religious categories: Christian, Jewish, and Muslim. To submit religion as a variable we would create two new variables (one fewer than the number of categories) and enter each of these into the regression analysis. These variables are coded as 1 for presence, 0 for absence. These are best created using the RECODE procedure, as in:

i. Point-and-Click Method:

- Transform

- Recode

- Into Different Variables . . .

Using this procedure, create one fewer new variables than categories in the original religious affiliation variable. Each of the new variables will be entered into the regression analysis as independent variables. So, in the example of a three category religious affiliation variable (Christian, Jewish, and Muslim) one would make one variable CHRI with a coding of 1 for Christians and everyone else coded 0; a second variable, JEWI, would be coded 1 for the Jews and 0 for everyone else. The third religious category, Muslim, is taken into account in the residual category of the two previous categories. One has to be cautious in interpreting the results when dummy variables are used. These variables are at some disadvantage in explaining variance since they have only two values, 0 and 1. In short, we might some-what underestimate the importance of the variable religion in such an analysis.

B. SOME CAUTIONS

CAUTION 1 ENSURE VARIABLES ARE THEORETICALLY INDEPENDENT OF ONE ANOTHER.

What this means is that one cannot use aspects of the dependent variable as independent variables. Include only meaningful potential causes of the dependent variable—not alternate measures of it.

CAUTION 2 WATCH OUT FOR HIGHLY CORRELATED INDEPENDENT VARIABLES.

The weightings that will be attached to the variables will be unstable if the independent variables are strongly correlated with one another. The program will print out a warning if there is a problem in this area.

CAUTION 3 INTERPRET WEIGHTINGS WITH CARE.

Understand that the weightings are for the particular combination of independent variables for a particular sample and these weightings might not apply reliably to other samples.

CAUTION 4 MONITOR THE NUMBER OF CASES CAREFULLY.

By default, SPSS will delete a case if it has a missing value in any of the variables in the equation. Thus, if there are several variables in an analysis there is a danger of losing many cases. And, as the number of cases drops closer to the number of variables, the R^2 will increase dramatically. *To determine the number of* cases used in the analysis, add 1 to the total degrees of freedom reported in the table. If a large number of cases have been dropped, try running the analysis using PAIRWISE treatment of missing cases; and if there are still many missing try MEANS (this will substitute the mean of the variable for any missing cases).

An additional possibility, after an initial narrowing down of the variables has been done, is to resubmit the analysis, naming only the significant variables, plus perhaps two or three that were dropped in the last few steps. This preserves those cases that were dropped because of missing values in variables not included in the final equation.

15. RELIABILITY: ASSESSING INTERNAL CONSISTENCY

Indexes combine two or more indicators to reflect complex variables such as socioeconomic status, quality of life, health status, or an attitude toward some nursing issue. Frequently, the researcher constructs sub-indexes that can be treated alone or combined with other sub-indexes to form a composite measure. For example, a researcher measuring attitudes toward abortion might construct a sub-index for "soft reasons" (economically inconvenient, preference for having a baby later, etc.) and "hard reasons" (pregnancy as a result of rape, severely handicapped, etc.). These sub-indexes might also be combined to form an overall index. In each case, however, the researcher will have to ensure that appropriate items are included in each sub-index.

Chapter 13 presented a discussion of item analysis and introduced the principles of index construction. The RELIABILITY procedure evaluates which items should go into an index. RELIABILITY examines the components of a proposed additive index providing a variety of diagnostics for each item. The procedure does not actually compute the index, but rather provides an assessment of each item; the actual index would be constructed with a COMPUTE command. Of particular note for the beginning researcher is that RELIABILITY computes item means and standard deviations, inter-item correlations, a series of item-total comparisons, and *Cronbach's alpha* for index reliability.

The RELIABILITY procedure in SPSS uses the internal consistency approach to reliability. The method that is used to calculate the *standardized* alpha involves the number of items going into the index and the average inter-item correlation among the items, as in:

$$\text{Alpha} = \frac{N \text{ (average inter-item correlation)}}{1 + (\text{average inter-item correlation } (N - 1))}$$

Where:

N is the number of items proposed for the index being tested
average inter-item correlation is the average of the correlations between the items: this value is printed when the SUMMARY options MEANS is selected

The standardized alpha for the index evaluated in Box A.14 would be as follows:

$$\text{Alpha} = \frac{5 \, (.3507)}{1 + (.3507 \, (5 - 1))}$$

Alpha $= 1.7535 \div 2.4028$
Alpha $= .7298$

Cronbach's alpha varies with the average inter-item correlation, taking into account the number of items that make up the index. If there is an increase in either the inter-item correlation or the number of items, alpha increases. For example, with 2 items and a .4 mean correlation, the alpha value would be .572; with 8 items and a .4 mean inter-item correlation, the alpha would be .842. With .6 inter-item correlations, the alpha for 2 versus 8 items would be .750 and .924, respectively. Table 13.2 on p. 374 summarizes the relationship between items and inter-item correlations. (See Chapter 13 for more details.)

In examining Box A.14, note that we are examining five 9-point Likert-type liberal gender attitude items, known as v29, v30, v31, v32, and v33. Note that v30 to v33 are inverse measures (the higher the score the *less* liberal the attitude). Let us go through the steps to evaluate these items.

STEP 1

Reverse-score any items that are negative (in this case: v30 to v33) using the RECODE procedure.

STEP 2

Point-and-Click Method

- Analyze

- Scale

- Reliability

Identify variables for which you want procedure run (V29, V30R, V31R, V32R, and V33R); Click on **Statistics**, click to place a check mark on all items in the Descriptives pane; in Summaries pane check **Means** and **Correlations**; in Inter-Item pane check **Correlations**; in ANOVA pane check **None**. Once this is done click on **Continue**. At the Reliability Analysis window check **OK**.

STEP 3

Examine the results shown in Box A.14.

As a rule of thumb, you have an acceptable index if:

- the *correlation matrix* indicates that the correlations between the items are positive (all are positive; they vary from .13 to .56);

- the *mean inter-item correlations* should be above .25 (in the case we are examining the value is .3507); note here, however, that if you were using items based on Likert items with fewer than 9 points you might want to accept slightly lower mean inter-item correlations, perhaps as low as .20;

- examine the *item-total statistics*; this part of the analysis examines the individual items, comparing each to the total score for the index being evaluated; the *corrected item-total correlation* presents the correlation between the item and the total index score with the effects of the individual item removed. Generally, you would expect each of these items to be above .25;

- at the bottom of the table two alphas are reported; earlier the calculation for the standardized item alpha was demonstrated; we attempt to get as high an alpha as possible when constructing an index. The alpha reported in Box A.14 is .7268;

BOX A.14   RELIABILITY ANALYSIS: SAMPLE OUTPUT

RELIABILITY ANALYSIS — SCALE (ALPHA)

		Mean	Std Dev	Cases	
1.	V29	4.4341	2.4435	182.0	
2.	VR30	7.2143	2.2773	182.0	
3.	VR31	6.7253	2.4430	182.0	❶
4.	VR32	7.6209	1.9845	182.0	
5.	VR33	5.4341	2.8291	182.0	

CORRELATION MATRIX

	V29	VR30	VR31	VR32	VR33	
V29	1.0000					
VR30	.1331	1.0000				
VR31	.3135	.3185	1.0000			❷
VR32	.1629	.5046	.4422	1.0000		
VR33	.3043	.3740	.5569	.3975	1.0000	

N of Cases = 182.0

Statistics for Scale	Mean	Variance	Std Dev	N of Variables		
	31.4286	69.4507	8.3337	5		
Items Means	Mean	Minimum	Maximum	Range	Max/Min	Variance
	6.2857	4.4341	7.6209	3.1868	1.7187	1.7480
Inter-item Correlations	Mean	Minimum	Maximum	Range	Max/Min	Variance
	.3507	.1331	.5569	.4238	4.1837	.0173

❸

ITEM-TOTAL STATISTICS   ❹   ❺

	Scale Mean if Item Deleted	Scale Variance if Item Deleted	Corrected Item-Total Correlation	Squared Multiple Correlation	Alpha if Item Deleted
V29	26.9945	52.4696	.3110	.1227	.7464
VR30	24.2143	49.8599	.4479	.2908	.6947
VR31	24.7033	44.2098	.5932	.3880	.6367
VR32	23.8077	50.6203	.5274	.3508	.6714
VR33	25.9945	40.2596	.5901	.3773	.6358

Reliability Coefficients   5 items

Alpha = .7268   Standardized item alpha = .7298

cont'd

NOTES:

① Lists the means, standard deviations, and number of cases for variables

② Shows the correlation matrix (check to see that all are positive)

③ Note especially the mean inter-item correlation (should be above .25)

④ The "Corrected Item-Total Correlation" is a measure of the correlation between the item and the total score minus the item score

⑤ Provides the Standardized Alphas if the item were deleted (suggests we should drop item V29 because that would result in a higher Alpha)

- the *alpha if item deleted column* reports on what the alpha would be if the item were deleted; in Box A.14 we note that if we dropped v29 the alpha would be .7464; for all other cases the alpha would be lowered if the item were deleted; our decision will be to drop v29 when the final index is calculated using the COMPUTE procedure.

STEP 4

If two or more items are to be removed from the final index it will be necessary to resubmit another RELIABILITY job. If one or no items need to be eliminated, then one can go immediately to step 5.

STEP 5

Having decided which items are to be included in the index, a new job should be run adding the items together using a COMPUTE command. (Either point-and-click or syntax commands can be used.) The Syntax command would look like:

COMPUTE sexatt = v30r + v31r + v32r + v33r.
VARIABLE LABELS sexatt "Sex Role Attitude".

The system file should be updated, saving the new index scores with a **File/Save** command. There are many other options available within the RELIABILITY procedure. It is possible to compute split-half coefficients and various coefficients proposed by Louis Guttman (1950). Consult the SPSS User's Guide for additional models and options.

16. SPEARMAN CORRELATION: CORRELATION FOR ORDINAL DATA

Spearman correlations are used when ordinal-level measurement has been attained. They can be reported and interpreted in the same manner as Pearson correlations. Like Pearson correlations they vary from −1.00 to +1.00 and measure the strength of an association.

i. Point-and-Click Method

- Analyze   • Correlations   • Spearman

In the Correlation Coefficients box click on **Spearman**. Identify the variables for which you want the procedure run; Click **OK**.

17. *T*-TEST: COMPARING MEANS OF TWO GROUPS

The *T*-TEST procedure tests whether the difference in the means between two groups is statistically significant. For a between-subjects design use the Independent Samples *t*-Test; for a within subjects design use the Paired Samples *t*-Test. (Recall that a between-subjects test involves the comparison of two groups of subjects—typically one group is exposed to a treatment, the other group is not exposed to it. A within-subject test is used when the same subject is exposed to the different treatments—these are also known as repeated measures designs.)

i. *Point-and-Click Method*

- Analyze
- Compare Means
- Independent Samples *t*-Test

    or

- Paired Samples *t*-Test

The following steps need to be taken to complete the analysis:

- For the between-subjects design (using the Independent Samples *t*-Test) move the test variable to the Test Variables window. Next, place the Grouping Variables in its window. You will need to then enter the values for the Grouping (usually 1 and 2, or 0 and 1). Click **OK**.

- For the within subjects design (using the Paired Samples *t*-Test) move the paired variables to the window and click **OK**.

ii. *Sample Output and Notes*

Box A.15 shows sample output from two *T*-TEST analyses. The first shows the command format and results from a between-subjects design; the second shows how to set up a job to do a within-subject analysis.

18. Z SCORE: USING Z SCORES TO CREATE AN INDEX

Z scores are used to standardize variables so that each variable will have a mean of 0 and a standard deviation of 1. Suppose you wanted to create an index that adds mother's educational category to her occupational prestige, equally weighting the two elements. One way to proceed (dealing with the different range of variables involved) would be to standardize the scores (Z scores) and then add the standardized scores together. Z scores

BOX A.15   *T*-TEST SAMPLE OUTPUTS

① PAIRED SAMPLES STATISTICS

		Mean	N	Std. Deviation	Std. Error Mean
Pair 1	time 1 speed	13.260	10	.324	.102
	TIME2	13.160	10	.267	8.459E-02

PAIRED SAMPLES CORRELATIONS

		N	Correlation	Sig.
Pair 1	time 1 speed & TIME2	10	.941	.000

② PAIRED SAMPLES TEST

		Paired Differences					t	df	Sig. (2-tailed)
		Mean	Std. Deviation	Std. Error Mean	95% Confidence Interval of the Difference				
					Lower	Upper			
Pair 1	time 1 speed - TIME2	1.000E-01	.115	3.651E-02	1.740E-02	.183	2.739	9.	.023

NOTES:

① The mean times at time 1 and time 2 shown here

② The correlation of the measures at the two times is .941

③ The t-test value

④ The degrees of freedom

⑤ The two-tailed test of significance

⑥ Conclusion: Reject the null hypothesis; there is a statistically significant difference in the speeds at the two times.

cont'd

versions of variables are available in the DESCRIPTIVES procedure by simply naming the relevant variables and clicking on the box called **Save standardized values as variables**.

A **Z** will be prefixed to the name of the variable. Next, one would simply do a COMPUTE adding together the new standardized variables. The compute could be done as follows:

BOX A.15 CONTINUED

BETWEEN-SUBJECTS SAMPLE OUTPUT
GROUP STATISTICS ❶

	Type of Tire	N	Mean	Std. Deviation	Std. Error Mean
TIME	Standard	10	18.390	2.168	.685
	Experimental	10	18.060	2.447	.774

INDEPENDENT SAMPLES TEST

		Levene's Test for Equality of Variances		t-test for Equality of Means						
									95% Confidence Interval of the Difference	
		F	Sig.	t	df	Sig. (2-tailed)	Mean Difference	Std. Error Difference	Lower	Upper
TIME	Equal variances assumed	.524	.478	.319	18	.753	.330	1.034	−1.842	2.502
	Equal variances not assumed			.319	17.741	.753	.330	1.034	−1.844	2.504

❷   ❸   ❹❺

NOTES:

❶ The mean lap times for the "standard" and "experimental" tires shown here

❷ Computed *t* value

❸ Degrees of freedom

❹ Two tailed test of significance

❺ Conclusion: Accept the null hypothesis: there is no statistically significant difference between the lap times on the different tires.

COMPUTE newses = zv62.1 + zv64.
VARIABLE LABELS newses "Ses Score: Education plus Prestige".

Incidentally, if you wanted to weight the elements so that two-thirds of the final scores were based on occupational prestige and one-third on educational level, the COMPUTE command would be altered to:

COMPUTE newses = (zv62.1 * .33) + (zv64 * .67).

The previous section presented the basic commands for examining relationships. The SPSS package contains a broad range of options, statistics, and file-management and analysis procedures. The chances are that most analyses you want to do are possible within SPSS. After you have mastered the basic procedures, you will be ready to begin exploring SPSS in greater detail.

C. SPSS MANUALS

There are many manuals currently available for SPSS for Windows versions 10.0 to 14. For students taking an introduction to research methods course, the introduction provided in this Appendix is likely sufficient. There are more detailed user guides available, ranging from brief user guides to books outlining how to use SPSS for advanced statistical models. They can be purchased online from the SPSS Store at **www.spss.com/estore/softwaremenu/index.cfm?source=homepage&hpzone=nav_bar** or through major bookstores and university bookstores.

PINEO AND PORTER'S CANADIAN OCCUPATIONAL PRESTIGE INDEX

Students will note that the terminology in this appendix reflects job titles from the 1960s, some of which reflect the more gender differentiated nature of the labour force in that period. More recent research has incorporated gender neutral language (e.g., mailman was changed to mail carrier, draftsman was changed to draftsperson, auto repairman became auto repairer; see John Goyder, 2005). Goyder's research also suggests that some occupational prestige rankings have changed somewhat since the mid-sixties, and he encourages further research on occupational scaling to track the changes.

National N=**793**

OCCUPATION	SCORE
Professional	
Accountant	63.4
Architect	78.1
Biologist	72.6
Catholic Priest	72.8
Chemist	73.5
Civil Engineer	73.1
County Court Judge	82.5
Druggist	69.3
Economist	62.2
High School Teacher	66.1
Lawyer	82.3
Mathematician	72.7
Mine Safety Analyst	57.1
Mining Engineer	68.8
Physician	87.2
Physicist	77.6
Protestant Minister	67.8
Psychologist	74.9
Public Grade School Teacher	59.6
University Professor	84.6
Veterinarian	66.7

Semi-Professional	
Airline Pilot	66.1
Author	64.8
Ballet Dancer	49.1
Chiropractor	68.4
Commercial Artist	57.2
Computer Programmer	53.8
Disc Jockey	38.0
Draughtsman	60.0
Funeral Director	54.9
Journalist	60.9
Medical or Dental Technician	67.5
Musician	52.1
Musician in a Symphony Orchestra	56.0
Physiotherapist	72.1
Playground Director	42.8
Professional Athlete	54.1
Professionally Trained Forester	60.1
Professionally Trained Librarian	58.1
Registered Nurse	64.7
Research Technician	66.9
Sculptor	56.9

Social Worker	55.1
Surveyor	62.0
TV Announcer	57.6
TV Cameraman	48.3
TV Director	62.1
TV Star	65.6
YMCA Director	58.2

Proprietors, Managers and Officials, Large

Administrative Officer in Federal Civil Service	68.8
Advertising Executive	56.5
Bank Manager	70.9
Building Contractor	56.5
Colonel in the Army	70.8
Department Head in City Government	71.3
General Manager of a Manufacturing Plant	69.1
Mayor of a Large City	79.9
Member of Canadian Cabinet	83.3
Member of Canadian House of Commons	84.8
Member of Canadian Senate	86.1
Merchandise Buyer for a Department Store	51.1
Owner of a Manufacturing Plant	69.4
Provincial Premier	89.9
Wholesale Distributor	47.9

Proprietors, Managers and Officials, Small

Advertising Copy Writer	48.9
Beauty Operator	35.2
Construction Foreman	51.1
Driving Instructor	41.6
Foreman in a Factory	50.9
Government Purchasing Agent	56.8
Insurance Claims Investigator	51.1

Job Counsellor	58.3
Livestock Buyer	39.6
Lunchroom Operator	31.6
Manager of a Real Estate Office	58.3
Manager of a Supermarket	52.5
Member of a City Council	62.9
Motel Owner	51.6
Owner of a Food Store	47.8
Public Relations Man	60.5
Railroad Ticket Agent	35.7
Sawmill Operator	37.0
Service Station Manager	41.5
Ship's Pilot	59.6
Superintendent of a Construction Job	53.9
Trade Union Business Agent	49.2
Travel Agent	46.6

Clerical and Sales

Air Hostess	57.0
Bank Teller	42.3
Bill Collector	29.4
Bookkeeper	49.4
Cashier in a Supermarket	31.1
Clerk in an Office	35.6
File Clerk	32.7
IBM Keypunch Operator	47.7
Insurance Agent	47.3
Manufacturer's Representative	52.1
Post Office Clerk	37.2
Real Estate Agent	47.1
Receptionist	38.7
Sales Clerk in a Store	26.5
Shipping Clerk	30.9
Stenographer	46.0
Stockroom Attendant	25.8
Telephone Operator	38.1
Telephone Solicitor	26.7
Travelling Salesman	40.2

Truck Dispatcher	32.2	Bookbinder	35.2
Typist	41.9	Bus Driver	35.9
Used Car Salesman	31.2	Cod Fisherman	23.4
		Firefighter	43.5
Skilled		Fruit Packer in a Cannery	23.2
Airplane Mechanic	50.3	Logger	24.9
Baker	38.9	Longshoreman	26.1
Bricklayer	36.2	Loom Operator	33.3
Butcher in a Store	34.8	Machine Operator in a Factory	34.9
Coal Miner	27.6	Newspaper Pressman	43.0
Cook in a Restaurant	29.7	Oil Field Worker	35.3
Custom Seamstress	33.4	Oiler in a Ship	27.6
Diamond Driller	44.5	Paper Making Machine Tender	31.6
Electrician	50.2	Policeman	51.6
House Carpenter	38.9	Private in the Army	28.4
House Painter	29.9	Production Worker in the	
Locomotive Engineer	48.9	Electronics Industry	50.8
Machine Set-up Man in a Factory	42.1	Professional Babysitter	25.9
Mucking Machine Operator	31.5	Quarry Worker	26.7
Plumber	42.6	Sewing Machine Operator	28.2
Power Crane Operator	40.2	Steam Boiler Fireman	32.8
Power Lineman	40.9	Steam Roller Operator	32.2
Pumphouse Engineer	38.9	Steel Mill Worker	34.3
Railroad Brakeman	37.1	Textile Mill Worker	28.8
Railroad Conductor	45.3	Timber Cruiser	40.3
Saw Sharpener	20.7	Trailer Truck Driver	32.8
Sheet Metal Worker	35.9	Troller	23.6
TV Repairman	37.2	Worker in a Meat Packing Plant	25.2
Tool and Die Maker	42.5		
Typesetter	42.2	**Unskilled**	
Welder	41.8	Carpenter's Helper	23.1
		Construction Labourer	26.5
Semi-Skilled		Elevator Operator in a Building	20.1
Aircraft Worker	43.7	Filling Station Attendant	23.3
Apprentice to a Master Craftsman	33.9	Garbage Collector	14.8
Assembly Line Worker	28.2	Hospital Attendant	34.9
Automobile Repairman	38.1	Housekeeper in a Private Home	28.8
Automobile Worker	35.9	Janitor	17.3
Barber	39.3	Launderer	19.3

Mail Carrier	36.1
Museum Attendant	30.4
Newspaper Peddler	14.8
Railroad Sectionhand	27.3
Taxicab Driver	25.1
Waiter in a Restaurant	19.9
Warehouse Hand	21.3
Whistle Punk	18.4
Worker in a Dry Cleaning or Laundry Plant	20.8

Farmer

Commercial Farmer	42.0
Dairy Farmer	44.2
Farm Labourer	21.5
Farm Owner and Operator	44.1
Hog Farmer	33.0
Part Time Farmer	25.1

Not in Labour Force

Someone who lives off inherited wealth	45.8
Someone who lives off property holdings	48.7
Someone who lives off stocks and bonds	56.9
Someone who lives on social assistance	7.3

Source: This table represents a portion (national scores only) of Peter C. Pineo and John Porter (1967). "Occupational Prestige in Canada," *The Canadian Review of Sociology and Anthropology*, 4(1), 36–40.

GLOSSARY

action research The systematic collection and analysis of data for the purpose of taking action and making change. Action research provides practitioners, organizations, or communities with tools to solve their problems.

advocacy research Social research that advocates social changes or advances the personal or collective agendas of its practitioners.

aggregation A group rather than an individual. Studying aggregations means that research is focused on groups (e.g., professional athletes), institutions (e.g., families, hospitals), communities (e.g., municipalities), or nations. For example, one might conduct research comparing the distribution of wealth in different nations.

analysis of variance (ANOVA) A procedure for deciding if a ratio-level dependent variable is significantly associated with a nominal or ordinal independent variable.

analytic files Files relating to a specific topic or relationship explored in a field study.

androcentricity A tendency to view things exclusively from a male perspective.

anecdotal evidence Evidence for a generalization based on one incident or a small handful of incidents that do not make up a representative sample.

antecedent variable model A causal model proposing a variable that causes variation in an independent variable, which, in turn, influences the dependent variable in the model. Thus, the antecedent variable is one that precedes both the main independent and dependent variables.

appeal to authority Using the opinion of a person of high status rather than relying on actual evidence relevant to the issue. For example, we could state that capital punishment is bad because physics Nobel Prize winner, Dr. X., claims that it is.

applied research Focuses on figuring out how to bring about specific changes in society.

audit trail Documenting all the raw data generated as well as methods and sources of data generation and analysis decisions.

axiomatic derivation A method of logically deriving new statements of relationship from a given set of assumptions and propositions.

b coefficient A coefficient associated with regression analysis. The b coefficient is an unstandardized measure of the influence of an independent variable on the dependent one.

baseline measure A measure taken at the beginning of a set of observations, once stability has been achieved in the dependent variable.

baseline stability See *baseline measure*.

beta weight A standardized measure of the relative influence of an independent variable on the dependent one; associated with regression analysis.

between-subjects design A type of classical experimental design. The between-subjects design is also known as the pretest, post-test control group design because subjects are randomly assigned to treatment or control groups, and the results for each group are compared before and after members of the treatment group are exposed to the treatment under study. This design contains the three crucial elements of the classical experiment: control over extraneous variables, methods of dealing with pre-treatment similarity of groups, and manipulation of a treatment.

bias A preference or predisposition to favour a particular conclusion.

bi-modal distribution A distribution with two peaks.

blocked design An experimental design in which subjects have been grouped together on some variable that needs to be controlled and are then randomly assigned to treatment and control conditions.

bracketing A cognitive process used by the researcher to set aside personal biases about the research topic. Its purpose is to make known what the researcher believes about the research topic so that such beliefs will not unconsciously influence the research.

candidate variable model A model that proposes several independent variables as possible causes of variation in a dependent variable.

causal explanation An explanation in which an event, or sequence of events, is explained by making reference to preceding, influencing events.

causal model A diagram showing the causal connections between variables.

Chi-Square test (X^2) A test of statistical significance associated with contingency table analysis, in which the dependent variable is a nominal one.

classic experimental design The classic experimental design is an experiment designed to demonstrate the effect treatment variable(s) have on the dependent variable. There are two types of classic experimental designs: the between-subjects design and the within-subject design (or control by comparison design).

cleaning the data The systematic search for errors in a data set in order to correct the errors before analysis of the data begins.

coefficient of reliability A measure of agreement between the coders on the categorization of the items being analyzed. The proportion of times there is agreement is reflected in the coefficient.

comparative research Research that typically involves cross-cultural or historical analyses of social behaviour.

componential analysis A form of analysis that looks for all the contrasts among the cultural categories in the domains. Componential analysis is the systematic search for the *attributes* (components of meaning) associated with cultural categories.

concept A general idea referring to a characteristic of an individual, a group, or a nation.

conceptual hypothesis A statement of the relationship between two or more conceptual variables.

conceptual level The stage of the research at which the researcher defines the concepts and concept relationships that are to be studied.

conceptual variable An idea that has a dimension that can vary.

concurrent validity A type of criterion validity. A measure is said to have concurrent validity if it correlates highly with a different measure of the same construct. For example, if two different measures of depression are highly correlated, the measures have concurrent validity.

conditional variable A variable that accounts for a change in the relationship between an independent variable and a dependent variable when the general conditions change.

confirmability The objectivity of the data. If two or more independent researchers would agree about the meanings emerging from the data, the conclusions are confirmable.

confounding variable A variable that could unintentionally obscure or enhance a relationship.

consequentialist A view of research ethics that bases ethical judgments about a research project on the consequences for the subject, for the academic discipline, and for society. In contrast to the *deontological* view.

constant comparative method A method of data analysis in which each piece of data is coded and compared to other pieces to reveal similarities and differences in the lives of those interviewed.

construct validity A situation in which a theoretically derived hypothesis turns out as predicted.

content analysis A technique for making inferences by objectively and systematically coding information.

content validity The extent to which the measure reflects the dimension(s) implied by the concept.

contingency table A table that cross-classifies variables so that the relationship between a nominal-level dependent variable can be related to an independent variable.

control by constancy The technique in within-subject designs where the same subject experiences different levels of the treatment; hence the subject acts as his/her own control.

control group The group in an experiment that is not exposed to the treatment, in order to allow comparison with the experimental group, which is exposed to the treatment.

control group design An experimental design in which the researcher uses randomized assignment to groups (or precision matching) to adjust for known and unknown variations between the two groups.

control variable A variable taken into account in exploring the relation between an independent and dependent variable. There are three basic types of control variables: the intervening variable, the conditional variable, and the source of spuriousness (or confounding) variable.

controlled observations Observations in which other confounding factors are minimized or taken into account.

convenience sample A non-probability sampling procedure that involves selection on the basis of ease or convenience.

core variable A variable that focuses the theory and accounts for most of the variation in a pattern of behaviour that is both relevant and problematic for the participants.

correlation analysis A procedure for measuring how closely two ratio-level variables co-vary.

correlation coefficient (*r*) A measure of the strength of association between two variables; a correlation may vary from +1 to –1.

counterbalancing A technique in experimental designs that involves introducing, changing, maintaining, and then returning to the first level of the experimental treatment to control for effects of learning on the subject's performance.

covert participant A researcher who enters and studies a group from within; group members are not informed that they are the subject of a research project.

credibility The accuracy of the description of the phenomenon under investigation. To be credible, the portrayal of the reality must be faithfully represented and plausible to those who have experienced that reality.

criterion validity The extent to which a measure is able to predict accurately.

critical approach An approach that views human behaviour as essentially characterized by certain social groups attempting to enhance their interests at the expense of other less powerful groups. The fundamental goal of the critical approach is to counteract this tendency and bring about a truly egalitarian society—one in which there is equality of opportunity *and* equality of result.

critical research Research aimed at empowering participants and/or improving social conditions for marginalized members of society.

Cronbach's alpha A commonly used method of assessing internal consistency or the intercorrelations of all the items in an instrument measuring a construct.

cultural scene An ethnographic term used to refer to the culture under study.

cultural themes Recurrent patterns in the data that are used to connect domains.

culture A way of life belonging to a designated group of people. Culture includes all the ways a group of people solves problems, as reflected in their language, dress, food, traditions, and customs. It is a pattern of living that guides the group's thoughts, actions, and sentiments.

curvilinear relationship A relationship in which the plot between the variables first goes in one direction and then switches to another one.

data massaging The practice of playing with the data until the analysis producing the strongest association is identified and retained. In massaging the data, the bias will usually be towards finding evidence supporting expected or preferred outcomes.

debriefing Researchers explaining studies to subjects after the data have been collected and, in particular, noting any deception and why the deception was necessary and reassuring subjects that their participation was appreciated and helpful.

deductive explanation An explanation in which the phenomenon to be explained is a logically necessary consequence of the explanatory premises. As in: if A = B and B = C, then A = C.

degree of freedom Degree of freedom (df) = (Number of rows – 1) × (Number of columns – 1).

demand characteristic A distortion introduced in the course of data collection when respondents give the answers that they think are expected (i.e., "demanded") by the researcher.

deontological A view of research ethics that proposes absolute moral strictures that must never be violated. In contrast to the *consequentialist* view.

dependability Both the stability and the trackability of changes in the data over time and conditions. The issue of dependability in qualitative investigations reflects the reality that situations constantly change and people's realities differ.

dependent variable A variable that is viewed as being influenced by other variables. It is the "effect" in a cause–effect relationship.

descriptive research Research that describes *what* and how many of *what*.

descriptive statistics A branch of statistics that includes various tools, conventions, and procedures for describing variables or the relation between variables. (For instance, means, standard deviations, normal distributions, and Z scores are used to describe individual variables and crosstabulations, means across categories, and correlations are some of the procedures used to describe relationships between variables.)

discriminant function analysis A mode of analysis used in situations in which the dependent variable is measured at the nominal or ordinal level and the researcher wants to examine the impact of several independent variables simultaneously. This procedure provides weightings maximizing the likelihood of correctly predicting the category of the dependent variable into which each case will fall.

domain analysis Moving from observing a *social situation* (a set of behaviours carried out by people in a social situation) to discovering a *cultural scene.*

double blind An experimental design in which neither experimenters nor subjects are aware of which experimental condition is being applied to which subject.

double standard When a researcher uses different means of measuring identical behaviours, attitudes, or situations for each gender, the researcher is guilty of using a double standard.

dummy variable A variable that is coded 1 for presence and 0 for absence of a characteristic and that represents one category of an independent variable. Dummy variables are used in multiple regression and in discriminant analysis to enable the researcher to incorporate nominal variables.

empathetic explanation An explanation in which the experience of how the subject comes to see, comes to understand, is stressed.

equivalence of concepts The idea that while different cultures may have concepts that seem to be the same, the researcher must understand that there may be subtle differences in the content and meaning of concepts as we cross from culture to culture.

ethical guidelines The use of ethical rules, such as providing informed consent and protecting confidentiality, to guide the development of research protocol.

ethnography A qualitative research method that attempts to understand human behaviour in the cultural context in which it is embedded.

ethnomethodology A research method that typically involves a detailed examination of a single event or case; associated with the interpretative and critical traditions.

evidence Information drawn from the world that is used to test a hypothesis about the relationship among variables. When social scientists ask "What is your evidence?" they are asking you about the type and quality of data collected to shed light on a subject under investigation.

expectancy An anticipation of particular research results. Expectancy can lead to a distortion of results in the direction of expectations.

experimental group The group in an experiment that is exposed to a treatment intervention (also known as the treatment group). The outcomes for this group are then compared to the outcomes for the control group, which is not exposed to the intervention.

experimenter effect A tendency to produce findings that are consistent with the experimenter's expectations.

explanatory research Research that seeks to provide answers to *why* questions.

external validity The extent to which results can be extrapolated from the particular study to other groups in general.

***F* distribution** A test of significance used to compare means using a ratio-level dependent variable and a nominal-level independent variable.

face validity An evaluation of an indicator that, on inspection, appears to reflect the concept you want to measure.

false dilemma When the researcher argues (erroneously) that something is caused by either A or by B and then, having provided some evidence that B is not responsible, falsely concludes that A must be the cause.

familism A special case of gender insensitivity that involves treating the family as the unit of analysis when, in fact, it is individuals within the family unit that engage in a particular activity or hold a certain attitude. Familism is also a problem when we assume that some phenomenon has an equal impact on all members of the family when, in fact, it may affect different family members in different ways.

feminist research Research that is organized to expose the social causes of women's oppression and promote women's empowerment.

feminism A belief that one cannot adequately understand human societies without paying attention to the universal role of patriarchy—which refers to the domination of social groups by males, who have greater power and privilege than women and children.

field experiment An experiment in which the researcher intervenes in a natural setting and which, in contrast to most participation observation studies, can be simple and quickly completed.

field notes In participant observation studies, notes that attempt to capture the essence of the group being studied. Field notes include descriptions of events and people and their surrounding context, as well as the interpretations of the researcher and the participants.

file The name for a data set, or the text of a report, entered into a computer.

focus group A focus group brings together six to twelve individuals, who discuss the research topic. The researcher observes the interactions among focus-group members and solicits the individuals to talk about the research topic.

folk wisdom Ideas passed down from generation to generation; these can be an important source of ideas for the social researcher. Such ideas should not, however, be accepted as true until tested in some rigorous scientific fashion.

formal theory There are three elements in a formal theory: concepts, propositions stating the relations between the concepts, and the propositions that form a deductive system.

functional explanation An explanation in which the presence of some phenomenon is explained in terms of the role it plays in maintaining some system.

gatekeeper In participant observation studies, an individual with special group status who can lead the researcher to other *key informants.*

gender insensitivity A disregard of the differential impacts of research conclusions or of social policy on men and on women.

generalization A statement describing a pattern of behaviour or a relationship that can be applied to a variety of situations.

grounded theory The idea that the conclusions of a participant observation study should be grounded in the data—that is, based on direct and careful observations of everyday life within the group.

Hawthorne effect Any variability in a dependent variable that is not the direct result of variations in the treatment variable (see also: *source of spuriousness, confounding variable*).

history In a pre-experimental design, concurrent events that could be influencing variation in the dependent variable, along with the experimental manipulation. The possible influence of historical events on the outcome of the study is a flaw of the pseudo-experimental design.

independent variable The "cause" in a cause–effect relationship. The independent variable is a variable that has been selected as a possible influence on variations in a dependent variable.

in-depth interviews Personal interviews in which probing is used to explore issues in detail.

index A combined score based on two or more indicators.

individually delivered questionnaires Questionnaires that are handed to the respondent by a researcher.

inferential statistics Statistics that deal with making extrapolations from a sample to the population from which it was drawn.

informant Participant in an ethnographic investigation.

informed consent The right of a potential respondent to be informed as to the nature of the study, the kinds of issues that will be explored, how the respondent was selected, and who is sponsoring the research. In studies involving children, the infirm, or incompetent adults, the organization or individual responsible for the prospective respondent should provide consent in writing.

informed opinion An opinion based on evidence that has been collected under controlled circumstances.

insufficient evidence Evidence that is insufficient to confirm or disconfirm a hypothesis. To draw theoretical conclusions, appropriate evidence must be obtained. Evidence from one case or from a poorly selected sample would, for example, constitute insufficient evidence.

instrument decay A deterioration in the measurement instrument over the course of measurements in a study.

internal consistency The ability of the items in an instrument to measure the same variable. *Homogeneity* is often used to refer to the internal consistency of an instrument; that is, the items taken together measure one construct. A homogenous instrument contains items that are strongly correlated with each other. The higher the intercorrelations among the items, the greater the internal consistency of the instrument.

internal consistency approach to reliability An approach that involves comparing an individual item's correlation to the total index score: if an item is consistent with the total score it will correlate with it.

internal validity When the researcher has demonstrated that the treatment, in fact, produced the changes in the dependent variable.

internet-based survey A survey posted on the internet that the respondent can complete online and to which the respondent is usually directed by an email invitation.

interpretive approach An approach that relies mainly on field studies, with an emphasis on participant observation studies (joining a group and participating in it), in-depth interviews with people, and ethnomethodology (typically a detailed examination of a single event or case). Each of these studies typically involves a few cases that are described in detail. A key question for these researchers is: does the explanation offered make sense to the people whose behaviour is being explained? Communication of the results of such studies usually emphasizes verbal descriptions rather than numerical analyses.

intersubjectivity In phenomenology, a process for reaching subjective awareness and understanding in a common world.

intervening variable A variable that links an independent variable to a dependent one. An intervening variable represents an explanation of how the independent variable influences the dependent variable.

interview schedule A document that outlines the major questions that are to be raised in an interview. Within the guidelines provided by the interview schedule, the interviewer has autonomy in choosing which questions to explore in detail.

institutional ethnography A multi-method approach used by critical researchers interested in studying how people's lived experiences are organized by institutional practices.

Jackson's rule of thirds When testing to control the intervening variable in three-variable relationships, if the original difference between the categories increases by one-third or more, we will interpret this as an *increase*, or a strengthening, of the original relationship; if the difference remains within one-third of the original, we will interpret this as an indication that the relationship has *remained the same*; if the difference decreases by more than one-third, we will interpret this as a *decrease/disappearance* of the relationship; finally, if the relationship is markedly different when different control categories are compared to one another (e.g., it disappears in one category, but stays the same in the other), the result is *mixed*.

key character files In the analysis of data from participant observation studies, files established on key players in the organization or group being observed. Items are drawn from the master file to provide clues as to the personality and manner of operation of each individual.

key informants In participant observation studies, group members who are most knowledgeable about the study phenomenon.

Lambda A statistic measuring the *proportionate reduction in error* that occurs in estimating a dependent variable given knowledge of the independent variable.

leptokurtic distribution A distribution with little variability—a small standard deviation relative to the magnitude of the values—and sharply peaked.

lifeworld In phenomenology, a term that refers to the world of lived experience.

Likert-based index A measure for a construct that is based on a set of Likert-type questions. Likert-based indices are widely used in social science research because they can be shown to have high content validity and internal reliability.

Likert-type questions Questions that ask respondents to state their opinion on an issue by indicating whether they strongly disagree, disagree, are undecided or neutral, agree, or strongly agree with the statement.

linear regression equation An equation that describes a relationship between a number of independent variables and a dependent variable and provides for the best linear (additive) weightings of the independent variables and a constant calculated so as to maximize the prediction of the dependent variable.

lived experience In phenomenology, the everyday human experiences that are real to the individuals who experience them.

longitudinal data Data collected from the same sample (i.e., panel) over a period of time. Longitudinal data is also called time-series data, especially the sort of data employed by economists.

magnitude estimation procedure A procedure in which a respondent estimates the magnitude of a series of stimuli compared to some fixed standard. Magnitude estimation procedures are useful when comparative judgments are required.

master field file In the analysis of data from participant observation studies, a file made up of the complete journal of field notes.

master table A table recording all the data collected in the course of a study; any required tables for data analysis can be derived from the master table without going back to tally sheets.

maturation Changes that occur in an individual subject over the course of an experiment that could, along with the experimental manipulation, influence the outcome of the experiment. The possible influence of maturation is a flaw of the pseudo-experimental design.

mean More formally known as the *arithmetic mean* and less formally known as the *average*, a figure that is computed by summing the values of a variable and dividing the result by the total number of cases.

measurement The process of reflecting abstract concepts with empirical indicants.

measurement error The extent to which indicants fail to reflect the true underlying values of variables.

measures of central tendency Measures that use one number to typify a set of values.

median A figure that represents the mid-point of a distribution.

missing evidence Evidence that is necessary for the argument to be true and that is missing.

missing value code A value assigned to a variable to be used in cases where the information is absent or not applicable.

mode The most frequently occurring response to a nominal variable.

mortality Subjects selecting themselves out of a study.

multicollinearity The extent of the correlation among the independent variables.

multiple methods A combination of survey administration strategies used to encourage participants to complete and return the survey. For example, researchers may begin with a mailed survey and follow-up with a telephone survey to encourage those who have not completed the survey with the option of doing so on the telephone.

multiple regression analysis An analysis that identifies an equation to predict variations in a dependent variable from two or more independent variables.

multi-stage area sample A sample developed by stages when attempting to reflect a large unit such as a state, province, or country when no list of the population is available. At each stage of the sampling process, every individual (or unit) must have a known chance of being selected.

multivariate models Models that involve numerous variables.

mutually exclusive categories Categories established with boundaries that ensure that no category overlaps with another one.

natural setting experiments Experiments in which everyday situations can be manipulated, allowing for the researcher to observe reactions of people to the intervention.

naturalistic observational study A study in which people are observed in a natural setting without their knowledge that their behaviour is being recorded.

nominal measurement A quantitative measure in which the numbers are arbitrarily assigned to categories of the variable.

non-probability sampling techniques Techniques that do not provide potential respondents with a known chance of being asked to participate in a study. Convenience, quota, and referral (snowball) are examples of non-probability sampling techniques.

nonreactive studies Studies that involve indirect data collection—situations in which there is no opportunity for the person being studied to react to the observations.

normal distribution A distribution that approximates a bell-shaped curve, with few cases on the extremes and the majority clustered at the mean of the distribution.

null hypothesis A hypothesis that states there will be no relation between the variables.

objective Free from bias.

official statistics Data collected by formal public offices, such as hospitals, police, and coroners.

one-tailed test A test of significance done when the researcher is predicting which particular tail of the normal distribution the result will fall into if the null hypothesis is to be rejected.

open-ended question A question for which no preset response categories are provided.

operational level The stage of a research study consisting of the measurement of variables, as well as the collection and analysis of data.

operationalization The selection of indicators (measures) to reflect conceptual variables, and the implementation of a research project.

ordinal measurement Measurement in which there is an order in the values assigned, but the intervals between the values are not equal.

output (.spo) files The files that contain the results of the analysis conducted, when using SPSS to conduct statistical analysis.

overgeneralization A statement that claims to refer to all people but is based on evidence that does not represent all people.

overspecificity Using single-sex terms when members of both sexes could potentially be meant: for example, "The doctor . . . he . . . "

overt participant A researcher who enters and studies a group from within; group members know that they are the subject of a research project.

panel studies Studies that monitor specific organizations or individuals over time.

partial correlation A correlation that measures the strength of association between two ratio-level variables while simultaneously controlling for the effects of one or more additional variables.

partial theory A theory that explains an assumed or known relationship by specifying a testable causal model.

participant Individual who informs the study in qualitative investigations. Qualitative study participants are viewed as active participants in the research process and equal partners with the investigator.

participant observation studies Studies in which the researcher is involved in the daily lives of the study group, observing and recording as much as possible about their lives.

participatory action research Resarch that uses critical social theory methods; participatory action research is done for the purpose of taking action and creating change.

path model A graphic representation of a complex set of proposed interrelationships among variables.

patriarchy The domination of social groups by males who have greater power and privilege than women and children.

percentage A proportion multiplied by 100. Thus, a percentage represents *how many* for every 100 of something.

phenomenology A qualitative research method that describes the meaning of a lived experience from the perspective of the participant. Lived experiences are the everyday human experiences that are real to the individuals who experience them. Phenomenology seeks to achieve a deep understanding of the phenomenon being studied through a rigorous, systematic examination of it. Its purpose is to describe the essences of lived experiences.

pilot study A study in which a small sample of respondents completes the prepared questionnaire or undergoes the interview in order to test the questionnaire or interview schedule. Pilot studies are used to determine items to be included in indexes, and to determine, from open-ended questions, what categories should be used in a fixed choice format.

plagiarism The unacknowledged borrowing of other authors' ideas or words.

platykurtic distribution A distribution with a great deal of variability that will tend to be flat and wide.

point-in-time data Data that is collected at one point in time; point-in-time data cannot be used to measure change over time.

population That collection of individuals, communities, or nations about which one wishes to make a general statement.

positivist approach The approach to knowledge largely adopted in the physical sciences. In the early development of the social sciences some theorists attempted to model the new disciplines on the physical sciences. The French scholars Auguste Comte (1798–1857) and Emile Durkheim (1858–1917) were leaders in encouraging positivist approaches to understanding social behaviour.

precise communication Information that is unambiguous.

pre-coded single choice questions Questions that ask the respondent to select the appropriate answer from a list of pre-set response categories.

prediction In regression analysis, the extent to which variation in a dependent variable can be accurately estimated with knowledge of the independent variables.

predictive validity A type of criterion validity. A measure has predictive validity if it predicts the outcome. For example, if a graduate student entrance exam successfully predicts successful completion of a graduate program, the test has predictive validity.

presence-absence questions Questions that ask respondents to check off which items in a list do or do not apply to them.

primary sampling units Units of division of a larger area or population, such as census tract areas or other similar units, used when developing a multi-stage area sample in order to study a large unit such as a province, state or country. Primary sampling units normally number several hundred.

probabilistic explanation An explanation that involves arguing that a particular case will be similar to others in the same general category.

probability sampling procedures Techniques for selecting sampling units so that each has a known chance of being included.

pronoun problem A problematic use of language that encourages stereotypic thinking—by referring, for example, to doctors and managers as *he* and nurses as *she*.

proportion That part of 1 which is represented by a category; for example, how many females there are in a population compared to the total population. Proportions always begin with a decimal point.

proportionate reduction in error The reduction of error that occurs in estimating a dependent variable, given knowledge of the independent variable. If two variables are strongly associated, then errors in predicting variations in the dependent variable will be considerably reduced if information on the independent variable is taken into account. The proportionate reduction in error is measured by the statistic *Lambda*.

provincialism The tendency to see things narrowly as one's culture sees them.

proxemics The study of the norms surrounding personal space and the conditions under which such space will or will not be violated.

pseudo-experimental design An experimental design that does not permit clear causal inferences about the impact of a treatment on the dependent variable. Although these designs share some of the elements of the experiment, their structures inhibit clear causal interpretations.

pure research (also known as **descriptive research**) Research that focuses on understanding social relationships.

purposive sampling A process in qualitative research whereby participants are selected on the basis of whether they have a particular experience or group membership related to the phenomena under investigation. Thus, the researcher considers the purposes of the investigation in the selection of participants. Purposive sampling is sometimes called theoretical sampling.

qualitative research Research using concepts, classifications, and attempts to interpret human behaviour reflecting not only the analyst's view but the views of the people whose behaviour is being described. The emphasis is on verbal descriptions as opposed to numerical ones.

quality control monitoring system A system that ensures that interviewers are following established standard procedures for selecting respondents, asking questions, and entering the data.

quantitative research Research that seeks to quantify, or reflect with numbers, observations about human behaviour.

quasi-experimental design A design in which it has not been possible to do any or all of the following: (i) randomly assign subjects to a treatment or control group; or (ii) control the timing or nature of the treatment. The quasi-experiment comes as close as possible to experimental design in order to measure the impact of a treatment.

questionnaire A series of set questions that either have a space provided for an answer or offer a number of fixed alternatives from which the respondent makes a choice.

quota sample A sample for which respondents are selected on the basis of meeting certain criteria: the first respondent to meet the requirement(s) is asked to participate; sampling continues until all the categories have been filled—that is, until the quota for each has been reached.

r^2 A measure of the amount of variation in the dependent variable that is explained by an independent variable.

R^2 A measure of the amount of variation in the dependent variable that is explained by the combination of independent variables (regression analysis).

random error Inconsistencies that enter into the coding process but that have no pattern. In contrast to *systematic errors*.

random sample A sample that provides each unit (usually a person) in the population with an equal chance of being selected for participation in a study.

random variable A variable that varies without control but is taken into account by the way groups are set up in an experiment.

range The gap between the lowest and highest value in a distribution.

rank-ordering questions Questions in which a respondent is asked to indicate an ordering of response items, usually from most preferred to least preferred.

rate The frequency of some phenomenon for a standard-sized unit (such as incidence per 1,000 or per 100,000).

ratio measurement A quantitative measurement in which intervals are equal and there is a true zero point.

ratios Measures used to compare rates or other measures across categories.

reflexivity The critical thinking required to examine the interaction occurring between the researcher and the data during analyses. In critical research, researchers strive to understand how their ideas and value system can influence the collection and analyses of the data. The researcher needs to be reflexive so that she or he can uncover and provide a full account of deep-seated views, thinking, and conduct.

regression analysis A method for analyzing the relation between a ratio-level dependent variable and independent variables. This form of analysis provides weightings that may be used in an equation to describe the relationship; standardized weightings provide a means for estimating the relative impact of independent variables on the dependent one.

regression line A straight line describing the relation between an independent and dependent variable drawn so that the vertical deviations of the points above the line equal the vertical deviations below the line.

reliability The extent to which, on repeated measures, an indicator will yield similar readings.

replacement of terms Replacing general theoretical concepts by specific instances of these concepts.

research bias Systematic distortions in research outcomes.

research hypothesis The statement of relation between variables.

researcher affect A process whereby the researcher, having fallen in love with a particular explanation for some relationship or view of the world, may inadvertently engage in procedures that lead to conclusions supporting the preferred explanation.

response bias Bias that occurs when a respondent gives an untrue answer for any number of reasons—for instance, wanting to appear consistent (giving the same answer they gave the first time) or trying to help the researchers (suspecting they know what the study is about and, therefore, answering in a way that they believe satisfies the researcher's interests).

response rate The percentage of delivered questionnaires that are completed and returned.

response set A situation in which a respondent tends to answer similarly to all items.

review of the literature A section of a paper that tries to provide an overview of the current "state of scientific knowledge" on the topic being researched.

salience The degree of interest of the research topic to the respondent; the greater the salience of the topic to respondents, the greater the response rate.

sample A segment selected from a population; the sample is then interpreted to represent that population.

sampling fraction The sample size in relation to the population.

sampling frame The list from which the researcher draws a sample.

saturation A term used in qualitative investigations to refer to a situation in data collection whereby the participants' descriptions become repetitive and confirm previously collected data.

scale A complex combination of indicators in which the pattern of the responses is taken into account.

secondary data Information collected by persons other than the researcher.

secondary data analysis Data analysis conducted on existing data (e.g., official statistics) or on data originally collected for other purposes (e.g., survey data collected for another project).

selected evidence Evidence chosen because it supports a particular point of view; evidence that runs counter to what the researcher is attempting to demonstrate is ignored.

selection Subjects selecting themselves into a study.

self-administered questionnaire A questionnaire that is completed by the survey respondent without any interaction with the researcher who designed the questionnaire. There are four types of self-administered questionnaires: individually delivered questionnaires, group administered questionnaires, mailed questionnaires, and internet-based surveys.

sexual dichotomism Treating the sexes as discrete social, as well as biological, cohorts rather than two cohorts with shared characteristics.

simple random sample A sample that provides each unit (usually a person) in the population with an equal chance of being selected for participation in a study.

skip interval An interval determined by dividing the total sample requirement into the total number of units in the population being surveyed; this number should then be rounded to the nearest, but lower, round number.

snowball sampling A referral sampling procedure. As you complete one interview you ask if there is anyone else known to the respondent who might be appropriate for the study.

source of spuriousness A variable that is viewed as possibly influencing both the independent and the dependent variable in such a way that it accounts for the relationship between them.

source of spuriousness model A model in which a variable is identified as a possible influence on both the independent variable (X) and the dependent variable (Y) in such a way that it accounts for the relationship between them. In other words, the relationship between X and Y may be "spurious" because it is produced by the influence of S/S on each of them.

Spearman correlation A statistic that is used to measure the strength of association between two ordinal-level variables.

split-half method A method for testing reliability that involves randomly splitting index items into two groups, computing the indexes, and then correlating the resulting scores. Internal reliability would be indicated by a high correlation between the two indexes.

SPSS The Statistical Package for the Social Sciences (SPSS) is the most popular and widely used computer based statistical program used by social researchers.

standard deviation A measure that reflects the average amount of deviation from the mean value of the variable.

standard error of the means A measure of variability in the means of repeated samples.

statistical regression A tendency towards less extreme scores. Statistical regression is demonstrated when a sample is selected on the basis of extreme scores and upon retesting shows less extreme scores.

statistical significance The probability that an observed association or difference is reflective of some "real" difference in the population from which the sample has been taken and not merely the result of sampling fluctuations.

stratified sample A sample that will give individuals within designated categories an equal chance of selection.

structured interviews Face-to-face interviews in which questions are read to the respondents. Such interviews ordinarily will provide for in-depth probes on some of the questions.

summary tables Tables that compress the results of many analyses into one table.

surveys A method for collecting information by having respondents complete questionnaires.

symbolic interactionism An examination of how people define events or reality and how those beliefs shape their actions. Symbolic interactionism focuses on the meaning of events to people in everyday settings.

syntax (.sps) files The files that contain instruction commands specifying which statistical procedures should be computed for specific variables, when using SPSS to conduct statistical analysis.

system (.sav) files A file that contains all of the data and all of the labels describing the variables in the file, when using SPSS.

systematic errors Errors that distort the data in one particular direction. In contrast to *random error*.

systematic sample A sample that provides each unit (usually a person) in the population with an equal chance of being selected for participation in a study by choosing every nth unit, starting randomly.

tally sheets Sheets used to record information during the data-collection phase of observational studies.

taxonomy A set of categories organized on the basis of a single semantic relationship.

telephone survey A survey that relies on information reported by the respondent over the telephone.

test of significance A test reporting the probability that an observed association or difference is the result of sampling fluctuations and not reflective of some "real" difference in the population from which the sample has been taken.

texts In institutional ethnography, texts are defined as organizational features of institutions, such as schools, the workplace, hospitals, and government bureaucracies. Texts are studied to explicate the "ruling relations" that frame the interactions of individuals within organizations.

themes Recurrent ideas or patterns that emerge in the data and that represent common threads of meaning in the narrative of participants.

theoretical coding A system of coding data in ethnographic data analysis that forms theoretical linkages or connections between the data categories.

theoretical level The most abstract, general conceptualization of the research problem in a project.

theoretical memos The ideas the researcher holds about codes and the relationships as they strike the researcher during analysis.

theoretical sampling A process whereby the researcher collects, codes, and analyzes the data simultaneously and then decides what additional data are needed to develop the theory.

theory An idea or system of ideas that explains the behaviour of humans, or human institutions.

time-series data See *longitudinal data*.

transferability The ability of study results to be transferred to other settings, populations, and contexts and still hold true; also known as *generalizability*. In assessing transferability of findings the research consumer hopes to show that the results are not context bound.

treatment level The number of different categories of a variable that will be exposed to the subject in an experiment. A study, for example, with three treatment levels might compare the effects of seeing a short, medium, or long film.

treatment variable A variable whose effect on some dependent variable is being assessed in an experiment.

true value The underlying exact quantity of a variable at any given time.

trustworthiness The validity and reliability of qualitative research.

t-test A test of significance usually used with small samples.

two-tailed test A test of significance done when the researcher is not predicting which particular tail of the normal distribution the result will fall into if the null hypothesis is to be rejected.

type I error An error that results when a null hypotheses is rejected when it should be accepted.

type II error An error that results when a null hypothesis is accepted when it should be rejected.

unilineal model A model in which the same patterns of development are followed by all societies.

unit of analysis The basic type of object under investigation. Usually researchers define the unit and deal with only one unit at a time: it may be a speech, or a paragraph from the speech; it may be a number of individuals or a number of groups. The information collected describes the unit under investigation.

unwarranted conclusion A conclusion that is based on flawed reasoning. For example, if a researcher suggests that one variable causes a change in another variable simply because the two variables are correlated, there has been an error in reasoning, and the conclusions of the research are therefore unwarranted.

validity The extent to which a measure reflects the concept. The measure reflects nothing more or less than that implied by the conceptual definition.

variables Those concepts that we intend to measure.

variance The average amount of deviation from the mean value of the variable; the variance is the standard deviation squared.

verifiable Confirmable by tests conducted by others.

Verstehen A German word meaning the empathetic understanding of behaviour.

web survey A survey that is located on a website is called a web survey. A common way to solicit participation in a web survey is through an invitation received by email. The message contains the web address and the participant's password for doing the survey.

within-subject design An experimental design that exposes one subject to the different experimental treatments. Since the subject is the same person, background characteristics, attitudes, and intelligence are all perfectly controlled.

Z score A measure that expresses an observation's location relative to the mean (in standard deviation units) within a normal distribution.

BIBLIOGRAPHY

Abrahamson, Mark (1983). *Social Research Methods*. Englewood Cliffs, NJ: Prentice-Hall.

Adams, Tracey L. (2005). "Feminization of Professions: The Case of Women in Dentistry." *Canadian Journal of Sociology*, 30(1), 71–94.

Anderson, Nels (1961). *The Hobo*. Chicago: Phoenix Edition, [1923].

Arnold, Stephen, and Douglas J. Tigert (1974). "Canadians and Americans: A Comparative Perspective." *International Journal of Comparative Sociology*, 15, 68–83.

Atkinson, P., and M. Hammersley (1994). "Ethnography and Participant Observation." In N.K. Denzin and Y.S. Lincoln, eds., *Handbook of Qualitative Research* (248–261). Thousand Oaks, CA: Sage.

Babbie, Earl (1992). *The Practice of Social Research*. 6th ed. Belmont, CA: Wadsworth Publishing Company.

Baer, Doug, Edward Grabb, and William A. Johnston (1990). "The Values of Canadians and Americans: A Critical Analysis and Reassessment." *Social Forces*, 68(3), 693–713.

Bailey, Kenneth D. (1970). "Evaluating Axiomatic Theories." In Edgar F. Borgotta and George W. Bohrnstedt, eds., *Sociological Methodology 1970*. San Francisco: Jossey-Bass Inc.

Bakalar, Nicholas (2005). "Ugly Children May Get Parental Short Shrift." *New York Times* (3 May), F7.

Barnsley, J., and D. Ellis (1992). *Research for Change: Participatory Action Research for Community Group*. Vancouver, BC: Women's Research Centre.

Baron, Stephen W. (1989). "The Canadian West Coast Punk Subculture: A Field Study." *Canadian Journal of Sociology*, 14(3), 289–316.

Baumrind, D. (1964). "Some Thoughts on Ethics of Research: After Reading Milgram's 'Behavioral Study of Obedience.'" *American Psychologist*, 19, 421–423.

Beck, C.T. (1993). "Qualitative Research: The Evaluation of Its Credibility, Fittingness, and Auditability." *Western Journal of Nursing Research*, 15(2), 263–265.

Becker, Howard S., Blanche Geer, Everett C. Hughes, and Anselm L. Strauss (1961). *Boys in White*. Chicago: The University of Chicago Press.

Begley, Sharon (1993). "The Meaning of Junk." *Newsweek* (23 March), 62–64.

Berman, Helene, Marilyn Ford-Gilboe, and Jacquelyn C. Campbell (1998). "Combining Stories and Numbers: A Methodologic Approach for a Critical Nursing Science." *Advances in Nursing Science*, 12(1), 1–15.

Berreman, Gerald D. (1973). "Behind Many Masks: Ethnography and Impression Management in a Himalayan Village." In Donald P. Warwick, and Samuel Osherson, eds., *Comparative Research Methods*. Englewood Cliffs, NJ: Prentice-Hall, Inc., 268–312.

Beshers, James M. (1958). "On 'A Critique of Tests of Significance in Survey Research.'" *American Sociological Review*, (23 April), 199.

Blalock, Hubert M. Jr. (1979). *Social Statistics*. Toronto: McGraw-Hill Book Company.

——— (1969). *Theory Construction*. Englewood Cliffs, NJ: Prentice-Hall, Inc.

——— (1964). *Causal Inferences in Nonexperimental Research*. Chapel Hill, NC: The University of North Carolina Press.

Blau, Peter (1964). *Exchange and Power in Social Life*. New York: John Wiley & Sons, Inc.

Blishen, B.R. (1968). "A Socio-economic Index for Occupations in Canada." *Canadian Review of Sociology and Anthropology*, (February), 41–53.

Blishen, B.R., and H. McRoberts (1976). "A Revised Socioeconomic Index for Occupations in Canada." *Canadian Review of Sociology and Anthropology*, 13(1), 71–79.

Blumer, Herbert (1969). "Symbolic Interactionism: Perspective and Method." In W. Chenitz and J. Swanson, eds., *From Practice to Grounded Theory: Qualitative Research in Nursing*. Menlo Park, CA: Addison-Wesley.

——— (1951). "Collective Behavior." In A.M. Lee, ed., *Principles of Sociology* (167–222). New York: Barnes and Noble.

Bohrnstedt, G.W. (1969). "A Quick Method for Determining the Reliability and Validity of Multiple-Item Scales." *American Sociological Review*, 34, 542–548.

Bonnar, Anne Marie (1992). "To Signal or Not to Signal: A Study of Personal Space and Behaviour." Antigonish: St. Francis Xavier University, Sociology 100 paper.

Bottomore, T.B., and Maximilien Rubel (1988). *Karl Marx: Selected Writings in Sociology and Social Philosophy*. London: Penguin Books.

Boutlier, M., R. Mason, and I. Rootman (1997). "Community Action and Reflective Practice in Health Promotion Research." *Health Promotion International*, 12(1), 69–78.

Braithwaite, R.W. (1960). *Scientific Explanation*. New York: Harper Torchbooks.

Brennan, Andrea (1985). "Participation and Self-Esteem: A Test of Six Alternative Explanations." *Adolescence*, 20(78), 445–466.

Broussard, Michelle (1991). "Unwanted Intimacy in Female University Students." Antigonish: St. Francis Xavier University, Research Methods Paper.

Browne, G., C. Byrne, J. Roberts, A. Gafni, S. Watt, S. Haldane, I. Thomas, B. Ewart, M. Schuster, J. Underwood, S. Flynn-Kingston, and K. Rennick (1999). "Benefitting All the Beneficiaries of Social Assistance: The 2-Year Effects and Expense of Subsidized versus Nonsubsidized Quality Child Care and Recreation." *National Academies of Practice Forum*, 1(2), 131–142.

Browne, G., C. Byrne, J. Roberts, A. Gafni, S. Watt, B. Ewart, M. Schuster, J. Underwood, S. Flynn-Kingston, K. Rennick, I. Thomas, and S. Haldane (1998). *When the Bough Breaks: Provider-Initiated Comprehensive Care Is More Effective and Less Expensive for Sole Support Parents on Social Assistance*. Hamilton, ON: System-Linked Research Unit, McMaster University.

Browne, M.N., and S.M. Keeley (1990). *Asking the Right Questions*. Englewood Cliffs, NJ: Prentice-Hall, Inc.

Bunting, S.M., and J.C. Campbell (1994). "Through a Feminist Lens: A Model to Guide Nursing Research." In P. Chinn, ed., *Advances in Methods of Inquiring for Nursing*. Gaithersburg, MD: Aspen Publications.

Campbell, Brian (2003). "Student Technology Use Survey: Comparing the Response Rates for Web and Mailed Formats." Unpublished paper.

Campbell, Donald T., and Julian C. Stanley (1966). *Experimental and Quasi-experimental Designs for Research*. Chicago: Rand McNally & Company.

Campbell, Marie, and Frances Gregor (2002). *Mapping Social Relations: A Primer in Institutional Ethnography*. Aurora, ON: Garamond Press.

Carmines, Edward G., and Richard A. Zeller (1979). *Reliability and Validity Assessment*. Beverly Hills, CA: Sage Publications.

Chenitz, W.C., and J. Swanson (1986). *From Practice to Grounded Theory: Qualitative Research in Nursing*. Menlo Park, CA: Addison-Wesley.

Cheyn, Efian (1972). "The Effect of Spatial and Interpersonal Variables on the Invasion of Group Controlled Territories." *Sociometry*, 477–488.

Christiansen-Ruffman, Linda (2002). "Atlantic Canadian Coastal Communities and the Fisheries Trade: A Feminist Critique, Revaluation and Revisioning," *Canadian Woman Studies*, (Spring/Summer), 21(4)/22(1).

Collins, Randall (1975). *Conflict Sociology: Toward an Explanatory Science*. New York: Academic Press.

Comte, Auguste (1875). *System of Positive Polity*. London: Burt Franklin [1851].

Corbin, Juliet, and Anselm Strauss (1990). "Grounded Theory Research: Procedures, Canons, and Evaluative Criteria," *Qualitative Sociology*, 13(1), 3–21.

Coser, Lewis A. (1956). *The Functions of Social Conflict*. London: Free Press of Glencoe.

Costner, R.L., and R.K. Leik (1964). "Deductions from 'Axiomatic Theory.'" *American Sociological Review*, 29 (December), 819–835.

Counts, Dorothy Ayers, and David R. Counts (2001). *Over the Next Hill: An Ethnography of RVing Seniors in North America*. 2nd ed. Toronto: Broadview Press.

Crawford, Craig, and James Curtis (1979). "English Canadian–American Differences in Value Orientations." *Studies in Comparative International Development*, 14, 23–44.

Creswell, J.W. (1998). *Qualitative Inquiry and Research Design: Choosing among Five Traditions*. London: Sage.

——— (1994). *Research Design: Qualitative and Qualitative Approaches*. Thousand Oaks, CA: Sage.

Curtis, James (1971). "Voluntary Association Joining: A Cross-National Comparative Note." *American Sociological Review*, 36 (October), 872–880.

Curtis, James, Ronald D. Lambert, Steven D. Brown, and Barry J. Kay (1989). "Affiliation with Voluntary Associations: Canadian-American Comparisons." *Canadian Journal of Sociology*, 14(2), 143–161.

Czerny, Michael, Jamie Swift, and Robert G. Clarke (1994). *Getting Started on Social Analysis in Canada*. 3rd ed. Toronto: Between the Lines.

Dahrendorf, Ralf (1958). "Out of Utopia: Toward a Reorientation of Sociological Analysis." *American Journal of Sociology*, 64.

Daly, Kerry (2002). "Time, Gender, and the Negotiation of Family Schedules." *Symbolic Interaction*, 25(3), 323–342.

Davidoff, Henry (1953). *A World Treasury of Proverbs*. London: Cassell & Company.

Deagle, G., and C. McWilliam (1992). "Developing Healthy and Supportive Community Environments: A Strategy for Action." Paper presented at Prevention Congress V. London, ON, 27 April.

Denzin, N., and Y. Lincoln (2000). *Handbook of Qualitative Research,* 2nd ed. London: Sage.

Desroches, Frederick J. (2002). *Force and Fear: Robbery in Canada*. Toronto: Canadian Scholars Press Inc.

——— (1990). "Tearoom Trade: A Research Update." *Qualitative Sociology*, 13(1), 39–61.

Deutscher, Irwin (1966). "Words and Deeds: Social Action and Social Policy." *Social Problems,* 13, 235–254.

Deutskens, Elisabeth, Ko De Ruyter, Martin Wetzels, and Paul Oosterveld (2004). "Response Rate and Response Quality of Internet-Based Surveys: An Experimental Study." *Marketing Letters*, 15(1), 21.

Dietz, Mary Lorenz, Robert Prus, and William Shaffir, Eds. (1994). *Doing Everyday Life: Ethnography as Human Lived Experience*. Mississauga, ON: Copp Clark Longman Ltd.

Dillman, Don A. (1978). *Mail and Telephone Surveys: The Total Design Method*. New York: John Wiley & Sons.

Dillman, Don A., James A. Christenson, Edwin H. Carpenter, and Ralph M. Brooks (1974). "Increasing Mail Questionnaire Response." *American Sociological Review,* 39(5), 744–756.

Driver, H.E., and W.C. Massey (1957). *Comparative Studies of North American Indians*. Philadelphia: The American Philosophical Society.

Dunk, Thomas (1991). *It's a Working Man's Town: Male Working-Class Culture in Northwestern Ontario*. Montreal: McGill-Queen's University Press.

Durkheim, Émile (1976). *Suicide*. Glencoe, IL: Free Press [1915].

——— (1954). *The Elementary Forms of Religious Life*. New York: The Free Press [1912].

——— (1951). *Suicide: A Study of Sociology*. Translated by J. Spaulding and G. Simpson. New York: The Free Press, [1897].

——— (1938). *The Rules of Sociological Method*. New York: The Free Press, [1895].

Easthope, Gary (1974). *History of Social Research Methods*. London: Longman Group.

Eichler, Margrit (1997). "Feminist Methodology." *Current Sociology*, 45(2), 9–36.

——— (1988). *Nonsexist Research Methods*. Boston: Allen & Unwin.

Eichner, Klaus, and Werner Habermehl (1981). "Predicting Response Rates to Mailed Questionnaires." *American Sociological Review,* 46, 361–363.

Erdos, Paul L. (1983). *Professional Mail Surveys*. Malabar, FL: Robert E. Krieger Publishing Company.

Erickson, M. (1968). "The Inhumanity of Ordinary People." *International Journal of Psychiatry*, 6, 277–279.

Etzioni, A. (1968). "A Model of Significant Research." *International Journal of Psychiatry*, 6, 279–280.

Fain, J.A. (1999). *Reading, Understanding, and Applying Nursing Research: A Text and Workbook*. Philadelphia: F.A. Davis.

Fay, Brian (1987). *Critical Social Science: Liberation and Its Limits*. Ithaca, NY: Cornell University Press.

Featherman, David L., and Gillian Stevens (1982). "A Revised Index of Occupational Status: Application in Analysis of Sex Differences in Attainment." Chapter 7 in R.M. Hauser, D. Mechanic, A.O. Haller, and T.S. Hauser, eds., *Social Structure and Behavior: Essays in Honor of William Hamilton Sewell*. New York: Academic Press.

Fern, E.F. (1982). "The Use of Focus Groups for Idea Generation: The Effects of Group Size, Acquaintanceship, and Moderator on a Response Quality and Quantity." *Journal of Marketing Research*, 19, 1–13.

Festinger, L., H.W. Riecken, and S. Schachter (1956). *When Prophecy Fails*. New York: Harper & Row.

Feurstein, M. (1988). "Finding the Methods to Fit the People: Training for Participatory Evaluation." *Community Development Journal*, 23, 16–25.

Fisher, Doug (1993). "Fed Up with Too Many Questions, Canadians Are Hanging Up on Pollsters." *Montreal Gazette* (24 September), A8.

Ford-Gilboe, M., and J. Campbell (1996). "The Mother Headed Single Parent Family: A Feminist Critique of the Nursing Literature." *Nursing Outlook*, 44, 173–183.

Fougere, Annette (1992). "Effects of Eating Breakfast on Grade Performance." Antigonish: St. Francis Xavier University, Research Methods Paper.

Gibbs, J.P. (1972). *Sociological Theory Construction*. Hinsdale, IL: The Dryden Press, Inc.

Gibbs, J.P., and W.T. Martin (1964). *Status Integration and Suicide: A Sociological Study*. Eugene, OR: University of Oregon Press.

Gillis, Amy (1998). "The Trends and Variations in Smoking." Antigonish: St. Francis Xavier University, Nursing 300 paper.

Gillis, A., and W. Jackson (2002). *Research for Nurses: Methods and Interpretation*. Philadelphia: F.A. Davis.

Glaser, Barney G. (1978). *Theoretical Sensitivity*. Niel Valley, CA: Sociology Press.

Glaser, Barney G., and Anselm Strauss (1967). *The Discovery of Grounded Theory*. Chicago: Aldine Press.

Goffman, Erving (1962). *Asylums*. Chicago: Aldine Press.

Gold, David (1958). "Comment on 'A Critique of Tests of Significance.'" *American Sociological Review*, 23 (February), 85–86.

Gottschalk, S. (1999). "Speed Culture: Fast Strategies in Televised Commercial Ads." *Qualitative Sociology*, 22(4), 311–329.

Government of Canada (2006). "Tri-Council Policy Statement: Ethical Conduct for Research Involving Humans." Retrieved 24 February 2006 from http://www.pre.ethics.gc.ca/english/policystatement/policystatement.cfm.

Goyder, John C. (2005). "The Dynamics of Occupational Prestige: 1975–2000." *Canadian Review of Sociology and Anthropology*, 42(1), 1–23.

——— (1985). "Nonresponse on Surveys: A Canada–United States Comparison," *Canadian Journal of Sociology*, 10 (Summer), 231–251.

——— (1982). "Further Evidence on Factors Affecting Response Rates to Mailed Questionnaires." *American Sociological Review*, 47 (August), 550–553.

Goyder, John C., and Jean McKenzie Leiper (1985). "The Decline in Survey Response: A Social Values Interpretation." *Sociology*, 19(1), 55–71.

Grabb, Edward, and James Curtis (2005). *Regions Apart: The Four Societies of Canada and the United States*. Don Mills, ON: Oxford University Press.

Grabb, E., J. Curtis, and D. Baer (2001). "On Accuracy and Big Pictures: Reply to Lipset." *The Canadian Review of Sociology and Anthropology*, 38(1), 101–103.

——— (2000). "Defining Moments and Recurring Myths: Comparing Canadians and Americans after the American Revolution." *The Canadian Review of Sociology and Anthropology*, 37(4), 373–419.

Groves, Robert M., and Robert L. Kahn (1979). *Surveys by Telephone: A National Comparison with Personal Interviews*. New York: Academic Press.

Guba, E.G., and Y.S. Lincoln (1981). *Effective Evaluation*. San Francisco: Jossey-Bass.

Guttman, Louis (1950). "The Basis for Scalogram Analysis." In S.A. Stouffer, L. Buttman, E.A. Suchman, P.F. Lazarfeld, S.A. Star, and J.A. Clausen, eds., *Measurement and Prediction*. Princeton, NJ: Princeton University Press.

Habermas, Jurgen (1984). *The Theory of Communicative Action*, Vol. 1. Boston: Beacon Press.

Hacker, Diana (1990). *A Canadian Writer's Reference*. Scarborough, ON: Nelson Canada.

Hamblin, Robert L. (1974). "Social Attitudes: Magnitude Measurement and Theory." In H.M. Blalock Jr., ed., *Measurement in the Social Sciences* (61–120). Chicago: Aldine Publishing Company.

———— (1971a). "Mathematical Experimentation and Sociological Theory: A Critical Analysis." *Sociometry*, 34, 423–452.

———— (1971b). "Ratio Measurement for the Social Sciences." *Social Forces*, 50, 191–206.

———— (1966). "Ratio Measurement and Sociological Theory." Paper read at the American Sociological Association meetings, Miami, FL.

Harding, S. (1991). *Whose Knowledge? Whose Science? Thinking from Women's Lives*. Ithaca, NY: Cornell University Press.

———— (1987). "Is There a Feminist Method?" In S. Harding, ed., *Feminism and Methodology*. Bloomington, IN: Indiana University Press.

Harrell, W. Andrew (2005). "Are Prettier Kids Protected Better: A Field Observational Study of Child Safety in Grocery Carts." Unpublished paper.

———— (2003a). "Safety of Children in Grocery Carts: Adults' Personal Health and Safety Habits." *Psychological Reports*, 92, 908–914.

———— (2003b). "Dangerous Activities by Children in Grocery Carts: Is Adult Supervision Important?" *Psychological Reports*, 92, 957–962.

———— (1994). "The Impact of Shopping Cart Restraints and Adult Supervision on Near Injuries to Children in Grocery Stores." *Accident Analysis & Prevention*, 26(4), 493–500.

Harrell, W. Andrew, and E. Elaine Reid (1990). "Safety of Children in Grocery Stores: The Impact of Cart Seat Use in Shopping Carts and Parental Monitoring." *Accident Analysis & Prevention*, 22(6), 531–542.

Hart, E., and M. Bond (1998). *Action Research for Health and Social Care*. Philadelphia: Open University Press.

Heberlein, Thomas A., and Robert Baumgartner (1978). "Factors Affecting Response Rates to Mailed Questionnaires." *American Sociological Review*, 43.

Heise, David R., and George W. Bohrnstedt (1970). "Validity, Invalidity, and Reliability." In Edgar F. Borgatta and George W. Bohrnstedt, eds., *Sociological Methodology 1970*. San Francisco: Jossey-Bass Inc.

Henry, Frances, and Effie Ginzberg (1990). "Racial Discrimination in Employment." In James Curtis and Lorne Tepperman, eds., *Images of Canada* (302–309). Scarborough, ON: Prentice-Hall Canada Inc.

Henshel, Richard L. (1976). *On the Future of Prediction*. Indianapolis, IN: The Bobbs-Merrill Company, Inc.

Hochschild, A.R. (1983). *The Managed Heart: Commercialization of Human Feeling*. Berkeley: University of California Press.

Holden, Constance (1979). "Ethics in Social Science Research." *Science*, 206 (November), 537–540.

Holsti, Ole R. (1969). *Content Analysis for the Social Sciences and Humanities*. Don Mills, ON: Addison-Wesley Publishing Company.

Homans, George C. (1964). "Bringing Men Back In." *American Sociological Review*, 29, 809–818.

———— (1961). *Social Behavior: Its Elementary Forms*. New York: Harcourt, Brace and World.

Horowitz, Irving Louis (1973). "The Hemispheric Connection: A Critique and Corrective to the Entrepreneurial Thesis of Development with Special Emphasis on the Canadian Case." *Queen's Quarterly*, 80 (Autumn), 327–359.

Horowitz, Irving Louis, and Lee Rainwater (1970). "Journalistic Moralizers." *TransAction*, 7(7), 5–7.

Huber, Peter W. (1991). *Galileo's Revenge: Junk Science in the Courtroom*. New York: Basic Books.

Humphrey, Charles, and Elizabeth Hamilton (2004). "Is It Working?: Assessing the Value of the Canadian Data Liberation Initiative." *The Bottom Line*, 14(4), 137–146.

Humphreys, Laud (1970). *Tearoom Trade*. Chicago: Aldine Press.

Hunter, Alfred A. (1985). "Doing It With Numbers." *The Canadian Review of Sociology and Anthropology*, 22(5), 645–672.

Im, E. (2000). "A Feminist Critique of Research on Women's Work and Health." *Health Care for Women International*, 21, 105–119.

Jackson, Winston (1995). *Methods: Doing Social Research*. Toronto: Prentice Hall.

––––––– (1988). *Research Methods: Rules for Survey Design and Analysis*. Scarborough, ON: Prentice-Hall Canada Inc.

––––––– (1973). *University Preferences and Perceptions of Pictou County Students*. Antigonish: St. Francis Xavier University.

Jackson, Winston, and Nicholas W. Poushinsky (1971). *Migration to Northern Mining Communities: Structural and Social Psychological Dimensions*. Winnipeg: Centre for Settlement Studies, University of Manitoba.

Johnson, Ronald W., and John G. Adair (1970). "The Effects of Systematic Recording Error vs. Experimenter Bias on Latency of Word Association." *Journal of Experimental Research in Personality*, 4, 270–275.

Johnson, Ronald W., and Brenda J. Ryan (1976). "Observer Recorder Error as Affected by Different Tasks and Different Expectancy Inducements." *Journal of Research in Personality*, 10, 201–214.

Kahane, H. (1988). *Logic and Contemporary Rhetoric*. Belmont, CA: Wadsworth.

Kaplowitz, Michael D., Timothy D. Hadlock, and Ralph Levine (2004). "A Comparison of Web and Mail Survey Response Rates." *Public Opinion Quarterly*, 68(1), 94–102.

Kaufman, H. (1967). "The Price of Obedience and the Price of Knowledge." *American Psychologist*, 22, 321–322.

Kirby, Sandra L., and Kate McKenna (1989). *Experience Research Social Change: Methods from the Margins*. Toronto: Garamond Press.

Krahn, Harvey (1991). "Sociological Methods of Research." In Lorne Tepperman and R. Jack Richardson, eds., *The Social World: An Introduction to Sociology* (34–66). Toronto: McGraw-Hill Ryerson Limited.

Lambert, Ronald D. (1993). "Publications, Theses and Scholarly Papers Based on the Canadian National Election Studies, 1965–1988." Unpublished paper.

Lapiere, Richard T. (1934). "Attitudes vs. Actions." *Social Forces*, 13, 230–237.

Lastrucci, Carlo L. (1967). *The Scientific Approach*. Cambridge, MA: Schenkman Publishing, Inc.

Lazarsfeld, Paul F., Bernard Berelson, and Hazel Gaudet (1968). *The People's Choice: How the Voter Makes up His Mind in a Presidential Campaign*. New York: Columbia University Press.

Lecompte, Margaret D., and Judith Preissle Goetz (1982). "Problems of Reliability and Validity in Ethnographic Research." *Review of Educational Research*, 52(1), 31–60.

Lee, Michelle (1992). "Smoking Behaviours." Antigonish: St. Francis Xavier University, Research Methods paper.

Levin, Jack, and James Alan Fox (1991). *Elementary Statistics in Social Research*. 5th ed. New York: HarperCollins Publishers Inc.

Lewin, K. (1951). *Field Theory in Social Sciences*. New York: Harper and Row.

Liebow, Elliot (1967). *Tally's Corner: A Study of Negro Streetcorner Men*. Toronto: Little, Brown and Company.

Likert, Rensis (1931). "A Technique for the Measurement of Attitudes." *Archives of Psychology*. New York: Columbia University Press.

Lincoln, Y.S. (1995). "Emerging Criteria for Quality in Qualitative and Interpretive Research." *Qualitative Inquiry*, 1, 275–289.

Lincoln, Y.S., and E.G. Guba (1994). "Competing Paradigms in Qualitative Research." In N.K. Denzin and Y.S. Lincoln, eds., *Handbook of Qualitative Research* (105–117). Thousand Oaks, CA: Sage.

––––––– (1985). *Naturalistic Inquiry*. Beverly Hills, CA: Sage.

––––––– (1981). *Effective Evaluation: Improving the Effectiveness of Evaluation Results through Responsive and Naturalistic Approaches*. San Francisco: Jossey-Bass.

Lindsey, E., and K. Stajduhar (1998). "From Rhetoric to Action: Establishing Community Participation in AIDS-Related Research." *Canadian Journal of Nursing Research*, 30(1), 137–153.

Lipset, S.M. (2001). "Defining Moments and Recurring Myths: A Reply." *The Canadian Review of Sociology and Anthropology*, 38(1), 98–100.

––––––– (1990). *Continental Divide*. New York: Routledge.

––––––– (1986). "Historical Conditions and National Characteristics." *Canadian Journal of Sociology*, 11(2), 113–155.

——— (1964). "Canada and the United States: A Comparative View." *The Canadian Review of Sociology and Anthropology*, 1, 173–185.

Lodge, Milton (1981). *Magnitude Scaling: Quantitative Measurement of Opinions*. Beverly Hills, CA: Sage Publications.

Lofland, John (1971). *Analyzing Social Settings*. Belmont, CA: Wadsworth Publishing Company, Inc.

MacDonald Lara (1991). "Attitudes toward the Elderly." Antigonish: St. Francis Xavier University, Research Methods report.

Malinowski, Bronislaw (1954). *Magic, Science and Religion*. New York: Doubleday [1925].

Marshall, C., and G.B. Rossman (1995). *Designing Qualitative Research*. 2nd ed. Thousand Oaks, CA: Sage.

Martin, David W. (1991). *Doing Psychology Experiments*. 3rd ed. Pacific Grove, CA: Brooks/Cole Publishing Company.

Marx, Karl (1977). *Capital*. New York: Vintage Books [1867].

McCabe, C. (1991). "Job Satisfaction: A Study of St. Martha Regional Nurses." Antigonish: St. Francis Xavier University, Sociology 300 project report.

McGinnis, Robert (1958). "Randomization and Inference in Sociological Research." *American Sociological Review*, 23 (October), 408–414.

McIver, John P., and Edward G. Carmines (1981). *Unidimensional Scaling*. Beverly Hills: Sage Publications.

McMaster University and Affiliated Health and Social Service Agencies. (2005). "Interview with Dr. Gina Browne." Retrieved 29 November 2005 from http://www.fhs.mcmaster.ca/slru/interview.htm.

Mead, George H. (1934). *Mind, Self, and Society*. Chicago: University of Chicago Press.

Mead, Margaret (1966). *An Anthropologist at Work: Writings of Ruth Benedict*. New York: Harcourt Brace Jovanovich.

——— (1935). *Sex and Temperament in Three Primitive Societies*. New York: Morrow.

Miles, M., and A. Huberman (1994). *Qualitative Data Analysis*. London: Sage Publications.

Milgram, Stanley (1974). *Obedience to Authority*. New York: Harper Colophon Books.

——— (1964). "Issues in the Study of Obedience." *American Psychologist*, 19, 848–852.

——— (1963). "Behavioural Study of Obedience." *Journal of Abnormal and Social Psychology*, 67, 371–378.

Mill, John Stuart (1925). *A System of Logic*. 8th ed. London: Longmans, Green and Co.

Miller, Delbert C. (1977). *Handbook of Research Design and Social Measurement*. 3rd ed. New York: Longman.

Mills, C. Wright (1959). *The Sociological Imagination*. New York: Oxford University Press.

Mitchell, Mark, and Janina Jolley (1992). *Research Design Explained*. 2nd ed. Orlando, FL: Harcourt Brace Jovanovitch College Publishers.

Monette, Duane R., Thomas J. Sullivan, and Cornell R. DeJong (1990). *Applied Social Research: Tool for the Human Services*. 2nd ed. Fort Worth, TX: Holt, Rinehart and Winston, Inc.

Morrison, E. Denton, and Ramon E. Henkel, Eds. (1970). *The Significance Tests Controversy*. Chicago: Aldine Press.

Moustaka, C. (1994). *Phenomenological Research Methods*. Thousand Oaks, CA: Sage.

MRC, NSERC, SSHRC (1998). "Context of the Ethics Framework." *Tri-Council Policy Statement*. Retrieved 22 March 2006 from http://www.ncehr-cnerh.org/english/code_2/intro03.html#B.

Munhall, P.L., and C.O. Boyd (1993). *Nursing Research. A Qualitative Perspective*. New York: National League for Nursing Press.

Munhall, P.L., and C.J. Oiler (1986). *Nursing Research: A Qualitative Perspective*. Norwalk, CT: Appleton-Century-Crofts.

Murdock, George P. (1960). *Social Structure*. New York: Macmillan.

Nachmias, David, and Chava Nachmias (1981). *Research Methods in the Social Sciences*. 2nd ed. New York: St. Martin's Press.

Nagel, Ernest (1961). *The Structure of Science: Problems in the Logic of Scientific Explanations*. New York: Harcourt, Brace & World.

Nettler, G. (1970). *Explanations*. New York: McGraw-Hill Book Company.

Nunnally, J.C. (1978). *Psychometric Theory*. 2nd ed. New York: McGraw-Hill.

Oakley, A. (1981). "Interviewing Women: A Contradiction in Terms." In H. Roberts, ed., *Feminist Research Methods: Exemplary Readings in the Social Sciences* (44–62). San Francisco: West View Press.

O'Connell, K. (2000). "If You Call Me Names, I'll Call You Numbers." *Journal of Professional Nursing*, 16(2), 74.

Olesen, V. (1994). "Feminisms and Models of Qualitative Research." In N.K. Denzin and Y.S. Lincoln, eds., *Handbook of Qualitative Research* (158–174). Thousand Oaks, CA: Sage.

Omery, A. (1983). "Phenomenology: A Method for Nursing Research." *Advances in Nursing Science*, 5(2), 49–63.

Orne, Martin T. (1962). "On the Social Psychology of the Psychological Experiment: With Particular Reference to Demand Characteristics and Their Implications." *American Psychologist*, 17, 776–783.

Osgood, C.E., G.J. Suci, and P.H. Tannenbaum (1957). *The Measurement of Meaning*. Urbana, IL: University of Chicago Press.

Palys, Ted (1992). *Research Decisions: Quantitative and Qualitative Perspectives*. Toronto: Harcourt Brace Canada Inc.

Parahoo, K. (1997). *Nursing Research: Principles, Process, and Issues*. London: Macmillan Press.

Parse, R., A.B. Coyne, and M.J. Smith (1985). *Nursing Research: Qualitative Methods*. Bowie, MD: Brady.

Piliavin, J.A., and I.M. Piliavin (1972). "Effect of Blood on Reactions to a Victim." *Journal of Personality and Social Psychology*, 23, 353–361.

Pineo, Peter C., and John Porter (1967). "Occupational Prestige in Canada." *Canadian Review of Sociology and Anthropology*, 24–40.

Platt, John R. (1964). "Strong Inference." *Science*, 146(3642), 347–353.

Prus, Robert (1996). *Symbolic Interaction and Ethnographic Research: Intersubjectivity and the Study of Human Lived Experience*. New York: State University of New York Press.

Prus, Robert, and Scott Grills (2003). *The Deviant Mystique: Involvement, Realities, and Regulation*. Westport, CT: Praeger Publishers.

Prus, Robert C., and C.R.D. Sharper (1977). *Road Hustler: The Career Contingencies of Professional Card and Dice Hustlers*. Toronto: Gage Publishing Limited.

Psathas, George (1973). *Phenomenological Sociology: Issues and Applications*. New York: Wiley.

RAND Corporation (2001). *A Million Random Numbers with 100,000 Normal Deviates*. Santa Monica, CA: RAND Corporation [1955].

Reinharz, S. (1992). *Feminist Methods in Social Research*. New York: Oxford University Press.

Reynolds, Paul Davidson (1982). *Ethics and Social Science Research*. Englewood Cliffs, NJ: Prentice-Hall Inc.

Ribbens, J. (1989). "Interviewing—An Unnatural Situation?" *Women's Studies International Forum*, 12(6), 579–592.

Ritzer, G. (1988). *Sociological Theory*. 2nd ed. New York: Alfred A. Knopf.

Roethlisberger, F.J., and W.J. Dickson (1939). *Management and the Worker*. Cambridge, MA: Harvard University Press.

Rose, Damaris (2001). *Revisiting Feminist Research Methodologies: A Working Paper*. Submitted to the Status of Women Canada, Research Division. Retrieved 29 November 2005 from http://www.swc-cfc.gc.ca/pubs/pubspr/revisiting/revisiting_8_e.html.

Rosenthal, Robert (1979). "The 'File Drawer Problem' and Tolerance for Null Results." *Psychological Bulletin*, 86(3), 638–641.

——— (1966). *Experimenter Effects in Behavioral Research*. New York: Century.

Rosenthal, Robert, and K.L. Fode (1963). "The Effect of Experimenter Bias on the Performance of the Albino Rat." *Behavioral Science*, 8, 183–189.

Rosenthal, Robert, and Ralph L. Rosnow (1991). *Essentials of Behavioural Research: Methods and Data Analysis*. 2nd ed. New York: McGraw-Hill, Inc.

Rothe, J.P. (1994). *Qualitative Research: A Practical Guide*. Heidelberg, ON: RCI Publications.

Rugg, Harold O. (1917). *Statistical Methods Applied to Education*. Boston: Houghton Mifflin Company.

Sandelowski, M. (1993). "Rigor or Rigor Mortis: The Problem of Rigor in Qualitative Research Revisited." *Advances in Nursing Science*, 16 (2), 1–8.

——— (1986). "The Problem of Rigor in Qualitative Research." *Advances in Nursing Science*, 8(3), 27–37.

Sandelowski, M., and S. Pollack (1986). "Qualitative Analysis: What It Is and How to Begin." *Research in Nursing and Health*, 18, 371–375.

Saunders, E. (1988). "Women and Canadian Society: The Sociological Frame." In D.P. Forcese and S. Richer, eds., *Social Issues: Sociological Views of Canada* (pp. 151–185). Scarborough, ON: Prentice-Hall Canada Inc.

Schatzman, Leonard, and Anselm L. Strauss (1973). *Field Research: Strategies for a Natural Sociology.* Englewood Cliffs, NJ: Prentice-Hall, Inc.

Schmitt, R. (1972). "Phenomenology." In Paul Edwards, ed., *The Encyclopedia of Philosophy*, Vol. 6 (135–151). New York: Macmillan-Free Press.

Schonlau, Matthias, Beth J. Asch, and Can Du (2003). "Web Surveys as Part of a Mixed-Mode Strategy for Populations That Cannot be Contacted by Email." *Social Science Computer Review*, 21(2), 218.

Schuman, Howard, and Stanley Presser (1981). *Questions and Answers in Attitude Surveys.* New York: The Academic Press, Inc.

Schutz, A. (1954). "Concept and Theory Formation in the Social Sciences." *Journal of Philosophy*, 51(9), 257–273.

Sellin, J.T., and M.E. Wolfgang (1964). *The Measurement of Delinquency.* New York: John Wiley.

Selvin, Hanan C. (1957). "A Critique of Tests of Significance in Survey Research." *American Sociological Review*, 22 (October), 519–527.

Selvin, Hanan C., and Alan Stuart (1966). "Data Dredging Procedures in Survey Analysis." *Journal of the American Statistical Association*, 61, 20–23.

Senn, Charlene, Norine Verberg, Serge Desmarais, and Eileen Wood (2000). "Sampling the Reluctant Participant: Studying Men and Sexual Coercion." *Journal of Applied Social Psychology,* 30(1): 96–105.

Sheppard, Robert (1993). "Yes, No, Undecided or Just Hangs Up?" *Globe and Mail* (23 August), A11.

Shields, Stephanie A. (1988). "Functionalism, Darwinism, and the Psychology of Women: A Study in Social Myth." In Ludy T. Benjamin Jr., ed., *A History of Psychology*. New York: McGraw-Hill Book Company.

Siegel, S. (1956). *Nonparametric Statistics.* New York: McGraw-Hill.

Silverman, D. (1997). *Qualitative Research: Theory, Method and Practice.* London: Sage.

Silverstein, Brett, Lauren Perdue, Barbara Peterson, and Eileen Kelly (1986). "The Role of the Mass Media in Promoting a Thin Standard of Bodily Attractiveness for Women." *Sex Roles*, 14(9/10), 519–532.

Simon, Herbert A. (1957). *Models of Man.* New York: John Wiley & Sons.

Simon, Julian L., and Paul Burstein (1985). *Basic Research Methods in Social Science.* 3rd ed. New York: Random House.

Skipper, James K., Anthony L. Guenther, and Gilbert Nass (1967). "The Sacredness of.05: A Note Concerning the Uses of Statistical Levels of Significance in Social Science." *American Sociologist*, 2, 16–18.

Smith, Dorothy E. (2005). *Institutional Ethnography: A Sociology for People.* Toronto: Altamira Press.

——— (2002). "Institutional Ethnography." In T. May, ed., *Qualitative Research in Action.* London: Sage.

——— (1999). *Writing the Social: Critique, Theory and Investigations.* Toronto: Toronto University Press.

——— (1993). *Texts, Facts and Femininity: Exploring the Relations of Ruling.* London: Routledge.

——— (1987). *The Everyday World as Problematic: A Feminist Sociology.* Toronto: University of Toronto Press.

Smith, Michael D. (no date). "Effects of Question Format on the Reporting of Woman Abuse: A Telephone Survey Experiment." Toronto: Institute for Social Research, York University.

Smith, P. (1997). *Research Mindedness for Practice: An Interactive Approach for Nursing and Health Care.* New York: Churchill Livingstone.

Solchany, J.E. (1998). "Anticipating the Adopted Child: Women's Preadoptive Experiences." *Canadian Journal of Nursing Research,* 30(3), 123–129.

Spiegelberg, H. (1975). *The Phenomenological Movement.* The Hague, Netherlands: Martinus Nijhoff.

Spradley, James P. (1980). *Participant Observation.* San Diego, CA: Harcourt Brace College Publishers.

——— (1979). *The Ethnographic Interview.* New York: Holt, Rinehart and Winston.

Statistics Canada (2005). "What Is the Data Liberation Initiative?" Statistics Canada Home Page, Data Liberation Initiative (DLI). Retrieved 8 March 2006 from http://www.statcan.ca/english/Dli/whatisdli.htm [posted 31 December 2001].

Sterling, T.D. (1959). "Publication Decisions and Their Possible Effects on Inferences Drawn from Tests of Significance—or Vice Versa." *Journal of the American Statistical Association*, 54, 30–34.

Sterling, T.D., W.L. Rosenbaum, and J.J. Weinkam (1995). "Publication Decisions Revisited: The Effect of the Outcome of Statistical Tests on the Decision to Publish and Vice Versa." *The American Statistician*, 49, 108–112.

Stern, P.N. (1980). "Grounded Theory Methodology: Its Uses and Process." *Image*, 12(1), 20–23.

Stevens, S.S. (1966a). "A Metric for the Social Consensus." *Science*, 151, 530–541.

———— (1966b). "Matching Functions between Loudness and Ten Other Continua." *Perception and Psychophysics*, 1, 5–8.

———— (1951). "Mathematics, Measurement, and Psychophysics." In S.S. Stevens, ed., *Handbook of Experimental Psychology*. New York: Wiley.

Strauss, A.L. (1987). *Qualitative Analysis for Social Scientists*. New York: Cambridge University Press.

Strauss, A., and J. Corbin (1990). *Basics of Qualitative Research: Grounded Theory Procedures and Techniques*. Newbury Park, CA: Sage.

———— (1997). *Grounded Theory in Practice*. Thousand Oaks, CA: Sage.

Streubert, H.J., and D.R. Carpenter (1999). *Qualitative Research in Nursing: Advancing the Humanistic Imperative*. 2nd ed. Philadelphia: J.B. Lippincott.

———— (1994). *Qualitative Research in Nursing: Advancing the Humanistic Imperative*. Philadelphia: J.B. Lippincott.

Sudman, Seymour (1967). *Reducing the Cost of Surveys*. Chicago: Aldine Publishing Company.

Sudman, Seymour, and Norman Bradburn (1983). *Asking Questions*. San Francisco: Jossey-Bass Publishers.

Sussman, S., D. Burton, C.W. Dent, A.W. Stacy, and B.R. Flay (1991). "Use of Focus Groups in Developing an Adolescent Tobacco Use Cessation Program: Collection Norm Effect." *Journal of Applied Social Psychology*, 21, 1772–1782.

Sykes, Gresham M. (1968). *The Society of Captives*. New York: Atheneum.

Tanner, Julian, and Harvey Krahn (1991). "Part-Time Work and Deviance among High School Seniors." *Canadian Journal of Sociology*, 16(3), 281–302.

Tawney, R.H. (1926). *Religion and the Rise of Capitalism*. New York: Harcourt, Brace and Company, Inc.

Thibaut, John W., and Harold H. Kelley (1959). *The Social Psychology of Groups*. New York: Wiley.

Travers, K. (1997). "Reducing Inequities through Participatory Research and Community Empowerment." *Health Education and Behavior*, 24(3), 344–356.

Turner, Jonathan H. (1991). *The Structure of Sociological Theory*. 5th ed. Belmont, CA: Wadsworth Publishing Company.

Von Hoffman, Nicholas (1970). "Sociological Snoopers." *TransAction*, 7(7), 4–6.

Walby, Kevin (2005). "How Closed-Circuit Television Surveillance Organizes the Social: An Institutional Ethnography." *Canadian Journal of Sociology*, 30(2), 189–214.

Warwick, Donald P. (1973). "Tearoom Trade: Means & Ends in Social Research." *Hastings Center Studies*, 1(1), 27–38.

Warwick, Donald P., and Samuel Osherson, Eds. (1973). *Comparative Research Methods*. Englewood Cliffs, NJ: Prentice-Hall, Inc.

Waterman, A., L. Webb, and W. Williams (1995). "Parallels and Contradictions in the Theory and Practice of Action Research in Nursing." *Journal of Advanced Nursing*, 22, 779–784.

Webb, C. (1993). "Feminist Research: Definitions, Methodology, Methods and Evaluation." *Journal of Advanced Nursing*, 18, 416–423.

Weber, Max (1964). *Sociology of Religion*. Boston: Beacon Press.

———— (1904). *The Protestant Ethic and the Spirit of Capitalism*. New York: Charles Scribner & Sons.

Weinberg, Eve (1971). *Community Surveys with Local Talent*. Chicago: National Opinion Research Center.

Whyte, W.F. (1955). *Street Corner Society: The Social Structure of an Italian Slum*. 2nd ed. Chicago: University of Chicago Press.

Whyte, W.F., D. Greenwood, and P. Lazes (1991). *Participatory Action Research: Through Practice to Science in Social Research*. Newbury Park, CA: Sage.

Zetterberg, Hans L. (1965). *On Theory and Verification in Sociology*. Totowa, NJ: The Bedminster Press.

Zhang, Yin (2000). "Using the Internet for Survey Research: A Case Study." *Journal of the American Society for Information Science*, 51(1), 57–68.

INDEX